# WILLIAM GODWIN

From a Painting by Thomas Kearsley.    Engrav'd by Roberts

*William Godwin, Esqr.*

I. Godwin, aged 38, by Thomas Kearsley, 1794. Engraved by P. Roberts.

# WILLIAM GODWIN

Peter H. Marshall

Yale University Press · New Haven & London · 1984

Designed by Caroline Williamson
Set in VIP Baskerville
by Clavier Phototypesetting Ltd, Southend-on-Sea, Essex
Printed in Great Britain at The Pitman Press, Bath

**Library of Congress Cataloging in Publication Data**
Marshall, Peter H., 1946–
   William Godwin

Bibliography: p.
  Includes index.
   1. Godwin, William, 1756–1836. 2. Novelists, English – 19th century – Biography. 3. Philosophers – England – Biography. 4. Revolutionists – England – Biography.
I. Title.
PR4723.M3 1984   828'.609 [B]   83-19823
ISBN 0-300-03175-0

*For Dylan, Emily and Jenny*

# CONTENTS

# ILLUSTRATIONS

# ACKNOWLEDGEMENTS

I would like to thank Dr. John W. Burrow who followed the early stages of this book. Without his excellent advice and warm encouragement, it would never have been undertaken. The comments of Professor Gwyn A. Williams also proved invaluable. No serious student of William Godwin could fail to be indebted to the bibliographical labours of Professor Burton R. Pollin.

I should like to acknowledge the assistance of the staff of the University of Sussex Library, the University of London Library, the British Library, the British Museum, Dr. Williams's Library, the Bodleian Library, the Victoria and Albert Museum Library, the Norfolk Central Library, and the National Portrait Gallery.

I am indebted to Lord Abinger for permission to use and quote from the manuscripts in his possession. I have also been helped by Mrs. Mary Claire Bally-Clairmont, Professor Marion K. Stocking, Professor Don Locke, Mr. Kenneth Garlick and Lady Mander in locating the portraits of Godwin and his circle.

I would especially like to thank Jenny Zobel for her great help and understanding. The enthusiasm of my brother Michael has been much appreciated. I am indebted to Yvonne Carmichael for typing different drafts of the manuscript and to Caroline Williamson for seeing the work through the press. And to my friends who have been both inspired and irritated by my interest in William Godwin, thank you.

Croesor, Gwynedd, July 1983

# INTRODUCTION

William Godwin died in April 1836, virtually unknown except to a small
coterie of intellectuals. His writings formed the creed of no organized body
of followers, and his grave in St. Pancras Churchyard remained unvisited.
Yet, according to Hazlitt, forty years before,

> He was in the very zenith of a sultry and unwholesome popularity; he
> blazed as a sun in the firmament of reputation; no one was more talked
> of, more looked up to, more sought after, and wherever liberty, truth,
> justice was the theme, his name was not far off . . . No work in our time
> gave such a blow to the philosophical mind of the country as the cele-
> brated *Enquiry concerning Political Justice.* Tom Paine was considered for
> the time as a Tom Fool to him, Paley an old woman, Edmund Burke a
> flashy sophist.[1]

When Godwin's principal treatise appeared in 1793 it was avidly read by
young intellectuals like Southey, Coleridge and Wordsworth, by radical
leaders like Francis Place and John Thelwall, and by many artisans who
clubbed together to pay its high price. His novel *Things as They Are; or, The
Adventures of Caleb Williams,* published in the following year, was considered no less of a masterpiece.

It was Godwin's misfortune to have his name closely linked to the French
Revolution. As the reaction against Jacobinism in Britain grew, so his
reputation waned. He was at first vilified and then rapidly forgotten. By
1812 his eclipse was so great that it was with 'inconceivable emotions' that
his future son-in-law Shelley found the author of *Political Justice* to be still
alive.[2] He continued to write prolifically and to recruit the occasional
disciple, but apart from the temporary notoriety of his *Of Population* in
1820, he was unable to recapture the public imagination. The prejudice

against the heroic veteran of the 1790s was too great. De Quincey spoke on behalf of the ruling class when he declared 'most people felt of Mr Godwin with the same alienation and horror as of a ghoul, or a bloodless vampyre, or the monster created by Frankenstein'.[3]

This was, of course, an exaggeration. His doctrines quietly influenced the early socialists Robert Owen, William Thompson and Thomas Hodgskin, and through them his vision of a free and classless society reached Marx. The growing labour movement also took note of what he had to say. In the 1830s and 1840s the Owenites and Chartists printed in their journals many extracts from Godwin's works and published a new edition of *Political Justice* in 1842.

It was not however until Kegan Paul brought out the excellent biography *William Godwin: His Friends and Contemporaries* (1876) that he began to receive serious scholarly attention. It was soon recognized that 'the seeds of all the ideas of recent Socialism and Anarchism' were to be found in his work.[4] Even the eminent Victorian Leslie Stephen expressed a keen interest in the 'gorgeous bubbles' of the 'venerable horseleech'.[5]

Yet the Tory image of Godwin still held away, particularly amongst literary historians. He continued to be remembered more for his disastrous family connections as the husband of Mary Wollstonecraft, the father of Mary Shelley, and the step-father of Byron's mistress Claire Clairmont; more for his baneful influence on Southey and Wordsworth; more for his strange friendship with Coleridge, Lamb and Hazlitt; and more for his sponging off Shelley than for any contribution to philosophy or literature. When not dismissed as a Utopian crank, he was described as an icy rationalist who held outrageous opinions on government, property and marriage. His chief opponent, Malthus, it was felt, had answered him once and for all.

Legends are notoriously difficult to change. In our own century, however, changed circumstances and careful research have led to a considerable measure of reappraisal. Godwin is now recognized as the first and most capable exponent of anarchism, a prominent figure in the history of ethics, and a pioneer in socialist economics and progressive education. His novels have been praised for their powerful psychological insight and acute social observation.

Apart from his stature as a philosopher and novelist, Godwin is important as a representative figure. He was brought up as a Calvinist but like many Dissenters lost his faith and became a radical. He drew the extreme conclusions of eighteenth-century rationalism only to help create the new cult of sensibility associated with Romanticism. He was at the centre of the radical intellectual and literary circles in London during the French Revolution. From his birth in 1756 to his death in 1836 he straddled two centuries, and his thought and action reflect some of the most momentous changes in British history. And he looked both backwards and forwards: one of the last great Commonwealth Men, he became the most eloquent prophet of modern anarchism.

At the same time, Godwin is not merely of historical interest. His arguments have never been so relevant. As a moral philosopher, he imaginatively challenges the crumbling orthodoxy in contemporary ethics by arguing that facts about human nature are relevant to values and that moral principles can be supported by sound reasoning and truth. In so far as utilitarianism is a living tradition, Godwin provides better arguments than Bentham and anticipates the best of John Stuart Mill.

In political philosophy, he questions many fundamental assumptions in his treatment of government, democracy and law. He will be of interest to all those who believe that politics is inseparable from ethics and that independence, individuality, rationality and happiness are central concerns of political enquiry. Above all, he speaks directly to the new radicalism which has emerged in the last decade which seeks a libertarian way between the bureaucratic centralism of communist states and the organized lovelessness of the capitalist world. What Locke is for liberalism and Marx is for communism, Godwin is for anarchism.

A great deal of the extensive commentary on Godwin is uneven. Amongst recent studies, Burton R. Pollin has brought out well the role of *Education and Enlightenment in the Works of William Godwin* (1963). John P. Clark has given a useful general exposition of *The Philosophical Anarchism of William Godwin* (1977), although it is based only on a few books. Don Locke's *A Fantasy of Reason: The Life and Thought of William Godwin* (1980) is a lively and substantial work but it defies chronology and neglects the historical context. He presents Godwin as a philosopher's philosopher but underestimates him as a novelist's novelist. While he recognizes his importance as a moral thinker, he unjustly claims that Godwin is 'unquestionably dead' as a political theorist.[6] And as the title of his work suggests, he tries to demonstrate the unreasonableness of Godwin's reason and narrates the 'massive misjudgments' of his life and writings.[7] For his part, Jean de Palacio in his *William Godwin et son monde intérieur* (1980) rigidly separates Godwin's political concerns from his inner world. Inspired by Freud, he relentlessly tracks him down in his fiction in order to present him dubiously in a 'retraite autistique à l'intérieur de soi'.[8] Finally, B. J. Tysdahl has written a mainly formal and stylistic account of *William Godwin as Novelist* (1981).

My own work is a study of both Godwin's life and writings. It is particularly important to consider the relationship between the two since he elaborated his ideas directly from his own experience: 'the philosophy of the wisest man that ever existed', he wrote, 'is mainly derived from the act of introspection . . . the analysis of the individual may stand in general consideration for the analysis of the species'.[9] Similarly, his novels are largely autobiographical, indeed confessional; he believed that every author 'puts much of his own character into his work; and a skilful anatomist of the soul before he reaches the perusal of the last page, will have formed a very tolerable notion of the dispositions of the writer'.[10] It is equally advisable to take a chronological approach to a study of his work, not only because it helps to explain the apparent inconsistencies and contradictions, but because he himself admitted that every four or five years he would look back 'astonished at the stupidity & folly of which I had a short time before been the dupe'.[11]

While tracing his fundamental assumptions and specific borrowings, I have tried as far as possible to place Godwin in his personal, social and historical context. His ideas and feelings were after all only part of his activity as a whole living being, and he belonged to a specific social group in a particular time and place. In order to give a clear account of the origins, nature and evolution of his thought, I have shown the gradual emergence and subsequent revision of his major themes. I also give a critical estimate of his work, recognizing the equal importance of his philosophy and literature and their mutual illumination.

My study of Godwin's life and work, based on the largely untapped Abinger Manuscripts and extensive new published and unpublished materials, offers the following arguments. First, the most important context of his philosophy was the Dissenting tradition. While he borrowed much from the liberal thinkers of the English and French Enlightenment, his early exposure to Calvinism and his contact with the Dissenters played a crucial role in his development. Secondly, many of his fundamental beliefs were developed well before the publication of *Political Justice* in 1793, and despite his subsequent revisions, the spirit and outline of his system remained intact. Thirdly, Godwin's influence, both on his contemporaries and in the nineteenth century, was much greater than is usually assumed. And finally, Godwin is not merely a man of two books: there is a great deal of his enormous output which continues to be of burning interest and real value today.

It will become apparent that the traditional image of Godwin as a naive and abstract philosopher, living in a frozen ivory tower, is fundamentally wrong. His roots were in rural Norfolk and he came to live in the metropolis only in his late twenties. He had a close knowledge of practical affairs and participated in some of the major controversies of the day. He was no visionary but made a clear distinction between theory and action, between what we may accept in the 'sobriety of the closet' and what we may assume in 'actual life'.[12] Far from being the 'bloodless vampyre' of popular mythology, he recognized the importance of the imagination and valued the heart as well as the head.

A study of Godwin is no easy task. He was active, if not always competent, in many fields. At different times in his life, he was a journalist, literary critic, satirist, political philosopher, psychologist, economist, educationalist, biographer, historian, novelist, playwright, essayist, grammarian, lexicographer, fabulist, and writer of sermons and children's books. Yet behind this varied and vuluminous output, Godwin had an overriding sense of purpose. In all his writings, he insisted, 'the study to which I had devoted myself was man, to analyse his nature as a moralist, and to delineate his passions as an historian, or a recorder of fictitious adventures'.[13]

Godwin has been chiefly remembered as a philosopher and novelist. But he was also a revolutionary, albeit a peaceful one, in that he called for a thorough transformation of human relations. In his last major work, *Thoughts on Man*, he summarized inadvertently his own achievement: 'If I devote my energies to enlighten my fellow-creatures, to detect the weak places in our social institutions, to plead the cause of liberty, and to invite others to engage in noble actions and unite in effecting the most solid and unquestionable improvements, I erect to my name an eternal monument'.[14] Like Rousseau, Godwin sought to produce the whole person who would make the ideal society. This profound humanism inspired all that he thought and did.

# CHAPTER I

## *Childhood*

William Godwin was born in 1756, four years before the accession of George III and at the outset of a period of profound changes. Since the settlement of 1688 the landed gentry had been in power, and under Walpole the House of Commons had become the dominant political body. There was little to distinguish between the major parties, and the names 'Whig' and 'Tory' related as much to tradition and descent as to political ideology. But as John Wilkes and his followers made clear in the following decade, parliament was corrupt, unrepresentative and dependent on the Crown. Abroad, Britain was expanding her Empire in India and America, and in the year Godwin was born Chatham declared war – the Seven Years War – on her chief rival France.

Britain was still primarily a society of peasants earning a subsistence from strip farming and of artisans working independenntly or in small workshops. Enclosures by Act of Parliament, however, were gathering momentum, turning the English countryside into the now familiar pattern of hedges, fields and scattered farms. The factory system had yet to appear but the first British canal had just been opened in Lancashire. At Godwin's birth, Britain was thus about to experience the Industrial Revolution which not only produced violent changes in agriculture and industry, but fundamentally transformed the whole structure of society.

It was at the back of the castle in Wisbech, in a new brick house in Knowe's Acre, that William Godwin was born on 3 March 1756. In the middle of the century, Wisbech, the capital of North Cambridgeshire, was an assize and race-town. It was a flourishing market for the sheep, cattle, and corn from the fertile Fens, while the tidal river Nene had turned it into a bustling port. It was an attractive town, with the broad sweep of its river and its imposing architecture.

The district had a long tradition of political dissent. The local peasantry

II. Wisbech, engraved in 1756 by Dr. Massey.

and craftsmen no doubt retained something of the spirit of staunch independence which had inspired the revolt in 1549 of twenty thousand men led by Robert Kett against enclosures of common land. In the following century, East Anglians formed the nucleus of Cromwell's New Model Army, organized the Independent movement, and listened enthusiastically to the teachings of the Levellers.

The religion of Godwin's family, however, was probably more important to his subsequent development. His family had been Dissenters for several generations. Although officially tolerated since 1689, the Dissenters were unable to participate freely in English life. Unless he was ready to conform to the articles of the Anglican Church, William Godwin would be unable to register his birth, marry officially, or be buried in consecrated ground. The national universities and all public offices would be closed to him. Not surprisingly, the Dissenters came to form a separate group and constituted a 'great, permanent undercurrent of dissatisfied criticsm of the State of England'.[1]

As with most Dissenters, both sides of Godwin's family came from the prosperous middle class. His paternal great-grandfather Edward had been an attorney in Newbury, where he was elected Mayor in 1706, and became the Town Clerk until his death in 1719. The wig of this illustrious ancestor remained as a relic in the family, and as a boy Godwin wore it several times, dressing himself up as Cato: the role of heroic republican was one which he readily assumed in later life.

Godwin was even more proud of his grandfather Edward, whom he consciously took as a model. Born in 1695, he was sent to the Dissenting academy directed by Samuel Jones at Tewkesbury and trained for the ministry. Among his fellow pupils were Isaac Watts, the hymn writer, Thomas Secker, later Archbishop of Canterbury, and Joseph Butler, the moral philosopher. In this excellent company, Edward Godwin was not, as his grandson put it, 'wholly unworthy'.[2] After a short period as joint tutor of an academy in Hungerford he became the minister at Little St. Helens, Bishopsgate Street, London, and turned the fashionable congregation into one of the most popular in the capital.

Godwin's grandfather was a man of great learning and pious disposition. He was a close friend of some of the leading Dissenting intellectuals: he supervised the printing of the Dr. Philip Doddridge's *The Family Expositor*, an abridged version of the New Testament, and Robert Blair asked him to criticize the manuscript of his poem *The Grave*. He published at least six volumes of sermons, a small volume of hymns, and a collection of Christian tales. At his funeral in 1764 Dr. William Langford declared that 'few have been more generally esteemed and loved by good Men of all Denominations than he was'.[3]

Both his two sons became ministers. The elder, Edward, having run a 'career of wildness & dissipation', was eventually converted by the Methodist George Whitefield.[4] He became a distinguished preacher and published many devout allegories, accounts of religious experiences, and hymns, but died young in 1764.

The other son, John, Godwin's father, was born on 21 February 1723. He attended the Dissenters' academy at Northampton, which was noted for its excellent scholarship and freedom of enquiry. He was lucky in having his father's friend Philip Doddridge as a tutor, and he not only adopted his moderate Calvinism but retained for him throughout his life a 'more affectionate veneration than for any other human being'.[5] Doddridge had a long-standing connection with the congregation in Wisbech, and he no doubt arranged his pupil's appointment as a minister there in 1746.

The Dissenters were a powerful group in Wisbech — the most active Christian body, without whom the town would have been 'utterly heathen'.[6] They were however in decline, and it may well have been a reduced congregation as much as an increase in his family that persuaded John Godwin to leave Wisbech two years after the birth of his seventh child, William.

The family moved in 1758 to the small market town of Debenham in Suffolk. The new congregation was not however an easy one: it had seen seventeen ministers in sixteen years.[7] A schism concerning Arianism soon broke out and forced the Trinitarian John Godwin to apply again in the midsummer of 1760 to the Independent Church of Christ in Guestwick, a remote village sixteen miles north of Norwich. It was a tiny place: there was no main street and its few inhabitants were scattered thinly for about a mile

III. Guestwick Old Meeting House, sketched in 1850 by Joseph Davey.

around. Here Godwin's father was to remain for the last twelve years of his life.

The chapel in Guestwick reflected the simple faith of its adherents. Built between 1672 and 1695, it was a plain rectangular structure of about twelve yards by sixteen, with a balcony on three sides and sash windows. It had strong republican roots and was founded by the Puritan Richard Worts in 1652, whose signature appears amongst the political papers of John Milton.[8] Godwin's father would also have sat in the pulpit in a finely carved oak chair known as Cromwell's chair. It may well have been presented by the Lord Protector himself, or by his son-in-law General Fleetwood, who lived at Irmingland Hall six miles away.

The area was among the most prosperous in the country. Norfolk was the chief producer of grain and Norwich the centre of the worsted industry. The prosperity, however, was not shared by the labourers and artisans of John Godwin's congregation. In the second half of the eighteenth century, the enclosure movement had an adverse effect on the peasantry. Unemployment increased. Despite higher productivity, the wages of the labourers rose about a quarter while the average price of purchases increased by at least 60 per cent.[9]

John Godwin's small congregation would travel up to eight miles from some thirty-seven villages around Guestwick. It did not prove a great success. During the twelve years of his rule, the congregation of seventeen members and forty or so subscribers more than halved.[10] Yet he seems to have been quite content to remain in this rural backwater, earning £60 a year, little more than the wages of a skilled artisan.

He was certainly not a man of learning. His son recalled that he spent little time studying:

> His sermon, for in my memory he only preached once on a Sunday, was regularly begun to be written in a very swift short-hand after tea on Saturday evening. I believe he was always free from any desire of intellectual distinction on a large scale; I know that it was with reluctance that he preached at any time at Norwich, in London, or any other place where he suspected that his accents might fall on the ear of criticism.

All the same, he discharged his duties conscientiously and spent much of his time visiting his congregation on horseback. He was, as his son remarked, regarded by his neighbours 'as a wise as well as a good man, and he desired no more'.

Godwin's attitude to his father seems to have been somewhat ambivalent. Although his father was extremely affectionate to the rest of his family, Godwin felt that he was singled out for ill-treatment: 'to me, who was perhaps never his favourite, his rebukes had a painful tone of ill humour and asperity'.[11] Godwin moreover recalled his death in 1772 with apparent indifference, merely commenting that he showed considerable reluctance to quit this world.

On the basis of this scanty evidence, it has been argued that Godwin reacted to his father's real or imagined antagonism by the contrary impulses of wanting first to become a minister, and then by rejecting his religion.[12] The recurrent theme of rebellion against a father figure in his novels is also put down to a badly resolved Oedipus complex.[13] Such an interpretation rests however on ambiguous evidence and runs counter to Godwin's own assertions. He described his father as 'a man of a warm heart and unblemished manners, ardent in his friendships, eager for the relief of distress whether of mind or circumstances, and decent and zealous in the discharge of his professional duties'.[14] He may have resented his father's rebukes, but his subsequent atheism and anarchism cannot be explained simply in terms of an unconscious parricide wish.

Nevertheless, his father was responsible for the atmosphere of austere piety which prevailed at home. A man of great temperance, 'extremely nice in his apparel, and delicate in his food', he was a strict Calvinist and steadfast Dissenter. He was scrupulous about religious observances. Godwin recalled that one Sunday, as he was walking in the garden, he took the family's cat in his arms: 'My father saw me, and seriously reproved my levity, remarking that on the Lord's day he was ashamed to observe me demeaning myself with such profaneness'.[15] When his son later expressed a desire to become a minister, he declared that he had 'a sort of pride & unsubmittingness' in him which was incompatible with the humility of the gospel. He always reproached him for his 'aristocracy' and for his 'want of religion'[16]

While he was a minister in Wisbech, John Godwin had married Ann Hull. Her family had originally owned landed property in Durham, but her father had settled in Wisbech after retiring from the Merchant Navy. He owned several vessels in King's Lynn, which plied their trade as far as the Baltic. In his short memoirs, Godwin makes only a passing reference to her family.

Godwin's mother received a scanty education, but she was a warm and affectionate person, moderating her husband's austerity. 'Some of the villagers', Godwin recalled, 'were impertinent enough to allege that she was too gay in her style of decorating her person. She was facetious, and had an ambition to be thought the teller of a good story, and an adept at hitting off a smart repartee. She was most obliging, submissive, and dutiful wife'.[17] After her husband's death, however, she became deeply religious, converted to Methodism, and grew extremely parsimonious. Her one worry was the infidelity of her offspring: 'How cuting a stroke it is', she lamented, 'to be the means of bringing Children into the world to be the subjects of the kingdom of Darkness to dwell with Divils and Damned Spirits . . .'[18] She would pray for Godwin three times a day, as well as during the sleepless hours of the night.

Godwin later rejected on utilitarian grounds the ties of consanguinity, and argued that it was the duty of the enlightened man to save in a fire a great benefactor like Archbishop Fénelon before his chambermaid, even if she were his mother or wife. He shocked his contemporaries by asking: 'What magic is there in the pronoun "my"' to overturn the decisions of everlasting truth? My wife or my mother may be a fool or a prostitute, malicious, lying or dishonest. If they be, of what consequence is it that they are mine?'[19] It was not, however, through maternal neglect that he later condemned the domestic affections. He always remembered his mother with great affection and warmth. He regretted that on doctor's advice he was sent from home for two years to be 'nourished by a hireling', but this was more from a hurt sense of dignity than a feeling of being spurned.[20] He believed that she always protected him in a mysterious way, and it was only when she died in 1809 that he felt truly alone for the first time.

Godwin was an exceptional child. Neither his eleven brothers nor his only sister seem to have excelled in any way. They became tradesmen, and for the most part, were poor, sick and unsuccessful. Through them he was able to experience vicariously the world of the farm, the small business, and the prison, as well as the lives of the sailor, the labourer, the journeyman, the clerk, the seamstress and the servant. Although Godwin was later to move amongst the leading intellectuals in the metropolis, there was a real personal basis to his social criticism and imaginative writing.

He was seventh of thirteen children and the third to survive infancy. Only eight were alive when their father died in 1772. Nothing is known of Edward, except that he died in Shoreditch in April 1776. Equally shadowy remains Conyers Jocelyn, who was born on 24 November 1769, assumed the name of John Hull, and died on board the 'Fox' on an unknown date.

The date of birth of Godwin's younger brother John is also unknown. He apparently hid successfully in 1788 from the press gang in Norfolk, and afterwards went to London to work in a low capacity in a firm. Although he boasted 'Seneca's morals', as his mother put it, he died almost starving in December 1805.[21] Nathaniel, born 19 February 1768, was the youngest. After a seven-year stint at sea, he too decided in 1799 to go into business but was forced to take a journeyman's place in 1805. He eventually returned to the navy, and probably died at sea. A closer brother was Joseph, whose dates of birth and death are also unknown. He chiefly distinguished himself by going to prison and by ill-using his wife Mary.

The only sister was Hannah, born on 7 April 1762. She became a dressmaker by trade but turned her hand to poetry and after Godwin was the best educated member of the family. Like her brothers, she was a constant worry to her mother. 'Poor dear Hannah', she lamented in 1788, 'once made it [religion] her Chief concern and happiness but I now fear it is otherwise'.[22] Hannah later saw Godwin regularly in London and discussed knowledgeably the principles of political justice. Her faith revived however before she died unmarried on 27 December 1817.

Godwin's closest brother was Philip Hull, born 13 March 1765, who called himself Hull. He remained a farmer in Norfolk, first on his father's estate in Wood Dalling, which he purchased in 1799, and then at East Bradenham. He became the most prosperous member of the family. He married on 6 March 1793 and had a large family of seven children – some of whose descendants were still alive in the neighbourhood in 1862.[23] The two brothers maintained an irregular but friendly correspondence, mainly about family affairs. Hull would sometimes send the odd ham or turkey from his farm and Godwin would forward little presents of books for the children.

An additional member of Godwin's large family was his father's first cousin Hannah, an ex-schoolmistress who came to live in the same household. Godwin's mother later told her son that she was 'a person you ought to Rever as your second Mother, who nurtured you in your infancy'.[24] Her whole time was spent in solitary devotion, reading religious books, and cultivating a garden.

Cousin Hannah was entrusted with the initial education of Godwin and probably exerted the greatest influence on him. There was little time for fun or games. Although Godwin had the honour to share her bed, she instructed him to make himself ready for sleep 'with a temper as if I were never to wake again in this sublunary world'.[25] The lesson made a deep impression on him. It was confirmed by reading five or six times at the age of five Bunyan's *Pilgrim's Progress,* with its gloomy Calvinist stress on human depravity and predestination.

The second book Godwin read was James Janeway's *A Token for Children* (1676), an 'Account of the Conversion, Holy and Exemplary Lives, and Joyful Deaths of Several Young Children'. If anything, its impact was even greater. The 'premature eminence' of the children, Godwin recalled, 'strongly excited my emulation. I felt as if I were willing to die with them, if I could with equal success engage the admiration of my friends and mankind.'[26] It helped trigger off a love of fame which became the ruling passion of Godwin's life.

His school life only confirmed the religious and moral influences which surrounded him at home. When he was four, he and a younger brother became the pupils of an old woman called Mrs Gedge who had seen twenty years of the previous century and was deeply religious. Godwin remembered her bitterly lamenting the adoption of the Gregorian calendar in September 1752, which dropped eleven days in the year, altered Christmas day, and led to riots throughout the country. Under her tuition, he read through the Old and New Testaments and acquired a close knowledge of their contents.

He was a precocious child. At the age of six he was able to write, enjoyed reading poetry, and wanted to be a poet. Bred after the strictest form of the Christian religion, he was regarded by many 'as a saint, and set apart for the public service of God from my mother's womb'.[27] Religion became the most essential part of his existence, and rendered him 'one of the gravest and most serious boys that ever lived'.[28] He was a stranger to the carefree joys of the village lads. Since he was endowed with a 'remarkably puny constitution', he was unable to play games.[29] Those about him were more solicitous for the health of his soul than for the health of his body. Indeed, he later felt that he never experienced childhood in the usual meaning of the term.

By the time he was eight he had already decided to become a minister. He began to preach sermons 'in the kitchen every Sunday afternoon, and at other times, mounted in a child's high chair, indifferent as to the muster of persons present at these exhibitions, and undisturbed at their coming and going'.[30] Later he became more concerned about his audience but his desire to reform his fellows never weakened.

On the death of his schoolmistress, Godwin went in April 1764 to a nearby school at Hindolveston. It was run by a self-educated journeyman tailor, Robert Akers, and had about a hundred pupils, a third of whom were boarders. Godwin again was isolated from his fellows since he was alone in liking his schoolmaster. He was also deeply disturbed by their religious laxity and tried to convert one poor village lad named Steele by preaching sin and damnation so effectively that he drew tears from his eyes. He even obtained secretly the key of his father's meeting house in order to preach and pray over the boy from the pulpit.

Akers was a man of extraordinary talents for such an obscure spot. He was not only an adept mathematician but a master of calligraphy: anyone who has read the neat script of Godwin's manuscripts must feel indebted to him. He had a smattering of Latin which he proceeded to teach to his docile pupil, thereby exciting a lifelong passion for the classics. He also encouraged emulation and competition amongst his pupils by offering prizes. They had an indelible effect upon Godwin's character, for rapid and easy success encouraged his 'overweening vanity & conceit'.[31] The astonished Akers declared that such a child had never come under his observation before.

The intellectual curiosity of the 'young Solomon', as his mother called him, was truly insatiable. He first read all the books in his father's library, which he imagined contained everything that it would be necessary for him to know. Even when he realized the extent of existing literature, he still looked forward 'with terror to the ample field of human life', wondering what he would do after having read all the books that had been written.[32] The most memorable works he read between the age of five and eleven were Watts's hymns, Gay's fables, and a history of England.

In the winter Godwin would stay in lodgings in Hindolveston, but in the summer he would walk to school from Guestwick across two and a half miles of fields and hedgerows. He made the journey in all weathers, accompanied by one of his brothers, from the age of six to eleven. Although he later said that he experienced 'exquisite feelings from the scenes of nature', he made no mention of these walks, and the vast sky and rolling plains of North Norfolk seem to have made little impression on him.[33] His mature taste was for more rugged and wilder landscapes.

It was not all religious meditation and scholarly study, however. When he was nine he went with his parents and his cousin on a tour of Norwich, King's Lynn and Wisbech to visit relatives. In Norwich his cousin took him to see Thomas Otway's play of political conspiracy *Venice Preserved* at a time when the theatre was frowned upon by the Dissenting community. In Wisbech they went to the races. He followed them with great interest, but never again was he to enjoy so profane a diversion. The village fair at home proved to be the happiest event of his childhood.

When Godwin was eleven, it was decided to send the rural prodigy to Norwich to develop his exceptional talents. He became the sole pupil of the Reverend Samuel Newton, an Independent Minister who preached at the Old Meeting House. Godwin later recalled that

> It was scarcely possible for any preceptor to have a pupil more pene-trated with curiosity and a thirst after knowledge than I was when I came under the roof of this man. All my amusements were sedentary; I had scarcely any pleasure but in reading; by my own consent, I should sometimes not so much as have gone into the streets for weeks together . . . . Add to this principle of curiosity a trembling sensibility and an insatiable ambition, a sentiment that panted with indescribable anxiety for the stimulus of approbation.[34]

He had therefore already developed the three features which he later felt were the principal indications of early genius: curiosity, candour, and love of distinction.[35] His austere upbringing, based more on strictness than love, on learning than play, on duty than pleasure, also left an indelible mark. Godwin may have appeared undemonstrative, but beneath a cool veneer he was full of passionate feeling. His apparent self-sufficiency masked a deep longing for friendship and his outward pride was a defence against self-doubt.

In fact childhood for Godwin was no lost golden age; it was rather a prolonged period of torture. When his cousin told him that the life of a child was happier than that of an adult, he remembered listening to her 'with much the same sort of sensation, as if she had told me that it was more eligible to partake the fate of the damned, than to go to heaven'.[36] Unfortunately, his stay in Norwich was only to confirm this view.

# CHAPTER II

# *Norwich*

When Godwin arrived in Norwich in 1767, it was the third largest city in England, with a population of over 35,000. It was a market for a great area, and had important leather and brewing industries. Keels and wherries sailed along the River Yare to Yarmouth, taking corn and malt to London and the North and returning with coal and fish.

For many centuries Norwich had also been the centre of the worsted trade in England, and most of the population were employed in the industry. It was controlled by a few big merchants, although most of the weavers were nominally independent and worked in their own homes. There had been high profits in the middle of the century but soon after the industry entered a period of recurrent depression and crisis.[1] A year before Godwin's arrival in the city, a serious bread riot occurred, during which the New Mills and many houses were attacked. Two of the rioters were later executed.[2] With the absence of local supplies of coal and flowing water, and growing competition from the textile manufacturers of West Riding and Lancashire, things could only get worse.

Not surprisingly, there was a renewed interest in politics in the region. In the year that Godwin arrived in Norwich, Charles Townsend as Chancellor of the Exchequer introduced the American Import Duties which caused so much discontent amongst the colonists and bitter remonstrance by the Opposition at home. Then in 1768, after the resignation of Chatham, the Whig Sir Edward Astley ousted one of the two Tory representatives of Norfolk in the first election for thirty-four years.[3]

In the same contest the celebrated reformer John Wilkes was elected for Middlesex. Considerable unrest broke out in Norfolk when he was arrested for libel under a general warrant and there was great rejoicing on his release from prison in April 1770. It marked a turning-point. Wilkes brought Parliament into disrepute, demonstrating both its unrepresentative nature

IV. Old Meeting House, Norwich.

and its potential threat to personal liberty. As elsewhere in the country, the campaign in his favour in Norfolk saw the rise of organized public opinion as a major force in public affairs.

Despite the apparent attraction of a bustling city for an eleven-year-old boy from a tiny hamlet, Godwin complained of the 'odiousness of the Norwichers'.[4] His world does not seem to have extended much beyond the congregation of his tutor at the Old Meeting House in Claygate. He was, however, at the centre of the Dissenters who were a very powerful force in the city.[5] The chapel, founded in 1643, counted John Cromwell, near relation of the Lord Protector, amongst its past ministers, and had remained the mother church of Norfolk Nonconformity.[6]

The Old Meeting House itself, built in 1693 and still standing today, is the first important example of Free Church architecture, a handsome, dignified building. Inside, the broad gallery, the plain family pews and the imposing pulpit speak of the confident prosperity and austere rectitude of the congregation. Clearly, religion for them was a deeply serious matter.

Samuel Newton had succeeded his father-in-law Dr. Samuel Wood in

1768. He had been educated for the ministry at Mile End, afterwards the Homerton Academy. He was apparently

> an interesting and respected character , a man of extraordinary vivacity, and a communicative, intelligent, entertaining companion. His features were well-formed and a strong interest was given to his whole countenance by an eye that was benignant, quick, penetrating, and which, when his mind was affected by any extraordinary emotions, seems to dart living fires in all those that surrounded him.[7]

The only surviving portrait of Newton bears out this description, although it does not show the strong marks of smallpox which disfigured his face.

Godwin has left us an unpleasant picture of Newton. His chief passion was polemics and he proved 'the most wretched of pedants'. Godwin found the expression in his eyes 'singularly cold & glaring' and felt it marked 'the greatness of his self complacency, & indifference to the sensations of others'. Indeed, Newton delighted to contemplate cruelty and torture, rather 'like a butcher, that has left off trade, but would with transport travel fifty miles for the pleasure of felling an ox'.

As for his wife, Godwin compared her to 'an animated statue of ice'. She would never, like Newton, 'put herself out of the way for the delight of giving anyone pain, but she was indifferent to their pleasures, as she might be said, in a popular sense, to be indifferent to her own'.[8] To stay with them as their only boarder was to prove a devastating experience for so sensitive a youth.

Previously Godwin had received only constant praise from his tutors which had encouraged a sense of self-esteem. Newton however complained of his proud stubbornness, and made 'detestable tirades' about his 'stiff neck'. Then one day during an angry dispute Newton suddenly birched his pupil. It came as a terrible shock.

It had never occurred to Godwin that his person could suffer such 'ignominious violation'. 'The idea', he wrote, 'had something in it as abrupt as a fall from heaven to earth. I had regarded this engine as the appropriate lot of the very refuse of the scholastic train.'[9] The injustice of the assault, coupled with the invasion of his physical integrity, left Godwin with an indelible hatred of coercion and violence.

Excessive reprimand, he later wrote, will only embitter the mind of an ingenious youth: 'He shuts up the sense of this despotism in his own bosom; and it is the first lesson of independence and rebellion and original sin.'[10] It was the experience of being the sole pupil of a severe tutor which also led Godwin to reject Rousseau's system of solitary instruction, and to recommend a middle path between private and public education in order to

V. Samuel Newton, artist unknown.

soften the 'slavery' of the 'tyrant' preceptor.[11]

Godwin's rebellion against Newton took the form of violating the symbol of his rule: his library. When his tutor was out, he would borrow his books without asking permission. Analyzing his own motives, he later wrote: 'I never asked for a thing then, when there was a chance of being refused. I was under the control of a despot; & I resolved he should not be a despot to me, where I could avoid it. Never mortal felt more energetically the sentiment, "My mind, my mind shall be the master of me!" '[12]

Indeed, Godwin seems to have drawn on this experience with Newton in his novels. In *Caleb Williams*, for example, the situation of Caleb and his master Falkland neatly parallels the relationship between Godwin and Newton. Like Godwin, Caleb is possessed by an insatiable curiosity. There is an obvious analogy between Godwin's clandestine invasion of the library and Caleb's opening of his master's secret trunk which precipitates his downfall. In both cases, their pursuit of knowledge is a means of over-throwing their oppressors, and their actual rebellion is marked by feelings of triumph and guilt. It is perhaps more than a coincidence that Godwin compares both Newton and Falkland with Nero and Caligula.[13]

Again, in *Mandeville* the protagonist's tutor Hilkiah Bradford appears to be a direct portrait of Newton. A man of utmost integrity, he is nevertheless, imbued with all the prejudices that belong to 'the most strait-laced of the members of his sacred profession'. As a tutor he is inflexible and austere; he demands submission, humility, and hard work. He reprimands with great vigour his pupil's defects, particularly his conceit and 'carnal pride of an unregenerate nature'. Like Godwin, the young Mandeville submits outwardly but retains 'the principle of rebellion entire, shut up in the chamber' of his thoughts.[14]

Although forced into submission, Godwin managed to escape from his unhappy and lonely situation into the world of the imagination. He later wrote that he was given to 'reveries' and during his walks he would compose books of 'fictitious adventures in the mode of Richardson' and of 'imaginary institutions in education and government, where all was to be faultless'.[15] He was moreover undoubtedly referring to himself when describing the solitary schoolboy who

> hovers on the brink of the deepest philosophy, enquiring how came I here, and to what end. He becomes a castle-builder, constructing imaginary colleges and states, and searching out the businesses in which they are to be employed, and the schemes by which they are to be regulated. He thinks what he would do, if he possessed uncontrolable strength, if he could fly, if he could make himself invisible. In this train of mind he cons his first lessons of liberty and independence. He learns self-reverence, and says to himself, I also am an artist, and a maker.[16]

Newton's varied and extensive library provided ample material for Godwin's imaginary voyages. The books which had the greatest impact on his mind between the age of twelve and thirteen were Rollin's *Ancient History,* Rapin's *History of England*, an abridgement of Richardson's *Clarissa Harlowe,* Fielding's *Tom Jones,* Swift's *Tale of a Tub,* and Smollett's *Roderick Random.* Between the age of fourteen and fifteen, they were Locke's *Some Thoughts concerning Education,* Addison's *Cato*, Milton's *Paradise Regained,* an abridgement of Collier's *Short View of the Immorality and Profaneness of the English Stage,* Plato on the death of Socrates and a biography of Alfred. Swift, Richardson, Smolett, Addison, Locke and Milton all remained favourite authors.

Godwin particularly remembered how he read the early volumes of the English translation of Charles Rollin's *Ancient History* with the 'greatest transport'. It was from Rollin that he 'drank in the love of liberty and of public virtue'.[17] It proved to be the third most important experience of his childhood:

The first impulse I received was from Calvinism: the unrighteous shall scarcely be saved &c. The second from eulogium: Mrs. Sothren, Akers &c. The third from Rollin, History of the Invasion of Greece by the Persians. The first infused a solemn tone of mind, the second self-esteem, the third enthusiasm.[18]

Newton seems to have given his pupil an advanced education for his tender years. Unlike Godwin's father, he was a man of learning. He published many works and articles for the theological journals.[19] The catholicity of his reading and the extent of his knowledge may be indicated by his later praise for some of his pupil's ideas in *Political Justice* which he felt surpassed in 'simplicity, elegance, force and utility' all that he had ever read in Tacitus, Polybius, Montesquieu, Grotius, Robertson, Price or Priestley. He encouraged Godwin in particular to read the American philosopher Jonathan Edwards. His correspondence also shows that he was familiar with the writings of Hume and Johnson, and advocated the philosophy of necessity, the association of ideas, and the immutability of truth.[20]

In his religion and politics, Newton professed extreme views. He was both an uncompromising disciple of the ultra-Calvinist Robert Sandeman and an ardent supporter of John Wilkes. Hitherto the malleable Godwin had adopted his father's moderate Calvinism and Whiggism, but placed under the stern guidance of Newton, he was unable to defend his position: 'I was his single pupil', he recollected, 'and his sentiments speedily became mine.'[21]

Newton was no religious bigot. He condemned the 'intemperate zeal' with which most religious controversies were treated, and addressed his arguments to the 'impartial Reader'.[22] He tried to base them on the Scriptures, reason and common sense. He extended the principle of religious toleration to Quakers, and even deists.

Yet Newton followed the teaching of Robert Sandeman, the most radical Calvinist in the eighteenth century. Sandeman was a disciple and son-in-law of the Scottish minister John Glas, but his followers broke away from the Scottish Establishment after 1762.[23] They seemed to have attracted more notoriety than converts.[24] Their churches were never very numerous in England; and outside London, societies were formed only in Norwich, Nottingham, Liverpool, Whitehaven and Newcastle. Indeed, Newton's own congregation declined during his fifty-six-year rule to 'the mouldering ruins of a noble edifice' because of the 'perpetual earnestness' with which he enforced Sandemanian principles.[25]

In practice, Sandeman applied the most literal interpretation of the New Testament: he advocated the abstinence from blood and strangled meat, the washing of feet, the weekly observance of the Lord's supper, and the distribution of wealth to the needy. In theory, he restricted the possibility of grace to a tiny minority. Furthermore, and this is perhaps the most radical aspect of Sandeman's thought, grace could not be achieved by good works or faith, but only by the rational perception of divine truth.[26]

After Calvin had damned ninety-nine in a hundred of mankind, Godwin joked bitterly, Sandeman had

> contrived a scheme for damning ninety-nine in a hundred of the follow-
> ers of Calvin. Calvin has sufficiently guarded against the merit of good-
> works, but Sandeman undertakes to show a flaw in his passport for the
> elect, & demonstrates that, after we have dispossessed the devil of the
> battery of good-works, he gains possession of the citadel by imposing
> upon us the merit of faith. In a word, he incontestibly shows that many
> repented orthodox divines have represented faith as an act of the will or a
> disposition of the heart, *whereas God works to save or damn a man but
> according to the right or wrong judgment of his understanding.* Hence he
> infers, that these repented orthodox divines in addition to the acknow-
> ledged corps of heretics, pagans, & infidels, shall without doubt perish
> everlastingly. This scheme for damning the good, simple souls, who
> never suspected a word of the matter, but thought themselves cock-sure
> of everlasting life, was the favourite topic of Newton's discourses.[27]

Godwin's exposure to Sandemanianism under Newton's roof ruthlessly reinforced his early Calvinist upbringing and he was to remain an adherent to the rigid and gloomy creed until he was twenty-five. Ever since he was a boy, the Calvinist doctrine of predestination had weighed on his spirits. He had heard his father and other ministers preach, 'Lord, we put our hands on our mouths, and our mouths in the dust, and cry out, Guilty, guilty, Unclean, unclean.'[28] Now his worst fears about his future state were confirmed by his Sandemanian tutor who insisted that 'Christianity supposes mankind to be degenerate, totally lost and miserable.'[29] He became convinced that if he died, he would go straight to the Devil.

Fate, guilt, and fear later became common ingredients of his novels. In *Caleb Williams,* a terrifying tale of flight and pursuit, he transposed all the horror he felt as a boy for the Calvinist God. Falkland, the pursuer, warns Caleb, his victim: 'You might as well think of escaping from the power of the omnipresent God, as from mine!' For his part, Caleb describes Falkland's pursuit 'like what has been described of the eye of omniscience pursuing the guilty sinner'.[30] The novel *Mandeville* shows that twenty-five years later Godwin was still living emotionally in the Calvinist universe. Mandeville feels convinced that he was linked for evil with his rival Clifford: 'I saw as plainly the records of the BOOK OF PREDESTINATION on this subject, as the Almighty being in whose single custody the BOOK for ever remains

. . . The letters glowed and glittered, as if they were written with the beams of the sun, upon the dark tablet of Time that Hath not yet Been.'[31]

The Calvinist doctrines of the omnipotence and inscrutability of God and the nothingness and depravity of man seem to have encouraged feelings of deep loneliness in Godwin. Throughout his schooldays, he felt cut off from his fellows and was considered by them as something 'odd and unaccountable'.[32] The central characters in all his novels are significantly lonely individuals who crave for companions. Indeed, in his adult life, his friendships became affairs of passion, full of jealousies, hurt feelings, and quarrels. Friendship, he knew, is a 'necessity of our nature, the stimulating and restless want of every susceptible heart.'[33]

He suffered, even more, from a permanent sense of anxiety. The Sandemanians were notorious for the 'chill' which seized their devotions.[34] Godwin recalled that their creed 'paralysed' the understanding: if a man feels he is of the elect, he experiences a 'sacred horror and a nameless fear of that God who has thus miraculously rescued him'; if he thinks he is damned, he looks forward to a future 'with emotions of indescribable horror, and not seldom has the faculties of his mind utterly subverted with the anticipation of the dreadful sentence that awaits him in another world'.[35]

In his fragments of self-analysis, Godwin admitted that no one was 'less like what is vulgarly called a man of courage'.[36] Indeed, in a moment of insight, he recognized that one of the sources of his excessive love of fame was probably his 'timidity and embarrassment'.[37] Psychologically, in Godwin's case, it seems that to be socially esteemed was not very different from being in a state of divine grace. Just as the young Calvinist Godwin searched for assurance of divine justification in the innermost recesses of his heart, so he tried later to overcome his feelings of anxiety by trying to win the stamp of social approval.

Godwin then was never able to free himself emotionally from his early Calvinism. But while the experience may have caused him permanent psychological damage, it did have its advantages. Much of the imaginative power of the novels may be traced to its impact. His Calvinist training probably disciplined his personality to such an extent that he was later able to entertain sanguine hopes for all mankind to live in a society without laws and government. Above all, had Godwin not been such an extreme Calvinist in his youth he would probably never have developed by reaction such a profound humanism and so radical a philosophy.

In a more specific way, Calvinism and its more extreme Sandemanian form helped shape some of the most characteristic aspects of Godwin's mature philosophy. As Hazlitt rightly observed, Godwin was 'a mixture of the Stoic and of the Christian philosopher', and *Political Justice* was a 'metaphysical and logical commentary on some of the most beautiful and striking texts of Scripture'.[38] Godwin himself moreover acknowledged in a notebook how strongly its three principal errors were connected with 'the Calvinistical system, which had been wrought into my mind in early life, as to enable these errors long to survive the general system of religious opinion of which they formed a part'.[39]

The first error which Godwin apprehended was 'Stoicism, or the inattention to the principle, that pleasure & pain are the only bases upon which morality can rest'.[40] In the austere separation between God and his creatures, it was natural for the Calvinist to see the world as permanently lost and steeped in sin. It therefore became his duty to practice self-discipline and self-control in a life devoted to obeying the will of God. Indeed, Newton argued that a religious society was a cause 'totally distinct from all worldly schemes of ambition, pleasure and interest', and sternly warned his congregation against 'Pharisaical Ostentation' and intemperance.[41]

In the first edition of *Political Justice*, Godwin maintained that it grows out of a clear and unanswerable theory of the human mind that our 'only true felicity consists in the expansion of our intellectual powers, the knowledge of truth, and the practice of virtue'. He tried to justify this preference on utilitarian grounds, but it is clear that he condemned sensual pleasure for its own sake. He was simply unable to escape from his Calvinist conviction that the voluptuary is 'the bane of the human species'.[42]

'Sandemanianism, or an inattention to the principle that feeling, and not judgment, is the source of human action', was the second error a wiser Godwin detected.[43] A suspicion of all emotion is, of course, central to the Calvinist tradition as a whole, since it was thought that it would divert God's creatures from salvation and promote idolatrous superstitions. But the Sandemanians were notorious even among Calvinists for the abstract and intellectual nature of their creed, and their leader made it the chief article of his faith that all the 'divine power' which operated in the minds of men is 'the forcible conviction of Truth'.[44]

Godwin was undoubtedly thinking of the Sandemanians when he referred in *Political Justice* to certain religionists who see 'a close and indissoluble connection' between a man's internal sentiments and his external conduct.[45] In fact, Godwin came to rest his whole theory of perfectibility on the belief that 'The Voluntary Actions of Men Originate in their Opinions': by changing their opinions, one would inevitably transform their behaviour.[46] Ironically enough, the most characteristic and extravagant of Godwin's doctrines, the lynch pin of his entire rationalist system, finds its source in the fanatical creed of an obscure eighteenth-century divine.

The final error that Godwin felt was srongly connected with his early Calvinism was the 'unqualified condemnation of the private affections'.[47] The Sandemanians took Christ's golden rule as a universally applicable natural law; Newton even argued that one should love one's neighbour not through any 'partiality' or 'natural affection' but only for the 'truth's sake'.[48] Sandemanian congregations would hold love-feasts every Sabbath to celebrate the Last Supper, and members would imitate Christ and wash each other's feet.

Universal benevolence was no new development in morals in the eighteenth century, but Godwin's exposure to the ritualized brotherly love of Newton's congregation helped make him the most implacable enemy of private affections, exclusive friendships, and gratitude. He reached these outrageous conclusions, as Hazlitt remarked, by making a 'literal, rigid, unaccomodating, and systematic interpretation of the text . . . "Thou shalt love thy neighbour as thyself" '.[49] Indeed, Godwin later held 'morality principally to depend, agreeably to the admirable maxim of Jesus, upon our putting ourselves in the place of another, feeling his feelings, and apprehending his desires; in a word, doing to others, as we would wish, were we they, to be done unto.'[50]

The Sandemanianism which Godwin imbibed under Newton's roof in Norwich further shaped his mature thought in ways which he never overtly recognized. Although many accused the Sandemanians of being antinomians, their leader stoutly defended the doctrine of natural law on the evidence of the Scriptures: the conscience of man conceives its duty from the impressions formed by natural relations so that round the globe 'No tradition, no custom, can ever shake our approbation of this maxim [the golden rule], however much we depart from it in practice.'[51] The idea of a universally recognizable natural law is at the heart of Godwin's philosophy. Just as Sandeman asserted that the conscience of man has a universal ability to discover the moral law, so Godwin upheld the power of reason to discern 'immortal and ever present truth'.[52] Godwin did not have to go to Plato or his disciples for his belief in eternal truths.[53]

This belief in natural law had an important corollary for man-made laws. Sandeman affirmed that men everywhere, in all ages, had 'by far too much law and too little righteousness'.[54] Godwin entirely agreed. Right transcends law: there can be no 'authority so paramount, as to have the prerogative of making that to be law, which abstract and immutable justice had not made to be law previously to that interposition'.[55] This conviction is the cornerstone of Godwin's philosophical anarchism.

The influence of Sandemanianism on Godwin was no less important in his economic thought. In their effort to follow every precept of the Scriptures, the Sandemanians practised a form of communism similar to that of the early Christian Churches. While they engaged in trade outside the sect, every member had to consider his property subject to the claims of the body, and no one was allowed to accumulate a fortune, which was termed 'laying up treasures on earth, in defiance of the Redeemer's prohibition'.[56]

Godwin specifically stated in *Political Justice* that religion had inculcated the 'pure principles of justice' and and that a condemnation of accumulated property had been the foundation of all religious morality.[57] Referring to Mark X, 21 and Acts II, 44-5, he affirmed that the most energetic religious teachers had also taught the rich that they are strictly accountable for 'every atom of their expenditure'.[58] And like the Sandemanians he proposed a voluntary communism of use: since all human beings are partakers of a common nature, it follows upon the principle of justice that the 'good things of the world are a common stock, upon which one man has as valid a title as another to draw for what he wants'.[59]

In a more diffuse way, Godwin's period with Newton encouraged the egalitarian and democratic tendency of his thought. The Sandemanians were noted for their belief that 'no one of mankind has the least room to glory over another' since 'all men are equally fit for justification, or equally destitute of any plea for acceptance with God'.[60] They therefore considered the distinctions of civil life to be annihilated in the church. Not only were their officers elected from the congregation but deaconesses could be elected from the aged widows. Even public worship was not exclusively conducted by the elders, and any member of the sect could take his or her turn.

Newton's entire congregation would decide in matters concerning its organization and discipline. In all important questions the whole church had to be unanimous, since they felt that to decide by a majority supposed in the minority a dissatisfaction which would be contrary to charity or the love of brethren. On two occasions, in 1782 and 1803, Newton's assistants went off with the minority to form separate chapels after failing to reach complete agreement on doctrinal issues. There is no vice more wicked, Newton told his congregation, than 'the love and abuse of power and authority', and he offered to resign his pastoral office whenever a majority of the members required it.[61]

Each member of the congregation was also subject to the surveillance of his brethren, and had a duty to inform his neighbour of his transgressions. Anyone who fell into gross sin on more than one occasion would be excommunicated. This happened in Newton's congregation for sins ranging from adultery and the neglect of worship, to fraud. In the stricter sects, it was held unlawful to eat, drink or converse in civil life with an excommunicated member or atheist.

Godwin was clearly impressed. He became greatly concerned with the moral status of the outvoted minority, and felt that a majority has no more right to coerce a minority, even a minority of one, than a despot has to coerce a majority. If a minority, moreover, is obliged to carry out the decisions of a majority, it 'inevitably renders mankind timid, dissembling, and corrupt'.[62] He equally believed in perfect sincerity and mutual inspection, and thought public opinion is a force on man 'not less irresistible than whips and chains' to reform his conduct.[63]

Unlike the Sandemanians, however, Godwin saw the dangers of the unchecked power of the congregation over its members. His remedy for contention was not expulsion from the body politic but further discussion, for the omnipotence of truth would eventually ensure agreement. Similarly, he was opposed to the Sandemanians' emphasis on godly watchfulness. Whatever the stress he placed on the educative role of public opinion, Godwin was utterly opposed to its tyranny, and made the right of private judgment the basis of his moral and political philosophy. Thus while he developed the liberal and democratic aspects of Sandemanianism, he uncompromisingly rejected its repressive tendencies.

Many of Sandeman's followers were criticized for practising their beliefs only in their sects and for neglecting the 'poor, ignorant, perishing multitude'.[64] Newton, however, extended his radicalism from the religious to the political sphere. Christianity, he maintained, is the 'most friendly system to the equality and liberty of mankind that ever was published'.[65] Godwin recalled that he was an enthusiastic supporter of Wilkes and an 'ardent champion' of political liberty.[66] In the 1790s, Newton was not actively involved in politics, but many of the leading radicals in Norwich were members of his congregation.[67]

But the awesome Newton did not spend his entire time inculcating religious and political beliefs into his sole pupil. There were some profane pursuits: Godwin was sent to dancing classes for a while, although he did not enjoy them. He was naturally clumsy and his legs were too short. He often recalled however the kindness of a fellow pupil who arranged for him to dance with Miss Carter, a 'very plain' girl but a good dancer who was at the head of the school.[68] His pleasure seems to have been derived more from a sense of ambition than from any personal attraction.

At the same time, Godwin's religious zeal did not diminish in intensity. He contracted smallpox at the age of twelve, having steadfastly refused on religious grounds to allow himself to be inoculated. During the illness he experienced ringing in the ears, a bursting head and languor. He was conscious of being entirely detached from life and ready to die. When he recovered, he rapidly took up his proselytizing again. To his supreme delight, his tutor's son Samuel, who had much difficulty in praying before others, agreed to come into his room and pray with him.

Although Godwin left an unpleasant picture of the cold and sadistic Newton, it must be said that his pupil was not exactly without faults himself. It is difficult to defend the young Godwin from the charge of being a prig.

He was certainly very conceited and had an exalted view of his own dignity. When he was thirteen or fourteen, for instance, he went by himself to the Sessions House in Norwich during the Assizes. Having his choice of seat, he placed himself immediately next to the Bench where Lord Chief Justice De Grey presided. 'As I stayed some hours', he recalled characteristically,

> I at one time relieved my posture by leaning my elbow on the corner of the cushion placed before his lordship. On some occasion, probably when he was going to address the jury, he laid his hand gently on my elbow and removed it. On this action I recollected having silently remarked, if his lordship knew what the lad beside him will perhaps one day become I am not sure that he would have removed my elbow.[69]

Godwin does not seem to have changed a great deal later. When he looked back to his youth in his seventies, he felt that for all his changes in opinion he had remained the 'same individual all through'.[70] This is borne out by the interesting correspondence which arose between Newton and Godwin after the publication of *Political Justice*. The old Calvinist naturally disapproved of his atheist views but confessed that 'it has such a cast of character in it from its author, that I am inclined to think I should have known it to have been yours, had not your name stood in the title page'.[71]

The disputes between Godwin and Newton reached a head in June 1770. Under the pretext of no longer wanting to become a minister, the unhappy and self-righteous pupil was sent back to the school in Hindolveston run by Akers. A servant's bawdy stories proved the most notable experience during this period. Godwin returned to Newton in the following March, hoping for fairer treatment, and was not wholly disappointed. Newton however dismissed him abruptly in December 1771, declaring that he had nothing more to teach him. Godwin was now approaching his sixteenth birthday. Akers took him on once again, this time not as a pupil but as an assistant master in writing and arithmetic. The experience stood Godwin in good stead; he was able to try out a libertarian approach in teaching the village children and began to develop his own educational theories.

When not teaching, he indulged in his favourite pastime — reading. He devoured Fielding's *Tom Jones,* Defoe's *Robinson Crusoe,* Fénelon's *Dialogues of the Dead* and *Telemachus,* Janeway's *Token for Children,* a *Life of Aesop,* and a *Life of Doddridge,* as well as the works of Spenser, Pope, and Sterne, and the whole of Shakespeare.[72] He still lived in a world of his own making and read books not so much for their moral import as for their tendency to excite his imagination. He followed up his early passion for poetry and anticipated his later moral and political concerns by planning an epic poem on Brutus, the founder of the Roman Republic who allowed his sons to be put to death for conspiracy against the Commonwealth.

At Hindolveston, Godwin began to read in his leisure the *Gentleman's Magazine*, paying particular attention to the records of the parliamentary debates. As a result his politics underwent a great revolution: 'being struck with the intemperance of all oppositions, & the repeated assertion that, if such a measure were adopted, our liberties were gone, I extracted a spirit of confidence, for the most part, in the wisdom and rectitude of the administration'.[73] He was to remain a Tory and a supporter of the aristocracy for the next seven years. It is worth noting, however, that Godwin became a Tory, a unique position amongst the Dissenting community, because of a regard for 'our liberties' and a fear of the 'intemperance' of the Wilkite opposition. This change in his political opinions may also have been prompted by a partial reaction against Newton: Godwin possibly associated his former tutor's enthusiasm for Wilkes with his eager use of the birch.

When Godwin's father died on 12 November 1772, his mother moved to a small property he had left her in Wood Dalling, a few miles from Guestwick. Although by no means rich, she decided to send her most gifted son to a Dissenting academy in London so that he might realize his childhood ambition to become a minister. An interview was arranged at Newton's old college, Homerton Academy. Godwin set off with his mother in April 1773, a month after his seventeenth birthday.

The journey, which took three days by coach, was a memorable one. They spent some days at Hide Hall near Subridgeworth, the residence of Sir Conyers Jocelyn, where Godwin was later to pass two or three weeks each year during his student life. The interview at Homerton however was a failure. The tutors John Stafford and Noah Hill suspected him of Sandemanianism and rejected his application.

Godwin decided to remain in London and lodged from April to May with one John Jacob, a druggist in Fish Street Hill in the City. The household was alive with political discussion. His host, like his former tutor Newton, was 'a most zealous champion of the Wilkite party', and not surprisingly the young Tory Godwin 'immediately conceived a warm attachment & profound deference' to his brother Joseph, who was 'politically in total hostility, without any breach of fraternal accord'.[74]

Godwin then spent the summer with some of his mother's relatives at Gravesend and Stockbury in Kent. One of the first things he did was to procure from the circulating library in Rochester the works of Robert Sandeman in order to compare his new principles with his previous habits of thinking and to find out the exact grounds of Stafford's accusation. He also wrote a harmony of the gospels, without the assistance of any commentator.

The diligent Godwin did not forget his other studies. He read Voltaire's plays and two volumes of Hume. He was inspired by his beloved Rollin to plan two tragedies: one on the subject of Iphigenia in Aulis, and the other on the death of Caesar. But he was unable to complete them, for in September the New College at Hoxton accepted him as a student.

At the age of seventeen and a half, Godwin was an unusual adolescent. Never having played games, he was intellectually precocious and almost entirely concerned with religious matters. The absence of companions and the harsh treatment of his preceptor had forced him to escape into a world of the imagination and to find his principal joy in reading. He had already developed the leading features of his adult character. He possessed an inquisitive and sceptical mind which did not shrink from extreme conclusions and yearned for fame and applause. His love of liberty and public virtue was matched by his hatred of intemperance and violence. He had decided to become a minister and a writer. But as he entered Hoxton Academy, a Sandemanian and a Tory, there was little external indication that he would one day become the greatest exponent of philosophical anarchism.

# CHAPTER III

## *Hoxton Academy*

Just as Godwin's early Calvinist upbringing had indelibly shaped his personality, so Hoxton Academy was to give a permanent and distinctive tenor to his thinking. Godwin was doubly fortunate in going to the Dissenting academy at Hoxton: it was one of the best academic institutions in England in the eighteenth century and its tutors Andrew Kippis and Abraham Rees were leading representatives of the English Enlightenment.

The Dissenters, excluded from the national universities by the demand for subscription to the articles of the Anglican Church, had been compelled to provide higher education for themselves. 'While your universities', Joseph Priestley wrote in 1787, 'resemble pools of *stagnant water* secured by dams and mounds and offensive to the neighbourhood, ours are like *rivers*, which, taking their natural course, fertilize a whole country.'[1] They not only produced many distinguished professional men, but some of the leading controversialists of the day.[2]

The education of their children was an overriding concern of the Dissenters. Their approach was based on the Lockean notion of the mind as a *tabula rasa* formed by experience. The recurrent theme of their educational writings was the precept: 'Train up a child in the way he should go, and when he is old, he will not depart from it.'[3] In general, the academies believed that sound learning was the first ally of true religion. But in Godwin's youth, they were taking an increasingly utilitarian turn, and Kippis at Hoxton wanted to convey a 'knowledge which invigorates the understanding, which inspires noble and enlarged sentiments of liberty, and tends to form a manly character'.[4]

The excellence of the academies lay in the width and novelty of their curriculum. They tended to pursue the ideal of universal science and at Hoxton Godwin's studies included the classics, Hebrew, logic, ethics, divinity, rhetoric, mathematics, natural philosophy and pneumatology. Particular importance was given to history and politics. Unfortunately, the very breadth of the curriculum meant a loss in depth, and the academies were sometimes criticized for trying to make students digest 'the whole *Encyclopedia* in *three* years'.[5]

The principal method of teaching was extraordinarily liberal in the sense of being quite undogmatic. Priestley recalled that the academies were 'exceedingly favourable to free inquiry' and that the students were referred to authors on both sides of every question, and were even required to give an account to them.[6] Doddridge, the most famous Dissenting pedagogue in the eighteenth century, further decided to substitute English for Latin as the language of the lecture room at Northampton Academy. Since there were very few textbooks written in English, tutors were obliged to write their own or to circulate the manuscripts of their lectures. A singular kind of scholarship therefore developed within the academies, and the tutors exerted a pervasive influence on their pupils.

Hoxton Academy was originally founded in 1701 and had been supported by the Coward Trust from 1738.[7] When it moved to Hoxton in 1762 the philosopher Richard Price declined the offer of a post, but its director Samuel Morton Savage was joined by Rees and Kippis. Despite their different ages, the three men were 'distinct and unsubordinate tutors', in the theological, mathematical and philological departments respectively.[8] A homely atmosphere was encouraged and the thirty-odd boarders were able to get to know each other well and receive personal tuition.

Godwin made good use of his time and the facilities at Hoxton. He had a passionate love of truth and a strong awareness of the contingency of his own opinions:

> 'Why should I,' such was the language of my solitary meditations, 'because I was born in a certain degree of latitude, in a certain century, in a country where certain institutions prevail, and of parents professing a certain faith, take it for granted that all this is right? — This is a matter of accident.'[9]

He therefore tried to take a survey of the world of knowledge during his five-year stay at the college. Deeply impressed with the Horatian maxim that *'art is long*, and *life is short'*, he thought it best to read a few things but read them well.[10] He decided to divide each day into several parts and to devote each one to a particular subject. It was a rule of study to which he adhered without interruption for most of his life.

The fundamental text at Hoxton was Doddridge's *Course of Lectures on the Principal Subjects in Pneumatology, Ethics and Divinity.* Jewish antiquities and ecclesiastical history were also studied, as well as the principal commentaries on the Scriptures.[11] When not working from their own notes, the tutors would have referred to William Wollaston's *Religion of Nature Delineated* (1724) (with its appeal to reason and mathematical demonstration), Francis Hutcheson's *System of Moral Philosophy* (1755) (with its emphasis on benevolence and utility as the cornerstones of virtue), and Isaac Watts's *Logick: or the Right Use of Reason in the Enquiry after Truth* (1725) (with its celebration of reason and hatred of prejudice).

Doddridge was a major influence in Godwin's education in more ways than one. Godwin's grandfather had been Doddridge's intimate friend and helped publish his *Family Expositor*. His father had been Doddridge's pupil at Northampton Academy and had adopted his tempered Calvinism. And now at Hoxton, Godwin came in daily contact with Kippis who compared Doddridge to Cicero and considered him no less than 'my benefactor, my tutor, my friend, and my father'.[12]

Doddridge's course of *Lectures* made a profound impression on Godwin. Its method was mathematical: the doctrine to be discussed was first stated as a proposition, and then followed by demonstration, scholium, corollary and lemma. Both sides of each question were presented and the students were encouraged to abridge the chief controversies for themselves.[13] Godwin was later to follow this approach very closely in *Political Justice* by first stating the question of each chapter, then discussing the arguments for and against it, before finally drawing a conclusion. He did not add, like Doddridge, Q.E.D., but that is the implication.

The lectures on pneumatology were principally concerned with the study of human nature, but stretched from the investigation of the mechanism of the brain to knowledge of ethical and metaphysical systems. Doddridge drew heavily on Locke, whose works at the time were banned at Oxford, but were venerated alongside the Bible in the academies. Godwin therefore received a thorough grounding in sensationalist psychology. In a chronological list of his philosophical principles, he included for the year 1779 whilst at Hoxton: 'mind is a substance of perfect simplicity: its faculties, modifications of that substance'.[14] He always considered Locke's *Essay concerning Human Understanding* to be 'the foundation of every thing of value which has since been written on the subject'.[15]

Doddridge also seems to have influenced Godwin's views of ethics and politics. He argued with Shaftesbury that virtue is founded on the *'eternal measure* and immutable *relation of things'* and followed Hutcheson and Balguy in defining it as the 'law of universal benevolence'.[16] Godwin dutifully recorded amongst his philosophical principles for 1776: 'human actions do not constantly originate in self love'.[17] Again, Doddridge devoted ten lectures of his course to politics and through them Godwin would have become acquainted with Pufendorf, Grotius, Sidney and

Locke. Doddridge embraced the social contract theory and grounded obedience in hedonistic utilitarianism: 'Every man is born in a *state of freedom*' and is no further obliged to submit to a government unless he judges that it will be 'for the good of the whole'.[18] Godwin followed suit and was to make the right of private judgment and the principle of utility the cornerstones of his political philosophy.

As well as psychology, ethics and politics, the academies distinguished themselves in science and mathematics. Abraham Rees was Godwin's tutor in this area, and drew on the lectures of his former tutor John Eames, who had been a friend of Isaac Newton and a member of the Royal Society. Godwin later lamented that his decision to limit his studies led him to ignore every branch of 'natural philosophy' and 'useful knowledge'.[19] He was, however, apt at arithmetic and geometry. He learned enough of Newtonian science to conceive of the universe as a vast system of interrelated events and to recognize that Newton had done for matter what Locke had done for mind.[20] Despite his lack of scientific qualifications, Godwin moreover felt able in his old age to discuss problems in astronomy, geography and phrenology, and to quote, among others, Buffon, Herschel, Newton, Copernicus, Kepler, Halley, Lavater, and Gall.[21]

Of all his tutors, it was undoubtedly Andrew Kippis who most influenced Godwin at Hoxton. Kippis was a leading Dissenter as well as a renowned scholar. He was elected a Fellow of the Society of Antiquarians and of the Royal Society. His sympathy for parliamentary reform led him to join the Whig Club, the Society of Friends of the People, and the Revolution Society. He founded the Whig journal *The New Annual Register* and devoted the last years of his life to the editorship of the mammoth but incomplete *Biographia Britannica*. Richard Price and Joseph Priestley were his intimate friends. He represented everything that was best in Dissenting culture, and as Rees observed, he united an 'inflexible integrity and an independence of spirit, which disdained every thing that was mean, selfish and servile'.[22]

Kippis was Godwin's tutor in philosophy, classics, *belles-lettres* and chronology. His favourite subject was *belles-lettres,* which covered the study of literature, the history of taste, universal grammar and practical criticism. By studying the best works of ancient and modern literature, he wished to make the sentiments of his students 'accurate and enlarged' and to develop their 'implanted' sense of 'Beauty, Harmony and Proportion'.[23]

As far as Godwin's 'implanted' aesthetic sense was concerned, Kippis must have been disappointed. It was, Godwin confessed, his peculiar character 'to strike out nothing, but to expand with no contemptible felicity the suggestions of others'.[24] He put this fault down to his early reading habits, which were motivated by a concern for feeling rather than criticism.

Contemplating the 'immense library' that might be filled with English

VI. Andrew Kippis, artist unknown.

writers, Godwin resolved to be selective and to confine his reading to modern authors.[25] His taste, like his tutor's, remained predominantly Augustan, and he looked in literature for 'unity, consistency of design, of proportion & arrangement of parts'.[26] He greatly admired the prose of Swift, Shaftesbury, Bolingbroke and Rousseau, but thought the best model was a 'due mixture and medium' of Burke and Hume.[27]

In his lectures, Kippis maintained that 'polite arts' gradually 'arrive to perfection' and that in the eighteenth century a 'just taste had been formed in polite learning'.[28] Godwin concurred with Kippis, and argued that there was 'no art that may not be carried to a still higher perfection'.[29] Indeed, in an essay on style, he opposed prevailing opinion by claiming that the English language was never in 'so high a state of purity and perfection' as in the reign of George III.[30] It was only after his discovery of the Elizabethan writers in 1799 that he altered his view, and admitted that progress in science was not necessarily paralleled by improvements in literature.

Kippis's lectures on oratory, eloquence and grammar also seem to have found fertile ground in the young Godwin. The aim of oratory, Kippis affirmed, was to cultivate 'the happiest Method of delivering Truth' and should be addressed primarily to the understanding.[31] He therefore insisted that language ought to be 'natural, clear, and capable only of one signification'.[32] Again, Godwin entirely agreed with Kippis: style should be the 'transparent envelop of our thoughts' and find its basis in a 'decisive and ardent thirst after simplicity'.[33] He tried to realize this ideal in his own philosophical style, which exhibited all the Augustan qualities of 'clearness, propriety, and compression'.[34]

This emphasis on clarity and precision was not only for aesthetic reasons. Godwin's whole scheme of perfectibility rests on the full communication of truth, and it was his firm conviction that 'accuracy of language is the indispensable prerequisite of sound knowledge'.[35] To this end he later compiled a school dictionary which gave the 'genuine, original and most customary use' of a word and a school grammar which encouraged the dissection of works to reveal 'the primary and secondary ideas they represent'.[36] For Godwin, the science of thinking is 'little else than the science of words', so he constantly recommended the study of languages to promote clear and rigorous thought.[37]

Kippis further encouraged Godwin's passion for the classics which had been first awakened by the books in Newton's library. In his lectures, Kippis offered an accurate survey of the works of Aristotle, Cicero, Xenophon, and Plato, and warmly recommended the ancient historians. Inspired by Kippis's enthusiasm, Godwin resolved to read the classics thoroughly. He devoted a part of each day to their study, and took about six months to read the works of one author. He worked his way through Virgil, Horace, Cicero, Livy, Sallust and Tacitus among the Romans, and Homer, Sophocles, Xenophon, Herodotus and Thucydides among the Greeks.[38]

Godwin never lost his enthusiasm for ancient literature and for the greater part of his life spent at least one hour reading some Greek and one hour reading some Latin every day. He warmly recommended the study of the classics to the young and later wrote for them some lively histories of Greece and Rome. Indeed, he felt ancient history provided the best models and the 'most excellent things of which human nature is capable'.[39]

But it was in the subject of history that Kippis had the greatest influence on Godwin. The study of history was one of the most important pedagogic innovations made in the Dissenting academies. Kippis would probably have drawn on Priestley's famous *Lectures on History and General Policy* (composed for delivery at the Warrington Academy), and like him had several axes to grind. History he felt, tends not only 'to enlarge the Mind, to nourish and strengthen the Understanding', but presents '1000 illustrious Characters, Actions and Events highly deserving our attention'. Above all, it demonstrates the incessant improvements in the arts and sciences and the 'progress of human Reason'.[40]

True to his Dissenting tradition, Kippis delighted in the Reformation and felt the Revolution of 1688 was undoubtedly the 'most illustrious and happy era in the British Annals'. Henceforth there had been a 'series of public Happiness which we may challenge any nation to parallel'.[41]

Godwin recalled that whilst at Hoxton, history was a study for which he felt a particular vocation. His boyish passion had been for poetry, but he now hesitated between history and moral philosophy as a means of achieving his early passion for literary distinction, 'dreading that I had not enough of elaborate exactness for the former, or of original conception for the latter'.[42] Although Godwin became famous for his moral philosophy, he spent the greater part of his life in the study and writing of history.

In a sermon written soon after leaving Hoxton, Godwin borrowed Bolingbroke's celebrated definition of history as 'philosophy teaching by example' and proclaimed in virtually the same terms as Kippis that it serves 'to enlarge and ennoble the human mind, to fill it with the sublimest attachments to its most generous benefactors, the patrons of virtue and liberty'.[43] In an unpublished essay written in 1797 he divided the subject up into two principal branches: 'general history' and 'individual history'. The first branch is concerned with the study of 'mankind in the mass, of the progress, fluctuations, the interests & vices of society', and its importance lies in the attempt to ascertain the causes that operate universally upon men under given circumstances. The second branch is biography and has the advantage both of inspiring the reader to noble deeds and of allowing him to appreciate the possible development of society. Whereas general history can furnish us with precedents, individual history permits us to observe the 'empire of motives' and be able to add to the knowledge of the past 'a sagacity that can penetrate into the depth of futurity'.

Although Godwin never treated facts with disdain in his historical writing, his concern for the edifying purpose of history led him to prefer inaccurate history with great moral truth to a dry factual chronicle. Indeed, he argued that the novel or 'romance' is the noblest species of history. In a lengthy comparison, he contended:

> The historian is confined to individual incident & individual man, & must hang upon that his invention or conjecture as he can. The writer of romance collects his materials from all sources, experience, report, & the records of human affairs; then generalizes them; & finally selects, from the various elements & various combinations they afford, those incidents he is best able to portray, & which he judges most calculated to impress the heart & improve the faculties of his readers.

Since historical evidence is doubtful and fragmentary, Godwin even suggested that the man of discrimination is more likely to prefer the 'reality of romance' to the 'falseness & impossibility of history'.[44]

Godwin's view of the past itself was not so clear cut as Kippis's. He was painfully aware of the moral decline of the moderns in comparison with the ancients: 'The ancients were giants but we, their degenerate successors, are pigmies.'[45] He was only too ready to assert with Voltaire that the history of mankind is 'little else than a record of crime' and with Maupertius that 'the whole history of the human species, taken in one point of view, appears a vast abortion'.[46] From another perspective, however, Godwin discerned a degree of real improvement in the world since the fall of Constantinople and the discovery of printing. These two circumstances had greatly favoured the Reformation, which shook 'the empire of superstitition and implicit obedience', and from that time the improvement of the arts and the sciences had been incessant.[47]

As a Dissenter, he naturally looked on the seventeenth century as marking an expansion of English freedom. The Commonwealth before Cromwell's usurpation, he maintained, could challenge any period of English history in 'the glory of its rule'.[48] After its collapse, he welcomed the Glorious Revolution, but he could not look on the eighteenth century with the same kind of optimism as Kippis:

> From the moment that the grand contest excited under the Stuarts was quieted by the Revolution our history assumes its most insipid & insufferable form. It is the history of negotiation & trickery; it is the history of revenues & debts; it is the history of corruption & political profligacy; but it is not the history of genuine, independent man.[49]

It was to transcend such a sorry state of affairs that Godwin dedicated the rest of his life.

In addition to the normal curriculum at Hoxton, Godwin devoted much of his time to metaphysics. For one whole summer he rose at five and went to bed at midnight in order to have sufficient time for its study. It marked the beginning of a lifelong interest in the subject, as his notebooks amply illustrate. He believed that metaphysics — the 'theoretical science' of the mind, the universe and causation — must settle the first principles of natural religion. Moreover, it excels all other studies as 'a practical logic, a disciplining and subtilising of the rational faculties'.[50]

Godwin wrote in 1808 or after that during the period at Hoxton, he formed 'from reading on all sides, a creed upon materialism and immaterialism, liberty and necessity, in which no subsequent improvement of my understanding has been able to produce any variation'.[51] This is an important statement. At Hoxton Godwin was drawn to immaterialism. Despite his disbelief in the immortality of the soul in 1788 and his adherence to atheism in 1792, he never became a materialist. It is a fact which has been widely overlooked and has led to a profound misunderstanding of his influence.

Although the controversy between Priestley and Price on materialism and immaterialism was raging at the time, Godwin seems to have formed his immaterialist creed by reading the works of Samuel Clarke, James Beattie and Andrew Baxter. At the beginning of the century, Samuel Clarke and Anthony Collins had entered into a public debate on the immateriality of the soul. Godwin's notebooks show that he carefully considered the issues. Like Clarke, he argued: 'Thought is the most important phenomenon. Can it be the accident of a certain arrangement of particles, not one of which separately has the property of thought? This is an argument in favour of immaterialism.'[52]

Not surprisingly, Godwin also felt that James Beattie's commonsense arguments against immaterialism in an *Essay on the Nature and Immutability of Truth* (1770) were 'at once superficial and confused, feeble and presumptuous'.[53] Instead, he was drawn to Andrew Baxter, who claimed that all those effects commonly ascribed to certain 'natural powers residing in matter are immediately produced by the power of an immaterial Being'.[54] Godwin's record of his philosophical principles for 1776 and 1778 shows that at Hoxton he also believed that 'powers are incompatible with matter' and that 'time and space are the attributes of the Deity'.[55] Many years later, he maintained that no young man could read Baxter's *Enquiry into the Nature of the Human Soul* (1733) 'without being the better for it'.[56]

Although his religious faith slowly eroded after leaving Hoxton, Godwin recorded in 1786 that he still believed 'that matter is an ideal existence'.[57] Six years later, he was an atheist, but he spoke in *Political Justice* of mind and matter as forming parallel interactive schemes, both subject to the laws of necessity. He emphasized, moreover, that the mechanism of the mind is determined by mental rather than physical causes. To any 'material system' which explains thinking in terms of matter in motion, he resolutely opposed the 'intellectual system' which finds in thought the source of physical action. Whilst borrowing Hartley's associationist account of the causality, he therefore rejected his theory of vibrations which 'unnecessarily clogged' his principal doctrine with a 'scheme of material automatism'.[58]

Godwin recollected that he had long arguments at Hoxton on necessity as well as on immaterialism. He formed his creed in this instance by reading the libertarian Samuel Clarke and the necessitarian Jonathan Edwards. Clarke in his *Boyle Lectures* (1704-5) had asserted that man must be a free agent because freedom is implied in intelligence and is necessary for moral responsibility. Although he addressed the Arminian Jeremy Taylor rather than Clarke, it was precisely this view that the New England Calvinist Edwards combated in *A Careful and Strict Enquiry into the Modern Prevailing Notions of that Freedom of the Will, which is supposed to be essential to Moral*

*Agency, Vertue and Vice, Reward and Punishment, Praise and Blame* (1754). Edward's writings, Godwin recalled, 'had great weight with me, & their effects may be traced even in the Enquiry concerning Political Justice'.[59] Amongst his philosophical principles for the year 1776, he also significantly listed 'That human actions are necessary'.[60]

When Godwin came to write *Political Justice*, he frankly acknowledged in his chapter 'Of Free Will and Necessity' that the argument for the impossibility of free will was treated 'with great force of reasoning in Jonathan Edwards's Enquiry into the Freedom of the Will'.[61] Like Edwards, Godwin's fundamental objection to the notion of free will is that rather than ensuring moral responsibility, it actually destroys it. He conceived of liberty in this sense as equivalent to acting in 'a foolish and tyrannical manner'. As such, it was as dangerous as materialism to his scheme of rational progress:'so far as we act with liberty, so far as we are independent of motives, our conduct is as independent of morality as it is of reason, nor is it possible that we should deserve either praise or blame for a proceeding thus capricious and indisciplinable'.[62] And just as Edwards argued that man's 'will is guided by the dictates or views of his understanding', so Godwin maintained that the 'voluntary actions of man originate in their opinions'.[63]

Hoxton was no exception to Priestley's dictum that the youth in the academies were taught the 'most liberal principles, both in religion and politics'.[64] Even though Savage, Godwin's tutor in theology, was a moderate Calvinist, he was famous for being guided 'by candour in his intercourse with his brethren of all denominations'.[65] Kippis, on the other hand, was a Socinian who denied the divinity of Christ and original sin. He wished to encourage 'a sincere, fervent, and at the same time, rational religion', based not on 'a slavish and servile dread of the Supreme being'. but on a 'rational sense of his authority'.[66]

Rees, however, was the most latitudinarian of the three tutors. He subscribed to the Unitarian creed of Price, who maintained that religious worship was sacred to One Being and that the divine government would comprehend the final happiness of the whole intelligent creation. Like Kippis, he felt that true religion ought to be voluntary and promoted a 'rational system of faith' based on the Scriptures.[67]

These liberal ministers encouraged Godwin in his theological studies. In his 'indefatigable search after truth' he read at Hoxton 'all the authors of greatest repute, for and against the Trinity, original sin, and the most disputed doctrines', but as his understanding was not yet sufficiently ripe for 'impartial decision', his enquiries terminated in Calvinism.[68] It was not without trying , however. In the last year of his academic life, he entered into 'a curious paper war' with a fellow-student, Richard Evans, on the question of the existence of God. Their papers have been lost but Godwin recalled that he took

> the negative side, in this instance, as always with great sincerity hoping
> that my friend might enable me to remove the difficulties I
> apprehended. I did not fully see my ground as to this radical question,
> but I had little doubt that grant the being of God, both the truth of
> Christianity, & the doctrines of Calvinism, followed by infallible infer-
> ence.[69]

Godwin, moreover, was even prepared to assert that virtue could exist
without Christianity. Rees maintained in conversation that an ambiguous
and obscure style was wisely kept up in the New Testament, since less than
the absolute belief in eternal suffering would never retain 'the lower orders
of the community in the path of duty'.[70] No doubt on the basis of his recent
study of the classics, Godwin boldly replied that he

> was persuaded there was more virtue and less crime in the best ages of
> Greece and Rome than in any period of the Christian dispensation, and
> was therefore satisfied that the doctrine of eternal punishment in hell
> was not absolutely required to prevent men from running out into
> excesses that would be destructive of the social system.[71]

In politics, Hoxton was as liberal as in religion. Savage was unusual in
supporting George III but he was still held to be an '*upright* man, uninflu-
enced by *court* favour, which he scorned to solicit'.[72] Both Rees and Kippis
on the other hand were firm supporters of the Whigs. One of the advantages
of knowledge, Rees argued, was that it made the pupil 'the strenuous and
inflexible assertor of the rights of mankind'.[73] Kippis equally felt that one of
the noblest employments of human liberty was 'to defend and promote the
civil and sacred rights of mankind'.[74] He followed Locke in his view of the
ends and limits of government and maintained that the British Constitution was an excellent combination of democracy, aristocracy, and monarchy: 'a plan of power which produces more true freedom than, perhaps, has
yet been enjoyed by any community, in any period'.[75]

Kippis's central concern in his politics was undoubtedly the legal and
political restrictions suffered by the Dissenters. As Godwin entered Hoxton
in the spring of 1773, Kippis was actively engaged in the campaign to widen
the Toleration Act. He spoke on behalf of his co-religionists when he
declared:

> We dissent, because we deny the right of any body of men, whether civil
> or ecclesiastical, to impose human tests, creeds, or articles; and because

we think it our duty, not to submit to any such authority, but to protest against it, as a violation of our essential liberty to judge and act for ourselves in matters of religion.[76]

Because of his regard for existing liberties and his fear of the intemperance of all oppositions, Godwin remained a Tory at Hoxton. He later developed, however, his tutors' staunch defence of the freedom of enquiry and belief. In *Political Justice*, he devoted a whole book to the question 'Of Opinion Considered as a Subject of Political Institution', and in separate chapters dealt with religious establishments, the suppression of erroneous opinion in religion, tests and oaths. The existing form of religious conformity, he maintained, was not only a 'system of blind submission and abject hypocrisy' but unjustly treated the Dissenter as an unsound member of society.[77] He went even further to ask: 'Is it not strange that men should have affirmed religion to be the sacred province of conscience, while moral duty is to be left undefined to the decision of the magistrate?'[78] Indeed, Godwin's anarchism, with its rejection of all forms of established authority, is little more than a strict application of the Dissenters' 'sacred and indefeasible right of private judgment'.[79]

During his last summer vacation at Hoxton Godwin successfully preached at Yarmouth every Sunday morning and at Lowestoft in the afternoon. He then graduated in the spring of 1778, having just turned twenty-two. His tutors certified that

Mr. William Godwin, having gone thro' a regular Course of Studies preparatory for the Christian Ministry, wth. great diligence & good Proficiency, in Mr. Coward's Academy at Hoxton, did, on the 26th January last, perform much to our Satisfaction the usual Exercises of exhibiting & defending a Theological Thesis, in Latin & delivering a Sermon in English. — that he was in Communion with a Christian Church & that he maintain'd a good Report, as to his religious Temper & moral Conduct, during the whole Course of his Academical Education. And we do therefore judge him to be very well qualified for entering on the sacred work of the Ministry & do most heartily recommend him to the Blessing of God & to the Service & Acceptance of the Churches of Christ.[80]

It still seems extraordinary that Godwin should have attended for five years one of the most liberal centres of higher education in Britain and yet have left with his Sandemanian beliefs and Tory principles apparently intact. There appear to be two main explanations. In the first place, Godwin's mind was habitually cautious. In his old age, he wrote that during his college life:

I read all sorts of books, on every side of any important question, or that were thrown in my way, that I could hear of. But the very passion that determined me to this mode of proceeding, made me wary and circumspect in coming to a conclusion. I knew that it would, if any thing, be a more censurable and contemptible act, to yield to every seducing novelty, than to adhere obstinately to a prejudice because it had been instilled into me in youth.[81]

Secondly, Godwin was extremely unhappy as a boarder at Hoxton. In his novel *Mandeville*, he bitterly criticized boarding-schools for trying to achieve a false uniformity of speech and conformity of thought. Boarders, like prisoners, are governed much like a machine:'the machinist has to touch a spring only, and the whole is obedient'.[82] Added to this, Godwin recalled that although famous for 'calm and dispassionate discussion' and for 'the intrepidity of my opinions and the tranquil fearlessness of my temper', his fellow students 'almost with one voice, pronounced me to be the most self-conceited, self-sufficient animal that ever lived'.[83] Godwin was undoubtedly trying to justify his position at Hoxton when describing Mr. Godfrey at Oxford in his first novel *Damon and Delia*. Although considered 'indisputably' superior to his contemporaries, Mr. Godfrey was not courted, for he

had a stiffness and unpliableness of temper, that did not easily bend to the submission that was expected of him. He could neither flatter a blockhead, nor pimp for a peer. He loved his friend indeed with unbounded warmth, and it was impossible to surpass him in generousness and liberality. But he had a proud integrity, that whispered him, with a language not to be controled, that he was the inferior of no man.[84]

Both Godwin's character and opinions isolated him at Hoxton. He confessed that 'my finding myself alone both in my political and religious opinions and the continued opposition I sustained on that account did not operate to diminish my singularity'.[85] He seems to have suffered deeply from the persecution of his fellow students and found it necessary to defend his beliefs as a means of upholding the integrity of his personality. For all his 'indefatigable' search after truth, to agree with his opponents at this stage would have been too painful an admission of defeat. It was only after leaving Hoxton, when the opposition was removed, that he could consciously acknowledge the validity of their arguments. He had thus 'no sooner gone out into the world' than his political and religious sentiments began to give way: 'my toryism did not survive above a year, and between my twenty-third and my twenty-fifth year my religious creed insensibly degenerated on the heads of the Trinity, eternal torments, and some others'.[86]

Godwin's education at Hoxton then clearly laid the foundation of his mature thought. In the lectures of Doddridge, he was introduced to the principles of Lockean psychology, the altruistic moralists, and the natural right school of politics. With Rees, he became acquainted with the rudiments of Newtonian science. Kippis played an important role in shaping his views on literature and history. In his own free time, he formed a creed upon immaterialism and necessity which subsequently underwent no fundamental change. And although the effect was delayed, he was indelibly influenced by the latitudinarian religion and radical politics of the academy.

More important perhaps than actual doctrines was the prevailing atmosphere of the place. It encouraged free enquiry and rational examination and trained Godwin systematically to question his inherited beliefs and to doubt existing orthodoxies. Above all, the living example of Savage, Kippis and Rees, men of outstanding integrity and candour, who called for justice and liberty and practised what they preached, showed that mankind could be enlightened and free. The importance of Godwin's five-year stay at Hoxton, which has hitherto been virtually ignored, can indeed hardly be overestimated.

# CHAPTER IV

## *The Ministry*

Godwin left Hoxton Academy in 1778, a dedicated Christian apostle. He intended to enter the ministry like his father and grandfather before him and spent the next five years in obscure rural congregations as a candidate minister. It was a crucial stage in his intellectual development, yet in his autobiographical fragments he passed it over in almost complete silence. The young minister, arrogant and diffident by turns, continued to experience the miseries of solitude and found himself increasingly in conflict with his former beliefs and with his congregations. It was a difficult and painful period and he no doubt felt that it was best forgotten.

His start in the world was far from auspicious. On leaving Hoxton in the spring, he contracted a 'putrid fever' which almost killed him. He then preached a trial sermon at Christchurch in Hampshire and was rejected by the congregation. He was a little more successful at the Independent chapel in the little village of Ware in Hertfordshire, but was still obliged to leave in the following summer of 1779.

The members of the congregations probably disliked the narrow Calvinism and Tory politics of their young candidate minister. In a volume of sermons published a few years later, Godwin insisted that we have 'forfeited the exemptions and immunities of an innocent being'.[1] A good Christian has 'no will but that of God, not a passion, nor a thought, that is not subdued into silence before him'.[2] As for existing social inequalities, Godwin defended them on the traditional principle of the need for a maximum variety or plenitude: 'A world of derived beings, an immense wide creation, requires an extended scale with various ranks and orders of existence.'[3] It was a hard pill for struggling artisans and farm labourers to swallow, disabled as they were by the Test and Corporation Acts.

Whilst at Ware, however, Godwin met Joseph Fawcett, a young man of his own age who had just left Priestley's academy at Daventry. After the isolation at Hoxton, a new world now opened up for Godwin. They soon became the best of friends. Fawcett was the first person whom he felt compelled to respect and who carried with him the 'semblance of original genius'.[4] He became the first of the 'four principal oral instructors' to whom Godwin felt his mind indebted for improvement.[5] As late as 1820, he remembered him with gratification as 'my first companion of imaginative soul and luxuriant ideas'.[6]

Fawcett later became a celebrated poet and a popular preacher. Hazlitt, who was his friend as a young man, recollected that the conversations he had with him on the subjects of taste and philosophy gave him 'a delight, such as I can never feel again'. Of all the persons he had ever known, Fawcett was 'the most perfectly free from every taint of jealousy or narrowness'.[7] As for Godwin, Hazlitt claimed that Fawcett spoke of his writings 'with admiration, tinctured with wonder'.[8]

The two young friends spent hours together in their poor lodgings discussing philosophy and literature. Godwin had been reading Jonathan Edwards's *Dissertation on the Nature of True Virtue* (1765) which argued that it most essentially consists in 'benevolence to Being in general', and consequently excludes friendship, domestic affections, and gratitude.[9] A declamation against the domestic affections proved to be one of Fawcett's favourite topics of conversation. It not only 'admirably coincided' with the dogmas of Jonathan Edwards, Godwin recalled, but being 'well adapted to the austerity & perfection which Calvinism recommends, had undoubtedly a great influence on me'. He significantly recorded amongst his philosophical principles for the year they met: 'That gratitude is not a duty of external obligation'.[10]

Like Godwin, Fawcett also proved to be a necessitarian and a rationalist. Soon after their meeting, they disputed for a whole day the question whether a motive be necessary to virtue — only to conclude that it was. Again, Fawcett upheld the Socratic doctrine that vice only results from 'intellectual deficiency' and Godwin duly recorded amongst his philosophical principles for the year of their meeting: 'That superior virtue must be the fruit of superior intelligence'.[11] The two young candidate ministers doubtlessly saw themselves as part of the enlightened council of 'rationals' celebrated later by Fawcett who meet to form 'some fair and beauteous plan of public good' and stand

> Serene and solemn!   mind illumining mind!
> Reason's confederated rays thrown out
> In intellectual alliance firm![12]

Philosophy was not Godwin's only preoccupation at this time. Having been rejected by two congregations, he decided to go to London in August and resided with great economy for some months at a little lodging in Coleman Street, near Cripplegate. Alone and unemployed in his small room, his thoughts eventually turned to politics. But the unexpected happened: his sentiments suddenly underwent a great revolution and he was converted from Toryism to the Whig opposition. The liberal influence of his Dissenting upbringing and education had at last had its effect.

The colonists in America had been waging a war of independence for several years, and had just been joined by Spain and France in their struggle against Britain. The command of the sea had been lost. The opposition in parliament called for American independence in the name of justice and humanity while Lord North and his administration blindly insisted on the letter of the Constitution. It was a grand contrast.Godwin considered it the great fortune of his life that the minds of the public were so preoccupied when he first took an active interest in politics:

> It was auspicious for me, not that a question of finance & taxes, of customs & excises, of commercial monopolies & preferences, not even of ordinary peace & war, engaged the attention at that period, but a question involving eternal principles, a question of liberty and subjugation, & a question that seemed to embrace one half of the world.[13]

Nevertheless, he did not let himself get carried away. He followed the debate closely and chose his party with great sobriety, deciding on the one which sought 'to improve or adapt to new circumstances, as they arose, the principles of our government'.[14] A reading of the newspaper reports of the speeches of Edmund Burke and Charles James Fox greatly influenced him, and he immediately conceived for these Whig leaders an 'ardent attachment' which no lapse of time was able to shake.[15] His choice of party was further confirmed by his first visit to the House of Commons at the opening of parliament on 25 November 1779, when he heard Fox's celebrated speech in which he condemned the principle that the king might be his own minister and so violently attacked William Adam that it led to a duel.

Despite his new friendship with Fawcett and the sudden change in his political opinions, Godwin remained in London only for about six months. His funds quickly ran out and he was forced in December 1779 to resume his profession as a candidate minister, this time at the market town of Stowmarket in Suffolk. Situated on the River Gipping, which provided osier for basket-weaving and transport for the tanning industry, the town was surrounded by rich pasture and cornfields. It was famous for its hops and hempen fabrics. Godwin, however, was preoccupied with his own thoughts and troubles and later regretted not having observed the scenes of nature during his two-year stay at Stowmarket.

It was probably the most difficult period in his life. His rural congregation did not like his prickly manner or his learned sermons, and made no secret of it. The more he tried to please, the less he succeeded. Once again, he was shunned and found himself living in a hostile environment. Indeed, the only pleasant acquaintance he had was a Mrs. Alice Munnings, and her son Leonard, a captain of the Suffolk Militia and a 'lively, well bred and intelligent man'.[16]

In his enforced solitude, Godwin turned in on himself and began to examine his beliefs. The ministry was rapidly receding as a desirable vocation, and after his daily pastoral duties, he returned to his study determined to follow truth wherever it led him. It must have been with excitement and trepidation that he took down his treasured books from his shelf. The result of his careful analysis was a momentous upheaval in his opinions which marked a turning-point in his life.

He had only just moved from Toryism to Whiggism in politics, but a perusal of the Roman historians and the political writings of Swift made him a republican overnight. He had of course been interested in Roman history ever since he had read Rollin's *Ancient History* in Norwich. He had also made a close study of Livy, Sallust and Tacitus at Hoxton. Although he would not have found a direct critique of monarchy in their works, his present situation probably encouraged him to identify strongly with the great Roman republicans who had selflessly opposed corruption and despotism. 'One would have thought no man could have perused the history of Rome and the history of England', he wrote later, 'without seeing that in the one was presented the substance of men, and in the other the shadow.'[17]

The second impulse which made Godwin a republican at Stowmarket came from the Tory Dean Swift. Although Swift went over to the Tories in 1710, he never surrendered his allegiance to the principles of the 1688 Revolution, and in his political writings he mordantly criticized existing practices and became the ardent champion of Irish independence.

Godwin was profoundly impressed by his views. He later described the author of *Gulliver's Travels* (1726) as a man 'who appears to have had a more profound insight into the true principles of political justice, than any preceding or contemporary author'.[18] He was particularly taken by the Houyhnhnms, the dignified horses who believed that Reason was sufficient to govern rational creatures and that in a society practising universal benevolence and perfect sincerity there would be no need for government, law, coercion, commerce or religion. Indeed, Godwin described the 'Voyage to the Hoynhnms' as 'one of the most virtuous, liberal and enlightened examples of human genius that has yet been produced'.[19] It became his life's task to inspire Yahoo humanity to imitate Houyhnhnm excellence.

When Godwin was twenty-six there came to Stowmarket a tradesman from London called Frederick Norman. Their encounter was to spark off indirectly another great revolution in Godwin's opinions. Norman was deeply read in the French philosophers, and put into the hands of the young Calvinist minister the works of D'Holbach, Helvétius and Rousseau — the most subversive writers of the French Enlightenment, whose banned works were causing an uproar on the other side of the Channel. When Godwin closed their covers, the universe and his fellows no longer appeared the same. The books not only shook his faith in Christianity, but completely undermined his Calvinist view of man.

In a sense, the culture of Rational Dissent based on Lockean psychology and Newtonian science which Godwin had imbibed at Hoxton Academy had already prepared him for a reading of the *philosophes*. But where the Rational Dissenters remained Christian if unorthodox, the *philosophes* were militantly anti-Christian, and had developed Cartesian philosophy in a naturalist direction. Godwin's strict Sandemanianism had insensibly degenerated after leaving Hoxton, but he still believed that the majority of mankind were objects of divine condemnation and that their punishment would be eternal.

The radical critique of original sin in D'Holbach's *Système de la nature* (1770), Helvétius's doctrine of the intellectual equality of human beings at birth in *De l'esprit* (1758), and Rousseau's defence of the natural goodness of man in his *Discours sur l'origine de l'inegalité de l'homme* (1775) and *Émile* (1762), all combined to give the final blow to Godwin's Calvinist beliefs. He did not immediately become an atheist, and took refuge in deism. But, more important, he became convinced that political solutions could be found for ills which he had hitherto considered endemic in human nature. In 1782, he concluded 'That human depravity originates in the vices of political constitution'.[20] His whole world view had changed.

Godwin of course did not accept uncritically all the opinions of D'Holbach and Helvétius. He was impressed by their views on necessity and utility and their unsparing criticism of unjust institutions. At the same time, he conducted a lifelong crusade against their egoistic psychology in the name of universal benevolence.

Rousseau, on the other hand, was a man after his own heart and he went on to collect all his works. He entirely endorsed his emphasis in *Émile* on the power of education and commended warmly the attack in the *Discours* on the evils of private property and the artificiality of modern civilization. Above all, he recognized in Rousseau the first thinker to teach that the 'imperfections of government were the only perennial source of the vices of mankind'.[21] Not surprisingly, Godwin was disappointed by Rousseau's idea of the general will and advocacy of political imposture in his *Contrat social* (1762), but he still proved to be a great inspirer of his later anarchism.

The radical works of the French Enlightenment must have stood somewhat incongruously next to the Bible and edifying sermons on Godwin's shelf. His own position was also ambivalent — a republican and deist in theory, he continued to perform his ministerial duties to a pious, conservative, and ignorant flock. To make matters worse, a dispute broke out on a question of Church discipline. Godwin had decided at Hoxton that a candidate minister should administer communion and baptism before he was ordained and his congregation at Stowmarket had consented to his doing this. When the time came for his ordination, however, the neighbouring ministers, led by the learned Thomas Harmer of Wattisford, refused to attend.

Godwin was deeply troubled; his failure to be ordained could mean that he would have to spend the rest of his life at Stowmarket. In the meantime, one member of the congregation, who 'insinuated himself much among the lower people', refused to accept the sacraments from Godwin and drew up a list of twenty of his faults.[22] In the dispute which followed the congregation became divided and Godwin was at length dismissed.

Godwin probably drew on the experience in his first novel *Damon and Delia*, written in the following year. The 'enthusiasm of virtue' had at first led the talented young divine Mr. Godfrey to try and be 'the friend and the father of the meanest' of his flock. He conducted himself

with the most unexceptionable propriety, and the most generous benevolence. But there were men in his audience, men who loved better to criticise, than to be amended; and women, who felt more complacency in scandal, than eulogium. He displeased the one by disappointing them; it was impossible to disappoint the other. He laboured unremittedly, but his labours returned to him void.[23]

After his dismissal, Godwin returned in April 1782 to London where he found cheap lodgings in Holborn. In some ways, he was pleased; his increasing religious doubts made his position as a candidate minister uncomfortable. He also now had an opportunity to realize his childhood ambition to become a writer. Encouraged by his friend Fawcett and helped financially by a printer and publisher called John Paul, he planned a series of biographies of English political figures.

Godwin began to write *The History of the Life of William Pitt, Earl of Chatham* in July, but it soon grew to the size of a volume and he did not finish it until 30 November. It was eventually published by G. Kearsley at his own expense of £40 on 20 January 1783, with a dedication to Lord

Camden, then President of the Privy Council. He sent a copy to Burke, but was particularly disappointed when the one man 'whose favour he most wished to engage' failed to look into it.[24] Other copies were dispatched to Lord Camden, Dr. Johnson and the Duke of Richmond.

The biography is little more than a meandering sketch of the political life of the elder Pitt (who had died four years before), written in a style which is alternately pedestrian and mannered. Only occasionally is there a glimpse of the vigorous eloquence of the mature Godwin. The many asides, which contribute to its failure as a biography, give it value however as a source of Godwin's ideas at an obscure but crucial period in his development.

In the introduction, Godwin argues that the historian should be a personally disinterested but morally engaged commentator of human affairs. As a 'citizen of the world' his task is to reveal virtue and vice to humanity so that 'by imperceptible, never ceasing advances', they might be won over to the 'restoration of paradise'.[25] From this perspective, he welcomes Chatham's first Tory administration which attempted to restore the vigour of the constitution after the corrupt pragmatism of Walpole. He is naturally disappointed when Chatham exchanges reform for the 'trophies of conquest', and sternly castigates him for his determined opposition to American Independence.[26] Nevertheless, in Godwin's final estimate of his character and career, Chatham stands out as an upright champion of liberty: 'While all, around him, were depressed, by the uniformity of fashion, or the contagion of venality, he stood aloof. He consulted no judgment, but his own; and he acted, from the untainted dictates of a comprehensive soul.'[27]

Despite his attempt at a balanced account of Chatham, Godwin could not restrain his new republican sympathies. Responsibility, he argues, is the first principle of a free government and the confidence of the people the only basis of a good administration. After tracing the gradual decline of the 'independency, and the sturdy virtue' of the House of Commons since the Glorious Revolution of 1688, he declares: 'The combination of monarchy and republicanism is clearly artificial: and, I believe, we should lie open to very few exceptions, should we establish it as a maxim; that the prince is never averse to disengage himself from the shackles of control.'[28]

Godwin must have been delighted by the reception of his first book. The *Gentleman's Magazine* declared that 'The author of this volume is a poet, a painter, a philosopher, a friend of freedom, and a lover of mankind. His painting and philosophy give a spirit to the work; but his poetry we could have dispensed with.'[29] The *Critical Review* said it was animated and able, the *Edinburgh Weekly Magazine* concurred but found the language affected, and *The New Annual Register* felt that although derived from common records, it had energy and spirit.[30] The work ran into four editions in one year, two in London and two in Dublin. Godwin's friend John Paul also managed to pay for the insertion of the characters of Walpole, Carteret and Pelham in the papers. His 'Character of Chatham' was reprinted in *The New Annual Register for 1783*.

His *Life of Chatham* brought Godwin no money, and unable to find employment in London, he returned reluctantly in December 1782 to the ministry, this time at Beaconsfield in Buckinghamshire. It was not undertaken lightly. He was still troubled by the 'infidel principles' which he had recently imbibed from the French philosphers. But a reading of Priestley's *Institutes of Natural and Revealed Religion* (1772-4) enabled him to find a temporary rest in Socinianism which accepted the existence of God but denied the divinity of Christ. In a long entry in his notebooks, Godwin recorded at this time:

> I believe in this being, not because I have any proper or direct knowledge of His existence,
> But, I am at a loss to account for the existence and arrangement of the visible universe,
> And, being left in the wide sea of conjecture without a clue from analogy or experience,
> I find the conjecture of a God, easy, obvious, and irresistible.[31]

Godwin remained a Socinian for another four years. The strain however of having to work as a minister whilst privately entertaining radical political views and profound religious doubts was too great for him. He experienced the first attack of an 'apoplectic complaint' in 1783 which returned periodically during the rest of his life. It usually took the form of a 'fit of entire insensibility' for about a minute which returned several times during three or four days.[32] Although Godwin's constitution was always weak, the fits tended to occur at times of great stress in his life, and therefore probably had a psychological as well as a physical origin.

It did not prevent the taciturn and diffident young minister in Beaconsfield from taking a keen interest in the political life of the metropolis. In May 1783, he wrote *A Defence of the Rockingham Party, in their late Coalition with the Right Honourable Frederic Lord North*. It was inspired by Fox's apparent betrayal of principle in accepting a post as Secretary of State with his former opponent Lord North who had been responsible for the American war.

Godwin's *Defence of the Rockingham Party* might appear a strange production for a self-confessed republican and one of the most trenchant critics of political imposture in the history of thought. Yet, as in the case of his *Life of Chatham*, the work is in keeping with Godwin's lifelong attitude to practical politics. In a long and important note to be found amongst his papers, Godwin made his position clear:

> My political creed may be stated with great brevity & clearness. It consists of two parts, speculative and practical. In speculative politics, I indulge with great delight to my own mind (& I cannot easily persuade myself with injury to others), in meditating on what man can be, on all the good which our nature taken in the most favourable point of view, seems to promise, & in endeavouring to trace in the wide & unexpected sea of future events, through what adventures & by what means that good (certainly in many of its branches exceedingly remote) may ultimately be brought home to man.
>
> In practical politics, my path is mapped with many a beacon, which is wanting to me in the tracks of speculation, & therefore I may hope is less exposed to error. In the first place, I am an enemy to revolutions. I abhor, both from temper, & from the clearest judgment I am able to form, all violent convulsions in the affairs of men. I look to the understanding alone for all real & solid improvements in the structure of human society . . . [33]

It is thus as a Whig, a friend of the Constitution, and an advocate of gradual change, that Godwin came to defend the coalition. His argument was based on a belief that only the Rockingham party could successfully serve the country: they were steady in their love of freedom and disinterestedness, eager to establish equal representation, and above all led by 'that wonderful man' Fox and the 'unrivalled genius' Burke.[34] Since it was desirable for them to be in power, Godwin concluded that there was no alternative but to unite with Lord North and his followers, the least pernicious of the other factions.

As a topical pamphlet, it was well-argued, lively, and to the point. The preacher of sin and damnation was clearly on his way to becoming the advocate of political justice. His republican sympathies are clear in his attack on aristocracy as the 'most intolerable' form of despotism and in his praise of those 'patriots of former ages' who sacrificed their fortunes and their lives for the welfare of their fellow citizens.[35] And although he laments that 'disinterested affection' had taken up her last refuge 'in a few choice spirits', he is confident that the 'general diffusion of science' will continue to enlighten the minds of all men.[36]

A Defence of the Rockingham Party was published by J. Stockdale who gave Godwin five guineas. It had a mixed reception. It provoked at least one hostile pamphlet and the Critical Review and The New Annual Register rejected the validity of Godwin's argumentation.[37] On the other hand, the

*Monthly Review* thought it a 'sensible, temperate enquiry' and the *London Magazine* praised its 'just and pertinent ideas' and the 'elegant and lively style'.[38]

In the meantime, Godwin could not settle down at Beaconsfield: his congregation became hostile once again, and after six months he was forced to leave. He was both disappointed and anxious. He told his mother that the 'character' of Dissenting minister 'quitted me when I was far from desiring to part with it'.[39] Although his aspiration after truth had been 'vehement & continuous', he had for years been 'entangled in the fetters' of his profession because of the 'dreadful denunciations' of the Gospel hanging over him.[40] There were also the uncertainties of employment and the reproaches of his acquaintances to consider.

But while Godwin was obliged to leave the ministry, he always remained a preacher. Hazlitt observed that he later reminded those who knew him of 'the Metaphysician engrafted on the Dissenting Minister'.[41] Even in his old age, Godwin spoke of his 'vocation as a missionary'.[42] Instead of praising the glory of God, he devoted his life to the benefit of mankind. As he wrote to his mother soon after leaving the ministry: 'I know nothing worth the living for but usefulness and the service of my fellow-creatures. The only object I pursue is to increase, as far as lies in my power, the quantity of their knowledge and goodness and happiness'.[43]

When Godwin in June 1783 returned to London and took lodgings first in Porter Street and then in the Strand, he had just turned twenty-eight. His career as a minister had been a disaster, and his Calvinist beliefs had inexorably lapsed. But his political views were taking firmer shape and he had already published a book and a pamphlet which had been moderately praised. He therefore decided to try and realize his second boyhood ambition, to become a writer.

# CHAPTER V

## *London*

When Godwin settled in London in 1783 it contained six hundred thousand people, one-eighth of the country's population. It was a rigid and prejudiced society, with its marked class differences, its exclusive trades and corporations, and its ferocious hatred of foreigners. In the recent past, there had been a slight improvement in the standard of living, but life for the majority remained an uncertain affair. Work was insecure, health precarious, and poverty a constant threat. In the circumstances, Francis Place claimed he was not exaggerating when he complained of the 'ignorance, the immorality, the grossness, the obscenity the drunkenness, the dirtiness, and depravity of the middling and even of a large portion of the better sort of tradesmen, the artizans, and the journeyman tradesmen of London'.[1]

Politics did not escape the general corruption. George III was on the throne and used his wealth to buy seats and support in Parliament. The House of Commons had already settled the first instalment of the huge debts incurred by the Prince of Wales. Burke was still a Whig, and with Fox and Sheridan led the Opposition. But the notorious coalition defended by Godwin, which made the Tory Lord North and his opponent Fox Secretaries of State, showed how easily political differences could be reconciled. When it fell, a year after Godwin's arrival in London, Pitt became Prime Minister at the age of twenty-four.

There was, however, a growing demand for reform. Although the cry of the mob in the Gordon Riots of 1780 was 'No Popery', they were expressing a keen dissatisfaction with their lives. The struggle over Wilkes, expelled from parliament for libel, was not forgotten. The gentlemanly County Associations called for a reduction of State sinecures, places and pensions. In April 1780 the M.P. John Dunning put down his famous motion that 'the influence of the Crown has increased, is increasing and ought to be diminished'.[2] The more radical Society for Constitutional Information, led by John Jebb, Major Cartwright and John Horne Tooke, was formed in the same year to educate the 'free-born Englishman' in his rights and to restore the Constitution to its original purity of the reign of Alfred the Great. Two years later, Burke succeeded in passing the Economical Reform Act, which dealt with some of the worse abuses in the House of Commons. Above all, the protracted War of American Independence ended in 1783, demonstrating that the spirit of the Glorious Revolution was still alive and that a people could be equal and free.

Having failed for the fourth time to keep a congregation, Godwin turned to the natural alternative for one trained for the ministry: teaching. It was not considered a noble profession, often being the resource of the ruined and discredited artisan or shopkeeper.[3] Nevertheless Godwin borrowed some money, hired a furnished house, and wrote in June 1783 *An Account of the Seminary that will be opened on Monday the Fourth Day of August, at Epsom in Surrey, for the Instruction of Twelve Pupils in the Greek, Latin, French and English Languages*. T. Cadell published the prospectus for Godwin and it was advertised in the *Morning Herald* on 2 July. It was however much more concerned with Godwin's general views on society and education than with the practical details of a school. The opening is uncompromisingly radical:

> The state of society is incontestibly artificial; the power of one man over another must be always derived from convention, or from conquest; by nature we are equal. The necessary consequence is, that government must always depend upon the opinion of the governed. Let the most oppressed people under heaven once change their mode of thinking, and they are free.[4]

Godwin was clearly beginning to form some of the fundamental ideas of *Political Justice*. For the present he felt that government is very limited in its power of making men either virtuous or happy, but that 'our moral dispositions and character depend very much, perhaps entirely, upon education'.[5] He is convinced that 'nothing is so easily proved, as that the human mind is pure and spotless, as it came from the hands of God'.[6] Indeed, man is naturally capable of virtue, and Godwin argues with the 'very elegant philosopher' Francis Hutcheson that self-love is not the source of all our passions, for 'disinterested benevolence has its seat in the human heart'.[7]

When it comes to the curriculum, Godwin is no less radical. Grammar could be dispatched within a fortnight, but particular attention should be paid to the early study of the Greek, Latin, French and English languages. Most important of all is history, particularly the history of men and manners, which gives sound moral training. But wherever possible, Godwin prefers to have recourse to the 'book of nature to any human composition'.[8]

Godwin also has extreme views on teaching methods. He feels it is absurd to use force to inculcate knowledge:

> Modern education not only corrupts the heart of our youth, by the rigid slavery to which it condemns them, it also undermines their reason, by the unintelligible jargon with which they are overwhelmed in the first instance, and the little attention, that is given to the accommodating their pursuits to their capacities in the second.[9]

He therefore criticizes the inflexibility of Rousseau's system and outlaws all harsh treatment in favour of fostering the particular talents of the child. The tutor should use a 'gentle yoke' and harmonize his directives as much as possible with the 'eternal laws of nature and necessity'.[10] Instead of inciting competition, he should encourage discreetly the latent sympathy of his pupils: 'Benevolent actions should not directly be preached to them, they should strictly begin in the heart of the performer.'[11] Above all, it should be remembered that the 'intuitive faculty' of the imagination is the grand instrument of virtue, and that the *'chef d'oeuvre* of a good education is to form a reasonable human being.'[12] To this end Godwin rejected Rousseau's scheme of solitary education, preferring to teach in small groups.

Only two journals bothered to review the prospectus. The *Monthly Review* dismissed it as an experiment derived from Rousseau despite stated differences and disliked the laboured attempt at 'ostentatious elegance'.[13] The *Gentleman's Magazine*, on the other hand, felt it was not only 'ingenious' and 'deeply speculative', but also 'strictly practicable', and suggested that the author would give perfect satisfaction to pupils and parents alike.[14]

Unfortunately for Godwin not enough pupils applied at one time, and he was forced to drop the project. Nevertheless, *An Account of the Seminary* remains an unduly neglected work. It shows just how rapidly Godwin had evolved in the five years since leaving Hoxton Academy: a decade before *Political Justice* he had already formed the main outline of his philosophy. Above all, by drawing on his own unhappy experience as a pupil, he developed the ideas of Rousseau to write one of the most eloquent and incisive essays on libertarian education.

When it became clear that not enough pupils would enrol in his seminary in Epsom, Godwin began to write furiously. By the following spring he had revised a volume of sermons, written two pamphlets, and composed three novels. It was the busiest period of his life. He wanted to prove to himself once and for all whether he had any talent as a writer. He also needed the money — he later acknowledged that the choice of all his works before *Political Justice* was moulded by 'some view to profit', although he was fortunate enough to be able to unite his 'tendencies & talents' to the 'economic laws of circumstances'.[15]

Godwin first chose six of his best sermons and published them in his own name under the title *Sketches of History,* with an eulogistic dedication to the 'Dissenter's Bishop' Richard Watson. Although a Socinian at the time, he still presents Jesus as the Son of God and discusses his character, arraignment, crucifixion and resurrection. But on re-reading his old sermons, Godwin could not entirely silence his critical mind. He condemns the Old Testament God for being a 'political legislator' in a theocratic State, and maintains that 'the right of the creator does not extend to the making of an innocent being, in a comprehensive sense, and with a view to the whole of his existence, miserable. God himself has not a right to be a tyrant.'[16]

In general, however, Godwin's revamped sermons offer a pedestrian justification of the ways of God to man. Only occasionally do they transcend the mannered style of a Dissenting academy graduate. Even so, the *English Review* and the *European Magazine and London Review* both praised their style and content.[17] The *Monthly Review* regretted the remark on the tyranny of God, but felt the sermons were like the animated style of the French orators: 'They are picturesque, and therefore entertaining: they are declamatory, but the declamation is not destitute of thought or good sense.'[18]

After revising his sermons in August, Godwin immediately returned to a pamphlet entitled *The Herald of Literature* begun a month earlier. It was finished in October and the publisher John Murray advertised it in the *Morning Chronicle* on 17 November 1783. The work purports to review 'The Most Considerable Publications that will be made in the Course of the Ensuing Winter'. In fact, it was an elaborate hoax: Godwin invented both the titles and the extracts of the works reviewed.

*The Herald of Literature* is a remarkable *tour de force*. Its lively banter shows that there was another side to Godwin than the gloomy Calvinist. The vivid forays into history, biography, the novel, drama, and poetry all reveal his wit and stylistic ingenuity.

Godwin includes in the pamphlet 'extracts' from the entirely fictitious works by the 'noble author of the Modern Anecdote', by a 'Shandean', and by Fanny Burney. Their composition must have been invaluable practice for Godwin as he was about to write three novels of his own. He also realizes his youthful passion for poetry by imitating William Hayley in an extract from 'An Essay on the Novel' and James Beattie in a poem entitled 'Inkle and Yarico'. In the latter, based on Steele's love story of a British soldier and a Red Indian girl, Godwin makes a characteristic plea for racial harmony. His sensual description of Yarico seems strangely at odds with the stoicism of his sermons:

> Her limbs were form'd in nature's choicest mould,
> Her lovely eyes the coldest bosoms sway'd.
> And on her breast ten thousand Cupids play'd . . .
> What though her skin were not as lilies fair?
> What though her face contest a darker shade?[19]

The wittiest piece though is the extract from 'The Alchymist, a Comedy, altered from Ben Jonson, by Richard Brinsley Sheridan'. It was inspired by one of Sheridan's parliamentary sallies: being taunted by the twenty-three-year-old Pitt for his dramatic works, Sheridan replied by comparing him to the 'angry boy' Kastril in Jonson's comedy *The Alchemist*. While Captain Face (the deposed Fox) has gone about some business, Kastril asks Subtle (Sheridan) to teach him the 'art of brawling'.

In the other spurious extracts, Godwin makes no effort to conceal his own opinions. In a passage on Saladin by Gibbon, he lauds Mahomet's 'sublime' doctrine (reflecting his own Socinianism) of the 'unity of God, the innocence of moderate enjoyment, the obligation of temperance and munificence'.[20] But it is for Burke that Godwin has the highest esteem. Two extracts on the American question are given to illustrate his 'originality of genius, and sublimity of conception'.[21] Thomas Paine also comes in for praise: for all his stern sentiments and rough style, he speaks with energy to 'the sturdy feelings of uncultivated nature' and is the best of the political writers in America. Godwin offers as proof some of Paine's reflections on the American revolution — the 'most important event' in the century, whose principal actors 'exhibit a combination of wisdom, spirit and genius, that can never be sufficiently admired'.[22]

Modern readers may have missed Godwin's irony, but contemporary reviewers, who were pilloried in the preface, certainly did not. The *Critical Review* praised its 'rancour mixed with mirth' and urged the authors to follow up the prophecies; the *Monthly Review* spoke mockingly of its useless ingenuity; and the *Gentleman's Magazine* objected to its 'wantonness of satire'.[23]

The second pamphlet Godwin wrote in late December 1783 was entitled *Instructions to a Statesman* and 'humbly inscribed to the right Honourable George Earl Temple'. It was published by Murray on 5 January 1784. The incident which provoked the pamphlet was the part played by George Grenville, Earl Temple, in bringing down the coalition of the Rockingham Party and Lord North which Godwin had already defended earlier in the year. Fox's East India Bill had been passed in the House of Commons by a two to one majority early in December, but George III, who never fully approved of the coalition, persuaded Temple to warn the House of Lords that he would regard anyone who voted for the bill as an enemy. His intervention had its desired effect. The coalition fell on 13 December and Pitt formed a Tory ministry.[24] Godwin reacted by attacking sarcastically Temple in particular and unprincipled statecraft in general.

In his dedication, Godwin claims that the pamphlet was written by a hermit living near Temple's country estate. The *Instructions* themselves are a practical guide for establishing one 'simple and god-like system' of despotism.[25] The advice falls into two parts: how to persuade the king, and how to win over the House of Commons. To achieve the first, the hermit offers sound advice on bribery, disguises, back stairs, lanterns, and invisible ink. For the second, he argues that the statesman must purchase a majority, govern in defiance of the House of Commons, or simply dissolve it altogether. There may of course be difficulties, for the people must be persuaded that

> It is he, most noble patron, who can swallow the greatest quantity of porter, who can roar the best catch, and who is the compleatest bruiser, that will finally carry the day. He must kiss the frost-bitten lips of the greengrocers. He must smooth the frowzy cheeks of the chandlers-shop women. He must stroke down the infinite belly of a Wapping landlady . . .[26]

Godwin's irony in the pamphlet made all the more effective the implied condemnation of secret influence, ambition, and political intrigue. He boldly exposes the corruption and venality of contemporary politics, and represents the monarchy and the aristocracy as potential threats to parliamentary democracy. For all the clever sarcasm and banter, it is clear that Godwin considered the Machiavellian *Instructions* to be 'the darkest and most tremendous scheme for the establishment of despotism that ever was contrived'.[27]

The ironic purpose of the pamphlet was not missed by contemporary reviewers. The *Critical Review* thought it provided no important political lessons, and, referring to the hermit who carved pipe stoppers, suggested that it be used for that purpose.[28] The *Monthly Review*, on the other hand, considered it the production of a 'wicked wit', and praised its 'bold and animated' conclusions.[29] Nevertheless, it proved the last of Godwin's pamphlets to be published with such bitter sarcasm and party venom.

In the meantime, Godwin was trying hard at novel writing. In November 1783, he wrote in ten days a short tale called *Damon and Delia*, for which Thomas Hookham gave him five guineas. The theme is that of ill-fated love. The protagonists are torn between their affection for each other and their duty to their tyrannical fathers who are more concerned with wealth and reputation than with their children's feelings. But after a series of misadventures, true love triumphs and marriage is celebrated as the 'sweet-est, and the fairest of all the bands of society'.[30]

But while Godwin borrows sentimental devices from Comtesse de La Fayette, Fielding and Goethe (whom Delia reads), he adds much robust satire. The action takes place in high society in provincial Southampton. Prettyman, Squire Savage and Mr. Prattle make absurd appearances. Fops are humiliated, amazons have crackers in their skirts, and lords sprawl in the mud.

There is also some memorable characterization. Moreland is the first of many noble misanthropes. Mr. Godfrey is clearly autobiographical: driven by a love of fame, he becomes minister, tutor and then writer. The most interesting character, however, is Sophia Cranley, a steady republican who claims that women are not born to be controlled and who inveighs against the effeminacy and depravity of modern times: 'We wcrc slaves, and we deserved to be so. In almost every country there now appeared a king, that puppet pageant, that monster in creation, miserable itself, a combination of every vice, and invented for the curse of human kind.'[31]

Godwin's first novel is of great interest. The plot is slight and conven-tional. The narrative is uneven. Yet there is a fluent urgency in the style and the dialogues are well-handled and vigorous. The fate of Delia effectively excites our sympathy and the affectation of her entourage earns our scorn. For a first attempt written so quickly, it was a real achievement.

Godwin must have been pleased by its reception. The *English Review* admired its 'philosophical sensibility' and recommended it as 'indisputably superior' to the common run of novels.[32] The *Critical Review* called it an amusing little tale and the *Westminster Magazine* found it agreeable and interesting.[33] Only the *Monthly Review* thought the wit insipid, and the pathos dull.[34]

Immediately after *Damon and Delia*, Godwin wrote in three weeks another novel called *Italian Letters: or, The History of the Count de St. Julian*. Despite its small compass, George Robinson gave him twenty guineas for it — twice the normal sum. It had a similar didactic purpose and equally exploited the literature of sensibility. He used the epistolary form and the theme of seduction and betrayal developed by Richardson. Many details of the plot came from Henry Mackenzie's *Julia de Roubigné* (1777), and the names of the protagonist the Marquis de Pescara, his bride Matilda della Colonna, and his friend Ferdinand San Severino were borrowed from Castiglione's *The Book of the Courtier* (1561). All these influences were absorbed by Godwin however to create a novel which was characteristically his own.

*Italian Letters* explores the sentimental education of two young aristocrats who attended Palermo University together. The plot is very simple. The stoic Count de St. Julian adopts the role of mentor to his friend the Marquis de Pescara and tries to prevent him from being made the 'dupe of artifice' and misled by the 'sophistry of vice' in fashionable Naples.[35] Tragically, he fails to take into account the insidious influence of the Marquis de San Severino, a dissolute and Machiavellian noble. In the meantime, St. Julian, deprived of his inheritance by his younger brother, falls in love with the peerless Matilda. But when Matilda's father dies, she insists on a year of mourning — time enough for the unscrupulous Pescara to send St. Julian on business to Spain and to marry his fiancée. On hearing the news, the inconsolable St. Julian kills Pescara in a duel, after which Matilda decides to devote the rest of her life to her maternal duties.

While the plot is trite, Godwin uses it to express some of his major moral preoccupations. Gallantry, we are told, casts down 'all the sacred barriers of religion' and scorns that 'suspicious vigilance' and that 'trembling sensibility' which constitute the essence of virtue.[36] The conscious aim of the novel is thus to increase the number of those 'noble and elevated spirits, that rise above the vulgar notions and the narrow conduct of the bulk of mankind, that soar to the sublimest heights of rectitude'.[37]

In *Italian Letters*, Godwin also offers some very real social criticism. There is a constant contrast between the simplicity and innocence of rural Palermo and the elegance and depravity of the court at Naples. All the leading characters are aristocrats, and their position prevents rather than encourages virtue: 'A man of rank is a poor shivering, exotic plant, that cannot subsist out of his native soil. If the imaginary barriers of society were thrown down, if we were reduced back again to a state of nature, the nobleman would appear a shiftless and a helpless being . . .'[38] For his part, St. Julian had read his Rousseau and declares that he would rather dwell in a cottage than be master of the proudest palace that Naples could boast.

As a whole the novel suffers from the implausibility and melodrama often found in the literature of sensibility. As Mary Shelley later observed, there is scarcely any 'anatomy of heart'.[39] While the epistolary approach allows the protagonists to reveal their motives, Godwin's style does not vary according to their characters. His portrayal of love rings hollow, and he relies on superlatives to describe mental states. His rhetoric is often strained and the many solecisms reflect only too well the speed with which the novel was written.

Most of Godwin's contemporaries, however, were impressed. The *Critical Review* applauded the refined sentiments and elegant language while the *English Review* commended the morality.[40] The *Monthly Review* was the most generous this time: it found the story 'pathetic and interesting', written in 'a chaste, easy and perspicuous style' and intermixed with reflections 'equally sensible, benevolent and moral'.[41] Godwin's cousin, now Mrs.

Sothren, felt it was his best novel — 'vastly prettier' than *Caleb Williams*.[42] Only the *Gentleman's Magazine* thought the incidents and pathos common.[43]

Having finished two novels in quick succession, Godwin immediately set about composing a third. He wrote *Imogen: A Pastoral Romance* in the first five months of 1784. John Lane bought it for ten pounds, and it was advertised in the *Morning Herald* on 11 July. It proved to be the best of Godwin's early fiction.

In his preface, Godwin acknowledges his debt for the plot to Milton's *Comus*, but as its sub-title 'From the Ancient British' indicates, he was also reflecting a growing interest in native mythology. Godwin parodies Macpherson's spurious translation of the poems of Ossian by first supposing that *Imogen* was a translation of a novel written in 'Welch' by the ancient bard 'Cadwallo', and then concluding that it was written by Rice ap Thomas who lived in the reign of William III.[44]

The plot is based on the stratagems of a magician Roderic who misuses his powers to seduce the innocent shepherdess Imogen and to confound her lover Edwin. It turns on the prophecy pronounced by a refractory goblin at Roderic's birth:

> 'When Roderic', cried he, 'shall be overreached in all his spells by a simple swain, unversed in the various arts of sorcery and magic: when Roderic shall sue to a simple maid, who by his claims shall be made to hate the swain that once she loved, and who yet shall resist all his personal attractions and all his power; then shall his power be at an end. His palaces shall be dissolved, his riches scattered, and he himself shall become an unpitied, necessitous, miserable vagabond.'[45]

This revolutionary scenario inexorably reaches its climax when Imogen rejects the advances of Roderic who impersonates Edwin. The lordly despotism of the land-owning magician is then destroyed and the common people return once again to their harmonious living.

The novel begins with a description of society in the Welsh valleys in ancient times which is strongly reminiscent of Rousseau's ideal:

> All was rectitude and guileless truth. The hoarse din of war had never reached its happy bosom; its rivers had never been impurpled with the stain of human blood. Its willows had not wept over the crimes of its inhabitants, nor had the iron hand of tyranny taught care and apprehension to seat themselves upon the brow of its shepherds. They were strangers to riches, and to ambition, for they all lived in a happy equality.[46]

Such men and women have no knowledge of the 'degeneracy of modern times'.[47] In their society before government, no one claims dominion over another, and relations are completely open and sincere.

In opposition to them, Godwin places the lustful magician Roderic. His mother has forced 'crowds of degenerate shepherds' to build a grand and commanding mansion which is filled with artificial luxuries and witnesses 'one uninterrupted scene of ingenious cruelty and miserable despair'.[48] Roderic has also enclosed his fields and with the help of the iron plough practises agriculture.

While virtue is associated with the pastoral Imogen and Edwin, the enterprising Roderic is the embodiment of vice. He is irredeemably attached to sensuality, luxury and lust. He misuses his learning for selfish ends, and is devoured by spleen. Roderic is clearly intended to represent the eighteenth-century despotic landowner while Imogen and Edwin possess the enlightened morality of a reborn humanity living in harmony with nature.[49]

Godwin thus carefully draws the contrast between the sophisticated decadence of the castle and the simple virtue of the country. It is in the open valleys of the shepherds that innocence, simplicity, and tranquillity are to be found. Even Roderic in a moment of insight confesses: 'How gladly would I quit my sumptuous palace, and my magic arts, for the careless, airy, and unreflecting joys of rural simplicity!'[50]

But while the shepherds scorn luxury and wealth, they are not ignorant. Roderic is perplexed to find in Imogen so much simplicity, judgment and gaiety in union. When he fails to seduce her by his eloquence and riches, he exclaims in exasperation that she is 'too well fortified with the prejudices of education, and the principles of an imaginary virtue'.[51] Inevitably, his sinister attempt to overthrow the Celtic paradise is defeated by the Godwinian principles of 'unblemished truth' and 'omnipotence in virtue'.[52]

Although Godwin uses the pastoral convention and sets his ideal society in the past, his romance is not merely a nostalgic yearning for a lost Golden Age. He may exploit the vogue for primitivism with skill and charm, but he ultimately pictures his society without government in pre-Christian Wales as a real and ever-present possibility. 'The Gods', Imogen declares, 'have made all their rational creatures equal. If they have made one strong and another weak, it is for the purpose of mutual benevolence and assistance, and not for that of despotism and oppression.'[53] Anticipating the collapse of Roderic's empire at the end of the novel, Imogen significantly recalls the Druids' teaching that virtue 'may be obscured for a moment, but it shall only be to burst forth again more illustrious than ever'.[54]

In form *Imogen* takes its place with other minor pre-Romantic works of literature of the period, but it was Godwin's most sustained piece of literary creation to date. He skilfully intermingles plot, character and theme to form a coherent whole. The style is somewhat stilted but it has an elegance which on occasion reaches a majestic rhetoric.

Like his two previous novels, it was favourably received. The *Critical Review* did not hesitate to pronounce that it abounds 'with tender sentiments, pleasing description, and innocent simplicity of manners'; the *Monthly Review* felt that for all its lack of verisimilitude it is 'of a chaste and virtuous tendency'; while the *English Review* argued that it leaves 'a pleasing impression, and is calculated to revive ideas of the days of pastoral purity and innocence'.[55]

The well-known publisher L. A. H. de Cavitat said it was popular in America as late as 1804 and it may even have influenced Edgar Allan Poe in *The Fall of the House of Usher*.[56] Mary Shelley, however, felt it was somewhat forced and saw its value, like that of the other early novels, mainly as a stylistic exercise. It remained for Godwin to find a subject worthy of his genius — 'a subject to support his style, which hitherto had supported his subject'.[57] This did not happen readily, and it was ten years before Godwin returned to novel writing.

Godwin in the meantime saw much of James Marshal, whom he had first met when he was seventeen at Hoxton. He too was engaged in hack work — translating, indexing and correcting for the publishers — but he lacked originality and never emerged from Grub Street. Although Godwin found him a dull companion, and according to his daughter was 'from an earnest sense of being in the right, somewhat despotic on occasions', they remained close friends for life.[58] Marshal admired Godwin from the beginning and once prophesied that he would become a Secretary of State or a High Chancellor. The chief thing against it, he declared, is

> the weight of your political virtue, which has hitherto & always will if you retain it bear you down. Could you prevail with yourself to part with one half of this ponderous quality that pervades your little frame, you would ascend [?] like a feather into the region of places and pensions & get a secure and quiet retreat, from the poverty of an author, the [vio]lence of booksellers, & the duns of creditors, in the Red Book.[59]

Marshal acted as a literary agent for Godwin, but when he went to the West Indies to seek his fortune in 1784, Godwin was forced to deal with editors and publishers directly.

On the strength of his pamphlet *The Herald of Literature*, he became a contributor in February to John Murray's *English Review*. The journal, established in 1783, reviewed British, American and European literature, and gave memoirs of the more celebrated authors. It was set up to rival the

Tory *Annual Register* and the Whig *New Annual Register*, but was moderate in both politics and religion. Godwin probably wrote the review of *Imogen* which appeared in the August issue. He also reviewed the controversy which followed Priestley's *A History of the Corruptions of Christianity* (1782). He told Priestley privately that as a Socinian he was perfectly satisfied that Christianity would 'not stand the test of philosophical examination, unless stripped of its doctrinal corruptions'. He was unwilling, however, to make himself a party since it was the business of a review 'to represent candidly the arguments of both sides'.[60]

It is impossible to identify with any certainty Godwin's other articles, but they cannot have been many for he was only paid two guineas a sheet and he could not hope for more than twenty-four guineas a year. He was reduced to doing whatever work came along. Murray offered him twenty guineas for translating the French manuscript of the *Memoirs of the Life of Lord Lovat* but it was only published after extensive revisions in 1797. Godwin thus remained in dire straits, and for most of the time did not eat his dinner 'without previously carrying my watch or my books to the pawnbroker'.[61]

There were, however, new openings. He had several professional dinners at Murray's house with the other contributors of the *English Review*. When his volume of sermons appeared, Richard Watson, to whom it was dedicated, declared that 'there is the animation of youth in many parts of it, held in, however, by the judgement of a more advanced age in all'.[62] As a result Godwin met him about half a dozen times.

More important, he made the acquaintance of the wealthy radical Dissenter Timothy Hollis who was famous for his patronage of promoters of 'knowledge, truth and liberty'.[63] At his dinners held twice a week at his house in Great Ormond Street, Godwin met 'several respectable people, but above all, Mr. Barry, the painter, whose conversation afforded me extreme delight, & with whom I became exceedingly intimate'.[64] James Barry, Irish protegé of Burke and tutor to William Blake, combined the grand style in painting with extreme republicanism in politics. When Godwin first met him, he had just finished his monumental murals for the great hall of the Royal Society of Arts, which illustrated the progress of human culture and were dedicated to the *'melioration, liberties,* and reform of mankind'.[65] Godwin and Barry remained close friends for many years.

Godwin's reputation as a competent writer continued to grow in liberal and Dissenting circles. In July 1784, the publisher George Robinson and his old tutor Andrew Kippis offered him ten guineas to complete the last three chapters of the 'British and Foreign History' section of *The New Annual Register* for 1783. His work being well-received, a permanent contract was sealed by a dinner with Robinson and Kippis at the Crown and Anchor tavern in the Strand. He continued to write for the journal until the summer of 1791, when he began composing *Political Justice*.

The 'British and Foreign History' section of *The New Annual Register* covered on average one hundred and fifty double-columned closely-printed pages. It demanded a detailed knowledge of leading events and personalities in Britain, Europe, India and America, as well as first-hand acquaintance with the parliamentary debates. In the next seven years Godwin was therefore to acquire a thorough understanding of contemporary history and politics.

Although Godwin's narrative is predominantly descriptive, he does not hesitate to make his own views known. In the edition for 1783 he roundly condemns British policy in India, and in a discussion of the Mahratta War gives tempered criticism of the 'illustrious culprit' Warren Hastings and moderate praise to the 'humane' and 'equable' Hyder Ali.[66] On the other hand, he hails America as the 'first enlightened people who have formed for themselves an independent government in the Western hemisphere'.[67]

In the following year Godwin once again expresses his enthusiastic support for the Rockingham Whigs and his admiration for their leaders. In his account of Fox's East India Bill, for example, he describes Burke's speech as the 'most sublime and finished composition that his studies and labours produced' and speaks of Fox's 'superior and unequalled abilities, his manly, rapid and astonishing eloquence'.[68] In subsequent volumes, which focus principally on parliamentary affairs at home and political developments in Ireland, France, the United Provinces and India, Godwin consistently supports the cause of 'justice, equality and truth'.[69]

His work was evidently much appreciated for he assumed increasing responsibility for the production of the journal. The money was not however great and Godwin's shyness and delicacy made it difficult for him to solicit more work. His old tutor Kippis came to his aid once again in March 1785 and recommended a private pupil called Willis Webb. Godwin much appreciated the gesture and later wrote: 'I reflect at all times with pleasure on the memory of Dr. Kippis, as having been sincerely my friend, & having with much kindness assisted me in conquering the difficulties of an adventurous situation.'[70]

Webb stayed with Godwin for about two years before going on to a large private school at Hitcham, near Eton. Godwin was thus able to put his own educational theories in practice and Webb became the first of many young disciples who regarded him with genuine esteem. After experiencing the 'liberality' of Godwin's private tuition, Willis was later very unhappy with the restrictions at Hitcham since 'the same vices that flourish at Eton or Westminster are practised at Hitcham, with this *glorious* addition that here deceit is necessary to conceal them'.[71] When he eventually entered St.

John's, Cambridge in 1788, he warmly thanked his old tutor for his help.

Willis brought Godwin about eighty guineas a year. His income was further increased in July 1785 by an invitation from Dr. Gilbert Stuart to join Dr. William Thomson and John Logan on a new Whig journal called the *Political Herald, and Review*. Since his colleagues were already well-known authors, Fox and Sheridan clearly thought of Godwin at this stage as a competent writer and useful partisan. Thanks to his new appointment, Godwin, who had moved to Norfolk Street in January 1785, and thence to Tavistock Row in March, was able on 24 June to move from a second floor to a first floor in Broad Street, Soho.

Godwin became editor of the journal in August when Stuart died, but he was never entirely happy with the political nature of his appointment. In a letter to Sheridan, he insisted: 'I disdain the prospect of any private & personal advantage; & am desirous, if my efforts be of the smallest service, to retain the consciousness of their having been disinterested and sincere.'[72] Unfortunately the journal soon began to lose money and after refusing a regular salary from Whig party funds, Godwin arranged its closure in 1787. That his efforts were appreciated however is clear from a letter he later wrote to Lord Holland in which he declared that he had a 'much more favourable opinion' of the service of the administration of 1786 than 'some with whom I was accustomed to converse', and that he knew it was 'in the contemplation of Mr. Fox's friends, & particularly yourself, to have made some provision for my latter days . . .'.[73]

Amongst Godwin's contributions to the *Political Herald, and Review*, it is now only possible to identify with any certainty seven letters signed 'Mucius' and three unsigned articles.[74] Since they were written on his own initiative they can truly be said to represent his own views. They follow the familiar pattern of enthusiastic support for the Whigs (particularly Burke, the 'foremost of the human species') and unqualified condemnation of the Tories (especially Pitt's career of 'naked, honest, unplausible despotism').[75]

Godwin also wrote indignantly about foreign affairs. The impeachment of Warren Hastings and the Rohilla War highlighted British colonial policy, and Godwin began some 'Memoirs of the Administration of the Government of Madras during the Presidency of Lord Macartney'. He managed to publish three articles on the complicated history of the events in India from 1749 to 1782, but was forced to discontinue the series after his request for materials to Lord Macartney and Sir George Stanton had been refused. He therefore only partly realized his aim of examining the charge that those responsible for Indian affairs were guilty of 'cruelty, tyranny, usurpation and avarice'.[76]

Nearer home, but no less concerned, Godwin addressed an open letter to the 'Freemen and Citizens of Ireland', warning them not to jeopardize their claim to national independence in exchange for Pitt's offer of free trade. They were not only competing like America with 'the most illustrious' periods of Athens and Rome but offered the 'wonderful exhibition' of an army of eighty thousand United Volunteers. 'What might we not promise from beginnings like these?', Godwin mused.[77] He intended to bring out more letters addressed to the 'People of Ireland', but the collapse of the *Political Herald, and Review* in December 1786 made it impossible.

Godwin's articles to the journal show that he was deeply disturbed by repression in India and Ireland. But although he hinted at violent measures, he was the first to recognize that reform is inevitably slow and that the 'harvest cannot be reaped on the same day which the seed is committed to the earth'.[78] A few years before the composition of *Political Justice*, he was thus primarily committed to the Whig programme of parliamentary reform: 'The creed of a whig, Sir,' he told Pitt, 'necessarily taught me to imagine the house of commons the first power in the constitution.'[79]

With the collapse of the *Political Herald, and Review*, Godwin began writing a *History of the Internal Affairs of the United Provinces*. It owed its specific origins to the recent revolution of the Dutch against William V, the Stadtholder. Godwin carefully narrates the principal events of the upheaval from 1780. While impressed by the attempt of the Dutch cities to govern themselves by popular councils, he does not openly advocate them. He believes at this stage that aristocracy should remain in Holland as long as there is economic inequality, since political authority must inevitably accompany wealth.

In his conclusion, however, Godwin shows just how near he is to forming the fundamental ideas of *Political Justice*. The great aim of the political thinker should be the 'morals, the liberty, and the equal government of the people'.[80] Above all, two years before the French Revolution, Godwin is able to conclude: 'a new republic of the purest kind is about to spring up in Europe; and the flame of liberty, which was first excited in America, and has since communicated itself . . . to so many other countries, bids fair for the production of consequences, not less extensive than salutary'.[81]

The work was praised by the *English Review* for its 'clear and masculine understanding' and Godwin himself probably wrote the fulsome review in *The New Annual Register* which focused on its appeal to 'truth and reason'.[82] As Thomas Brand Hollis, the reformer, wrote in 1791, the history certainly demonstrated Godwin's 'attachment to public liberty'.[83] But it had little effect in preventing foreign intervention, for William V was rapidly re-established by the Prussians with British approval.

Godwin must have been very lonely living on his own in cheap lodgings and devoting his time to solitary study and political journalism. He was shy and aggressive by turns and did not easily make friends. There were clearly

times when he regretted his bachelor independence. Although his prospects
were uncertain, he asked his sister Hannah in the spring of 1784 to find him
a wife.

She immediately recommended a friend called Miss Gay whom she
considered in every sense formed to make him happy:

> She has a pleasing voice, with which she accompanies her musical
> instrument with judgment. She has an easy politeness in her manners,
> neither free nor reserved. She is a good housekeeper and a good
> economist, and yet of a generous disposition. As to her internal accompl-
> ishments, I have reason to speak still more highly of them, good sense
> without vanity, a penetrating judgment without a disposition to satire,
> good nature and humility, with about as much religion as my William
> likes, struck me with a wish that she was my William's wife. I have no
> certain knowledge of her fortune, but that I leave for you to learn.[84]

The cautious Godwin, however, took his time. Some months passed before
he inquired after the lady's age and opinions, and two more before he called
on her. But he was not impressed and sought no further interviews. He
resigned himself to living on his own, and declined his sister's suggestion
that they live together.

He was still unhappy with his lodgings. On 24 June 1786, he first moved
to Newman Street, and then on 29 September to Upper Berkeley Street,
Portman Square. But at least his circle of acquaintances was slowly expanding. He became a regular member of the literary parties of the publisher
George Robinson, where he saw Thomas Warton, the poet, James Heath,
the engraver, and James Perry and William Woodfall, the newspaper
editors. He also met Thomas Holcroft, the playwright, William Nicholson,
the scientist, and William Shield, the composer, all of whom became close
friends.

During the negotiations over the *Political Herald, and Review*, Godwin
moved closer to the Whig patricians. Sheridan proposed introducing him to
the Duke of Portland and invited him to dinner with General Fitzpatrick
and Richard Tickell, although neither meeting took place. He did, however, dine at Sheridan's in June with George Canning and the Royal Burghs
of Scotland. Canning was still a schoolboy at Eton at the time, but Godwin
recalled with pride that the future Prime Minister was 'very pressing' to
make his acquaintance.[85] He also met the twenty-year-old George Grey,
who seemed more worried about his gold buckles and his legs than his
recently acquired constituency. But the auspicious openings all proved
disappointing. With the collapse of the *Political Herald, and Review*, Sheridan soon dropped Godwin, and he was never able to meet the admired

Burke.

There were other consolations. His improved financial position enabled Godwin on 25 March 1787 to move yet again to more commodious lodgings in New Norfolk Street, Grosvenor Square. After reading his articles in *The New Annual Register,* Henry Beaufoy, the Dissenters' most consistent supporter in the House of Commons, invited Godwin to his house, where he renewed his acquaintance with Richard Watson, the Bishop of Llandaff, and met the young reformer William Wilberforce. Towards the close of the year, Kippis's beautiful protegée Helen Maria Williams also welcomed him at her tea-time literary coteries, which were attended by the poet Samuel Rogers and Mrs. Piozzi, Dr. Johnson's intimate friend.

More important for his political development, Godwin became increasingly friendly in 1788 with the wealthy republican Thomas Brand Hollis. He had actively supported the American Cause and helped John Jebb to establish the Society for Constitutional Information (S.C.I.). Tom Paine was soon to entrust him with the keys of the Bastille to forward to George Washington. At Thomas Brand Hollis's, Godwin met some of the leading intellectuals of the day: John Adams, the American ambassador, Samuel Romilly, the future penal reformer, Richard Sharp, the friend of Dr. Johnson and Burke, Capel Lofft, the co-founder of the S.C.I., Thomas Taylor, the Platonist, Gilbert Wakefield, the Unitarian scholar and polemicist, and George Walker, the Unitarian mathematician. Just before the outbreak of the French Revolution, Godwin was thus exposed to a tradition of republicanism which dated from the Commonwealth, and was on friendly terms with some of the leading veterans of the campaign for American Independence and parliamentary reform. Many of these new acquaintances were to become the most prominent radicals in the following decade.

Godwin's most important relationship at the time was undoubtedly with Thomas Holcroft, whom he had first met at Timothy Hollis's parties three years before. Holcroft rapidly became his closest friend and the second of his four principal oral instructors. In many ways, they were ill-suited. There was ten years difference in age between them. Where Godwin was highly educated and sedentary, Holcroft was self-taught and widely travelled. The son of a cobbler, he had successively earned his living as bootmaker, ostler, village schoolmaster, strolling player, reporter, playwright, and novelist. He had also spent three years in Paris as a correspondent for the *Morning Herald*, where he read the French *philosophes*, translated Voltaire's memoirs and pirated Beaumarchais's *Le Mariage de Figaro*.

Despite their different backgrounds and ages, Godwin and Holcroft remained, except for a short period before the latter's death, the firmest of friends. Mary Shelley recalled that Holcroft was a man of 'stern and irascible character' — but then her father was not entirely placid either.[86]

VII. Thomas Holcroft, *c.* 1782, by John Opie.

Each became the other's most respected critic. They practised perfect sincerity, and although it often led to *'démêlés'*, as Godwin recorded in his diary, their friendship proved a 'delightful mingling of souls'.[87] Godwin probably modelled the rugged but warm-hearted Mr. Forester in *Caleb Williams* on Holcroft and all his life kept his portrait painted by John Opie alongside Mary Wollstonecraft's in his study. In a note, he later commented: 'I was favoured by Sheridan, courted by Canning, & estimated to my real worth by Holcroft.'[88]

Holcroft's immediate impact was on Godwin's religious beliefs. Since 1783 he had remained a Socinian. He had entertained doubts two years later but Joseph Priestley's arguments and his fear about a future life had kept him from disbelief in the revealed truth of the Bible and miracles. But now he was exposed to the militant Holcroft, who, according to Coleridge, was: 'Fierce, hot, petulant, the very High priest of Atheism, he *hates* God "with all his heart, with all his mind, with all his soul & with all his strength".'[89] Religion, Holcroft declared to a friend, was the 'scourge of mankind' and the true heaven was only to be found in the 'improvement of the mind'.[90]

Not surprisingly, Holcroft reawakened all Godwin's doubts about the truth of miracles. As was his wont, he read on both sides of the question, first in Hume's *Essay on Miracles* (1748) and then in George Campbell's reply *Dissertation on Miracles* (1762). He recognized the latter to be the 'most complete & consummate exhibition' of the Christian argument, but the work had the opposite of its desired effect and Godwin lapsed into disbelief.[91] For the year 1788, he recorded amongst his principles: 'That miracles are the creatures of the imagination; That the varieties of mind are the produce of education'.[92] For the time being, however, Godwin only lost his faith in Christianity, not in a God. It was not until 1792 when he was writing *Political Justice* that his conversations with Holcroft and his reflections on the doctrine of necessity made him an atheist.

In politics the influence was mutual. Five years earlier Holcroft had written that there are 'no good governments'. In their place, he boldly called for a rational society of 'absolute freedom' in which equals have their property 'sole, and undivided, to their own use', and are 'not shackled by the degrading recollection of dependence, nor deterred by the rapacity of power'.[93] But he felt that the prevailing intellectual inequality of mankind made such a scheme impractical, and in his poem *Human Happiness; or, the Sceptic*, and in his other writings, displayed royalist sentiments. He was moreover thoroughly disillusioned with practical politics. During the famous Westminster by-election of 1788, he wrote to Godwin that electioneering is 'a trade so despicably degrading, so eternally incompatible with moral and mental dignity, that I can scarcely believe a truly great mind capable of the dirty drudgery of such vice'.[94] It was some years before Godwin managed to make Holcroft a republican, but he retained his disdain for practical politics.

Godwin missed the Westminster by-election because he was in Guildford from July to September, banished, as he put it, 'from human society, and condemned to eat grass with the beasts'.[95] He was in fact looking after a second cousin Thomas Cooper, whose father had just died in India and whose inheritance had been lost at sea. Godwin had stayed with the Coopers during some of his holidays whilst at Hoxton, and he now decided to repay their kindness by taking charge of their eldest son. When they returned to London together, Godwin's debts forced him to move on 29 September into a cheaper lodging with his friend Marshal in Great Marylebone Street.

Although Godwin was poor and had little spare time from his writing, it was an ideal opportunity to develop his educational principles sketched in *An Account of the Seminary* and only briefly practised on Willis Webb. In his notebook Godwin carefully defined his aim: 'It is of no consequence whether a man of genius have learned either art or science before twenty-five: all that is necessary, or even desirable, is that his powers should be unfolded, his emulation roused, and his habits conducted into a right channel.' As to the method: 'Give energy, and mental exertion will always have attraction enough.' Godwin aimed at 'gentleness, kindness, cordiality', but it did not prevent him from chiding Cooper for being rude to his old friend Marshal or for not apologizing when coming home too late.[96]

For his part, the spirited and wilful Cooper also kept notes. On one occasion, the fourteen-year-old boy complained that his tutor had called him a 'Brute', a 'Viper', a 'Tiger', with a 'black heart' and 'no proper feelings'.[97] He left the memorandum for Godwin, who replied with warmth: 'There is in this paper a degree of sensiblity that has great merit. The love of independence and dislike of unjust treatment is the source of a thousand virtues. If while you are necessarily dependent on me I treat you with heaviness and unkindness, it is natural you should have a painful feeling of it.'[98] He clearly valued the sincerity of Cooper's outburst more than his personal animosity.

Cooper later recalled that at this time Godwin still dressed in clerical garb: 'a black suit, large cocked hat, his hair frizzed at the sides and curled stiffly behind'. He was a 'small well-made man, with a thin face, large nose, blue eyes, and most placid countenance'. But the appearance belied Godwin's passionate nature, for he readily explained and read to the young Cooper *Clarissa Harlowe* and all of Shakespeare's plays. Despite their altercations, Cooper felt Godwin was 'one of the most pure and benevolent of men', and later told William Dunlap that 'much more than a common father is he to me; he has cherished and instructed me'.[99]

Holcroft also took a part in Cooper's education. The boy followed his example, and with Godwin's full approval went on the stage in 1792. At first he had little success as a strolling player but when he went to America four years later he became a great celebrity and made Holcroft's plays popular in the New World. He never forgot his debt to the two men who had launched him on his illustrious career.

In the meantime, Godwin had been following political events closely at home and abroad. In *The New Annual Register* he covered the impeachment of Warren Hastings, and the debates on the slave trade. He reported with enthusiasm the bitter campaign to repeal the Test and Corporation Acts which handicapped the Dissenters so severely. He wrote extensively about the revolution in the United Provinces, which he felt had been inspired by the creed of America and the example of Ireland. Above all, he studied the attempts to reform the *ancien régime* in France and declared Turgot to be a 'most enlightened minister' and Mirabeau an 'extraordinary genius'.[100]

At home, the clamour for reform grew inexorably louder. On 4 November 1788, fires were lit throughout England to commemorate the centenary of the Glorious Revolution. At the Revolution Society in London, Godwin's former tutor Kippis gave a resounding address, and in the London Tavern afterwards forty-one toasts were proposed, beginning with 'The Majesty of the People!' and ending with 'May Truth and Liberty prevail throughout the World!' The Society also moved three declaratory principles: '(i) That all civil and political authority derives from the people; (ii) That the abuse of power justifies resistance; (iii) That the right of private judgment, liberty of conscience, trial by jury, freedom of the press, and the freedom of election ought ever to be held sacred and inviolable'.[101] Godwin could well write in *The New Annual Register* for 1788:

> It was long a kind of problem in philosophy, whether or not the human species collectively, like the intellectual powers of the individual, were in a state of gradual progress ... This problem is hastening fast to a decision. Liberty, humanity, and science are daily extending, and bid fair to render despotism, cruelty, and ignorance subjects of historical memory.[102]

# CHAPTER VI

# *The French Revolution*

When the French Revolution broke out in 1789 it was not entirely unexpected. Godwin was thirty-three at the time, and his long exposure to the Lockean individualism of the Dissenters and his careful reading of the French *philosophes* had prepared him for the event. He had been gladdened by the American Declaration of Independence and the libertarian struggles in Ireland and the United Provinces, and was therefore delighted when the oppressive *ancien régime* in France collapsed at last. On the day following the fall of the Bastille, he recorded in his diary 'King of France submits to the National Assembly'.[1] The bald statement fails to express his joy; he later wrote:

> My heart beat high with great swelling sentiments of Liberty. I had been for nine years in principle a republican. I had read with great satisfaction the writings of Rousseau, Helvetius, and others, the most popular authors of France. I observed in them a system more general and simply philosophical than in the majority of English writers on political subjects; and I could not refrain from conceiving sanguine hopes of a revolution of which such writings had been the precursors.[2]

It was to have a profound effect on his opinions and to shape the rest of his life.

He continued for the time being writing the historical section of *The New Annual Register*, but moved closer to the radical Dissenting circles. That he was now considered one of their number is clear by his presence at the dinner on 6 May at the London Tavern to celebrate the opening of the notorious academy at Hackney. He also joined his old tutors Kippis and Rees at the dinner of the Society for Commemorating the Glorious Revolution on 5 November 1789. At the Old Jewry Meeting House, Price had delivered the night before *A Discourse on the Love of our Country* which summarized many of the fundamental beliefs of the Rational Dissenters. The peculiar blend of rationalism, millenarianism, Christian ethics, and radical politics anticipates *Political Justice* and shows just how far Godwin was indebted to their culture.

Taking his cue from the parable of the Good Samaritan, Price rejected the narrow ties of family or country and argued that the noblest principle in our nature is the regard for 'general justice' and that 'good-will which embraces all the world'.[3] He then developed the Socratic view that vice is error and emphasized the need for enlightenment: 'Ignorance is the parent of bigotry, intolerance, persecution and slavery. Inform and instruct mankind and these evils will be excluded.'[4] Finally, he called for the realization of the principles of the Glorious Revolution, an end to aggressive wars, and the creation of a representative federation of sovereign states to enable mankind to determine its destiny and to reach moral perfection. Referring to the recent events in France, he perorated enthusiastically: 'And now, methinks, I see the ardor for liberty catching and spreading; a general amendment beginning in human affairs; the dominion of kings changed for the dominion of laws, and the dominion of priests giving way to the dominion of reason and conscience'.[5]

Godwin, like his fellow Dissenters, was inspired by such eloquent prophecy. He kept amongst his papers for the rest of his life a copy in Marshal's hand of a congratulatory message sent by the Revolution Society to the National Assembly in Paris. It declared confidently:

> The inhabitants of Great Britain in particular may expect to derive the most essential benefit from the Revolution of France; and united as we are to you by congeniality of sentiment, by the cultivation of science and truth, and by the love of that freedom for which our ancestors bled, we trust it is scarcely possible for any occasion to offer that can lead two such nations to engage in mutual hostilities.[6]

Initially, Godwin quietly watched political developments in France and at home. He hoped the French Revolution would trigger off a reform movement in Britain, and listened regularly to the debates in the House of Commons to see if there were any propitious signs. He was soon to be disappointed. On 13 February 1790 he attended a dinner of the 'Anti-Tests' — the leading Dissenters and their parliamentary allies who were campaigning to repeal the Test and Corporation Acts. The year before, their Bill had been narrowly defeated, but when Fox tried again on 2 March, it was resoundingly outvoted. Worse still, Burke took the opportunity to make an unexpected and inflammatory attack on Dissenters as disaffected citizens. Nothing could have made his claim more probable.

Godwin was also present at the celebration at the Crown and Anchor Tavern on Bastille Day in July. Price spoke again, praising France for its wish to abandon war and calling for a United States of the World. The Whig leaders Stanhope and Sheridan were there, and Godwin was pleased by his own warm reception. He quoted in a rare note in his diary: 'We are particularly fortunate in having you among us; it is having the best cause countenanced by the man, by whom we most wished to see it supported.'[7] The last great occasion of the year which Godwin attended was the annual dinner of the Revolution Society on 5 November. France had already begun to dismantle feudalism and on 19 June abolished the nobility. It was decided to debate the issue: the old campaigner John Horne Tooke proposed the abolition of the nobility in Britain, and eventually carried the day.

Godwin in the meantime was finding it increasingly frustrating as the writer of the historical section for *The New Annual Register*. In the spring of 1790, he therefore applied for a post in the Department of Natural and Artificial Productions in the British Museum. No doubt he felt that the post would give him greater independence to press his own views, but he was quite willing to make use of his respectable past. In a letter to Lord Robert Spencer, asking for a recommendation, he still signed himself 'Rev. William Godwin'.[8] This was probably to identify himself, but it seems odd for one who had long left the ministry and was a confirmed unbeliever. In another letter, he claimed that Lord Robert Spencer was 'extremely disposed to serve him', that the M.P. Henry Beaufoy had espoused his interest 'with particular warmth', and that Richard Watson, the Bishop of Llandaff, had spoken on his behalf in the House of Lords.[9] The Bishop declined however to write to the Archbishop of Canterbury in Godwin's favour since '*my* appearing in support of a *Dissenter* would rather have tended to obstruct than to promote your wishes'.[10]

Unable to obtain a post in the British Museum, Godwin returned to his writing. He composed in 1790 a drama based on St Dunstan, 'being desirous, in writing a tragedy, of developing the great springs of human passion', and 'of inculcating those principles on which I apprehend the welfare of the human race to depend'.[11] The work was never acted, and has since been lost, but its subject matter suggests how Godwin's imagination was afire with hopes of reform.

Godwin moved his lodgings once again on 4 January 1791 to Titchfield Street. It was a symbolic start to the year which was to see the main crisis in his life. Burke's *Reflections on the Revolution in France* had been published in November 1790, with its passionate attack on the French Revolution, abstract rights, Dissenters and the 'swinish multitude' — all in the name of prescription, prejudice, and the British Constitution. Like Burke, Godwin

rejected the doctrine of the Rights of Man discussed by the French Con-
stituent Assembly, but not through a fear of innovation or a lack of faith in
human nature. He was therefore bitterly disappointed by Burke's defec-
tion. It was, he exclaimed in *The New Annual Register,* 'a circumstance
sufficiently to be wonderful that a man of so comprehensive an intellect, of
such astonishing ability, and of so great natural and acquired powers,
should have committed a mistake in so great and essential a point'.[12]

Burke quickly became the *bête noire* of the radicals. Mary Wollstonecraft's
*Vindication of the Rights of Men,* published by Joseph Johnson, heralded a
whole spate of anti-Burkean works. But Johnson soon faltered: because of
its inflammatory nature, he withdrew the publication of the first part of
Paine's *Rights of Man* which was due to appear on 22 February 1791.
Godwin, Holcroft and Brand Hollis however came to the rescue. They
formed a committee and arranged its publication with J. S. Jordan. In his
diary, Godwin noted on 27 February 'Call on Paine' and on 3 March
'Borrow Paine' after a dinner at Brand Hollis's. He was very impressed.
'The pamphlet', he wrote,

> has exceeded my expectations & appears to be nearly the best possible
> performance that can be written on the subject. It does not confine itself,
> as an injudicious answer could have done, to a cold refutation of Mr.
> Burke's errors, but with equal discernment & philanthropy embraces
> every opportunity of impressing the purest principles of liberty upon the
> hearts of mankind . . . The seeds of revolution it contains are so vigorous
> in their stamina, that nothing can overpower them.[13]

Paine sent a preface and Jordan published the work with a few grammatical
corrections on 16 March. Holcroft sent a characteristic note to Godwin
expressing wild excitement:

> I have got it — If this do not cure my cough it is a damned perverse mule
> of a cough — The pamphlet — From the row — But mum — We don't
> sell it — Oh, no — Ears and Eggs — Verbatim, except the addition of a
> short preface, which, as you have not seen, I send you my copy — Not a
> single castration (Laud be unto God and J. S. Jordan!) can I discover —
> Hey for the New Jerusalem! The millennium! And peace and eternal
> beatitude be unto the soul of Thomas Paine.[14]

Holcroft and Godwin were by now intimate friends. The suicide of
Holcroft's sixteen-year-old son William in November 1789 had brought
them closer together and they were seeing each other almost every day.[15]
Holcroft had, under Godwin's guidance, become a republican, and in turn

provided 'stimulus and excitement' to his rather lethargic comrade.[16]

After helping to publish Paine's *Rights of Man*, the two friends decided to try and influence directly the Whig leaders. In a debate on the bill for a new constitution for Canada, Fox argued against the introduction of the House of Lords. Godwin and Holcroft then wrote on 29 April 1791 two anonymous letters to Sheridan and Fox respectively, urging them 'to presevere gravely and inflexibly' in their career.

Although it still shows a confidence in government to implement reform, Godwin's long unpublished letter to Sheridan offers an uncompromising denunciation of monarchy, clergy, laws and oaths, and calls upon the British to imitate the French revolutionaries. Thanks to men like Rousseau, Raynal, Helvétius, D'Holbach and Paine, Godwin declares, there has been a steady progress in the 'estimate of liberty, truth, & right principles of government'. It is therefore time for those who 'take things as they are' to be 'swept away with the rest of the insects of the day' and to make room for a new order. After a devastating survey of British institutions, Godwin concludes:

> Liberty strips hereditary honours of their imaginary splendour, shows the noble & the king for what they are — common mortals . . . Liberty leaves nothing to be admired but talents & virtue . . . Pursue this subject to its proper extent, & you will find that — give to a state but liberty enough, & it is impossible that vice should exist in it.[17]

The letter to Sheridan shows just how deeply Godwin had drunk the spirit of the French Revolution. It also demonstrates his total confidence in the moral integrity of human beings and his unreserved commitment to social liberty. As Mary Shelley later commented, her father's belief that no vice could co-exist with perfect freedom was 'the very basis of his system, the very keystone of the arch of justice, by which he desired to knit together the whole human family'.[18]

As Godwin and Holcroft attempted to influence the course of events through the Whig leaders, the reformers were already beginning to suffer setbacks. On 18 April 1791 Godwin heard the debate instigated by Wilberforce on the slave trade which ended in defeat. Price died the next day, Godwin heard Priestley's funeral sermon on 1 May which symbolized the passing of an era. Five days later, he listened to the famous dispute between Fox and Burke which finally broke their long-standing political alliance. Henceforth, parliament was in the firm control of Pitt and the die-hard Tories.

Throughout the country the issue of reform was rapidly undermining old friendships and forcing the politically conscious to take sides. The poor, hit by high prices, took to the streets and attacked French sympathizers, especially in provincial towns. The Dissenters were becoming increasingly suspect. When Priestley formed in June a Constitutional Society in Birmingham and planned to celebrate the anniversary of the French Revolution local Tories encouraged a riot which led to the destruction of Priestley's house, library, and unique laboratory.

In the meantime, republicanism was growing in France. The king clearly disapproved of the Civil Constitution of the Clergy and the abortive attempt in June of the Royal family to escape from Paris — the flight to Varennes — only made matters worse. On 14 July, Godwin celebrated the second anniversary of the French Revolution at the Crown and Anchor Tavern. Three days later, a republican petition in Paris led to the celebrated massacres in the Champs de Mars. Godwin wrote ominously in his diary 'Tumults at Paris'.

These developments made Godwin all the more impatient to be his own master, and he found his writing for *The New Annual Register* both dull and irksome. In March, the publisher George Robinson proposed to Godwin a work on Natural History, but when he replied asking for the princely sum of £1050 for two volumes, they had a row and the project was dropped. On 30 June, however, Godwin proposed at dinner to Robinson a treatise on 'Political Principles', and on 10 July 1791 a generous agreement was reached. Robinson was to advance his expenses so that he could dedicate himself entirely to the task, and eventually paid him a thousand guineas. Godwin finished writing for *The New Annual Register* on 4 September. He immediately sat down to work, and began recording in his diary his daily reading and writing.

It was no easy task that he had set himself. While Burke was the prime target for most of the other radicals, Godwin's original conception proceeded on a feeling of the imperfections and errors of Montesquieu's *Esprit des Lois*, and a desire of supplying a less faulty work. Godwin could not accept Montesquieu's attempt to ascribe to physical causes, and especially climate, the different types of government to be found in different regions. Instead, he felt that the best social arrangements are applicable to all humanity and that political truth is universal. In the first fervour of his enthusiasm, he therefore entertained

the vain imagination of 'hewing a stone from the rock', which, by its inherent energy and weight, should overbear and annihilate all opposition, and place the principles of politics on an immoveable basis. It was my first determination to tell all that I apprehended to be truth, and all that seemed to be truth, confident that from such a proceeding the best results were to be expected.[19]

To achieve this end, Godwin felt that he would have to collect whatever was 'best and most liberal in the science of politics, to condense it, to arrange it more into a system, and to carry it somewhat farther, than had been done by any preceding writer'.[20] He therefore systematically devoted a part of each day to a study of his favourite authors. They included the historians Thucydides, Livy, Sallust, Plutarch and Rollin, who had first inspired his republicanism. The French *philosophes* Montesquieu, Voltaire, Rousseau, D'Holbach, Helvétius, Condillac, Mably, Raynal, Mirabeau and Turgot, who had shattered his Christian faith and helped him believe in progress through enlightenment, were consulted afresh. The thinkers Locke, Clarke, Collins, Edwards, Hume, Price and Priestley were revisited to clarify his views on necessity and immaterialism. A re-reading of Plato confirmed his belief in eternal and immutable truths. Beccaria enabled him to clarify his views on law and punishment; Swift to sketch his view of political justice. And then he made himself familiar with the contemporary political debate sparked off by the French Revolution in the works of Burke, William Paley, Paine, Holcroft, James Mackintosh, Joel Barlow, and Dr. Samuel Parr.[21]

Godwin worked with great care, writing never more than six or seven pages a day, and sometimes only a single paragraph. These he carefully revised as he proceeded. Although he would only work three or four hours a day, the sedentary habits of a lifetime began to have their effect, and he often experienced bouts of giddiness and attacks of headache and eyeache. When not writing or reading, he received or visited friends.

The book which emerged — *An Enquiry concerning Political Justice, and its Influence on General Virtue and Happiness* — took Godwin sixteen months to write. The polished style and exacting argumentation show little sign of haste, but Robinson set the type and even began printing the sheets long before the composition was finished. They both felt that much of the benefit of the work would depend upon its early appearance. Godwin, however, was not a man to flinch from extreme conclusions and would follow truth wherever it led him. The experience of the French Revolution had already reconciled him to the 'desirableness of a government of the simplest construction', but as his enquiries advanced so his ideas became 'more perspicuous and digested'. The result, Godwin acknowledged in his preface, was

an occasional inaccuracy of language, particularly in the first book, respecting the word government. He did not enter upon the work, without being aware that government by its very nature counteracts the improvement of the individual mind; but he understood the full meaning of this proposition more completely as he proceeded, and saw more distinctly into the nature of the remedy.[22]

Godwin's political development was therefore tremendous during the writing of *Political Justice*. He set out very close to the English Jacobins like Paine only to finish a convinced and outspoken anarchist — the first great exponent of society without government.

Godwin's composition of *Political Justice* did not prevent him from commemorating once again on 5 November 1791 the Glorious Revolution of 1688 at the London Tavern. Not only did his Dissenting acquaintances Kippis, Rees, Priestley, and Brand Hollis attend, but also the radicals Horne Tooke and Thomas Paine, and the French ambassador Jérôme Pétion. Brand Hollis introduced Godwin at his own request to Paine, but in the hurry and confusion of the large meeting, Godwin was unable to talk to him personally. When he breakfasted with the French ambassador the next day, Godwin therefore asked him for Paine's address. Two days later, he wrote to him:

> I have wished for an occasion of expressing to you my feeling of the high obligation you have conferred upon Britain & Mankind by your late publication of the Rights of Man: I believe few men have a more ardent sense of that obligation than myself; & I conceive that it is a duty incumbent upon persons so feeling to come forward with the most direct applause of your efforts. I regard you, Sir, as having been the unalterable champion of liberty in America, in England, & in France, from the purest views to the happiness & the virtue of mankind . . . I am, sir, already the ardent friend of your views, your principles & your mind.[23]

On 11 November, Godwin re-read Paine's *Common Sense* and received a reply to his letter. A dinner was arranged at the publisher Joseph Johnson's two days later. It was to prove an eventful occasion in more ways than one.

Godwin found both Paine and Mary Wollstonecraft at Johnson's Sunday dinner. Paine at the time was absorbed in writing the second part of his *Rights of Man* and in his general habits was no great talker. Though he threw in occasionally some 'shrewd and striking remarks', Mary Wollstonecraft, to Godwin's annoyance, dominated the conversation.[24]

It was hardly a propitious first meeting between Godwin and his future wife. He did not like the style of her recent *Vindication of the Rights of Men* and had barely bothered to look into it. Moreover, he detected in her 'in a very blameable degree, the practice of seeing every thing on the gloomy side, and bestowing censure with a plentiful hand'.[25] Thus when he lauded Horne Tooke, Dr. Johnson, and Voltaire, she declared prescription, prejudice, and the British Constitution. Like that such lavish praise disagreed on religion; Godwin was a sceptical unbeliever, while Wollstonecraft still remained a Deist. As the conversation proceeded — it touched upon monarchy and pursuits — Godwin became increasingly dissatisfied with his own share. In the end, he not only missed a unique opportunity to get to know Paine, but left Wollstonecraft on bad terms. He only met her three times in the course of the following year before she went over to France, and it was not until 1796 that they became intimate.

Although Godwin never met Paine again, he paid tribute to him in *Political Justice* as a 'most acute, original and inestimable author'.[26] He was particularly impressed by Paine's opening declaration in *Common Sense* (1776) that 'Society in every state is a blessing, but government even in its best state is but a necessary evil' and helped supervise the ninth edition of the pamphlet published by Jordan in August 1792.[27] He must have been all the more delighted to find in January that Paine had developed along similar libertarian lines when he declared in the second part of *The Rights of Man* that 'the more perfect civilization is, the less occasion has it for government'.[28] They disagreed about natural rights and written constitutions but they were fighting a common cause.

Whilst composing *Political Justice*, Godwin continued to see his friends and discussed its principles with them. In the process, many of his ideas were clarified or developed. Fawcett, fresh from his widely popular series of lectures delivered at the Old Jewry, was in town in the autumn of 1791 and they talked enthusiastically of genius, virtue, Christianity, property, Helvétius, and the ministry. Godwin also met on 5 September a young man called George Dyson who was to become a regular visitor at his house and his third principal oral instructor. They had several discussions in October about self-interest during which, Godwin noted on the 23rd in his diary, 'Dyson owns himself convinced'. The hedonistic Dyson, however, was later to wean Godwin from his Calvinist stoicism and to persuade him that pleasure was the only good.

Although his work was still unfinished and unseen, Godwin's reputation grew apace in radical circles. On 4 March 1792 he was introduced to the young Scotsman James Mackintosh, a member of the French Assembly, the honorary secretary of the Friends of the People, and the celebrated author of *Vindiciae Gallicae* (1791). During their five subsequent meetings they discussed self-love, necessity, Hartley, laws, property, revolution, war, and God.[29]

They had good grounds for debate. In *Vindiciae Gallicae*, Mackintosh had insisted that it was time that men should 'shrink from no novelty to which reason may conduct'.[30] He condemned Burke's advocacy of complex government based on '*political imposture*' in favour of simple political truths that all could understand.[31] Above all, Mackintosh defined justice as 'expediency' and gave a clear utilitarian definition of government. While still using the language of natural rights, he nevertheless maintained that:

> When I assert that a man has a right to life, liberty, &c. I only mean to enunciate a MORAL MAXIM founded on *general interest*, which prohibits any attack on these possessions. In this primary and radical sense, all rights, natural as well as civil, arise from expediency.[32]

It was only a short step for Godwin to apply more rigourously the principle of utility and abandon natural rights altogether.

Godwin also met the American poet Joel Barlow, who had just returned from France with introductions from Thomas Jefferson to Priestley and Johnson. Godwin saw him ten times from March to October, and their many conversations ranged from self-love, laws, revolution, property, marriage, immortality, and perfectibility.[33] To appreciate fully Barlow's arguments, Godwin made a careful study of his writings.

In March he read his *Advice to the Privileged Orders* (1792) and his *Conspiracy of Kings* (1792). Then in October he re-read his *Advice* and studied his *Letter to the National Convention* (1792). There was much in them to reinforce Godwin's own opinions, particularly the trenchant criticism of the church, the military system, and the administration of justice. He entirely endorsed Barlow's libertarian view that 'society has hitherto been curst with governments, whose existence depended on the extinction of truth'.[34] He would doubtless have been disappointed by the *Letter to the National Convention*, with its Painite emphasis on natural rights, constitutions and state education, but the vigorous republicanism of *The Conspiracy of Kings*, which attacked the 'Drones of Church and the harpies of the State', was of great inspiration.

Godwin was most indebted during the composition of *Political Justice*, however, to 'the conversation & advice of two friends from [sic] whose talents & character he has the highest esteem, Mr. Holcroft & Mr. William Nicholson'.[35] Godwin had first met Nicholson in 1786 at the literary parties of the publisher Robinson. Although lacking in formal education, he became a competent translator, an ingenious inventor, and a famous scientist. He constructed with Anthony Carlisle the first voltaic pile in England and thereby discovered electrolysis. From 1797 he edited the *Journal of Natural Philosophy* and his *Encyclopedia* was later used by Shelley. When Nicholson died in 1815, Godwin wrote a memorial of his old and trusted friend.

The exact nature of Nicholson's influence on Godwin however is difficult to establish. They discussed at their regular meetings, about once every fortnight, all the leading topics of *Political Justice*, and especially taxation, necessity, abstraction, and government. Nicholson was also the only one to criticize the manuscript, and helped Godwin revise the preface, introduction and conclusion.[37] Yet for all this close collaboration, Godwin did not include Nicholson among his principal oral instructors. His role seems to have been chiefly in stimulating Godwin's mind and editing his prose.

It was Holcroft who undoubtedly had the greatest effect on Godwin during the composition of *Political Justice*. The two men would dine alone together in each other's lodgings almost every other day. Godwin's diary records that they discussed constituents, oaths, property, law, government, self-love, passivity, marriage, immortality, libel, powers of the mind, language, necessity, automatic motion, sleep, majorities, promises, abstraction, division of labour, chastisement, poetry, religion, infinite liberty, optimism, French and Spartan virtue, sympathy, perfectibility, obedience, war, revolution, history, coercion, co-operation, Plato, Burke, Paine and Pitt — in short, all of Godwin's major preoccupations whilst writing his *magnum opus*.[38]

At the time, the two friends were also members of a small debating club called the Philomathean Society. According to John Binns, chairman of the London Corresponding Society, Godwin and Holcroft were so prolix that the committee had to use fifteen-minute glasses whenever one of them rose to speak.[39] This debating society seems to have been the only one Godwin joined and it was probably at Holcroft's instigation.

Their collaboration did not end there. Godwin diligently read and corrected Holcroft's works. After editing his translation of the *Posthumous Works of Frederick II, King of Prussia*, Godwin published an anonymous article in the *Monthly Review* in November which praised the translation and summarized the work.[40] He next revised in the following month Holcroft's first directly political play — *The School for Arrogance*, which aimed at exposing the 'weakness of pride, as it is founded on the prejudice either of wealth or ancestry'.[41] At the same time he began reading the manuscript of Holcroft's philosophical novel *Anna St. Ives*, which was intended to show how one ought 'to act in the present state of society'.[42] Once it was published in February 1792, Godwin turned to Holcroft's play *The Road to Ruin*, which contrasted the 'domestic virtues of a city life' with the 'vices of city manners'.[43] Godwin therefore not only immersed himself in Holcroft's best and most radical works but played an intimate part in their composition.

In fact, Holcroft and Godwin largely worked out together the New Philosophy which promised so much. It is not surprising that a reading of Holcroft's novels should have prepared the young Henry Crabb Robinson to accept the doctrines of *Political Justice* for they express the same message: the omnipotence of truth, universal benevolence, and the perfectibility of man.[44] With his heroine Anna St. Ives, Holcroft asked his contemporaries:

Dare you think that riches, rank, and power, are usurpations; and that wisdom and virtue only can claim distinction? Dare you make it the business of your whole life to overturn these prejudices, and to promote among mankind that spirit of universal benevolence which shall render them all equals, all brothers, all stripped of their artificial and false wants, all participating the labour requisite to produce the necessaries of life, and all combining one universal effort of mind, for the progress of knowledge, the destruction of error, and the spreading of eternal truth?[45]

Indeed, *Anna St. Ives* has been called a 'novelized *Political Justice*, and most critics have been content to see Holcroft as 'a system-monger of Godwin's school'.[46]

The debt, however, is not so clear-cut: Holcroft was eleven years older than Godwin, more experienced and just as adamant. They thrashed out their views in many quarrels. Godwin certainly was the more systematic and powerful thinker, but Holcroft held original views, particularly on mind, marriage and government. In this area, at least, he seems to have been the intellectual leader.

The unlimited powers of the mind were Holcroft's favourite theme. He was convinced that pain is an illusion and that death and disease exist only through mental weakness: 'it is nonsense to say that we must all die; in the present erroneous system I suppose that I shall die, but why? because I am a fool!'[47] Convinced by this reasoning, Godwin developed in *Political Justice* Franklin's 'sublime conjecture' that mind would one day become omnipotent over matter, and went so far as to suggest that 'We are sick and we die, generally speaking, because we consent to suffer these accidents.' He even speculated that the present race of men might possibly live to see the abolition of disease, anguish and death 'in part accomplished'.[48]

Holcroft was also a stern critic of the existing institution of marriage. He had already been married three times, and was in the process of becoming estranged from his third wife. It is not therefore so surprising that in *Anna St. Ives* he should argue: 'All individual property is an evil — Marriage makes woman individual property — Therefore marriage is evil — Could there be better logic?'[49]

At first, Godwin was worried by such argument. After reading *Anna St. Ives* in its manuscript form, he told Holcroft that he had two insuperable objections to the last volume: it would not only impress on his readers 'an abhorrence of the very name of Political Philosophy' but also rendered 'sophistry victorious'. In particular, he condemned Holcroft's advice to women 'to make laws for themselves in direct contradiction to the institutions under which they live . . . It is at least very problematical whether, when property & all its modes be abolished, the commerce of the sexes will be accomplished by any species of marriage.'[50]

When Godwin came to discuss marriage in *Political Justice*, however, he declared like Holcroft that marriage is 'law, and the worst of all laws . . . So long as I seek to engross one woman to myself, and to prohibit my neighbour from proving his superior desert and reaping the fruits of it, I am guilty of the most odious of all monopolies.'[51] The bachelor Godwin was no libertine. The evidence is that he was sexually inexperienced when he met Mary Wollstonecraft. It was not therefore personal considerations which persuaded Godwin of the folly of marriage but the validity of Holcroft's abstract arguments.

Finally in *Anna St. Ives*, Holcroft remarked that the deepest thinkers inform us that 'every thing in which governments interfere is spoiled'.[52] In 1790, Godwin had not changed his view 'That governments are omnipotent; the reform of government the one thing needful' and 'That the reform of individuals is an undertaking of inferior importance'.[53] When he began writing *Political Justice* a year later he still argued with Helvétius that 'a sound political institution was of all others the most powerful engine for promoting individual good'.[54] But as he acknowledged in the preface, it was only as he proceeded that he gradually realized that government by its very nature counteracts the 'improvement of individual mind' and that Reason should be 'the only legislator'.[55]

It was Holcroft who helped him realize these truths. He was the only reviewer of *Political Justice* to point out Godwin's inconsistent treatment of government. Godwin, he argued, should have recognized from the beginning that 'while men continue to have vices the coercion of government is an inevitable consequence, but in proportion as they acquire virtue and restraint, coercion becomes pernicious'.[56] A general diffusion of knowledge, not legislation, was the remedy for the existing oppression of mankind. As Holcroft wrote in his novel *The Adventures of Hugh Trevor* in the following year, the idea that there must be government and governors is a 'radical mistake in politics'.[57] Holcroft therefore played a crucial role in helping Godwin develop his system of anarchism.

Another important acquaintance Godwin made while writing *Political Justice* was John Horne Tooke. He had seen Horne Tooke at the annual dinners of the Revolution Society but it was not until 24 November 1792 that they dined together at Horne Tooke's house in Wimbledon. The veteran and the rising radical talked of 'politics & morals'. They met again on 23 December when there was 'talk of ideas & revolution'.[58]

Horne Tooke had been a member of the Association Movement, a former associate of Wilkes, and a leading light of the Society for Constitutional Information. He was also an able philologist, and in his witty medley *Epia*

*Pteroenta, or the Diversions of Purley* (1786–1805) tried to demonstrate that the nature of words has no connection with the nature of things or the objects of thought. Godwin later owned that he was greatly indebted to Horne Tooke's 'etymological conversation and various talents' although these came too late to be of any use to him in the concoction of *Political Justice*, which was nearly printed off before he had the pleasure of meeting 'this extraordinary and admirable man'.[59]

Towards the end of 1792, Godwin also met the former actress Elizabeth Inchbald. He had admired her portrayal of the improper education of women in her best novel *A Simple Story* and corrected the manuscript for the publisher Robinson the year before. When they met at Robinson's on 29 October, she gave him the manuscript of her tragedy *The Massacre*. It was inspired by the September massacres in France and was intended to staunch the bloodshed. Godwin read the work on 1 November but advised her against publishing it the following day. She acknowledged that there was 'so much tenderness mixed with the justice of your criticism' and eventually withdrew the printed edition.[60] Godwin then went on to revise on 26 and 27 November her comedy *Every One has His Fault* which was successfully produced at the end of January 1793. They soon became close friends. Although she was three years older than Godwin, he could not, his daughter later wrote, fail to admire her since 'Her talents, her beauty, her manners were all delightful to him. He used to describe her as a piquante mixture between a lady and a milkmaid, and added that Sheridan declared that she was the only authoress whose society pleased him.'[61]

While Godwin was working out the principles of *Political Justice* in his Titchfield Street rooms with clockwork regularity, events on both sides of the Channel were becoming more unpredictable. The Girondins came to power in the spring of 1792 and abolished the monarchy in September after the massacres. In London the Society for Constitutional Information reorganized itself early in the year and began regular meetings. The spring also saw the foundation of the more radical and popular London Corresponding Society (L.C.S.), which called for annual parliaments and universal suffrage. The French victories at Valmy and Jemappes against the Prussians and Belgians in the autumn were greeted by them with wild enthusiasm. The membership of the popular clubs throughout the country mushroomed, and by November the L.C.S. alone numbered at least 800 committed militants, about 1,500 members, with 5–6,000 'hearers'. The more radical part II of Paine's *Rights of Man*, published in February, could be had for 4p. The people may be said to have entered politics for the first time during this year.[62]

The counter-revolutionary forces in Britain were not, however, dormant. In November, John Reeves founded with the connivance of the government the 'Association for Preserving Liberty and Property against Republicans and Levellers' which sparked off hundreds of Loyalist associations in the provinces. A spate of pamphlets, hand-bills, and ballads were distributed accusing the reformers of treason. Godwin attended Paine's trial *in absentia* for seditious libel on 18 December, and was sufficiently enraged by the poor defence to write to Paine's counsel Thomas Erskine and to upbraid him for betraying his client and failing to argue that 'such writings & such enquiries ought to be permitted in a free society'.[63]

As Godwin was writing the conclusion and introduction of *Political Justice*, he felt compelled to protest against the mounting government oppression. On 8 January 1793 Daniel Crichton, a journeyman tallow-chandler from Scotland, was imprisoned for three months for seditious and treasonable words, having allegedly declared during a drunken visit to the Tower of London: 'Damn the king! We have no king in Scotland, and we will soon have no king in England.'

Godwin thought the action was so serious that he referred to it in a footnote in the preface to *Political Justice*.[64] On 16 January he also wrote a letter signed 'Mucius' to the editor of the *Morning Chronicle*, defending the 'old, boasted privilege of Englishmen; liberty of speech'. The real conspirators against the Constitution, Godwin argued, were the loyalist spies and informers. Indeed the foundation of John Reeves's Association at the Crown and Anchor Tavern on 20 November had marked the beginning of a 'reign of despotism' in Britain.[65]

Godwin wrote two more letters to the *Morning Chronicle* on the following day. He addressed the first to Reeves, the 'assassin of the Liberties of Englishmen', condemning his scurrilous and violent campaign.[66] In the second he warned Archibald MacDonald, the Attorney General, that his proposed restriction of the freedom of speech could involve the 'whole fabric of the English Government in conflagration'.[67] Godwin then urged in a fourth letter, written on 18 January, the prospective jurors of trials for seditious and treasonable words to deliberate impartially and intrepidly. As the trial of Crichton made clear, it was for them to defend the freedom of speech and the freedom of the press which alone held absolute power at bay. Liberty, Godwin asserted,

consists in allowing every man, in the way of enquiry and argument, to speak what he thinks. It consists in delivering us from the empire of spies and informers, in not subjecting us to perpetual watchfulness and reserve, in not putting an instrument of vengeance into the hands of every man who may think proper to quarrel with us.[68]

As Godwin was finishing *Political Justice,* he had therefore ample evidence of the tyranny of government and good reason to believe that his own contribution to the cause of Freedom and Equality could prove his own undoing. Godwin knew the odds, but the unassuming scholar was also a man of great courage. In his preface to *Political Justice*, dated 7 January 1793, he boldly challenged the government to put an 'end to the disquisitions of science' and concluded: 'it is the fortune of the present work to appear before a public that is panic struck, and impressed with the most dreadful apprehensions respecting such doctrines as are here delivered. All the prejudices of the human mind are in arms against it.'[69] A week later Louis XVI was guillotined. Godwin nevertheless completed *Political Justice* on 29 January and Robinson published it on 14 February, a fortnight after France had declared war on Britain. Its appearance could not have been more untimely.

# CHAPTER VII

## *Political Justice*

Godwin set out in *Political Justice* to express himself with the frankness of a 'Catholic penitent' and to place the principles of politics on an immovable basis.[1] But the project was not undertaken in a cold and calculating manner. 'No man', he recalled

> perhaps has at any time been animated with a more earnest spirit of philanthropy, than I was in the composition of that work ... My enthusiasm was so great, that I often thought it shall be scarcely possible for anyone to advocate narrow principles, & at the same time to conciliate to himself disciples after the book is published.[2]

This did not however detract from the rigidly deductive nature of his approach. Politics, he felt, is a subject like mathematics which must proceed by argument and demonstration. He therefore did not proceed as Locke did to trace historically the origins of government and society, but preferred to examine them philosophically, that is to say, to consider the 'moral principles on which they depend'.[3] To this end, he first stated a proposition in each chapter, demonstrated it by reasons and evidence, considered possible objections, and then drew a conclusion.

As he considered accuracy of language to be the 'indispensable prerequisite of sound knowledge', he further carefully defined his terms and made his ideas as clear and precise as possible.[4] Apart from some passages of fervent rhetoric, the whole is written in a chaste, lucid and balanced prose. The tone is polite, the diction latinate. Godwin was writing for the sober and thoughtful citizen, the calm friend of truth.

For all his love of order and clarity, Godwin however was unable to present his principles as clearly and consistently as he would have liked. His desire to publish early meant that the printing was begun long before the composition was finished. Since his ideas became more 'perspicuous and digested' as his enquiries advanced, it led in the first edition to a few contradictions, especially respecting government.[5] The early printing also adversely affected the chronology. At the end of volume one, for instance, Godwin discussed metaphysical and moral principles assumed from the beginning.

Godwin first and foremost conceives politics to be the 'proper vehicle of a liberal morality'.[6] As the subtitle of his enquiry indicates, he is primarily concerned with the influence of 'political justice' on 'general virtue and happiness'. In addition, while his political theory can stand on its own, it is 'most intimately connected' with his more 'abstruse speculations' in metaphysics and psychology.[7] The eight hundred and ninety-five pages of *Political Justice* therefore add up to more than a political treatise: the political conclusions are firmly derived from ethical principles which in turn are based upon a particular view of nature and man.

In his metaphysics, Godwin adopts the Newtonian view of the universe as a machine governed by necessary and universal laws. Man and nature are both subject to the strict laws of necessity, so that 'In the life of every human there is a chain of causes, generated in that eternity which preceded his birth, and going on in regular procession through the whole period of his existence, in consequence of which it was impossible for him to act in any instance otherwise than he has acted.'[8] But Godwin is no dogmatic determinist. He is well aware of Hume's scepticism about the principle of causality: strictly speaking all that we know of the material universe is a 'succession of events' and no experiment of reasoning can show their necessary connection.[9] Like Hume, however, and using his arguments, Godwin is ready to accept the causal assumption on practical grounds. History, the notion of character, social policy and moral discipline would be meaningless without it.

Nor is Godwin a materialist. The universe is not merely matter in motion as D'Holbach had argued, for 'mind is a real cause, an indispensable link in the great chain'.[10] It is a fact of experience that mind affects matter, and matter affects mind. As in the case of causation, we may not be able to know how they interact, but this does not mean that they do not affect each other.

Godwin in fact freely adopts Hume's criticisms of Montesquieu's theory of climate to demonstrate that our actions are determined primarily by psychological rather than physical causes. He also rejects Hartley's theory of vibrations to explain our actions since it 'unnecessarily clogged' his account of the mind with a scheme of 'material automatism'.[11] To any 'material system' which explains thinking in terms of matter in motion, Godwin resolutely opposes his 'intellectual system' in which thought remains a real and efficient source of physical movement.[12] Indeed, Godwin even entertains the 'sublime conjecture' of Franklin that 'mind will one day become omnipotent over matter' and suggests that men will not only abolish sleep but the 'accidents' of death and disease.[13]

It was due to his reflections on the doctrine of necessity during the composition of *Political Justice* that Godwin became an atheist. Although he does not deal directly with religious questions in the work, his position is clear. Religion in all its parts, he declares, is an 'accommodation to the prejudices and weaknesses of mankind'.[14] Rather than offering a body of absolute truth, it provides instruction only for children in understanding. As for life after death, Godwin comments drily: 'all that can be told me of a future world, a world of spirits or of glorified bodies . . . is so foreign to the system of things with which I am acquainted, that my mind in vain endeavours to believe or to understand it'.[15]

At the same time, Godwin is unable to accept the relativity of the French empiricists D'Holbach and Helvétius who have no external standard of value. He holds secure to the Platonic notion of universal, eternal and immutable truths which are discoverable by the unaided use of reason. Such truths taught the 'creator of the world the nature of his materials' and preceded 'either substantially or in the nature of things, the particular existences that surround us, and are independent of them all'.[16] God might not exist, but in this way Godwin is able to proceed with certainty in his investigation of metaphysics, morals, and politics. In any argument, he is always able to appeal to the 'omnipresent and eternal volume of truth' as the ultimate criterion of objectivity.[17]

What Newton had done for our understanding of matter, Godwin believed, Locke had done for man. He therefore stands firmly within the tradition of sensationalist psychology. Following Locke, Hartley and Rousseau, he rejects categorically the theory of innate ideas and instincts. Man is born equal and innocent: there is no 'mystical magazine, shut up in the human embryo' and we are 'neither virtuous nor vicious as we first come into existence'.[18] It is our environment and culture which shape us, or, as Godwin puts it in his chapter title: 'The Moral Characters of Men Originate in their Perceptions.'

Two important corollaries follow from this fundamental premise. In the first place, the absence of innate differences means that all human beings are 'partakers of a common nature' and share a 'great and substantial equality'.[19] Godwin dismisses the possible effects of breed compared to cultural influences and maintains that all mankind, including Indians, negroes and women, are equally capable of exercising reason. Since existing inequalities are entirely the result of social arrangements, it follows that there are no grounds for hereditary distinctions and slavery, and the improvement 'to be desired for the one is to be desired for the other'.[20]

Secondly, Godwin's rejection of original sin and innate differences enables him to argue for the perfectibility of man, that is to say, man as a morally and intellectually progressive being. Certainly the past appears from one point of view 'little else than the history of crimes'.[21] But it is only necessary to contrast man's original state of ignorance with modern civilization to recognize that his inventions are capable of perpetual improvement. Since he has done so much in the arts and sciences, why then should he not be able to advance in wisdom and justice? Perfectibility, Godwin concludes, 'is one of the most unequivocal characteristics of the human species, so that the political, as well as the intellectual state of man, may be presumed to be in a course of progressive improvement'.[22]

Godwin's theory of perfectibility, the linchpin of his system of political justice, rests on the potential rationality of all human beings. But it is not a simplistic or reductionist belief. He recognizes the importance of dreams, reveries, unperceived impressions and non-conscious actions. The mind is presented as constantly thinking and capable of a rapid succession of single ideas. Human motives are so inscrutable that history must always remain doubtful and uncertain. Indeed, consciousness must be a 'sort of supplementary reflection' and appears as 'one of the departments of memory'.[23]

Yet for all the emphasis on the subtlety and complexity of the mind, it is true that for Godwin reason remains supreme. The understanding is a 'faculty distinct from sensation' and while physical impressions provide materials for thought, they 'sink into nothing' when compared with the 'great and inexpressible operations of reflection'.[24] What distinguishes human beings from animals is precisely their power of abstraction and the 'greater facility with which we arrange our sensations, and compare, prefer and judge'.[25]

It is reason in Godwin's scheme of things which also ensures that we can act altruistically. Godwin is eager to rebut both Helvétius's view that man is solely motivated by calculations of self-love, and Locke's view that he acts to reduce a sense of uneasiness. Psychological egoism cannot explain a child's instantaneous impulse of sympathy, or account for an adult's deliberate intention to contribute to the general good.

Instead, Godwin attempts to derive benevolence from hedonism via reason. Now, it 'immediately' results from the nature of human beings that pleasure is agreeable and pain odious, that pleasure is to be desired and pain obviated.[26] The cries of another will no doubt prompt our first impulses of sympathy because they excite by association painful feelings in us. But what is at first a spontaneous feeling can become a rational principle. Reason soon recognizes that we share a common nature with our neighbours and have an equal claim to happiness. It is therefore only mistaken ideas of self-interest, and not any inherent psychological drives, which prevent us from benevolence.

Godwin goes on to give a central place to reason in his account of human behaviour. Under the doctrine of necessity all our conduct is determined, but he distinguishes between involuntary and voluntary actions. The former are dictated by past experience and unaccompanied by design; the latter are determined by a judgment of future consequences and are 'subjects of reflection and foresight'.[27] Reason moreover both evaluates the end of an action and irresistibly moves the agent to perform it. The traditional distinction between the intellectual and active powers of the mind is therefore false and there is an indissoluble connection between judgment and outward behaviour. Under normal circumstances Godwin believes people actually *do* what they *think* is right: 'That which we can be persuaded clearly and distinctly to approve, will inevitably modify our conduct.'[28]

Godwin therefore denies in a bold and original move the independent operations of reason and passion. Indeed, he defines passions as 'vivid' thoughts and desire as another name for preference, or a 'perception of the excellence real or supposed of any object'.[29] The will thus becomes, as Clarke and Hartley maintained, the 'last act of the understanding, one of the different cases of the association of ideas'.[30]

Not only does reason have an appetitive power, but it can also perceive in an intuitive way. Like Price's reason, it has a natural affinity for truth which it apprehends instantaneously. And like Blake, Godwin feels that truth is omnipotent, capable of conquering 'the most obstinate prepossessions'.[31] Indeed, he has such faith in its power that he devotes the whole of Book VI to condemning the superintendence of opinion. Even by the collision of prejudices, truth is elicited. And since 'all vice is nothing more than error and mistake reduced into practice' a sober display of truth will ensure that 'oppression, injustice, monarchy and vice will tumble into a common ruin'.[32]

It would appear from the foregoing account that Godwin's metaphysics and psychology are more subtle than is usually assumed. In his metaphysics, he is no crude materialist or determinist. Although he admitted that their relation remains mysterious, he went beyond D'Holbach's epiphenomenonism to assert that mind and matter form parallel interactive schemes. Again, like Hume he recognized that there can be no certain knowledge of the necessary connection between events and that determinism must therefore be based on high probabilities. And by introducing reason as an essential link in the chain of causes and effects and by making volition the last act of the understanding, he came close to the traditional upholders of free will.[33]

In his psychology, he traces the history of the mind from the raw material of sensation recorded by memory and arranged by association. But as soon as the understanding develops, human beings can compare and judge their sensations and gradually extend the province of voluntary action. We are endowed with reason, capable of recognizing truth and acting accordingly. We may be products of our circumstances but we can also change them. Godwinian man thus stands potentially equal, rational, benevolent and perfectible.

While Godwin suggests that the reader of *Political Justice* could overlook with impunity some of his more abstruse speculations in metaphysics and psychology, he insists that there is an indissoluble connection between politics and ethics. As there is no concern of a rational being which falls outside the province of morality, politics must be 'the proper vehicle of a liberal morality' and political enquiry 'strictly speaking a department of the science of morals'.[34]

In his ethics, Godwin is a thoroughgoing utilitarian. Inspired by Jonathan Edwards but using the contemporary language of utility, he defines virtue as that 'species of operations of an intelligent being, which conduces to the benefit of intelligent beings in general'.[35] Justice then is 'coincident with utility' and declares that 'I am bound to employ my talents, my understanding, my strength and my time for the production of the greatest quantity of general good'.[36]

For Godwin, morality is not relative but 'fixed and immutable', and we must prefer 'a general principle to the meretricious attractions of a particular deviation'.[37] But while Godwin argues that general moral rules are psychologically and practically necessary, he warns against too rigid an application of them. Since no action of any man is ever the same as another action, there can be no clearer maxim than 'Every case is a rule to itself.'[38] It is therefore the duty of the just man to contemplate all the circumstances of each individual case in the light of the sole criterion of general utility. By applying the criterion of utility to each individual act rather than to classes of acts, Godwin is therefore a qualified act-utilitarian rather than a rule-utilitarian.

His ethics, he claims, are not undermined but reinforced by his philosophy of necessity. This may at first seem strange. If man be a passive being through which certain causes operate, he cannot be held responsible for his actions: 'the assassin cannot help the murder he commits any more than the dagger'.[39] And since there is no essential difference between animate and inanimate substances, the ideas of 'guilt, crime, desert and accountableness' can have no place in ethics.[40] According to Godwin, however, such a conclusion does not make morality impossible. It is rather the doctrine of free will that is the true subverter of morality: 'so far as we act with liberty, so far as we are independent of motives, our conduct is as independent of morality as it is of reason, nor is it possible that we should deserve either praise or blame for a proceeding thus capricious and indisciplinable'.[41]

While moral determinism may deny individual responsibility, it does not overturn the distinction between vice and virtue. A man, just like a knife, has a capacity to be employed in the purposes of utility and both are the affair of necessity. We approve a sharp knife rather than a blunt one, because its capacity is greater; in the same manner, we will continue to approve of a man according to the application of his 'capacity to the general good'.[42] On the other hand, there will be no room for condemning the vicious who could not have acted otherwise than they did: 'our disapprobation of vice will be of the same nature as our disapprobation of an infectious distemper'.[43]

The doctrine of necessity has further moral advantages for Godwin. It may well deny the possibility of exertion, but it makes persuasion all the more effective. The task of the moral reformer becomes simply 'the exhibition of motives to the pursuit of a certain end, and the delineation of the easiest and most effectual way of attaining that end'.[44] If he employs real antecedents, he has a right to expect real effects. Above all, the necessitarian need not be prey to the 'tumult of passion' since he can reflect on the moral concerns of mankind 'with the same clearness of perception, the same unalterable firmness of judgment, and the same tranquility as we are accustomed to do upon the truths of geometry'.[45]

In his definition of the good, Godwin, like the philosophical radicals Helvétius and Bentham, endorses hedonism:

> The nature of happiness and misery, pleasure and pain, is independent of all positive institution: that is, it is immutably true that whatever tends to procure a balance of the former is to be desired, and whatever tends to procure a balance of the latter is to be rejected.[46]

But while Godwin often uses 'happiness' as synonymous with 'pleasure', he does not equate the good with all types of pleasures. On the very first page of *Political Justice*, he introduces a qualitative scale: 'intellectual and moral happiness or pleasure is extremely to be preferred to those which are precarious and transitory'.[47] He then goes on to depreciate systematically both the strength and value of sensual pleasure: the 'true perfection of man is to divest himself of the influence of passions; that he must have no artificial wants, no sensuality, and no fear'.[48] Sexual intercourse is a 'very trivial object' which apart from the delusions of intellect would be nearly the same in all cases.[49] Just as reasonable men now eat and drink only because it is essential to their health, so they will propagate the species not for the accompanying pleasure but because it is 'right' that the species should be propagated.[50]

True happiness, Godwin concludes, does not lie in 'luxurious accommodations' but 'in the expansion of our intellectual powers, the knowledge of truth, and the practice of virtue'.[51] He illustrates this by a simple scale of happiness. On the lowest level is the brute who spends the greater part of his life in listlessness and is but one remove from a plant. On the next level is the licentious man whose pleasure is momentary and is followed by endless weariness and disgust. It is only the virtuous man who possesses a perpetual source of enjoyment: not only will he be impervious to poverty and disgrace, but he will experience 'the positive satisfaction of a mind conscious of rectitude, rejoicing in the good of the whole'.[52] It is not a developed felicific calculus like Bentham's but shares his aim of defining pleasure and anticipates John Stuart Mill's qualitative distinctions.

Godwin appears to depart from the utilitarianism of the philosophical radicals by emphasizing like Mill the importance of intentions as well as consequences in his account of virtue. He first distinguishes between the disposition of an agent and the action he performs. Now in Godwin's moral arithmetic a wrong action performed from a right disposition is no more virtuous than a right action performed from the wrong disposition. Virtue demands that both the agent be genuinely motivated by disinterested benevolence and that his action really will contribute to the general good. But as the criterion of virtue is always utility, Godwin lays the main stress upon a virtuous disposition since it will in the majority of instances be productive of virtuous actions.

It is Godwin's rigorous application of the principle of utility which leads him to proscribe many of the traditional values of liberal morality. In the first place, he rejects the fashionable doctrine of rights. Men have no inalienable rights in a discretionary sense, only a duty to practise virtue and to tell the truth. Godwin is adamant on this point and rejects both Locke's right to property and Paine's right to choose a government. I can only have discretion in matters of total indifference, like whether I shall sit on the right or the left side of the fire. Otherwise, my property and my person are merely held as trusts on behalf of mankind. Every shilling has already 'received its destination from the dictates of justice', and if I can promote the general good by my death more than by my life 'justice requires that I should be content to die'.[53]

The same holds true for society. Social clubs and religious congregations have no right, any more than individuals do, to adopt statutes and provisions which trample on reason. Conscience and the press should remain unrestrained not because there is such a thing as the right of free speech but simply because society has no right to assume the 'prerogative of an infallible judge'.[54] The sole exception Godwin allows is the right to the assistance and co-operation of our neighbours, but this is only in the sense of a 'strict claim' and is merely the counterpart of their duty to help us.[55]

Godwin's strict utilitarianism also leads him to object to the view that promises form the foundation of morality. Promises themselves are based on a prior obligation to do justice: I should do something right not because I promised, but because justice prescribes it. In all cases I ought to be guided 'by the intrinsic merit of the objects, and not by any external and foreign considerations'.[56] A promise in the sense of a declaration of intent is relatively harmless, but Godwin maintains that one should make as few of them as possible and recognize that they do not morally bind future conduct. 'It is impossible to imagine', he declares, 'a principle of more vicious tendency, than that which shall teach me to disarm future wisdom by past folly . . .'[57]

Combined with the principle of impartiality, Godwin's view of utility takes him to other original conclusions. The need for impartiality arises from the fundamental equality of mankind and is axiomatic of reason. It demands that we transcend all personal considerations and perceive ourselves and others in the 'eye of an impartial spectator'.[58] But while Godwin believes that all human beings are entitled to equal consideration, it does not follow that they should be treated equally. When it comes to distributing justice the impartial person must discriminate in favour of the more worthy, that is, those who have the greatest capacity to contribute to the general good. Godwin illustrates this principle by the case of the Archbishop Fénelon and his chambermaid: faced with the inescapable choice of saving only one of them in a fire, I ought to prefer the philosopher, even though the chambermaid might be my wife, my mother, or my benefactor. 'What magic', Godwin asks, 'is there in the pronoun "my," to overturn the decisions of everlasting truth? My wife or my mother may be a fool or a prostitute, malicious, lying or dishonest. If they be, of what consequence is it that they are mine?'[59]

Godwin therefore insists that we should prefer universal benevolence to self-interest. Sentiments like family affection or gratitude which might interfere with our duty as impartial spectators have no part in virtue. It is even of no consequence that I am the parent of a child when it has been once ascertained that the child will receive a greater benefit under the care of a stranger. No doubt the present unequal distribution of property and the ignorance of the worth of strangers make it more practical for me to prefer my friends and relatives but this does not, Godwin asserts, turn error into right.

Such Olympian impartiality naturally demands a profound understanding of justice and a clear perception of truth. Since vicious conduct is always the result of narrow views, there is an indissoluble connection between knowledge and morality. The truly virtuous man must therefore be highly developed: he must grasp the general principles of morality, understand the workings of human nature and society, and appreciate the necessary consequences of his actions. On these grounds, Cato was clearly more virtuous than the honest ploughman, and because of his talents Milton's devil must be recognized as a 'being of considerable virtue'.[60]

The virtuous man must also be independent, that is, free 'from all constraint except that of reason and argument'.[61] It is justifiable to rely on those with superior knowledge, as when, for instance, I employ a builder to construct a house. It might also be necessary to comply with superior force, as with a 'wild beast, that forces me to run north, when my judgment and inclination prompted me to go south'.[62] To act, however, from the hope of reward or the fear of punishment is always wrong. Without the free exercise of private judgment there can be no proper understanding of moral truth while to defer to another is to blunt all discrimination: 'Man, when he surrenders his reason, and becomes the partisan of implicit faith and passive obedience, is the most mischievous of animals.'[63] It is on these grounds that Godwin goes on to proscribe coercion, law, punishments, censorship, oaths, co-operation and even marriage.

As well as being intelligent and independent, the virtuous man must be sincere. Sincerity, or a 'strict adherence to truth', is the grand instrument for improving the mind and perfecting virtue.[64] As such, it is one of those 'paramount and general rules' which should never give way to the affairs of the day.[65] It is therefore right to tell a dying woman the news of the accidental death of her husband and wrong to lie to save one's own life. In the case of a reformer in a despotic country, his duty is to leave it rather than to conceal his true opinions. It naturally follows that a master should never direct his servant to say that he is not at home. All religious tests or oaths and all libel laws should also be abolished. The benefits of sincerity would be so great, Godwin claims, that if everyone told all the truth they knew, in three years there would be scarcely a falsehood 'of any magnitude remaining in the civilised world'.[66]

From this account of Godwin's ethics, it might appear that he was an unfeeling rationalist who would quite happily let his mother perish in order to follow an abstract principle. Hazlitt's *bon mot* that Godwin's definition of morals was the same as 'the admired one of law, *reason without passion*' has had a widespread currency.[67] But this is the result of a superficial reading. Godwin insists that 'earnest desire' is essential to virtue: it not only improves the understanding but generates capacity.[68] His definition of justice is based moreover on universal love: a mind without benevolence is a 'barren and a cold existence' while the love of our neighbour is the 'great

ornament of a moral nature'.[69] For all his impartiality and intelligence, the
genuine moralist is no cool calculator. He tries to overcome his partial
affections and selfish desires, but is powerfully moved by compassion and
sympathy. Ultimately, Godwin calls for an expansion not a contraction of
love:

> Animated by the love of truth, and by a passion inseparable from its
> nature, and which is almost the same thing under another name, the love
> of my species, I should carefully seek for such topics as might most
> conduce to the benefit of my neighbours, anxiously watch the progress of
> mind, and incessantly labour for the extirpation of prejudice.[70]

Godwin would therefore appear to be a serious and sensitive moral
philosopher who deserves a prominent place in the history of ethics. His
departures from utilitarianism are more apparent than real. Certainly he
sometimes treats knowledge, independence and sincerity as if they were
absolute values. He differs from the philosophical radicals Helvétius and
Bentham in maintaining that man is capable of altruism, that disposition is
an essential part of virtue, and that there are qualitative differences in
pleasures. To their system of education by rewards and punishments, he
insists on the free exercise of private judgment. His doctrine of universal
benevolence also owes much to the Moral Sense school of Shaftesbury and
Hutcheson and to the calm rationalism of Price. But whatever he borrows
from different and incompatible traditions, he consistently tried to base his
principles on the utilitarian ethic. By doing so, he not only reveals imaginatively the strengths and weaknesses of utilitarianism at the time of its
inception, but anticipates many of the innovations made later by John
Stuart Mill and Henry Sidgwick.

In his politics, Godwin is thus primarily motivated by his concern with
morality. As man is a product of his circumstances and a morally progressive being, he wants to find the kind of society which would fit the moral
man. He believes it possible to establish a 'science of politics' on the firm
principles of human nature and deduce from them the 'one best mode of
social existence'.[71] Hence the enquiry into 'political justice'.

The term 'political justice' however is somewhat misleading. Godwin
defines it as 'the adoption of any principle of morality or truth into the
practice of a community'.[72] He does not believe that justice is political in the
traditional sense but social: his idea of a just society does not include
government. He therefore carefully distinguishes between government
and society and argues that they have different origins and purposes.
Human beings associated at first for the sake of 'mutual assistance' and it
was only the 'errors and perverseness of a few' which made the restraint of

government necessary.[73] Quoting Paine's pamphlet *Common Sense*, he concludes that 'Society is in every state a blessing; government even in its best
state but a necessary evil'.[74]

Society, for Godwin, is essentially atomistic, nothing more than an
'aggregation of individuals'.[75] He explicitly rejects Rousseau's notion that it
creates a 'real' or a 'moral' individual, and denies that there is such a thing as
the general will.[76] At the same time, he insists that man is a social being, and
that it is only in society that he can reach his full moral stature.

Godwin begins his enquiry by investigating the foundations and influence of government and then considers the type of social organization
which would best permit moral growth and promote general happiness. He
quickly dismisses as plainly immoral Hobbes's and Filmer's arguments that
government is founded on superior strength or divine right. He deals more
carefully with the idea of an original social contract, which had wide
currency at the time, but he is no less dismissive. Extending Hume's
criticisms of its ambiguous nature and applying his own moral reservations
about promises, he wonders who formed the contract and what were its
conditions. At the same time, if tacit consent is considered sufficient
acquiescence, as Locke argued, it would make all existing governments,
however tyrannical, legitimate. As for Rousseau's attempt to solve the
problem by making the people sovereign, they would in practice be still
denied the power to draw up measures and only asked to express assent to
the legislator's decrees.

Having rejected the social contract theory, Godwin finds the true foundation of government in 'common deliberation'. As government is a 'transaction in the name and for the benefit of the whole' and all human beings
have an equal claim to happiness, it follows that every member of the
community ought to have some share in its administration.[77] At this stage,
Godwin is prepared to accept the practical need for delegation and majority
decisions, but he insists that unlike the social contract theory this creates no
formal obligations: if a measure be just, 'it is entitled both to my chearful
submission and my zealous support. So far as it is deficient in justice, I am
bound to resist.'[78] Furthermore, government strictly speaking has no legislative but only an executive function: 'Reason is the only legislator, and her
decrees are irrevocable and uniform. The functions of society extend, not
to the making, but the interpreting of law.'[79] It follows for Godwin that the
only ground for obedience is voluntary consent. While it may be practically
necessary on some occasions to rely on delegates, such confidence in others
should be made as seldom as possible. It is not men but the rules of
immutable justice that I must obey.

At the beginning of *Political Justice*, Godwin suggested that a political
institution might be a 'most powerful engine' for promoting individual

good.[80] It has a universal influence and appears to be the cause rather than the effect of the manners of a nation. He soon recognized, however, that hitherto the rich had been 'directly or indirectly the legislators of the state' and that government had reduced oppression into a system.[81] Above all, it tends to give permanence to our errors, and instead of 'suffering us to look forward, teaches us to look backward for perfection'.[82] The more he thought about it, the more he became aware that government by its very nature counteracts the improvement of the individual mind. By the time he reached Book III, he had become convinced that it is morally preferable for every individual to govern himself without the imposition of any compulsory restraint. Since government even in its best state is an evil, he concluded that 'we should have as little of it as the general peace of human society will permit'.[83] Thereafter, Godwin devoted himself to making government not less evil but less necessary.

He is first eager to rebut Montesquieu's claim that different societies require different forms of government and Burke's argument that the English constitution peculiarly suits the English temper. Since truth is universal and all human beings share a common nature, liberty can flourish in every soil: 'if an equal participation of the benefits of nature be good in itself, it must be good for you and me and all mankind'.[84] Godwin then proceeds in Volume II to examine monarchy, aristocracy and democracy in order to discover the best form of society.

Godwin's reading of the Latin historians and the political writings of Swift had convinced him twelve years earlier that monarchy is a species of government which is unavoidably corrupt. By his isolated education, his inordinate power, and his luxurious life style, every king is not only a despot in his heart, but the 'bitterest and most potent of all the adversaries of the true interests of mankind'.[85] Whatever its form, monarchy is an absolute imposture which conceals truth and overthrows the equality of mankind. It is, and always will be, the 'bane and the grave of human virtue'.[86]

Godwin makes the same arguments against aristocracy. It is the outcome of the 'ferocious monster' of feudalism and is based on false hereditary distinctions and the unjust distribution of wealth.[87] It perpetuates the unintelligible burden of titles and honours. Above all, it finds it well that a majority of the community 'should be kept in abject penury, rendered stupid with ignorance and disgustful with vice, perpetuated in nakedness and hunger, goaded to the commission of crimes, and made victims to the merciless laws which the rich have instituted to oppress them'.[88]

Democracy on the other hand treats every man as an equal and restores to him 'a consciousness of his value, teaches him by the removal of authority and oppression to listen only to the dictates of reason, gives him confidence to treat all other men as his fellow beings'.[89] A democrat moreover is opposed to offensive war, and will only fight to defend liberty. Yet Godwin does not accept uncritically all types of democracy. He recognizes that it can enable the ignorant to outnumber the wise and the crafty demagogue to wield power.

His defence of democracy, then, is essentially negative. It is neither an ideal nor an end in itself, but merely preferable to other existing political systems. Indeed, Godwin criticizes the theory of complex and balanced government which Montesquieu so admired and which Burke found in the English constitution. He is against two houses because they create social divisions, and opposes the separation of legislative and executive powers because there should be no positive limits to a representative assembly. The only check he recognizes is a 'slow and deliberate proceeding'.[90]

He is even less happy about representation. In the first place, elections bring out the worst in people: the great mass are often purchased by obsequiousness and bribery, or driven by threats of poverty and prosecution. Secondly, since it encourages timidity and hypocrisy, the secret ballot must be the 'direct and explicit patronage of vice'.[91] Thirdly, given the uniqueness of human beings, no one can be truly represented. And finally, the practice of voting itself inevitably has pernicious consequences.

Godwin's arguments against voting are among his most trenchant. In practice, it always creates a fictitious unanimity since the outvoted minority is obliged to execute the decisions of the majority. It produces an unnatural uniformity of opinion by limiting debate and reducing contentious disputes to simple formulae. It encourages rhetoric and demagoguery rather than the cool pursuit of truth. Above all, it involves 'an intolerable insult upon all reason and justice', for the casting of numbers cannot decide on truth.[92] Though opposed by millions, a solitary thinker may well be the true apostle of truth. It follows for Godwin that morally a majority has no more right to coerce a minority, even a minority of one, than a despot has to coerce a majority.

Despite the weakness of representative assemblies, Godwin recognizes for the time being that they are the least pernicious form of government. They have the advantage over primary assemblies in that they are able to call upon the most enlightened part of the nation to deliberate for the whole. The powers of the representatives, however, should be limited to executive ones such as financial details and specific emergencies. They should remain accountable to their electors and merely enact their wishes. Government as a whole can have no more than two legitimate purposes: the suppression of injustice against individuals within the community, and the organization of defence against external invasion.

But while Godwin at this stage allows a limited role to a transitional government, he is utterly opposed to its interference in the intellectual life of the community. Indeed, his defence of freedom of thought and expression is one of the most convincing and eloquent in the language and anticipates many of John Stuart Mill's central arguments. All political superintendence of opinion is ineffective, since law cannot influence the manners of a country; pernicious, because it undermines mental capacity; and unnecessary, as truth and virtue are competent to fight their own battles. If I accept a truth on the basis of authority or prejudice rather than by understanding its terms and weighing its evidence, it will appear 'flaccid and lifeless' and be 'weakly and irresolutely embraced'.[93] The same is true of religious establishments. The system of religious conformity in England is one of 'blind submission and abject hypocrisy'.[94] Subscription to the Thirty-nine Articles can only create a clergy who are incapable of enquiry or action. All tests, oaths, and libel laws are plainly pernicious.

The moral improvement of the species is not therefore to be found in multiplying regulations but in their repeal. Truth and virtue will flourish most when least subjected to 'the mistaken guardianship of authority and laws'.[95] The only legitimate interference with the freedom of speech Godwin would allow is in the case of a specific preparation for a riot. Otherwise, it would appear that excesses are never the offspring of free enquiry but rather 'of power endeavouring to stifle reason and traverse the common sense of mankind'.[96]

Although Godwin shares with the French reformers their faith in education as the means of reform, he is also aware that in the hands of the state it can only too easily degenerate into indoctrination or propaganda. Like all public institutions, state schools produce permanence and uniformity of thought and become the mirror and tool of government. No wonder that knowledge taught in the national universities is a century behind that of the 'unshackled and unprejudiced' members of the community, while the chief lessons given in Sunday schools are 'a superstitious veneration for the church of England, and to bow to every man in a handsome coat'.[97] All this must be unlearned, Godwin argues, before we can begin to be wise.

Having rejected all superintendence of opinion, Godwin then considers the role of government in shaping opinion through a system of rewards and punishments. He dismisses Burke's advocacy of pensions for public benefactors since they appeal to personal gain rather than to disinterested zeal. It is even better for functionaries to subsist on private liberality than on public salaries. His most biting criticisms, however, are reserved for punishment as a motive to action. He considers it the most fundamental subject in the science of politics and devotes the whole of Book VII to its refutation.

Godwin defines punishment as the 'voluntary infliction of evil upon a vicious being' and can find no justification for its use.[98] In the first place, under the system of necessity, there can be no personal responsibility: the assassin cannot help the murder he commits any more than the dagger can. Secondly, coercion annihilates the understanding. It is always a 'tacit confession of imbecility', since the chastiser punishes because his argument is weak.[99] It follows that punishment for retribution is among the 'wildest conceptions of untutored barbarism'; punishment for reformation over-looks the nature of mind which cannot be convinced by force; while punishment for example is not only ineffective but unjustly treats its victim with 'supercilious neglect'.[100] Godwin concludes that coercion absolutely considered is an evil and that private individuals should only use restraint as a temporary expedient when all else fails for defence against an invading despot or a 'domestic spoiler'.[101]

In his treatment of law and punishment, Godwin touches further on some central problems in the liberal tradition. Where Locke called for settled and known laws, for Godwin all laws are arbitrary. The rule of law does not protect human freedom, but rather is the greatest threat to free-dom. Far from embodying the wisdom of ancestors, law is nothing else but a venal compact of superior tyrants. Like the bed of Procrustes, it tries to reduce the multiple actions of men to one universal standard. Once estab-lished, it never stops growing and heaps confusion on ambiguity. No wonder that its practitioners are professionally dishonest, 'perpetually con-versant in quibbles, false colours and sophistry'.[102]

Godwin follows Beccaria in suggesting that the only just criterion to administer punishment would be to consider the 'motives of the offender and the future injury to be apprehended'.[103] But given the inscrutability of motives, the uncertainty of evidence, and the unreliability of witnesses, this would be extremely difficult to judge. Any attempt moreover to classify crimes and correlate punishments is plainly unjust since no two crimes are ever alike. Indeed, there can be no clearer maxim than 'Every case is a rule to itself'.[104] And since jails are nothing but 'seminaries of vice', Godwin concludes that the wrongdoer should be restrained with as much kindness and gentleness as possible.[105]

Godwin clearly draws on Beccaria in his specific criticisms of the existing legal system, but cannot accept his justification of punishment for crimes as violations of governmental contracts. Similarly, while Godwin shares Bentham's desire to reform the penal code, he is completely opposed to his rigid classification of crime and punishments. Where the philosophical radicals called for a wise legislator to inaugurate the millennium via the statute book, Godwin looked for the gradual replacement of all man-made laws by the 'laws of eternal reason that are equally obligatory wherever man is to be found'.[106]

Given Godwin's criticism of government and positive laws, it is under-standable that he should oppose contemporary reformers like Paine and

*Hanya Chlala*

*Robert Saxton*

Monday 13 February 1989 at 7.45 pm

# Robert Saxton
# ELIJAH'S VIOLIN

*First performance of a new work commissioned
by the English Chamber Orchestra*

FULL PROGRAMME:

**Elgar** – Introduction and Allegro, Op 47
**Bridge** – There is a willow grows aslant a brook
**Saxton** – Elijah's Violin
**Britten** – Symphony for Cello and Orchestra, Op 68

YO YO MA *cello*
ENGLISH CHAMBER ORCHESTRA
*Conducted by* JEFFREY TATE

## ▦ Barbican
## ▦ Centre

Owned, funded and managed
by the Corporation of London
*Director* Henry Wrong CBE

Booking from 7th January 1989 at Barbican Centre Box Office,
telephone 01-638 8891 (10 am-8 pm daily including Sundays)
£12, £10, £8, £6, £4

*For further information about this and other concerts
please contact English Chamber Orchestra and Music Society,
2 Coningsby Road, London W5 4HR (telephone 01-840 6565)*

Arts Council Funded

Barlow who called for a new constitution. He is particularly critical of the French Assembly of 1789 which, having just broken loose from the 'thick darkness of an absolute monarchy', assumed to prescribe lessons of wisdom to all future years.[107] Institutions should not be fixed by constitution but allowed to change as political knowledge improves. Moreover, as the French Assembly was willing to submit the draught constitution to districts for their approbation, Godwin cannot understand why they did not take the further step of allowing the districts to make laws for themselves.

Although Godwin feels that as republicanism gains ground, men will come to be estimated for what they are, he does not believe that a republic by itself is enough to eradicate social evils. 'The true reason', he insists,

> why the mass of mankind has so often been made the dupe of knaves, has been the mysterious and complicated nature of the social system. Once annihilate the quackery of government, and the most homebred understanding will be prepared to scorn the shallow artifices of the state juggler that would mislead him.[108]

He therefore looks to a simplified and decentralized form of society based on the principles of justice and equality and which would provide enough security for the free development of all. He found the answer in a loose federation of 'parishes', or small face-to-face communities where 'the voice of reason would be secure to be heard'.[109]

Godwin did not offer a blue-print of future society in *Political Justice*. Indeed, had he done so, it would have been directly opposed to his notion of moral and intellectual progress. He makes clear, however, the broad directions in which he would like to see society develop.

In the first place, there would be no more nation states. Colonies and dependencies would be given their independence. Neighbours are best informed of each other's concerns and justice is more likely to be found in a limited circle. But this need not mean insularity, for without nation states the whole of the human species would constitute in a sense one great republic.

Secondly, law and government would be gradually abolished. If a society be content with the rules of justice, then positive laws are superfluous. In a free and equal society, motives to offence would become rare while friendly advice given in perfect sincerity would suffice to reform the wrongdoer. Any disputes which might arise in the community could be dealt with by temporary, non-professional juries.

There would be no need for a permanent national assembly. On extraordinary occasions, a general congress, rather like the amphictyonic council of ancient Greece, could be elected to solve differences between districts or to repel a foreign invasion. Although at first such congresses and juries might issue commands, they would gradually lose their political authority. Soon it would be enough to invite individuals to co-operate for the common advantage. All vestiges of government would eventually be dissolved and society become a free and voluntary association of autonomous, self-reliant, and independent individuals. 'With what delight', Godwin perorates,

> must every well informed friend of mankind look forward to the auspicious period, the dissolution of political government, of that brute engine, which has been the only perennial cause of the vices of mankind, and which, as has abundantly appeared in the progress of the present work, has mischiefs of various sorts incorporated with its substance, and no otherwise to be removed than by its utter annihilation![110]

Thirdly, in Godwin's regenerated society, there would be an equalization of property. The established system of property, he believes, harms the rich and the poor alike. Like Rousseau, he argues that the first offence was committed by the man who took advantage of the weaknesses of his neighbours to secure a monopoly of wealth. Since then, the effects of property have been disastrous. It not only creates a 'servile and truckling spirit' but encourages the 'narrowest selfishness'.[111] It multiples vice by generating the crimes of the poor, the passions of the rich, and the misfortunes of war. Far from promoting civilization and prosperity, as Hume argued, or public virtue, as Mandeville claimed, the system of private property turns society into nothing less than 'a state of war, an unjust combination, not for protecting every man in his rights and securing to him the means of existence, but for engrossing all its advantages to a few favoured individuals, and reserving for the portion of the rest want, dependence and misery'.[112] Godwin refers to the writers Plato, More, Swift, Mably, Ogilvie, and Wallace, and also to the examples of Crete, Sparta, Peru and Paraguay to back up his case.

In place of the prevailing system of property, Godwin proposes a form of voluntary communism. His starting-point is that since all men share a common nature it follows on the principle of impartial justice that 'every man is entitled, so far as the general stock will suffice, not only to the means of being, but of well being'.[113] Justice further obliges every man to regard his property as a trust, and to consider in what manner it may best be employed for the increase of liberty, knowledge, and virtue. At the same time, justice is reciprocal: every man has a duty to assist his neighbour as well as a claim to his assistance.

In Godwin's new society everyone would therefore receive the product of his industry. After taking what was necessary for his own subsistence, he would then distribute the remainder to the most needy. Personal accumulation would rapidly cease since there would be no need to protect oneself against accidents or infirmity. Exchange being unknown, perishability would limit any individual's appropriation. The word property might remain, but only in the sense of possession and not as an exclusive right: 'Every man would be welcome to make every use of my accommodations, that did not interfere with my own use of them.'[114] By making a distinction between property and possession Godwin thus anticipates Proudhon, while his communism is reminiscent of Kropotkin's. He fails, however, to suggest a way of organizing production and distribution beyond individual initiative.

The benefits of an equalization of property, Godwin argues, would be inestimable. Without the present manufacture of luxuries and the maintenance of courts, armies, and government officials, labour would be considerably reduced. If all worked equally, half an hour's labour a day might suffice to meet the basic needs of a person, thereby freeing him to cultivate his intellect and to practise virtue. In such a society,

> the narrow principle of selfishness would vanish. No man being obliged to guard his little store, or provide with anxiety and pain for his restless wants, each would lose his own individual existence in the thought of the general good. No man would be an enemy to his neighbour, for they would have nothing to contend; and of consequence philanthropy would resume the empire which reason assigns her. Mind would be delivered from her perpetual anxiety about corporal support, and free to expatiate in the field of thought which is congenial to her. Each man would assist the enquiries of all.[115]

With its frugal economy and its face-to-face relationships, there is much in Godwin's ideal of the parish society of old England which was being threatened by the Industrial Revolution. But *Political Justice* is not an exercise in rural nostalgia or a Rousseauist lament for lost times. It is not backwards but forwards that we must look for perfection. Godwin specifically criticizes the 'romantic notions of pastoral life and the golden age' and those disappointed individuals who recur in imagination to 'the forests of Norway or the bleak and uncomfortable Highlands of Scotland in search of a purer race of mankind'.[116] Godwin's regenerated men may have simple tastes, but they are cultivated nonetheless. Ignorance, he insists, does not lead to virtue.

Similarly, far from ignoring the technological advances of the Industrial Revolution, Godwin is distinctly impressed by the 'various sorts of mills, of weaving engines, of steam engines' which were appearing.[117] He admits that such inventions were causing alarm and distress among the labouring part of the community but he does not overlook their potential liberating effect. In a state of equal labour their utility would be indisputable. An automatic plough is not beyond the limits of the imagination, while machines might extinguish the need for manual labour and become the helots of the future.

Godwin sees no threat from an increase in population to upset his new order. Certainly, the existing system of property strangled many children in the cradle but Godwin dismisses Wallace's contention that common property would result in excessive population. In the first place, there is no evidence for natural scarcity: three-quarters of the habitable globe was still to be cultivated, and land already cultivated could be considerably improved. Secondly, there is, Godwin believes, a 'principle' in human society which keeps population down to the means of subsistence.[118] Even if the population did threaten to outgrow the food supply, Godwin suggests that the sexual passions of enlightened men and women would be reduced and eventually extinguished. People would simply cease to propagate if their needs could not be met. It was a persuasive argument that Malthus could not leave unanswered.

Godwin's vision of a free and equal society is ultimately based on the Greek notion of individual self-fulfilment. He values liberty and equality chiefly as means of personal growth in wisdom and virtue. Liberty is a necessary condition for the exercise of the intellect and imagination, while equality would permit the emancipation of the whole species. Although he thinks it desirable, he does not call so much for a career open to talents, as the lawyers of the French Revolution, but equal opportunity for all to develop freely their full potential as rational and moral beings.

But personal growth is not a private affair. Godwin repudiates what was to be one of Mill's major principles by arguing that all have a duty to amend the errors and promote the welfare of their neighbours. Every person is to practise perfect sincerity and become an 'ingenuous censor'.[119] Indeed, in Godwin's new order persuasion would replace public authority and 'general inspection' provide a force 'not less irresistible than whips and chains' to reform conduct.[120]

Now all this may sound distinctly illiberal. Godwin certainly denies the discretionary right to do as we please and insists on our duty to correct others. But he is no less adamant that 'coercion cannot convince, cannot conciliate, but on the contrary alienates the mind of him against whom it is employed'.[121] The censure he advocates is a gentle and friendly appeal to reason, not mental torture or personal abuse. Godwin might have been more sensitive to the tyranny of government than of opinion, but it cannot be said that he was 'anti-liberal'.[122] His whole system is based on the free exercise of private judgment.

It is precisely to safeguard the autonomy of the individual that Godwin maintains 'every thing that is usually understood by the term co-operation, is in some degree an evil'.[123] There is therefore no need for common meals, common stores, or common labour. It may be necessary at present to work together and specialize in a particular trade, but it is quite possible that technology will make 'the most extensive operations' within the reach of one man.[124] Enlightened humanity may even find it intolerable to repeat words and ideas which are not their own, or play music composed by others. As for schools, they would no doubt disappear and mind would be free to expand as it wishes.

Godwin's stress on the autonomy of the individual further leads him to condemn marriage. In the first place, it involves cohabitation which inevitably subjects a couple to some degree of 'thwarting, bickering and unhappiness'.[125] Secondly, it often renders a thoughtless relationship permanent through 'the worst of all laws'. Thirdly, it is 'an affair of property, and the worst of all properties' and as such turns human beings into objects. 'So long as I seek to engross one woman to myself', Godwin concludes, 'and to prohibit my neighbour from proving his superior desert and reaping the fruits of it, I am guilty of the most odious of all monopolies.'[126]

Godwin sees no evil consequences following from the abolition of marriage. Each person would feel kindness towards another in exact proportion to his or her worth and their relations would be regulated not by force but by 'the unforced consent of either party'.[127] It would of course mean that the father of each child could not be definitely known, but it is only aristocracy, self-love, and family pride that teach us to set a value on such things. The spirit of democracy would lead to the abolition of surnames. Each mother would probably look after her infants with the help of her neighbours, while food and clothing would flow spontaneously to where they were most needed.

Godwin feels that these principles would not lead to a sullen selfishness but to a genuine concern for others. The individuality he recommends tends to the good of the whole and is valuable 'only as a means to that end'.[128] But while Godwin does not give 'absolute value' to autonomy, neither does he want the individual to be 'submerged in communal solidarity'.[129] In the final analysis, it is his love of personal independence which leads him to develop the libertarian aspects of traditional liberalism and to become a founding father of modern anarchism. 'No doubt man is formed for society', he writes,

But there is a way in which for a man to lose his own existence in that of others, that is eminently vicious and detrimental. Every man ought to rest upon his own centre, and consult his own understanding. Every man ought to feel his independence, that he can assert the principles of justice and truth, without being obliged treacherously to adapt them to the peculiarities of his situation, and the errors of others.[130]

Having established his political principles and sketched an alternative society, Godwin was still left with the problem of social change. He was uncertain of the best means of reform, and changed his views during the composition of *Political Justice*. As he points out in his preface, this leads to a few contradictions. He did not enter the work without being aware that 'government by its very nature counteracts the improvement of individual mind', but he understood the full meaning of this proposition as he proceeded, and saw more distinctly into the nature of the remedy.[131]

In a discussion of reform in the early part of the work, Godwin thus rejected the use of literature because it only reaches a privileged few, and education, because it raises the problem of educating the educator and has uncertain results. Instead, he favoured 'political institution' as the most effective means since it has such an extensive influence. By the time he reached Book III, however, he became convinced that the 'grand instrument for forwarding the improvement of mind is the publication of truth through discussion'.[132] Godwin then aimed the whole of Book IV against the political superintendence of opinion and proscribed any scheme of national education. It is not for the school-house or parliament to bring about change, he concluded, but a dedicated elite who would shape public opinion: 'give to the people guides and instructors; and the business is done.'[133]

But such guides are not to be found amongst the artisan leaders of the popular societies. Godwin recognizes the value of associations in times of revolution to protect the oppressed individual, and lauds the 'most liberal views' of their leaders, but he insists that human beings should meet together not to enforce their will but to enquire.[134] The new political associations not only produce a fallacious uniformity of opinion, but can easily lead to the 'depredations of a riot'.[135] Clubs in the old English sense of a periodical meeting of small and independent circles are all that Godwin will allow.

Like all the Enlightenment *philosophes*, Godwin places his faith in an intellectual elite. Since persuasion and argument, not violence or resentment, are the proper mode of effecting a revolution, Godwin turns to the men of 'study and reflexion' to act as catalysts of change.[136] For such a task, they must be capable of 'sober thought, clear discernment and intrepid discussion'.[137] They should be utterly disinterested and perfectly sincere, and, if necessary, be ready to accept martyrdom. One such man, Godwin declares, 'with genius, information and energy, might redeem a nation from vice'.[138]

Although Godwin looked to an elite to diffuse truth and dissolve the spell of government, he cannot strictly speaking be called an elitist. Certainly he feels that it is inevitable for ideas to descend in 'regular gradation from the most thoughtful to the most unobservant'.[139] But he is totally opposed to dividing men into classes, 'one of which is to think and reason for the whole, and the other to take the conclusions of their superiors on trust'.[140] He disdains Burke's and Rousseau's advocacy of political imposture and is an implacable enemy of implicit faith. In the long run, fundamental change cannot come from the authority of a chief magistrate, or the persuasion of a few enlightened thinkers, but from the 'serious and deliberate conviction of the community at large'.[141] For this reason, Godwin appeals to all classes of society.

Nothing could be more inaccurate than to accuse Godwin of believing 'as firmly as an early Christian in the speedy revelation of a new Jerusalem, four-square and perfect in its plan'.[142] Time and time again, he insists that progress has been and should be gradual. He is unable to share the pacifist faith of the Quakers precisely because 'we are not yet wise enough to make the sword drop out of the hands of our oppressors by the mere force of reason'.[143] Again, he does not naively picture his fellow men as perfectly rational beings inexplicably oppressed by evil institutions. He is only too aware that he is dealing with men who are 'imperfect, ignorant, the slaves of appearances' and whose virtues are alloyed with 'weakness, fluctuation and inconstancy'.[144]

If anything, Godwin would rather postpone than incite a political revolution. He recognizes that anarchy, in the negative sense of disorder which might follow the immediate dissolution of government, has a 'distorted and tremendous likeness, of true liberty', but he fears that it would suspend intellectual enquiry and personal security.[145] In order for anarchy to be the 'seed plot of future justice, reflexion and enquiry must have gone before, the regions of philosophy must have been penetrated, and political truth have opened her school to mankind'.[146] Indeed, Godwin feels that his contemporaries are not yet enlightened enough for a state of equality and that the reformer should therefore suffer the 'lapse of years' before reducing his theory into action. In this long transitional period, the 'delusive' love of distinction may also prove a necessary motive before people become truly capable of justice.[147]

Godwin thus looks to a revolution in opinion, not on the barricades. He opposes the traditional right of resistance in the sense of making violent changes which had been recognized by Locke and espoused by the

Dissenters. If a whole nation faces an unavoidable choice between tyranny and liberty, then armed struggle might be permissible, but the duty of the reformer is to make every attempt to resist injustice by reason not force. *Political Justice*, Godwin claims in his preface, has the express purpose of dissuading 'all tumult and violence'.[148] It is the power of example and persuasion that Godwin advocates, not the force of arms: non-violence is his strategy of liberation.

This did nothing, however, to interfere with his hopes for the future. He perceived clear signs in modern Europe of progress from barbarism to refinement. Commerce and learning had loosened the feudal bonds and moral and political truth was gaining ground. He was confident that 'inevitable progress' would insensibly lead towards an equalization of property.[149] All the prejudices of the human mind might be up in arms against the doctrines of *Political Justice*, but, Godwin wrote in his preface, 'it is the property of truth to be fearless, and to prove victorious over every adversary. It requires no great degree of fortitude, to look with indifference upon the false fire of the moment, and to foresee the calm period of reason which will succeed.'[150]

Godwin's system of *Political Justice* is clearly both profound and imaginative. With Locke and Mill, his politics are an extension of his ethics, and he tries to find the form of society which will best promote human happiness. His view of society is essentially atomistic and he carefully draws the distinction between society and government. He goes beyond liberalism, however, to question the very basis of political authority and suggest that there can be no obligation except to the dictates of one's understanding. He criticizes the social contract theory, finds a close link between government and class, and believes that it perpetuates rather than suppresses injustice. He concludes like Thoreau that while government may be at present a necessary evil, it is best when it governs least, and that the ultimate goal must be its total dissolution.

At the same time, Godwin offers a most eloquent defence of the freedom of thought and expression. In his analysis of punishment, he can find no justification for coercion except in the benevolent restraint of wrongdoers. In place of man-made laws, which falsely assume moral responsibility and try to reduce the diversity of human actions to one common standard, he appeals to the universal authority of reason. In his economics, he develops the labour theory of value, shows the psychological and moral effects of unequal distribution, and calls for a form of voluntary communism.

Godwin reserves some of his most trenchant criticisms for representative democracy, although he finds it preferable to monarchy or aristocracy. He shows the dangers of majority rule, the practice of voting, and the division of powers. As a temporary measure, he would prefer a periodic assembly in which wise delegates have executive powers in order to maintain security. But it would be best to simplify and decentralize society into a federation of face-to-face communities. Technology would increase leisure and allow all to develop their potential.

While replacing law with the force of public opinion to modify conduct, Godwin is well aware of its potential dangers. Although he rejects enforced co-operation he does not encourage a selfish individuality. Like Kropotkin, he wishes to avoid the claustrophobia of traditional societies and to combine mutual aid with personal independence.

Godwin is no idle visionary. He does not believe that the immediate abolition of government would lead to perfect harmony and his gradualism extremely cautious. His confidence in the power of truth is tempered by his stress on the influence of environment in shaping human nature. In the long term, however, he believes that all can run the generous race of improvement and that education and enlightenment could bring about a better order of things on earth.

Godwin thus came to challenge in *Political Justice* some of the fundamental assumptions of moral and political philosophy. Drawing on the experience of the American and French revolutions and developing the liberal tradition of the English and French Enlightenment, his bold reasoning led him to elaborate the most consistent and thorough exposition of anarchism. It was an achievement of extraordinary intellectual and imaginative power, and one which places Godwin alongside Hobbes, Locke, Rousseau and Mill in the history of political philosophy.

# CHAPTER VIII

## *Political Justice Triumphant*

The early 1790s were a heyday for political debate. The French Revolution and Burke's *Reflections* had triggered off a plethora of radical literature. But when Godwin's *Political Justice* appeared on 14 February 1793, it was to sweep the field. 'The booksellers' counters', wrote a contemporary,

> groaned under the weight of new views of the state of the representation, theories of reform, and philosophical treatises on the constitution. Every day brought forth its bundles of pamphlets and broadsheets. Every man who had anything to say, or nothing to say, put it into print . . . And in the midst of this shoal of minor speculators, suddenly appeared a great leviathan in the shape of Godwin's *Political Justice*.[1]

Hitherto Godwin was unknown except to a few Whig politicians and journalists. Literally overnight he became a celebrity. *Political Justice* was an immediate success and its author was ranked at once among men of the highest genius. 'Perhaps no work of equal bulk', Godwin's first biographer John Fenwick wrote in 1799, 'ever had such a number of readers; and certainly no book of such profound inquiry ever made so many proselytes in an equal space of time.'[2]

Godwin was naturally keen to get as wide a circulation as possible. He took the sheets of *Political Justice* on 26 January 1793 to Chauvelin, the French ambassador in London, together with a dedicatory letter to the National Convention in which he described himself as 'un des admirateurs les plus zélés de la révolution française'.[3] A couple of weeks later, he also asked his friend John Fenwick, who was going to Paris, to take a copy to General Francisco Miranda, the founder of the republics of Colombia and Venezuela, and to try and arrange a French translation.[4] No translation appeared in France although *Political Justice* was known there and excited at least one reply in Jean-Baptiste Salaville's *De la perfectibilité* (1798). It was given further notoriety by a translation of Elizabeth Hamilton's satirical *Memoirs of Modern Philosophers* (1800).[5] As late as 1804, Benjamin Constant considered *Political Justice* to be 'one of the Masterpieces of our Age', and only withheld his careful translation because of the unfavourable political climate.[6]

When the German radical Georg Forster visited Paris in July 1793 he copied as many extracts as possible from the copy of *Political Justice* which Chauvelin had delivered to the National Convention.[7] A translation by G. M. Weber appeared later in Würzburg, Germany, in 1803. Henry Crabb Robinson on a visit there at the turn of the century found that his oracle Godwin was an 'excellent bridge' between French philosophy and the German school since he had 'as much of Kant as of Mirabeau'.[8] He doubtlessly recommended it enthusiastically to Schelling and Salzmann when he met them. Another disciple of Godwin's, John Arnot, also visited Germany in 1799 and probably informed Wieland and Herder of the excellence of *Political Justice*.

In America, a pirated second edition appeared in Philadelphia in 1796 and in New York in 1804. James Ogilvie, the friend of Jefferson, became one of Godwin's most ardent champions, and his ideas played a central part in the controversy between the Jeffersonians and the Federalists at the turn of the century.[9] Benjamin Silliman in his satirical letters of Shah-Coolen observed that the New Philosophy 'is *inculcated*, and believed by multitudes in America', and in another pamphlet of 1802 remarked that while the author of *Political Justice* was hunted down in England, he was still admired by all the republicans in New England.[10]

The reviewers at home were almost unanimous in their praise. The *Monthly Review* and the *Analytical Review* both gave lengthy extracts. The former, written by Holcroft, pointed out some of the inconsistencies about government, but called it a 'bold and original work' written in a 'simple, clear and logical' diction.[11] The latter similarly praised the moral sentiments and clear language although it did object to the offensive religious speculations and found its ultimate goals utopian.[12] *The New Annual Register*, in a review possibly written by Godwin's former tutor Kippis, spoke warmly of the author's 'well informed, bold, and vigorous' mind and considered the work a 'liberal and unrestricted enquiry'.[13] The *Literary and Biographical Magazine and British Review* complained about the extraneous metaphysical matter in the book but still felt Godwin was 'a very persuasive advocate for a pure democracy'.[14] Even the conservative *Critical Review*, which called the philosophy of necessity 'an irreligious and monstrous absurdity', was able to recommend the enquiry as informative and entertaining.[15] Only the *British Critic* attacked him as a 'wildly extravagant'

VIII. Frontispiece of an unidentified pamphlet.

philosopher who had attempted to systematize the irony of Swift and Burke in a 'perfectly chimerical' book.[16] Yet it too recognized his talents and praised his style. Despite its high price, over three thousand copies of the first edition were sold.

Godwin's influence was not limited to a small and highly literate circle. The price of the book was fixed at £1 16s 0d (more than half the average monthly wages of a labourer), and it was for this reason that Pitt decided not to prosecute the author.[17] Yet pirated editions appeared in Ireland and Scotland and the 'people of the lower classes were the purchasers'. In many places, perhaps 'some hundreds in England and Scotland', mechanics and labourers banded together to buy it by subscription and read it aloud at their meetings.[18] George Robinson issued a second edition in octavo in 1796 at fourteen shillings to capture this market — which again was pirated in Ireland — and demand was sufficiently great to warrant a third edition two years later. The radical publishers Symonds, Spence and Eaton moreover all issued lengthy extracts in cheap collections.[19]

Godwin clearly became a leading symbol of reform in the popular imagination. The frontispiece of an unidentified pamphlet protesting against Pitt's attack on the freedom of speech pictures a female figure of Liberty against a glorious dawn and surrounded by Paine's *Rights of Man*, Thelwall's *Lectures* and Godwin's *Political Justice*.[20] According to the ex-radical Reid, heads of hitherto industrious families remained at home in their 'working dresses' on the Sabbath, and got Paine's *Age of Reason* and Godwin's *Political Justice*, which 'have remained upon their shelves, and full in sight of the possessors the whole time!'. To Reid's horror, fanatics who called themselves disciples of Godwin blindly insisted that 'the time is fast approaching, and will infallibly arrive, when men and nature will be perfect in all their relations; and the former will be able to live without government, without laws, and without submission!!!'.[21]

Godwin was soon to be regarded as one of the most dangerous enemies of established society. For the time being, however, he was at the very zenith of his reputation. In London, he could not walk the streets without being gazed at as a wonder. When he made a visit to the west of England in 1794 he hardly found a person in town or country who had any acquaintance with modern publications who was not familiar with the contents of *Political Justice*:

> I was nowhere a stranger. The doctrines of that work (though if any book ever contained the dictates of an independent mind, mine might pretend to do so) coincided in a great degree with the sentiments then prevailing in English society, and I was everywhere received with curiosity and kindness. If temporary fame ever was an object worthy to be

coveted by the human mind, I certainly obtained it in a degree that has seldom been exceeded.[22]

All the same, the abstract nature of *Political Justice* made it a book for intellectuals. The Dissenting community immediately recognized the value of a work produced by one of their ranks. Joseph Priestley told Godwin that it contained a 'vast extent of ability' and would be 'uncommonly useful', although he could not follow him in all his conclusions.[23] Despite his disapproval of some of his moral sentiments, Godwin's tutor Newton was also charmed with his 'general idea of political justice and liberty'.[24] Gilbert Wakefield read *Political Justice* 'with pleasure and improvement; with admiration of the philosophical composure, the temperate but vigorous ratiocination, the perspicuous energetic stile, the clear discernment, and the unreserved investigation, of the author'.[25] Thomas Belsham was sufficiently impressed with his view of justice to give long extracts in his *Elements of the Philosophy of the Mind, and of Moral Philosophy* (1801).

Of Godwin's acquaintances, only the cantankerous veteran Horne Tooke told him that it was a 'bad book' and would do a great deal of harm.[26] Charles Fox found he could not read it and merely returned it to the bookshop, while Burke not surprisingly dismissed its 'extravagant and absurd theories', which he put down to Godwin's vanity and desire 'of appearing deep, when really shallow'.[27] On 25 May 1793, Pitt and his cabinet discussed its prosecution but decided against it because 'a three guinea book could never do much harm among those who had not three shillings to spare'.[28]

The price certainly did not deter young radicals. The doctrines of *Political Justice* were eagerly debated by John Stoddart, Thomas Fragnall Dibdin and John Horseman at Oxford; by William Frend at Cambridge; and by Thomas Chalmers and his friends at St. Andrews University.[29] Henry Crabb Robinson recalled that no book ever made him feel 'more generously': he gave up the study of law, wrote a critique of his profession which was an 'abridgement' of Godwin's morality, and signed a defence 'Philo-Godwin' which he sent to Benjamin Flower's radical *Cambridge Intelligencer*.[30] Equally enthusiastic were William Hazlitt, Thomas Wedgwood, Mary Hays, and Basil Montagu, all of whom became Godwin's acquaintances. Even Charles Lamb was affected for a while, and according to Charles Lloyd was like him a believer 'in the doctrine of philosophical necessity, and in the final happiness of all mankind'.[31]

When Daniel O'Connell, later known as the 'Liberator' of Ireland, read *Political Justice,* he admired it way beyond any work he had ever met with. 'It has enlarged and strengthened my understanding', he wrote in his diary, 'and infused into my mind a serenity never before enjoyed.' The best government, he concluded, was that 'which laid fewest restraints on private judgment'.[32] Godwin also helped the radical satirist William Hone to over-come his childhood religion and look forward to a time when 'governments would disappear, and every individual would be self-governed'.[33] The great labour leader Francis Place acknowledged that he owed everything he most valued in himself to the 'sole perusal' of Godwin's writings, while John Thelwall, a leader of the London Corresponding Society, called *Political Justice* 'the most extensive plan of freedom and innovation in the language'.[34]

Godwin's most celebrated disciples however were the Romantic poets Southey, Coleridge, and Wordsworth. Southey first became acquainted with his ideas at the Oxford debating club attended by the Godwinians Stoddart, Dibdin, and Horseman. Late in 1793, he took out *Political Justice* twice from the library in Bristol where he was staying. He immediately recommended it to a friend, lamenting that society makes the crime and then punishes it.[35] In the summer of the following year, he urged Coleridge to write a sonnet in honour of its author. In the autumn, he wrote to Grosvenor Bedford that the philosophical principles which formed the basis of his character were 'ably elucidated' in Godwin.[36] Indeed, Southey's play *Wat Tyler*, written in 1794 but suppressed, shows clear signs of the philosopher's influence; as does *The Fall of Robespierre* which he wrote in collaboration with Coleridge in the same year.

Godwin's influence moreover was not only theoretical. By the autumn of 1794, Southey, Coleridge, and Robert Lovell were planning their scheme of Pantisocracy — an example of human perfectibility to be set up on the banks of the Susquehanna where all would be equal and property held in common. Southey enthusiastically wrote in November to his brother that Joseph Gerrald, Holcroft and Godwin — 'the three first men in England, perhaps in the world' — highly approved of their plan.[37] But Southey and Coleridge only got as far as Bristol, fell out, married, and rapidly turned against all radical innovation.

Coleridge later wrote to Godwin that Southey 'just looked enough into your books to believe you taught Republicanism and Stoicism — ergo, that you were of his opinion, & he of your's and this was all. Systems of Philosophy were never his Taste or his Forte.'[38] But although Godwin's influence on Southey was short-lived, it was not superficial. Southey told Grosvenor Bedford in October 1795 that the 'frequent and careful study of Godwin was essential service. I read, and all but worshipped.'[39] In the following month, he asserted that for all its faults *Political Justice* has a 'mass of truth in it that must make every man think'.[40] But he found its doctrines distasteful on religious grounds, and in the following year wrote to Bed-ford: 'Do not despise Godwin too much . . . He will do good by defending Atheism in print, because when the arguments are known, they may be easily and satisfactorily answered.'[41]

When Southey met Godwin in 1797 there was a natural antipathy: he never liked Godwin and Godwin never liked him. Turned Poet Laureate and orthodox in politics and religion, Southey later affirmed that he called on Godwin only about half a dozen times and found him 'intolerably dull and tho without any harm equally good-for-nothing'. In proportion as he valued what was true in *Political Justice*, he abominated 'the cursed mingle-mangle of metaphysics and concubinism and atheism with which he polluted it'.[42] In private conversation, he was more to the point: he told Coleridge that Godwin was like 'a close Stool pan, most often empty, & better empty than when full'.[43] Southey summed up Godwin's influence on him in a letter to William Taylor of Norwich in 1799: 'Once, indeed, I had a mimosa sensibility, but it has long ago been rooted out. Five years ago I counteracted Rousseau by dieting upon Godwin and Epictetus; they did me some good, but time has done more.'[44]

Coleridge, like Southey, played down in later life his youthful interest in Godwin. He was initially drawn to him because of his radical reputation. At Southey's earnest request, he addressed the author of *Political Justice*:

> O form'd t'illumine a sunless world forlorn,
>     As o'er the chill and dusky brow of Night,
> In Finland's wintry skies the Mimic Morn
>     Electric pours a stream of rosy light,
> Pleas'd I have mark'd OPPRESSION, terror-pale,
>     Since, thro' the windings of her dark machine,
>     Thy steady eye has shot its glances keen —
> And bade th' All-lovely 'scenes at distance hail'.
>
> Nor will I not thy holy guidance bless,
>     And hymn thee, GODWIN! with an ardent lay;
>     For that thy voice, in Passion's stormy day,
> When wild I roam'd the bleak Heath of Distress,
>
>     Bade the bright form of Justice meet my way —
> And told me that her name was HAPPINESS.[45]

It was first published in the *Morning Chronicle* on 10 January 1795, despite Coleridge's reservations about its mediocrity.

Coleridge however soon grew critical of Godwin's rational benevolence and as early as July 1794 told Southey that the 'ardour of Private attachments makes Philanthropy a necessary *habit* of the Soul'.[46] Their religious views were also at odds: in September, he wrote again that Godwin was writing a book on atheism, and added 'I set him at Defiance — tho' if he convinces me, I will acknowledge it in a letter to the Newspapers.'[47] Nevertheless, he claimed in the following month to have read Godwin with the 'greatest attention' and intended to write a book on Pantisocracy in which he hoped 'to have comprised all that is good in Godwin — of whom and whose book I will write more fully in my next letter'.[48] The work, according to his notebooks, was to be entitled 'A Practical Essay on the Abolition of Individual Property'.[49] Unfortunately, neither the letter nor the book was written. But Coleridge's contribution to *The Fall of Robespierre* written in the same year suggests that he saw the Terror in France primarily as the result of an excessive reliance on reason; the courtesan Adelaide significantly defends the value of domestic affections in a most un-Godwinian fashion.

Coleridge's personal acquaintance with Godwin late in December 1794 at first confirmed his doubts about his philosophy. Having read his sonnet on Kosciusko in the *Morning Chronicle*, Holcroft invited him to dine with Godwin and the famous scholar Richard Porson. Coleridge was still over-awed by Godwin's reputation and later hazily recalled his excitement on meeting

> the sublime Philosopher, the aweful Legislator and the Grand Justiciary for all rational Natures, whose works I had never seen indeed, but which Southey, my more than Delphian Oracle, had read, and recommended as the very apex of Philosophy, and immoveable Basis of Morality and Liberty — to meet with *him* — . . . The giant-making Mist, thro' which I looked forward to the meeting, and the anxious self-doubting & inward perplexity which accompanied it's gradual rarefaction and final evanescence, has never ceased to give an interest to the name of Godwin.[50]

Their conversation, which according to Godwin's diary, touched on 'self-love & God', proved a great disappointment. 'My God', Coleridge wrote to Southey soon afterwards, 'to hear Porson *crush* Godwin, Holcroft &c — They absolutely tremble before him!'[51] He also told Thelwall that Godwin appeared to him 'to possess neither the strength of intellect that discovers truth, or the powers of imagination that decorate falsehood — he talked futile sophisms in jejune language'.[52]

Nevertheless, Coleridge took Godwin's views seriously enough to discuss them in his lectures delivered in Bristol in 1795. In *A Moral and Political Lecture*, he referred early in the year to 'that small but glorious band' of disinterested patriots who believe that 'vice originates not in the man, but in the surrounding circumstances; not in the heart, but in the understanding' and who look forward to 'that glorious period when Justice shall have established the universal fraternity of love'.[53] He would seem to be referring to Godwin and his disciples here, but in another *Political Lecture* delivered in 1795 and published later in *The Friend*, he criticized Godwin for looking to 'private societies' as a means of reform rather than being '*personally* among the poor' and insisted that we must feed on the truths of necessity as 'insects on a leaf', till the 'whole heart be coloured by their qualities'.[54] Again, in his *Conciones ad Populum* (1795), Coleridge warned against that 'proud Philosophy, which affects to inculcate Philanthropy while it denounces every home-born feeling, by which it is produced and nurtured'.[55]

Yet *Political Justice* was still the main inspiration behind Coleridge's *Lectures on Revealed Religion, its Corruption and Political Views* (1795). He continued to agree with Godwin that the system of private property must be removed, that vice is a product of circumstances, that government is a source of evil, that the necessary revolution should be bloodless and the result of gradual enlightenment. But he increasingly tended to give a Christian interpretation to Godwin's teaching and repeatedly criticized his rational view of universal benevolence.[56]

Coleridge's opinion of Godwin soon developed from qualified approval to outright opposition, mainly on account of their differing religious views. A reading of Cudworth and Berkeley further undermined his belief in necessity: by late 1795 or early 1796, he was planning to write 'a dissection of Atheism — particularly the Godwinian System of Pride', which made man an 'outcast of blind Nature ruled by a fatal Necessity — Slave of an ideot Nature!'[57] His growing dissatisfaction with his philosophy was reinforced by some unpleasant rumours he heard from Walter Scott about Godwin's rudeness to the Welsh poet Edward Williams, his 'gross adulation' of a money-lender called John King, and his 'endeavours to seduce' Maria Reveley.[58] He admitted to Thelwall in the summer of 1796 that 'it is not his Atheism that has prejudiced me against Godwin; but Godwin who has perhaps *prejudiced* me against Atheism'.[59]

He returned to a public attack of Godwin in the third number of *The Watchman* in the spring of 1796. In an essay on 'Modern Patriotism', he arraigned the would-be patriot who reads *Political Justice* and thinks 'filial affection folly, gratitude a crime, marriage injustice, and the promiscuous intercourse of the sexes right and wise'.[60] When he was criticized in the *Bristol Gazette* by one 'Caius Gracchus' who defended *Political Justice* as a 'deep Metaphysical Work' written in a 'manner unequalled in the English language', Coleridge replied that an examination of Godwin's 'Sensuality' would appear shortly in *The Watchman* in a series of essays. In the meantime, he resorted to abuse and ridicule: 'I am not quite convinced with yourself and Mr. Godwin that mind will be omnipotent over matter, that a plough will go into the field and perform its labour without the presence of the Agriculturist, that man may be immortal in this life, and that Death is an act of the Will!!!'[61] His friend Thelwall could well upbraid him for his 'sledge-hammer of abuse', but Coleridge merely reaffirmed in a long letter his belief in the indissolubility of marriage and that a sensualist is not likely to be a patriot.[62]

Coleridge still planned to write a more sustained and coherent reply to Godwin. On 2 November 1796, he wrote to Benjamin Flower that he would 'shortly' be delivered of an 'Examination of Godwin's political Justice'.[63] Later in the month he even informed Thelwall that a chapter on 'The origin of Property, & the *mode of removing it's* evils' would be the last one of his 'Answer to Godwin' which would appear in a few weeks.[64] In December, however, he told Flower that it would appear in a six-shilling octavo shortly before Christmas and its scope was widened to show 'not only the absurdities and wickedness of *his* System, but to detect what appear to me the defects of all the systems of morality before & since Christ'.[65] He was by now unreservedly Godwin's opponent and told Thelwall emphatically early in 1797 'for thank heaven! I abominate Godwinism'[66] But like so many of his projects, Coleridge's 'Answer to Godwin' was never written.

Despite Coleridge's increasing conservatism in politics and Christian inspiration in morals, he continued to criticize the evils of private property and in his notebooks planned some 'Essays on Property as the Basis of Government'.[67] Moreover, when Coleridge and Godwin met again in December 1799, they soon became close friends, and Godwin was to acknowledge Coleridge as his fourth and last 'principal oral instructor'.[68] For his part, Coleridge admitted in 1811 that when he had read his writings

> religious bigotry, the but half-understanding of your principles, and the *not* half-understanding of my own, combined to render me a warm & boisterous Anti-Godwinist. But my Warfare was open; my unfelt and harmless Blows aimed at an abstraction, I had christen'd with your name; and you at that time if not in the World's *favor,* were among the Captains & Chief men in it's admiration.[69]

Having mellowed with time, he could now call Godwin the philosopher who gave the 'first system in England that ever dared reveal at full that most important of all important Truths, that Morality might be built up on it's own foundation, like a Castle built *from* the rock & *on* the rock . . .'[70]

In fact, Godwin's influence on Coleridge was much deeper and more enduring than is usually recognized. Coleridge summed up his fundamental objection to Godwin in a Latin tag from Hobbes: 'Rationem Defectus esse defectum Rationis'.[71] In other words, Coleridge found the reason for the flaw in Godwin's philosophy to be the flaw in his reason. Godwin was undoubtedly at the back of his mind in his celebrated distinction between reason and understanding. Godwin, he told Hazlitt, was a man of 'mere understanding'.[72] By that he meant that his mind could generalize and arrange the phenomena of perception, but did not possess 'reason' as the 'organ of the Super-sensuous' which is the source and substance of transcendental truths.[73] Moreover, Coleridge came to criticize Godwin's philosophy of necessity which had a tendency 'to deaden the feelings of will and free power, to extinguish the light of love and of conscience, to make myself and others worthless, soul-less, God-less'.[74] In short, Coleridge rejected Godwin's metaphysics and turned him into a symbol of all that was bad in determinism, atheism, and utilitarianism.

Nevertheless, the impact of *Political Justice* is still evident in *The Friend* of 1809 where Coleridge borrowed, in his essay 'On the Communication of Truth', his definition of truth from Godwin's treatment of sincerity. He clearly continued to respect Godwin for his psychological insights.[75] Moreover, while his later notion of the 'clerisy' clashed with Godwin's egalitarianism and faith in the people, his grounding of political philosophy upon obligation rather than individual rights, his denial of the authority of the State over the individual as a moral person, his dislike of political associations, and his conception of property as a trust are all characteristically Godwinian doctrines.[76]

With Wordsworth, Godwin's influence was much more lasting and played a crucial part in his emotional and intellectual growth. Godwinism for the poet was no mere temporary disease or unfortunate aberration but a profound experience which helped shape some of his most characteristic beliefs. The poetry of the Great Decade was as much a development from as a reaction to his early Godwinian discipleship.

Exactly when Wordsworth first read Godwin is difficult to establish but it seems likely that it was not before the summer of 1794. He had of course written the fiery *Letter to the Bishop of Llandaff* but it was probably through his experience of the French Revolution and his reading of Rousseau and Paine rather than Godwin that he had developed a passion for justice and equality.[77] Godwin however was to confirm these sentiments.

The first hard evidence of Wordsworth's reading *Political Justice* comes in a letter to his friend Mathews in June 1794 about his proposed magazine *The Philanthropist*. Many of the views and phrases are lifted directly from *Political Justice*. Any writer who has the welfare of mankind at heart, Wordsworth declares, 'should diffuse by every method a knowledge of those rules of political justice, from which the farther any government deviates the more effectually must it defeat the object for which government was ordained'. He further recommends like Godwin the 'freedom of

IX. Samuel Taylor Coleridge in 1795, by P. Vandyke.

X. William Wordsworth in 1798, by R. Hancock.

inquiry' as the best means of reform and condemns all addresses which might inflame the passions of men.[78] There are even parallels in imagery. Just as Godwin laments that in a state of social chaos the wisest would bid farewell to the 'labour of the midnight oil' and mind would appear 'like the coruscations of the meteor, not like the mild illumination of the sun', so Wordsworth asserts: 'I would put into each man's hand a lantern to guide him, and not have him to set out upon his journey depending for illumination on the abortive flashes of lightning or the coruscations of transitory meteors.'[79]

When Wordsworth came to revise his poem *Guilt and Sorrow* in 1795 he developed the Godwinian aim 'partly to expose the vices of the penal law and the calamities of war as they affect individuals'.[80] The portrayal of the Sailor in the same work further appears as a perfect example of Godwin's doctrine that society creates the criminal, and there are many parallels with *Caleb Williams*.[81] But by this time, Wordsworth was maintaining with difficulty his faith in the French Revolution, suffering the double agony — so movingly described in Book X of *The Prelude* — of apparently supporting the Terror and resisting patriotic feelings. The death of Robespierre in July 1794 temporarily raised his hopes, but when France changed a war of self-defence to one of conquest, it proved traumatic. He reacted by undertaking a systematic study of Godwin's philosophy.

Wordsworth seems to have become a wholehearted Godwinian in the spring of 1795 during his third long stay in London. He met the philosopher on 27 February 1795 at William Frend's, and the very next day he called at his home. By the middle of March he even became for a short time Godwin's neighbour at 15 Chalton Street, Somers Town. They met nine times between February and August, on all but two occasions unaccompanied. It was probably during these conversations that Godwin converted Wordsworth, as he claimed later, from the 'doctrine of self-love to that of benevolence'.[82] Basil Montagu, with whom Wordsworth shared rooms, was also probably the student at the Temple who, according to Hazlitt, was told by the poet to throw aside his books of chemistry, and 'read Godwin on Necessity'.[83] Montagu himself became a Godwinian and later recalled how it was 'scarcely possible' to conceive the 'extensive influence' of Godwin at the time, and that his friends discussed his ideas on reason, benevolence, gratitude and marriage.[84]

For Wordsworth, the new-found moral freedom based on the dictates of Godwinian reason was heady indeed. 'How glorious', he recalled, to

> Build social freedom on its only basis,
> The freedom of the individual mind
> Which, to the blind restraints of general laws
> Superior, magisterially adopts
> One guide, the light of circumstances, flash'd
> Upon an independent intellect.[85]

But the mood did not last long. The attempt 'to abstract the hopes of man/Out of his feelings', the worship of 'Reason's naked self', the probing of 'the living body of society/Even to the heart' and the violation of 'Nature's holiest places' only lead to terrible doubt and devastating confusion.[86] 'Sicked, wearied out with contrarieties', he yielded up moral questions in despair and turned to mathematics.[87] It was not until he joined his sister in the West Country in the autumn of 1795 and experienced the healing presence of Nature that he was able to recover from his crisis.

The period of Wordsworth's crisis is usually marked by his acceptance and rejection of Godwinism. It would appear, however, that his discipleship was never so intense nor his repudiation so absolute as is usually assumed. Godwin was not the only thinker whose 'wild theories' Wordsworth had listened to. The description of his moral investigations in *The Prelude* where he recalls 'Dragging all passions, notions, shapes of faith,/Like culprits to the bar' seems more applicable to Helvétius or Paley than Godwin.[88]

Similarly, Wordsworth's tragedy *The Borderers*, begun soon after his personal acquaintance with Godwin in the autumn of 1795, is not so much an exposure of Godwinism but of the misuse of reason and the dangers of pride. As Wordsworth makes clear in his preface, the central character Oswald 'disguises from himself his own malignity by assuming the character of a speculator in morals' and he is intended to demonstrate 'the dangerous use which may be made of reason when a man has committed a great crime'.[89] It is not the calm benevolence of Godwin but the assertive selfishness of a restless ego that Oswald demonstrates. Power is 'life to him' and 'where he cannot govern/He will Destroy'.[90] Wordsworth moreover drew on Godwin's novel *Caleb Williams* for his central situation in which a repeated crime springs from the intense relationship between two protagonists.[91]

Wordsworth then did not simply react against Godwinian 'naked reason' and lay a Romantic stress on feeling. Although he became critical of reason as an analytical tool — the 'humbler power' referred to in *The Prelude* whose function is 'rather proud to be/The enemy of falsehood, than the friend/Of truth' — he continued to value reason in its higher function as a faculty of intuition.[92] It is normal to attribute this distinction to Coleridge but Wordsworth could equally have found in Godwin a view of reason not merely as a faculty of comparison and analysis but as an intuitive power capable of discerning immutable and necessary truths.

On the other hand, Wordsworth certainly rejected the abstract humanism of Godwin's doctrine of universal benevolence. He would never have sacrificed his sister Dorothy for Fénelon, and he emphasized the value of domestic affections for developing virtue. We must therefore learn to appreciate:

> What there is best in individual Man,
> Of wise in passion, and sublime in power,
> What there is strong and pure in household love,
> Benevolent in small societies . . .[93]

He further turned away from city intellectuals, from Godwin's dictum that an honest ploughman could not be as virtuous as Cato, to treat in the *Lyrical Ballads* low and rustic life precisely because in that condition the 'essential passions of the heart find a better soil in which they can attain their maturity'.[94]

Yet Wordsworth continued like Godwin to find the ideal moral agent in the man of rational benevolence. In *The Old Cumberland Beggar,* he still offers a Godwinian account of virtue:

> Where'er the aged Beggar takes his rounds,
> The mild necessity of use compels
> To acts of love; and habit does the work
> Of reason; yet prepares that after-joy
> Which reason cherishes.[95]

Moreover, in the *Lines left upon a Seat in a Yew-tree,* Wordsworth emphasizes the need for cheerful and altruistic participation in society. It is the 'labours of benevolence' which give meaning to the human world, and the recluse must be

> Instructed that true knowledge leads to love;
> True dignity abides with him alone
> Who, in the silent hour of inward thought,
> Can still suspect, and still revere himself,
> In lowliness of heart.[96]

The theme of benevolent necessity, with its stress on tranquillity and cheerfulness, remained central to Wordsworth's mind.

Finally, Wordsworth in the *Lyrical Ballads* did not react violently against Godwin's view of property. In *Political Justice*, Godwin had not condemned the institution of property, but only its unequal distribution which corrupted the rich and oppressed the poor. The treatment of property in poems like *Michael* and *The Last of the Flock* is not therefore incompatible with Godwin's view of the right to subsistence. Indeed, in his letter to Fox, Wordsworth makes it clear that his aim is not to defend the rich but rather to urge that 'the most sacred of all property is the property of the Poor'.[97]

What Wordsworth disliked in Godwin was not so much his doctrines, which clearly helped shape his own views, but the manner in which he tried to change human behaviour. It was a case of the poet preferring figurative description and example to the logical argument of the philosopher. Thus in 1796 he complained that the preface of the second edition of *Political Justice* was a 'piece of barbarous writing' with 'scarce one sentence decently written'.[98] Again, in an incomplete 'Essay on Morals', probably written in late 1798, he argued that books like Godwin's were impotent to all their intended good purposes: 'Now I know no book or system of moral philosophy written with sufficient power to melt into our affections, to incorporate itself with the blood & vital juices of our minds, & thence to have an influence worth our notice in forming those habits of which I am speaking.'[99] It is a more extended version of the argument in the preface to the *Lyrical Ballads* that it is the poet rather than the mere logician who is the true philosopher.

Godwin's influence on Wordsworth was therefore neither as clear-cut nor as temporary as most critics assume.[100] On the one hand, his initial allegiance to naked reason in ethics was not purely of Godwinian inspiration. On the other, Godwin converted him to a system of rational benevolence which he developed in the poetry of the Great Decade. Although the abstract nature of Godwin's philosophy made Wordsworth more fully aware of the value of domestic affections, their view of reason as an intuitive faculty was similar. They both continued to attack the unequal distribution of wealth and were inspired by a humanitarian concern for the poor.

Although Wordsworth continued to see Godwin whenever he was in London until his death, their personal acquaintance never developed into friendship. 'The said Mr. G.', he wrote to Coleridge in 1799, 'I have often heard described as a puppy, one of the fawning, flattering kind in short, a polite liar, often perhaps without knowing himself to be so.'[101] But while he found little to revise his view of the man, he still retained some admiration for his philosophy. As late as 1804, when he had turned away from social questions to explore his own personal feelings, he could write of his 'Godwinian' period:

> A noble aspiration, yet I feel
> The aspiration, but with other thoughts
> And happier . . .[102]

Godwin has been most remembered as the revolutionary mentor of the young Romantic poets, but he also had an important influence on the radical movement in the 1790s through his personal contact with some of its leaders and his eloquent public defence of freedom and justice. He remained aloof from the popular agitation because of his fear of tumult and his disapproval of political associations. Reserved by disposition, the composition of *Political Justice* had nevertheless inspired him

> to tell my neighbour whatever it might be of advantage to him to know, to shew myself the sincere and zealous advocate of absent merit and worth, and to contribute by every means in my power to the improvement of others and to the diffusion of salutary truth through the world. I desired that every hour that I lived should be turned to the best account, and was bent each day to examine whether I had conformed myself to this rule.[103]

The first occasion which presented itself was the trials of Thomas Fyshe Palmer and Thomas Muir. They had attended in December 1792 a Convention held in Edinburgh which gave a fillip to the reform movement in Scotland. The government became increasingly anxious. In February 1793 war was declared on France. Three months later the House of Commons refused to consider petitions of reform, thereby closing the last constitutional channel. A severe crack-down on the reformers themselves then followed.

Muir, a moderate lawyer who had even gone to France to prevent the execution of the king, and Palmer, a unitarian minister and a fellow at Cambridge, were arrested and charged with sedition. At their trials, Muir was sentenced to fourteen years' transportation to Botany Bay and Palmer to seven years. It was further ruled that they should not be treated as political prisoners but as felons of the worst sort.

Godwin was incensed. He was no friend of popular agitation or political associations, but he could not let such injustice go unopposed. While revising the preface to *Political Justice*, he wrote on 7 December 1793 to the *Morning Chronicle* complaining bitterly of their treatment: 'a punishment the purpose of which is to inflict on such men slavery, degradation of soul, a lingering decay and final imbecility — can do nothing but exasperate men's minds, and wind up their nerves to decisive action.'[104] Despite his eloquence, the prisoners were duly shipped to Botany Bay. All Godwin could do was to visit them on 20 and 28 January 1794 whilst they were awaiting transportation in the hulks on the Thames.

The Scottish reformers replied to these sentences by calling another Convention at short notice in Edinburgh in November 1793. The aim was shorter parliaments and universal suffrage, but the manner was more histrionic — they adopted French styles and dated the minutes 'The First Year of the British Convention'. When the meeting was broken up forcibly in December the secretary William Skirving and the members of the London Corresponding Society — Maurice Margarot, Joseph Gerrald and Charles Sinclair — were arrested. The first two were sentenced to fourteen years' transportation at the trials which followed, but Sinclair under suspicious circumstances was discharged. Gerrald managed to secure bail, and returned to London to report to the L.C.S. He went back to face trial in March 1794.

Gerrald was perhaps the ablest theorist of the L.C.S. He had contacted Godwin in August to express his admiration for *Political Justice*, and they rapidly became friends. When Godwin heard of his arrest, he immediately came to his aid and throughout January he visited him regularly to help prepare his case. In a long letter dated 23 January 1794, he urged Gerrald not only to establish the lawfulness of the meeting, but to appeal to an 'authority paramount to the English constitution, to all written Law and parchment constitutions; the Law of universal Reason'. Above all, he stressed the importance of the occasion — 'it may be the means of converting thousands, and, progressively, millions, to the cause of reason and public justice' — and the need for calm and reasoned argument. 'Farewell;' he concluded, 'my whole soul goes with you. You represent us all.'[105]

At the trial, Gerrald followed Godwin's advice closely. While basing his case on the constitutional right to agitate for reform, he also appealed to that 'moral light' which is 'as irresistible by the mind, as physical by the eye'.[106] And despite deliberate provocation from the notorious judge, 'hanging' Braxfield, he conducted himself with great calmness and fortitude. Needless to say, Gerrald was found guilty of sedition and committed to Newgate Gaol. He refused a pardon by the Secretary of State and was shipped in May 1795 to New South Wales, where he died five months later. By his example, Gerrald may well have helped avoid a White Terror in England.[107]

Godwin visited him in prison and in the hulks, and noted his departure on 2 May 1795 in his diary. He always spoke of him afterwards with affectionate admiration. The epitaph inscribed on a brass plate on the tomb in Sydney of this 'Martyr to the Liberties of his Countrymen' is also said to have come from Godwin's pen: 'He was too sincere, and generous to an extreme. The magnanimity of his spirit, and purity of his sense of honour, could only be completely understood by those who made them the subject of personal observation.'[108] All Godwin could do after the trial was to write to the discharged Charles Sinclair asking him to refute the accusation that he was a government spy but he declined to reply.[109]

The immediate effect of the trials was to increase rather than dampen agitation for reform. Thelwall began a series of lectures to provide funds for the prisoners' defence. An ailing L.C.S. sprang back into life and new clubs emerged up and down the country. At the end of March the London committee sent out a call for a British Convention.

Pitt, supported by Burke, acted immediately. He suspended Habeas Corpus on 12 May 1794 and arrested Thomas Hardy, the shoemaker secretary of the L.C.S., on a charge of High Treason. Within a week Horne Tooke, Thelwall and eight others were taken to the Tower or Newgate. On 2 October the Lord Chief Justice Eyre presented a charge to a grand jury who returned a bill of indictment enabling the trial to proceed. When Holcroft heard that he too was named a traitor, he boldly entered the court room and gave himself up. It was a memorable epoch in the history of English liberty: if the accused had been convicted they would certainly have been hanged.

Godwin had been dining with Thelwall at Horne Tooke's the day before Hardy was arrested. He watched the preparations of the trial of his friends with growing concern. During the spring and summer of 1794 he met Holcroft frequently and visited Horne Tooke and Thelwall's wife. When he heard of the news of the indictment during a visit to Dr. Parr in Warwickshire, he immediately returned to London to help his friends. He knew that he was himself in danger, but he went to Newgate with Marshal to visit Holcroft on 14 and 16 October.

The next two days Godwin locked himself at home and wrote some

*Cursory Strictures on the Charge delivered by Lord Chief Justice Eyre to the Grand Jury, October 2, 1794*. It appeared in the *Morning Chronicle* on the 21st and was immediately copied by the opposition papers. On receiving a menace from the Treasury, Kearsley, who first published the pamphlet for a shilling, discontinued its sale, but the intrepid Daniel Isaac Eaton reprinted it at half the price. It proved to be one of Godwin's most eloquent and effective works.

Eyre's charge attempted to prove by circumstantial evidence that there had been a conspiracy to 'bring the people together in convention in imitation of those National Conventions which we have heard of in France in order to usurp the Government of the country'.[110] Such a charge in Godwin's view, was made up of 'hypothesis, presumption, prejudication, and conjecture'.[111] Eyre had simply tried to construct out of many overt facts, no one of which was capital, a capital crime. Given the extreme gravity of the charge, however, Godwin no longer appeals to the laws of universal Reason (the trial of Gerrald had shown how many were blind to its light) but focuses on the particular legal argument. The accused must be proved guilty of a crime against the law as it stands — it is not enough simply to bring a guilty verdict by the 'mere names of Jacobin and Republican'.[112] As for Eyre's call for the jury to bring in a bill to settle the legality of 'constructive treason', the plain English of his recommendation is:

'Let these men be put on trial for their lives; let them and their friends through the remotest strainers of connection, be exposed to all the anxieties incident to so uncertain and fearful a condition; let them be exposed to ignominy, to obloq[u]y the partialities, as it may happen, of a prejudiced judge, and the perverseness of an ignorant jury; we shall then know how we ought to conceive of similar cases.'[113]

The pamphlet could not have been more timely. Its effect was immediate. Instead of the guilt of the accused, little was heard of but the flagrancy of the charge. When Horne Tooke met another prisoner on Tower Parade, he held up Godwin's pamphlet, broke the rule of silence and declared: 'By God, Joyce, this lays Eyre completely on his back.'[114]

The crown was, however, unwilling to leave it at that. An *Answer* to the *Cursory Strictures* first appeared in the *Morning Chronicle* on 21 October and then on the 25th in *The Times*, three days before the trial was to begin. It was immediately reprinted by Eaton. The author was said to be 'Judge Thumb' — Sir Francis Buller, who had ruled that it was legitimate for a man to beat his wife with a stick, as long as it was no thicker than his thumb. He accused the author of the *Cursory Strictures* of being 'most impudent, false and unconstitutional' — impudent because he attacked a 'high Judicial Character'; false because he misstated the 'learned Chief Justice's positions'; and unconstitutional because he tried to influence the minds of the jury.[115] The *Answer* rather lamely tried to restate Eyre's charge, proceeded by abuse rather than argument against the 'officious and unprincipled scribler' who dared to raise objections, and finally called for his prosecution.[116]

Initially, Godwin felt the *Answer* was so unsatisfactory and superficial that it only deserved silence. Nevertheless, possibly because he feared prosecution himself, he began a reply on 23 October. It was refused insertion in the *Morning Chronicle*, so Eaton published it as a pamphlet. Once again, Godwin went over the essential points of his interpretation of Eyre's *Charge*, protesting that a more nefarious proceeding can scarcely be imagined

> than that a man should be hanged upon an action which he did not know to be High Treason, which he could not know to be High Treason, which the Judges of the land did not know to be High Treason, and which was not High Treason till it was made so by the adjudication under which he is executed![117]

Godwin also rehearsed with great candour, and no doubt to the relish of his enemies, the arguments which he would use in full court if the *Cursory Strictures* were prosecuted. The pamphlet, he claimed, was one of 'close, severe and accurate investigation'. Above all, it was aimed at influencing the minds of the jury far less than Eyre's *Charge* and the innumerable 'Bills, hand-bills, songs, pamphlets, and even printed pocket handkerchiefs' which had appeared against the accused in the last six months.[118]

Despite Godwin's intervention the trial went ahead as planned. Hardy was first selected to be placed at the bar on 28 October. The atmosphere was tense in the court room, and Godwin with his friends Fawcett, Dyson and Marshal looked on with bated breath. The building was beleaguered by great crowds, and throughout the country men had given up work to await the news. Some radicals expected wholesale arrests to follow and were ready to go into exile. The Attorney General opened with a speech nine hours long, dwelling for a full hour on Godwin's pamphlet. Erskine, who had defended Paine, replied with a speech nearly as long. But as the trial dragged on the evidence proved increasingly slender and after only three hours' deliberation the jury returned a verdict of Not Guilty. There was immediate rejoicing; in Colchester, Crabb Robinson, then a lad of nineteen, ran from house to house shouting the news. The trials of Horne Tooke and Thelwall followed, but the prosecution, having spent all their energy, failed once again. After Thelwall's acquittal, the crowd outside the court unharnessed the horses from Erskine's coach, and he was dragged through the streets in triumph. The case against the rest of the accused was

XI. Godwin and Thomas Holcroft at the 1794 Treason Trials, sketched by Sir Thomas Lawrence.

dropped, much to Holcroft's chagrin. It proved a landmark in the history of English liberty by establishing the principle that Englishman could not be convicted of treason for what they said and wrote.

Although Godwin knew that he was a marked man he did all he could for the accused. He visited Newgate every day just before Hardy's trial and was present for part of each day during the trials. As soon as he heard that Holcroft had been arrested he asked his wife to tell Erskine that 'I am Mr. Holcroft's principal friend upon whom he chiefly depends, & that I prefer his happiness to every earthly consideration.'[119] He went on to help Holcroft arrange his defence and was asked to collect for him statements from the prosecution witnesses.[120] When Holcroft was discharged without trial and denied the opportunity to speak in court, he immediately left the dock and sat beside Godwin. Thomas Lawrence, struck by the juxtaposition of the two friends, made a spirited sketch, contrasting Godwin's bent and meditative profile with Holcroft's more aggressive figure.

To demonstrate that he stood above faction and held no personal animosity, Godwin wrote a friendly letter to Chief Justice Eyre who had presided at Horne Tooke's trial. He praised his summing up as 'fair & manly' but still objected to his exposition of the law of treason. While insisting that he had been inspired in his *Cursory Strictures* by a 'sense of deep iniquity' at the conviction of the prisoners, he apologized for the warmth of some of his expressions, adding 'I cannot believe that truth will ever be injured by a sober & benevolent style.'[121]

Godwin did not sign his *Cursory Strictures* and for a time it was thought to be the work of Miles Vaughn, a liberal attorney. When it became known who was the true author, Godwin was widely acclaimed. It marked the high-point of the fragile alliance between the radical intellectuals and the artisans of the popular clubs. As Hazlitt wrote later, Godwin had possibly saved the lives of twelve innocent individuals, 'marked out as political victims to the Moloch of Legitimacy, which then skulked behind a British throne, and had not yet dared to stalk forth'.[122]

Dr. Parr, who strongly disapproved of the activities of the L.C.S., nevertheless felt that Godwin's pamphlet was 'luminous in style, powerful in matter, and solid in principle'.[123] It was Horne Tooke's response, however, which most moved Godwin. He had frequently rallied Godwin on the visionary nature of his politics, but when at a dinner on 21 May 1795 he heard that he had written the pamphlet, he requested him to give his hand. Godwin recalled:

> I had no sooner done this than he suddenly conveyed my hand to his lips, vowing that he could do no less by the hand that had given existence to that production. The suddenness of the action filled me with confu-

sion; yet I must confess that when I looked back upon it, this homage thus expressed was more gratifying to me than all the applause I had received from any other quarter.[124]

Although Godwin had helped check the Moloch of Legitimacy, he was soon to fall out with the more impatient elements in the L.C.S. The blissful dawn of revolution was almost over, and the quarrel took a particularly bitter turn. It centred on a disagreement between Godwin and John Thelwall, who had replaced Gerrald as the most accomplished theorist of the L.C.S., on the means of reform.

Thelwall was an extraordinary man — journalist, pamphleteer, lecturer and playwright. He became a close friend of Colcridge and was no mean poet himself. Godwin had exerted a considerable influence on him: Thelwall publically called him his 'philosophical father' and praised the 'daring excellencies' of *Political Justice*.[125] They shared the same views on reason, truth, necessity, universal benevolence, marriage and property.[126] Indeed, part of the evidence used against Thelwall in the Treason Trials was that he had read aloud and commented on passages from *Political Justice*. Unlike Godwin, however, he gave a positive role to government and encouraged direct action. He was more concerned with attacking particular abuses and bringing about immediate change — so much so that he took Jacobinism to the border of revolutionary socialism.[127]

A preliminary skirmish occurred whilst Thelwall was awaiting trial in the Tower. Godwin refused to visit him. He considered that it would be a matter of 'personal gratification', inconsistent with his decision 'to carry my life in my hand; not to indulge a particle of selfish retrospect to life or its pleasures, or the fear of pain and death; but to expend this treasure, which does not belong to me, but to the public, with all the wisdom I am able . . .'. To Thelwall, Godwin's heroic resolve no doubt appeared as pusillanimity or indifference. Moreover, Godwin went on to advise Thelwall to appeal to 'that eternal law which the heart of every man in common-sense recognises immediately', to reprimand 'the spirit of resentment and asperity' against his persecutors in his letters, and to remind him of the 'Divine principle of loving our enemies'.[128] Thelwall took little heed of Godwin's words and after his acquittal, he devoted himself in his political lectures to shake 'the pillars of corruption till every stone of the rotten edifice trembled'.[129]

In the meantime, a serious split occurred in the L.C.S. between those who like Thelwall supported unlimited popular agitation to compel the government to grant reform, and those who saw its function as mainly educational through discussions and publications. Prominent among the latter was the artisan Francis Place, who was to become a leading historian of the early labour movement. He too had been strongly influenced by *Political*

*Justice* which had undermined his belief in abstract rights and had encouraged him to become an honest and independent tailor.[130] Unlike Thelwall, Place believed with Godwin that the calm diffusion of truth was the best means of reform. When many in the L.C.S. called for meetings in order to 'force the House of Commons to consent to radical reform in the state of representation', he resigned along with twenty other members.[131] As firm Godwinians, they deplored the 'increase in factitious spirit, the preference given to measures the most inconsiderate and violent'.[132]

The year 1795 was to prove a turning-point in the radical campaign in more ways than one. There were food riots throughout the country. Citizen Lee in Soho issued tracts with titles like the *Happy Reign of George Last*, or *King Killing, the Reign of the English Robespierre*. On 26 October 1795, Thelwall and John Binns, but not Place, addressed a meeting in Copenhagen Fields of nearly 150,000 people. Three days later the king's coach was stopped on the way to parliament by a mob shouting: 'Down with Pitt!' 'No War!' 'No King!' Perhaps some 200,000 Londoners thronged the streets. When a stone broke a window, George III is said to have exclaimed 'My Lord, I, I, I've been shot at!'[133] The government acted swiftly. Pitt introduced his notorious Anti-Sedition Acts which abrogated the freedom of speech, of assembly, and of the press. Habeas Corpus was suspended for the next eight years.

Godwin responded to these events with the pamphlet *Considerations on Lord Grenville's and Mr. Pitt's Bills, concerning Treasonable and Seditious Practices, and Unlawful Assemblies*. It appeared on 21 November during the parliamentary debates and Johnson fixed the price at one shilling and sixpence. It was signed by 'A Lover of Order' and aimed at the mind 'untainted with the headlong rage of faction'.[134] Setting himself above the political struggle, Godwin condemns both extremes — Pitt's policy of repression and Thelwall's strategy of agitation. On the one hand, he denounces the proposed legislation as abrogating the Bill of Rights, overthrowing the hard-won liberties of recent centuries, and encouraging a 'national militia of spies and informers'.[135] On the other hand, he accuses the Jacobin agitators of the L.C.S. of encouraging tumult by sending missionaries to propagandize amongst the people and by holding huge rallies. Thelwall in particular is described (although his name is not directly mentioned) as an 'impatient and headlong reformer' who simmers the 'cauldron of civil contention'.[136] He may well urge the practice of universal benevolence and utter remonstrances against violence, but such 'saving clauses' are like 'lord George Gordon preaching peace to the rioters in Westminster-Hall' or 'Iago adjuring Othello not to dishonour him by giving harbour to a thought of jealousy'.[137]

Godwin was not of course defending Pitt in the pamphlet but rather his own view of reform through the gradual enlightenment of mankind in small friendly circles. Godwin exclaims 'Oh, Reform! Genial and benignant power!' but insists that it 'is a delicate and an awful task. No sacrilegious hand must be put forth to this sacred work. It must be carried on by slow, almost insensible steps, and by just degrees.'[138] It was no different from the message he had preached in *Political Justice*, but coming at a crucial stage in the government's persecution of the radicals, it was bound to have repercussions. Moreover, in no uncertain terms he declared:

> The London Corresponding Society is a formidable machine; the system of political lecturing is a hot-bed, perhaps too well adapted to ripen men for purposes, more or less similar to those of the Jacobin Society of Paris. Both branches of the situation are well deserving the attention of the members of the government of Great Britain.[139]

The statement destroyed in one stroke the delicate alliance Godwin had forged with the Jacobins during his campaign for civil liberties in the two previous years.

Thelwall, whom Godwin had helped save by his pamphlet on the Treason Trials only a year before, was both disappointed and indignant. He immediately sent an angry letter to Godwin, challenging him to confess authorship of the pamphlet. He found it difficult to believe that the man who had been his 'private panegyrist' should join in the 'warhoops of slanderous misrepresentation against an individual whom every engine of Tyranny and Falsehood is at work to destroy'.[140] Godwin replied that there was nothing in the pamphlet which he had not pressed upon him 'again and again with earnest anxiety'.[141] To Thelwall's still more bitter response, Godwin wrote on the following day that it was impossible to answer his 'farrago of abusive language'.[142]

Thelwall did not leave it at that. He presented his public answer in the preface of the second volume of the collected numbers of *The Tribune*. He felt particularly distressed that the author of *Political Justice* should reprobate moderate reform and mount such a malignant public attack. Above all, he considered Godwin's pamphlet as proof of the dangers of a 'life of domestic solitude' and concluded that effective reform cannot be achieved by writing quarto volumes and conversing with a few speculative philosophers.[143]

Godwin's reply, a dignified restatement of his doctrine of non-violent persuasion, was published in the next volume. He claimed that he did not intend to impute sinister motives to Thelwall, but merely to point out the consequences of his actions.[144] Thelwall was unconvinced and in a commentary on the letter, declared that Godwin mistook vanity for principle and had been unjust to a beleaguered friend in his zeal for candour.[145]

The dispute between Godwin and Thelwell was short-lived but symbolic. It marked the final break between the radical middle-class intellectuals and the Jacobin artisans of the L.C.S. It also came at a time when the reform movement was rapidly beginning to lose its momentum. The L.C.S. had collapsed by the end of 1796. Apart from the ill-fated naval mutinies in the following year, Jacobinism was all but dead.

As for the two disputants, Godwin recorded in his diary that he had an explanation with Thelwall on 22 December 1795. Whatever their differences on the means of reform, they had too much in common to remain enemies. In the spring of 1796, Thelwall was again defending Godwin against the young Coleridge.[146] In the summer, a friend of Crabb Robinson's witnessed their reconciliation at William Taylor's in Norwich:

> I have since seen them walking together around our Castle Hill. Of course the former will no longer be accused of 'cherishing a feebleness of spirit', nor will the latter be again compared to Iago. Like Gog & Magog or the two kings of Brentford they will now go hand in hand in their glorious schemes.[147]

# CHAPTER IX

## *Terror was the Order of the Day*

Having finished writing *Political Justice*, Godwin left his old friend James Marshal and moved late in 1792 to a small house at 25 Chalton Street, Somers Town, where in keeping with his principles he lived frugally and alone. His daughter later left a sketch of his methodical life at this time:

> He rose between seven and eight, and read some classic author before breakfast. From nine till twelve or one he occupied himself with his pen . . . The rest of the morning was spent in reading and seeing his friends. When at home he dined at four, but during his bachelor life he frequently dined out. His dinner at home at this time was simple enough. He had no regular servant; an old woman came in the morning to clean and arrange his rooms, and if necessary she prepared a mutton chop, which was put in a Dutch oven.[1]

If guests came, they would have to help Godwin prepare their dinner and serve themselves.

The thousand guineas that Godwin eventually received from Robinson for *Political Justice* left him comparatively well off but he was anxious not to spend a penny which was not calculated to render him 'a more capable servant of the public'.[2] Rather than re-distribute the money immediately, he decided to use it to subsist while writing for the common good. He furnished only part of his house, and in the following three years lived on £110, £120, and £130 respectively at a time when the average price of labour was about a shilling a day.

His phenomenal success naturally drew many admirers and the exalted state of his spirits made him more of a talker than before or after. He grew friendly with Dr. Samuel Parr, 'the Whig Dr. Johnson', the vegetarian scholar Joseph Ritson, the Della Cruscan poet Robert Merry, the scholar

Richard Porson, and the young Thomas Wedgwood of Etruria. At one time Godwin and Wedgwood even contemplated making a common household together 'on the most economical plan', but Wedgwood suffered from an incurable disease and the plan fell through.[3]

Godwin also met the first of several women who found the philosopher's company strangely attractive. Amelia Alderson, later the wife of the painter John Opie, was the beautiful and accomplished daughter of a Norwich physician well-known in Dissenting circles. Godwin made a visit to Norfolk in June 1794, and spent much of the time in her company. She introduced him to many of her liberal friends, including Capel Lofft, the old campaigner, John Taylor, a successful manufacturer who was later to help Godwin, and William Taylor, the first translator of Goethe and the German Romantics.

Despite his frugal manner of living, Godwin for a short time began to take note of contemporary fashion. He changed his black minister's suit to 'a blue coat, yellow cassimere breeches, very blue white silk stockings'. His hair was 'plaited behind, instead of the single clerical curl, and the large cocked hat was dismissed and replaced by a round one'.[4] For all his abstract philosophy, Amelia Alderson found him surprisingly elegant and gallant:

> We arrived at about one o'clock at the philosopher's house, whom we found with his hair *bien poudré*, and in a pair of new, sharp-toed, red morocco slippers, not to mention his green coat and crimson under-waistcoat. He received me very kindly, but wondered I should think of being out of London – could I be either amused or *instructed* in Southgate? How did I pass my time? What were my pursuits? and a great deal more, which frightened my protector, and tired me . . . In short, he convinced me that his theory has not yet gotten entire ascendancy over his practice.[5]

Holcroft also introduced Godwin in September 1793 to Maria Reveley, who after a childhood in Constantinople had married the radical architect who drew up the plans for Bentham's model prison, the Panopticon. She painted, had an enquiring spirit, and expressed no objection to serving as Pitt's hangman. Mary Shelley, who knew her later as Maria Gisborne, wrote:

> There was a gentleness, and yet a fervour in the minds of both Mrs. Reveley and Godwin that led to sympathy. He was ready to gratify her desire for knowledge, and she drank eagerly of the philosophy which he offered. It was pure but warm friendship, which might have grown into another feeling, had they been differently situated.[6]

Godwin continued to visit Reveley for the next six years despite her husband's disapproval, and he experienced for her more tenderness than for his other women friends. For her part, she later confessed that she had loved him for years.

But after the publication of *Political Justice* Godwin did not only spend his life in social rounds. No doubt inspired by the republican victory in France, he proposed to Robinson a Roman history from the building of the city of Romulus to the battle of Actium. Deeply impressed by the magnitude of the undertaking, he wanted to portray the 'great characters of Rome, their virtues & their errors, the causes that produced them, & the consequences of which they are the source'.[7] The history however was put aside and only saw light as a children's book in 1809.

A much more exciting project was on Godwin's mind. Immediately after finishing *Political Justice* early in January 1793, he began to put down hints for a story which was to become his best novel: *Things as They Are; or, The Adventures of Caleb Williams*. Ten days later he wrote the first page and soon after was methodically writing several pages each day. It took fifteen months to complete. Benjamin Crosby bought it for £840 and published it on 26 May 1794.

The story, Godwin later wrote, was the 'offspring of that temper of mind' in which the composition of *Political Justice* had left him and was produced in a state of great 'fervour' of spirit.[8] His philosophical treatise had been the work of imagination controlled by intellect; now he could allow his imagination free rein. He therefore only composed when the 'afflatus' was upon him, hoping that the tale would 'constitute an epoch in the mind of the reader, that no one, after he has read it, shall ever be exactly the same man that he was before'.[9] Indeed, he did not write the novel to have a temporary effect on the reader but wanted it to be 'incorporated in the very fibres of his soul'.[10]

Godwin's initial idea was for a tale of a 'series of adventures of flight and pursuit' in which a man is hunted down. He then worked backwards to provide the circumstances which led up to the climax. He organized the novel in three parts. The last, which he wrote first, deals with Falkland's pursuit of Caleb, 'the fugitive in perpetual apprehension of being overwhelmed with the worst calamities'. The second, which he wrote next, presents the causes of the conflict between Falkland and Caleb by the discovery of a secret murder. He then tried in the first part to make the pursuer appear both powerful and virtuous so that his act of murder would evoke the deepest regret. In this way, Godwin hoped to fuse incident and feeling in an 'entire unity of plot'.[11]

Nearly all critics have attested to the strange power of *Caleb Williams*, although they have failed to agree on its exact status. It has been variously interpreted as a psychological study, metaphysical tale, moral fable, and political allegory.[12] Godwin himself complicated the matter: in 1794 he called the novel *Things as They Are* and stressed its political purpose in a preface, only to change its title in 1831 to *Caleb Williams* and to give in 1832 a thoroughly psychological account of its genesis. It was however precisely Godwin's ability to fuse psychological, moral and social insights into a consistent whole which makes *Caleb Williams* one of the great imaginative achievements of the late eighteenth century.

It is easy to see why *Caleb Williams* should be called the first psychological novel. What delighted Godwin in writing fiction was the imaginative freedom to analyse 'the private and internal operations of the mind, employing my metaphysical dissecting knife in tracing and laying bare the involutions of motive'.[13] There is also a strong confessional element in the novel. Godwin began his narrative in the third person, but quickly became dissatisfied and found it easier to write in the first person. He doubtlessly drew on his own experience in depicting the relationship between Caleb and Falkland: an obvious parallel exists between the servant and the master and the young Godwin and his tutor Newton.

There is also the possibility that Godwin identified strongly with Caleb because of his own position after writing *Political Justice*. In the original preface to the novel which was withheld because of the 'alarms' of the booksellers, Godwin remarked that 'Terror was the order of the day' and that it was feared that the 'humble novelist might be shown to be constructively a traitor'.[14] Having exposed the truth in *Political Justice*, the naturally timid Godwin seems to have been appalled by the consequences of his subversive thought, and feared like Caleb that he would be 'cut off from the whole human species'.[15]

At a deeper level, his early experience of Calvinism undoubtedly inspired his writing. In his description of Falkland, Godwin transposed all the contrary feelings of respect and horror which he felt as a child for the Calvinist God.[16] Having decided on the main outline of his story, Godwin looked for any book which might bear on his subject: it is significant that he should be struck by a 'tremendous compilation' entitled *God's Revenge against Murder* in which 'the beam of the eye of Omniscience was represented as perpetually pursuing the guilty, and laying open his most hidden retreats to the light of day'.[17]

After the sweet reasonableness and optimism of *Political Justice*, a reader might be surprised to learn that *Caleb Williams* was written by the same author. The dramatic opening sets the dominant tone:

> My life has for several years been a theatre of calamity. I have been a
> mark for the vigilance of tyranny, and I could not escape. My fairest

prospects have been blasted. My enemy has shown himself inaccessible to intreaties and untired in persecution. My fame, as well as my happiness, has become his victim.[18]

We are plunged into a terrifying world, a world of manic evil and destructive obsessions. Apart from the poet Clare who dies early, the other main characters — Falkland, Forester, Tyrrel, Gines and even Laura — all fail to see things as they are and misjudge Caleb's honesty. The innocent — Emily Melville and the Hawkins — are ruthlessly crushed. In the long run, it is prejudice and passion, not truth and reason, which seem omnipotent.

The core of the novel is the dynamic and reciprocal relationship of Falkland and Caleb. They are both men of considerable merit — Falkland a just landowner, Caleb a loyal autodidact. But both are possessed by a ruling passion which inevitably brings about their downfall. In Falkland's case, his excessive love of fame makes him feel disgrace to be 'worse than death'.[19] To maintain his public image, he is prepared to murder an opponent, allow two innocent men to be executed, and hound his servant to the ends of the earth. At the same time, Caleb's curiosity is even stronger than his love of independence. He is irresistibly drawn to spy on his master and finds an 'alluring pungency' in breaking his commands.[20]

Both men realize that they are playing with fire, but their monomania drives them to mutual persecution which cuts them off from the rest of society. In fits of insanity, Falkland tries to find solace for his troubled soul amongst the wildest scenes of nature. Caleb is forced underground, symbolically disguising himself as a beggar, Irishman, Jew and freak. At length, he exclaims 'Here I am an outcast, destined to perish with hunger and cold. All men desert me. All men hate me.'[21] Every incident deepens the despair of Falkland and Caleb until they are forced at the end of the novel into the very confrontation which they hoped to avoid.

In writing *Caleb Williams*, Godwin drew on his own experience, only to create a fable which has the fascination of myth. In his image of a hunted man, he touches on one of the most common dreams. In his choice of a discovered secret as the cause of conflict, he alluded to the Fall of Man. Indeed, Godwin consciously had in mind the tale of Bluebeard, the classic allegory of the guilt complex: 'Falkland was my Bluebeard, who had perpetrated most atrocious crimes, which if discovered, he might expect to have all the world roused to revenge against him. Caleb Williams was the wife, who in spite of warning, persisted in his attempts to discover the forbidden secret . . .'[22]

Reading *Caleb Williams* is like entering a nightmare. The supernatural force of Falkland and the Herculean but futile labours of Caleb do not belong to the everyday. Caleb is trapped; he can move neither to the left nor to the right; he is totally alone. Terrible coincidences occur; a malign destiny unfolds; the world is ruled by some malevolent Deity. As Forester observes on leaving Falkland House: 'there was some ill destiny that hung over it, which seemed fated to make all its inhabitants miserable, without its being possible for a bystander to penetrate the reason'.[23] It is undoubtedly Godwin's ability to explore the problems of sin and guilt, expiation and punishment, in a mythical situation which gives *Caleb Williams* its peculiar and lasting power.

But while *Caleb Williams* may be interpreted in psychological and metaphysical terms, Godwin himself emphasized its moral and political significance. In *Political Justice*, he maintained that there is no type of composition 'in which the seeds of a morality too perfect for our present improvements in science, may more reasonably be expected to discover themselves, than in works of imagination'.[24] In an unpublished essay, 'Of History & Romance', he went further to argue that the novel is a superior species of history, since it displays the manner in which 'character acts under successive circumstances'.[25] It therefore comes as no surprise that in *Things as They Are*, to give the novel its original title, he intended to offer 'a study and delineation of things passing in the moral world' and to demonstrate the truth that 'the spirit and character of the government intrudes itself into every rank of society' to people who are unlikely to read books of philosophy and science. Accordingly, the story was a vehicle to convey 'a general review of the modes of domestic and unrecorded despotism, by which man becomes the destroyer of man'.[26]

The conflict between the characters is clearly drawn on class lines. Falkland stands for the feudal values of the *ancien régime*, having imbibed in his youth in Italy the 'poison of chivalry'.[27] Like Burke, he has been ruined by a corrupt system of government.[28] He believes that the distinction in ranks is necessary for peace, but maintains that it is the duty of the rich to do everything in their power to lighten the yoke of the lower orders. Caleb, on the other hand, represents the artisans like Thomas Paine and Francis Place who were beginning to assert their rights. He is the ambitious son of a peasant who attempts to improve himself through education, and although forced to become a servant, he demands the 'privilege of an Englishman to be sole judge and master of his own actions'.[29] Tyrrel is a member of the middle-class squirearchy: he brutally exploits his tenants and clashes unashamedly with the aristocratic Falkland. Hawkins, who is evicted for refusing to vote according to his landlord's wishes and is subsequently destroyed, draws Godwin's moral: 'if we little folks had but the wit to do for ourselves, the great folks would not be such maggoty changelings as they are. They would begin to look about them.'[30]

When Godwin began writing *Caleb Williams*, it was in an atmosphere of increasing repression and his love of history naturally led him to interpret contemporary events in terms of the past. The whole struggle between Caleb and Falkland can in fact be seen as an allegory of Dissenting history: Falkland's persecution of Caleb reflects the government's oppression of Dissenters, while Caleb's demands for personal autonomy and respect for truth mirrors the Dissenters' claim for the right of private judgment. Significantly Godwin was inspired at the time by *The Adventures of Mademoiselle de St. Phale*, a book he first read as a boy, which narrates the 'utmost terror' of the Protestant Huguenots who fled persecution in France.[31]

A more obvious parallel was the English Civil War. Much of the debate on the French Revolution was seen in terms of the old struggle between the Royalists and the Republicans. Godwin, who had sat in Cromwell's chair in his father's pulpit, always had the struggle close to mind. Both the names and the dispositions of the characters in *Caleb Williams* reflect this interest.

Ferdinando Falkland was undoubtedly modelled on Lucius Cary, Second Viscount Falkland, who imbibed the chivalric code of honour, remorselessly persecuted to death the Earl of Strafford, and eventually committed suicide at the battle of Newbury. Caleb, on the other hand, was one of the spies sent by Moses into the Promised Land, and meant either 'dog' or 'bold'.[32] More significantly, Godwin would have known that the leader of the Republicans was registered at his marriage 'Oliver Cromwell, alias Williams'.[33] It is also probable that Godwin himself identified with his near namesake.

Contemporary reviews did not miss the propagandist intention of the work. The *British Critic* thought it was 'a striking example of the evil use which may be made of considerable talents, connected with such a degree of intrepidity as can inspire the author with resolution to attack religion, virtue, government, laws'.[34] When an anonymous lawyer sent to the review a detailed account of the legal errors in the novel, Godwin replied that his object was not only to attack bad laws but 'to expose the evils which arise out of the present system of civilized society; and . . . to disengage the minds of men from prepossession, and launch them upon the sea of moral and political enquiry'.[35]

Godwin's biting social criticism is only too evident. He carefully traces the inextricable relationship between government, law, prisons, and property. The tenant farmer Hawkins is unjustly but legally expelled from one farm only to be ruined and have his son imprisoned by his new landlord Tyrrel. His case demonstrates only too well that 'law was better adapted for a weapon of tyranny in the hands of the rich, than for a shield to protect the humbler part of the community against their usurpations'.[36] It is moreover the existing distribution of wealth which forces men of energy and integrity like Raymond into banditry, and the intractable nature of the law which prevents their reformation.

As for Caleb, his whole story demonstrates how the rich and powerful manipulate the law and the courts for their own ends. He is not only framed by Falkland and arrested on the capital charge of theft, but he is later mistakenly arrested for mail robbery. In the many trial scenes, it becomes increasingly clear that the accused is held guilty until he can prove his innocence, and that the word of a gentleman of £6000 per annum will always be believed before that of his servant. Caleb draws the inevitable conclusion: 'the law has neither eyes, nor ears, nor bowels of humanity; and it turns into marble the hearts of all those that are nursed in its principles'.[37]

Godwin saved his greatest indignation for the prisons, which he felt, like Blake, were built with Stones of Law. The historian in Godwin even led him to use footnotes to authenticate his vivid description of 'their unwholesomeness, their filth, the tyranny of their governors, the misery of their inmates' and to demonstrate his thesis that England too had her Bastille.[38] When Caleb manages to escape from Newgate, he exclaims with all his soul:

> Turn me a prey to the wild beasts of the desert, so I be never again the victim of man dressed in the gore-dripping robes of authority! Suffer me at least to call life and the pursuits of life my own! Let me hold it at the mercy of the elements, of the hunger of beasts or the revenge of barbarians, but not of the cold blooded prudence of monopolists and kings![39]

Unfortunately Caleb was only experiencing the illusion of freedom, for he is soon hunted down ruthlessly by Falkland's agent Gines. When he tries to leave for Holland, he learns that Falkland has turned Britain into one vast prison and will not allow him to go beyond its boundaries. After all his efforts to lead an ordinary life have failed, Caleb finally decides to announce publicly the secret of Falkland's crime.

There are, however, two endings to the novel. In the original one, Caleb's attempt to incriminate his master in a court of law fails once again. He is imprisoned and poisoned. Before his reason completely collapses, he recognizes that 'it too plainly appears in my history that persecution and tyranny can never die!' and concludes pitifully that 'true happiness lies in being like a stone'.[40] But while in keeping with what preceded, such a deeply pessimistic conclusion would have overthrown Godwin's most cherished beliefs and implied that *Political Justice* was written in vain.

It was also perhaps too prophetic of the actual course of events. Whilst Godwin was writing *Caleb Williams*, his friend Joseph Gerrald had been found guilty of sedition and was awaiting transportation in Newgate Gaol. Godwin took his leave of Gerrald on 29 April and finished the manuscript of the novel on the following day. From 4 to 8 May, however, he rewrote the ending. In the new court scene, Caleb reveals his soul to his hearers and is convulsed with anguish at accusing his master. Falkland, for his part, recognizes Caleb's sincerity, confesses his guilt, and dies of a broken heart three days later. In this second and published ending, there is a definite concession to sentimental utopianism. While most of the novel demonstrates the ambiguity and the impotence of truth, the new ending enacts the triumph of justice which failed to take place at Gerrald's trial. It is almost schizophrenic in its reversal.[41]

The revised ending is however in keeping with the principles of *Political Justice*. Just before Caleb's final meeting with Falkland, the necessitarian Collins tells him: 'I consider you as a machine . . . you did not make yourself; you are just what circumstances irresistibly compelled you to be.'[42] It is precisely Falkland's failure to recognize that Caleb's curiosity is the result of circumstances which makes him employ the law (which falsely assumes individual responsibility) to hunt him down. Caleb's reluctance to heed Collins's words equally leads him to make the 'hateful mistake' of resorting to the law to expose Falkland. In both cases they should have relied on the 'sovereignty of truth' and tried privately to provide new motives to change their opponent's conduct. Too late, Caleb recognizes that Falkland in a personal interview would not have been able to resist a 'frank and fervent expostulation'.[43] Truth and law, Godwin implies, simply cannot be reconciled.

The revised ending also brings together the psychological, metaphysical, moral and political themes in a way which reaches the heights of tragedy. Godwin does not merely offer us a contrived fictional ending to show the triumph of virtue over vice or the dangers of a false education: the pursuer and the pursued, impelled by a common condition, confuse their roles and dramatically suffer a similar fate. Just as Caleb had been the conscience of Falkland, so Falkland becomes the conscience of Caleb. They recognize their mutual errors and symbolically fall into each other's arms. But tragically it is too late: consumed with guilt and remorse, Falkland dies and Caleb is condemned to a kind of death-in-life. Their fate is not only psychologically convincing and morally illuminating, but shows just how easily the 'corrupt wilderness of society' can poison the most noble talents and sentiments.[44] Never again would Godwin be able to combine philosophy and fiction to create a work of such extraordinary intuitive depth and imaginative power.

*Caleb Williams* is not, however, without its faults. Godwin's attempt to work backwards in order to explain the genesis of the central pursuit was not entirely happy. In the first part, the description of the conflict between Tyrrel and Falkland is unnecessarily long. Elsewhere the plot visibly falters:

its twists and turns are insufficiently prepared for and the chance encounters are hardly credible. Furthermore, the many incidents borrowed from picaresque and sentimental novels — such as Emily Melville's story, Caleb's prison escape, and the robber band — are not properly woven into the narrative.

Godwin was clearly more interested in psychology than plot. But while his principal characters are complex and memorable, he was unable to match his contemporary Jane Austen in subtlety and depth. His style too is quite different from the chaste lucidity of *Political Justice*: the dialogues are lively and the descriptions of mental states vivid but the rhetoric is often mannered and the rhythm uneven. Yet whatever its structural weaknesses and stylistic infelicities, *Caleb Williams* undoubtedly achieves an organic unity and possesses superb energy and weight. It not only stands out as the most impressive novel of the 1790s, but remains a masterpiece.

Ironically, Godwin very nearly failed to complete the work. When he had written about seven-tenths of his first volume he showed the manuscript to his old friend Marshal. It was sent back with the note: 'I return to you your manuscript, because I promised to do so. If I had obeyed the impulse of my own mind, I should have thrust it in the fire. If you persist, the book will infallibly prove the grave of your literary fame.'[45] Godwin was flabbergasted. It cost him at least two days of deep anxiety before he recovered from the shock. All his previous novels had fallen still-born from the press, and he had high hopes for his new tale. As usual when faced with criticism he turned into himself: 'I had nothing for it but to wrap myself in my own integrity. By dint of resolution I became invulnerable.'[46]

It was just as well. When he sent the proofs to Elizabeth Inchbald, she replied rapturously that 'fine ladies, milliners, mantua-makers, and boarding-school girls will love to tremble over it, and that men of taste and judgment will admire the superior talents, the *incessant* energy of mind you have evinced'.[47] Gerrald, whom Godwin considered 'one of the most accomplished readers and excellent critics', received the novel late one evening in Newgate, and read through the three volumes before he closed his eyes.[48] Henry Crabb Robinson recalled how he 'idolized' the book for 'the eloquence and moral dignity which pervade the whole'.[49] Anna Seward, the 'Swan of Lichfield' and friend of Walter Scott, was also electrified. 'Have you read Caleb Williams?' she wrote to a friend, 'where expectation is excited to breathless ardour, and where the terrible Graces extend their petrifying wands. The style of this extraordinary work is manly, compressed, animated, and impressive, in a degree which vies with that of the best writers of this period . . .'[50]

As for the reviews, only the conservative *British Critic* found *Caleb Williams* an evil work.[51] The *Analytical Review* praised it as a singular novel written by a 'genius' and the *Monthly Review* concurred that it was full of 'genius and philosophy'.[52] The *Critical Review* went so far as to claim that it ranked above all novels save those of Fielding, Smollett, and Burney and was even superior to them in its narrative form.[53] 'We conceive', Hazlitt wrote many years later, 'no one ever began *Caleb Williams* that did not read it through: no one that ever read it could possibly forget it, or speak of it after any length of time but with an impression as if the events and feelings had been personal to himself.'[54]

Few books made a greater impression on their first appearance. Godwin's reputation, already great after *Political Justice*, was raised to the highest pitch. Mary Shelley recalled how its influence extended into every grade of society: 'those in the lower classes saw their cause espoused, & their oppressors forcibly & eloquently delineated — while those of higher rank acknowledged & felt the nobleness, sensibility & errors of Falkland with deepest sympathy'.[55] The painter James Northcote told Godwin that even George IV was very interested and read it more than once.

It went through three editions by 1797 and appeared in Dublin and Baltimore in 1795. It was translated twice into French in 1794, and another version appeared in the following year. Samuel Constant published his translation in Geneva in 1795. Although the philosopher André Morellet lamented its revolutionary distortion and Marie Joseph de Chénier found it vulgar, over 5000 copies were sold in a very short time. Chateaubriand recognized its importance, Madame de Staël praised it, and Stendhal read it with great pleasure. Two German translations appeared in 1795 and 1797. According to Mackintosh, it was *Caleb Williams* which most needed to be replaced in continental libraries.[56] Henry Crabb Robinson also remarked in 1830 that the adoption of legal incidents as the source of romantic and dramatic interest begun by Godwin had run from one end of Europe to the other.[57]

*Caleb Williams* also had considerable success on the stage. George Colman's dramatization *The Iron Chest* (1796) gave Edmund Kean one of his most powerful roles as Falkland, and in America it became one of the most famous performances of Godwin's former ward Thomas Cooper. In Jean Louis Laya's French version *Falkland, ou la conscience* (1798), Talma took the leading part and received wide praise.[58] Godwin, the philosopher, had clearly triumphed once again as a novelist.

# CHAPTER X

## *Political Justice Revisited*

The downfall of the Jacobin dictatorship in France, Pitt's repression at home, and his own dispute with Thelwall and the L.C.S. all made politics in 1795 a major preoccupation with Godwin. He continued to work on his history of the Roman republic but the booksellers were unwilling to publish it. He therefore began planning some 'Observations on the Revolution in France' in order 'to ascertain in what part it is to be considered as an example to imitate & in what part as a beacon to warn'.[1] Ritson the antiquarian had no doubt that the work would be a 'parcel of lies and sophisms' with a view, perhaps, 'to wash the blood off his favourite Robespierre'.[2] Godwin certainly told a correspondent that 'I like you, will weep over his errors; but I must still continue to regard him as an eminent benefactor of mankind.'[3] The work on the French Revolution however never went beyond a few notes.

Godwin also planned in 1795 a 'Life of Alexander the Great' but it likewise never saw the light of day. He picked up, only to drop, his old tragedy on Dunstan. Three tales planned on 'The Coward', 'The Lover' and 'The Adept' were left incomplete, although they found their way in some guise in his next two novels in 1799 and 1805.

Instead, Godwin devoted most of his time in 1795 to preparing new editions for George Robinson of *Political Justice* and *Caleb Williams* which had been a phenomenal success. They appeared at the end of the year, both dated 1796. He made about five hundred changes in *Caleb Williams* but they were all minor, intended to improve the style or clarify the narrative rather than to change the substance of the novel. There was some attempt to make the dialogue more convincing and the characterization sharper. Names of some of the minor characters were changed: Doctor Arnold to Doctor Wilson, Gines (Falkland's caretaker) to Warnes, Jones (Caleb's pursuer) to Gines, Barton to Jeckels, and Wilson to Larkins. Again, these emendations did not affect the meaning.

The only important addition was the Laura episode in Volume III where Caleb is befriended by an accomplished and virtuous mother in Wales and becomes the tutor to her children. It provides the only real sentimental note in the novel and reflects Godwin's changing attitude to the domestic affections: Laura's whole family, we are told, composed a group with which 'a lover of tranquillity and virtue would have delighted to associate in any situation'.[4] At the same time, the political significance of *Caleb Williams* was underlined by Godwin's inclusion of the original preface, which had been withdrawn in compliance with the alarm of the booksellers.

The changes in *Political Justice* were much more radical. Godwin wrote soon after that he was 'an uninstructed tyro, exposed to a thousand foolish and miserable mistakes' when he began the work, and only properly understood the subject when he had completed it.[5] The haste in bringing out the first edition also meant that there were several unavoidable contradictions and inconsistencies. Godwin therefore welcomed the opportunity to undertake a careful and thorough revision for the new octavo edition.

In his metaphysics, he still retained his parallel scheme of mind and matter and his doctrine of necessity, but there is now a greater sceptical emphasis in his epistemology. Our faculties, he now recognizes, are severely limited:

> We cannot penetrate into the essences of things, or rather we have no sound and satisfactory knowledge of things external to ourselves, but merely our own sensations. We cannot discover the cause of things, or ascertain that in the antecedent which connects it with the consequent, and discern nothing but their contiguity.[6]

The only thing we can be certain of is the existence of our own ideas and sensations, which linked together, produce 'the complex notion of unity or personal identity'.[7] Beyond the knowledge of our mental processes, we can therefore only deal with probabilities.

In the first edition, Godwin thought it advisable not to press matters of 'close and laborious speculation' at the outset, but he found that the inferences from Book I were materially injured by such a procedure.[8] He therefore greatly expanded the old chapter iii, 'The Moral Characters of Men Originate in their Perceptions', into a more profound and logical chapter iv entitled 'The Characters of Men Originate in their External Circumstances', and added chapter v 'The Voluntary Actions of Men Originate in their Opinions'. Without fundamentally changing his position, he thus made his premises more explicit and clearer.

He is still eager to demonstrate that the dispositions of mankind are the offspring of their circumstances, but he is prepared to allow that there are character differences at birth due to antenatal impressions. Again, he admits that the mind may well fix for itself 'resting places' in the form of habits rather than review all the reasons for every action.[9] But this does nothing to affect his scheme of rational progress. The forces of sense cannot overwhelm those of reason; indeed, they pass through the same medium, and assume the same form: 'It is opinion contending with opinion, and judgment with judgment.'[10] While delusive passions like ambition, envy or lust can and ought to be restrained, passion in the sense of ardour is 'so far from being incompatible with reason, that it is inseparable from it'.[11] It follows for Godwin, then, that to follow nature is not to consult our appetites, to worship God, or to wage war, but 'to employ our understandings and increase our discernment'.[12] The perfection of human character is still to approach as nearly as possible the completely voluntary state and reason remains 'the sufficient instrument for regulating the actions of mankind'.[13]

Where Godwin merely affirmed human perfectibility in the first edition, he now attempts to give a proof of this central doctrine. It is deducible from the very nature of man and truth:

> Sound reasoning and truth, when adequately communicated, must always be victorious over error: Sound reasoning and truth are capable of being so communicated: Truth is omnipotent: The vices and moral weakness of man are not invincible: Man is perfectible, or in other words susceptible of perpetual improvement.[14]

All the same, Godwin does not claim that progress will be easy or inevitable. 'Vicissitude' appears to be the leading characteristic of nature and there is a 'vast portion of pain and calamity' in the world.[15] A state of luxury and inequality might be a stage through which it is necessary to pass in order to arrive at the 'goal of civilisation'.[16] It may be even doubted whether the human species will ever be emancipated from their 'present subjection and pupillage'.[17] As for the omnipotence of mind over matter, Godwin drops the conjecture that sleep and death may one day be banished and suggests that it is only 'in a certain sense' that we consent to the accidents of sickness and death.[18] The doctrine of perfectibility does not therefore mean that man will inevitably reach perfection but rather that he possesses the faculty of 'being continually made better and receiving perpetual improvement'.[19]

The most noticeable change in the second edition is the toning down of the Platonic rationalism of the first. Godwin significantly drops the passage which referred to Plato and those eternal and immutable truths which exist independent of the Creator and act as a formal cause in the process of creation. He also introduces a Humean note in reply to those critics who had objected to his notion of immutable truth as having an independent and separate existence: 'He that speaks of its immutability, does nothing more than predict with greater or less probability, and say, "This is what I believe, and what all reasonable beings, till they shall fall short of me in their degree of information, will continue to believe."'[20] But he does not entirely surrender to a subjective and relativist concept of truth and maintains that truths describe the real relations of things and are true whether we like it or not.

There is also a distinct move towards a more consistent form of hedonistic utilitarianism. The first principal error Godwin discerned in the first edition was 'Stoicism, or the inattention to the principle, that pleasure & pain are the only bases upon which morality can rest'.[21] He put it down to the influence of his early Calvinism and said it was rooted from his mind in 1794 principally by the arguments of George Dyson who became the third of his four principal oral instructors. Although Godwin complained of the 'deviousness' of his conduct and the 'fermentation' of his passions, Dyson remained one of his 'prime favourites' — until 1800, that is, when he assaulted Godwin's housekeeper in a drunken frenzy.[22]

The young hedonist convinced Godwin that 'Pleasure and pain, happiness and misery, constitute the whole ultimate subject of moral enquiry. There is nothing desirable, but the obtaining of the one, and the avoiding of the other. All the researches of human imagination cannot add a single article to this summary of good.'[23] Godwin therefore defends in a new chapter 'Of Good and Evil' the epicurean maxim that 'pleasure is the supreme good' against the animadversions of the Stoics.[24] Moreover, he does not now advocate in a regenerated society a state of 'Stoical simplicity' and sees no reason why a state of equality should not be incompatible with 'considerable accommodation and even in some sense with splendour'.[25]

Nevertheless, Godwin's new stress on hedonism does not fundamentally undermine his doctrine of rational altruism. In a new and shorter chapter 'Of Self Love and Benevolence', he gives a more precise and convincing account of deriving benevolence from egoism via reason. It is true that the good of my neighbour is a passion and could not have been chosen but as the means of agreeable sensation. But it is equally the nature of the passions to convert what at first were means into ends. Like the miser and his gold, we soon begin to love benevolence for its own sake. But unlike the miser, 'once we have entered into so auspicious a path as that of disinterestedness, reflection confirms our choice'.[26] And the more we reason, the more we feel sympathy for those beings who share the same nature as ourselves. We are thus able to become 'impartial spectators' and estimate the relative worth of our own and others' needs. Ultimately, it is not therefore the maximum amount of personal pleasure but the rational principle of impartiality — 'the beacon and regulator of virtue' — which makes us prefer benevolence to egoism.[27]

Similarly, Godwin retains in the second edition his qualitative distinction between pleasures. While everything in man is related to pleasure and pain, some pleasures are more 'exquisite' than others.[28] Indeed, he calls for a 'science of pleasure' and develops a scale of happiness which stretches from the peasant and artisan, via the man of wealth and the man of taste, to the man of benevolence.[29] The true equalization of mankind therefore is not to reduce all to a 'naked and savage equality' but to make all men capable of a 'liberal and comprehensive benevolence'.[30]

In keeping with the shift to hedonistic utilitarianism, Godwin rewrote his chapter on duty to clarify his definition of virtue. In the first edition, he had loosely distinguished between the quality of an action and the disposition with which it is performed, and while he maintained that a virtuous action must contribute to the general good, he laid the greatest stress on a virtuous disposition. In the second edition, the stress falls more on the consequences of the action.

A distinction is now drawn between the virtue of actions in general and the virtue of a particular agent. In the first case, a virtuous action must proceed from a 'kind and benevolent intention' as well as have a 'tendency to contribute to general happiness'.[31] In the second case, we must also compare the agent's performance with his capacity. Duty is now defined as 'that mode of action on the part of the individual, which constitutes the best application of his capacity to the general benefit'.[32] Nevertheless, morality, Godwin insists, is 'nothing but a calculation of consequences' and intention is of no further value than as it leads to utility: 'it is the means and not the end'.[33]

The move towards utilitarianism is also discernible in the rewritten and considerably extended chapter on promises. Godwin still argues that promises are not the foundation of morality, but recognizes that they may be a necessary evil in some cases. He also qualifies his belief in perfect sincerity by stressing that while it takes first place in the catalogue of human virtues it is founded on the principle of utility and should not be valued for its own sake. As a general moral rule it is useful because the remote consequences of an action depend chiefly on general circumstances, and not upon particulars. In special circumstances, however, it should be superseded, as for instance in the case of a drunken bigot who holds a pistol at my breast and demands assent to his creed. Godwin therefore concludes: 'wherever a great and manifest evil arises from disclosing the truth, and that evil appears to be greater than the evil to arise from violating in this instance the general barrier of confidence and virtue, there the obligation is suspended.'[34]

The second principal error that Godwin apprehended in the first edition of *Political Justice* was 'Sandemanianism, or an inattention to the principle that feeling, and not judgment, is the source of human actions'.[35] It owed its destruction to a perusal of Hume's *Treatise of Human Nature* in 1795 whilst the second edition was nearly printed off. The Sandemanians were undoubtedly the religionists mentioned who define faith as the 'lively persuasion of the understanding' and who saw 'a close and indissoluble connexion' between man's internal sentiments and his external conduct.[36] Hume, on the other hand, had endeavoured in his *Treatise of Human Nature* to prove '*first*, that reason alone can never be a motive to any action of the will; and *secondly*, that it can never oppose passion in the direction of the will'.[37] It is the prospect of pain or pleasure which moves us to action by arousing the passions and reason can only inform the passions as to the means of securing or avoiding their prospective objects. Thus, in Hume's celebrated dictum, 'Reason is, and ought only to be the slave of the passions, and can never pretend to any other office than to serve and obey them.'[38]

Godwin was impressed and did his best to rehabilitate feeling in the sheets of the work which had not already been sent to the printers. At the end of volume one, he therefore inserted the claim that 'Voluntary action cannot exist but as the result of experience. Neither desire nor aversion can have place, till we have had a consciousness of agreeable or disagreeable sensations.'[39] In a new footnote, he further praised Hume's 'unsurpassed profoundness of logical distinction' which ranked him with 'the most illustrious and venerable of men'.[40]

It was a perusal of Hume's *Treatise of Human Nature* that also destroyed the third principal error of the first edition of *Political Justice*: 'The unqualified condemnation of private affections'.[41] Hume had, of course, argued that 'sympathy is the chief source of moral distinctions' but felt that 'the generosity of man is very limited, and that it seldom extends beyond their friends and family, or, at most, beyond their native country'.[42] In the early part of volume one, Godwin had merely made a concession to outraged public opinion by replacing in the famous fire cause Fénelon's chambermaid (who might be my wife or my mother) by a valet (who might be my brother or father). This did nothing to interfere with his doctrine of universal benevolence. Under Hume's influence, however, he added at the end of the volume that it is only 'after having habituated ourselves to promote happiness of our child, our family, our country or our species, [that] we are at length brought to approve and desire their happiness without retrospect to ourselves.'[43]

Godwin also toned down his strictures on marriage. In the first edition it was left in doubt whether the relations between the sexes in a reasonable state of society would be promiscuous or permanent. In the second edition he makes it clear that he is in favour of the latter: a voluntary attachment in some degree permanent between two persons of opposite sex is right, but marriage as practised in European countries is wrong. Marriage however is still 'a monopoly, and the worst of monopolies', while inconstancy, when not practised in a clandestine manner, may be compatible with a 'character of uncommon excellence'.[44]

In his politics, the first inconsistency Godwin eradicated was the central one concerning government. Inspired by Helvétius, he had originally set out to see whether it could be proved that a 'sound political institution' is the 'most powerful engine for promoting individual good' and it was only as he proceeded that he became aware that it inevitably checks the mind and gives permanence to error.[45]

In the second edition he therefore rewrote the introduction and asked rhetorically: 'May it not happen, that the grand moral evils that exist in the world, the calamities by which we are so grievously oppressed, are to be traced to its defects as their source, and that their removal is only to be expected from its correction?'[46] He next deleted chapter iv and in a new one argued that 'politics and modes of government will educate and infect us all'.[47] He then dropped or changed those passages giving a positive function to government: the 'power of social institutions' in changing the character of nations is replaced by the 'power of reasonable and just ideas'; the 'power of legislation' becomes the 'compass of human ability'.[48] In this way, Godwin moved from the artificial identification of interests by government to the harmonious fusion of interests through free discussion. He thus made his anarchism consistent throughout the work. As he became primarily concerned with the effects of political *injustice*, the title of his *magnum opus* therefore stands as an ironic reminder of his original Helvétian intention.

Since Godwin believed, like Hume, that government is founded in opinion, it follows that reform can best be achieved by slowly changing people's opinions. The second edition, if anything, is even more fearful of sudden change. As in his *Cursory Strictures*, Godwin affirms that the great cause of humanity has but two enemies: 'those friends of antiquity, and those friends of innovation, who, impatient of suspense, are inclined violently to interrupt the calm, the incessant, the rapid and auspicious progress which thought and reflexion appear to be making in the world'.[49] He consequently rewrote his chapter on resistance. The emphasis is now less on the duty to resist injustice than on the dangers of armed rebellion. 'To dragoon men into the adoption of what we think right', Godwin asserts, 'is an intolerable tyranny'.[50] Indeed, Godwin argues that external freedom is of little value without the internal sentiments of magnanimity, energy and firmness. Civil liberty then is chiefly desirable not as an end in itself but 'as a means to procure and perpetuate this temper of mind. They therefore begin at the wrong end, who make haste to overturn and confound the usurped powers of the world. Make men wise, and by that very operation you make them free.'[51]

On these grounds, Godwin in two greatly revised chapters argues that the wise man and true politician will endeavour to postpone revolutions and prevent the formation of political associations. Events in France had shown him that while revolution is engendered by an indignation against tyranny, it is itself 'evermore pregnant with tyranny'.[52] Moreover his dispute with Thelwall had only confirmed his view that political associations, however well-intentioned, are inevitably attended with party spirit and tumult.

In his treatment of rights, however, Godwin moved closer to the radicals. He had rejected all rights in a discretionary sense in the first edition in favour of duty, but he rewrote the whole chapter on rights to give a clearer and more consistent account. He now distinguishes between positive and negative rights. The positive right to do as we please, even with our own lives, is still outlawed, but Godwin allows two negative rights — the right of private judgment and the right to the assistance of our neighbours. They derive their force however not from some notion of natural right but from the principle of utility: they may be superseded whenever a greater sum of pleasure will result from their infringement rather than from their observance.

As long as government exists, Godwin argues, its first object should be to preserve the right of private judgment. Every person has a 'certain sphere of discretion' which should not be infringed.[53] While public opinion might replace punishment as a means of correcting behaviour in an enlightened society, 'No man must encroach upon my province, nor I upon his. He may advise me, moderately and without pertinaciousness, but he must not expect to dictate to me. He may censure me freely and without reserve; but he should remember that I am to act by my deliberation and not his.'[54]

Godwin deals with the second negative right to the assistance of our neighbours in a greatly revised and systematized Book VIII on property. His starting-point is still that the good things of the world are of a common stock and that justice obliges us to consider our property as a trust to be used to produce the greatest quantity of general good. But he now carefully distinguishes between four classes of things: the means of subsistence, the means of intellectual and moral improvement, inexpensive pleasures, and luxuries. It is the last class that is the chief obstacle to a just distribution of the previous three.

Three degrees of property rights are then deduced from this classification. The first is 'my permanent right' in those things 'the use of which being attributed to me, a greater sum of benefit or pleasure will result, than could have risen from their being otherwise appropriated'.[55] This includes the first three classes of things. The second degree of property is the empire every man is entitled to over the produce of his own industry. This is only a negative right and in one point of view a sort of usurpation for any produce in excess of my entitlement based on the first degree of property must be distributed in the most beneficial way. The third degree, which corresponds to the fourth class of things, is the 'faculty of disposing of the produce of another man's industry'.[56] It is entirely devoid of right since all value is created by labour and it directly contradicts the second degree.

Godwin thus condemns the appropriation of another man's labour and advocates an equal distribution of the good things of life. But just as I have the right to the assistance of my neighbour, he has the right of private judgment. It is his duty to afford me the supply of my needs, but equally it is my duty not to violate his sphere of discretion. Property then is founded on the 'sacred and indefeasible right of private judgment' and as such is the 'palladium of all that ought to be dear to us'.[57] Only in exceptional circumstances may I take goods by force from my neighbour's store in order to save myself or others from distress. In the long run, Godwin believed that his scheme of personal possession and voluntary distribution would 'come to the same thing as what is vulgarly conceived under the idea of a community of property'.[58]

De Quincey, never a careful reader or profound thinker, later claimed that the second edition of *Political Justice* as regards principles is 'not a recast, but absolutely a travesty of the first; nay it is all but a palinode'.[59] Godwin's own statement in his preface, however, that 'the spirit and the great outlines' of the work 'remain untouched' is more accurate.[60] The major changes were only to be found in the first four books on the powers of man, the principles of society and government, and the operations of opinion, and in the last book on property. Godwin more or less rewrote these books not so much because he changed his mind drastically, but because he wished to reason with more accuracy from his premises and fundamental positions. The increasing scepticism and move to hedonistic utilitarianism were an outcome of his more thoroughgoing empiricism, while his treatment of government and property became more consistent and radical. Whatever it may have lost in urgency and daring, the second edition of *Political Justice* therefore offers a more substantial and convincing exposition of Godwin's philosophical anarchism.

Whilst revising *Political Justice*, Godwin began writing a series of essays which were published in 1797 under the title *The Enquirer. Reflections on Education, Manners, and Literature*. But where his *magnum opus* proceeded on close deductive reasoning from fundamental premises, Godwin now decided to investigate truth in self-contained essays with 'an incessant recurrence to experiment and actual observation'.[61] He presented them 'not as *dicta*', but 'as the materials of thinking' and as 'hints of enquiry'.[62]

Godwin did not treat explicitly any political themes in *The Enquirer*, but it did not mean that he had turned his back on politics. In his preface, he observes that while the 'principles of Gallic republicanism were yet in their infancy', the reformers including himself were somewhat 'too imperious in their tone'. But while he felt himself more patient and tranquil, he insisted that he had 'as ardent a passion for innovation as ever'.[63]

In fact, while writing essays for *The Enquirer* in 1796, Godwin considered entering parliament for the first and last time in his life. 'I ought to be in parliament,' he wrote in a note,

> My principles of gradual improvement are particularly congenial to such a situation. It is probable that in the course of the next six years circumstances may occur in which my talents, such as they are, might be of use. I am now forty years of age; the next six years will be six of the most vigorous years of my life. I would be no infrequent speaker. I would adhere to no party. I would vote for no proposition I did not wish to see carried. I would be an author of motions; thus endeavouring to call public attention to salutary ideas.[64]

It may seem a strange consideration from an implacable opponent of government and Godwin was well aware of the ridicule he would excite if he were to become an M.P. But he had always supported the Whig programme of parliamentary reform in his practical politics, and he was uncertain whether he should spend a speculative or an active life. As things turned out, he wisely decided not to go ahead with the plan and soon recognized where his true talents lay:

> I am ill-calculated for a practical politician, in however confused a sense of that term. I have little skill in seizing the passions of others, and thus moulding them imperceptibly to the purposes I have myself conceived. I have small pretensions to the gift of foresight; & when events arise contrary to my wishes, am apt to be mortified & confused. My abilities are better adapted for contemplation than action.[65]

Yet for all Godwin's moderate and pragmatic emphasis in politics, the first part of *The Enquirer* offers the most remarkable and advanced treatise on education to appear at the end of the eighteenth century. He develops the arguments of his *Account of the Seminary* and of *Political Justice* and goes beyond the teachings of Helvétius and Rousseau to anticipate what is best in progressive education today.

Godwin's revived interest in education is clearly a recognition of the power of prejudice and the force of habit. Truth had simply not been so omnipotent as he had envisaged. He therefore found it necessary to look among the new generation for 'the long-looked-for saviours of the human race' to point out the defects of society and to propose the remedy.[66] It was, Godwin wrote to his young American disciple James Ogilvie, from the 'agency' or 'lucubrations' of such persons that the amelioration of human institutions must be expected to proceed.[67]

The aim of such educators, Godwin asserts in *The Enquirer*, is to generate general happiness: since man is a social being he should learn to produce happiness for himself and for others. Nevertheless, Godwin argues that this is to be achieved not by inculcating any particular species of knowledge but by forming a sound judgment and clear habits of thinking. In a word, the first lesson of a judicious education is to learn 'to think, to discriminate, to remember, and to enquire'.[68]

Godwin believes that all members of the human species are capable of developing such abilities. In keeping with the Lockean psychology of *Political Justice*, his starting-point is that we are primarily what our environment makes us. A man may bring a 'certain character' into the world with him, and even have a 'certain predisposition for wisdom', but genius is something acquired not given.[69] Education should therefore begin at a very early age when the mind is more pliable and retentive.

There still remains the problem how best to develop talents in young children. Having experienced both private and public education in his youth, Godwin argues that while the former provides sympathy, it produces a sort of 'unripened hermit'.[70] Society, which public education offers, is on the other hand the 'true awakener of man'.[71] As a temporary measure, Godwin therefore suggests a compromise of educating children in small groups.

An 'adventurous and undaunted philosophy' however would perhaps reject formal schooling altogether and allow the child to learn only through desire at his or her own pace.[72] The plan would change entirely the face of education:

> The whole formidable apparatus which has hitherto attended it, is swept away. Strictly speaking, no such characters are left upon the scene as either preceptor or pupil. The boy, like the man, studies, because he desires it. He proceeds upon a plan of his own invention, or which, by adopting, he has made his own. Everything bespeaks independence and equality. The man, as well as the boy, would be glad in cases of difficulty to consult a person more informed than himself. That the boy is accus-

tomed almost always to consult the man, and not the man the boy, is to be regarded rather as an accident, than any thing essential.[73]

Such a bold system, based on the desire of the autonomous learner rather than the will of the authoritarian teacher, would not only replace the drilling practised by traditional teachers but also the supposedly progressive methods of Rousseau who wished to manipulate the mind of the child. Such an approach, Godwin hopes, would end at a stroke the slavery of the young, strengthen their judgment, and encourage them to study.

Godwin would not have children pass their days in indolence. He lays great stress on the benefits of an early taste for literature: 'He that loves reading, has everything within his reach. He has but to desire; and he may possess himself of every species of wisdom to judge, and power to perform.'[74] He particularly recommends the study of the classics, since it was from them that the moderns learned to think. The Latin historians in particular provide the purest models of virtue. A reading of Latin literature will also help us with the philosophy of language (a perusal of Virgil and Horace is worth a 'thousand treatises on universal grammar') and with the nature of logic (the science of thinking is 'little else than the science of words').[75] Contrary to Rousseau, Godwin concludes that our early years would be more advantageously spent in acquiring a knowledge of words rather than of things.

At the same time, he is utterly opposed to any form of censorship. To set up an Index Expurgatorius as does the Church of Rome not only erects a wall between children and adults but is counter-productive by exciting curiosity and deceit. He further argues that the author's conscious moral intention in his work is very often different from its moral tendency, and books rarely produce vice in a mind unless it is already present. The child should therefore be allowed to choose freely his own course of reading which may lead him into new trains of thinking.

The most original and radical element in Godwin's philosophy of education is his stress on the need for respect, honesty and toleration in dealing with children. He recognizes that education inevitably involves some form of despotism but every child is entitled to a 'little sphere of empire and discretion'.[76] There is simply no need for Rousseau's 'puppet-show exhibition' in which the master holds the wires of the pupil, nor for the threat of punishment, even including angry looks or words of rebuke.[77] Instead, Godwin argues that in our relations with a child,

we should make ourselves as much as possible his equals, that our affection towards him should display itself in the most unambiguous colours, that we should discover a genuine sympathy in his joys and his sorrows, that we should not play the part of the harsh monitor and austere censor, that we should assume no artificial manners, that we should talk in no solemn, prolix and unfeeling jargon, that our words should be spontaneous, our actions simple, and our countenance the mirror to our hearts.[78]

In this way, Godwin hoped the parent or tutor would become a friendly guide rather than a dictatorial task-master and that children would not be schooled into passive obedience but allowed to develop fully and freely their potential. Education, he recognizes, is the basis of freedom, just as freedom must be the basis of education. Godwin was thus the first to defend systematically the freedom of children and to make the end of education the cultivation of their happiness rather than their preparation as a work-force.

In other essays, Godwin took up and explored some of the new themes which appeared in the second edition of *Political Justice*. The rehabilitation of feeling is immediately apparent: 'Man has not only an understanding to reason, but a heart to feel.'[79] Far from being a cold ratiocinative process, morality should appeal to the 'strongest and most unalterable sentiments of the human heart'.[80] At the same time, Godwin shows a greater awareness of the complexity of motives and the depth of human frailty. Impartiality, the great rule of morality, is, alas, 'a virtue hung too high, to be almost ever within the reach of man!'[81] We are forever prey to the unconscious influences of passion and interest, and can easily be misled to embrace the 'shadow of reason'.[82]

We must not therefore be too severe in our moral judgment of men. A man of uncommon moral endowments (Godwin himself?) stands in need of great allowances, whether it be in punctuality or repaying debts. Even irreligion, swearing, loose conversation, gaming, excessive drinking and fornication should not entirely condemn a man.

Godwin also qualifies his advocacy of sincerity as a means of moral improvement by arguing that there is no need to be abrupt and austere in the treatment of others. Real toleration requires not only an absence of laws to restrain opinion, but that 'forbearance and liberality shall be moulded into the manners of the community'.[83] Thus while frankness is always recommended, and we should talk about people in the same way whether they be absent or present, perfect sincerity is not at present to be expected. True politeness, Godwin concludes, is not something only to be associated with courts but is the 'corner-stone' upon which virtue rests.[84] The moralist of *Political Justice* is clearly not intended as a priggish moralizer or an interfering busybody.

But while Godwin stresses the need for polite toleration, he tries to make his ethics more consistently utilitarian and hedonistic. 'Virtue', he insists, 'is a calculation of consequences, is a means to an end, is a balance carefully adjusted between opposing evils and benefits.'[85] Thus while sincerity should be given first place, it is not to be valued for its own sake but only as a means, and is valuable in so far as it answers the purposes of benevolence. The same is no less true of temperance, activity, and perseverance.

Godwin endorses a qualified hedonism by taking the Stoics to account for their belief that riches are no benefit and poverty no evil. He that is born poor is born a slave, for poverty not only shortens life but denies that leisure which is the 'genuine wealth of man'.[86] In a vigorous essay 'Of Self Denial', Godwin further insists that 'pleasure or happiness is the sole end of morality' and condemns the 'visionary and repulsive' extremes of those religious sectarians (presumably the Sandemanians) who preach the vanity of all earthly things.[87] While the pleasures of virtue and the intellect are undoubtedly superior to those of the body, the wise man will cultivate every part of his nature, including the 'animal economy annexed to the commerce of the sexes'.[88] Godwin never went so far in *Political Justice*.

When he turns to economic and social questions, Godwin makes few compromises. In an essay entitled 'Of Avarice and Profusion', he gives a trenchant account of exploitation and defends the claim of every individual to the fruits of his labour. Labour is the sole source of value: 'What is misnamed wealth, is merely a power vested in certain individuals by the institutions of society, to compel others to labour for their benefit.'[89] Since wealth consists of the commodities created by human labour, Godwin concludes that the rich man who encourages industry only offers 'added expedients for grinding the poor'.[90] It follows that the avaricious man is preferable since he only locks up pebbles and rejects that luxury which is 'the principal source of all the oppression, ignorance and guilt which infest the face of the earth'.[91] But in the place of both avarice and profusion, Godwin would have his voluntary scheme of cultivated equality in which all would share in the production of the necessaries of life.

The just distribution of wealth however is no easy task for there is always the danger of creating dependence and encouraging indolence. Thus in an essay 'Of Beggars', Godwin admits the need to help those who are victims of 'overwhelming calamity' but considers professional beggars as 'injurious to society' and the 'opprobrium of human nature'.[92] Yet Godwin is no cold-hearted utilitarian. He will not countenance the extreme argument that since the existence of beggars is a reproach to the government, the evil must be allowed to grow: 'I cannot consent to lending even my passive assistance, to the starving of men to death, that the laws may be reformed'.[93]

The position of domestic servants also worried Godwin. He found the idea of having servants living in a separate and dingy part of the house absolutely abhorrent. Indeed, such a monstrous association of wealth and poverty together in a rich man's home made him want to 'plunge in the depth of groves and the bosom of nature, and weep over the madness of artificial society'.[94] But while he recognizes that the condition of a servant is infinitely more pitiable than a day-labourer and only marginally preferable to a West Indian slave, all he could do was to encourage his readers to exercise a mild empire over them.

While Godwin is full of sympathy for the lot of the genuine beggar and servant, he gives a devastating survey 'Of Trades and Professions' in one of his most incisive essays. He was never happy dealing with tradesmen, and added a radical edge to traditional satire. He is astonished that a human being could stoop so low to become a tradesman, and cannot understand how 'this supple, fawning, cringing creature, this systematic, cold-hearted liar, this being, every moment of whose existence is centred in the sordid consideration of petty gains, has the audacity to call himself a man'.[95]

He is no less dismissive of the professions. The lawyer's great object is to puzzle and perplex. Rather than appeal to the 'touchstone of reason' and the 'volume of nature', he prefers the endless tomes of those written laws which are the 'prejudices of a barbarous age' and are intended to strengthen the usurpation of the few.[96] Again, the physician reaps a harvest from 'pain, sickness, and anguish' and pretends to be most wise when he is most ignorant.[97] As for the soldier, he is inevitably a 'depraved and unnatural being' and acts like the puppet of a showman.[98] The most vitriolic abuse, however, is reserved for the clergy whose ranks Godwin nearly joined. Nothing, he suggests, has contributed more to 'the introduction and per-petuating of bigotry in the world, than the doctrines of the Christian religion'.[99] No wonder then that we find in the clergyman 'study rendered abortive, artificial manners, infantine prejudices, and a sort of arrogant infallibility'.[100]

Godwin appends to his survey the reservation that if there be any extra-ordinary characters who have managed to escape the prevailing contagion, they have no right to be offended. He counted, after all, lawyers, physicians, and ministers amongst his friends. It is an appalling picture of things as they are, nonetheless. 'What sort of scene then', Godwin asks hopelessly, 'is that in the midst of which we live; where all is blank, repulsive, odious; where every business and employment is found contagious and fatal to all the best characteristics of man, and proves the fruitful parent of a thousand hateful vices?'[101] In *Political Justice*, he had tried to alert the population to the danger of government and the injustice of inequality. In *Caleb Williams*, he had wanted to portray the modes of domestic and unrecorded despotism. But his voice was beginning to be drowned by the din of war and the strident tones of the Anti-Jacobin campaign. Despair was an enemy he had constantly to repel.

But for all his preoccupation with social and economic matters, and his concern about the political state of Europe, Godwin found solace in reading. He devoted the last quarter of *The Enquirer* to an essay 'Of English Style' which shows his curious taste and aesthetic canon. The works of the best authors, he claims, constitute a 'well arranged and beautiful whole' and possess a 'flowing eloquence of language, and an exquisite propriety of diction'.[102] Celebrating the Augustan values of clarity and simplicity, he insists that style should be the 'transparent envelop' of our thoughts.[103]

Yet Godwin is not merely content to describe the characteristics of great literature; he must have a thesis and demonstrate its validity. His progressive impulses compel him to prove by examples that the English language was never in so high a state of perfection as in the reign of George III. He therefore gives long extracts from the Elizabethan writers onwards, studding his pages with asterisks to indicate offensive phrases. He warms to his favourite authors Shakespeare, Milton and Swift, but on his own principle he is forced to admit that Fielding is their superior even though his style is feeble. It was only a couple of years later when he discovered in Beaumont and Fletcher a 'museum of untried delights' that he abandoned his shaky thesis.[104] The second edition of *The Enquirer* which appeared in 1823 was revised accordingly.

Apart from his unhappy detour into literary criticism, *The Enquirer* contains some of Godwin's most incisive writing and perceptive thoughts. While increasing in sensibility and being more sympathetic to hedonism, he remains as radical as ever. His views on education are profoundly original, and his observations on manners and men always provoking. The relaxed mode of the essay clearly suited his talents. It was a form he was to return to with added vigour in his old age.

Robinson published *The Enquirer* early in 1797, and editions appeared in Dublin and Philadelphia during the year. The reviews were generally favourable once again. The *Monthly Magazine*, the *Monthly Review*, the *Monthly Visitor*, and the *Scots Magazine* were all impressed.[105] The *Analytical Review* and the *Critical Review* went out of their way to agree with Godwin's view of style.[106] Even the conservative *British Critic*, which considered Godwin a dangerous and extravagant author, praised his original and useful hints.[107] The Dissenters' *New Annual Register*, not surprisingly, objected in an otherwise friendly review to his bitter attack on Christianity.[108]

Unfortunately for Godwin the favour of the public did not warrant another volume. Nevertheless *The Enquirer* was to play an important role in labour history. A discussion of the essay 'Of Avarice and Profusion' with his Godwinite father inspired Thomas Malthus to write his attack on all improvement in the *Essay on the Principle of Population* (1798). On the other side, it was Godwin's trenchant criticism of the division of labour and man in the essay of 'Trades and Professions' which led the Chartists to reprint it as a pamphlet in 1842 and the *English Chartist Circular* to praise extravagantly his comprehensive and penetrating mind.[109]

# CHAPTER XI

## *The Most Odious of All Monopolies*

After the publication of *Caleb Williams*, Godwin was at the height of his reputation. The reaction against Jacobinism was not yet triumphant, and he was nowhere a stranger. It was, as Hazlitt observed, 'a new and startling event in literary history for a metaphysician to write a popular romance', and Godwin was thought 'a man of powerful and versatile genius'.[1]

In society, however, he was sometimes ill-at-ease and often appeared cold, uninviting and intractable. He considered himself to be bold and adventurous in his opinions but not in life. In a remarkable piece of self-analysis, he put this down to his 'nervous character' which often deprived him of self-possession when he wanted to repel an injury or correct an error. Experience of this rendered him 'in the first case, a frightened fool, and in the last, a passionate ass; in both my heart palpitates and my fibres tremble; the spring of mental action is suspended; I cannot deliberate or take new ground; and all my sensations are pain and aversion — aversion to the party, impatience with myself'.[2] He felt he was unfit to be alone in a crowd, a circle of strangers, in an inn, and almost in a shop.

Godwin had a passion for what he called 'colloquial discussion'.[3] Hazlitt maintained, however, that his talk was 'as flat as a pancake' and compared him to an 'eight-day clock that must be wound up long before it can strike'.[4] Godwin's own comments seem to confirm this; he universally hated to speak to an unwilling listener, and scarcely ever began a conversation without a preconceived subject. He recalled once meeting a man in the street who was prone to the same liability: they stood looking at each other for the space of a minute, each listening for what the other would say, and eventually parted without either uttering a word.[5]

And yet there was something in him which attracted the greatest talkers of the age and some of the most accomplished women. His frankness could give offence, but his obvious sincerity was endearing. He was seldom

XII. Godwin, aged 39, by Sir Thomas Lawrence, 1795. Engraved by W. Ridley.

envious and always ready to praise others. He cultivated benevolence as part of his theory, yet it was spontaneous and warm for all that. His strong moral sense, his egalitarian spirit, his discerning intellect and his unusual sensibility all combined to make him a welcomed guest.

The period from 1795 to 1797 proved to be the happiest in Godwin's life.

He had finally broken from the intellectual fetters which had restricted him in his youth. He had at last realized his ambition of becoming a famous writer. He no longer had to worry about where his next meal was coming from. Above all, in achieving personal freedom, he had the conscious satisfaction of contributing to the cause of liberty and justice.

Friends proved a constant delight. He continued to take a fatherly interest in his ward Thomas Cooper who was finding his way as a strolling player. Holcroft was still his boon companion, and they happily corresponded on their mutual beliefs: Holcroft ready to describe how after a fall from a ladder he tried to convince himself that pain is an illusion; to complain jokingly about 'Tyrant Necessity'; and to question the rights and wrongs of declaring sentiments of personal affection.[6]

There were also some new acquaintances. Godwin was particularly pleased in 1795 by a request from the Earl of Lauderdale to meet him. He became almost a regular guest at his 'most select parties', where he met the Whig patricians Fox, General Fitzpatrick, Lord Derby, Sir Philip Francis, Dudley North, William Smith, Robert Adair and others.[7] He became friendly with the physician Anthony Carlisle, the actor John Kemble, the actress Sarah Siddons, and the Welsh bard Edward Williams. Wordsworth's friend Basil Montagu became a regular visitor at his home.

An odder acquaintance was the Jewish John King, a notorious money lender, who was married to the Countess Dowager of Lanesborough. Walter Scott gave a disparaging account of the affair to Coleridge.[8] But Godwin's motive was simple — as a moralist and novelist, he believed he could learn some lessons from King and his visitors which he was unlikely to acquire in any other quarter. Godwin, however, soon became unhappy about the relationship, and when King was arrested for fraud, he refused to give testimony on his behalf.

The forty-year-old celibate philosopher also very much enjoyed the company of his female friends. He continued to see regularly the young and pretty Amelia Alderson and the novelist Elizabeth Inchbald. When he took his leave before setting off to visit Dr. Samuel Parr in the summer of 1795, Alderson wrote to a friend:

> He wished to salute me, but his courage failed him . . . 'Will you give me nothing to keep for your sake, and console me during my absence', murmured out the philosopher, 'not even your slipper? I had it in my possession once, and need not have returned it!' This was very true; my shoe had come off, and he had put it in his pocket for some time. You have no idea how gallant he is become; but indeed he is much more amiable than he ever was. Mrs. Inchbald says, the report of the world is, that Mr. Holcroft is in love with her, *she* with Mr. Godwin, Mr. Godwin

XIII. Amelia Opie, née Alderson, in 1798, by John Opie.

XIV. Elizabeth Inchbald, by Sir Thomas Lawrence. Engraved by Freeman.

with *me*, and I am in love with Mr. Holcroft! A pretty story indeed![9]

Godwin could clearly be gallant and playful in his own peculiar way. But it was not through strong sensual desire. His daughter insisted that he was 'in a supreme degree a conscientious man, utterly opposed to anything like vice or libertinism'.[10] He declared moreover that 'I do from my heart & soul, abjure & detest coquetry' and complained that he knew several admirable women who 'put on & off the flirt' and thereby 'put in & out a heart'.[11]

A more ardent but less coquettish admirer was Mary Hays. A self-taught feminist of considerable talent, she had championed Mary Wollstonecraft in her *Letters and Essays, Moral and Miscellaneous* (1793) and soon became her close friend. She had first become interested in *Political Justice* after reading the lengthy analysis in the *Analytical Review*. William Frend, Coleridge's tutor at Cambridge, also enthusiastically recommended it to her, forecasting that it would 'in a few years operate as great a change in the political sentiments of our nation as Locke's famous treatise on government'.[12] But since she could not afford a copy or obtain one from several circulating libraries, she took the characteristically bold step in October 1794 of applying to the author direct. She described herself uncompromisingly as 'disgusted with the present constitutions of civil society', a believer in the 'ultimate perfection of the human mind', and a 'disciple of truth'.[13]

Godwin not only acceded to her request but subsequently visited her early in 1795. Because he was so busy, they agreed that she would communicate her sentiments by letter, and he would reply in person. She was delighted with the arrangement. In 1795 and 1796, she sent a stream of letters, largely unanswered, which moved from the discussion of religious and political questions to the confession of her most intimate feelings. She suffered from unrequited love, at first it seems for William Frend and then for the poet Charles Lloyd. Godwin tried to console her, but it was to no avail. She sought relief in the writing of the *Memoirs of Emma Courtney* (1796), one of the best novels of the day, in which Godwin appears as the sage and steady Mr. Francis.

Godwin, for his part, did not want to get too involved with Hays. He praised the first sheets of her novel but later she denounced him as a 'savage-hearted and barbarous' critic.[14] He was particularly worried about her uncontrollable passion and complained of her 'morbid madness' and 'misanthropical gloom'.[15] Nevertheless, he still called on her regularly, and his letters show that he was ready to discuss moral philosophy, advise her on literature, and inspire her with fortitude — so much so that she considered his friendship one of her 'greatest, and most unmixed consolations'.[16] She became permanently stigmatized as a Godwinian.

The most important event in 1796 for Godwin was his renewed acquaintance with Mary Wollstonecraft. They had first met at dinner with Tom Paine at Joseph Johnson's in 1791, but both had been disappointed. Godwin heard her when he wished to hear Paine, and although he recognized in her an independent thinker, their conversation was desultory and antagonistic. They had met two or three times in the following year but the initial impression was not dispelled. Thus when Mary Hays suggested they meet again at her place on 8 January 1796, Godwin replied that he would be happy to meet 'Mrs. Wollstonecraft of whom I know not that I ever said a word of harm, and who has frequently amused herself with depreciating me'.[17]

Mary Wollstonecraft has rightly been called the first major feminist. A self-taught farmer's daughter, she had decided at the age of fifteen never to marry for interested motives or to endure a life of dependence. Consequently she was obliged to work at different times as a lady's companion, school-teacher, governess and even seamstress. Her ambition was to be the first woman to achieve economic independence through writing, and with the help of the publisher Joseph Johnson she eventually became novelist, historian, essayist, reviewer, translator and philosopher. When Godwin first met her in 1791, she had just completed her *Vindication of the Rights of Men*, the first reply to Burke, and was working on her celebrated *Vindication of the Rights of Woman*, the first sustained argument for female emancipation.

Engraved by Ridley from a Painting by Opie.

Mʳˢ. WOLLSTONECRAFT.

Pubᵈ for the Proprietors of the Monthly Mirror, by T.Bellamy, King Sᵗ Covent Garden Febʸⁱ 1796.

XV. 'Mrs. Wollstonecraft', c. 1796, by John Opie. Engraved by W. Ridley.

Partly to console herself for a hopeless love-affair with the married painter Henry Fuseli and partly to gain first-hand knowledge of the French Revolution, she went to Paris in the following year. She rapidly became acquainted with the expatriate radicals Helen Maria Williams, Thomas Christie, Tom Paine, and Archibald Hamilton Rowan, and began to move in Girondin circles. Although deeply disappointed by the Terror, she could express a guarded confidence, in her *Historical and Moral View of the Origin and Progress of the French Revolution* (1794), that the 'people are essentially good' and that 'out of this chaotic mass a fairer government is rising than has ever shed the sweets of social life on the world'.[18]

During her stay in Paris in 1793 she met the American radical Gilbert Imlay, with whom she had an illegitimate daughter Fanny. After a trip to Scandinavia as his business agent, she returned calling herself Mrs. Imlay only to find that another had replaced her in his affections. Her despair was so great that she attempted to commit suicide for the second time by jumping off Putney Bridge in London at night. It was whilst she was recovering that she met Godwin at Mary Hays's little dinner party.

There was much in Wollstonecraft's writing that Godwin would have agreed with. She was, after all, a courageous moralist and original thinker — one of the half-dozen or so leading radical intellectuals in the 1790s. In her first work on female education, written in 1787 under the influence of her friend Richard Price, she had shown herself a warm advocate of the rational control of the instincts and a firm believer in universal benevolence. Marriage, she declared, is 'too often a state of discord' and strongly urged her readers to find rational grounds for loving a person.[19] In her first novel *Mary*, published a year later, she depicted a worthy heroine who becomes a victim of an arranged marriage and dies hoping to enter a country where *'there is neither marrying,* nor giving in marriage'.[20]

After the French Revolution she revealed herself in her two *Vindications* as an implacable enemy of hereditary distinctions and the established Church and State. Moreover, as a woman she had experienced the full force of property rights, and she linked radicalism and feminism in a new and powerful way. Her attack on Rousseau's view of woman as a plaything created for man's pleasure, her notion that mind has no sex, her impassioned plea for the new woman to become man's rational and independent companion rather than a passive and indolent mistress would have struck a chord of sympathy in Godwin's heart. Above all, she maintained like Godwin that 'from the exercise of reason, knowledge and virtue naturally flow'.[21]

There were, nonetheless, fundamental differences between the two. The whole system of abstract rights on which Wollstonecraft based her case, Godwin felt was muddle-headed. Whereas she defended domestic affections, he outlawed them. Her scheme of national education as the means of reform was according to him quite impossible. Above all, while he admitted that her *Vindication of the Rights of Woman* was a 'very bold and original production', he felt that it was 'eminently deficient in method and arrangement' and in parts revealed a 'rigid, and somewhat amazonian temper'.[22]

When Mary Wollstonecraft and Godwin renewed their acquaintance in 1796 she was thirty-seven and he thirty-nine. Fuseli had called her a 'philosophical sloven' with her lank hair and black worsted stockings, but the portrait by Opie in the following year shows a remarkably handsome woman in a simple dress.[23] Her glance appears serene and compassionate, if a little sad. Mary Hays has perhaps left the best general description of her at this time:

> Her person was above the middle height, and well proportioned; her form full; her hair and eyes brown; her features pleasing; her countenance changing and impressive; her voice soft, and, though without great compass, capable of modulation. When unbending in familiar and confidential conversation, her manners had a charm which subdued the heart.[24]

Godwin also described her as 'lovely in her person, and, in the best and most engaging sense, feminine in her manners'.[25] She was given to bouts of despair, and could be impulsive and occasionally tetchy. But Godwin saw in her a person with a generous mind and a passionate nature. He was fascinated both by her past independence and by her breadth of vision.

Godwin for his part did not cut a very impressive figure. His body was slim, but his legs were on the short side. Most striking was his large head and massive brow, as well as his nose which Southey called 'most abominable' and longed to cut off whenever he saw it.[26] Years of study had impaired his eyesight, and his hair was thinning. He continued to dress soberly, very much like the Dissenting minister he had aspired to be, although his radical sympathies had led him to discard his wig.

As a man, he was somewhat slow of perception, poor in conversation, and pedantic in manner. A sedentary celibate, he had little of Wollstonecraft's experience of love and the world. Yet she found in him a penetrating intellect and warm heart, and his mild temper was a pleasant foil to her own. At home, he was comfortable and relaxed. Indeed, a peculiar weakness of his constitution increasingly obliged him to take a nap in the afternoon, much to the amusement of his guests.

Wollstonecraft was coming to the end of her relationship with Imlay when they met at Mary Hays's. She made one last effort to win him back but

XVI. Mary Wollstonecraft in 1797, by John Opie.

XVII. Godwin, aged 42, by J. W. Chandler, 1798.

to no avail. She departed with dignity once and for all in March, although Hays informed Godwin that she was broken-hearted. She took some furnished rooms with her two-year-old daughter in Cumming Street in Pentonville, not far from Godwin's house in Somers Town, planning to earn some money through her writing in order to travel to Italy or Switzerland.

In the meantime, Godwin had been pleasantly surprised by their meeting. 'Sympathy in her anguish', he wrote later, 'added in my mind to the respect I had always entertained for her talents.'[27] Moreover, he read her *Letters written during a Short Residence in Sweden, Norway, and Denmark* which peculiarly suited her imagination and combined a love of nature with a hatred of injustice. 'If ever there was a book calculated to make a man fall in love with its author', Godwin wrote, 'this appears to me to be the book'.[28] When she unexpectedly called on him on 14 April, he was therefore extremely pleased. A week later, on the 22nd, he invited her to join a party of friends at his house which included Holcroft, Elizabeth Inchbald, Dr. Parr and his two daughters, and James Mackintosh and his wife. It was a great success and only reinforced their growing esteem.

Wollstonecraft was not, however, the only woman on Godwin's mind at that time. The poet Robert Merry introduced him in the spring of 1796 to Mary Robinson, former actress and mistress of the Prince of Wales, and a popular writer of sentimental prose and verse. Godwin not only thought her the most beautiful woman he had ever seen, but found her an accomplished and delightful companion. She was later attacked by the *Anti-Jacobin Review* as a disciple of Godwin for her portrayal of vicious lords and virtuous peasants, but their acquaintance did not develop into an intimate friendship.

There was also Amelia Alderson. According to his diary, Godwin made a 'proposal' — exactly what of is not clear — to her father on 10 July 1796 during a visit with Robert Merry to Norfolk. His proposal rejected, he spent his time seeing Thelwall and helping Merry to raise £200 to pay off his debts. On his return to London, he continued to see Elizabeth Inchbald, whom a somewhat jealous Wollstonecraft dubbed 'Mrs. Perfection'.

Nevertheless, Godwin soon began courting Wollstonecraft in earnest. Already in June, he had sent her a poetical tribute which is unfortunately lost. She replied enclosing a copy of the last volume of Rousseau's *La Nouvelle Héloïse* with the note:

> I do not give you credit for as much philosophy as our friend, and I want besides to remind you, when you write to me in *verse*, not to choose the easiest task, my perfections, but to dwell on your own feelings — that is to say, give me a bird's-eye view of your heart. Do not make me a desk 'to write upon', I humbly pray — unless you honestly acknowledge yourself *bewitched*.[29]

Whilst Godwin was away in Norfolk, she gave up the idea of going to the Continent and moved — 'probably without knowing exactly why', Godwin later wrote — to 16 Judd Place West, on the outskirts of Somers Town where he lived.[30] On his return, their relationship developed rapidly. By 13 July he could write that her company infinitely delighted him: 'I love your imagination, your delicate epicurism, the malicious leer of your eye, in short everything that constitutes the bewitching tout ensemble of the celebrated Mary'. He could even be witty and passionate at the same time:

> Shall I write a love letter? May Lucifer fly away with me, if I do! No, when I make love, it shall be with the eloquent tones of my voice, with dying accents, with speaking glances (through the glass of my spectacles), with all the witching of that irresistible, universal passion. Curse on the mechanical, icy medium of pen & paper. When I make love, it shall be in a storm, as Jupiter made love to Semele, & turned her at once to a cinder. Do not these menaces terrify you?[31]

Apparently not. The subsequent notes they sent each other were warm, bantering and down to earth. She had been clearly touched by Godwin's frank and whimsical declaration, and three weeks after his return from Norfolk they became lovers. On 21 August, he wrote in his diary: 'chez moi, toute'.

It has been suggested that Wollstonecraft turned to Godwin on the rebound from her liaison with Imlay, that he was merely 'a consolation prize of a superior kind'.[32] Godwin certainly found in her a wounded heart, but the love which developed between them was genuine and profound — a love based on mutual esteem and not without passion. Theirs was, Godwin wrote, 'the purest and most refined style of love. It grew with equal advances in the mind of each. It would have been impossible for the most minute observer to have said who was before, and who was after . . . It was friendship melting into love'.[33]

But it was not without its problems. She was worried that she had yielded too quickly to Godwin and anxious that he might abandon her like Imlay. On the morrow of their first night together, she spoke of her emotions bordering on agony, of how she only encountered the thorns of life, and ended: 'Consider what has passed as a fever of imagination; one of the slight mortal shakes to which you are liable — and I — will become again a *Solitary Walker*. Adieu! I was going to add God bless you! —'[34] Godwin, however, quickly reassured her that there was nothing in her that would 'in the slightest degree authorise the opinion, that, *in despising the false delicacy, you have lost sight of the true*. I see nothing in you but what I respect & adore.'[35] Her fears were quickly allayed. When on 19 August she sent him a fable about a sycamore tree which put its leaves out too early and was frost-bitten, he replied in the language of the anxious lover: 'Your fable of to day puts an end to all my hopes. I needed soothing, & you threaten me. Oppressed with a diffidence & uncertainty which I hate, you join the oppressors, & annihilate me.'[36]

Marriage was not considered. In keeping with their views of personal independence, they chose not to cohabit: they would write during the day in their present lodgings, send notes to each other, and then meet in the evening. They also decided to continue to meet their old friends separately. She saw John Opie, and kept her relationship with Godwin so secret that it was rumoured as late as December that she was to marry the painter. Godwin for his part still saw Inchbald; on one occasion, there was a mix up about some theatre tickets, and when Wollstonecraft from her poor seat saw Godwin and Inchbald in comfort, she could not prevent herself from threatening: 'I am determined to return to my former habits, and go by [my]self and shift for myself'.[37]

These misunderstandings merely added to the joy of an increasingly tender relationship. Beneath the timid and somewhat cool exterior, she found in Godwin a 'tender considerate creature' and felt 'sublime tranquillity' in his arms.[38] 'Let me assure you that you are not only in my heart, but in my veins', she wrote one morning,

> I turn from you half abashed — yet you haunt me, and some look, word or touch thrills through my whole frame — yes, at the very moment when I am labouring to think of something, if not somebody, else. Get ye gone Intruder! though I am forced to add dear — which is a call back.
>
> When the heart and reason accord, there is no flying from voluptuous sensations, I find, do what a woman can — Can a philosopher do more?[39]

Godwin could not. And in addition to passion, he was beginning to know the delights of domestic affections. Wollstonecraft's daughter Fanny took a great liking to her mother's new friend whom she called 'Man'. Out on a walk one day, she insisted 'go this way Mama, me wants to see Man'.[40] One of her real treats was to dine with 'Man' — although her mother had to persuade him not to give her butter with her pudding.

As they were both writing for a living, they regularly exchanged their manuscripts for criticism. Godwin sent her some of the essays which were to make up *The Enquirer* and the first drafts of the tragedy *Antonio*. She was reviewing regularly for the *Analytical Review* and serving as Johnson's editorial assistant, but found time to begin a largely autobiographical novel to be entitled *The Wrongs of Woman: or, Maria*. Its aim is to exhibit 'the misery and oppression, peculiar to women, that arise out of the partial laws and customs of society'.[41] The heroine literally becomes a prisoner of her sex and is locked up in a madhouse by a brutal husband who attempts to seize her fortune. Male tyranny is lashed and the laws which reduce marriage to 'a mere affair of barter' are condemned. Above all, a woman's right to sexual feelings is asserted: 'we cannot, without depraving our minds, endeavour to please a lover or husband, but in proportion as he pleases us'.[42]

Unfortunately, the work was never finished. Godwin later praised it as 'pregnant with passion and distress' and felt that it placed in a striking point of view 'evils that are too frequently overlooked'.[43] Yet when she first showed him the manuscript his criticisms of her style were so severe that she was almost forced to give up writing. She counter-attacked by warning Godwin against being too extreme: 'do not make too many philosophical experiments, for when a philosopher is put on his metal, to use your own phrase, there is no knowing where he will stop . . .'[44] In addition, she persuaded him on the advantages of small day schools as a temporary expedient in *The Enquirer*. But her greatest help was her warm encouragement: on reading his essays, she always experienced 'a pleasureable movement to the sensations' whenever she reminded herself that the author loved her.[45]

But the laws of nature were rudely to interrupt their growing love and mutual inspiration. At the end of 1796, five months after the beginning of their affair, Wollstonecraft found that she was pregnant again. Godwin's 'chance-medley system' of contraception, which seems to have been a kind of rhythm method, had clearly failed.[46] Her immediate reaction, as so often before in times of difficulty, was one of cold independence: 'I can abide by the consequences of my own conduct, and do not wish to envolve any one in my difficulties.'[47] She did not feel well and became irritable and depressed. After dangling her petticoats in the snow on her way to visit Godwin, she was prompted to exclaim: 'But women are born to suffer.'[48]

Godwin, as usual, was patient and stood by her, declaring that his sole concern was to study her happiness. Unwilling to face once again the social ostracism of bringing an illegitimate child into the world, Wollstonecraft suggested that they should marry. Godwin reluctantly agreed. He knew what his critics would make of it but he felt compelled to sacrifice a general moral principle for the well-being of an unhappy individual. Besides, he was already developing a taste for domestic life.

So on 29 March 1797, the man who had declared that marriage was 'the most odious of all monopolies' was duly wed at St. Pancras Church to the woman who had prided herself that she had given herself to a lover 'without having clogged my soul by promising obedience &c &c'.[49] The witness and only guest was Godwin's old friend Marshal. Godwin made no note of the occasion in his diary. It was only after moving on 6 April to a joint home in the Polygon that they informed their friends. Mary Hays was one of the first to know. 'My fair neighbour', Godwin wrote to her on the 10th,

> bids me remind you of the earnest way in which you pressed me to prevail upon her to change her name . . . we found there was no way so obvious for her to drop the name of Imlay, as to assume the name of Godwin. Mrs. Godwin — who the devil is that? — will be glad to see you at No. 29, Polygon, Somers Town, whenever you are inclined to favour her with a call.[50]

It was an act which delighted his enemies and puzzled his friends. However hard he tried, Godwin was unable to live down the apparent contradiction between his philosophy and practice. In a letter to the young Thomas Wedgwood asking for a loan of £50 to pay off his wife's debts, he tried to justify his position:

> The doctrine of my 'Political Justice' is, that an attachment in some degree permanent, between two persons of opposite sexes is right, but that marriage, as practised in European countries, is wrong. I still adhere to that opinion. Nothing but a regard for the happiness of the individual, which I had no right to injure, could have induced me to submit to an institution which I wish to see abolished, and which I would recommend to my fellow-men, never to practise, but with the greatest caution. Having done what I thought necessary for the peace and respectability of the individual, I hold myself no otherwise bound than I was before the ceremony took place.[51]

It was at least in keeping with the doctrine of *Political Justice* that general moral rules must give way to the urgency of special circumstances. Besides, as Godwin told another correspondent, every day of his life he was obliged to comply with institutions and customs which he wished to see abolished. Morality, he added, 'is nothing but a balance between opposite Evils. I have to draw between the Evils social & personal, of compliance & non compliance'.[52]

When Holcroft heard the news, he was delighted: 'From my very heart and soul I give you joy. I think you the most extraordinary married pair in existence. May your happiness be as pure as I firmly persuade myself it must be.'[53] As for his mother, she piously wrote, 'Your broken resolution in regard to mattrimony incourages me to hope that you will ere long embrace the Gospel . . .' She wished them joy, sent a box of eggs, offered a feather bed, and advised them not to make 'invitations and entertainments'.[54] Of his intimate female friends, Maria Reveley was at first uncertain, but on becoming acquainted with his wife found, she told Mary Shelley later, that 'instead of losing one she secured two friends, unequalled, perhaps, in the world for genius, single-heartedness, and nobleness of disposition'.[55]

Only Elizabeth Inchbald, whom Godwin had continued to see at the theatre and private parties, was hurt. She reacted sharply and asked him to find someone else to give him theatre tickets, adding 'If I have done wrong, when you next marry, I will act differently.'[56] Unperturbed, Godwin turned up with his new wife, whereupon Inchbald took the opportunity of being 'base, cruel and insulting' to her in the company of Amelia Alderson, Maria Reveley, and the Fenwicks.[57] Like Sarah Siddons, she soon broke off her friendship, not wishing to compromise herself by appearing in Mary Wollstonecraft's society now that she had publicly acknowledged that she had never been married to Imlay.

As for the young Amelia Alderson, she wrote to a friend: 'Heigho! what charming things would sublime theories be, if one could make one's practice keep up with them'.[58] She later contented herself with ridiculing the couple in a satirical novel Adeline Mowbray (1804). The Times also happily but inaccurately announced on 15 April the marriage of 'Mr. Godwin, author of a Pamphlet against the Institution of Matrimony, to the famous Mrs. Wolstonecroft, who wrote in support of the Rights of Women'.

Neither felt entirely happy about the marriage. 'A very suitable match', Anna Barbauld wrote to a friend, 'but numberless are the squibs that are thrown out at Mr. Godwin on the occasion, and he winces not a little on receiving the usual congratulations.'[59] For her part, Wollstonecraft declared to Alderson that 'I still mean to be independent, even to the cultivating sentiments and principles in my children's minds, (should I have any more,) which he disavows.' She signed herself 'Mary Wollstonecraft femme Godwin'.[60] True to their ideas of personal independence, they continued to receive friends of either sex, and made visits as separate individuals rather than as man and wife. They also decided not to cohabit entirely. Their joint home was at 29 The Polygon, a ring of handsome houses four stories high which were built around gardens and situated near open fields. But Godwin also took rooms at No. 17, Evesham Buildings in Chalton Street, about twenty doors away, where he would work and sometimes sleep. They would rarely see each other until dinner, and sent messages to each other via Wollstonecraft's maid.

Mary Wollstonecraft's relationship with Godwin proved to be the most fruitful experience in her life. At last she had met someone who loved her deeply and at the same time treated her as an equal and recognized her independence. Yet she was unable to accept completely such a relationship based on mutual tolerance and individual autonomy. When Godwin criticized her writings, she became defensive and even competitive. If he did not deal directly with the tradespeople, she became domineering. And when he seemed to be spending a great deal of his time with a Miss Pinkerton, she broke their original agreement, played the traditional role of the possessive wife, and demanded that they stop seeing each other. They could not avoid some bickering: she saw in Godwin's readiness to speak his mind the 'coquetish candour of vanity', while he later maintained that she was 'too quick in conceiving resentments'.[61]

But despite all this they were in general exceedingly happy in their growing love and comradeship. When Godwin set off with Basil Montagu on a trip in the summer to visit the Wedgwoods of Etruria, she admitted jokingly that a 'husband is a convenient part of the furniture of a house'. Not to be outdone, he confessed that 'after all one's philosophy' the knowledge that there is some one who takes an interest in our happiness is 'extremely gratifying'.[62]

Godwin's trip with Montagu was a great success. They set off 'as gay as larks' on 3 June and took a route via Oxford, where John Horseman gave them a grand dinner and declared that Godwin and his wife were the 'two greatest men [sic] in the world'; to Stratford, where Dr. Samuel Parr rallied him on his marriage but forbad a visit because his daughter had just eloped; to Birmingham, where they saw the ruins of two large houses demolished during the riots of 1791; and thence to Etruria.[63] The Wedgwood family treated him very cordially. He visited their china 'manufactory' (more interested in the 'countenances of the workpeople, than the wares they produced'), travelled through Brindley's Harecastle Tunnel on the Grand Trunk Canal, and spent a miserable evening at the theatre in Stoke-on-Trent.[64] After a week, they returned via Derby, hoping to see Dr. Erasmus Darwin but he was out. They were luckier when they met at the mills in Elford the self-educated paper manufacturer turned radical novelist Robert Bage. Godwin spent a delightful day in his company, learned his life's story, and remarked that he was a memorable instance of 'great intellectual refinement, attained in the bosom of rusticity'.[65] Dr. Parr received them at Hatton this time, but Godwin could not persuade Montagu to indulge in the 'divine enthusiasm' he felt coming over his soul when they visited nearby Kenilworth Castle.[66] After a look at Coventry Fair, they arrived back in London on 20 June.

Godwin's letters during the trip contain many entertaining anecdotes and lively descriptions. The temporary exile only increased his happiness.

'Separation', he wrote, 'is the image of death; but it is Death stripped of all that is most tremendous, & his dart purged of its deadly venom. I always thought St Paul's rule, that we should die daily, an exquisite Epicurean maxim. The practice of it, would give to life a double relish.'[67] He was secure in his wife's love, growing fonder of his new two-year-old stepdaughter Fanny, and was looking forward to the birth of little William.

For her part, she felt that his absence at first made her affection more alive, but complained later of the impersonal tone of his letters and his delay in returning. They soon made up; their last notes to each other show them happily awaiting the birth of what turned out to be a daughter. It was to prove fatal to the mother.

The child was delivered with the help of a Mrs. Blenkinsop, matron and midwife of Westminster Lying-in Hospital, on Wednesday 30 August at 11.20 p.m. Wollstonecraft believed too much fuss was made of childbirth and deliberately went against fashion by deciding on a midwife rather than a male doctor to help her. For the sake of decorum, however, she preferred Godwin not to be in the house. At first all seemed well, but it was found necessary to call Dr. Poignard, a physician at the Westminster Hospital, to remove the placenta which had broken into pieces. The process was agonizing; there was a great loss of blood, and Wollstonecraft told Godwin afterwards that she would never have lived through the night if she had not been determined to stay with him.

The next day Godwin's old friend Dr. George Fordyce called and pronounced all was well. On the Friday, Godwin happily visited his friends George Robinson, William Nicholson, and Mary Hays. His wife's old friend and publisher Joseph Johnson called to offer his congratulations. Anthony Carlisle, one of the best physicians of the day and a friend of the family, was kept informed of developments. Visits continued on Saturday, but in the evening the mother was suddenly worse and a nurse was called. The next day, Godwin was still sufficiently sanguine to walk with Montagu as far as Kensington to visit friends, but he was to regret it. When he returned, he learned that his wife had been having violent shivering fits. It marked the onset of septicaemia; she was doomed.

She stopped feeding her daughter and puppies were applied to take off the excess milk. Her situation deteriorated rapidly. On Tuesday, Dr. John Clarke, a well-known women's physician, called to see if any operation could be performed but found the patient too weak. The next day Carlisle came and remained at her bedside for the next four days and nights. Godwin, almost driven to distraction, was given the job of supplying her sips of wine to dull the pain. With a great effort of will, she lingered on until Sunday morning, 10 September. She remained till the end gentle, tranquil, and courageous. In her last words she said of Godwin: 'He is the kindest,

XVIII. Godwin's Diary, 27 August–9 September 1797.

best man in the world.'[68] In his diary, which so meticulously recorded the visits of the last days, he could only write '20 minutes before eight . . .' and filled in three lines with strokes of his pen.[69]

He was heart-broken. 'My wife is now dead', he wrote to Holcroft on the same day, 'I firmly believe that there does not exist her equal in the world. I know from experience we were formed to make each other happy. I have not the least expectation that I can now ever know happiness again.'[70] His immediate reaction was to seek solitude and attach himself to those objects and employments he associated with his dead wife. He found, he wrote to a friend, a pleasure difficult to describe in the cultivation of melancholy: 'It weakens indeed my stoicism in the ordinary occurrences of life, but it refines and raises my sensibility.'[71]

In an attempt at reconciliation, he informed Elizabeth Inchbald: 'I always thought you used her ill, but I forgive you.'[72] It led to a short exchange of letters. Inchbald tried to refute the charge, coldly assured Godwin that he would get over his loss, and finally insisted that their acquaintance should end forever: 'I respect *your prejudices*, but I also respect my *own*.'[73]

Eliza Fenwick, Mary Hays, and Basil Montagu, who had stayed to the end, wrote the necessary letters. On 15 September, the body of Mary Wollstonecraft Godwin was buried in the quiet churchyard of St. Pancras not far from Somers Town, in the presence of a few intimate friends. Godwin stayed away, from grief rather than principle. As his wife's remains were being lowered into the earth, he wrote a letter from Marshal's lodgings to Carlisle thanking him for all he had done. Fawcett kept him company in the evening.

Godwin's first move was to transfer all his books and papers into the room which had been his wife's. He hung Opie's portrait of her which was to remain in his study until he himself died forty years later. He was determined to look after Fanny and the new-born baby, who had been in Maria Reveley's care during their mother's illness, and brought them home. Louisa Jones, a friend of his sister's, came to help and soon became part of the family.

For the time being Godwin rarely went out. His closest friends constantly visited him — Holcroft, the Fenwicks, and Maria Reveley — but they could not dispel his melancholy and anxiety. Seven weeks after the death of his wife, he wrote to one of her friends that he had seen 'one bright ray of light that streaked my day of life only to leave the remainder more gloomy, and, in the truest sense of the word, hopeless'.[74]

His one consolation was reading his wife's writings. Within two weeks of her death, he began writing her memoirs which he was to publish with a four-volume edition of her works and correspondence in the following year. It proved to be one of his most impressive and lasting works and stands as a minor masterpiece of biography. The sisters of Mary Wollstonecraft refused to help him, but her friends Joseph Johnson and Hugh Skeys did as much as they could. For the most part, he made use of his own recollections. The result was a simple, frank and honest recreation of Mary Wollstonecraft's life and ideas.

Godwin makes no attempt to conceal the less respectable aspects of her life — her affairs with Fuseli the painter, Imlay, and himself, her two suicide bids, and her emotional weaknesses. On the other hand, he eloquently describes her talents and achievements and humbly records his own indebtedness. Indeed, his readiness to explore his own feelings and to present her as a 'female Werter' shows how deeply she had affected his way of thinking and makes the work an important Romantic document.[75] Above

Engraved by J. Chapman from an original Painting.

M<sup>RS</sup> GODWIN.

XIX. 'Mrs. Godwin', artist unknown. Engraved by J. Chapman.

all, Godwin offers a magnificent tribute not to 'poor Mary' of the popular biographies but to 'a woman, with sentiments as pure, as refined, as delicate, as ever inhabited a human heart!'[76]

Godwin's emotional and intellectual debt to Mary Wollstonecraft was enormous. In the *Memoirs*, he suggests that they carried to an uncommon degree the traditional characteristics of the sexes to which they belonged: where he had been more accustomed to exercise his reasoning powers, she had relied on her feelings. But each corrected the weakness in the other, and Godwin gladly acknowledged that 'Her taste awakened mine; her sensibility determined me to a careful development of my feelings. She delighted to open her heart to the beauties of nature; and her propensity in this respect led me to a more intimate contemplation of them.'[77]

In philosophy, her belief in a God undoubtedly prepared the ground for Coleridge's conversion of Godwin to a form of pantheism three years later. Her influence further coincided with Hume's to make him conclude that 'moral reasoning is nothing but the awakening of certain feelings'.[78] Above all, she was a 'worshipper of domestic life' and had argued in their correspondence that 'the exercise of the domestic affections' was the foundation of virtue.[79] His intense but short-lived experience with her thus made him realize that while cohabitation may be 'pregnant with ill-humour', true wisdom will recommend us to individual attachments,

> since the man who lives in the midst of domestic relations, will have many opportunities of conferring pleasure, minute in the detail, yet not trivial in the amount, without interfering with the purposes of general benevolence. Nay, by kindling his sensibility, and harmonizing his soul, they may be expected, if he is endowed with a liberal and manly spirit, to render him more prompt in the service of strangers and of the public.[80]

Godwin made his revised views even more explicit in his next novel *St. Leon* which contained an idealized picture of Mary Wollstonecraft.

Godwin's memoirs of his wife were published on 29 January 1798 together with four small volumes of *Posthumous Works,* mainly consisting of the incomplete novel, *The Wrongs of Woman: or, Maria* and letters to Imlay. Johnson issued a second edition within a few months in which Godwin omitted the most explicit references to his wife's relations with her lovers. It was translated into German by Salzmann in 1799 and into French in 1802. Two editions appeared in Philadelphia in 1799 and 1804. The public reaction, however, offered Godwin little consolation.

The *Analytical Review* defended Wollstonecraft's conduct and doctrines, but offered the sort of patronizing apology which Godwin deliberately avoided.[81] Although the *Monthly Magazine* found the memoirs written with truth and simplicity, it did not think it advisable to examine her frailties so soon after her death.[82] The *Monthly Review* lamented that Godwin 'neither looks to marriage with respect, nor to suicide with horror'.[83] Not surprisingly, the *Anti-Jacobin Review* resorted to scurrilous abuse of her life rather than her opinions, and in the index to the magazine put under the heading of 'Prostitution': '*See* Mary Wollstonecraft'.[84] No other work contributed more extensively to the increasing horror polite society felt for Godwin. The *European Magazine* was undoubtedly correct when it prophesied that it would be read

> with disgust by every female who has any pretensions to delicacy; with detestation by every one attached to the interests of religion and morality; and with indignation by any one who might feel any regard for the unhappy woman, whose frailties should have been buried in oblivion.[85]

It became the fashion to abuse Godwin violently for his attempt to tell the truth about his dead wife. The biographer William Roscoe summed up the general reaction in his verses:

> Hard was thy fate in all the scenes of life,
> As daughter, sister, mother, friend, and wife;
> But harder still thy fate in death we own,
> Thus mourn'd by Godwin with a heart of stone.[86]

One of the few exceptions was the poet Anna Seward who thought the memoirs bore 'strong marks of impartial authenticity' and were 'highly valuable'. To reveal the motives on which Mary Wollstonecraft had acted was surely, she wrote to a friend, 'not injury but justice to a deceased wife'.[87] Unfortunately, Godwin did not know of Seward's response, and felt that the public outcry was yet another sign of the inveterate prejudice and hardened reaction of his contemporaries.

# CHAPTER XII

## St. Godwin

The death of Mary Wollstonecraft was a turning-point in Godwin's life. Bliss had been snatched away at the very moment that it was in his grasp for the first time. He seems to have felt in some way responsible for her death, for the heroes of his subsequent novels are consumed with guilt for murdering the perfect mothers of their children.[1] The opposite of Don Juan, they appear as knights errant longing for and yet fearing family life. It is almost as if his novels were to become acts of compensation for her death.

After editing her papers and writing her memoirs, Godwin did his best to return to his daily routine of writing and reading in the morning and visiting or receiving friends in the afternoon. His health was not good — his diary records many attacks of fainting or 'deliquim' — and he could not work for more than a few hours at a time. He still managed to read though a classical author every day, particularly the Latin poets, and a little French, usually the older and standard authors.

He had, except for his beloved Shakespeare, mainly confined himself for years to reading modern English literature. In 1799 however this methodical routine was suddenly changed. Considering drama as a possible means of subsistence, he picked up one day Beaumont and Fletcher. It proved a revelation — 'it was as if a mighty river had changed its course to water the garden of my mind'.[2] It led to the discovery of the old English authors which opened up for him a whole new field of improvement and pleasure.

There was also the delight of bringing up his two young children. Louisa Jones supervised the household at the Polygon and a nurse was called in to look after Mary. Godwin's sister Hannah would occasionally come round to lend a hand. And although Godwin did not like to be disturbed in his cosy study, he became a playful, affectionate and caring father. He treated Fanny no differently than if she had been his own daughter. As they grew up he practised on them his own scheme of voluntary education: rather than inculcating his own beliefs, he waited until they expressed a desire to learn.

Despite Godwin's waning reputation, he attracted the admiration of individual enthusiasts, particularly amongst the young. Thomas Wedgwood, who had contacted Godwin in 1795 after reading *Political Justice*, still kept up a regular correspondence. The heir to the Etruria potteries told Godwin that he was 'almost the only person whose judgment is valuable to me on speculative points', and on that account continually felt the need of his sanction.[3] He sent his manuscripts to him, although Godwin's careful corrections were mainly stylistic, more in the manner of the schoolmaster than the philosopher. His notebooks show him a convinced Godwinian — a believer in associationist psychology, an advocate of perfectibility, a lover of liberty, and an enthusiast for 'Child-study'.[4] In 1797, he even proposed to Godwin a 'practical nursery of genius' which would be run on these principles and be supervised by a committee of philosophers composed of Godwin, Thomas Beddoes, Holcroft, Horne Tooke and himself, with Wordsworth and Coleridge acting as superintendents.[5] But the scheme never went beyond an idea, and Wedgwood's fragile health rapidly grew worse. Just before his early death, he wrote warmly to Godwin: 'I passed your life hastily in review, and renewed my assurance . . . of the goodness of your moral feelings, your subjection to the dictates, erroneous or otherwise, of a moral conscience.'[6]

Another young disciple was John Arnot, a Scotsman who walked from Edinburgh to London to see the philosopher. He stayed long enough in London to fall in love with his housekeeper Louisa Jones, but decided to leave for a tour of Northern Europe which took him from St. Petersburg, via Warsaw and Vienna into Germany. The two men kept up an irregular correspondence. Godwin complained of Arnot's intemperance, but sent him money and kept him informed of political events. He also gave him an introduction to Holcroft, who was in Germany at the time, and recommended that he look out for Coleridge and Wordsworth who had landed at Hamburg — 'both extraordinary men, and both reputed men of genius. Coleridge I think fully justifies the reputation. . .'[7]

Arnot, for his part, was an out-and-out Godwinian. During his travels in Europe, he often thought of Godwin's household 'as the centre of virtue & happiness to the race of man'.[8] Whilst in Germany, he visited Goethe but was not admitted, although he was luckier with Wieland and Herder. Wieland had not read *Caleb Williams*, but according to Arnot 'he had heard much of it & had long been desirous of procuring it'.[9]

But male friends and disciples did not satisfy Godwin completely. His short experience of domestic happiness with Wollstonecraft and the responsibility of bringing up two girls led him to invite rather than to guard himself against the feelings of love. He was therefore very pleased to meet Harriet Lee during a short holiday in Bath in the spring of 1798. She ran a girls' school with her sister Sophia, with whom she wrote a popular series of contemporary *Canterbury Tales*. She was also a poet and a dramatist. Despite 'a little of coxcomb in her manners', Harriet proved to be lively and sensible.[10]

On his return to London, Godwin immediately invited her to stay at his house next time she came up to the metropolis. When no reply came, he wrote in great agitation three drafts of a letter, the first a simple announcement of his intention to visit Bath, the second a fervent confession of his feelings, and the third, of which he made three copies, an amalgam of vanity and boldness. He wanted to know the cause of her silence: 'It might mean simply that I had not been long enough your knight, to entitle me to such a distinction. But it might mean disapprobation, displeasure, or offence, when my heart prompted me to demand cordiality and friendship.'[11]

She consented in a formal note to see him the following week in Bath, and he enjoyed what he called in his diary a 'conference' with her on 5 June. She does not seem to have been opposed to marriage, but was worried about the reaction of her sister and friends to a match with such a notorious infidel. Godwin was not easily dissuaded, and in a flood of letters tried to deflect her scruples. At first, he argued that 'Celibacy contracts and palsies the mind, and shuts us out from the most valuable topics of experience', and that she possessed the materials to make 'the most illustrious and happiest of all characters, when its duties are faithfully discharged — a wife — a mother'.[12]

Lee, however, was not to be won over by his rhetoric and preferred to discuss matters of theology. But when she argued that a God and a future state of reward and punishment are necessary for virtue, Godwin quickly accused her of bigotry. Virtue, he insisted, is not a form of external conduct, but a sentiment of the heart: 'If Omnipotence itself were to annex external torments to the practice of benignity and humanity, I know not how poor a slave I might be terrified into; but I know that I should curse the tyrant, while I obeyed the command.'[13] All this was too much for the pious lady, and she decided to end the correspondence. She bid Godwin farewell, hoping that he would one day accept the doctrine of 'a just and all-powerful Deity'.[14]

The knight of love might have failed, but the philosopher in Godwin was still ready to pick up the lance. He returned to the attack in a series of letters in one week which offer a singular account of his religious beliefs at the time. Deism, he declared, is more a matter of taste than reason. The origin of the universe and a future state are veiled in impenetrable mystery, while it is patently absurd 'to infer the character of infinite benevolence from what we see in a world where despotism, and slavery, and misery, and war continually prevail'.[15] Unfortunately, Godwin's tirade only confirmed Lee's initial estimate, and on 7 August she finally dispelled any remaining hopes he might have cherished. They still occasionally corresponded but it was esteem not love that they expressed for each other.

Although Godwin was put out by Harriet Lee's refusal of marriage in the summer of 1798, he by no means resigned himself to celibacy. Thus when Gilbert Reveley died suddenly on 6 July 1799 of a stroke, his hopes of a closer attachment with his wife Maria were suddenly revived. Only a few weeks after his death, he dismissed the 'cowardly ceremonies' of bereavement and exclaimed: 'Is woman always to be a slave? Is she so wretched an animal that every breath can destroy her, and every temptation, or more properly every possibility of an offence, is to be supposed to subdue her?'[16] When she refused to see him, Godwin wrote more to the point: 'You are invited to form the sole happiness of one of the most known men of the age . . . I offer you a harbour, once your favourite thought . . .'[17] Reveley still remained unconvinced. When he heard that her reluctance was due to his excessive mental powers, he forgot the arguments of Mary Wollstonecraft and wrote:

> We are different in our structure; we are perhaps still more different in our education. Woman stands in need of the courage of man to defend her, of his constancy to inspire her with firmness, and, at present at least, of his science and information to furnish to her resources of amusement, and materials for studying. Women rightly repay us for all that we can bring into the common stock, by the softness of their natures, the delicacy of their sentiments, and that peculiar and instantaneous sensibility by which they are qualified to guide our tastes and to correct our scepticism.[18]

But his special pleading was to no avail for early in December she began seeing John Gisborne whom she married soon after.

During all this time, Godwin's thoughts were not only preoccupied with thoughts of love and marriage. In the spring of 1797, he revised *Political Justice* for a third edition with an index. It appeared in December but was dated 1798. The principal object was to remove a 'few of the crude and juvenile remarks', but although Godwin did not rewrite any chapters or change his fundamental view of political justice, his recent reading and experiences led him to make some significant philosophical revisions.[19] In addition, he provided a 'Summary of Principles' which is not always consistent with the text.

In his metaphysics, Godwin had been moving towards immaterialism ever since reading Berkeley's *Principles of Human Knowledge* in the summer of 1795. He commented in a notebook that Berkeley's argument against an 'unknown, imperceptible substratum' was 'incomparably excellent'.[20] In the spring of 1797, he further wrote to Wedgwood that a belief in the absolute existence of matter is 'merely presumptive', although he avoided complete solipsism by arguing that the 'plurality of minds or sensations' exists on the principle of analogy: 'It is the only thing the existence of which I really know.'[21] In *Political Justice*, he could not change his dualist scheme of mind and matter without upsetting its whole framework, but he substituted Berkeley and Hume for Boscovich in a note denying the objectivity of the primary qualities of matter.[22]

In his treatment of necessity, the influence of Hume is even more apparent. 'Necessary connexion' becomes 'regularity and conjunction' while 'chance' is changed to 'the appearance of irregularity'.[23] Where Godwin had originally placed the emphasis on the lack of choice in human behaviour, he now stresses its predictability. It is not so much that an intelligent being 'could not in any moment of his existence have acted otherwise' but that we are qualified 'to predict the conduct he will hold, with as much certainty, as [we] can predict any of the phenomena of inanimate nature'.[24]

Hume, as well as Mary Wollstonecraft, is behind the important shift in Godwin's psychology towards a recognition of the feelings. A motive, for instance, is no longer defined as 'the idea of certain consequences' but the 'hope or fear of a certain event'.[25] In his 'Summary of Principles', Godwin is unashamedly Humean in his belief that the voluntary actions of men are under the direction of their feelings: 'Reason is not an independent principle, and has no tendency to excite us to action; in a practical view, it is merely a comparison and balancing of different feelings.'[26]

This is a major concession, and Godwin recognized that the statement was inconsistent with the text. In a notebook, he observed that in the crucial chapter 'The Voluntary Actions of Men Originate in their Opinions', there was still 'too little given to passion'. He planned a new chapter entitled 'Provinces of Feeling & Judgment Considered' to replace iv and v of Book I, but it was never written.[27]

Godwin did not, however, entirely abandon his first principles or contract a 'disease' of feeling.[28] In an analysis of Hume's philosophy in his notebooks, he rejected categorically his attempt to prove that 'reason is not the source of morality or immorality, but that the whole is referable to original passions & sentiments'. Moreover, while he fully admitted his definition of belief as the 'vivacity of perception', he maintained that men are not accustomed to call 'a vivid apprehension on any subject a belief, unless they conceive that apprehension to be rational'.[29] In short, he still held in the third edition that 'Reason, though it cannot excite us to action, is calculated to regulate our conduct, according to the comparative worth it ascribes to different excitements.'[30] There is no simple Humean opposition between reason and passion, and it is to the improvement of reason that we are to look for the improvement of our social condition.

Another important addition in 1798 was Godwin's modification of Helvétius's doctrine of the intellectual equality of human beings at birth. In the second edition he had allowed the possibility of character differences due to the effect of antenatal impressions. In the meantime, conversations with his friend Nicholson, a disciple of Lavater, and observations of his own baby Mary, led him further to consider the likelihood of congenital differences and genetic improvement: 'children certainly bring into the world with them a part of the character of their parents; nay, it is probable that the human race is meliorated, somewhat in the same way as the races of brutes'.[31] He immediately adds, however, that these causes operate too uncertainly to afford any just basis of hereditary distinction, and progress is still to be achieved through education and enlightenment.

In his ethics, Godwin gave an even greater emphasis to hedonistic utilitarianism in his 'Summary of Principles'. The true object of moral and political disquisition is 'pleasure or happiness'. He divides pleasures into two classes, physical and mental. But rather than depreciate physical pleasures as he had done in the first edition, the aim is now to maximize all types of pleasure: 'The most desirable state of man, is that, in which he has access to all these sources of pleasure, and is in possession of a happiness the most varied and uninterrupted.'[32] Independence and soundness of understanding are not therefore to be valued for their own sake but for the 'right cultivation of all our pleasures'.[33] Moreover, his experience with Mary Wollstonecraft had made him realize that happiness must 'necessarily be individual', and that marriage might be a 'salutary and respectable institution' if there be room for liberty and repentance.[34]

There are also some important changes in Godwin's view of government. He is far less certain about the benefits of anarchy. In 1793 and 1796, he had argued that anarchy had a tremendous likeness to true liberty, but he now insists that it cannot immediately lead to the best form of society. Again, he still recognizes that 'Government was intended to suppress injustice, but its effect has been to embody and perpetuate it.'[35] Yet although the most desirable state of mankind is the maximum amount of individual independence, he allows a negative role to government in maintaining general security. Indeed, he goes farther than the arguments of his text to assert in the 'Summary of Principles' that while the exertions of men should *ordinarily* be trusted to their discretion, their forbearance is in certain cases 'the direct province of political superintendence'.[36] Godwin thus began *Political Justice* with confidence in good government, then rejected it in the second edition, only to give it a qualified approval in the third.

Finally, Godwin paid greater attention in the third edition to the problem of population as a threat to his scheme of progress. He is still confident that there is a 'principle in the nature of human society, by means of which everything seems to tend to its level, and to proceed in the most auspicious way, when least interfered with'.[37] But even if there were not a spontaneous readjustment of population to food supply, Godwin points out that improvements in agriculture and the use of the uncultivated three-quarters of the habitable world would provide sufficient means of subsistence for 'myriads of centuries'.[38] And, although he does not recommend them, there are artificial methods of checking population such as the exposure of children, abortion, the promiscuous intercourse of the sexes and systematic abstinence.

There are therefore some important changes in the subsequent editions of *Political Justice*. In his metaphysics, there is a move to Berkeleyan immaterialism and Humean scepticism; in his psychology, a greater recognition of the importance of feeling; in his morality, an increased emphasis on hedonistic utilitarianism. In his politics, he toned down his view of anarchy, gave a limited role to government, but found no obstacle to his scheme of rational progress.

Political events and his own experience had helped modify his philosophy and with perfect candour he wished to deliver his changed sentiments to the public. His revisions were made with painstaking care in an attempt to make his system more consistent, precise and convincing. But while this tampering with the foundations of his philosophical edifice made it totter, it did not 'come crashing down'.[39] In a sense, this was Godwin's tragedy, for he was never able to reconstruct his philosophy but only to qualify and develop it here and there. In *Political Justice* he had presented all he knew; he could go no further.

Godwin soon realized however that his piecemeal emendations in the third edition of *Political Justice* were inadequate and often not in keeping with the rest of the text. He therefore planned in 1798 a book to be entitled 'First Principles of Morals' in order to make his new position clear. In the first place, he wrote in a notebook, his account of reason in *Political Justice* was essentially defective in not

yielding a proper attention to the empire of feeling. The voluntary actions of men are under the direction of their feelings: nothing can have a tendency to produce this species of action, except so far as it is connected with ideas of future pleasure or pain to ourselves or others. Reason, accurately speaking, has not the smallest degree of power to put any one limb or articulation of our bodies into motion. Its province, in a practical view, is wholly confined to adjusting the comparison between different objects of desire, and investigating the most successful mode of attaining those objects.

Secondly, in his treatment of benevolence, he had not sufficiently stressed that

every man will, by a necessity of nature, be influenced by motives peculiar to him as an individual. As every man will know more of his kindred and intimates than strangers, so he will inevitably think of them oftener, feel for them more acutely, and be more anxious about their welfare. This propensity is as general as the propensity we feel to prefer the consideration of our own welfare to that of any other human being. Kept within due bounds, it is scarcely an object of moral censure . . . The series of actions of a virtuous man will be the spontaneous result of a disposition naturally kind and well-attempered. The spring of motion within him will certainly not be a sentiment of general utility. But it seems equally certain that utility, though not the source, will be the regulator, of his actions; and that however ardent will be his parental, domestic, or friendly exertions, he will from time to time examine into their coincidence with the greatest sum of happiness in his power to produce.

Finally, Godwin wanted to retract the favourable opinion he had given of Helvétius's doctrine of the equality of intellectual beings as they are born into the world, and to subscribe to 'the received opinion, that, though education is a most powerful instrument, yet there exist differences of the highest importance between human beings from the period of their birth'.[40]

Godwin was particularly anxious to publish these changes since he was filled with grief at the possibility that 'any extravagances or oversights of mine should bring into disrepute the great truths I have endeavoured to propagate'.[41] In the following spring, he was still intending to write his treatise in one octavo volume to correct the errors of *Political Justice* but it never saw the light.

The other major book Godwin planned in 1798 was to be entitled 'Two Dissertations on the Reasons and Tendency of Religious Opinion'. No doubt inspired by his correspondence with Harriet Lee, its object was to sweep away 'the whole fiction of an intelligent former of the world, and a future state' and to lead men to apply their whole energy 'to practicable objects and genuine realities'. The first Dissertation would be applied:

(1) to shew that the origin of worlds is a subject out of the competence of the human understanding; (2) to invalidate the doctrine of final causes; and (3) to demonstrate the absurdity and impossibility of every system of Theism that has ever been proposed.

The second Dissertation would treat of

the injurious and enfeebling effects of religious belief in general, and of prayer in particular. The consideration would be wholly confined to the most liberal systems of Theism, without entering into superfluous declamation upon the pretences of impostors and fanatics.[42]

The dissertations however were never written and ironically Godwin was to be won over to a kind of theism by Coleridge eighteen months later.

Instead of philosophy, Godwin turned to fiction. After the success of *Caleb Williams,* he had hesitated for a long time, despairing of finding again a topic so rich in interest and passion. It struck him however roughly at the same time that Coleridge was urging Wordsworth in the *Lyrical Ballads* to give 'the charm of novelty to things of every day, and to excite a feeling analogous to the supernatural', that he could attain a sort of novelty by mixing 'human feelings and passions with incredible situations'.[43] The result was *St. Leon: A Tale of the Sixteenth Century*, a work in which Godwin used the supernatural devices of Gothic fiction to his own moral and political ends.[44]

The first hint of the plot came from a curious collection of tales by J. H. Cohausen called *Hermippus Redivius: or, The Sage's Triumph over Old Age and the Grave,* which was translated by John Campbell and published in 1744. The work had a natural interest for Godwin, since the idea of prolonging life had been one of his most notorious conjectures in *Political Justice*. In his preface to his novel, he referred particularly to the mysterious tale of one Signor Gualdi who was meant to have appeared in Venice in 1687 with a portrait of himself painted by Titian, who had of course been dead for a hundred and fifty years.

But *Hermippus Redivius* is also full of stories of necromancers. There is an interesting parallel between the hero of Godwin's novel and one Nicholas Flamel: from an aristocratic background, he falls on hard times, only to acquire occult powers from a Jew in the Spanish town of Leon. Both suffer from the suspicions of their neighbours, although Flamel succeeds in carrying out some of the philanthropic projects planned by Godwin's hero. Significantly, when Godwin began his novel at the end of December 1797, he first called it 'The Adept', then 'Opus Magnum', 'Natural Magic', and finally in July 1798, 'St. Leon'.

Like Godwin himself, and like Falkland and Caleb respectively, St. Leon possesses both a love of distinction and a fervent curiosity. These passions lead him to acquire the secrets of the philosopher's stone and the elixir vitae which bestow on him limitless wealth and eternal youth. But while this discovery gives St. Leon enormous power, it also isolates him from common humanity: his family disintegrates, the mob rise up against him, and the powerful try to acquire his knowledge. His attempts at philanthropy rebound. He is hunted, imprisoned, and finally condemned to an immortal death-in-life. His story is that of one who is finally cut off 'for ever from everything that deserves the name of human'.[45]

There are clear signs of a personal allegory in all this. The man who discovers the truth (the philosopher's stone) and then wishes to use it for the general good must expect to be rejected and forego the affection of family and friends. This had happened to Joseph Priestley, who was forced to emigrate to America after his house and laboratory had been destroyed in the Birmingham Riots in 1791, and it was beginning to happen to Godwin whilst he was composing *St. Leon*. When St. Leon's own house is destroyed by a superstitious Italian mob, his friend Filosanto (lover of holiness) exclaims in a transport of misanthropy:

> no innocence and no merit could defend a man from the unrelenting antipathy of his fellows. He saw that there was a principle in the human mind destined to be eternally at war with improvement and science . . . The midnight oil was held to be the signal of infernal machinations.[46]

At the same time, Godwin deliberately wanted to show that boundless wealth and immortality are poor substitutes for the affections and charities of private life. He now admits in his preface that he had been wrong to neglect them in *Political Justice*. Quoting his favourable opinion of them in the second edition of his memoirs of Mary Wollstonecraft, he now adds:

> I apprehend domestic and private affections inseparable from the nature of man, and from what may be styled the culture of the heart, and am fully persuaded that they are not incompatible with a profound and active sense of justice in the mind of him that cherishes them.[47]

The 'culture of the heart' was a phrase used by Mary Wollstonecraft and much of *St. Leon* is a moving tribute to her memory.[48] The spotless and accomplished Marguerite de Damville is clearly an idealized portrait of her. Godwin began the novel some months after her death, and in his description of the love between the hero and his wife, he seems to have developed his fondest memories and his deepest aspirations: 'never does man feel himself so much alive, so truly etherial, as when, bursting the bonds of diffidence, uncertainty and reserve, he pours himself entire into the bosom of the woman he adores'.[49] The passage reveals all the passion of an authentic love tragically cut short.

Marguerite tries tirelessly to reform St. Leon by the influence of the domestic affections. It is only when she dies in childbirth (like Mary Wollstonecraft) that St. Leon recognizes their value, and experiences a deep sense of remorse and guilt. But it is not too late. Having failed to improve the lot of the world at large, St. Leon defends at the end of the novel his preference for the happiness of his son:

> Philanthropy is a godlike virtue, and can never be too loudly commended, or too ardently enjoined: but natural affection winds itself in so many folds about the heart, and is the parent of so complicated, so various, and so exquisite emotions, that he who should attempt to divest himself of it, will find that he is divesting himself of all that is most to be coveted in existence.[50]

It is a far cry from the resolute stoicism of the first edition of *Political Justice*.

Godwin of course always had a heart as well as a head, and his profound intellect was matched by a powerful imagination. In *St. Leon*, however, there is a clear shift towards a Romantic stress on the importance of the emotions. 'Feeling', St. Leon exclaims approvingly, 'flows impetuously from the heart, without consulting the cooler responses of the understanding'.[51] There is also a new interest, almost Wordsworthian in its intensity, in the beauties of nature. When St. Leon is overcome by guilt his first impulse is to seek the mountains since 'the wildness of an untamed and savage scene best accorded with the temper of my mind'.[52] Again, during a tranquil journey through the Alps, he records: 'Everything was calculated to soothe and subdue the mind, to inspire a grand and expansive tranquillity. The enthusiasm it spoke, occupied every channel of my heart.'[53]

Godwin originally conceived *St. Leon* as a fable of an exceptional being who overstretches himself and ends in moral and social isolation. The denouement was to come in Volume III, with the hero preparing to spend the rest of his days in expiation for his wife's death. But the novel grew under Godwin's hands and he added a fourth volume in which a rejuvenated and immortal St. Leon wanders through a Hungary torn between Solyman the Turk and Charles of Austria. He makes an abortive attempt to revive its war-ravaged economy, falls foul of the blood-curdling Bethlem Gabor, and even becomes the rival in love of his own son Charles.

Godwin was nearly always too verbose, but what the novel lost in unity, it gained in psychological power and drama. The saintly Marguerite remains entirely one-dimensional in her innocent purity and long-suffering patience; St. Leon is more interesting in his ill-fated mixture of ambition and philanthropy; but Bethlem Gabor is a tremendous and unforgettable character.

As a historical figure, he was the leader of the Transylvanian Calvinists. Godwin came across him in the German Gothic novel *The Necromancer* and out of him created one of the most memorable villains of the period.[54] Like Skakespeare's Macduff, Bethlem Gabor is turned by the murder of his family into a vengeful and terrifying monster. This 'man-abhorring palatine' is St. Leon writ large, an exemplar of malevolence created in men by the society which oppresses them, and as such inspires a kind of horrified admiration and reluctant sympathy.[55] Godwin's daughter was to be inspired by him in her novel *Frankenstein*.

But *St. Leon* is more than a study of character or a philosophical tract extolling the virtue of the feelings. As its subtitle indicates, it is also 'A Tale of the Sixteenth Century'. Godwin had already attempted to show how the characters of men originate in their circumstances in *Caleb Williams* and he tried the same in his new novel with even greater success. Holcroft's daughters were right when they called St. Leon a 'second Falkland'.[56] Both come from aristocratic backgrounds and imbibe during their childhood the poisonous code of chivalry. St. Leon recalls that his mother loved his honour and his fame more than she loved his person. At the age of fifteen, he was greatly impressed by the meeting of Francis I and Henry VIII at Ardes in 1520. At nineteen, he took part in the siege of Pavia and the defeat of Francis I by the Holy Roman Emperor — an occasion, Godwin remarks in high Burkean spirit, which gave a deadly wound 'to the reign of chivalry, and a secure foundation to that of craft, dissimulation, corruption and commerce'.[57]

Like Falkland, St. Leon therefore starts life with a set of aristocratic ideals which are at odds with the temper and demands of the age. Godwin underlines their incongruity by comparing St. Leon's sense of military glory with all the real horrors of war. He shows how his luxurious upbringing leads him to gambling and a passion for gold which poisons every 'nobler and more salubrious feeling'.[58] It is only after a series of disastrous adventures in which he abandons his family and friends that he realizes the value of the simple but cultivated life.

The fable in fact is firmly set in the age of the Renaissance. Godwin describes how Marguerite was taught to draw by Leonardo da Vinci and had her poetic taste formed by Clement Marot. St. Leon meets in her father's house (the Marquis de Damville, who played an important part in the religious wars in France) some of the most eminent wits and scholars of the new Humanism, particularly Marot, Erasmus, Rabelais and Scaliger.

Godwin also takes his hero through a giddy tour of Europe which is torn by religious conflict. In Calvinist Constance, for instance, St. Leon complains of the 'gloomy temper and melancholy austerity' of the reformers.[59] When he is captured by the Inquisition in Spain, the Grand Inquisitor is given many pages to defend the movement only for St. Leon to explain that a religion which is supported by such means is 'viler than atheism'.[60] Godwin stresses the contemporary relevance by making his hero exclaim:

> Human affairs, like the waves of the ocean, are merely in a state of ebb and flow: 'there is nothing new under the sun:' two centuries perhaps after Philip the Second shall be gathered to his ancestors (he died in 1598), men shall learn over again to persecute each other for conscience sake; other anabaptists or levellers shall furnish pretexts for new persecutions; other inquisitors shall arise in the most enlightened tracts of Europe . . .[61]

Apart from his rehabilitation of feeling and historical purpose, there are many other themes in *St. Leon* close to Godwin's heart. He further qualifies the Helvétian doctrine of the intellectual equality of man at birth. Speaking from his own experience, St. Leon argues that children 'are not puppets, moved with wires, and to be played upon at will. Almost from the hour of their birth, they have a will of their own, to be consulted and negotiated with.'[62] Yet this concession does not interfere with Godwin's view that all human beings share a common nature. The turnkey Hector is deliberately depicted as a negro whose countenance indicates a 'sound understanding and an excellent heart', a man to whom 'kings might have confessed their inferiority'.[63] Even his dog Charron appears as a kind of noble savage. On the other hand, men of rank and power like St. Leon are cut off from the rest of the species since equality is 'the soul of all real and cordial society'.[64]

Godwin even gives an essay in political economy when St. Leon tries to stimulate the agriculture and industry of war-ravaged Hungary. At first he lays down a law to himself 'to commit the least practicable violence upon the genuine action of human society in pursuit of the means of subsistence'.[65] But he does not take his own advice. He sets himself up as a corn-dealer and architect, and by increasing the quantity of precious metals, he causes prices to rise. Famine and strikes follow, St. Leon fears for his personal safety, and then makes the disastrous mistake of calling in the occupying Turkish military government. From the failure of his economic intervention, St. Leon is forced to conclude that the man of wealth cannot replace the collective self-help of the people and that the cash-nexus is no substitute for the organic ties of local interests: 'I had no bonds of alliance but those which money afforded, the coarsest, the meanest, the least flattering, and the most brittle of those ligatures, that afford the semblance of uniting man with man.'[66]

With the failure of the French Revolution and the persecution of the English Jacobins, Godwin increasingly despaired of major social changes and looked to the family in a rural retreat as an immediate alternative to the postponed millennium. Godwin pictures St. Leon poor in wealth in his lakeside cottage in Constance, but rich in the confidence of every member of his family:

> I lived in the bosom of nature, surrounded with the luxuriance of its gifts, and the sublimity of its features, which the romantic elevation of my soul particularly fitted me to relish. In my domestic scene I beheld the golden age renewed, the simplicity of the pastoral life without its grossness, a situation remote from cities and courts, from traffic and hypocrisy, yet not unadorned with taste, imagination and knowledge. Never was a family more united in sentiments and affection.[67]

Coleridge, Wordsworth, and his sister Dorothy were reaching similar conclusions in the West Country, while Thelwall was retreating to a farm in South Wales.

The central theme of St. Leon is the Rousseauist one that riches and power cannot bring real and lasting contentment but that it is to be found in the simple, independent, and natural life. But Godwin does not recommend a return to nature or to some mythical past but a new age in which cultured individuals would live in small communities and work the land. Although she loves the sight of the peasants, Marguerite tells St. Leon that she would not be a peasant herself; she would put in a claim for the 'refinements and purifying of intellect, and the luxuries of uncostly, simple taste'.[68] Godwin's idea of progress thus combines a primitivist vision with a respect for the achievements of civilization.

St. Leon was published on 2 December 1799. The thousand copies of the first edition sold out immediately and a second one appeared on 3 February 1800. It not only boosted Godwin's flagging confidence, but earned the handsome sum of four hundred guineas from George Robinson. The Monthly Magazine declared that it had uneven literary merit and the Monthly Mirror complained of the absurd plot and its sickening Rousseauist sensibility.[69] Yet the Monthly Review praised the masterly drawing of St. Leon; the New London Review discovered much originality of thought and fervour of imagination; and the Critical Review felt that it evoked powers of invention and genius.[70] Even the conservative British Critic and the Anti-Jacobin Review were agreeably surprised, although both objected to some of the anti-Christian sentiments.[71] Nearly all appreciated the change in Godwin's view of the domestic affections. The general approval, however, did not prevent Edward Dubois from writing a satire, *St. Godwin: A Tale of the Sixteenth, Seventeenth and Eighteenth Century* (1800), by Count Reginald de St. Leon, which followed the plot in part and quoted the most extravagant lines.

Pirated editions of *St. Leon* appeared in Dublin in 1800, and in Alexandria, Virginia, in 1801 and 1802. It also inspired in America John Daly Burk's historical drama *Bethlem Gabor, Lord of Transylvania, or The Man-Hating Palatine* (1807). A German translation was published in Hamburg in 1800, while the French translation which appeared in Paris in 1799 was followed by another two in 1800.

Godwin's acquaintances were generally impressed. Ritson thought it 'excellent, a hundred times better than *Caleb Williams*'; Charlotte Smith was 'full of applause' and only Nicholson pronounced it 'a clear failure'.[72] Hazlitt declared *St. Leon* to be superior to Walter Scott's historical novels and hailed it as one of 'the most splendid and impressive works of the imagination which has appeared in our times'.[73] When Godwin in his old age told Byron that the effort of writing another novel would kill him, the poet is said to have replied: 'And what matter? We should have another St. Leon!'[74]

Coleridge told Godwin that it was 'of a better species than CW; because, though less impressive in a first reading, more acceptable in a second'.[75] He also made some jottings, possibly intended for a review. He objected to the occasional 'melodramatic exaggeration' and 'abominable' style, but found some passages 'very beautiful'. And while he felt the character of Bethlem Gabor was extravagant, he considered his friendship with St. Leon as 'sublime'.[76] He clearly read closely and it made him think that he and Southey could probably toss up a novel. It also marked the beginning of Coleridge's change of heart towards Godwin.

Holcroft informed Godwin that although his daughters Louisa and Fanny were delighted with Marguerite, they felt that the novel as a whole created less interest than *Caleb Williams*. For his part, Holcroft disliked the improbable incidents and the tendency to sermonize, but found Marguerite inimitable — 'knowing the model after which you drew, as often as I recollected it, my heart ached while I read' — and declared Bethlem Gabor to be 'wonderfully drawn'.[77] Anna Seward also found the story less interesting than *Caleb Williams*, but admired the 'striking and deep observations on human nature' and saw in them evidence that Godwin was moving in a Christian and conservative direction.[78]

The Holcrofts and Anna Seward were right. *St. Leon* was a bold undertaking, but Godwin was unable to capture again the unique combination of history, philosophy and fiction in *Caleb Williams*. There are still adventures of flight and pursuit but the coincidences tire and the new love theme remains static. The drama is gone, except in the episode with Bethlem Gabor. The organic unity of plot and character is absent, and Godwin relies too much for his effects on the Gothic apparatus of the supernatural, heroic and the picturesque. The imagery is more exuberant, and the style often inflated and at times downright bombastic.

Nevertheless, in *St. Leon* Godwin used Gothic paraphernalia to create another strange and powerful novel. It is moreover an important document in the history of Romanticism for it shows how the great rationalist philosopher of the English Enlightenment was succumbing with his contemporaries to the new cult of sensibility at the end of the eighteenth century.

# CHAPTER XIII

## *Reaction*

When Godwin told Harriet Lee in June 1798 that 'I believe no person who has so far run counter to the prejudices and sentiments of the world has ever been less a subject of obloquy', he was undoubtedly indulging in wishful thinking.[1] The excesses of the Terror in France, the wave of patriotism which followed Britain's declaration of war on the new Republic, and the persecution of the opposition at home, had all contributed to the wane of revolutionary hopes. By 1797 the L.C.S. had all but disbanded and even the resolute Thelwall was driven into retirement. The Jacobins, their fellow-travellers, and anyone else expressing opposition to Church and King were hounded by a virulent campaign of counter-propaganda. Indeed, Godwin wrote that down to the middle of the year 1797, he heard little else than the voice of commendation, but 'I was at length attacked from every side, and in a style which defied all moderation and decency. No vehicle was too mean, no language too coarse and insulting, by which to convey the venom of my adversaries.'[2]

The attack came in three principal forms: in abusive verse, in satirical novels, and in a series of lectures, sermons and pamphlets which contained more deliberate criticism. Taken together, they constituted a formidable and sweeping indictment and in 1801 Godwin was eventually forced to break his stoical silence and defend himself in his *Thoughts. Occasioned by the Perusal of Dr. Parr's Spital Sermon.*

In fact, the reaction against Godwin had begun earlier than he realized. As a result of his dispute with Thelwall an important faction of the practical reformers had turned against him. Place and the other Godwinian advocates of passive obedience and non-resistance had withdrawn from the L.C.S. in 1795. Meanwhile, Coleridge had attacked Godwin in his lectures in Bristol and in the following year offended many of his radical subscribers in *The Watchman* by his contemptuous treatment of the philosopher.

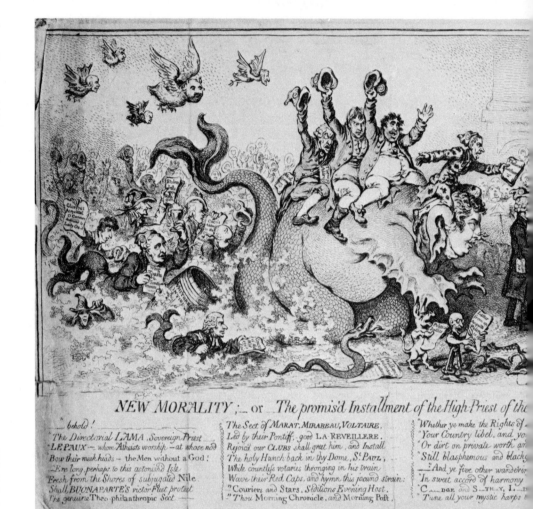

XX. 'New Morality', by James Gillray for the *Anti-Jacobin Magazine and Review* (1798).

Pub.d August 1.st 1798. by J.Wright N.o 169. Piccadilly, for the Anti Jacobin Magazine & Review

Js. Gilray, inv.t & fec.t

...ANTHROPES, with the Homage of Leviathan and his Suite.

"PR_TL_Y and W_F_LD, humble, holy men,   "And thou LEVIATHAN! on Ocean's brim;
"Give praises to his name with tongue and pen!   "Hugest of living things that sleep & swim;
"_TH_LW_L. and ye that Lecture as ye go,   "Thou in whose nose by BURKE'S gigantic hand
"And for your pains get Pelted, praise LE PAUX!   "The hook was fix'd to drag thee to the land
"Praise him each Jacobin, or Fool, or Knave,   "With ____, ____, and ____ in thy train,
"And your cropp'd heads in sign of worship wave!   "And W____ wallowing in the Yeasty main;
"— All creeping creatures, venomous and low,   "Still as ye snort, and puff, and spout, and blow,
"PAINE, W_LL_MS, G_DW_N, H_LC_FT, praise LEPAUX!   "In puffing, and in spouting, praise LEPAUX!"

Vide Anti Jacobin.

There had also been a slight skirmish in the *Cambridge Intelligencer* in 1795. A letter to the editor Benjamin Flower maintained that the ideas of *Political Justice* were so outrageous, so much worse than Paine's, that it must have been arranged by the ministry to deride the ideas of liberty and equality.[3] It was hastily answered by 'Philo Godwin' (Henry Crabb Robinson) who argued that despite its daring propositions, *Political Justice* had no compulsory element and was less dangerous than Paine's *Rights of Man* since it was abstract, expensive and impractical.[4] A friend of Robinson equally felt that Godwin was harmless in 1796:

> The present Government has nothing to fear from Godwinites, while they entertain such visionary ideas of approaching Perfection . . . He is still in a dream of Theory, but he does not *snore* loud enough to disturb the peace of his neighbours, or provoke any of Pitt's Watchmen to give him a tweak by the nose.[5]

The campaign of denigration really warmed up in the following two years. Godwin made a brief entrance as Mr. Vapour with Wollstonecraft as Miss Ardent in Elizabeth Hamilton's *Letters of a Hindoo Rajah* in 1796. In the following year, Isaac D'Israeli, the father of the future Prime Minister, attacked him in his satirical novel *Vaurien; or, Sketches of the Times*. Godwin is clearly Mr. Subtile, Holcroft probably Mr. Reverberator, and Thelwall Mr. Rant. Subtile is called the 'coldest-blooded metaphysician of the age' and in a summary of his work 'Prejudices Destroyed, or Paradoxes Proved', D'Israeli expounds Godwin's views on utility, gratitude, promises, property, punishment and perfectibility.[6] The chief criticism is aimed at Godwin's rationalism. 'Some of the most enlightened men', D'Israeli asserts, 'have been the tyrants of the world. Man has a heart influenced by the passions more frequently, than a head that combines ideas; and sensation is more potent than reason.'[7] Henry Crabb Robinson for one found the work 'well written & though false & unjust . . . highly amusing'.[8]

Ever since the publication of *Political Justice*, the *British Critic* had been calling Godwin dangerous and extravagant whenever one of his works appeared, but it was the *Anti-Jacobin*, founded in 1797 with a government subsidy, which now led the popular campaign against Godwin. In a putative letter from 'Mr. Higgins of St. Mary Axe', he was ridiculed as believing in, first, *'Whatever is, is WRONG'*, and secondly, the *'eternal and absolute PERFECTIBILITY OF MAN'*.[9] It set the tone for the next five years.

In a celebrated squib entitled the 'New Morality', Godwin, Paine and Holcroft were all called 'creeping creatures, venomous and low'.[10] Gillray caricatured him in an accompanying cartoon as a braying donkey, with *Political Justice* held in its hoofs. Out of a 'Cornucopia of Ignorance' topple works including *The Enquirer* and the *Memoirs* of Wollstonecraft. To make the message quite plain, Philanthropy is presented as a voracious woman encompassing a globe, treading on sheets of paper entitled 'Amor Patria' and the 'Ties of Nature', while Justice appears as an old hag with raised daggers and a pair of scales at her feet.

In September, George Canning, one of the editors of the renamed *Anti-Jacobin Review*, at least showed some knowledge of *Political Justice* in his ode to 'The Anarchists' (which also castigated Paine, Thelwall, Coleridge, Southey, Lloyd and Lamb), when he related:

But thou, O G-DW-N! meek and mild;
Speak thy metaphysic page:
Now it cheer'd a laggard age,
And bade new scenes of joy at distance hail;
When tyrant Kings shall be no more,
When human wants and wars shall fail,
And sleep and death shall quit the hallow'd shore.[11]

The *Anti-Jacobin Review* took every opportunity to recommend the anti-Godwinian verse and prose satires which poured from the presses from 1798 onwards.[12] Thomas James Mathias was highly commended for *The Shade of Alexander Pope on the Banks of the Thames* (1798). In the notes, he called Godwin's memoirs of his wife 'a convenient Manual of speculative debauchery', and in the poem itself declared:

Mark now, where bold, with fronts metallick shine
*William* and *Mary* on one common coin:
Full freedom to the genial bed restore,
And prove whate'er Vanini prov'd before.
Fierce passion's slave, she veer'd with every gust,
Love, Rights, and Wrongs, Philosophy, and Lust:
But some more wise, in metaphysick air,
Weigh the man's wits against the Lady's hair.[13]

Mathias further expressed his love of legitimacy in his vastly popular *Pursuits of Literature*, which contained the lines:

Godwin's dry page no statesman e'er believ'd,
Though fiction aids, what sophistry conceiv'd
Genius may droop o'er Falkland's funeral cry;
No patriot weeps when gifted villains die.[14]

In his extensive notes, he attacked *Political Justice* for its 'cold blooded indifference to all the mild, pious, and honourable feelings of our common nature', described *The Enquirer* as 'an alarum of nonsense', only to conclude that 'I really am fatigued with this man.'[15] Thomas Dutton tried to come to Godwin's defence in his satirical poem *The Literary Census* (1798) but to little effect.[16]

Charles Lloyd, a Godwinian apostate and former member of the Coleridge circle, was also praised by the *Anti-Jacobin Review* for his *Lines suggested by the Fast* (1799). Godwin, he asserts, is a 'spirit evil and foul' who has hatched an 'obstinate sedition/From pamper'd lust and infidel despair'.[17] Lloyd also included an extract from Charles Lamb's poem 'Living without God' (without a title but undoubtedly with the poet's permission) which was intended as 'a satire on the Godwinian jargon':

> Some braver spirits of the *modern sort*
> Affect a Godhead nearer; these talk loud
> Of mind and independent intellect;
> And energies omnipotent in man;
> And man, of his own fate, Artificer,
> Yea, of his own life, Lord![18]

The most scurrilous abuse however appeared in C. Kirkpatrick Sharpe's Spenserian poem entitled *The Vision of Liberty*. It was printed anonymously in the *Anti-Jacobin Review* in August 1801, which attacked all the leading radical intellectuals in turn:

> Then saw I mounted on a braying ass
> William and Mary, sooth, a couple jolly;
> Who married, note ye how it came to pass,
> Although each held that marriage was but folly? —
> And she of curses would discharge a volley
> If the ass stumbled, leaping pales or ditches:
> Her husband, sans culottes, was melancholy,
> For Mary verily would wear the breeches —
> God help poor silly men from such usurping b—————s.

> William hath penn'd a waggon-load of stuff,
> And Mary's life at last he needs must write,
> Thinking her whoredoms were not known enough,
> Till fairly printed off in black and white. —
> With wondrous glee and pride, this simple wight
> Her brothel feats of wantonness sets down,

Being her spouse, he tells, with huge delight,
How oft she cuckolded the silly clown,
And lent, O lovely piece! herself to half the town.[19]

If the verse was bad and forgettable, much of the prose satire which
attacked Godwin was worse. John Ferriar in 1798 set the pattern by his
*Dialogue in the Shades* between the Godwinian Neodidactus and the Burkean Lucian. With ample quotations from Godwin's works in the footnotes,
Neodidactus expounds his philosophy, only to be answered by Lucian that
it must be 'destructive of every estimable quality in his [man's] breast, and
must drive him again into savage solitude'.[20]

At the same time, Charles Lloyd published his novel *Edmund Oliver*. It
contained an unflattering portrait of Coleridge but was principally
intended to refute Godwin's attitude to universal benevolence and to
marriage. When the passionate Gertrude decides to dispense with the
marriage tie, her lover abandons her and she dies in childbirth. On the
other hand, Edmund, her spurned fiancé, rejects the advice of a Godwinian
friend to use his inherited fortune as a trust, and argues that the 'general
laws of Christianity produce the greatest possible happiness'.[21] When he
marries at the end of the novel, he is convinced that 'domestic relations are
the necessary and indispensable means of leading the soul to general
benevolence'.[22] Lloyd published soon afterwards a *Letter to the Anti-Jacobin
Reviewers* (who still found traces of radicalism in his novel) emphasizing that
his express purpose was to disparage the 'spurious progeny' of the Godwinian school.[23]

In the same year, Sophia King's *Waldorf; or, The Dangers of Philosophy* was
published. Waldorf, a true Godwinian, bases his principles on reason alone.
He mocks the ties of marriage and religion and converts the heroine to free
love.[24] After wrecking the lives of three women, however, he repents,
becomes a recluse in a forest, and eventually shoots himself. The plot was to
become a model for many pious female novelists.

Jane West drew on it in 1799 in her *Tale of the Times*. The villain
Fitzosborne, who witnesses the French Revolution, seduces the fair Geraldine by using Godwin's arguments against marriage and gratitude. Predictably, Geraldine is driven to the refuge of a premature grave while Fitzosborne commits suicide in prison while awaiting execution during the reign
of Terror in France.

A letter to the editor of Robert Bisset's *Historical, Biographical, Literary
and Scientific Magazine* in 1799, also related the adventures of Timothy
Newlight, a votary of Godwin's philosophy. Having read at Hackney Dissenting college *Political Justice* (which says 'whatever has been established is
bad'), Newlight uses it to justify a career of seduction and ends up as a

highwayman preying on his own uncle.[25]

George Walker, a London publisher who had already slavishly copied the plot of *Caleb Williams* in his own novel *Theodore Cyphon* (1796), produced a powerful and witty indictment in *The Vagabond* (1799). Stupeo, a vivid satirical portrait of Godwin, turns his benign benevolence into a ruthless creed of self-assertion: 'The great mass of mankind are fools, and no better than the callous sod on which we tread.'[26] *Political Justice* is paraphrased and quoted, with all its central doctrines deliberately misinterpreted. Gaming, Stupeo discovers, is a good way of equalizing property; since gratitude is wrong, he can seduce the wife of his protector; and having rejected domestic affections, there is no need to grieve when he shoots his mother whilst robbing a coach. To demonstrate his thesis, Walker transports his characters to a utopian republic in America based on the Godwinian principles of equality and political justice; inevitably, chaos reigns. It all goes to prove that man is worse than the 'savage hyena of the desert' and needs coercion and strong laws to restrain him.[27]

Mary Anne Burges was almost as specific in her satire of Godwin's ideas in her popular *The Progress of the Pilgrim of Good-Intent, in Jacobinical Times* (1800). Modelled on Bunyan, the allegory satirizes lamely the reign of reason and freedom. It ridicules in passing the unmistakeably Godwinian tenets of the abolition of age, sickness and death, the faults of all institutions, the weakness of gratitude, and the vanity of marriage.[28]

In the same year appeared the most consistently anti-Godwinian satire — *St. Godwin: A Tale of the Sixteenth, Seventeenth and Eighteenth Century* by Count Reginald de St. Leon (i.e. Edward Dubois). The work is based in part on the plot of *St. Leon,* but Dubois quotes the most absurd lines and adds his own comments to make a mockery of Godwin's opinions. When, for example, St. Godwin abandons his children, he asserts that it is 'the *noblest and most virtuous effort of my life*!!'[29] Although he submits to the fraud of marriage with Pandora because of the divinity of necessity, it does not change his view that 'women, like air, were by nature intended as a common advantage'.[30] After a series of disastrous adventures, Dubois locks St. Godwin up in the Bastille from 1612 to 1789. When he is released he studies Jacobinism and composes *Political Justice,*

in which, in the *'lawlessness* of my imagination,' with a terrible pother about what nobody could understand; namely; The *absoluteness of necessity*, the *perfectibility of man*, and *the omnipotence of truth*, I opposed all political and moral order, and endeavoured to overturn every system that time and experience had sanctioned and approved.[31]

Finally, he turns to fiction; the plan succeeded for a time, but at last St.

Godwin laments 'they burlesqued my works, and made me look a fool!'[32]

Bisset had already declared in his *Life of Edmund Burke* (1798) that Paine, Holcroft and Godwin had established 'three great banks of anarchy and infidelity'.[33] He returned to the attack in his novel *Douglas; or, The Highlander* (1800). His aim was to show that the 'steady pursuit and attainment' of private good most effectively promote the public welfare.[34] The plot recalls the tales of King and West. Godwin appears as Subtlewould and Holcroft, who 'learns' all his books from the philosopher, as one Tom Croft.[35] Vagabond's friend Sidney adopts the teachings of Wollstonecraft and Godwin, practises free love, and takes no responsibility for his illegitimate child.[36] It all ends in disaster and Vagabond can only conclude that Godwin's theory 'seems to me fit only for Bedlam' and when practised 'naturally leads to the gallows'.[37] It was a popular message and the novel went through three editions in as many years.

Equally popular but more intelligent was Hamilton's *Memoirs of Modern Philosophers* which appeared in the following year. The work made a frontal attack on the New Philosophy. Bridgetina is seduced by a reading of *Political Justice* at the age of five, while Vallaton offers a parody of its teaching: he rejects filial duty, gratitude and marriage, believes in necessity, and admires the guillotine. At one stage, Bridgetina decides to emigrate with the philosophers Myope and Glib (Godwin and Holcroft) but the Godwinian plan for a utopian colony is never realized.[38] As for Vallaton, after seducing the pure Julia, he receives his just deserts when he dies on the scaffold. At the end, Bridgetina's bemused mother is compelled to ask who is this 'General Utility' whose name is forever in her daughter's mouth:

> 'General Utility, my dear Madam', said Dr. Orwell, smiling, 'is an ideal personage, a sort of Will o' the wisp, whom some people go a great way out of the road to find, but still see him shining in some distant and unbeaten track; while, if they would keep at home, and look for him in the plain path of christian duty, they would never miss their aim.[39]

The work was translated into French and contributed to Godwin's notoriety abroad.

Two other novels, all on the dangers of rejecting the marriage tie, appeared in 1801. In the anonymous *Dorothea; or, A Ray of New Light*, the protagonists Dorothea Melville and Williams recall the names of Emily Melville and Caleb Williams in Godwin's most famous novel. The heroine is educated by a Godwinian governess but at the age of sixteen rejects her guidance as a form of despotism. For his part, when the unscrupulous Williams abandons his children and runs off with his wife's property, he exclaims:

Justice, immutable and unerring justice lifts me above all selfish ties and considerations: I am neither father, husband, or brother to any individual! My children are posterity in the aggregate! I am wedded only to universal philanthropy, and my brother is man![40]

It comes as no surprise that he is eventually stabbed by one of his victims while Dorothea is reconciled to the duties of a submissive wife.

Charles Lucas next made every attempt to denounce Godwin's teaching in *The Infernal Quixote* (1801) by referring constantly to his works in his footnotes. The central character Marauder excuses his vices by appealing to necessity, rejects the ties of friendship and gratitude, persuades Emily to forego marriage, and denounces the professions, not however for the sake of universal benevolence, but for 'HIS OWN INTEREST'.[41] Predictably, in the end Marauder goes insane and commits suicide, the 'wretched victim of Despair'.[42]

The anti-Godwinian verse and prose published between 1796 and 1801 clearly represent the reaction of the ruling class against Godwin's hopes for moral regeneration and social reform. The most bitter invective was reserved for his doctrine of universal benevolence which proscribed marriage and the domestic affections. If practised it would, the novels try to demonstrate, inaugurate an era of debauchery in which its adherents would inevitably be led to ostracism, madness or suicide. The Machiavellian sophist, they imply, can too easily make the doctrine into an excuse for ruthless egoism.

Godwin refused to discuss 'the vulgar contumelies of the author of the Pursuits of Literature, novels of buffonery and scandal to the amount of half a score, and British Critics, Anti-Jacobin Newspapers, and Anti-Jacobin Magazines without number'.[43] He had no choice. The extent and the bitterness of the attack reflect just how dangerous an influence Godwin was considered to be. To be a disciple of Godwin was, according to Jane Austen, to be held unavoidably 'raffish'.[44] The scurrilous counter-propaganda was however successful, and contributed more than anything else to make most people in polite society consider Godwin, as De Quincey put it, 'with the same alienation and horror as of a ghoul, or a bloodless vampyre'.[45]

Godwin felt differently about some of the more serious criticisms of his philosophy offered by divines and scholars. The first of two pamphlets which ushered in what Godwin called the 'tremendous war against philanthropy' was Thomas Green's *Examination of the Leading Principle of the New System of Morals*, published anonymously early in 1798.[46]

Green's work is the most able and serious reply to *Political Justice*. He takes Godwin as the leading and most consistent exponent of utility, but he criticizes the principle since it tends to extinguish those natural feelings 'ordained by Providence' and to dispose the mind either to a 'low and sordid selfishness' or to 'wild, daring, experimental projects of reform'.[47] Godwin's version of the principle of utility moreover is delusive and impracticable: firstly, because it is a law of nature that 'we proceed from personal affection to general regard'; and secondly, because it upsets traditional morality 'without furnishing any discoverable plan of action'.[48] Above all, it fails to recognize that 'our moral sentiments are original principles of action; and cannot therefore, as such, be derived from reason'.[49]

It was a telling criticism of the dangers of utilitarianism and ethical rationalism, but Godwin chose not to answer Green directly. He was also silent about the other pamphlet which appeared in 1798. In *Modern Philosophy and Barbarism*, William Proby made a direct comparison between the theory of Godwin and the practice of Lycurgus in Sparta, and attempted to demonstrate the injurious consequences which would result if the principles of modern philosophy were carried into practice. Both systems advocate the sacrifice of every sympathy resulting from man's 'feelings and sensibility to the general good'; both call for the abolition of wealth and the 'consequent equality of condition'; and both support the 'annihilation of an exclusive sexual intercourse'.[50]

Even their differences are superficial, Proby argued, and are merely due to dissimilar historical circumstances. Godwin looks to the omnipotence of mind over matter to replace slavery, and instead of physical coercion, he countenances 'a force of the most despotic nature, the tyranny of public opinion and public censure'.[51] In fact, duplicity pervades the whole of Godwin's system:

> It pretends to increase the powers of man, and enlarge his sphere of action, even unto universal benevolence, and narrows them to selfishness. It appears under the disguise of enlightened philosophy, whilst gloomy superstition and organized barbarism lurk beneath, and soon display themselves in all their horrors.[52]

Although somewhat exaggerated, Proby's criticism was at least intelligent and well-argued.

The same cannot be said of George Hutton who, in a dull sermon preached in September 1798, attacked Godwin's philosophy of necessity for confounding 'all distinction of virtue and vice'.[53] George Gleig also thundered from his pulpit two months later against those false teachers who 'with universal benevolence constantly in their mouths, are labouring to involve this country in all that confusion, uproar, and massacre, which have converted the politest people of Europe into something more savage than a herd of wild beasts'.[54] Robert Fellowes, in his pamphlet *A Picture of Christian Philosophy* (1798), was a little more rational. He contrasts the Christian temper with Godwin's system in order to show that while Christianity inspires universal benevolence it takes 'individual sympathies' as its foundation.[55] Like Green, he argues that Godwin's rule of the general good is 'a cold abstraction, intricate and embarrassing', which must be always difficult to understand, and on which it can seldom be safe to act.[56]

Godwin paid no attention to these ministers in his *Thoughts* but he was forced to answer his erstwhile friend James Mackintosh when he viciously and unexpectedly attacked him in his 'Lectures on the Law of Nature and Nations', delivered in Lincoln's Inn between February and June 1799. Mackintosh had helped Godwin clarify his principles during the composition of *Political Justice*, and they had remained on friendly terms ever since. But his opinions had been slowly changing since *Vindiciae Gallicae*, and when he met Burke late in 1796 he eagerly took up his challenge to become a 'faithful knight' and to destroy the exponents of the New Philosophy — 'the brood of that putrid carcass, that mother of all evil, the French Revolution'.[57]

Mackintosh presented his case in his preliminary *Discourse* to his lectures, and made no attempt to restrain himself. To begin with, he decries the 'multitude of superficial and most mischievous sciolists' who have given birth to a 'brood of abominable and pestilential paradoxes'.[58] Next, he focuses on the need to defend the great institutions of property and marriage: 'on them rests the whole order of civil life'.[59] Finally, he advocates the very theory of complex government whose existence he had denied in *Vindiciae Gallicae*.

Godwin had discussed Burke with Mackintosh on 16 January 1797 and continued to see him regularly during the next two years. He must have known of Mackintosh's changing opinions, but when he read the copy of the *Discourse* which Mackintosh sent him, he was flabbergasted by the violence of his apostasy and immediately demanded an explanation for being treated like a 'highwayman or an assassin'.[60] Mackintosh replied that he was not referring to Godwin in particular, and that in his lectures he intended to apply epithets to doctrines and not to men. But although he had always esteemed his 'acuteness and benevolence', he now admitted that Godwin had made speculative mistakes of 'the most dangerous tendency'.[61] In reply, Godwin welcomed the opportunity of a public discussion in which they would treat each other with a 'uniform liberality & respect', but still insisted that the criterion of accepting or rejecting a doctrine was not its practical effects but its truth or falsehood.[62]

When Mackintosh began his series of lectures, however, Godwin was sorely disappointed. It was his unequivocal intention, Mackintosh wrote to a friend, to 'abhor, abjure and forever renounce' the French Revolution, 'that conspiracy against God and man, the greatest scourge of the world, and the chief stain upon human annals'.[63] In his lecture notes, he combined the arguments of Proby and Green to declare that the New Philosophy is nothing less than 'Dogmatical, boastful, heedless of everything but its own short-sighted views, and intoxicated with the perpetual and exclusive contemplation of its own system of disorder, and demonstrations of insanity'.[64] But that was not all, for according to Godwin, Mackintosh three times a week expressed his 'contempt and abhorrence' of his person and his writings and represented him as 'a wretch, who only wanted the power, in order to improve himself as infernal as Robespierre'.[65]

Godwin did not attend the first lecture on 13 February but was present on the 20th and 23rd and on 2 March, and would have attended more if he and the other hearers had not felt that he was the object of Mackintosh's strictures. 'Poor Godwin', Hazlitt wrote, 'who had come, in the *bonhomie* and candour of his nature, to hear what new light had broken in upon his old friend, was obliged to quit the field, and slank away after an exulting taunt thrown out at "such fanciful chimeras as a golden mountain or a perfect man".'[66] Godwin complained to Samuel Parr that Mackintosh had loaded indiscriminately the writers of the New Philosophy with every epithet of contempt — 'absurdity, frenzy, idiotism, deceit, ambition, and every murderous propensity dance through the mazes of his glittering periods' — in order to procure them 'either to be torn in pieces by the mob, or hanged up by the government'.[67]

Godwin made the same point in his *Thoughts*, complaining that such lectures did not allow an opponent to reply and only incensed human passions. As he had made clear in his earlier dispute with Thelwall, political lectures are not the appropriate means of enlightening the people, and the intellectual elite have a responsibility to be moderate and clear in their language.[68]

Up to a hundred and fifty people attended the lectures, many of them lawyers, M.P.s, men of letters, and country gentlemen. Canning, Romilly and Pitt were there. Amongst Godwin's old disciples, Crabb Robinson was amused, Parr rapturous, and Basil Montagu converted. Others were not so impressed. Hazlitt felt the tendency of the lectures was 'to unsettle every principle of reason or of common sense'; Coleridge called them the 'Steam of an Excrement'; Lamb likened Mackintosh to Judas, 'an apostate black', in one of his more memorable epigrams.[69] In the autumn of 1800, Coleridge also tried to reassure Godwin that the fact that Mackintosh and his followers had the present 'flow' of opinion was greatly in his favour, for mankind at present are *gross* reasoners — they reason in a perpetual *antithesis*. Mackintosh is an oracle, & Godwin therefore a Fool . . . when he publishes, depend on it, it will all be over with him & then the minds of men will incline strongly in favor of those who would point out in intellectual perceptions a source of moral progressiveness.[70]

But this was over-optimistic. Mackintosh never published his lectures. As Hazlitt recalled, 'The Modern Philosophy, counterscarp, outworks, citadel, and all, fell without a blow by "the whiff and wind of his fell *doctrine*," as if it had been a pack of cards.'[71] Even Mackintosh was surprised by his success; he was only inconvenienced by 'a slight rumour or two, soon dispelled — a buzz among some very obscure partisans; — the attacks of the more extravagant republicans, and of the small sect of Godwinians'.[72] After Mackintosh repeated his lectures in the spring of 1800, Godwin acknowledged to Samuel Parr that it had become 'a sort of fashion with a large party to join in the cry against me'.[73]

A close friend of Mackintosh's, the Dissenting minister Robert Hall, also attacked Godwin in November 1799 in his widely popular sermon *Modern Infidelity considered with Respect to its Influence on Society*. Robert Hall had for long been a bitter opponent of Godwin; whenever he heard any incident of 'unnatural depravity or abandoned profligacy' mentioned, he would exclaim: 'I could not have supposed any man capable of such an action, except Godwin . . .'.[74] On learning that Crabb Robinson had defended Godwin's doctrine of universal benevolence at the Royston Book Club, he even tried to prevent a member of his congregation in Bury from entertaining him. When Crabb Robinson protested, Hall replied furiously that Godwin's speculations are 'big with inculculable mischief. They confound all the duties and perplex all the relations of human life.'[75]

In his sermon, Hall declared that it was the object of modern sceptics 'to obliterate the sense of Deity, of moral sanctions, and a future world, and by these means to prepare the way for the total subversion of every institution, both social and religious, which men have been hitherto accustomed to revere'.[76] To limit, moreover, virtue to an attachment to the general good would lead to the 'chilling frost of universal indifference' and the 'violation of every duty, and the perpetration of every crime'.[77] In his *Thoughts*, Godwin did not deign to reply to Hall directly and only commented that in his 'much vaunted' sermon 'every notion of toleration or decorum was treated with infuriated contempt'.[78]

It was followed in 1800 by dull and vicious attacks on Godwin and the New Philosophy in John Bowles's *Reflections on the Political and Moral State of Society* and in the ex-radical William Reid's *The Rise and Dissolution of the Infidel Societies in this Metropolis*.[79] In March, the Scottish divine Charles

Findlater also attacked the doctrines of liberty and equality which if adopted would only reduce men to the 'original state of savagism'.[80] In an appendix to the published version, he put down Godwin's 'boundless extravagance' to the unbalancing effect of the French Revolution.[81]

It was Dr. Samuel Parr's *Spital Sermon* in April 1800 which most upset Godwin. The 'Whig Dr. Johnson' had remained a close friend since 1794 and had even told Basil Montagu during their visit to his house at Hatton in 1797 that he considered Godwin 'more skilful in moral science than any man now living'.[82] In the same year, he had attended the trial of John Binns, a leader of the L.C.S., and was felt to be a powerful friend of reform.

The first sign Godwin had of his coolness was when he received no reply to a presentation copy of his novel *St. Leon*. Godwin therefore wrote to Parr early in 1800 for an explanation. Having heard that Parr had been seeing a great deal of Mackintosh, he presumed that he had 'settled accounts with him as to your opinion of his political lectures'.[83] He had, but not in the way Godwin expected. In fact they had planned their attack on Godwin and the New Philosophy together; Parr had earlier written to Mackintosh: 'I have something to tell you about the simplification of principles, or rather the simpleton-jargon about R-r-r-eason and let us do the business well.'[84]

Parr chose the annual *Spital Sermon* which was delivered before the Lord Mayor and other dignitaries on Easter Tuesday, 15 April, at Christ Church, Newgate Street, for his onslaught. His criticisms were by now commonplace, but virulent and effective for all that. His aim was to destroy the 'philanthropic system' which had been developed from 'certain romantic and even pernicious notions' in France and was accompanied by a 'long and portentous train of evils'.[85] Benevolence, Parr asserts, is best achieved in a narrow compass since men are incapable of doing good to all men: according to the law of association, the concern for oneself must precede that of others.

But Parr did not restrict himself to philosophical disquisition. Although Godwin is not named, he is clearly intended in the description of 'the capacious mind of a modern sage, who is accustomed to be rapt in beatific visions of universal benevolence' and uses his ideas as cloaks 'for insensibility where other men feel'.[86] In his notes, which swelled the sermon four times its original size, Parr specifically criticizes Godwin for misinterpreting Jonathan Edwards on benevolence, and warmly recommends Green's strictures of his utilitarianism.[87] He concludes by asserting that the advocates of the New Philosophy 'perplex the understanding in a dark and barren wilderness of metaphysics, and they cramp the affections by confused representations of their contrariety to the dictates of reason, perfected by a long series of triumphs over education and custom'.[88]

It was a formidable catalogue of crimes from an old and respected friend, but as Sydney Smith remarked in a witty review, Parr was 'certainly more remarkable for his learning, than his originality'.[89] While Smith defended Godwin, the Scottish philosopher Dugald Stewart wrote to thank Parr for his 'peculiarly seasonable' strictures since he knew no other book than *Political Justice* which had done so much mischief among half-informed readers.[90]

Godwin was understandably dismayed. Mackintosh was repeating his lectures in which he represented him three times a week as a 'wretch unworthy to live', and now Parr had joined the 'pack' against him. He therefore wrote to his erstwhile friend for an explanation of the crimes of which he was chargeable in 1800 but of which he had not been guilty six years earlier when Parr had sought his acquaintance with 'so much kindness and zeal'.[91] He also pointed out the revision of his doctrine of universal benevolence in *St. Leon*.

Five days later, Parr replied. He explained that he had laid aside and then lost Godwin's first letter about Mackintosh's lectures because he did not expect to find the contents agreeable. As for his novel, he had only looked at the preface, and on hearing an account of its contents from his wife, felt no desire to read any further. He then traced his change of mind to a reading of *The Enquirer*, where Godwin's criticisms of Jesus Christ reminded him of the 'impious effusions of Mr. Voltaire'. He had also been shocked like 'all wise and good men' by his memoirs of his wife, horrified by the dreadful effects of his opinions on two or three young men of virtue and talent, and dismayed by the 'eagerness and perseverance' with which he employed every kind of vehicle to convey his principles to all classes of readers.[92] The letter marked the end of their friendship. Parr requested Godwin not to trouble to write or to visit him and six months later returned his copy of *St. Leon* with the icy formality of the third person.[93]

What could Godwin do? He contented himself with making lengthy notes on Parr's letter and their relationship in case it was published.[94] He also draughted but did not finish a letter to Parr in which he observed:

> If I could ever be prevailed upon to present to the public the luxuriant but short-lived vegetation of your professions of regard, as they now lie by me in my closet, contrasted with the expressions of this letter, and the frivolous reasons by which they are attempted to be supported, your character would be placed in a light in which it was never yet the lot of a human being to be exhibited.[95]

He felt completely betrayed.

In his *Thoughts*, Godwin complained of the 'gall, intolerance and contempt' expressed in Parr's *Spital Sermon*, but deliberately avoided following his example. Instead, he restricted himself to a clarification of his own view of benevolence. After quoting from his preface to *St. Leon*, he adds to the original statement in *Political Justice*:

> I would now say that, ' in the generality of cases,' not only the external action, but the motive, ought to be nearly the same as in the commonly received cases of morality; that I ought not only, 'in ordinary cases, to provide for my wife and children, my brothers and relations, before I provide for strangers, p.132,' but that it would be well that my doing so, should arise from the operation of those private and domestic affections, by which through all ages of the world the conduct of mankind has been excited and directed.[96]

At the same time, in a discussion of justice, Godwin defends his notorious example of Fénelon and his valet. The criterion of virtue is still 'utility, or justice, or, more periphrastically, the production of the greatest general good, the greatest public sum of pleasurable sensation'.[97] We may be moved to act by our affections, but it is still reason which judges their worth and keeps them in bounds: 'I must take care not so to love, or so to obey my love to my parent or child, as to intrench upon an important and paramount public good.'[98] In fact, Godwin goes on to argue that although he stresses the criterion of virtue and Parr the importance of the motive, they share the same utilitarian creed. Christ, moreover, was one of the 'most conspicuous advocates' of the doctrine of universal benevolence.[99]

Godwin treated much more seriously the criticism of his views made by the Reverend Thomas Malthus in his *Essay on the Principle of Population*, which appeared anonymously in the summer of 1798. The essay originated in a discussion of the essay on 'Avarice and Profusion' in *The Enquirer* which Malthus had with his Godwinian father, but it grew to take in the arguments of *Political Justice* as well as those of other advocates of the perfectibility of man.

In fact, a third of Malthus's essay was devoted to a refutation of Godwin's philosophy. While he was undoubtedly impressed by the 'most beautiful and engaging' picture of his ideal society, he proclaimed that the vices and miseries of mankind do not originate in human institutions which are 'mere feathers that float on the surface' but in 'the fixed and unalterable laws of nature'.[100] These laws are 'First, That food is necessary to the existence of man. Secondly, That the passion between the sexes is necessary and will remain nearly in its present state.'[101] Since population increases in a geometrical ratio and subsistence only in an arithmetical one, there is a natural tendency for population to outgrow food supply unless necessity in the form of vice and misery operates as a check. If Godwin's system of equality were to be introduced, the pressure of population would reduce it within thirty years to the present form of society, that is, one 'divided into a class of proprietors, and a class of labourers, and with self-love as the main spring of the great machine'.[102]

Malthus was not content to leave it at that. In four more chapters he systematically attempted to destroy the foundations of Godwin's theory of progress. In the first place, he argues that although improved reason will always tend to prevent the abuse of sensual pleasures, it by no means follows that it will extinguish them. Secondly, great intellectual exertion is more likely to shorten rather than prolong life. Thirdly, while the voluntary actions of men may originate in their opinions, the passions will always disturb the decisions of the understanding. Finally, Malthus accepts the argument of the essay 'Of Avarice and Profusion' that the frugal man is preferable to the spendthrift, not, however, because he avoids oppressing mankind with unnecessary labour, but because he can accumulate money in order to maintain labour in the production of useful commodities. As for Godwin's scheme of voluntary communism, it would only encourage idleness, vice and dependence. In the great sea of political discovery, Malthus concludes, 'Reason would teach us to expect no other than winds perpetually adverse, constant but fruitless toil, frequent shipwreck, and certain misery.'[103]

It was clearly an important reply. Godwin began reading Malthus's *Essay* on 5 August 1798 and invited him to breakfast ten days later. Unfortunately, the letter Godwin wrote soon after their first meeting is lost but it seems likely that he counter-attacked with his doctrine of moral restraint or prudence as a means to check population. Malthus replied on 20 August, however, that the foresight of difficulties which prudence demands could equally result in 'such a competition as would destroy all chance of an equal division of the necessary labour of society'. Great improvements might take place in the state of society but he still could not see how the present form or system could be radically changed 'without a danger of relapsing again into barbarism'.[104]

Malthus's letter was extremely cordial and he welcomed the opportunity of hearing Godwin's response. They first met on 2 December 1800, when they were guests at their mutual publisher, Joseph Johnson. They saw each other again on 7 December 1800 and 2 January and 4 April 1801. They still remained on good terms. Indeed, when Godwin came to write his *Thoughts*, he expressed his 'unfeigned approbation and respect' for Malthus and maintained that he had made 'as unquestionable an addition to the theory of political economy, as any writer for a century past'.[105]

Godwin chose in the pamphlet to focus primarily on the principle of population as a threat to his theory of progress. He is ready to admit

Malthus's ratios in their full extent and even accepts that in all old-settled countries population is always in some degree in excess of the means of subsistence. It is Malthus's conclusions that he repels. Vice and misery are not the only checks to population. As in the third edition of *Political Justice*, he mentions abortion and the exposure of children, adding that he would rather see a child 'perish in the first hour of its existence, than that a man should spend seventy years of life in a state of misery and vice'.[106] In their place, however, he would prefer the powerful check of 'virtue, prudence or pride' which prevents early marriage and only operates less in the lower classes because of the 'oppression under which they groan'.[107]

Godwin decided to go no further in his criticism of his opponents in his *Thoughts*. In general, his tone was calm, polite, dignified and sincere. He was even charitable to the apostates of the French Revolution, recognizing that truth was not as omnipotent as he had hoped: 'Our creed is, ninety-nine times in a hundred, the pure growth of our temper and social feelings.'[108] Yet despite the fact that the tenets of Jacobinism were held in almost universal odium and that even the 'starving labourer in the alehouse' had become a champion of aristocracy, Godwin did not despair.[109] On the other side of the Channel, he saw in Buonaparte an 'auspicious and benefi-cent genius' and was confident that 'the future government of France will be popular, and her people free'.[110] Indeed, he still held firm to his belief in perfectibility and concluded that 'what the heart of man is able to conceive, the hand of man is strong enough to perform'.[111]

Godwin clearly felt his *Thoughts* clarified rather than altered the central doctrines of *Political Justice*. In a note dated June 1801, he recorded his will that in any future editions of his *magnum opus* the pamphlet should be renamed 'Defence of the Enquiry concerning Political Justice' and inserted after the prefaces, not so much 'to perpetuate the fugitive and obscure controversies which have been excited on the subject, as because it contains certain essential explanations and elucidations with respect to the work itself'.[112]

Godwin's pamphlet had a mixed reception. Southey was pleased with it except for the 'loathsome cursed passage' on infanticide, and felt Godwin was 'a good creature — brimfull of benevolence — as kind hearted as a child would wish'.[113] Coleridge wrote in the margin of his copy against Godwin's account of the reaction against him:

I remember few pages in ancient or modern authors that contain more just philosophy in appropriate, chaste & beautiful diction than the five following pages. They reflect great honour on Godwin's Head and Heart. Tho' I did it only in the Zenith of his Reputation, yet I feel remorse *ever* to have spoken unkindly of such a man. S.T.C.[114]

He also told Godwin 'I never remember to have read a pamphlet with warmer feelings of sympathy & respect.'[115] It struck him, however, that both in his *Thoughts* and in the second edition of *Political Justice*, Godwin's retractions had been more injudicious than the assertions or dogmas retracted, adding, 'To the World it would appear a Paradox to say, that you are all too persuadible a man; but you yourself know it to be the truth.'[116]

The reviewers were less fulsome. Even so the *Monthly Mirror* and the *Monthly Review* gave a balanced account and praised the vigour of his intellect, as did Sydney Smith in the *Edinburgh Review*.[117] The *Monthly Magazine* regretted the weakness of his defence but felt that just as *Political Justice* had been once overvalued, it was now undervalued.[118] Not surprisingly, the *Anti-Jacobin Review* spoke of Godwin's absurd ideas and poor style while the *British Critic* suggested the fate of Babeuf for him.[119] There was a slight ripple when Godwin sent a letter to the *Monthly Magazine* in order to refute a correspondent's charge of infanticide.[120] Although he claimed that it would never be necessary in an improved society, the correspondent was not satisfied and the accusation stuck in the public mind.[121]

Malthus continued to see Godwin after the publication of his *Thoughts*. He called on him on 17 March 1802 and they were both guests at Johnson's on 17 October. In the following year, Godwin met Malthus on 19 January and 2 February, and they were again at Johnson's on 12 May. In the greatly revised second edition of his *Essay on the Principle of Population* which appeared towards the end of 1803, Malthus incorporated Godwin's idea of moral restraint as a preventive check, but still maintained that the principle of population 'essentially alters the foundation of political justice'.[122] In a small chapter replying to Godwin's *Thoughts*, he argued again that benevolence is an inadequate motive to action and that the goal of cultivated equality is chimerical.

Despite the extent of his revisions and the clarity of his arguments, Godwin's *Thoughts* failed to stem the tide of abuse and ridicule. In 1802, the familiar 'Godwinian' themes of the absurdity of all laws, the coming empire of reason, the vice of filial duty, and the infamy of patriotism were all pilloried in the anonymous Eastern tale *Massouf; or, The Philosophy of the Day*.[123] An Oxford clergyman Philip Smyth also issued an anonymous book of poems entitled *Rhyme and Reason* which included one on 'The Modern Philosopher':

Tho' men of no minds call me madman and oaf,
Yet my friends all declare me un grand philosophe;
Religion I hate — for I hate all restraint,
And whatever I've been, I'm no longer a saint . . .
Should my liberal notions e'er meet with a stop,

And my lungs be clear'd up by that sophist — a *Drop*,
I still would maintain that my exit, forsooth,
Was 'political justice' contending with truth.[124]

The publishers were clearly more interested in the political orthodoxy of
the good clergyman than in his poetic genius.

The Dissenting minister Thomas Belsham, on the other hand, gave a full
and sympathetic analysis of *Political Justice* in his *Elements of the Philosophy of
the Mind, and of Moral Philosophy* (1801), while maintaining that it is only
religion which can reconcile self-love and benevolence.[125] Edward Maltby
took up the theme in his *Illustrations of the Truth of the Christian Religion*
(1802) and devoted a chapter to refute Godwin's representation of Jesus
and Christianity in *The Enquirer*. Although Maltby considered Godwin as
prejudiced against Christianity as Voltaire or Gibbon, he was at least
moderate and polite.[126] This cannot be said of Robert Hall, who returned to
the attack in the following year in his *Sentiments proper to the Present Crisis*
(1803). 'The patrons', he thundered from his pulpit, 'of purity and licentiousness have put on the cloak of the philosopher: maxims the most licentious have found their way into books of pretended morality, and have been
inculcated with the airs of a moral sage.'[127]

By now Godwin had fallen into one common grave with the cause of
liberty. At least four literary satires made sure that he stayed there. In 1803,
the *Christian Observer,* edited by Zachary Macaulay, a leading member of
the Clapham Sect, published a long anonymous poem entitled 'Modern
Philosophy, and the Godwynian System'. For all its Spenserian tone, it is
the only informed and talented verse satire of Godwin which appeared
during the Anti-Jacobin period:

By Socrates pourtray'd with matchless grace,
Philosophy display'd an angel's face.
Now with the frolic mimicry of apes,
The goddess takes a thousand forms and shapes . . .
Godwyn, arch-priest, her mystic lore expounds,
And gaping pupils catch the wond'rous sounds.
Far beyond Nature's bounds, he boldly springs,
And Man's *perfectibility* he sings;
Fashions a new Utopia's blest domain
Uncurst with laws, exempt from Custom's rein,
Where Reason reckless spurns at love and hate,
And Justice holds with Apathy her state.
Connubial ties, parental cares and fears,
And ever charity that life endears,

Love, friendship, gratitude, the pleasing glow
Of pity melting at a brother's woe,
The Philosophic Hierophant proclaims
Phantoms of weakness, visionary names;
Of *general happiness* arrays a plan,
Where man imparts no social bliss to man . . .
Ah! grieve not, Anarchists, if heav'n assign
A transient hour to visions so divine,
If Nature reassume her ravish'd right,
And Godwyn's goddess vanish into night.[128]

Godwin was no doubt most hurt by the attack made by his old friend
Amelia Opie (formerly Alderson) in her *Adeline Mowbray* (1804). Glenmurray and Adeline (like Godwin and Wollstonecraft) reject the marriage tie,
but the strain of their liaison contributes to his early death. She then on his
advice marries his friend Berrendale who soon reveals his true self, commits adultery and eventually marries an heiress in Jamaica. Adeline recognizes her faults, but it is too late and she dies in despair. Despite the
ambiguity of the tale — the lover Glenmurray appears noble while the
husband Berrendale is deceitful — the conscious intention of the novel is to
show that without the sacred institution of marriage all would degenerate
into 'unbridled licentiousness'.[129]

D'Israeli also returned to the attack in his *Flim-Flams!* (1805). In a
veritable *tour de force*, he mocks Godwin's views, of course, on marriage,
cohabitation, and utility.[130] At a dinner party, Caco-nous (Godwin)
recommends infanticide as a check to population only to make Too-many
(Malthus) cry: 'I am astonished that such a metaphysical Orpheus is not
already torn into fragments, by those mothers who meet you musing on the
annihilation of the unborn generations, every morning at Islington Spa.'[131]
It was hardly a fair charge.

In fact, Godwin had little to fear since he was no longer considered
dangerous. As Sydney Smith wrote in 1802 'Malthus took the trouble of
refuting him; and we hear no more of Mr. Godwin.'[132] In the summer
Thomas Robinson also wrote to his brother Henry Crabb:

> Some singular facts have occurred in our day. The famous new philoso-
> phy of the French which seemed to promise to revolutionise the world is I
> believe now almost without a disciple. The Political Justice rests quite at
> ease up on the bookseller's shelf. At Garnham's Auction I think it sold for
> less than two shillings — although there were booksellers present who
> came from Camb. & Norwich.[133]

In a chapter on the 'New Philosophy' in his *Modern Literature* two years later, Bisset considered Godwin (whom he calls St. Leon) sufficiently harmless to be kind to him. He bemoaned the misapplication of his great literary talents and recalled how his spirit at one time was diffused through books, pamphlets, and periodical publications: 'It met us at the theatre, or popt on us in the form of novels. Catching as it went the follies of its various bearers, it babbled in spouting clubs, howled from the tribune, or by its importunate prattle disturbed the tranquillity of private companies.'[134] Godwin was now part of history: the revolutionary era had well and truly ended.

As for Godwin himself, the concerted effort of the Anti-Jacobin campaign exhausted him. He never fully recovered his creative strength. Apart from an attempt to refute the triumphant Malthus in *Of Population* in 1820, he played an insignificant role in practical politics and did not try to reconstruct his political philosophy. The fiery advocate of liberty and equality, the skilful opponent of Pitt, and the bogeyman of the Anti-Jacobins was soon forgotten. Godwin remarried and put on his slippers. Sensitive to the demands of a growing family, he first unsuccessfully turned to drama and then settled down to become a publisher and writer of children's books. With the exception of his novels, which show some of his old fire, he spent most of his time writing a series of distinguished but unsensational biographies, histories and essays. He remained at the centre of an accomplished circle of friends, he never lost his radicalism, but he was unable to recapture the philosophical profundity and imaginative power of the early 1790s.

# CHAPTER XIV

# *Dramatic Interludes*

While Godwin was being pilloried and ridiculed from all directions, he withstood the onslaught as best he could by quietly studying and writing in his house in Somers Town. He lived modestly and 'solely with a view to the improvement and gratification' of his children. The five-year old Fanny Imlay and the three-year old Mary were his 'favourite companions and most chosen friends'.[1] The household, however, was gloomy, and when Coleridge dined there at the end of 1799, he wrote to Southey: 'the cadaverous Silence of Godwin's Children is to me quite catacomb-ish'.[2] Thinking of Mary Wollstonecraft, he became oppressed by it.

Godwin found some consolation in his disciples and friends. James Ballantyne, the famous Edinburgh printer whom Godwin had met at Holcroft's three years earlier, introduced Dr. James Bell to him in 1799. Ballantyne described Bell as an amiable and accomplished physician whose mind was filled with the 'most exalted respect for your talents, and affection for your heart'. Bell was about to set sail for Jamaica, where he was to take up an influential position and intended to exert his power 'to lighten the woes and diminish the horrors of slavery'.[3] Unfortunately, he died there soon after his arrival and was unable to put Godwin's teachings to good effect.

In the meantime, Godwin's disciple John Arnot was sending interesting but worrying letters about his travels in Europe. Godwin sent him advice and money and asked Holcroft, who was also in Germany, to take a fatherly interest in the young man. Holcroft himself had been continually persecuted since the presentation of his play *Love's Frailties* (1794). He had left England in 1799 with his two daughters, partly to escape the anger he excited and partly because he had sold all his property to repay his debts.

There had been a growing coolness between the two friends since Godwin's marriage. Their practice of perfect sincerity had its difficulties, particularly when it came to literary matters. To avoid painful argument, Godwin sent in January 1799 a detailed list of rules of criticism to Holcroft with the manuscript of his play *Antonio*, stressing that one should not find fault 'in such an absolute and wholesale style, as might at once kill your ardour'. When Holcroft showed Godwin however the manuscript of his play 'The Lawyer' (a sentimental comedy which achieved some success as *Hear Two Sides* in 1802), Godwin neglected his own rules and came to it with a 'sledge hammer of criticism'. He told Holcroft that it would be damned, that the characters and plot were but transcripts of himself, and that everybody would say that it was 'the garrulity of an old man'.[4] Not surprisingly, Holcroft was incensed. He recorded in his diary their subsequent row, in which Godwin admitted being 'cowed and cast down by rude and unqualified assault', accused him of 'triumphant banter', and declared him to be a 'man of iron'.[5]

But it was just another one of their frequent *démêlés* and they soon made up. In the summer Holcroft was writing that he would never cease to have 'an unequivocal and active friendship' for Godwin.[6] He replied that he thought of Holcroft continually and felt that 'one of the crying sins of society is that we do not sufficiently explain our feelings to one another'.[7] Although he had a growing family to support, and was heavily indebted to Tom Wedgwood, Godwin went out of his way to help his impoverished friend in Germany. On one occasion, Holcroft was genuinely moved and wrote in a burst of unphilosophical gratitude:

The ardour, firmness, and activity of your friendship, the true and simple dignity with which you feel and act, the embarrassment under which you are at this moment, and the relief which you find in the confidence that on the receipt of yours I shall immediately do my duty, — in short that delightful mingling of souls which is never so intimately felt as on such extraordinary occasions as these, are now all in full force.[8]

At the same time, Godwin asked Holcroft on behalf of his old friend Marshal, who had made a successful translation of Volney's celebrated infidel treatise *The Ruins, or A Survey of the Revolution of Empires*, to contact the author in France and request the sheets of his *Travels in America* before publication. Holcroft also helped Godwin by arranging a translation of *St. Leon* which appeared in Hamburg in 1800. His own scheme of buying art treasures for the English market, however, proved disastrous. Godwin managed his affairs as best he could: he was willing to clear the pictures at the Customs and contact Opie the painter but there was a limit to his patience. When he saw Holcroft heading for bankruptcy, he felt compelled to reprimand him on his 'madness' and warn him that it was better to be a prisoner in London than Hamburg.[9] To add to his troubles, a bottle of acid burst in Holcroft's face, severely testing their belief that pain is an illusion. His mind was sufficiently omnipotent over his matter, however, for him to support the burns with 'entire calmness'.[10] By frenzied writing, he managed to escape the debtors' prison.

Godwin also tried to renew his friendship with Elizabeth Inchbald who had refused to see him since the death of Mary Wollstonecraft. He sent her a copy of *St. Leon* and asked her whether she did not think two years of banishment and expiation sufficient for a reproach wrung from him 'at a period the most painful and agonizing in human life'.[11] She thanked him for the novel and wrote an elaborate critique, but although she was ready to meet him in company she refused to receive him as a 'familiar visitor' at her house.[12]

Following Maria Reveley's hasty marriage to John Gisborne and the unexpected attack of Dr. Parr in the spring, Godwin eagerly accepted a long-standing invitation to visit Ireland from the great barrister John Philpot Curran to do what he pleased 'as to idling, working, walking, eating, sleeping, &c'.[13] They had first met in 1797 and had seen each other intermittently ever since. In many ways, their characters were opposites. Curran was witty, temperamental, loose-living, a heavy drinker and a fighter of many duels. Yet the two men remained friends until Curran's death in 1817, when Godwin wrote an obituary praising his talents as an orator, his liberal politics, and his 'sincere and earnest heart'.[14] For his part, Curran was at first attracted to Godwin the novelist, but according to his son, he regarded him as 'a man of the most decidedly original genius of his time'.[15]

The letters Godwin sent home during his six-week tour were written half for Marshal and half to be read out to Fanny and Mary. At first he regretted leaving them and intended to cut his visit short. 'Tell Mary', he instructed his old friend who was looking after them, 'I will not give her away, and she shall be nobody's little girl but papa's. Papa is gone away, but papa will very soon come back again, and see the Polygon across two fields from the trunks of the trees at Camden Town.'[16] In his next letter home, he wrote: 'I depute to Fanny and Mr. Collins, the gardener, the care of the garden. Tell her I wish to find it spruce, cropped, weeded, and mowed at my return; and if she can save me a few strawberries and a few beans without spoiling, I will give her six kisses for them. But then Mary must have six kisses too, because Fanny has six.'[17]

In the meantime, Godwin was keeping aristocratic company, and dined with three countesses, including Lady Mountcashel who had spoken of him to Curran 'with peculiar regard'.[18] He found the future friend of the Shelleys 'a democrat and a republican in all their sternness, yet with no ordinary portion either of understanding or good nature'. She was 'uncommonly tall and brawny, with bad teeth, white eyes, and a handsome countenance'.[19]

Curran was usually busy during the day at the assizes, but Godwin acknowledged that his kindness was unceasing. There was, Godwin wrote to Coleridge, scarcely a man on earth with whom he ever felt so entirely at his ease: 'he is perpetually a staff and a cordial, without ever affecting to be either'.[20] He introduced him to Henry Grattan, who spoke without reserve but expressed not one word of esteem or kindness. Godwin considered Curran and Grattan as the two most eminent personages in Ireland:

> They are both somewhat limited in their information, and are deficient in a profound and philosophical faculty of thinking. They have both much genius. Grattan, I believe, is generally admitted to be the first orator in the British dominions; and variety and richness of picturesque delineation perpetually mask the slightest sallies of Curran's conversation. But Grattan is mild, gentle, polished, and urbane on every occasion on which I have seen him; Curran is wild, ferocious, jocular, humorous, mimetic and kittenish; a true Irishman, only in the vast portion of soul that informs him, which of course a very ordinary Irishman must be content to want.[21]

Godwin seems to have enjoyed himself in Ireland. He was received with kindness and cordiality wherever he went. No one he met was ignorant of his name and a few, including the antiquarian Joseph Cooper Walker and the painter Hugh Hamilton, were particularly friendly. The Lord Judge Michael Kelly, eighty years of age, asked Godwin to join him on the bench and made a grand speech because of his presence. *St. Leon*, moreover, was a much greater favourite everywhere in Ireland than *Caleb Williams*. The praise must have been heartening indeed for one whose reputation was at its nadir on the mainland.

During his stay he also visited the Skeys, who had provided him with materials for the memoirs of Mary Wollstonecraft, and her sisters Eliza Bishop and Everina Wollstonecraft, who had refused. He brought each of his daughters a present from them, and wrote to Marshal:

> I love Aunt Bishop as much as I hate (you must not read that word) Aunt Everina: and therefore Fanny, as the eldest, must, I believe, have the privilege of choosing Mrs Bishop's present, if she prefers it. Will not Fanny be glad to see papa . . .? Would pretty little Mary have apprehension enough to be angry if I did not put in her name?[22]

In Ireland, Godwin went out of his way to see the beautiful scenery of the county of Wicklow. He was particularly struck with the Scalp which he thought had a finer effect than Penmaenmawr in North Wales. He also visited with Lady Mountcashel the Devil's Glen which was the most stupendous scene he had ever seen: 'while cut off, on the one hand, from the whole world, your soul has room to expand in its desert, and savour its divinity'.[23] He returned via Conway in North Wales, walked to Llanrwst, and thence to Llangollen where he stayed with Lady Eliza Butler and Miss Ponsonby. He had ample opportunity to indulge in his growing taste for the sublime in nature.

This was undoubtedly encouraged by Godwin's deepening friendship at this time with Coleridge, who was to become his fourth and last principal oral instructor. Their relationship was based on a strange sympathetic antagonism. On their first meeting in 1794, Coleridge had found Godwin disappointing, but when they renewed their acquaintance at the end of 1799 they were both agreeably surprised. At first the young poet regarded the older philosopher with a kind of patronising amusement. After dining at Godwin's with the chemist Humphrey Davy, he wrote to Southey: 'To morrow Sara & I dine at Mister Gobwin's as Hartley calls him — who gave the philosopher such a Rap on the shins with a ninepin that Gobwin in huge pain *lectured* Sara on his boisterousness. I was not at home. Est modus in rebus.'[24]

The two families met for Christmas dinner and by the New Year Coleridge felt strongly drawn to Godwin. On 8 January he welcomed the opportunity to spend a 'Noctes Atticae' with him.[25] Godwin wrote in his diary on the 11th 'Tea, Coleridge's criticism', and immediately set about revising *St. Leon*. In March, Coleridge was apologizing for his tipsiness and extravagant talk at one of their dinners, and closed his letter affectionately: 'God bless you, & give your dear little ones a kiss a piece for me.'[26] By May, Coleridge could write from Nether Stowey: 'My dear Godwin! I remember you with so much pleasure, & our conversations so distinctly, that, I doubt not, we have been mutually benefited.' He added that Davy talked of Godwin with great affection, and invited him to join their band in Keswick in the autumn: '— and let me tell you, Godwin! four such men as you, I, Davy, & Wordsworth, do not meet together in one house every day of the year — I mean, four men so distinct with so many sympathies —'.[27]

As for Godwin, Coleridge gave the final blow to his atheist beliefs which had been already undermined by the influence of Mary Wollstonecraft. 'In my forty-fourth year', Godwin wrote,

I ceased to regard the name of Atheist with the same complacency I had done for several preceding years, at the same time retaining the utmost repugnance of understanding for the idea of an intelligent Creator and

Governor of the universe, which strikes my mind as the most irrational and ridiculous anthropomorphism. My theism, if such I may be permitted to call it, consists in a reverent and soothing contemplation of all that is beautiful, grand, or mysterious in the system of the universe, and in a certain conscious intercourse and correspondence with the principles of these attributes, without attempting the idle task of developing and defining it — into this train of thinking I was first led by the conversations of S. T. Coleridge.[28]

Coleridge's 'head' had of course for some time been with Spinoza and he had just returned from the West Country where he had found 'Religious meanings in the forms of Nature'.[29] Although he would not have entirely endorsed Godwin's kind of broad pantheism, it did show some resemblance to Wordsworth's famous notion of the mutual fitness between the human mind and the external world and was undoubtedly preferable to atheism.

Coleridge also helped Godwin to revise his attitude to the doctrine of necessity. While it may moderate 'the fury of political and private animosities', Godwin now felt that

We should lose the noblest emotions & sentiments of our nature by an indiscriminate application of the vulgar maxim 'it will be the same thing an hundred years hence', as the moral feelings of approbation & disapprobation, in their finest tones, would be extinguished within us, if we constantly viewed our fellow-men in the light of machines.[30]

At the same time, Godwin refused to give up his philosophical view of nature as *natura naturans,* or 'things as they may become', in favour of Coleridge's historical view of nature as *natura naturata*, or 'things as they now are or have become'.[31] Where Coleridge's cosmology led him to conservative conclusions, Godwin continued to believe that things would improve if nature were allowed to operate freely.

During the latter part of 1800 and for several years after, Coleridge and Godwin kept up a voluminous and regular correspondence. Unfortunately most of Godwin's letters have been lost, but Coleridge wrote some of his best prose and most valuable criticism for Godwin. They encouraged each other in their works and shared their most private experiences.

Godwin told Coleridge that he felt himself 'more natural and unreserved' with him than with others, and according to Lamb he was 'above all men, mortified' when Coleridge moved to the Lakes in the spring.[32] Coleridge was no less saddened, and he insisted that Godwin should come and join him and Wordsworth there. He also begged Godwin in the autumn to become a godfather to his new-born son Derwent, but the philosopher refused politely because of his opposition to Christian baptism.

Godwin was unable to join Coleridge and Wordsworth as he was putting the finishing touches to his tragedy *Antonio; or, The Soldier's Return* which had been occupying him for some years. Coleridge however was concerned that Godwin should not 'cease to appear as a *bold* moral thinker' and urged him to write a book 'on the power of words, and the processes by which the human feelings form affinities with them' in order to enquire whether thinking is impossible 'without arbitrary signs'.[33] When Godwin objected that the subject was not suited to his talents, Coleridge acutely remarked that he had not read enough travels and biographies and that he submitted too soon his notions to other men's censures in conversation: 'Dismiss, my dear fellow! your theory of Collision of Ideas, & take up that of mutual Propulsions.'[34]

Coleridge also introduced Charles Lamb to Godwin. Lamb had shown some sympathy for the New Philosophy but the arguments of Coleridge and his own religiosity and common sense quickly turned him against it. He was particularly repelled by Godwin's atheism. After learning that John Stoddart, Hazlitt's brother-in-law, was a 'cold hearted well bred conceited disciple of Godwin' and that his old school fellow Robert Allen had 'tamper'd' with Godwin and laughed at 'Superstition & Religion', he had written to Coleridge in July 1796: 'Why sleep the Watchman's answers to that *Godwin*?'[35]

But when Coleridge became friendly with Godwin in the beginning of 1800, Lamb too grew interested. They met for the first time at Coleridge's on 8 February. Although Lamb was the least politically conscious of the Coleridge circle, he had been portrayed as a toad with Lloyd as a frog in the famous 'New Morality' cartoon by Gillray in the *Anti-Jacobin* of July 1798. Godwin had remembered it and, according to Southey, when Lamb became disputatious during their first meeting he quietly said: 'Pray, Mr. Lamb, are you toad or frog?'[36] Coleridge, however, found them getting on handsomely the next morning. Lamb then wrote facetiously to his old friend Thomas Manning: '*Philosopher* Godwin! dines with me on your Turkey this day. = I expect the roof to fall and crush the Atheist.'[37] Lamb was agreeably surprised when it did not, and told Manning that he was a good deal pleased with Godwin: 'He is a well behaved decent man, nothing very brilliant about him or imposing as you may suppose; quite another Guess sort of Gentleman from what your Anti-Jacobins Christians imagine him —. I was well pleased to find he has neither horns nor claws, quite a tame creature, I assure you.'[38]

Lamb began to pass much of his time with Godwin, and in July wrote to Coleridge that 'he has shew'd me particular attentions . . . N.B. A thing I

XXI. Charles Lamb in 1804, by William Hazlitt.

much like!'[39] Several months later, he had christened Godwin the 'Professor' because of his pedantic manner, and joked with Manning about the 'explanations, translations, limitations' that he demanded whenever an assertion was made.[40]

But it was not all entertainment. Lamb played an important part in the production of Godwin's melodrama *Antonio* at Christmas 1800. The whole episode would appear farcical if it had not been a tragedy for Godwin. He spent more than three years writing it, called on all his friends (including Holcroft, Coleridge, Lamb and Sheridan) for criticisms and suggestions, and considered it his best piece of writing. It proved to be his worst, and an utter failure in performance.

Before he left for Germany, Holcroft, a skilful and successful dramatist, had seen the manuscript in its half-finished state but it was enough to make him 'irritably anxious' for its fate.[41] Godwin had also shown it to Sheridan in April 1799 and had been promised a performance at Drury Lane. When nothing happened he sent it as an anonymous work with his own recommendation to George Colman in June at the Haymarket Theatre. Colman, who had dramatized *Caleb Williams* as *The Iron Chest* without acknowledgement, turned it down. Godwin then revised it and approached Sheridan once again, who referred him to his manager John Kemble at the Theatre Royal. Kemble at first agreed to produce it, then read more and hesitated. He was eventually persuaded against his better judgment by a badgering Godwin to fulfil Sheridan's promise and the parts were assigned on 15 November. Kemble took the title role, and Sarah Siddons the leading female part Helena. Because of the political prejudices against him, Godwin took the precaution of asking John Tobin to appear as the author and to attend the rehearsal in his place.

In a voluminous correspondence, Godwin attempted to alley Kemble's growing fears. When he complained that the conduct of Antonio was unjustified and that the audience would not feel with him, Godwin replied irrelevantly with a long account of the literary condemnation and political persecution he had suffered, reminding him that 'Tragic writers are not the growth of every summer'.[42] Kemble was reduced to silence and even agreed not to advertise any other plays during the week preceding *Antonio*. Lamb undertook to write a prologue and epilogue. Coleridge was there in spirit — 'Be my Thoughts therefore sacred to Hope!' — but warned from the Lake District that it was not a time for tragedies to succeed.[43] But despite all the help and wishes from his friends, despite the best efforts of Kemble and Siddons, on 13 December 1800 *Antonio* was, Lamb noted on his programme, 'Damned with Universal Consent'.

The plot, as Lamb wrote in the epilogue, was simple:

Ladies, ye've heard how Guzman's consort died,
Poor victim of a Spaniard brother's pride . . .
In that romantic unenlighten'd time,
A *breach of promise* was a sort of crime.[44]

The heroine Helena is betrothed by her father on his death-bed to one

Roderigo, the best friend of her brother Antonio. But while they are abroad fighting wars, she falls in love with Don Gusman. Her guardian the king dissolves the original contract and the lovers marry. When Antonio returns, he is furious. He abducts his sister, demands that she enter a convent, and insists that the marriage be annulled. The king however refuses to change his mind, whereupon Antonio bursts through the guards and kills his sister.

Godwin considered drama useful because it is 'eminently subservient to the discovery & propagation of truth' and like sermons forms 'the link between the literary class of mankind & the uneducated'.[45] Not surprisingly, Antonio is unswervingly didactic. Like Falkland, the protagonist is consumed by an obsession with his reputation: 'Honour!', he exclaims,

> What is the world to me, if robb'd of honour?
> No kindred, no affection can survive.
> 'Tis the pure soul
> Of love, the parent of entire devotion,
> Without it man is heartless, brutish, and
> A clod. This was my infant creed; in this
> I'll die.[46]

Helena, on the other hand, is Godwin and Wollstonecraft rolled into one. She opposes her brother's outmoded code of chivalry and military prowess with a gospel of love:

> I am a wife, a sacred title,
> Fraught with all mysteries that adorn our nature . . .
> — Didst ever hear these themes?
> No, in good sooth: for thou, thou art a soldier;
> 'Gainst human feelings thy proud heart is steel'd;
> Thy hands are red with gore; and to thy darling fame
> Thou rushest on 'midst flaming cottages,
> The shrieks of widows, and poor infant blood.[47]

But unfortunately for Godwin the 'uneducated' in the pit were not ready, especially before Christmas, to be taught. They could not sympathize with Antonio, whose great passion seems unaccountable, nor with the neglected fiancé, who never reveals his vaunted qualities. There is a slight moment of drama in Act IV, when Gusman draws his sword in a dispute, but with invincible logic and halting verse Antonio warns that his death would only make matters worse. When at the end Antonio irrelevantly stabs his sister, Lamb recalled in one of his most memorable pieces:

the effect was, as if murder had been committed in cold blood. The whole house rose up in clamorous indignation demanding justice. The feeling rose far above the hisses. I believe at that instant, if they could have got him, they would have torn the unfortunate author to pieces.[48]

Godwin's first attempt at the theatre had proved a complete disaster. Even Lamb was implicated: the *Morning Post* described his epilogue and prologue as 'productions well suited to the piece, too bad to pass without censure except when they pass without observation'.[49] Coleridge received the *Morning Post* with a beating heart, and laid it down with a heavy one.[50] In Germany, Holcroft read the 'malignant and despicable triumph' of *The Times*.[51] Both offered their condolences. Kemble, shaken by the reception, nevertheless assured Godwin that he thought nothing of the trouble he had taken on his account.[52]

Lamb, for all his humour, realized what it meant to Godwin. He had accidentally seen on his table in his study a list of six people whom he had planned to invite to a sumptuous celebration supper, a list of newspapers to which he had intended sending an elaborate sketch of the story of his play, and a list of books which he had hoped to buy with the proceeds. 'The Professor has won my heart by *his* mournful catastrophe', Lamb wrote to Manning. As for his old friend Marshal, he looked in the lobby after the play 'like an angel; his face was lengthen'd and *all over sweat;* I never saw such a care-fraught visage'.[53]

Yet the indomitable Godwin was still unwilling to accept defeat and immediately asked Lamb to help him revise the play. He accordingly made over a hundred notes in an attempt to abridge it and urged Godwin to introduce some sensible images and some judicial pleadings. Eventually, however, his judgment got the better of him and he advised Godwin to give it up.

Godwin, still in the grip of what Lamb called 'o! monstrous & almost satanical *Pride*', felt that *Antonio* was the most finished of his works and was confident that its beauties would be appreciated when it appeared in book form.[54] But when an excited Anna Seward began reading a copy, she was forced to exclaim: 'O, my stars, what short-lived exultation! How are the mighty fallen, and the weapons of genius blunted! Is Godwin superannuated, that he could endure such stuff, as he wrote it? Is he mad, to commit, by its publication, this suicide on his fame?'[55]

The professional critics were no less disappointed. The *Critical Review* saw it as an example of a man of unquestioned abilities miscalculating the extent of his powers.[56] The other reviews were all disparaging. The *London Chronicle* found the plot offensive and the scenes too long; the *Monthly Review* called it a dramatic abortion, beneath all criticism and fit only for the flames; and the *British Critic* suggested that its author had turned the automatic plough of *Political Justice* into a pen.[57] The *Anti-Jacobin Review* recalled with great delight how it had been completely coughed down at its only performance.[58] Elizabeth Inchbald best summed up the general opinion when she wished Godwin joy for having produced a work which 'will hand you down to posterity among the honoured few who, during the past century, have totally failed in writing for the stage'.[59]

After the failure of *Antonio*, Godwin planned to write a life of Henry St. John, Viscount Bolingbroke, whom he saw as a martyr of moderation and tolerance and with whom he no doubt strongly identified. Coleridge, however, unwisely persuaded him against it and urged him to return immediately to play-writing. He suggested as a subject the death of Myrza as related in Holstein Ambassador's *Travels into Persia* which contained 'Crowd, Character, Passion, Incident & Pageantry'.[60] And lo and behold, two weeks after the performance of *Antonio*, Lamb was writing to Manning that the 'Professor' had actually begun

> to dive into Tavernier and Chardin's Persian Travels for a story, to form a new drama *for the* sweet tooth of this fastidious age — Has not Bethlehem College a fair action for non-residence against such professors? — Are Poets so *few* in this *age*, that He must write poetry? . . . Adieu, ye splendid theories! fairwell dreams of Political Justice! Lawsuits, where *I* was counsel for Archbishop Fenelon *versus* my own mother in the famous *fire* cause! —.[61]

Godwin, who was now writing in a frenzy out of financial and psychological necessity, managed to send the manuscript of the new play called 'Abbas, King of Persia' to Coleridge in the spring. Coleridge was in a bad state: he had spent 'many a sleepless, painful hour of Darkness by chasing down metaphysical Game' and felt that the poet was dead in him.[62] Nevertheless, he recommended the preface and the second volume of his and Wordsworth's *Lyrical Ballads*. He also found the energy to give a detailed criticism of Godwin's play — he greatly admired the plot but marked many passages written in 'false or intolerable English' and suggested that he reworked the first two acts.[63]

Godwin took Coleridge's advice into account and sent a revised manuscript in September to Thomas Harris, the manager and proprietor of Covent Garden. He refused it but proposed to pay Godwin for a plain domestic story. Godwin then sent it to Kemble and Sheridan, recognizing that it was too long but insisting that he had carefully avoided 'all the errors, which contributed, with certain external causes, to decide the fate of my piece last year'.[64] He also asked them not to name the author to the two readers who chose the plays for the Theatre Royal in Drury Lane.

Unfortunately the play was declined on 23 September. Godwin, utterly dismayed, wrote to Kemble asking whether his play was just put into the heap along with the production of 'sempstresses, hair dressers, and taylors' or whether it had received that 'vigilant and attentive perusal' due to the production of a known writer. He also proposed as a last resort to exhibit the principal character as 'sensitive, jealous, the slave of passion, bursting out on the most trifling occasions into uncontrollable fits of violence, at the same time that his intentions are eminently virtuous'.[65] Kemble replied that his play had received careful attention and invited Godwin to present a revised version for perusal. After an exchange of letters on the subject, however, Godwin was sufficiently disappointed to drop the project altogether.

But the irrepressible dramatist in Godwin was already searching after a theme for a new play even before 'Abbas' was rejected. Following Harris's suggestion, he turned for inspiration to Daniel Defoe's *Roxana; or, The Unfortunate Mistress*, a novel which had made a strong impression on him as a boy and which had remained a favourite. He drew up an outline based on an incident in the novel and showed it to Lamb. He replied at length urging Godwin to make it as like the life of the poet–murderer Richard Savage as possible, and above all to 'mix up some strong ingredients of distress to give a savour to your pottage'.[66] Godwin set to work in blank verse, but other projects intervened and he did not finish it for several years. He eventually decided to turn to prose and to follow his own instincts — which paid off, for his tragedy *Faulkener* was performed at Drury Lane in 1807. It was not, however, a great success. The philosopher may have triumphed as a novelist, but drama demanded different talents.

# CHAPTER XV

## *New Beginnings*

At the turn of the century, there was very little for Godwin to look forward to. His reputation was at a nadir: his *Thoughts* had failed to stem the abuse of the Anti-Jacobins and his tragedy *Antonio* had been a disaster. At home he felt the need for a companion and a mother for his growing daughters, but Harriet Lee and Maria Reveley had turned him down, and he did not see the willing housekeeper Louisa Jones as fitting the role. And there were serious money difficulties. He had received £100 from the sale of the family farm in Wood Dalling to his brother Hull and 400 guineas for his novel *St. Leon,* but this had already gone. Holcroft could well form in December 1800 'a thousand pictures of hovering distress of the dear children, the house you have to support, and the thoughts that are perhaps silently corroding your heart'.[1]

Godwin's difficulties only encouraged his natural propensity to introspection. He began his autobiography about this time, with the intention 'of being nearly as explicit as Rousseau in the composition of his Confessions', but unfortunately broke off when he reached his teens.[2] He also made some remarkable notes of self-analysis which show a profound insight into his own complex personality. His appearance as a somewhat pedantic, harsh, and cool ex-minister belies his tormented and doubting inner life; he emphasizes his diffidence, nervousness and embarrassment: the look of others was often torture to him. The notes also reveal the same peculiar mixture of abstract reasoning and deep feeling which characterizes his best work:

Too sceptical, too rational, to be uniformly zealous. Nervous of frame, mutable of opinion, yet in some things courageous and inflexible . . . I am tormented about the opinions others may entertain of me; fearful of intruding myself, and of co-operating to my own humiliation. For this

XXII. Godwin, aged 45, by James Northcote, 1801.

reason, I have been, in a certain sense, unfortunate through life, making few acquaintances, losing them *in limine*, and by my fear producing the thing I fear. I am bold and adventurous in opinions, not in life . . . I am feeble of tact, and occasionally liable to the grossest mistakes respecting theory, taste, and character; the latter experience corrects the former consideration; but this defect has made me too liable to have my judgment modified by the judgment of others . . . There is an evenness of temper in me that greatly contributes to my cheerfulness and happiness; whatever sources of pleasure I encounter, I bring a great part of the entertainment along with me; I spread upon them the hue of my own mind, and am satisfied. Yet I am subject to long fits of dissatisfaction and discouragement; this also seems constitutional.[3]

Godwin was now forty-five and sensed it was a turning-point in his life. He was preparing himself for a quiet old age with his two young girls. Then one day as he was sitting on his little balcony in the Polygon considering his reply to his enemies, a good-looking woman in her middle thirties with curly yellow hair and broad hips called from a neighbouring window: 'Is it possible that I behold the immortal Godwin?'[4] She knew perfectly well that it was, but Godwin in his present state was understandably flattered. It was an encounter worth recording; he wrote in his diary on 5 May 1801 *'Meet Mrs. Clairmont'*. She was soon to become his second wife.

She called herself Mary Jane Clairmont, and had two children named Charles Gaulis Clairmont and Mary Jane Clairmont. Her past however remains obscure, partly through her own efforts. According to what she told Godwin, she had emigrated to France at the age of eleven, and apparently witnessed the French Revolution.[5] She also claimed that a Charles Clairmont was the father of her two children but that he died of cholera in 1798 in Hamburg. Her son however was clearly named after Charles Gaulis, a Swiss merchant and the brother of Lady Clifton.[6] Although Charles Gaulis died in 1796 before Jane was born, she thought she had Swiss ancestry and even took his family name 'Trefusis' as her own.[7]

The identity of the father, or fathers, of Mary Jane's children therefore remains an impenetrable mystery. It would appear that before meeting Godwin she had never married: according to Henry Crabb Robinson, rumour had it that she had been abandoned and left destitute at the death of her 'keeper'.[8] Certainly when she married Godwin on 21 December 1802, she first underwent a ceremony 'by banns' at St. Leonard's, Shoreditch, under her assumed name 'Mary Clairmont, widow'. But then an hour later, no doubt worried about its validity, she obtained a marriage licence at St. Mary's, Whitechapel, in her true name and title: 'Mary Vial of the Parish of St. Mary-le-bone, Middlesex, spinster'. To darken the mystery,

XXIII. Godwin, aged 45, by James Sharples, 1801.

XXIV. Mary Jane Clairmont, by family tradition.

a birth certificate issued for her son the following year gives her name as Mary Jane, daughter of Andrew Peter Devereux.[9] It would appear that she too was illegitimate. The secrecy of the affair hardly throws a good light on either of the pair. Godwin seems to have countenanced the dissimulation in order to avoid another scandal, while the conduct of his wife only confirms her later reputation for dishonesty and hypocrisy.

Yet for all her shady past Mary Jane proved to have considerable talents. She had written a play in her youth which Godwin described as 'so firm its character, so far from any mark of a raw and puerile genius'.[10] She was a gifted linguist, and translated for George Robinson both Piccini's edition of the *Thoughts, Remarks, and Observations by Voltaire* (1802) and the African journals of the French explorer Sylvain Golbéry. And apart from being a competent secretary, she was a careful housekeeper and good cook.

Although they were both looking for partners, Mary Jane's calculated advances seem to have developed into a genuine and lasting affection, while Godwin soon found in her more than a housekeeper and a mother for his children. Four months after their first meeting, Lamb reported to his friend Rickman:

> I know no more news from here, except that the *Professor* (Godwin) is *Courting*. The lady is a Widow with green spectacles & one child, and the Professor is grown quite juvenile. He bows when he is spoke to, and

smiles without occasion, and wriggles as fantastically as Malvolio, and has more affectation than a canary bird pluming his feathers when he thinks somebody looks at him.[11]

By the autumn, Godwin was intimate enough with Mary Jane to advise her:

My dear love, take care of yourself. Manage and economize your temper. It is at bottom most excellent: do not let it be soured and spoiled. It is capable of being recovered to its primaeval goodness, and even raised to something better. Do not however get rid of your faults. I love some of them. I love what is human, what gives softness, and an agreeable air of frailty and pliability to the whole.[12]

It was not always to be the case.

Godwin's courtship however did not take precedence over his other activities. In November, he even thought of joining Holcroft in Paris, but Britain was at war with France and Godwin's reputation as a subversive was sufficient to make Lord Pelham refuse to grant him a passport. On hearing the news, he decided to get married instead. The local church at St. Pancras, where Mary Wollstonecraft was buried, clearly had too many associations so they travelled over to St. Leonard's, Shoreditch, where Marshal again was the only witness. They then went alone to the second ceremony at St. Mary's, Whitechapel. Godwin, with characteristic brevity, merely recorded in his diary: 'M. Shoreditch Church, &c., with C. & M.: dine at Snaresbrook: sleep.' As with Mary Wollstonecraft, nature may well have prompted Godwin to undertake a ceremony which he theoretically condemned. Less than five months after the wedding, an entry in his diary on 4 April 1802 reads '*William I, ½ after 11* . . . fetch Mary, Jane' — which may well refer to a miscarriage or still-born baby.[13]

It must have been difficult for Mary Jane to live with the portrait of Mary Wollstonecraft in Godwin's study and with her ghost in the house. But she possessed few of the feminist aspirations of the woman she replaced and lacked the universal benevolence and candour so dear to Godwin's heart. Where he treated Fanny and Mary impartially and welcomed Charles and Jane as his own, she continued to show a marked preference for her two children. She wanted to reserve their slender means to develop her daughter's talents, while leaving the household drudgery to Fanny and Mary. Not surprisingly, Mary reacted with keen resentment and Fanny felt increasingly unwanted.

Godwin's old friends who had known Mary Wollstonecraft were also bitterly disappointed with his new wife. Lamb, who had become a regular visitor, was the first to suffer. On one occasion, he had returned home from the 'Professor's' inspired with new rum but tumbled down and broke his nose. On another occasion, he had mischievously picked the pockets of the sleeping philosopher and carried off his snuff and spirits. But no less than seven weeks after his marriage, he wrote to Manning: 'The Professor's Rib has come out to be a damn'd disagreeable woman, so much so as to drive me & some more old *Cronies* from his House. If a man will keep *Snakes* in his House, he must not wonder if People are shy of coming to see him *because of the Snakes*.'[14] Seven months later, he wrote again: 'Godwin (with a pitiful artificial wife) continues a steady friend: tho' the same facility does not remain of visiting him often. That Bitch has detached Marshall from his house: Marshall, the man who went to sleep when the Ancient Mariner was reading, the old steady, unalterable, friend of the Professor —.'[15] Lamb remained her bitterest enemy, but she also succeeded in estranging Coleridge and Curran. Even the affable Henry Crabb Robinson found her possessive, back-biting, irritable, and scheming.

Even so, their marriage at first seemed happy enough. A boy named William was born on 28 March 1803. In the autumn, Godwin took his wife on a three-week holiday visiting his old friends in Suffolk, Norfolk and Cambridgeshire. They stopped off at Stowmarket where Godwin had been a candidate minister and met his old friend Norman who had played such an important role in his intellectual development. In Norwich he renewed his acquaintance with the Aldersons, the Opies, and other leading families. He also visited his mother and brother Hull in Wood Dalling for two days. The old lady was suitably impressed by her new daughter-in-law and wrote afterwards:

> The time we spent together was to me very pleasing, to see you both in such helth and and so happy in consulting to make each other so, which is beutiful in a married state, and, as far as I am able to judge, appears husifly which is a high recommendation in a wife: give her the fruit of her hands, and let her own hands praise her.[16]

But she was unaware of the true state of their relationship. Godwin's health had been bad during the summer — there are many records in his diary of fainting fits and bouts of vomiting which may have been encouraged by his strained domestic life. When they returned to London in October, a misunderstanding over a visit from Curran precipitated a serious row during which Mary Jane expressed a desire to separate. Characteristically, Godwin retired to his study, wrote a letter regretting her decision, but made no attempt to restrain her:

in order to be happy, you have nothing to do but suppress in part the excesses of that baby-sullenness for every trifle, and to be brought out every day (the attribute of the mother of Jane), which I saw you suppress with great ease, and in repeated instances, in the months of July and August last. The separation will be a source of great misery to me; but I can make up my resolution to encounter it . . . I have every qualification and every wish to make you happy, but cannot without your own.[17]

The letter remained incomplete, and there is no certainty that it was ever sent. At all events, Mary Jane preferred to stay with a prickly and down-at-heel philosopher rather than live a life of destitute and obscure independence.

Despite his wife's inhospitality, Godwin did his best to keep up with his friends. Holcroft was in Paris, still beset with financial difficulties but gradually improving his position. When he heard Godwin had married again, he wrote on New Year's Day 1802: 'I know you deserve the love and friendship of the whole earth, and I think you better calculated to find it in a married life than perhaps any man with whom I am acquainted.'[18]

In the following year, Godwin became embroiled in a momentous row Holcroft had with Lady Mountcashel. Godwin had given Lady Mountcashel a letter of introduction to Holcroft, and she was so impressed with him and his daughter Fanny that she quickly engaged Fanny, who had just married, as a governess for her children. In the meantime, a paragraph appeared in *The Times* of 26 January 1802 warning Englishmen in Paris against Holcroft as a spy. When Lord Mountcashel was informed that Holcroft had once been accused of high treason (he could never lose the title of 'acquitted felon') and that it would be prudent for loyal British subjects to avoid him, he insisted that the new governess be dismissed.

Holcroft was furious. He sent to Godwin the ensuing correspondence with Lady Mountcashel and asked him to publish immediately his first letter to her in the British press. He also intended taking an action for libel against *The Times*, though his name was not actually mentioned in the offending paragraph. But while Godwin was mulling over whether to publish Holcroft's letter, he received another one from Lady Mountcashel explaining the sequence of events which led to Fanny's dismissal. She had supposed Holcroft 'to be mild, moderate and rational' but he turned out to be 'selfish, violent and self-sufficient: beyond the power of cool argument, and utterly regardless of the feelings of any person but himself'.[19] Godwin not only agreed to postpone the publication of the letters but apparently never had them printed.

At the same time, Holcroft continued to help Godwin's friends. He sent a marmotte, and tried to obtain a loir, for the researches in comparative anatomy of Sir Anthony Carlisle. He also arranged with Madame de Staël to send on to Marshal the manuscript of her latest novel for translation. She insisted, however, that neither Godwin nor Holcroft should read it in such a partial manner.

Godwin suspected a growing coolness betwen himself and Coleridge in the winter of 1802. Coleridge had been unable to visit him when he was in London in November because of his ill-health and business commitments. But to Godwin's suggestion that he had altered his feelings and conduct since the summer, Coleridge replied in January that he had become a 'dreaming & therefore an indolent man —. I am a Starling self-incaged, & always in the Moult, & my whole Note is, Tomorrow, & tomorrow, & tomorrow'. At the same time, he had detected an altered tone in Godwin's letters — 'a want of interest in me, my health, my goings on'. But although he considered personal pride a great defect in his friend's character, he stressed that

> I have been really & truly interested in you, & for you; & often in the heat of my spirit I have spoken of your literary Imprudence & Self-delusions with an asperity, that if 'the good-natured Friends' have conveyed it to you [they] would have conveyed a bare story of the constancy of my friend-ship.[20]

Their friendship was strong enough for Coleridge to be the first to come and congratulate Godwin on the birth of his son William. In June, after his return to Greta Hall in Keswick, he sent Godwin a long letter expressing his 'strong feelings of affectionate Esteem' for him. He asked his advice about publishing a treatise entitled 'Organum verè Organum, or an *Instrument* of practical Reasoning in the business of real Life', and gave a detailed account of its contents.[21] He also asked Godwin to find a publisher for Hazlitt's abridgement of Abraham Tucker's *The Light of Nature Pursued*, to which he hoped to add an essay containing the whole substance of the first volume of Hartley's *Observations on Man*. The essay never saw the light of day but Hazlitt's work appeared in 1807.

Although Godwin lived a retired life, he still dined out occasionally and made new acquaintances. A memorable interview occurred on 2 March 1802 when Godwin visited the Earl of Lauderdale, the Whig politician, at whose house he met the Prince of Wales accompanied by Lord Spencer. Godwin left no comment of the occasion, but the encounter between the future king and the republican must have been tense, particularly as Godwin was one of the few friends who had attended the funeral of the Prince's former mistress Mary Robinson at the end of 1800.

In 1802, he also became friendly with a young Scotsman called David Booth with whom he agreed to write a work on etymology. He further proposed sharing any profits with Booth and suggested that the publisher Joseph Johnson, if not too old, might be interested.[22] Nothing came of the mutual undertaking, but Booth remained a close friend and both went on to prepare dictionaries separately.

Those who met the author of *Political Justice* at this time were often surprised by his modest and unassuming manner. Thomas Robinson wrote to his brother Henry Crabb that when he met the 'arch fiend Godwin' in November 1803, he found him 'as much like a man as any human being you ever saw'. He was even more impressed at the next meeting: 'His manners were much more those of a polite man of the world and he likewise seemed to possess more amiable feeling than I expected.'[23] Again, William Austin reported home that he was a mild fatherly figure rather than a dangerous ogre, a man 'whose ruddy, thoughtful, yet open countenance discovers both the temperature of health and philosophy'. In his family, he was 'affectionate, cordial, accommodating'; to his friends 'confidential, ready to make any sacrifice'.[24] Another American, Joseph Campbell, confirmed that he was a 'plain, decent, modest, smiling & agreeable little man'.[25]

With a greatly expanded family, Godwin however had to spend most of his time not entertaining but writing. After the failure to stage his second tragedy 'Abbas' in 1801, he decided to write a life of Chaucer. The initial impetus came from the republication of Thomas Tyrwhitt's edition of the *Canterbury Tales* in 1798 which contained an eight-page abstract of the poet's life. Despite the absence of materials, Godwin decided to follow Coleridge's advice and 'Make the Poet explain his age, and the Age explain the Poet'.[26] The project grew as Godwin researched into the fourteenth century, and what had started as a calculated money-earner rapidly became a labour of love.

Godwin worked with great industry, and despite his preference for working at home, attended the British Museum almost every day. He consulted all the known records in the Bodleian Library, Oxford, Caius College, Cambridge, the Exchequer Office, the Record Office of the Chapter to Westminster, the Heralds' College and the Tower of London. He corresponded with Horne Tooke on philological questions. He consulted Ritson about antiquarian details, and expressed his gratitude to the scholar in a warm obituary in the *Monthly Magazine* when he died in 1803. He even visited with his new publisher Sir Richard Phillips the building at Woodstock which was once thought to be Chaucer's home. The result was a scholarly but mammoth work: *Life of Geoffrey Chaucer, the Early English Poet: including Memoirs of his Near Friend and Kinsman, John of Gaunt, Duke of Lancaster: With Sketches of the Manners, Opinions, Arts and Literature of England in the Fourteenth Century* (1803).

Godwin's intention was 'to carry the workings of fancy and the spirit of philosophy into the investigation of ages past' and to enable the reader 'to feel for the instant as if he had lived with Chaucer'.[27] In the outcome, the work contained virtually all that was known at the time of fourteenth-century England, and a good deal on France and Italy as well. It is an antiquarian's feast day: descriptions of mysteries, pageants, hunting, hawking, archery, tournaments, architecture, arts, embroidery, painting and schoolboy amusements appear; the Battle of Crécy, the Plague of London, the fate of Wycliffe and the Black Prince are mentioned; the lives of Boccaccio, Dante and Petrarch given; education, law, religion and philosophy discussed — among many other subjects. The rest was devoted to a history and criticism of Chaucer's writings and an imaginative expansion of Tyrwhitt's sketch.

Godwin had a high opinion of Chaucer. He considered that no one in the 'history of the human intellect' had ever done more: he was not only the father of our language, but 'fixed and naturalised the genuine art of poetry in our island'.[28] Indeed, after the dramas of Shakespeare, Godwin claimed that

> there is no production of man that displays more various and vigorous talent than the Canterbury Tales. Splendour of narrative, richness of fancy, pathetic simplicity of incident and feeling, a powerful style in delineating character and manners, and an animated vein of comic humour, each takes its turn in this wonderful performance, and each in turn appears to be that in which the author was most qualified to excel.[29]

But apart from being a valuable contribution to the history and literature of the fourteenth century, the *Life of Chaucer* reveals its author's own intellectual and emotional development. He repeatedly stresses the importance of the imagination and the feelings. In a discussion of the schoolmen, for instance, he argues what so many had argued against him:

> The pure dialectician is soon bewildered in the labyrinth of his own terms; when he seems to be most accurate, he often becomes most absurd; strict deduction, even in mathematics, will sometimes lead to untenable conclusions. He who trusts much to sentiment, to impulse, to intuition will often be freest from absurdities, and be conducted to the most useful and beautiful modes of viewing either nature or man.[30]

The same recognition of the emotional springs of knowledge and action is to be found in his treatment of the religion and customs of the period. Thus while he criticizes the 'gloomy and despotic empire of papal superstition',

Godwin is ready to praise such practices as the singing of masses for the dead and the confession of sins.[31] He is even willing to recognize the peculiar beauty of Roman Catholicism: 'Religion is nothing, if it be not a sentiment and a feeling. What rests only in opinion and speculation, may be jargon, or may be philosophy, but can be neither piety toward God nor love to man.'[32]

Godwin's researches into the fourteenth century also led him to change his view of the age of chivalry. He praises John Bull and still condemns the feudal system for its warlike character and enormous inequalities of rank and wealth. Yet he values it for making us belong more to our families and less to the State. Indeed,

> The feudal system was the nurse of chivalry, and the parent of romance; and out of these have sprung the principle of modern honour in the best sense of that term, the generosity of disinterested adventure, and the more persevering and successful cultivation of the private affections.[33]

Fortunately, his publisher Phillips insisted on a limit to his writing and Godwin revised the last sheets of his *Life of Chaucer* on 23 September 1803. It was published in two volumes on 13 October. After the failure of *Antonio*, he awaited its reception with bated breath. He could not have been more disappointed with the principal reviewers. In the *Edinburgh Review*, Sir Walter Scott, no less, praised the 'considerable merit' of the critical discussions but condemned its 'most unfeeling prolixity'.[34] Southey, perhaps partly jealous of Godwin's friendship with Coleridge and Lamb, was even more offensive: it was a 'patchwork' of 'fine fustian', he wrote in *The Annual Review*, constructed chiefly of 'bloated' language and 'vile affectation'.[35] By trying to encompass so much, Godwin had failed in all.

Most of Southey's friends felt that he had gone too far in his attack on Godwin. Southey informed William Taylor of Norwich that the 'booby Godwin' had told Coleridge, to his great amusement, that there was 'nothing at all in William Taylor' and that he remembered this in reviewing his *Life of Chaucer*.[36] Taylor could not, however, thank Southey for so abusing Godwin. He had already reproached Mackintosh for forgetting Godwin's services in his *Cursory Strictures* to the cause of reform, and wrote nobly: 'Godwin is sincere, independent and disinterested, more than most men. What signifies it what he thinks of me?'[37] Southey was incapable of such high-mindedness, and replied that he had been further angered by Godwin's

> weathercock instability of opinion, and the odium which it brought upon the best principles and the best cause, and the want of all feeling in

stripping his dead wife naked, as he did, and such a wife, and taking such
another home, when the picture of *that first* hung up over his fireplace.[38]

He refused to withdraw one syllable.

Coleridge also roundly condemned Southey's party virulence and personal abuse, and put it down to the effects of the trade of reviewing. He later
addressed Godwin as the critic who in the *Life of Chaucer* had given 'if not
principles of AESTHETIC, or Taste, yet more & better Data for Principles
than had hitherto existed in our Language'.[39] He further suggested writing a
critique of Chaucer and of Godwin's biography in a series of letters to be
published in a small volume or in the *Morning Post* but unfortunately they
never saw the light of day.

As for Lamb, he tried to oblige Godwin by writing a review but after
repeated attempts could produce 'nothing but absolute flatness and  nonsense'.[40] But where Lamb put this down to his ill-health, Mary Jane Godwin
misreported the cause as his dislike of the work. Much hurt, Lamb wrote a
letter of explanation in which he acknowledged finding fault in Godwin's
'conjecturing spirit' but added that he was 'by turns considerably more
delighted than I expected'. Indeed, he thanked Godwin for 'some of the
most exquisite pieces of criticism' he had ever read in his life, especially that
on Troilus and Cressida and Shakespeare.[41] Nevertheless, the proposed
review, like Coleridge's, was never written.

The other reviews were generally laudatory. The *Literary Journal* and the
*Imperial Review* liked the way Godwin linked history with biography and
placed Chaucer in his circumstances.[42] The *Critical Review* and the *European
Magazine and London Review*, on the other hand, complained of his conjectures and irrelevant material.[43] But where the former found his style verbose, incoherent, and affected, the latter thought it generally correct and
sometimes elegant. The *Monthly Review* was full of high praise, while the
*Monthly Magazine*, whose editor was the publisher Phillips, naturally
recommended the work as showing 'labour, judgment, taste and talent'.[44]
The *Monthly Mirror*, however, was the most fulsome: it declared that it was
beyond doubt the masterpiece of Godwin, full of vigour of thought, richness
of imagination, and knowledge of the human heart.[45] As always the conservative *British Critic* dismissed it as ingenious but bad, though surprisingly
enough the *Anti-Jacobin Review* found it a 'rich entertainment, of which the
ingredients are equally substantial, and pleasing to the taste'.[46]

The success of the *Life of Chaucer* was more than Godwin could have
hoped. A thousand quarto copies vanished. 'I was at a loss to know how',
Scott wrote, 'till I conjectured that, as the heaviest materials to be come at,
they have been sent on the secret expedition . . . for blocking up the mouth
of our enemy's harbours.'[47] Another octavo edition of fifteen hundred

copies in four volumes appeared in 1804. It remained for many years the standard history of the poet and the age and was praised as late as 1835 by Charles Cowden Clarke in his celebrated edition of Chaucer. Even today it is worth reading for its remarkable scholarship and critical insights and stands as an outstanding example of Romantic history.

While Godwin was naturally pleased with its success, he considered the £600 he received from Phillips extremely mean. It in no way solved his financial difficulties. He had been receiving a small income from the rent of property owned by the Wollstonecraft family in Primrose Street which was divided between the survivors. But he had a wife and five children to support, and his brothers John and Nathaniel were constantly in need. Unable to repay a loan of £100, he was forced to apply once again to the ever-generous but ailing Tom Wedgwood who offered more if the need arose — 'I could not bear the idea of your struggling day after day with new perplexities.'[48]

Despite Godwin's even nature, the strain began to take its toll. In December 1803, for instance, he left Horne Tooke's house in Wimbledon in a fury because he had not been shown upstairs immediately. Tooke had been engaged in urgent business with Walter Scott and claimed afterwards that he had quite forgot that Godwin was waiting downstairs. When Godwin demanded a frank explanation, Tooke took him to task for such 'womanish jealousy'.[49]

Other people began to avoid him. Godwin was keen to make the acquaintance of the sculptor and designer John Flaxman who had supplied some details for his *Life of Chaucer*. In the autumn of 1803, he invited him to dinner with Curran and Horne Tooke but he declined. He still kept his distance after another invitation in the following year.[50]

A bitter dispute also took place with Coleridge at Lamb's before a large company of guests on 2 February 1804. According to the account Coleridge sent Southey, Godwin was the first to provoke him, although Mary Lamb's generous punch and Mrs. Godwin's jealous goading all played their part. Coleridge had apparently beeing outlining his plan for a regular review for an evening newspaper, when Godwin very coldly observed that it was something which 'no man, who had a spark of honest pride' could join with. To Coleridge's rejoinder that both Wordsworth and Southey approved, Godwin quickly declared: 'Yes — Sir! just so! — of Mr. Southey — just what I said.'

But this was only a skirmish. Godwin left the company for a while and returned to supper in a fighting mood. Coleridge in the meantime was 'disgusted at Heart with the grossness & vulgar Insanocaecity of this dim-headed Prig of a Philosophicide', and when he renewed the contest after supper 'did thunder & lighten at him' with frenzied eloquence for nearly an hour and a half, ending with a stinging contrast between Godwin as a man, a writer and a benefactor of society and those whom he had dared to criticize.[51]

The moment Coleridge awoke next morning however he felt a wretch. He immediately wrote to Godwin a profuse letter of apology, putting down his extravagant conduct to the intensity of his religious opinions and the 'poisonous excitement of nervous Feeling & the Punch'.[52] He was in fact genuinely contrite: to his wife he confessed, 'never can I wholly forgive myself', and to Wordsworth, 'Few events in my Life have grieved me more'.[53] Coleridge later learned from Lamb that Godwin would not have persisted in irritating him if Mrs. Godwin had not 'twitted him for his prostration' before him.[54] Southey was naturally delighted by the whole affair, and wrote to Coleridge: 'I am not sorry that you gave Godwin a dressing, and should not be sorry if he were occasionally to remember it with the comfortable reflection, *"in vino veritas"*'.[55]

The breach with Coleridge was patched up, but a more serious quarrel broke out with Godwin's closest friend Holcroft in the autumn of 1804 which eventually led to their estrangement. The cause of their dispute was initially over literary matters. Godwin's ward Thomas Cooper had in the previous year returned in triumph from America and replaced Kemble as theatre manager at the Drury Lane Theatre. Never a man to miss a good opportunity, Godwin immediately returned to his play which was to be called *Faulkener*. Unfortunately, Cooper decided to return to New York in 1804 and Godwin was obliged to send his work to his successor Richard Wroughton. When he refused to commit himself, Godwin sent the manuscript to Holcroft who had recently returned from Paris. Holcroft misunderstood his wishes and returned the play almost entirely rewritten. Godwin took it as a barbed comment on his own abilities as a dramatist and was so upset that he felt unable to see Holcroft when he came to town. For his part, Holcroft was sorry 'that a work which cost me such deep thought, and was, in my own opinion, so happily executed, should excite in your mind nothing but the chaos of which you inform me'.[56]

Godwin dropped the play and returned to a novel he had begun in March. But when Holcroft read in *Fleetwood; or, The New Man of Feeling* in the following year an account of a father (Mr. Scarborough) whose stern treatment led to his son's suicide, it was the last straw. Despite Godwin's insistence that he had taken his own relationship with his ward Thomas Cooper as a model, Holcroft interpreted it as a reference to his son's suicide in 1789.[57] He was so infuriated that he broke off all relations with Godwin until just before his death five years later.

Godwin's new novel was probably first conceived in 1798 as a story of 'common incidents and the embarrassments of lovers'.[58] Where *St. Leon* had been 'of the miraculous class', he tried in *Fleetwood* to return to the verisimilitude of *Caleb Williams*, and to present such adventures as have occurred to at least 'one half of the Englishmen now existing, who are of the same rank of life as my hero'.[59] Although there was little in the work to elevate and surpise, he believed that its merit lay 'in the liveliness with which it brings things home to the imagination, and the reality it gives to the scenes it pourtrays'.[60]

While the hero is hardly typical of the educated middle class as Godwin suggests, he is correctly called the 'New Man of Feeling'. Fleetwood's early career resembles the fate of the Romantic heroes in Rousseau's *La Nouvelle Héloïse*, Mackenzie's *Julia de Roubigné*, and Inchbald's *A Simple Story*, which Godwin knew well and read prior to composition. Echoes of *Othello* abound. There is an even closer parallel to be found in the lives of the Romantic poets Wordsworth, Coleridge and Thelwall, who, on becoming disillusioned with the possibility of progress, had retired to domestic life in the country.

Above all, Godwin found a model for Fleetwood in his own experience. Like Rousseau in his *Confessions*, whom he intended to imitate, and like Wordsworth in *The Prelude*, who was analyzing his past, Godwin had dwelt at the turn of the century on the growth of his own mind and tried to come to terms with himself in numerous autobiographical fragments. 'The proper topic of the narrative I am writing', Fleetwood declares, 'is the record of my errors. To write it, is the act of my penitence and humiliation.'[61]

By drawing on the literature of sensibility, by observing the progress of his contemporaries, and by analyzing himself, Godwin presented in *Fleetwood* the predicament of the Romantic artist who feels himself alone in a cruel and barren world. The hero turns away in despair from city life in order to seek personal salvation in contact with nature and a small circle of friends and family. But while Godwin develops his own brand of Romanticism, he offers at the same time a critique of Romantic sensibility and unlike most of his contemporaries does not entirely abandon hopes for radical social change.

Throughout the novel, Godwin develops a Rousseauist contrast between the scenes of nature which inspire virtue and the corrupting influence of city life. It is yet another illustration of his thesis that character is a product of circumstances and education. He sets his hero in the sublime landscape of Merionethshire which Godwin had visited on his way back from Ireland in 1800. 'My earliest years', Fleetwood recalls, 'were spent among mountains and precipices, amidst the roaring of the ocean and the dashing of waterfalls. A constant familiarity with these objects gave a wildness to my ideas, and an uncommon seriousness to my temper.'[62] It is amid such scenes that he learns sympathy for others and selflessly saves a peasant boy from drowning. But his instinctive benevolence is destroyed and his understanding brutified by life as a student at Oxford. It is followed up by a career of refined profligacy in Paris and London. By the age of forty-five, he has become a disillusioned misanthrope. It is only when he flees to the Alps where he meets his father's friend Ruffigny that he realizes the possibility of redemption. He then marries the daughter of Macneil, a cultivated philanthropist and friend of Rousseau who has retired to the Lake District. In spite of his jealousy of Kenrick, an innocent relative who enjoys his wife's company, Fleetwood is eventually reformed by domestic affections.

But while Godwin shares the Romantic poets' celebration of the healing effects of nature, he gives it less power than Wordsworth does, and carefully draws the dangers of a 'sickly sensibility' and a 'diseased imagination'.[63] The 'new man of feeling' can all too easily be devoured by ennui, despair and misanthropy. Fleetwood can find no satisfaction and his attempts to reform society prove abortive. But Godwin refuses to allow him to succumb to the Romantic agony and commit suicide. His distemper, the wise Ruffigny diagnoses, is not a result of the human condition but of his failure to commit himself to mankind: 'If you are now wayward and peevish and indolent and hypochondriacal, it is because you weakly hover on the outside of the pale of society, instead of gallantly entering yourself in the ranks, and becoming one in the great congregation of man.'[64]

The involvement that Godwin recommends is not, however, political martyrdom or even the isolated attempt to live an irreproachable life. He specifically states in his preface:

> The author of Political Justice, as appears again and again in the pages of that work, is the last man in the world to recommend a pitiful attempt, by scattered examples to renovate the face of society, instead of endeavouring by discussion and reasoning, to effect a grand and comprehensive improvement in the sentiments of its members.[65]

Where Godwin himself had been accused of trying to trample on the institutions of his country, he now urges his readers to participate in them. Far from proscribing the domestic affections, he presents marriage and the family as a haven in a crass and brutal world. A man must do the good that lies in his power and not despair because the ideal seems impossible. But while Godwin concludes in *Fleetwood* that charity begins at home, it must not stop there. The hero's marriage to Mary (another version of Mary Wollstonecraft) releases his repressed sympathy, but her father reminds him: 'I am a philanthropist in the plain sense of the word. Wherever I see a man, I see something to love, — not with a love of compassion, but a love of approbation.'[66]

With Godwin's celebration of family life comes his new attitude to women. Fleetwood's early affairs with aristocratic mistresses leave him with no favourable opinion of the female sex. He tries to educate his young wife, like Thomas Day and Horne Tooke had done, to his own taste, and is insanely jealous when she acts independently and offers to bring up her children on her own. Godwin makes him learn that to reap the 'unspeakable joys of social existence' it is necessary to live a 'life of accommodation'.[67] Yet for all this belated recognition of the dangers of male tyranny, Macneil tells Fleetwood as Godwin had told Maria Reveley:

> Man marries, because he desires a lovely and soothing companion for his vacant hours; woman marries, because she feels the want of a protector, a guardian, a guide and an oracle, someone to look up to with respect, and in whose judgment and direction she may securely confide.[68]

But as with all of Godwin's novels, Fleetwood does not merely offer a psychological study of misanthropy and an uplifting moral tale. There is much biting satire and trenchant criticism of 'Things as They Are', even though the whole is intended as fictitious history and set in the age of Louis XV. Both the original title of the novel 'Lambert' and 'Fleetwood' were names of famous republicans who lived on to witness the profligacy of the Restoration. Fleetwood was therefore associated in Godwin's mind with the great age of English liberty, all the more so since General Fleetwood, the son-in-law of Cromwell, had lived at Irmingland Hall only a few miles from Guestwick where Godwin had spent his early childhood.

Like Godwin himself, the Fleetwood of the novel admires fervently the leaders of the Commonwealth who decided 'perhaps for ever, on the civil and intellectual liberties of England.'[69] While he vaunts Switzerland as the country of freedom, moderation and good sense, he laments that the public character of England was gone: 'I perceived that we were grown a commercial and arithmetical nation; and that, as we extended the superficies of our empire, we lost its moral sinews and its strength.'[70] When he stands as an M.P., he finds that the first things to be sacrificed are personal integrity and freedom of thought. He must appeal to the vulgar taste of his electors and toast 'Church and King, and the wooden wall of old England'.[71] Above all, as a member of a party he is obliged to accept the prejudices of the majority and be made the tool and dupe of 'the vilest of the herd'.[72] Godwin had not at least changed his view about parliamentary representation and political parties.

Godwin also vividly describes the effects of the Industrial Revolution on the mental and moral well-being of the new working class. Godwin had visited Wedgwood's potteries at Etruria in 1797 and passed through the industrial parts of the Midlands, visiting Erasmus Darwin at Derby and Robert Bage's paper works at Elford. In September 1803, he saw the factory of his old friend Norman in Stowmarket during a visit to Norfolk. He then visited a silk mill in Spitalfields on 12 July 1804 to prepare materials for *Fleetwood*, just as he had visited Newgate to authenticate his descriptions of prisons in *Caleb Williams*.

Ruffigny, who describes his own experiences in a long sub-plot in the novel, denounces child labour in no uncertain terms. He relates how in the silk factories of Lyons children from four years of age are employed from six in the morning to six at night, sitting in front of the spinning wheels with a 'stupid and hopeless vacancy in every face'.[73] Liberty, he argues, is 'the school of understanding. This is not enough adverted to. Every boy learns more in his hours of play, than in his hours of labour . . . Put him into a mill, and his understanding will improve no more than that of the horse which turns it.'[74] Ruffigny then makes a plea to educate the 'lower orders of the people' to enable them to plan and provide for themselves, but he is only too well aware of the power of capital and the evangelical religion which sanctions it: 'the earth is the great Bridewel of the universe, where spirits, descended from heaven, are committed to drudgery and hard labour'.[75]

In many ways *Fleetwood* is an improvement in artistic terms on *St. Leon*. Godwin manages to forge together social criticism, moral teaching, and history in an allegory which demonstrates the dangers of Romantic alienation. He achieves a distinct unity of tone if not one of design. His style too is better: less extravagant and bombastic, more suited to the subject matter. The heroic epic on the fifth labour of Hercules in the Augean stables, said to be written by one of Fleetwood's friends at Oxford, shows that the poet in Godwin could transcend on occasion the flat verse of his tragedy *Antonio*. The descriptions of natural scenery in Wales and Switzerland are powerful and evocative. The macabre scene in which Fleetwood celebrates his anniversary with models of his wife and lover and then destroys them in a paroxysm of rage is superb. As usual, Godwin's heroine is too idealized but the minor characters Ruffigny, Macneil and Kenwick are vividly drawn.

But despite Godwin's more mature style, the novel suffers from his tendency to build a character out of one humour and explore its consequences. Little happens and there is virtually no dialogue. Hazlitt rightly observed that Godwin 'makes up by the force of style and continuity of feeling for what he wants in variety of incident or ease of manner'.[76] There is little of the white-hot pace of *Caleb Williams* or the sublime flights of *St. Leon*. It is a novel of quiet sense and fireside wisdom: the author appears horrified by existing abuses and the weaknesses of mankind, but can find a remedy only in tolerant family life.

Like Godwin's previous novels, *Fleetwood* was generally well-received. It gave great pleasure to Mackintosh (now made Sir James for his apostasy) who wrote from Bombay that it was 'far indeed above the limits of a vulgar fate'.[77] Walter Scott praised the Ruffigny episode in the *Edinburgh Review* and the treatment of Mary's derangement, but objected to the extravagant passion, credulity and egotism of the hero.[78]

The short piece in the *Monthly Review* praised Godwin's ability to analyze the human heart but the other reviews were more guarded.[79] The *Critical Review* felt the characters were all metaphysicians who reason when they should act.[80] The *Anti-Jacobin Review* called it mediocre, and felt the plot was poor and the conclusion absurd.[81] While praising Godwin's great skill, the *British Critic* felt his language was slovenly at times.[82] The *Imperial Review* simply found the plot too slight and gloomy, and the style Burkean and strained.[83] *The Annual Review* liked it more as it proceeded, but still recommended an abridgement.[84] An American edition was published in New York and Alexandria in 1805, a German translation in Frankfurt in 1806, and a French one in Paris in 1805 and 1807.

The relative success of *Fleetwood* helped Godwin's wounded self-esteem but it by no means solved his financial problems. In March 1805, he therefore concluded a contract with Phillips for a history of England which he hoped would replace Hume's, secure at least £2,000, and provide several years' pleasurable enjoyment. In the summer Phillips inserted in his *Monthly Magazine* a letter from Godwin dated 21 June requesting information and materials for his 'History of England from the Earliest Records of Events of this Island to the Revolution in 1688'.[85] But the work which Godwin intended to be 'a depository of inviolable truth' was unfortunately never completed.[86]

His wife had other ideas. Ever since their marriage they had been unable to meet their outgoings despite his writing and her translations. What would happen if ill-health or death should descend upon them? What would become of the five children? She had of late been editing a three-volume *Collection of Popular Stories for the Nursery* for the publisher Benjamin Tabart. It was a profitable market, and it suddenly occurred to her that with Godwin's talents and her business sense they could set up a rival publishing firm. Godwin had to acknowledge that they were broke and reluctantly turned away from his beloved historical research to begin the famous Juvenile Library. It was to cause him endless worry and financial difficulty for the next twenty years.

# CHAPTER XVI

## *The Juvenile Library*

While most people could hardly read or write at the time, there was a growing demand amongst the affluent middle class for children's books. For some years the Juvenile Libraries in Brook Street, St. Paul's Churchyard, Gracechurch Street and Paternoster Row had been turning out moral tales, grammars, histories and Christian tracts. Hannah More, Priscilla Wakefield, Mrs. Trimmer and other pious ladies and ministers had cornered the market. Godwin and his wife, with little business sense and less money, therefore set themselves a real challenge to break into the trade. Once committed to the idea, Godwin undertook the task with zeal; it would not only be a means of earning a living but provide an opportunity of shaping the next generation.

His first problem was to make sure that the public had no suspicion that he was connected with the concern: 'Reviewers & old women of both sexes, have raised so furious a cry against me as a seditious man & an atheist that the tabbies who superintend schools either for boys or girls would have been terrified to receive a book under the name of Godwin.'[1] He was lucky enough to find in one Thomas Hodgkins not only an experienced manager, but a person who was willing to give the firm his name. Godwin then decided to adopt the pseudonyms of Edward Baldwin and Theophilus Marcliffe to avoid detection.

Having borrowed another £100 from the dying Tom Wedgwood, he rented in the summer of 1805 a little house with a shop in Hanway Street, an alley which ran from Oxford Street to Tottenham Court Road. The rent was only £40 a year and lodgers brought in £35. It was just what he needed for his experiment. The shop was quickly stocked and the public invited to peruse their 'choice Collection of School Books; also Cyphering Books, Copy Books, Copper-plate Copies, Quills, Pens, Inkstands, Slates, Black-lead Pencils, Maps and Staionary [sic] of all kinds'.[2]

Godwin of course had a lifelong interest in education. Mary Wollstone-craft had pointed out to him the advantages of a public education, and after failing to find a place for his stepson Charles at Christ's Hospital School (which involved writing to Prince Hoare and others), he eventually got him into Charterhouse. Young William later followed him. But Godwin insisted that they should come and go as he pleased and that the authority of the teacher is derived only from that of the parent.[3]

Godwin educated his girls at home, which caused endless disputes with his wife. She believed that each child should be educated early to some definite position in life; he felt that they should learn through desire at their own pace. 'We should always remember that the object of education is the future man or woman', he wrote to a correspondent, 'and it is a miserable vanity that would sacrifice the wholesome and gradual development of the mind to the desire of exhibiting little monsters of curiosity.'[4] But he placed great stress on the growth of the imagination, without which he felt there could be no genuine morality, and he encouraged them to create their own stories. Jane for one came to resent the fact that in their family 'if you cannot write an epic poem or novel, that by its originality knocks all other novels on the head, you are a despicable creature, not worth acknowledg-ing'.[5] Nevertheless, the three girls generally got on well with their exacting father and became the most respected critics of the works of the Juvenile Library.

The first book which appeared under the pseudonym of Edward Baldwin was *Fables, Ancient and Modern*. It was written in five months and published on 21 October 1805, the same day as the Battle of Trafalgar. Drawing on Aesop, Perrault and La Fontaine, Godwin adapted some of the best known fables for very young children and deliberately contrived a happy and forgiving ending. But they are not mere dry homilies; he recognized that

> If we would benefit a child, we must become in part a child ourselves. We must prattle to him; we must expatiate upon some points; we must introduce quick, unexpected turns, which, if they are not wit, have the effect of wit to children. Above all, we must make our narrations pic-tures, and render the objects we discourse about, visible to the fancy of the learner.[6]

The result was a lively and informative collection of stories, written in a simple but elegant style and illustrated by seventy-three handsome copper-plates. Each leading object is introduced by a distinct explanation, so that the fables convey aspects of natural history as well as moral enlightenment. Children, he felt, improve twice as much by experience as they do by precept.

The radical in Godwin however comes through in his comments. In his adaptation of Phaedrus's 'The Wolf and the Dog', for instance, he makes the starving wolf declare to the well-fed but chained mastiff: 'Hunger shall never make me so slavish and base, as to prefer chains and blows with a belly-full, to my liberty.'[7] Again, in a fable entitled 'Washing the Black-amoor White', Godwin contributes to the anti-slavery propaganda by declaring that it is 'by no means impossible' for a young English lady to find her negro servant 'very handsome'.[8] And in 'The Cock and the Precious Stone', Godwin could not stop himself from exclaiming: 'How happy are children, and the inhabitants of certain nations where no people are rich, that they can live without a continual anxiety about jewels and wealth!'[9]

The reviews warmly received Baldwin's *Fables*, especially Godwin's arch-enemies the *Anti-Jacobin Review*, which declared that they were the best they had seen, and the *British Critic*, which recommended them without reserve.[10] Only the indomitable Mrs. Trimmers's *The Guardian of Education* found fault in his optimistic endings and in the 'terrifying' and 'amoral' tendency of many of the fables.[11] At all events the *Fables* went through ten editions by 1824 and Mary Jane translated them successfully into French.

It was an auspicious beginning. Godwin asked Lamb to contribute and he produced in 1805 *The King and Queen of Hearts*, a tiny book of verse with pictures, engraved by William Mulready. Godwin was so impressed by the young artist's success in overcoming his humble background that he wrote in 1805 his biography. He published it under the pseudonym of Theophilus Marcliffe as *The Looking Glass, A True History of the Early Years of an Artist*. Although Godwin had earlier condemned emulation, it was, as its subtitle indicates, 'calculated to awaken the emulation of young persons of both sexes, in the pursuit of every laudable attainment: particularly in the cultivation of the fine arts'. Most reviewers warmly recommended the little biography but the *Anti-Jacobin Review* felt there were too many excuses for the character's faults to provide a good model for others.[12] Mulready continued to work for Godwin for some time and remained a close friend. He taught Charles Clairmont to paint and introduced him in 1808 to the young painter John Linnell who was to become the friend of William Blake.

Godwin followed up the success of his *Fables* in 1806 with *The Pantheon; or, Ancient History of the Gods of Greece and Rome* by Edward Baldwin. Although Godwin tried to vindicate heathen mythology from misrepresentation, he claimed that it would not seduce 'one votary from the cross of Christ' and that nothing would be found in it 'to administer libertinism to the fancy of the stripling, or to sully the whiteness of mind of the purest virgin'.[13] A study of ancient mythology, he maintained, would help understand the poets of former times and awaken the imagination — 'the great engine of morality'.[14] The result was a lively survey of the principal Greek and Roman Gods, written in a simple and direct style, and illustrated by engravings taken from the remains of ancient statuary.

Godwin dedicated *The Pantheon* to Dr. Matthew Raine, headmaster of Charterhouse where Charles was a pupil, and his approval greatly increased sales. The *Monthly Mirror* approved of the way the tales had been stripped of their licentious colourings and the *British Critic* recommended it highly for schools, although the *Eclectic Review* castigated Godwin for not showing the baseness of the heathen religion.[15] *The Pantheon* proved so popular that it became the basic text on ancient mythology in schools and had gone through nine editions by 1836. When the Reverend Charles Burney complained of the revealing undress of the engravings, Godwin's sense of decorum got the better of his admiration of the human form, and he had some of them becomingly clothed in the third edition of 1810.

The year 1806 proved a busy one for Godwin. A *History of England* by Baldwin and a *Life of Lady Jane Grey, and of Lord Guildford Dudley, Her Husband* by Marcliffe appeared in quick succession. Although nothing like the great history he had intended to replace Hume's, the school text-book still contained some vigorous writing and touched upon the 'very principles and foundation of history and political society'.[16] As he traced the great landmarks of English history, he wrote largely from memory and in the Dissenting spirit imbibed at Hoxton. Cromwell, he asserts, governed the nation 'with more vigour and glory, than any king that ever sat upon the throne'.[17] Not surprisingly, he welcomed the Commonwealth, the Glorious Revolution, and the American War of Independence. He particularly defends the French Revolution: the revolutionaries may have been too eager, but the *ancien régime* had been 'singularly arbitrary and oppressive to the lower orders' and the confederacy of the European powers had only made matters worse.[18] Napoleon, he suggests, is the Cromwell of the French Revolution.

It was a comprehensive, informed, and stimulating English history, sufficiently muted for the *Anti-Jacobin Review* to recommend it for very young children.[19] The *British Critic* highly approved, although the *Critical Review* objected to some of his 'romantic ideas', and the *Monthly Review* felt it was too much in favour of the 'rights of the subject'.[20] It proved extremely popular and went through eight editions by 1836. Godwin also published an abridged version entitled *Outlines of English History* (1808) which went through three editions in his lifetime.

In the preface of his *History of England* Godwin refers the reader to his *Life of Lady Jane Grey, and of Lord Guildford Dudley, Her Husband* as a specimen of the manner in which his outline might be filled up. The *Life* is unashamedly didactic in intention and Romantic in spirit. The heroine, Godwin declares, is 'the most perfect model of a meritorious young creature of the female sex', and her tragic story is perfectly adapted 'to interest the affections, and to soften the heart'.[21] In his account of the young Catholic queen who was beheaded at sixteen, he praises the Reformation and condemns the isolation of kings. He makes, however, a strong plea for religious toleration to his young readers: 'A person may believe in transubstantiation, and say his prayers with a little ivory image standing before him, and yet be a very worthy man. There have been Roman Catholics in England, and other countries, who were an ornament to human nature . . .'[22] The *Anti-Jacobin Review* found it an interesting story narrated with plainness and sympathy, well suited for children.[23] The *Literary Journal* agreed, and with some reason assumed that Marcliffe was Baldwin but did not guess the real author.[24]

Godwin's interest in politics mainly found expression in these years in his histories for children. Since the turn of the century, popular radicalism, although not extinguished, had lost its coherence and the few Whigs who drifted back to parliament were unable to mount an effective opposition. Godwin made no protest in 1802 against the execution for high treason of Colonel Despard and his companions and took no part in the 'Burdett and no Bastille' election two years later. Across the Channel, Napoleon's acceptance of the crown as hereditary Emperor in 1804, his subsequent accommodation with the Vatican, and his elevation of a new hereditary nobility must have dashed Godwin's remaining republican hopes, but still he made no comment.

He joined the crowd however in January 1806 that saw Nelson's body being borne in state up the Thames from Greenwich to Whitehall to be buried at St. Paul's. When Fox died, he also broke his silence in the autumn and wrote a moving obituary of the great Whig leader for the *London Chronicle*. He presented him as a great advocate of liberty and a model parliamentary leader. As a man, he combined the 'best feelings of the human heart, with the acutest powers of the human understanding', while his public and private life formed 'beautiful parts of a consistent whole'. But Godwin also used the opportunity to celebrate the freedom which Fox had so enthusiastically defended — 'England has been called, with great felicity of conception, "The land of liberty and good sense"' — as well as to attack the bloody wars and the 'formidable innovations on the liberties of Englishmen' made so treacherously by Pitt.[25]

While Godwin's radicalism remained as firm as ever, his religious views had, under the influence of Coleridge, settled down to a kind of pantheism. He planned a work for the Juvenile Library to be called 'First Impressions of Religion' which was to include 'all that is pleasing in religion, & that only'. In a series of notes, he waxes almost mystically on the life-force in the universe which he calls God:

> Think of the living spirit that moves in Nature, that plays in the breeze, that grows & fructifies in the vegetable world.
> Think of the structure of vegetables, of animals, of man, the instinct of animals, is God.
> Think of man, the beauty of the world, the paragon of creation, all the wisdom of man, is God.
> The stars in their course, witness of God.[26]

He did not complete the work, but in another one entitled *Rural Works*, written for his son and published by the Juvenile Library, he developed the same theme. The work itself is lost, but in a long letter begun on 23 September 1806, he recalls a visit to the country and explains: 'By God then we mean the great invisible principle, acting everywhere, which maintains the life of everything around us: now is not this principle fitted to excite all our wonder, respect & admiration?' In a more lyrical mood, he describes all the motion, order, health and beauty in the world as the operation of a 'Great Spirit'. It is a good and beneficent principle: 'every wind that rustles around me, the waving of the grass, the shaking of every leaf of every tree reminds me of God; & I say to myself with an exaltation difficult for words to express "No, I am not alone!"'[27] Godwin moreover felt that the moral teachings of the Bible were sufficiently inspiring to publish under the name of Baldwin some *Scripture Histories, given in the Words of the Original* in two volumes. Unfortunately they too are lost.

While the Juvenile Library increasingly absorbed Godwin's precious time, he made a final effort to complete his tragedy *Faulkener* which he had begun in 1803. He developed an incident found in the 1745 edition of Defoe's novel *Roxana* but ignored both Lamb's suggestion to incorporate the life of Richard Savage and Holcroft's extensive revisions. It was accepted at last in 1806 by the Drury Lane Theatre for performance in January of the following year. The principal role of Countess Orsini was at first given to William Betty, the celebrated young 'Roscius', then thirteen years old, but he was unhappy with the part and it was eventually performed by Robert Elliston. Sarah Siddons played Lauretta. Lamb again wrote the prologue. Godwin's friend also Dr. John Walcot sent an extra epilogue but it came too late to be delivered. After many delays the première took place on 16 December 1807. All the signs were inauspicious. In 1806 Holcroft's play *The Vindicative Man* had failed, as had Lamb's farce *Mr. H.* Godwin's friends were in dismay. Mary Lamb wrote on 28 November that Godwin's new tragedy would 'probably be damned the latter end of next week'.[28] Two days before the first night, an anxious Coleridge told Southey that

'Poor Godwin is going to the Dogs, I fear.'[29] As it turned out, Godwin surprised himself and all his friends for *Faulkener* received some favourable notices and ran for six nights.

Godwin began writing his tragedy in poetry but wisely changed to prose except for a hundred lines. Whereas he had relied unsuccessfully in *Antonio* on his speeches for dramatic effect, he now concentrated on the action. There are elaborate masquerades, duels, prison and court scenes; mistaken identity, coincidences and secrets abound. In Act III, Godwin further exploits the contemporary taste for the macabre by staging a duel in what the directions describe as: '*A desolate and frightful Landscape: hanging Precipices and Caverns; a Visto opening to an interminable Glen of Rocks: Moonlight*'.[30] Godwin wanted to take no chances with dissatisfying the pit.

The plot, as Lamb pointed out in the prologue, is a 'real story of domestic woe' although it involves the highest in the land.[31] It takes place in Florence in the seventeenth century. Faulkener was the illegitimate son of the Countess Orsini, who became the mistress of King Charles Stuart after the death of her son's father. She is presented as a woman in whom 'frail and lavish action had disguised the colour of a virtuous mind', and in her marriage to Count Orsini she is genuinely afflicted by guilt for her former life.[32] As for Faulkener, he sees filial duty as the 'substance and reality of life' and the plot turns on his attempt to find out the identity of his mother.[33]

Lauretta, a discarded mistress of Count Orsini, and her accomplice Benedetto, a profligate relative of Orsini, are determined to prevent this from happening. But when Benedetto accuses Faulkener's mother of being the wanton mistress of Charles Stuart, he kills him in a fight. Unaware that it is her own son, Countess Orsini then demands punishment for the murderer of her husband's relative. In the meantime, Faulkener's friend Stanley asks the count for mercy, but they set to in a duel when Stanley tells him of his wife's past. The count is mortally wounded. In the final act in which Faulkener appears on trial for murder, his mother intervenes and recounts her past which has led to such disasters. The truth is out but there is no peace. On hearing of the death of her husband she falls to the ground and exclaims in utter anguish: 'And now the blood is on me! My hands are covered! — My robes are steeped!'[34] As Mrs. Siddons declared in the epilogue, it all goes to show how a devil may 'lure suspectless virtue to its ruin'.[35]

The *European Magazine and London Review* reported after the first night that there were some well-wrought scenes although the story did not possess strength and variety enough to engage the attention through five acts. Above all, the reviewer indignantly protested: 'the foundation is lewdness, the superstructure successful vice'.[36] The *London Chronicle* concurred that the characters were unnaturally depraved and the incidents improbable.[37]

As for the *Satirist or Monthly Meteor*, it took delight in damning the inadvertent broad farce 'written and *founded on fact* by Political Justice Godwin Esq.'[38] All the same, the play was heard throughout with occasional applause, and when the leading actor came forward at the end to announce it for repetition, the ayes won the day.

*Faulkener* was the last play Godwin wrote. It neither brought him the £800 he had expected, nor the fame he had hoped for; instead, he was forced to realize that his genius was not as a heroic tragedian. There was little conflict of real passion in his tragedy: it consisted essentially of a series of soliloquies spoken by cardboard characters. The stage business could not hide its hollowness. The excellent cast got as much out of *Faulkener* as they could, but when it was printed in the spring of 1808 the *Critical Review*, the *Literary Panorama* and the *Monthly Review* all noted the dullness and inspidity of the text.[39]

Godwin's last public statement on the theatre came after seeing Kemble's performance as Cardinal Wolsey in Shakespeare's drama *Henry VIII*. In a letter written to the *Morning Chronicle* on 3 April 1809 and signed 'Aristarchus', Godwin maintained that Shakespeare had tried to exhibit 'a great man sustaining himself with dignity amidst the storm of his fortune' (did Godwin identify with Wolsey?), while Kemble had represented him as 'a poor, broken-hearted wretch, robbed of office and spirit at the same time, and whimpering and wailing in the most pitiful strain'.[40] With scholarly precision, he quoted extensively from the play to back up his case. Where Godwin in *Political Justice* had suggested that enlightened humanity would refuse to repeat words and ideas not their own, as a playwright himself he insisted on fidelity to the author's intentions.

In the meantime, Godwin's relationship with his wife was far from perfect. During a trip to Southend in the summer of 1806, she complained of the 'sordid thoughts' which dominated their daily life in London, but all Godwin could do was to call on her to cultivate the 'firmness and equanimity' of philosophy.[41] They decided in the following year to move the Juvenile Library to larger premises at 41 Skinner Street, on the corner of Snow Hill, Holborn.[42] Godwin borrowed £300 from Curran and transferred the business on 18 May 1807. On 11 August, he took up residence and was joined by his wife and children late in the autumn. The family lived above the shop and a printing shop and warehouse were rented next door.

Although new, Skinner Street was not very salubrious. It was intended to improve access to the City but the houses were badly built and remained surrounded by a maze of decaying alleys. It never attracted much business. Only a hundred yards from their door public executions were performed at the Old Bailey, and in the very year the Godwins moved in, the hanging of the murderers Haggerty and Holloway drew a crowd of over 45,000 in

Vaughn del

Published June 1st 1803 by Tegg & Co.

Page sc

XXV. View of Skinner Street from Fleet Market, 1803.

which twenty-eight people were suffocated or trampled to death and sixty injured. In the early morning, animals would be drawn over the cobbles to Smithfield market while throughout the day prisoners would be taken from Giltspur Compter to Newgate. There would be a constant throng of people coming and going to the milliners, furriers, coffee-dealers, oil shops, floor-cloth manufacturers and oyster and orange warehouses in the street.

The rent of 41 Skinner Street at £150 a year was more than that of the Polygon and the Hanway Street rooms combined, but at least there was more room in the five-storeyed building. Over the entrance to the shop a stone carving of Aesop was placed relating fables to children. A passer-by could easily peer through the immense low display windows and see the counters laden with books, with Mrs. Godwin and her assistants organizing the business in a back room. One young enthusiastic reader recalled later how he lingered 'with loving eyes over those fascinating story-books, so rich in gaily-coloured prints; such careful editions of marvellous old histories'.[43]

Godwin for his part tried to avoid the shop as much as possible. He chose as his study a small room above it which gave onto the street. It was shaped like a quadrant, with windows in the arc and a fireplace in one radius. All the available wall space was taken up with shelves of rare books which he had been collecting. He hung above his desk Opie's portrait of Mary

Wollstonecraft which faced on the opposite wall Northcote's portrait of himself. It was small but comfortable, a haven in which he could escape temporarily the harsh demands of a debtor's life.

Whilst they were moving, Godwin very nearly lost the business. The manager Hodgkins, in whose name the Juvenile Library was registered to conceal Godwin's involvement, tried to claim that he was the legal owner. Godwin discovered the plan just in time and summarily dismissed Hodgkins. Although he continued to use a pseudonym for his own contributions to the Juvenile Library, it had sufficiently established a respectable reputation for him to have it registered in his wife's name.

The most pressing problem was to find a new manager. He asked Eliza Fenwick, the friend who had attended Mary Wollstonecraft on her deathbed, to recommend someone else as a manager. Being in desperate straits, with her husband in prison, she suggested herself. But the conditions were not good and she complained to Mary Hays: 'I suffer excessively from cold & long fasting, for as I cant have my meals there, I go everyday without dinner.'[44] She liked the work well enough however and wrote for Godwin a first grammar entitled *Rays from the Rainbow,* and the popular *Lessons for Children; or, Rudiments of Good Manners, Morals, and Humanity.* Unable to work under his wife, she eventually left for their publishing rival Benjamin Tabart in 1808.

Godwin also contacted Lady Mountcashel, the republican aristocrat whose acquaintance he had made during his trip to Ireland in 1800. She had left her husband and eight children to live in London as 'Mrs. Mason', a pseudonym used by Mary Wollstonecraft who had been employed in her family as a governess. She contributed to the Juvenile Library *Stories of Old Daniel: or Tales of Wonder and Delight,* the success of which warranted a *Continuation of the Stories of Old Daniel* and also encouraged Godwin to publish her *Stories for Little Girls and Boys in Words of One Syllable.*

But it was the Lambs who continued to be the best contributors. Early in 1807 Godwin paid them sixty guineas for their *Tales from Shakespear* which appeared in two volumes with illustrations designed by Mulready at the price of six shillings. It sold out immediately and was reissued separately in twenty parts. It became the most famous publication of the Juvenile Library and remains a classic. Lamb was pleased with the money but annoyed by Godwin's cavalier treatment of his text. He sent a copy to Wordsworth on 29 January 1807, apologizing for the plates, which had been chosen by the *'bad baby'*, and complaining of Godwin's 'egregious *dupery*' for having written the advertisement and the first part of the preface without consultation.[45]

The two friends continued to quarrel about literary matters. When Lamb sent in the following year the manuscript of *The Adventures of Ulysses,* Godwin objected to some of the more lurid descriptions on the grounds that 'it is children that read children's books (when they are read); but it is parents that choose them'.[46] Lamb replied that he was willing to make one alteration referring to a giant's vomit, but added 'Take the work such as it is, or refuse it.'[47] A month later Godwin complained that the preface was 'too naked' and asked him to add an introduction to Homer.[48] It was the final straw: 'I am *sick*', Lamb wrote, 'absolutely sick of that spirit of objection which you constantly shew, as if it were only to *teaze one*, or to warn one against having any more dealings with you in the way of trade.'[49] Godwin quickly recognized his fault however and replied next day: 'I am rightly served for having wanted any thing, In particularly for having expresse[d] my wants in so diffident a manner.'[50] He was also pleased to bring out in 1809 the Lambs' celebrated *Poetry for Children, Entirely Original* as well as *Mrs. Leicester's School; or, The History of Several Young Ladies, related by Themselves*.

But despite Godwin's industry and his wife's enthusiasm, the Juvenile Library never managed to become fully solvent. The cost of paper, printing, engraving and binding was great; the booksellers who took most of Godwin's publications were reluctant to pay; and the accounting was extremely haphazard. The £300 borrowed from Curran was quickly spent and profits did not meet the outgoings. By the spring of 1808, Godwin was desperate. He visited his mother and brother in Norfolk in May, and on his return called on Capel Lofft in Troston, but the trip failed to renew his spirits. He wrote to his wife despondently, 'I can bear prosperity, and I know I can bear adversity. The dreadful thing to endure is those uncertain moments, which seem to be the fall from one to the other, which call for exertions, and exhibit faint gleams of hope amidst the terrible tempest that gathers round.'[51]

The pressure seriously affected his health. He had been long subject to spells of sleepiness in the afternoon, which occasionally seized him even in company. His fainting fits however also returned with such severity that Godwin felt compelled to describe them to his friend Dr. Ash:

> the attacks were preceded by a minute's notice, and each fit (of perfect insensibility) lasted about a minute . . . If seized standing, I have fallen on the ground, and I have repeatedly had the fits in bed . . . in every instance each single fit seemed to find me and leave me in perfect health . . . The approach of the fit is not painful, but is rather entitled to the name of pleasure, a gentle fading away of the senses; nor is the recovery painful, unless I am teazed in it by persons about me.[52]

It is interesting that Godwin had sufficient power over himself to continue with his daily routine when these fits occurred. His self-discipline, however, might well have been the key to their recurrence. Their origin seems to have been psychosomatic, for they tended to occur in periods of greatest stress in Godwin's life: in 1783, when he was trying to leave the ministry; in 1800, when he was suffering from the public condemnation of his former friends; in 1803, when he was having difficulty in his second marriage; and now in 1808, as he was failing to make ends meet with the responsibility of a large family.

As a last resort, Godwin tried to raise enough capital to place the business on a sound footing by means of a public subscription. The publisher Joseph Johnson gave his advice and Marshal took the necessary arrangements in hand. Godwin was full of trepidation. 'I am prepared for the worst,' he wrote to Marshal, 'I will go to prison. I will be in the *Gazette*. I will move to a meaner situation, or anything else that is necessary.'[53]

Marshal approached many of the leading Whigs, but Godwin was sufficiently anxious to draw up himself a circular stating his case. He stressed above all that his books were

> so written as to be incapable of occasioning offence to any; as, indeed, Mr. Godwin would have held it an ungenerous and dishonourable proceeding to have insinuated obnoxious principles into the minds of young persons under colour of contributing to their general instruction. The books have accordingly been commended in the highest terms in all the reviews, and are now selling in the second and third editions respectively.[54]

The Whig patricians, spurred on by Lord Holland and the Earl of Lauderdale, rallied round the old friend of liberty, and with contributions from his acquaintances Curran, Johnson, Phillips, Grattan and Samuel Rogers, he eventually managed to raise some £1,600.

Godwin was thus saved from the debtors' prison. His wife took over the management of the business and spent the remainder of their capital on furnishings, equipment and stock. John Fairley, an umbrella maker in Edinburgh, agreed to act as their Scottish agent. This arranged, Godwin was able to return with renewed vigour to his study above the shop, and in 1809 published two works for adults, and a history, a grammar, a dictionary, and anthologies of prose and verse for children. Whatever the degree of his financial acumen, it cannot be said that he neglected his work and obligations.

Ever since reading Rollin as a boy, Godwin had been fascinated by Roman history, so it was only natural that after his *History of England* he should write a *History of Rome: From the Building of the City to the Ruin of the Republic*. He was less concerned with historical accuracy than with moral education, and felt Roman history was a proper study for the young precisely because it contained 'the finest examples of elevated sentiment and disinterested virtue, that are to be met with in the history of any country of the earth'.[55] Despite Godwin's claim in his circular that he would never insinuate 'obnoxious principles' into the minds of the young, his democratic and republican bias is obvious. He talks, for instance, of the possibility of virtue without religious dogma. He condemns the unequal distribution of property, and the respect paid to men on account of their wealth. Above all, he laments the fact that in the past rebellions have failed because the 'rich had dependents and friends among the poor, who though their interests were opposite, were ready to stand by their masters'.[56]

The *Monthly Review* found Godwin's attempt to inspire generous sentiments and appeal to the imagination congenial; the *European Magazine and London Review* felt it was in a higher class than a mere school-book; but the *Critical Review* objected to the lack of detail.[57] The public and schools were impressed and by 1835 it had reached six editions.

Godwin next published in 1809 *The Christ's Hospital Dictionary of the English Tongue* by W. F. Mylius. Mylius was not this time a pseudonym but the name of a schoolmaster at the Catholic Academy in Red Lion Square, High Holborn. Mylius may possibly have provided materials for the first edition of the dictionary but it was on Godwin's plan. Godwin also corrected the proofs and wrote the five-page preface. He had high hopes for its success and wrote on 12 July to Archibald Constable, the editor of the *Edinburgh Review*: 'this one publication might (in the phraseology of Garroway's Coffee-house) make a man of me for ever'.[58] The dictionary was published five days later. Godwin then immediately started to revise it to such an extent that he began to call it his own. 'I am just now writing,' he wrote to his fellow etymologist David Booth on 6 September, 'compelled by hard necessity & a concurrence of circumstances, something in your subject'.[59]

In the process of revising the dictionary, Godwin recorded in a rare note in his diary that he had made 'an entirely new discovery' as to the way of teaching the English language.[60] He then set about composing a grammar, and in the autumn the following work appeared: *Mylius's School Dictionary of the English Language . . . To which is prefixed A New Guide to the English Tongue by Edward Baldwin*. On 21 September, he wrote ironically to Henry Crabb Robinson:

Buonaparte is no more anxious for the success of his virtuous enterprises in Spain & Austria, than I am for the success of my School Dictionary . . . Mr. Baldwin (the celebrated author of Fables, Ancient & Modern, a Pantheon, a History of Rome, &c, alias W.G.) has done Mr. Mylius the favour to present him with a lucubration; & I am rendedered somewhat more sanguine by the weight of his name, & the *admirable perspecuity* of his discussions.[61]

In keeping with his liking for clarity and precision, Godwin stressed in the preface to the dictionary that he wanted to avoid the ambiguity of Dr. Johnson and give the original and most customary use of each word. By memorizing the definitions, the pupil would at once acquire 'clear, simple and accurate ideas', be imbued with 'the principles of taste', and have his mind stored with 'classical and elegant phraseology'. And by having the first meaning of a word in his thoughts which is the first in the reality of things, he would be made 'a logician and a philosopher'.[62]

The second edition of the dictionary was clearly the work of Godwin. True to the principles of *Political Justice*, politics is termed the 'science of government' and anarchy 'want of government; a nation without magistracy'. Again, truth is defined as a 'proposition which states things as they are', and justice as 'that which is due and equal in treatment between one living being and another'. It is difficult to see how the Catholic Mylius could define the Pope as merely 'the bishop of Rome', and God as 'the Supreme Being; a fictitious deity'. Even the definition of a novel — 'a fictitious history of ordinary life' — is in keeping with Godwin's view of fiction.[63]

The object of Godwin's grammar was to shorten the time necessary to obtain a competent knowledge of the English language. He wished to present a new method of declension in which the words are distributed into families, thereby showing how by easy rules the substantive, the verb, the adjective, the personal substantive, and the adverb are affiliated with each other. Such an approach would lead the pupil into the philosophy of language and inspire him 'with the inclination to dissect his words, and thus purify and clear, from incidental incumbrances, and the imaginary empire of lawless caprice, the primary and secondary ideas they represent'.[64] The *Anti-Jacobin Review*, the *European Magazine and London Review* and the *Monthly Review* all found the grammar ingenious and recommended it with the dictionary.[65] It became a standard text in schools. By 1819 it had sold more than 25,000 copies and was in its ninth edition. It was still being reprinted as late as 1853.

In the same year, Godwin published *The Junior Class Book; or Reading Lessons for Every Day of the Year*. Although it was ostensibly the work of Mylius, Godwin once again seems to have been responsible for the selection of the poetry and prose. Of the extracts from the 'most approved authors', twenty-nine come from Godwin's own pseudonymous works for the Juvenile Library and several from the Lambs' contributions. Many of Godwin's favourite themes and authors are also represented: Fénelon on

'The Triumph of Steadfast Integrity'; Addison on 'Benevolence Recompensed'; Goldsmith on 'Justice'; and Defoe on 'Give me neither Poverty nor Riches'. There is even the same extract 'Of Truth and Sincerity' from Tillotson's sermons which Godwin quoted in *The Enquirer*.[66]

Godwin still considered that there was a need for a more substantial school grammar than his *New Guide to the English Tongue*. He therefore turned to his young friend Hazlitt for one. Hazlitt had first met Godwin in 1794, but they did not become intimate until 1799. Hazlitt must have appeared to Godwin like a ghost out of his own past. Both were outstanding products of the culture of Rational Dissent: Hazlitt's father took over the congregation of Godwin's father in Wisbech; the young Hazlitt went to the New Dissenting College at Hackney which replaced Hoxton; and Godwin's old tutor Kippis became his sponsor. Hazlitt even became a close friend of Joseph Fawcett, Godwin's first principal oral instructor. Godwin for his part encouraged and helped the fledgeling writer who had come to London as a miniature painter. He had persuaded Joseph Johnson to publish his *Essay on the Principles of Human Conduct* (1804) (which defended disinterested benevolence on the ability of the imagination to foresee future events) and tried to find a publisher for his abridgement of Abraham Tucker's *Light of Nature Pursued*.

In 1807, they quarrelled however, when Hazlitt's *Reply to the Essay on Population, by the Rev. T. Malthus* appeared. Although Godwin felt Hazlitt had done an essential service to the public, he did not like the temper and arrangement of the work and was horrified to find himself misquoted on infanticide in a footnote. 'I can forgive this unjust attack upon me,' he wrote stiffly, 'but I must censure it.'[67] Hazlitt appeased him by insisting that the whole book was written on his side of the question and was first inspired by his anger against Malthus for having made 'unfair & uncandid use' of some of Godwin's unguarded expressions.[68]

When Godwin interfered with the manuscript of the grammar commissioned in 1809, it was Hazlitt's turn to be annoyed. He already had three of his books suppressed and 'to be dashed in pieces against the dulness of schoolmasters' was just too much.[69] Although Hazlitt set about revising the work, Godwin continued to be dissatisfied and in a string of letters in October and November they argued about its contents. In the end, Hazlitt told Godwin quite bluntly that he was wasting his powers with children's books: 'the works of William Godwin do not stand in need of those of E. Baldwin for vouchers and supporters. The latter (let them be as good as they will) are but dust in the balance compared with the former.'[70] But despite their acrimonious exchanges, the grammar was eventually finished in November and Godwin was able to recommend it to Archibald Constable as a work written by 'one of my inward friends, Mr. William Hazlitt.

He is a man of singular acuteness and sound understanding'.[71] For his part, Hazlitt was so sick of grammar and so disheartened by the changes that he never alluded to the book again except as one of Godwin's own productions.

*The New and Improved Grammar of the English Tongue* appeared at the end of 1809. When Godwin reissued it with his *New Guide to the English Tongue* in 1810, Lamb characteristically commented to Manning: 'Hazlitt has written a *grammar* for Godwin; Godwin sells it bound up with a treatise of his own on language, but the *grey mare is the better horse*. I don't allude to Mrs. Godwin, but to the word *grammar* . . .'.[72] Godwin, his eye for ever on the market, then published an abridgement of the two with some additions called *Outlines of English Grammar* in the same year. The *Anti-Jacobin Review* praised the introductory notes and the critical illustrations, while the *Critical Review* and the *Monthly Review* felt it was more suitable for schools than the existing ones.[73]

Although preoccupied with money worries and his publishing firm, Godwin still managed to express his personal opinions in the occasional essay. During the winter of 1808–9, he wrote and published at his own expense a curious *Essay on Sepulchres: or, A Proposal for erecting some Memorial of the Illustrious Dead in All Ages on the Spot where their Remains have been interred* in order to inspire others to noble deeds. He adopted the adage 'to write with fervour, and to revise with leisure' and the result was an elegant and whimsical essay.[74] His almost Burkean worship of ancestors and his new feeling for nature come together in a powerful passage when he exclaims: '*In new countries* we may discern the wilder and more romantic features of nature . . . But how much greater is it than this, to revert to the noblest of the creator's works, and to call up the nations and men who have formerly trod the earth which now I tread!'[75]

At the same time, the essay form allowed Godwin to range over many subjects, and he took the opportunity to make his views known to the public. In his metaphysics, he admits that he is 'more inclined to the opinion of the immaterialists, than the materialists', although he is unable to follow Bishop Berkeley in believing that the body — as the vehicle through which the knowledge of the thoughts and virtues of another are conveyed — is nothing: 'I cannot love my friend, without loving his person.'[76]

In his psychology, he rejects the division of human beings into the '*feeling*' and the '*unfeeling*'. Undoubtedly defending himself, and describing his own temperament, he insists that 'the sincerest warmth is not wild, but calm; and operates in greater activity in the breast of the stoic, than in that of the vulgar enthusiast'.[77] He further returns to a dominant theme of *Political Justice* and *The Enquirer* that 'man has an understanding to be matured, an imagination, or which is nearly the same thing, a moral sense, to be developed, and even a taste to be refined'.[78] Far from calling for a return to the 'savage state', he considers man 'a compound and heaven-born creature'.[79] Having pulled God down from the heavens, Godwin wished to elevate Man into a God, not place him on the par with animals.

The essay was the first piece of philosophical writing Godwin published since his *Thoughts* in 1801, and he had little hope for success. In his preface, he observed ironically:

> I am a man of no fortune or consequence in my country; I am the adherent of no party; I have passed the greater part of my life in solitude and retirement; there are numbers of men who overflow with gall and prejudice against me (God bless them!), and would strenuously resist a proposal I made, though it were such as from any other quarter they would accept with thankfulness.[80]

The proposal was never taken up, but the essay itself was generally well-received. The *British Critic*, the *Critical Review*, the *European Magazine and London Review*, and the *Literary Panorama* all found the project honour-able and the style pleasing, although the *Monthly Review* called it a 'play of genius' which was simply too sentimental and romantic.[81] Lamb, always given to whimsy, enjoyed it. He thought it was a 'very pretty, absurd, book' — better than James Hervey's *Meditations among the Tombs* but not as good as Sir Thomas Browne's *Hydriotaphia, or Urn-burial*.[82] His sister Mary also liked the sentiments although she felt the proposal itself was like 'throwing salt on a sparrows tail to catch him'.[83]

Although only fifty-two, Godwin no doubt imagined the recommended plain wooden cross over his own grave as one of the illustrious dead. In the following year, he began an 'Essay on Death'. He already felt himself to be only 'half' body, and longed for the very few years to pass when he would be 'all pure & unmingled mind'. He was deeply depressed by his fall from fame and the apostasy of his 'fellow-labourers' in the cause of humanity. 'Oh,' he exclaimed,

> when will the hour arrive, in which that only shall be remembered of me that is worthy to be remembered, & my follies & frailties, the sneers of my rivals & the misconceptions of my foes, shall be forgotten, like the blots & soil of the paper which now receives the record of my thoughts![84]

He dropped the essay however in dejection and turned to a well-tried remedy — fiction. He planned a new novel inspired by the Christian legend of the *Seven Sleepers of Ephesus* and by the tale of Sleeping Beauty in Perrault's *Mother Goose*. The idea was for a hero to fall asleep unexpectedly for many years at a time. It would allow Godwin to indulge both his love of history and invention, but he was keenly aware of the problem of unity it would pose and that such a canvas would demand 'a vast variety of figures, actions, and surprises'.[85] Nevertheless, he began the first episode, setting it in Spain in the twelfth century.

Written in the first person as usual, the noble hero describes his chivalrous upbringing. When he is a young man, his father and uncle go to fight the Moors, but while they are away the Moors storm and seize their castle. The narrative then breaks off — having finished one episode, Godwin did not feel up to the task of inventing anew a dozen or so times. It was left aside until 1833 when Godwin had it printed in the *New Monthly Magazine* as a 'Fragment of Romance'.

Apart from showing his interest in Spain — Wellington's Peninsular Campaign was on at the time — the fragment develops in embryo many of Godwin's favourite themes. The central idea of the sleeping narrator recalls Godwin's preoccupation in *Political Justice* and *St. Leon* with prolonging life and may well have been used to demonstrate the perfectibility of man. Like all Godwin's heroes, the sleeper is isolated from the rest of humanity by his exceptional gifts and has his benevolent nature corrupted by circumstances: 'In my childhood the world to me was innocent . . . but the injuries I am going to relate come from the hand of man . . . I was driven to entertain sentiments of suspicion, jealousy, and dislike . . .'[86]

Godwin also wishes to undermine the myth of the Dark Ages and the superiority of the North: the Spanish Christians might have excelled in military achievements, but the Moors who first came to Spain surpassed them in music, poetry and philosophy. And while he can celebrate the 'splendid feelings' which chivalry nourishes beyond any institution man ever conceived, he bemoans the fact that Christianity and war 'came united' from the lips of the hero's mother.[87]

This was perhaps the worst period in Godwin's life. The Juvenile Library demanded constant attention, he was endlessly forced to churn out children's books, and he was inexorably falling into debt. Many of his closest friends had dropped away. Fawcett had died in 1804, partly, according to Hazlitt, because of his disappointment at the failure of the French Revolution. The young Thomas Wedgwood died in the following year. Thelwall had become a teacher of elocution. Horne Tooke was in virtual retirement in Wimbledon. Maria Reveley and Amelia Alderson had become Mrs. Gisborne and Mrs. Opie respectively and had gone their different ways.

The rift with Elizabeth Inchbald was only partially healed. In 1805, Godwin had written to congratulate her on the success of her play *To Marry or Not to Marry*, signing himself 'votre ancien ami'.[88] She sent a printed copy in reply. But although she still had some affection for the philosopher, she could never forgive his conduct. 'Poor Godwin', she wrote to Mrs. Opie in 1809, 'is a terrific example for all conjugal biography; but he has marked that path which may be avoided, and so is himself a sacrifice for the good of others.'[89] Godwin called on her two years later, but she was not at home. They never re-established their personal acquaintance.

Although it had been expected, Godwin was deeply saddened when his oldest and most intimate friend Holcroft died on 23 March 1809 at the age of sixty-three. Throughout a long illness the tissues of his heart had hardened, but he confounded all the physicians by keeping himself alive by his extraordinary mental powers: it was a last and valiant demonstration of his favourite theory that mind might one day become omnipotent over matter.

Holcroft and Godwin had of course been estranged since 1805, but four days before he died, Holcroft expressed a wish to see his old comrade. According to Hazlitt, when Godwin came Holcroft's feelings were overpowered: 'He could not converse, and only pressed his hand to his bosom, and said, "My dear, dear friend!"' They met again the next day but he had not enough strength to hold a conversation. After taking an affectionate leave, he simply said that he had 'nothing more to do in this world'.[90]

Godwin was inconsolable. He attended the funeral with Nicholson, Paine, Thelwall, Lamb, Crabb Robinson and others. He then helped Marshal to raise a subscription for the widow and her children, and with his friends Tuthill and Nicholson agreed to supervise the publication of the incomplete memoir dictated by Holcroft in the last weeks of his life. Godwin would have been the ideal biographer, but he no doubt felt too close to his subject, and Hazlitt undertook to complete the life and edit the letters.

When Hazlitt published Holcroft's diary, however, Godwin was furious. He wrote indignantly to Mrs. Holcroft that if he had known that her husband recorded 'every idle word, every thoughtless jest' he made, he would never have called upon him at all. He could see no other purpose to the publication of the diary than 'to gratify the malignity of mankind, to draw out to view the privacies of firesides, and to pamper the bad passions of the idle and worthless with tittle-tattle, and tales of scandal'.[91]

But this was not the only shock Godwin was to have in 1809. Only five months after the death of his best friend, Godwin's mother died on 13 August. When he heard the news, he returned home immediately, and attended the funeral at Guestwick as chief mourner. The procession went three miles from his brother Hull's farm in Bradenham to the burial ground in Guestwick with four or five open chaises filled with friends and relations. John Sykes, the Methodist minister who had replaced Godwin's father, conducted the service. His mother was buried next to her husband and one of her children. Godwin had the following inscription made on a slab which covered the traditional brick stack:

> In memory of the Rev'd John Godwin who died November 12th 1772 in the 51st year of his age. Also Richard his son who died in his infancy. Also Anne the Wife of the above-mentioned John Godwin who remained 37 years his widow & affectionate Mother of his children & died Aug. 13th 1809 Aged 87 years.[92]

After the ceremony, Godwin was invited to dine at Hull's mother-in-law, but he preferred to be alone and returned to Hull's farm. He slept in the room where his mother's corpse had reposed the night before. He was strangely troubled, and wrote to his wife of profound feelings he rarely expressed:

> I was brought up in great tenderness, and though my mind was proud to independence, I was never led to much independence of feeling. While my mother lived, I always felt to a certain degree as if I had somebody who was my superior, and who exercised a mysterious protection over me. I belonged to something — I hung to something — there is nothing that has so much reverence and religion in it as affection to parents. The knot is now severed, and I am, for the first time, at more than fifty years of age, alone. You shall now be my mother.[93]

There were some bright spots however in these dark days. Godwin was flattered by a visit late in 1808 by Aaron Burr, the former Vice-President of America who had come to London after his acquittal for high treason. Burr had been accused of 'rank Godwinism' by his enemies and the two people he first sought out on his arrival were Godwin and Bentham.[94] He found the two daughters of Mary Wollstonecraft 'very fine children' but possessing 'scarcely a discernable trace of the mother'. He considered Godwin's son William a 'remarkably fine boy' and unlike nearly all who knew her, described his wife as a 'sensible, amiable woman'.[95] When he returned from the Continent in 1812 he came to be almost part of the family, and the penniless Godwin raised money for him by selling some of his books and his ring watch.

Despite his notorious reputation, most people were impressed by the mildness, politeness and affability of Godwin's character. Lamb's friend Robert Lloyd found Mrs. Godwin 'not a pleasant woman', but thought Godwin 'a most delightful Man — the modulation of his voice was beautiful, and his language uncommonly correct'.[96] About this time De Quincey also met Godwin. He waited with trepidation to meet the 'great mormo set up to terrify all England' but was pleasantly surprised to find a 'little man, with manners peculiarly tranquil, philosophic, and dignified'.[97]

Godwin could also still attract the occasional young disciple. He helped a student called Patrick Patrickson to obtain a place at Emmanuel College, Cambridge, and arranged a subscription for him among his friends. Godwin easily slipped on the mantle of moral guide and he warned Patrickson that he would inevitably meet at Cambridge young men who 'will tempt you to dissipation, and the only security you can have against infection is a severe frugality of your time, and, in subordination to that, of your money'.[98] But although Godwin encouraged Patrickson to express his intimate thoughts and feelings and continued to send him a great deal of advice and some money, he was unable to check his increasing morbidity which eventually led to his suicide.

When Henry Crabb Robinson got to know him better in 1810, he was not so impressed. Crabb Robinson had appointed himself a 'Knight Errant' of Godwin's 'beautiful and peerless System', but Mackintosh's lectures, his reading of the German idealist philosophers, and his growing religious belief had all tempered his enthusiasm.[99] A personal acquaintance then soon dispelled his admiration for Godwin as a man, for he took great liberties with him, and 'made me feel my inferiority unpleasantly'.[100] When Robinson, for instance, dared to argue in the spring of 1811 that Mandeville's *Fable of the Bees* made virtue a farce, Godwin, who thought it taught indirectly the doctrine of *Political Justice*, declared his disputant to be 'the most intolerant man he ever knew'.[101] On the other hand, Godwin did at least introduce Crabb Robinson to all his friends at his house, notably Curran, Lamb, Coleridge and Place, and the diarist admitted that he saw 'none but remarkable persons there'.[102]

Although Godwin and Coleridge saw less of each other, they were still on good terms. Godwin attended with great interest his lectures on Shakespeare, but thought they were 'infinitely' below his private conversation which always impressed him with 'the vast extent of his knowledge'.[103] He felt in particular that Coleridge's remark that Shakespeare's plays are only to be read, not acted, was absolutely false. He would also grow impatient with Coleridge's declaiming mood when he 'got upon the indefinite and infinite, viz. the nature of religious conviction'.[104]

Coleridge, however, continued to defend Godwin privately. When Crabb Robinson happened to meet him and Hazlitt at Lamb's on 30 March 1811, he spoke feelingly of the unjust treatment Godwin had met with. He criticized with severity those who were once his extravagant admirers but who turned against him as soon as his reputation declined. 'There was', Crabb Robinson heard Coleridge observe,

more in Godwin after all than he was once willing to admit, though not so much as his enthusiasts fancied. He had declaimed against Godwin openly, but visited him notwithstanding he could not approve even of Wordsworth's feelings and language respecting Godwin. Southey's severity he ascribed to the habit of reviewing.[105]

Coleridge further agreed with Crabb Robinson's view of the infinite superiority of Godwin over the French writers in moral tendency and feeling.

Coleridge took an active interest in the Juvenile Library. In the spring of 1811, he informed Godwin of a plan for a poem on a naval theme with little plates for children, and asked what metre he would like. He also suggested a school book in two octavo volumes of ancient and modern 'Lives' in the manner of Plutarch, or possibly a series from Moses to Buonaparte of great men who had been 'more or less distant causes of the present state of the world'. Unfortunately none of these works were written, for Coleridge intended his efforts entirely for his old friend's benefit:

> I shall consider the Work, as a small plot of ground given up to you, to be sown at your own hazard with your own seed (gold-grains would have been but a bad Pun, & besides have spoilt the metaphor) — if the Increase should more than repay your risk and labor, why, then let me be one of your guests at *Harvest-home*.[106]

The Lambs remained regular visitors at Skinner Street, despite the hostility between them and Mrs. Godwin. Mary Lamb could not stop herself maliciously telling Hazlitt's wife in 1809 how Mrs. Godwin was envious of her improved health and of Hazlitt's discovery of a well in his garden.[107] As for Charles, he wrote to his old friend Manning that she 'grows every day in disfavour with God and man. I will be buried with this inscription over me, Here lies C L the Woman *Hater:* I mean, that hated *one woman*.'[108] She was, he declared to Hazlitt, a 'damn'd infernal bitch'.[109] She undoubtedly inspired his sketch of Mrs. Priscilla Pry, and Godwin is recognizable in her husband Tom:

> He must know all about every thing, but his desires terminate in mere science. Now as far as the *pure mathematics*, as they are called, transcend the *practical*, so far does Tom's curiosity, to my mind, in elegance and disinterestedness, soar above the craving, gnawing, *mercenary* (if I may so call it) inquisitiveness of his wife.[110]

Nevertheless, Lamb was ready to be reasonably polite to Mrs. Godwin in order to see Godwin. When he was forced to ask them not to call in the morning because of his sister's delicate mental state, he insisted that 'Your friendship is as dear to me as that of any person on earth'.[111] And he continued to enjoy the philosopher's hospitality, returning home on occasion after a solitary rubber of whist 'brimfull of Gin & water & snuff . . .'.[112]

Nor did Lamb cease to contribute to the Juvenile Library. His *Prince Dorus: or Flattery Put Out of Countenance* appeared in 1811, with illustrations probably by Mary Ann Flaxman. He might also have written the poem *Beauty and the Beast: or a Rough Outside with a Gentle Heart*, published by Godwin in the same year with a song set to the music of John Whitaker. The latter was only undertaken after Wordsworth politely refused the commission:

> I cannot work upon the suggestions of others however eagerly I might have addressed myself to the proposed subject if it had come to me of its own accord. You will therefore attribute my declining the task of versifying the Tale to this infirmity, rather than to an indisposition to serve you.[113]

Like Coleridge, he was keen to make amends with Godwin and asked for a copy of his *Essay on Sepulchres* to be sent via Lamb.

Godwin in the meantime did not flag from publishing as many books as possible for the rising generation. In 1810, he brought out, under the name of Mylius, *The Poetical Class Book* which contained a selection of the most popular ancient and modern English poets for reading lessons. Once again, the preface and choice of poems betray Godwin's unmistakeable hand. As a new man of feeling, he had come to appreciate the value of poetry:

> Prose in its purest acceptation is the vehicle of truth, is geometry, is logic, is chronicle; but poetry represents to us the passions and feelings of the soul; it lays before us the sentiments and heart of the writer, or for the personages he introduces to our knowledge. Thus we are acquainted with the world in our early years, and before we are called upon to take an active part upon its theatre. Poetry is in this sense a school of morality.[114]

From amongst his contemporaries, poems by Helen Maria Williams, Charlotte Smith, Scott, Byron, Holcroft, Humphrey Davy, Samuel Rogers, Coleridge, Wordsworth and Mary Lamb were included. In the following year, Godwin also brought out under Mylius's name *The First Book of Poetry* which was intended as a series of reading lessons for younger children. He again ranges through the 'whole *parterre*' of British poets, but gives particular attention to the 'beautiful little pieces' of Dr. Isaac Watts and to some of

John Gay's fables.[115]

Godwin began in 1809 his last book for the Juvenile Library under the name of Edward Baldwin, a *History of Greece: From the Earliest Records of that Country to the Time in which it was reduced into a Roman Province*. It was written on the same plan as his histories of Rome and England, and was intended to replace Goldsmith's history. Godwin was overwhelmed by the achievements of the Greeks: not only did they possess like the Romans the 'simple sublime of moral magnanimity', but they excelled in 'subtlety of intellect' and 'all the graces of imagination'. Above all, whatever 'bold and admirable conception' occurred in their minds, they attempted to realize it.[116] He was particularly impressed by Sparta and devoted thirteen pages to a panegyric of its institutions for his young readers. The work however was not finished until 1821, when it went unreviewed, probably because the reputation of Baldwin was by then secure. At all events it sold well, and new editions appeared in 1828, 1829, 1836, and as late as 1862.

Apart from his *History of Greece*, Godwin took his leave of his young readers and wrote no more for the Juvenile Library. He published, however, a story written by his ten-year-old daughter Mary called *Mounseer Nongtongpaw* (1809). His wife, moreover, imitated from the French of J. L. Jauffret some *Dramas for Children* (1809).[117] The second edition of 1817 contained four plates by George Cruikshank. She made a notable coup by being the first to translate *The Family Robinson Crusoe* (1814), an abridgement of Johann Rudolf Wyss's celebrated *The Swiss Family Robinson,* which she also published complete for the first time two years later. Among other contributors, Alicia Lefanu, Sheridan's niece, wrote the poem *Rosara's Chain* (1812), and Caroline Barnard came up with *The Parent's Offering; or Tales for Children* (1813) and *The Prize: or, the Lace-Makers of Missenden* (1817).

Godwin's pen and his wife's enterprise thus managed to establish the Juvenile Library as one of the foremost publishers and distributors of children's books. Its list contained more than twenty volumes, with eight booklets in the Copperplate Series. He could be justly proud of them: they were clearly and entertainingly written, handsomely illustrated, well printed and bound, and admirably adapted to children of different ages. They continued to be reprinted long after the firm was fogotten and ensured that Godwin's radical influence reached generations of pupils.

When an agent investigated the Juvenile Library in 1813, he could well report to the Privy Council that

> The proprietor is *Godwin*, the author of *Political Justice*. There appears to be a regular system through all his publications to supersede all other elementary Books, and to make his Library the resort of Preparatory

Schools, that in time the principles of democracy and Theophilanthropy may take place universally.

But although the agent concluded after a lengthy analysis of his works that Godwin had tried by degrees to introduce to the young 'every principle professed by the infidels and republicans of these days', Lord Sidmouth decided to take no action.[118] He was no doubt aware that Godwin had eschewed all tumult and violence and still had some powerful friends in the Whig opposition.

Despite the literary success of the Juvenile Library, Godwin's financial affairs went from bad to worse. In the past he had received large subsidies from Tom Wedgwood, and after his death in 1805 he was given at least one sum of £500 by his brother Josiah. Curran was for ever generous, and John Taylor, who lived in Norwich, was always ready to fill the breach. But for all their generosity, and the handsome public subscription raised by Marshal in 1808, Godwin was forced more and more to borrow from anyone he met.

The punctilious Crabb Robinson could never forgive this in Godwin but even he ascribed his 'irregularities to distress and not want of principle'.[119] Other contemporaries like Thomas Noon Talfourd saw it as an example of Godwin's candour and simplicity. After meeting him at Lamb's, he tried to tap the impoverished Grub Street writer next day for a 'little bill' of £150. When he heard the reality of his finances, Godwin showed no signs of dismay: "Oh dear," said the philosopher, "I thought you were a young gentleman of fortune — don't mention it — don't mention it; I shall do very well elsewhere:" — and then, in the most gracious manner, reverted to our former topics.'[120] It was, after all, the doctrine of *Political Justice* that the rich should hold their wealth as a trust to be distributed to the most needy.

Yet for all his outward calm and detached air Godwin's affairs were in serious disorder. In December 1809, Godwin's old friend and publishing adviser Joseph Johnson died. In the New Year, he therefore turned in desperation to Francis Place, the former leader of the Godwinian faction in the L.C.S. and a master tailor of some standing. He readily agreed to help and immediately recruited the wealthy reformer Elton Hammond, and the shrewd business man John Lambert, both of whom admired *Political Justice*.

On seeing the books of the Juvenile Library, the three were agreeably surprised. Godwin's assets of about £7,700 seemed to exceed his debts by £3,000. They concluded that with another investment of £3,000 Godwin could not only be placed in comparative ease but that the growing business carried on by his wife would repay the loan. The money was raised: Hammond advanced £600, Lambert £250, and Place £250. The remaining £2,000 was borrowed, principally through Place's exertions. The transaction however proved disastrous. After four years Place and Lambert retired £365 out of pocket and Place considered at least £2,500 was wholly wasted.

His financial advisers were dumbfounded. Basing their calculations on Godwin's own statements, his income must have paid from year to year the greater part of his current debts. Since 1804 he had been receiving at least £400 a year from friends. He had not paid his rent of £150 a year from 1807 because the owner of his house was unknown. They were therefore unable to understand why the £3,000 raised did not make him solvent and could only conclude that he must have been spending the vast sum of about £1,500 a year.[121]

It would appear that Godwin never informed Place of the true extent of his indebtedness. Moreover, he continued to act independently — not only borrowing but lending money to those in need. Far from being deliberately deceitful, as Place accused him, Godwin's affairs were by 1811 so complicated and his accounts so confused that it was simply not possible to give an accurate statement of them.

The pressure of work, the financial worry, and his precarious health all took their toll. In the summer of 1811, Crabb Robinson felt that the fifty-five-year-old philosopher was more or less done for. He wrote in his diary:

> He looks ill, and I fear he is so broken in constitution that further intellectual exertion is not to be expected from him; perhaps not even the ordinary functions of an ordinary mind! Poor man! His latter days, if they be long, will be gloomy. He is not supported by enthusiasm, or the cheering hopes of a mild and sober faith. Nor will he be comforted by the kindness and respect of numerous friends . . .[122]

The strain of the Juvenile Library only worsened Godwin's difficult relationship with his wife. His heroic impatience broke at last in August: he told her that she was a 'burden' from which the law would not let him be free. She packed her bags and left. From lodgings, she wrote that 'in the hardest struggle that ever fell to the lot of woman', she had lost her youth and beauty, but added that her state of mind would be that 'to which 10,000 daggers are mild, till I hear you accept the reconciliation I now send to offer'.[123] Godwin, never one to bear malice and aware how essential she had become in his difficult life, accepted it. He went on a holiday immediately to clear his mind on the South Coast of England, where he met the poet William Hayley ('He has everything for the eye, and nothing for the heart. Damn him.') in Felpham, and saw his former disciple Stoddart in Ryde.[124]

In the following year, he apologized to his wife for not doing justice to her character, qualifications and exertions:

> You were perhaps destined by your intrinsic nature for something much better than my wife. Yet in reality nothing can more crown your merits than the readiness with which you have submitted to this, the cheerfulness with which you have applied yourself to plans for the common benefit and support of our united family and the courage with which you have stooped even to put yourself behind a counter.[125]

The family, however, was not to remain united for long.

# CHAPTER XVII

## *The Shelley Circle*

Despite the constant money difficulties in the Skinner Street household, Jane recalled that everyone led a lively and cheerful life there:

> All the family worked hard, learning and studying: we all took the liveliest interest in the great questions of the day — common topics, gossiping, scandal, found no entrance in our circle for we had been brought up by Mr. Godwin to think it was the greatest misfortune to be fond of the world, or wordly pleasures or of luxury or money; and that there was no greater happiness than to think well of those around us, to love them, and to delight in being useful or pleasing to them.[1]

The children were able to meet some of the best minds of the age. They listened behind the sofa to Coleridge reading his *Ancient Mariner*, they played with Lamb, met Curran, and went on walks with Aaron Burr. Godwin taught the girls Roman, Greek and English history, and they learned French and Italian from tutors. Fanny and Mary drew very well, but as Jane could never draw she learned music and singing instead. Charles knew Latin, Greek, French, mathematics and drawing. Even the nine-year-old William gave a weekly lecture. In 1812, Burr saw him present, with great gravity and decorum, a lecture written by one of his sisters from a little pulpit on 'The Influence of Governments on the Character of the People'.[2] After the lecture they had tea, and the girls sang and danced an hour.

Godwin regretted that he did not have the leisure to bring up Mary Wollstonecraft's two daughters strictly according to her ideas. Nevertheless, he was delighted with their development. Fanny, he observed 'is of a quiet, modest, unshowy disposition, somewhat given to indolence, which is her greatest fault, but sober, observing, peculiarly clear and distinct in the faculty of memory, and disposed to exercise her own thoughts and follow her own judgment'. He considered his own daughter Mary superior in capacity and the reverse of Fanny in many particulars: 'She is singularly bold, somewhat imperious, and active of mind. Her desire for knowledge is great, and her perseverance in everything she undertakes almost invincible. My own daughter is, I believe, very pretty; Fanny is by no means handsome, but in general prepossessing.'[3]

Mary was clearly Godwin's favourite, although he tried not to show it. For her part, Mary considered him her 'God' and remembered 'many childish instances of the excess of attachment' she bore him.[4] Her stepmother soon discovered this 'excessive and romantic' attachment and a potentially explosive situation developed between them.[5] This was all the more dangerous since Mrs. Godwin always gave preference to her own daughter Jane but was forced to admit that she did not have 'such first-rate abilities' and that Mary always considered her stupid.[6] The rivalry became so intense between stepmother and daughter that later Mary invariably referred to her as 'an odious woman' and felt 'som[e]thing analogous to disgust' whenever she mentioned her name.[7]

In the spring of 1811, Mary was ordered by her doctor to spend six months at the seaside because of an ailment in her arm. In the following summer, it was decided to send her to stay in Dundee with the family of William Baxter who had been first introduced to Godwin by David Booth. The ostensible reason was her health, but the growing tension with Mrs. Godwin was probably the real cause. Godwin informed the Baxters that Mary had 'nothing of what is commonly called vices' and possessed 'considerable talent', although he hoped she would receive no special attention: 'I am anxious that she sould be brought up (in that respect) like a philosopher, even like a Cynic.'[8] Mary was to stay in Dundee for two years.

Charles Clairmont still showed his stepfather deference, but was growing more independent. Godwin preferred, for instance, the work of Anthony Collins to the 'broad grins' of Tom Paine, but Charles insisted on reading the *Age of Reason*.[9] He left Charterhouse in the spring of 1811, and after a short period with a tutor of mathematics, took up an apprenticeship in the autumn with the bookseller Archibald Constable in Edinburgh. Godwin gave him a glowing reference, emphasizing his 'obliging and kind disposition' and his 'natural and unassuming manners'.[10] The Godwins hoped that he would eventually take over the Juvenile Library and prove their salvation. He stayed with Godwin's agent John Fairley and apparently gave Constable 'perfect satisfaction'.[11]

As for his own son William, Godwin had early discovered that 'from nature' he had 'great clearness and precision of understanding' and 'much quickness to study'. Not having enough time to educate him at home, Godwin sent him in 1811 as a day boy to Charterhouse when he was eight years old. He soon became impatient there however and was unable to brook the disdain of the boarders. Like his father, he had a 'somewhat fiery disposition' and was inclined to become reserved when he apprehended 'an opposition which came to him in the shape of authority'. But in general, Godwin recalled that he was early disposed to listen to reason and was a boy 'of warmest affection and most entire generosity of temper'.[12]

Godwin in the meantime was quietly working on his accounts for the Juvenile Library when he received a letter dated 3 January 1812 from an unknown young man called Percy Bysshe Shelley. It marked the beginning of a tempestuous relationship which was to change all the lives in the Skinner Street household.

Shelley was just twenty years old. He had already published some of his poetry and was the author of two novels, *Zastrozzi* (1810) and *St. Irvyne, or The Rosicrucian* (1811). He had been expelled from Oxford for issuing a pamphlet entitled *The Necessity of Atheism* (1811). Although he considered marriage the 'most despotic most unrequired fetter', he had married Harriet Westbrook, the daughter of a retired coffee-house keeper.[13]

Godwin was his idol. He probably read *Political Justice* as a pupil at Eton whilst suffering the tyranny and inanity of his masters and schoolfellows. He ordered a personal copy from Stockdale on 19 November 1810. He had also read Godwin's novel *St. Leon* before writing *St. Irvyne*, although he later claimed that 'the reasonings had *then* made little impression'.[14] At all events, by 1811 he was an ardent champion of Godwin: he discussed his principles enthusiastically with his friend Thomas Jefferson Hogg and tried to put them into practice in his own life. As a result, his wealthy baronet father Sir Timothy refused to correspond with him and reduced his allowance to £200 a year, complaining to a friend: 'I only wish I had to operate on an Ingenuous Heart and Sound understanding, but he is such a Pupil of Godwin that I can scarcely hope he will be persuaded . . .'[15]

Godwin's reputation was so low in 1811 that Shelley had already enrolled his name on the list of the 'honorable dead'. It was therefore with 'inconceivable emotions' that he learned, probably from Southey, that he was still alive in London. 'The name of Godwin', the young poet wrote from Keswick to the fifty-five year old philosopher,

has been used to excite in me feelings of reverence and admiration, I have been accustomed to consider him a luminary too dazzling for the darkness which surrounds him, and from the earliest period of my knowledge of his principles I have ardently desired to share on the footing of intimacy that intellect which I have delighted to contemplate in its emanations.[16]

The hard-pressed Godwin was delighted. He received Shelley's letter on 6 January and replied immediately, complaining apparently of its 'generalizing character'. Shelley quickly remedied the fault and on 10 January sent the following autobiographical details:

> I was haunted with a passion for the wildest and most extravagant romances . . . It is now a period of more than two years since first I saw your inestimable book on 'Political Justice'; it opened to my mind fresh & more extensive views, it materially influenced my character, and I rose from its perusal a wiser and a better man. — I was no longer the votary of Romance; till then I had existed in an ideal world; now I found that in this universe of ours was enough to excite the interests of the heart, enough to employ the discussions of Reason. I beheld in short that I had duties to perform.[17]

He added that he was writing an inquiry into the causes of the failure of the French Revolution to benefit mankind (an unfinished tale called 'Hubert Cauvin') and had resolved to lose no opportunity to disseminate truth and happiness.

Again, Godwin was fascinated. He replied on the very day he received the letter, declaring that he felt 'in a manner responsible' for his young disciple's conduct.[18] The idea that the author of *Political Justice* should become his personal friend and adviser produced 'the most intoxicating sensations' in Shelley.[19] 'Share with me', he wrote to his ardent correspondent Elizabeth Hitchener,

> this acquisition more valuable than the gift of Princes. — His letters are like his writings the mirror of a firm and elevated mind. They are the result of the experience of ages which he condenses for my instruction; it is with awe and veneration that I read the letters of this veteran in persecution and independence. He remains unchanged.[20]

In the meantime, Shelley was busy preparing to leave for Ireland to forward Catholic Emancipation and composing *An Address to the Irish People*. He was also preparing a broadside ballad called *The Devil's Walk* which Godwin later carefully copied out. Godwin offered Shelley a letter of introduction to his old friend Curran, but was fearful of his extremism and warned him against early authorship. Shelley, however, replied that a portrait of the growth of the mind could be worth 'many metaphysical disquisitions', and reassured Godwin that his pamphlet owned 'no religion but benevolence, no cause but virtue, no party but the world'.[21] What more could the philosopher of universal benevolence say?

When his pamphlet was published in Dublin on 24 February, Shelley sent it together with *The Necessity of Atheism* to Godwin, with a gracious invitation to meet him in North Wales on his return, in 'a spot like that in which Fleetwood met Ruffigny; that then every lesson of your wisdom might become associated in my mind with the forms of Nature'.[22]

Godwin carefully read Shelley's *Address to the Irish People*. It was chiefly inspired by *Political Justice* with a smattering of Paine's *Rights of Man*. It called for the repeal of the Union and the emancipation of the Catholics. It suggested that 'when all men are good and wise, government will of itself decay'.[23] It even argued that 'Temperance, sobriety, charity and independence will give you virtue; and reading, talking, thinking and searching will give you wisdom.'[24] All this was well and good. But Shelley had admitted privately to Elizabeth Hitchener that he intended 'to shake Catholicism at its basis' and he could not prevent the fiery language of revolution erupting from the calm rhetoric of Godwinian gradualism.[25] 'The discussion of any subject', Shelley declared to the oppressed masses, 'is a right that you have brought into the world with your heart and tongue. Resign your heart's blood before you part with this inestimable privilege of man.'[26] He also recommended the formation of political associations to facilitate the political education of the people.

Godwin immediately recognized the tone: it was that of the radical artisans of the L.C.S., of the disciples of Paine and Thelwall, of the revolutionary politics of the 1790s. However commendable he found many of the sentiments of Shelley's pamphlet, he felt sure that it would be either ineffective or light the flames of rebellion and war. Above all, the 'pervading principle' of *Political Justice*, he insisted, is that

> association is a most ill-chosen and ill-qualified mode of endeavouring to promote the political happiness of mankind . . . Discussion, reading, enquiry, perpetual communication: these are my favourite methods for the improvement of mankind, but associations, organized societies, I firmly condemn.

More Burkean than ever, he could calmly tell his impetuous disciple:

> every institution and form of society is good in its place and in the period of time to which it belongs. How many beautiful and admirable effects grew out of Popery and the monastic institutions in the period when they were in their genuine health and and vigour. To them we owe almost all our logic and literature. What excellent effects do we reap, even at this day, from the feudal system and from chivalry! In this point of view nothing perhaps can be more worthy of our applause than the English Constitution.[27]

Shelley responded with spirit to Godwin's remonstrances. He reiterated his esteem for Godwin but found little congenial in his armchair radicalism:

> I am not forgetful or unheeding of what you said of Associations. — But Political Justice was first published in 1793; nearly twenty years have elapsed since the general diffusion of its doctrines. What has followed? have men ceased to fight, has vice and misery vanished from the earth. — Have the fireside communications which it recommends taken place? — Out of the many who have read that inestimable book how many have been blinded by prejudice . . .?[28]

Godwin was only too well aware of his own eclipse and the failure of philosophical reform: he must have winced painfully at the accuracy of Shelley's observation. He must have been further put out by Shelley's *Proposals for an Association of Philanthropists* which observed that his writings had been 'totally devoid of influence' during the French Revolution.[29]

Godwin did not receive the pamphlet immediately, but when he read an extract in the *Dublin Weekly Messenger* his worst fears were confirmed. If the masses heeded Shelley's call, he warned, they would 'rise up like Cadmus's seed of dragon's teeth, and their first act will be to destroy each other'. The genuine reformer must learn 'to contribute by a quiet, but incessant activity, like a rill of water, to irrigate and fertilize the intellectual soil'. Godwin ended his homily by called Shelley back to London, adding seductively: 'You cannot imagine how much all the females of my family, Mrs. G. and three daughters, are interested in your letters and your history.'[30]

Shelley's failure to ferment revolt in Dublin and his growing horror of the abjectness of the poor combined to make Godwin's letter welcome. He decided to leave Ireland and to withdraw from circulation his two pamphlets. But he did not entirely give up his ground — his mind was 'by no means settled' on the subject of associations, and he had seen and heard enough to make him doubt 'the Omnipotence of Truth in a society so constituted as that wherein we live'.[31] Moreover, Shelley did not inform Godwin of the *Declaration of Rights* he was working on, which despite its Painite inspiration expressed a Godwinian belief in natural law, in the claims of leisure and liberty, and in the ultimate dissolution of government. Hereafter, Shelley was never completely open with Godwin about his political aims and means.

Godwin was naturally delighted with his apparent abandonment of popular agitation. He could now look upon him, he wrote on 30 March, 'not as a meteor, ephemeral, but as a lasting friend'. He even found Shelley's pessimism was going from 'one extreme to the other', although he reiterated that the thing most to be desired is 'to keep up the intellectual, and in some sense the solitary, fermentation, and to procrastinate the contact and consequent action'.[32]

Shelley left Dublin and arrived in Wales early in June 1812. He hoped that Elizabeth Hitchener and the Godwin family would join Harriet and Eliza Westbrook to form his longed-for community of enlightened spirits at a farm in Nantgwillt, near Rhayader. On 3 June, Shelley wrote to Godwin reaffirming his indebtedness and loyalty:

> I did not truly *think* & *feel* however, until I read Political Justice, tho my thoughts & feelings after this period have been more painful, anxious and vivid, more inclined to action & less to theory . . . I fear that I am waiting in that mild & equable benevolence concerning which you question me; still I flatter myself that I improve.[33]

And when Godwin's letter of 30 March sent to Dublin eventually caught up with Shelley in Wales on 11 June, the poet immediately replied: 'That it is most affectionate & kind I deeply feel & thankfully confess. I can return no other answer than that I will become all that you believe & wish me to be. I should regard it as my greatest glory should I be judged worthy to solace your declining years . . .'[34]

In his moments of self-doubt, Shelley clearly needed the reassurance of a fatherly figure like Godwin. He discussed his reading of ancient romances and Greek and Roman history, and asked for Godwin's remarks on *A Letter to Lord Ellenborough* that he was writing. It was inspired by Daniel Isaac Eaton's recent imprisonment for publishing the third part of Paine's *Age of Reason*, and contained a characteristically Godwinian defence of the freedom of the press and speech as essential to individual development. Godwin's view of the pamphlet is not known, but it was sufficiently inflammatory for the printer to burn almost all of his thousand copies in alarm.

Godwin kept up his end of the correspondence diligently, and wrote to Shelley on 1, 6, 17, and 24 June, but all the letters have been lost. In the last, he apparently suggested a house owned by a friend called Eton at Chepstow to the itinerant Shelleys, but they found it half-built and moved on to Lynmouth in North Devon. From there, Shelley again invited, on 5 July, Godwin and his family to join them.

Their letters crossed, for Godwin had expressed shortly before his impatience to see Shelley's face and was eager to know where he would settle. Shelley had clearly already conquered the Skinner Street household by his letters — from the moment his 'well-known hand was seen, all the females were on the tiptoe to know'. But although they had still not met, Godwin gave fatherly advice. Quoting from *Political Justice* on the need to employ all one's energy and property for 'the production of the greatest quantity of general good', he warned him against extravagant living and borrowing on his patrimony.[35] Shelley replied defending himself of the charge of unnecessary expense but he was quick to add that a certain standard of living was necessary for philanthropy: 'if I was employed at the loom or the plough, & my wife in [cu]linary business and housewifery we shou[ld] (in the present state of society) quickly become very different beings, & I may add, less useful to our species'.[36]

In the meantime, Elizabeth Hitchener had decided to throw her lot in with the Shelleys and stayed overnight with Godwin on 14 July on her way from Sussex. She brought bad tidings a few days later to Lynmouth: 'She has seen the Godwins', Harriet Shelley wrote to a friend, 'and thinks Godwin different to what he seems, he lives so much from his family, only seeing them at stated hours. We do not like that, and he thinks himself such a very great *man*.'[37] She was particularly disappointed that he would not let one of his own children visit them just because he had not seen their faces.

Godwin sent a letter to Shelley with Hitchener on the 15th and another by post on the 24th. Her description of the philosopher did not however prevent the two men from discussing in depth the implications of materialist philosophy. Godwin was now a Berkeleyan and argued that the loftiest disinterestedness is incompatible with the strictest materialism. Shelley, fresh from a reading of D'Holbach's *Système de la Nature*, saw no connection between the two doctrines and while sharing Godwin's hatred of the 'system of self love' was at this stage a thoroughgoing materialist. The two men also disagreed about the importance of a classical education and linguistic training. Unlike Godwin, Shelley felt that the evils in acquiring Greek and Latin during youth considerably overbalanced the benefits since words 'so eminently contribute to the growth & establishment of prejudice'. Nevertheless, he still assured Godwin: 'as I see you in Political Justice, I agree with you. Your Enquirer is replete with speculations in which I sympathise . . .'[38] Godwin also argued against Helvétius's opinion of the omnipotence of education and persuaded him that there are character differences at birth.

In August, Shelley began writing his first great poem *Queen Mab* — a creative alternative to popular agitation and political despair. His studies were interrupted, however, by the arrest of his servant Dan for posting up his *Declaration of Rights* and his ballad *The Devil's Walk* in Barnstable. Shelley correctly anticipated the enquiries of Sidmouth's spies and quietly left for Wales at the end of the month.

Godwin in the meantime had decided to combine his short summer excursion with a visit to the Shelleys. He wrote to him on 31 August and 7 September and set off on the 9th. Despite attacks of 'deliquium', he was determined to make the best of the trip, and travelled via Slough,

Beckhampton, and Bath to Bristol. On the 11th, he went to Chepstow and walked to the castle, and the following day made a round trip to Tintern by boat. Then on the 13th he returned by chaise to Bristol where he wrote again to Shelley. The next day he called on Joseph Cottle and heard the news that the French had reached Moscow. He sailed on the 16th to Lynmouth but arrived on the 18th only to find that the Shelleys had gone three weeks before. He went to console himself in the nearby Valley of Stones. He heard however from the Shelleys' servant that they would be in London in a fortnight. 'This quite comforts my heart', Godwin wrote to his wife.[39]

The Shelley band had crossed into Wales and by chance soon found themselves in the contemporary wonder of Wales, the New Town of Tremadoc set up by the Foxite Whig William Madocks. For Shelley, the new community and embankment project to hold back the sea and reclaim land appeared as a direct attempt to reform mankind and their circumstances. He eagerly took up the offer of the cottage 'Tan-yr-allt' on a mountainside and threw himself into the campaign to raise money. In the autumn he went to London to this end, and combined business with the pleasure of meeting Godwin and his family for the first time. They stayed in London for some five and a half weeks, from 4 October to 13 November, at a hotel in St. James's Street.

Shelley, Harriet, and Elizabeth Hitchener dined with Godwin on the day they arrived in London. It proved a great success. Harriet wrote to a friend that Godwin's manners were 'soft and pleasing' and that his head was like a bust of Socrates. He seemed to delight in Shelley's society and gave up everything to be with them. He was moreover 'quite a family man'. There was the nineteen-year-old Fanny, 'very plain, but very sensible', the nine-year-old William, who was 'extremely clever', and, of course, Mrs. Godwin, a woman of 'great fortitude and unyielding temper of mind'.[40] The other children were away from home at the time — Charles in Edinburgh working at Constable's publishing firm, Mary in Dundee with the Baxters, and Jane in Walham Green at a boarding school.

Shelley and Godwin in fact spent almost every day in each other's company, and apart from the principles of *Political Justice*, the subjects discussed ranged from matter and spirit, atheism, utility and truth, the clergy, church, government, and the characteristics of German thought and literature.[41] Godwin was pleased to find that Shelley had ostensibly given up revolutionary politics and was associating himself with the practical reforms of Madocks. He encouraged him to organize systematically his reading and studies. He was also ready to help him in his financial affairs, partly no doubt because, as Harriet put it, he was 'sometimes very much pressed for enough ready money' and required an 'immense capital'.[42]

In fact, Godwin's affairs were once again in a terrible mess. The £3,000 raised by Place with the help of Lambert and Hammond the year before had failed to put the Juvenile Library on a sound footing. In addition to his first investment of £250, Place had gone surety in part for a loan of £500 from Josiah Wedgwood, and became sole guarantor of another loan of £500. By the autumn of 1812 he was bitterly critical of Godwin's finances which forced the philospher to complain: 'you are a firm man, & I have no hopes of you'.[43] Place replied that on the contrary he was not firm enough and that 'all would be lost' unless a 'very large sum' was obtained from Godwin's 'young friend'.[44]

Whilst in London in the autumn of 1812, Shelley led a lively social life. He renewed his acquaitance with his student friend Hogg and met Peacock through his publisher Thomas Hookham. Godwin also introduced Shelley to his circle which included Place and Curran's daughter Amelia. A more important meeting took place on Guy Fawkes night when Shelley ran into the streets to see the fireworks with Godwin's son William, who led him to the family friend John Frank Newton, a Zoroastrian who was to help clarify Shelley's ideas on vegetarianism. Five days later, Mary returned with Christie Baxter from Dundee but the Shelleys made no mention of their meeting at dinner the next day on 11 November.

Christie Baxter later recalled how she was entirely happy in the Godwin household at this time. The four girls had plenty of liberty, with frequent visits to friends' houses and to the theatre. She retained a warm respect for Godwin who took a quiet pleasure in their girlish talk. Jane, she remembered,

> was lively and quick-witted, and probably rather unmanageable. Fanny was more reflective, less sanguine, more alive to the prosaic obligations of life, and with a keen sense of domestic duty, early developed in her by necessity and by her position as the eldest of this somewhat anomalous family. Godwin, by nature as undemonstrative as possible, showed more affection to Fanny than to anyone else. He always turned to her for any little service he might require.[45]

Shelley did not stay to get to know Mary and her friend. On 13 November the Godwins came to dine at the Shelleys' hotel only to find that they had departed for Wales in the morning. Nevertheless, while raising money for the embankment project in Tremadoc, Shelley began an intensive period of study under Godwin's direction. Undismayed by his sudden departure, Godwin wrote to him on 18 and 25 November. Then on 10 December, he warmly recommended the study of history as a means of becoming acquainted with 'whatever of noble, useful, generous, and admirable, human nature is capable of designing and performing' and argued that it is 'superior to all the theories and speculations that can possibly be formed'. He urged Shelley to read the contemporaries of Shakespeare, and judged Shakespeare and Milton to be the best English poets, and Bacon and Milton to be the best prose writers. He added however: '*You* have what appears to me a false taste in poetry. You love a perpetual sparkle and glittering, such as are to be found in Darwin, and Southey, and Scott, and Campbell.'[46]

Godwin's repeated emphasis on slow reform must also have irritated Shelley while he was engaged in writing his fiery philosophical poem *Queen Mab* in Tremadoc. The Socratic philosopher, whom Harriet had delighted to contemplate, was revealing his more humble dimensions. No doubt jealous of Shelley's involvement with him, she wrote to a friend early in the New Year of 1813:

Godwin, he, too, is changed, and [filled] with prejudices, and besides, too, he expects such universal homage from all persons younger than himself, that it is very disagreeable to be in company with him on that account, and he wanted Mr. Shelley to join the Wig party and do just as they pleased, which made me very angry, as we know what men the Wigs are now. He is grown old and unimpassioned, therefore is not in the least calculated for such enthusiasts as we are.[47]

Godwin continued to write to Shelley regularly throughout the winter — on 25 January, 11, 26 and 27 February and 30 March. Shelley's life took once again a tempestuous path, and after an attack by an unknown assailant on the night of 26 February, he went to Ireland to see Hogg only to follow his absent friend immediately to London. They arrived on 5 April but neglected to inform Godwin. The philosopher found on 8 June his most exasperating and impetuous disciple quietly taking tea and discussing vegetarianism at Newton's.

Shelley often neglected his friends and was deeply engaged in putting *Queen Mab* through the press. He probably did not want Godwin's stern judgment to interfere with his own creativity at this stage. He sent a copy of the long poem with its voluminous notes to Godwin, who was no doubt at turns exalted and depressed by Shelley's version of the ideal life based on atheism, free love, republicanism and vegetarianism.

Although there are many influences at work in the poem — Lucretius, Hume, Rousseau, D'Holbach, Volney and Paine — the overriding tone and conceptual framework are unmistakeably Godwinian. The cause of vice and misery is not to be found in fallen human nature or in external nature, but in the pernicious influence of Church and State. Man is not born, but made evil:

Kings, priests, and statesmen, blast the human flower
Even in its tender bud; their influence darts
Like some poison through the bloodless veins
Of desolate society . . .[48]

If left to itself, the principle of necessity will ensure that nature will take its
beneficial path: 'Spirit of Nature! all-suffering Power,/Necessity! thou
mother of the world!'[49] Man will then be free to grow to his full stature and
the Godwinian reign of peace, love, reason and longevity will be realized in
a world without law and government:

All things are void of terror: Man has lost
His terrible prerogative, and stands
An equal amidst equals: happiness
And science dawn though late upon the earth;
Peace cheers the mind, health renovates the frame . . .[50]

Shelley further underlined his indebtedness to Godwin in his notes by
quoting and referring to *The Enquirer* for the ridiculousness of the military
character; to *The Enquirer* and *Political Justice* for the labour theory of value
and the iniquity of luxury; and to *Political Justice* for the notion of time as
the consciousness of the succession of ideas in our mind.[51] He could also
have referred to Godwin for his claim that 'utility is morality', that happiness
is the 'object of all political speculation', and that marriage is a 'despotism'.[52]

In other essays written soon after, Shelley showed himself to be no less a
disciple of Godwin. In his incomplete *Treatise on Morals*, he takes a consistently necessitarian and utilitarian position: moral science is the 'doctrine
of the voluntary actions of man' and virtue is the action which produces 'the
highest pleasure to the greatest number of sensitive beings'.[53] Again, in his
*Essay on Christianity*, he defines God as the 'Power by which we are surrounded', declares that there is no original evil, and maintains that Jesus
taught every man is the 'steward and guardian' of the interests of the 'great
community of mankind'.[54] Above all, if mankind became wise, Shelley
suggests, there would be no need for coercive institutions and 'every man
would be his own magistrate and priest'.[55]

Godwin continued to see Shelley regularly throughout the summer of
1813 and between July and September wrote to him ten times. When the
poet visited his father at Field Place in Sussex, he apparently told an old
friend of the family that to Godwin he 'owed everything' and that from
*Political Justice* he had derived 'all that was valuable in knowledge and
virtue'.[56] He could not even escape the influence of his mentor. When for
instance he went to stay in July with Newton's sister-in-law Mrs. Boinville in

Bracknell, he met, according to Hogg, young men who 'sighed, turned up their eyes, retailed philosophy, such as it was, and swore by William Godwin and Political Justice; acting, moreover, and very clumsily, the parts of Petrarchs, Werters, St. Leons, and Fleetwoods'.[57]

It was probably during the summer of 1813 that Hogg met Godwin for the first time at Newton's. Their host and his family were called away suddenly to the country and the expected Shelley did not turn up. Hogg found

> a short, stout, thickset old man, of very fair complexion, and with a bald and very large head, in the drawing-room, where he had been for some time by himself, and he appeared to be rather uneasy at being alone. He made himself known to me as William Godwin; it was thus he styled himself. His dress was dark, and very plain, of an old-fashioned cut, even for an old man. His appearance, indeed, was altogether that of a dissenting minister . . .

> William Godwin, according to my observation, always ate meat, and rather sparingly, and little else besides. He drank a glass or two of sherry, wherein I did not join him. Soon after dinner a large cup of very strong green tea, — of gunpowder tea, intensely strong, — was brought to him; this he took with evident satisfaction, and it was the only thing that he appeared to enjoy, although our fare was excellent. Having drunken the tea, he set the cup and saucer forcibly upon the table, at a great distance from him, according to the usages of that old school of manners, to which he so plainly belonged. He presently fell into a sound sleep, sitting very forward in his chair, and leaning forward, so that at times he threatened to fall forward; but no harm came to him. Not only did the old philosopher sleep soundly, deeply, but he snored loudly.[58]

There was good reason for Godwin to be uneasy and tired — his financial state was in a sorry mess once again. 'Oh Place!', he wrote to his chief adviser on 5 September 1813, 'Why am I not a young man! & why have my habits been literary!'[59] His only hope was Shelley but he had turned twenty-one only to find that his father withheld his inheritance. He left for Scotland in the autumn. Godwin, as assiduous as ever, regularly sent him letters increasingly more concerned with raising money than with political justice. Shelley then suddenly turned up for breakfast at Godwin's on 10 December. Throughout the following months they met and corresponded regularly and tried to negotiate from George Nash a mammoth post-obit bond of £8,000 for £2,593.10s, half of which was to go to Godwin.[60]

But while Godwin was busy on his accounts, Shelley's thoughts were elsewhere. On 30 March 1814 Mary returned from Scotland, sixteen and a half years old, very pretty and blooming with health. She had an oval face, with fair skin, golden hair, and striking eyes. Her manners were gentle, but her imagination was full of extraordinary adventures and the wild landscapes of Scotland. Shelley was out of London at the time, but they met on 3 May when he dined at Skinner Street. The girl whom he had only briefly met two years before was now a young woman. She seemed to combine the keen sensibility of her mother with the intellectual force of her father: 'They say that thou wert lovely from thy birth,/Of glorious parents, thou aspiring Child', Shelley late wrote.[61] He was immediately electrified by the 'irre[s]istible wildness & sublimity of her feelings'.[62] For her part, she was fascinated by the young idealist who was on such intimate terms with her beloved father and was helping the family so generously. They rapidly fell in love.

Shelley at the time was under the threat of arrest for his debts, and although he kept on his lodgings in Fleet Street, Godwin invited him to make his house his principal home. Harriet waited anxiously in Bath with their new daughter, called Ianthe after the heroine of *Queen Mab*. From 19 June, Shelley dined at Skinner Street every day, and spent the afternoon walking with Mary and Jane. Shelley was soon composing an ode 'To Mary Wollstonecraft Godwin':

> Upon my heart thy accents sweet
>   Of peace and pity fell like dew
> On flowers half dead; — thy lips did meet
>   Mine tremblingly; thy dark eyes threw
> Their soft persuasion on my brain,
> Charming away its dream of pain.[63]

She in turn wrote in her copy of *Queen Mab* with its dedication to Harriet: 'I am thine, exclusively thine. I have pledged myself to thee and sacred is the gift.'[64] One of their favourite haunts was the old St. Pancras Churchyard where Mary Wollstonecraft was buried, and on 26 June Mary openly declared her love beneath the willow tree beside her mother's grave. Jane, as ever, looked on impatiently from a distant tombstone.

On the next day, Shelley told Godwin of their love. He was both astounded and horrified. Shelley was not only a married man, but it might appear to his enemies that he had sold his daughter for money. He tried to prevent their meeting and Shelley only took the odd meal at Skinner Street until 6 July when the negotiations with Nash were completed. On the same evening, Godwin managed to wring out of his benefactor a promise to give up his 'licentious love, and return to virtue'.[65] On 8 July, he had a 'Talk with Mary'.[66] He then shut himself up in his study during the next three days and wrote a ten-page letter to Shelley, now unfortunately lost.

Shelley however was unable to keep to his promise. He soon wrote to the pregnant Harriet that he had only felt brotherly love for her, and proposed a *ménage à trois*. 'I wish you could see Mary', he added, 'to the most indifferent eyes she would be interesting only from her sufferings, & the tyranny which is exercised upon her.'[67] Reacting to Godwin's restrictions with characteristic passion, he arrived at Skinner Street one day in the philospher's absence armed with a bottle of laudanum and a pistol: 'They wish to separate us, my beloved,' he exclaimed to Mary, 'but Death shall unite us.'[68]

On the 19th Shelley and Harriet both called on Godwin but he was not at home. Later in the day Godwin visited the disconsolate Harriet and probably urged her to write to Mary to ask her lover to calm himself. Godwin was at his wits' end — he even took Shelley out on a coach drive on the 16th to remonstrate with him privately. On the one hand, his reason told him that he desperately needed Shelley's money. On the other, all his emotions were in revolt against the threatening if not actual adultery. When he received on the 19th his share of the post-obit bond, he was determined to end the affair. He confined both Jane and Mary to the house, and wrote long letters to Harriet on the 22nd and to Shelley on the 25th. All seemed propitious. Then at 5 o'clock in the morning of 28 July he found a letter on his dressing table. Mary and — Godwin's eyes could not believe it — Jane had eloped with his greatest and best loved disciple!

Mrs. Godwin immediately set off in pursuit of the fugitives and tracked them down the following day to an inn in Calais. Shelley refused to allow her to see Mary, but Jane spent the night with her mother and was temporarily persuaded to return. She thought better of it, however, the next day and set off with Mary and Shelley to Paris, where they bought a mule which they rode in turns to Switzerland. Mrs. Godwin returned to London tired and empty-handed on 31 July.

Godwin was in despair. The whole episode seemed to confirm the criticisms of his enemies. Although he never advocated promiscuity and now celebrated the domestic affections, he had argued that marriage was the most odious of all monopolies and that lovers should remain together only as long as both wanted to. Shelley, it could be said, was merely putting his theory into practice; Harriet for one put his profligacy down 'entirely' to *Political Justice*.[69] Godwin's financial dependence on Shelley further complicated matters; indeed, it was later rumoured that he had sold Mary and Jane for £800 and £700 respectively.[70] And while he did his best to treat his children impartially, Mary had a special place in his heart.

There were other worries too. William was unhappy in the tense atmosphere at home, and on the 10 August he ran away and could not be found for two nights. It was the first of several such escapades. Then on the day following his son's disappearance, Godwin heard of the suicide of his young protégé Patrickson at Cambridge.

When the talented Patrickson had returned to Cambridge in July for his final term as a law student, he found his persecutors more active than ever. Godwin, a veteran at receiving abuse, advised him to read Seneca, sent £2, and urged him to regard his enemies 'no more than if you were "hush'd with buzzing night-flies to your slumber"'.[71] Patrickson dined with Godwin on 8 August but the call to stoicism was to no avail. On his return to Cambridge the next day, he wrote to Godwin: 'life has been a thing of no value to me, and I have been accustomed in times of sorrow to envy even the ground I trod on'.[72] The next day, 10 August, he shot himself in his rooms.

In the meantime, Godwin had come to yet another crisis in his financial affairs. Of the £600 he should have received of the Midsummer school accounts, only £200 had been sent. He therefore tried to persuade two brothers called Stone to take a half-share in the Juvenile Library, but although they appeared to take a great fancy to Godwin and his wife they wisely withdrew on learning the true state of the business. On 27 August, Godwin was therefore forced to write to John Taylor of Norwich, giving a long account of the elopement and begging yet another loan. Fearing bankruptcy, he then asked Place on 31 August to postpone the repayment of a loan of £300.

Place's patience at last gave out, and he complained bitterly of Godwin's 'most selfish' conduct which had prevented him from giving 'thousands instead of hundreds'.[73] The prospect was too much for Godwin. 'Oh, Place', he replied pathetically, 'After a life, spent to the best of my judgment in the cause of truth & mankind, I am overwhelmed with domestic calamities & with misfortune. Is it your wish to contribute your portion to my destruction?'[74] Place was not mollified. He made many remarks on Godwin's letter justifying his own behaviour but sent a brief note to Godwin charging him with 'false accusation and injustice and misquotation'.[75] To this, Godwin answered ironically: 'I am glad you can find so many better men than I, that you can afford to throw me away'.[76]

Place reflected for some days, and then wrote cuttingly that Godwin's chapter on 'Sincerity' in *Political Justice* led him to say that 'Men of rank — of power — of riches — of high reputation, shun you, so I have found it, because you are willing to be dependent.'[77] It was the last straw. Godwin reasserted his belief in perfect frankness, but added if the great had expressed their disapproval by dropping his society, they had at least left him 'to the blessings of sobriety, contemplation, & a mind habitually turned to tranquillity & contentment'.[78]

It was a noble letter which Place declined to answer, merely commenting later that Godwin either misunderstood or misinterpreted him in all points.

I doubt whether I should again take up the pen in this correspondence, if you had not in your last undertaken to quote my book against me.

This I own is provoking. For I ought surely to understand the doctrines of my own book (we will put out of the question for the present how far my own conduct is consistent with those doctrines); & if I do understand them, I take on me to decide that nothing can be more hostile to those doctrines, than your present proceeding.

The Enquiry concerning Political Justice inculcates a conduct void of fear & of resentment. I always approved that feature in the Bible, that Christ made himself a companion of publicans & sinners. I was always the advocate of sincerity, that we should tell men fearlessly (yet with affection & benignity) what we saw wrong in their judgments & actions; but I scorn the cowardice of expressing disapprobation by frowns & dropping their society. This is tyranny, & not the fair confronting of judgments, & opposing falshood with the manly, ingenuous, unwrinkled forehead of truth.

You say, you "had rather live alone, than" Not so the author of Political Justice, or any of its genuine disciples. It is our principle to seek the intercourse of

XXVI. William Godwin to Francis Place, 11 September 1814.

Yet Godwin was still willing to make amends and on 14 October gave the French political economist Jean-Baptiste Say a letter of introduction to Place.[79] He also called on Place twice and they had a long conversation each time, but Place refused to continue their acquaintance.

Place however was unable to avoid the consequences of their relationship: he repaid in 1815 the £500 borrowed from Josiah Wedgwood in 1811, and in 1824 heard for the first time from John Taylor of Norwich of an unpaid post-obit bond of 1814 for £300. In all fairness, the scrupulous Place commented in a note to their correspondence that Godwin had many good points and no one could know him without being benefited. 'Had Godwin been placed in different circumstances', he concluded,

> or had a prudent woman for a wife, instead of the infernal devil to whom he was married, his good qualities would have preponderated, and he would have been a man of extensive influence as well as personally as by his writings, and would have lived in ease and comfort and been a happy man.[80]

Godwin could at least draw some comfort from a more creative and lasting friendship which had begun early in 1813 with a philanthropic entrepreneur called Robert Owen. They first met on 24 January and continued to see each other almost twice a week until May, during which time Owen was composing the second, third and fourth essays of *A New View of Society*. Godwin later recorded that on one evening he converted Owen from the doctrine of 'self-love' to that of benevolence.[81] Although the next time they met Owen admitted that he had been too precipitate in his recantation, his attempt to derive benevolence from a desire for happiness is not very different from Godwin's.

Owen later listed Godwin among his principal literary companions and the philosopher has been rightly called his 'master'.[82] In fact, many of the fundamental ideas and sometimes the actual phrasing of Owen's works resemble the doctrines of *Political Justice*. Like Godwin, Owen built his theory of progress on the premises that characters are formed by their circumstances, that vice is ignorance, and that truth will ultimately prevail over error. Both men equated happiness with knowledge and spoke the language of utility. They stressed the primacy of the moral regeneration of mankind and advocated economic before political reform. They argued that the proper means of eradicating evils was not by a Benthamite system of punishments and rewards, but through rational education and universal enlightenment. They condemned political agitation and preached the voluntary redistribution of wealth. Their ultimate social ideal was that of a decentralized society of small self-governing communities.

Owen's experience and strong temperament naturally led him to differ from Godwin on the means of reform. Godwin tended to be like Owen's 'idle visionary — who *thinks* in his closet, and never *acts* in the world'.[83] Owen had initially more confidence in the positive function of government and in 'those who have influence in the affairs of men' to bring about change.[84] He continued to advocate a system of national education. Above all, he laid great stress on the advantages of co-operation. Yet even these differences were a question of degree rather than principle. Both men were friends of the British Constitution in their practical politics, and Owen was as concerned with protecting the freedom of private judgment as Godwin was in advocating the benefits of mutual aid.

After 1813, Owen and Godwin saw each other regularly, about eight times a year for the next five years, and then intermittently until Godwin's death. Fanny thought he was 'indeed, a very great and good man'. He told her that he wished Mary Wollstonecraft were still living, as he had 'never before met with a person who thought so exactly as he did'.[85] Godwin however was his real philosophical mentor; Owen did little more than restate the New Philosophy of the 1790s in different economic conditions with a more practical turn. The satirist William Hone, an ex-Godwinian himself, correctly accused him of having systematically attempted to diffuse the New Philosophy under the name of socialism.[86] Hazlitt was even more explicit in his review of *A New View of Society*:

> The doctrine of Universal Benevolence, the belief in the Omnipotence of Truth, and in the Perfectibility of Human Nature, are not new, but 'Old, old', Master Robert Owen . . . Does not Mr. Owen know that the same scheme, the same principles, the same philosophy of motives and actions . . . of virtue and happiness, were rife in the year 1793 . . .? Let his 'New View of Society' but make as many disciples as the 'Enquiry concerning Political Justice', and we shall see how the tide will turn about . . .[87]

But while Owen was to go on to win many converts, Godwin remained a neglected figure. A cartoon entitled 'The Genius of the Age' depicted him in December 1812 as a top hat floating on the waters of Lethe, with a pair of hands clutching at a passing copy of *Political Justice*.[88] In the following year Horatio Smith wrote with wit and truth:

> Our Temple youth, a lawless train,
> Blockading Johnson's window pane,
> No longer laud thy solemn strain,
>     My Godwin!

Chaucer's a mighty tedious elf,
Fleetwood lives only for himself,
And Caleb Williams loves the shelf,
    My Godwin!

No longer cry the sprites unblesst,
'Awake, arise! stand forth confess'd!'
For fallen, fallen is thy crest,
    My Godwin![89]

His old friend Lamb also noted his painful decline. The irony in a letter to Manning did not entirely disguise his genuine feeling: 'Poor Godwin! I was passing his tomb the other day in Cripplegate churchyard. There are some verses upon it written by Miss Hayes, which if I thought good enough I would send you.'[90]

But though eclipsed and preoccupied with money worries and his rebellious daughters, Godwin was not inactive. As his life grew more difficult, he increasingly turned in his imagination to the times of the Commonwealth when Britain had vied with the great republics of Greece and Rome. He had been collecting for many years pamphlets and books of the period, and realizing that he had more than forty works on the subject, he decided early in 1813 to write *Lives of Edward and John Philips, Nephews and Pupils of Milton. Including Various Particulars of the Literary and Political History of their Times*. It was published on 11 May 1815 at Godwin's own expense.

Godwin's interest in the Phillips's was chiefly because of their connection with Milton — 'the most advantageous specimen that can be produced of the English nation'.[91] Edward he preferred precisely because of his lasting respect for his uncle, while he had nothing good to say about John, who treated him with 'unnatural animosity'.[92] The fact that both brothers became royalists and wrote ribald satires could only disprove Helvétius and demonstrate that there is a 'power within us moulding up our different dispositions, independent of, and elder than, every species of education'.[93]

Their lives however were banal and their works mediocre. It is Godwin's political and literary observations which interest today. The Restoration was, he declares, an event of 'unmitigated calamity'. And even though the Glorious Revolution was achieved without loss of blood, it is probable that the 'nation has never recovered that tone of independence, strong thinking, and generosity, which the Restoration so powerfully operated to destroy.'[94]

In his literary remarks, Godwin makes an eloquent defence of obsolete translations, especially George Chapman's *Homer*. He is also one of the few writers of the age to recognize the value of Cervantes and to praise *Don*

*Quixote* as an 'incomparable monument of Spanish literature and genius'.[95] His most interesting judgment, however, is in his criticism of modern poetry for not conveying 'the real passions of the human heart' and for imitating at second or at twentieth hand the 'old, genuine poetry'.[96] The criticism recalls the preface to the *Lyrical Ballads*, but Wordsworth, who took it to refer to his own work, wrote in 'great wrath' in the margin of his copy of the *Lives*: 'That is false, William Godwin. Signed William Wordsworth.'[97]

The reviews generally felt like the *Monthly Review* that it was a valuable but uninspired historical work.[98] Its political nature did not go unnoticed. The *British Critic* complained about republican cant and prejudice and the *British Review and London Critical Journal* felt that its purpose was to justify regicide.[99] The most interesting review appeared in the *Edinburgh Review* by Sir James Mackintosh, now a Whig M.P. Making amends for his vicious attack in his lectures of 1799, he declared that *Political Justice* merited a more lasting fame and that all Godwin's subsequent works were 'fully respectable'.[100]

Since the turn of the century, Godwin had virtually retired from political activity. He continued to follow parliamentary elections with interest, noting them in his diary, but made no effort to join the new reform movement which began to emerge after 1810 under the leadership of Cobbett, Henry Hunt and Francis Burdett. Indeed, when Burdett was imprisoned in 1810 and Daniel Isaac Eaton, one of his own publishers, was put in the pillory two years later, he raised no voice in their defence. Luddism was something he never commented on.

He did however take a great interest in the career of Napoleon whom, like Hazlitt, he considered to be a child of the French Revolution. Despite his imperial conquests, Godwin was ready to defend Napoleon's execution of the incendiaries in Moscow in 1812.[101] Two years later, he admired Hazlitt's letters of 'Vetus' in *The Times* — his only writings that he considered 'worth a farthing' — which advocated a nation's right to self-determination, and an easy peace with France.[102] At first he was delighted with the moderation of the Allies in 1814 in allowing the French to choose leaders. But when Godwin read on 17 April 1815 that they had decided at the Congress of Vienna to outlaw and depose Napoleon after his triumphant return from exile on Elba, he was outraged. He immediately sat down and wrote a letter of protest which appeared in the *Morning Chronicle* on 25 May, the day war was voted in the Commons. It was then published with another letter in a pamphlet entitled *Letters of Verax*.

Talking as a 'citizen of the great commonwealths of England and mankind', Godwin argued eloquently that the Allies should not interfere in the internal affairs of France, since Napoleon had shown his readiness to accept a limited constitution and the people had declared themselves in his favour.[103] While Napoleon revealed himself an 'earnest votary of peace' and surrounded himself with the 'best patriots and republicans of France', the Allies were acting like that 'non-descript monster, called a statesman'.[104] If they proceeded with their war of conquest, he warned, they might well pull down 'the vast edifice of the political fabric upon the heads of all!'[105]

The pamphlet was published on 22 June, but on hearing the news of the battle of Waterloo, and the subsequent abdication of Napoleon, Godwin withdrew it — a move regretted by the *Monthly Magazine*, which admired its 'clear and convincing arguments'.[106] But patriotic fears were at their height, and Crabb Robinson for one was bitterly annoyed by Godwin for being 'passionate in his wishes' for the success of the French.[107] When Napoleon was defeated, Crabb Robinson further noted that amongst his acquaintances only Godwin, Tehwall, Capel Lofft and Hazlitt mourned the event.[108] Godwin may have fallen on evil days, and grown increasingly moderate in his old age, but he remained faithful to the hopes and principles of the French Revolution.

# CHAPTER XVIII

# The Fallen Eagle

When Shelley returned to England on 14 September 1814, Godwin would have nothing to do with the man whom, he felt, had seduced one daughter and corrupted the other. Shelley wrote a conciliatory letter on the 16th. On the same day, Mrs. Godwin called with Fanny at their lodgings, but when Shelley appeared they walked on refusing to speak. Later in the evening Charles threw stones at their window and stayed talking until 3 o'clock in the morning. But while Shelley was upbraiding Harriet for her 'wanton cruelty & injustice' in circulating a report that Godwin favoured his passion for his daughter, the philosopher himself refused on the 22nd 'with bitter invective' all communication with him.[1]

Thomas Love Peacock tried to heal the breach by visiting Godwin on 22 October but he refused to speak to anyone about Shelley except an attorney. Mary, who spent the day rereading *Political Justice* and *Caleb Williams*, exclaimed in her journal, on hearing the news, 'Oh! philosophy!'[2] Shelley was no less disappointed. He felt transformed by his love for Mary into a better man: 'a more true & constant friend, a more useful lover of mankind, a more ardent asserter of truth & virtue — above all, more consistent, more intelligible more true'.[3] And yet he had been cut off by the Godwins and the Boinvilles in London, forced to live apart from Mary in order to dodge his creditors, and under the constant threat of arrest.

'I confess to you', Shelley wrote to Mary on 24 October, 'that I have been shocked & staggered by Godwin's cold injustice.'[4] For her part, Mary was convinced that her father's intransigence must have been caused by her stepmother. When she received a letter from her on 28 October, she wrote enigmatically in her journal: 'she is a woman I shudder to think of. My poor Father! if — but it will not do.'[5] She then sent the note to Shelley: 'I detest Mrs. G[odwin] she plagues my father out of his life & then — well no matter — Why will not Godwin follow the obvious bent of his affections & be

XXVII. Godwin, aged 60, by G. Harlow, 1816.

reconciled to us —'[6]

In the meantime, Godwin and his wife were becoming frantic. Charles and Fanny were acting as intermediaries and were gradually becoming drawn into the Shelley orbit. To recover Jane, they used every means short of force: in September, they thought of sending her to a convent; in November, they sent a note saying that her mother was dying. When Godwin proposed sending her as a kind of governness to John Taylor of Norwich, she refused point blank. She reluctantly agreed to becoming a paying guest in the country, providing 'first, that she should in all situations openly proclaim, & earnestly support, a total contempt for the laws & institutions of society, — & secondly that no restraint should be imposed upon her correspondence & intercourse with those from whom she was separated'.[7] Since such conditions were unacceptable, the unrepentant Jane returned to her friends. Significantly, she began experimenting with a new name, which first became in her journal Clare, then Clara, until she finally decided on Claire.

Yet despite their estrangement, Godwin still borrowed from Shelley. He had no choice. The Juvenile Library, a precarious enterprise at best, was about to collapse once and for all. Lambert, who according to Claire was worth £300,000, was oppressing and insulting Godwin for £150 he owed him.[8] Shelley, on hearing the news, immediately offered Lambert a post-obit bond although he too was under the threat of arrest. With Charles as their go-between, the two enemies began to arrange the sale of another post-obit bond worth £10,000 which would bring them about £1,800 and £1,200 each. Whatever Mrs. Godwin may have felt about Shelley's corruption of her daughters, she happily informed John Taylor that he would pay off all their debts.[9]

Meanwhile, Shelley was as enthusiastic as ever in putting his ideas into practice. He attempted in the winter to set up once again his longed-for community of radical spirits. Mary and himself formed the centre, but he encouraged intimacies between Hogg and Mary and himself and Claire. Fanny and Charles remained satellite figures, fascinated by and jealous of the goings on in Kentish Town. But their parents remained implacable: when Mary gave birth on 22 February 1815 to a girl, who died two weeks later, Mrs. Godwin merely sent some linen, and Godwin said nothing.

Shelley's position dramatically improved in the New Year when his grandfather died, although he had deliberately tried in his will to prevent his grandson from squandering the family fortune. Godwin, fired by the news, warned Shelley on 5 February through Charles against making a rash settlement with his father. The two of them happened to bump into Mary and Shelley on 23 March, on which occasion Godwin remarked to Charles that 'Shelley was so beautiful, it was a pity he was so wicked.'[10] On 10 April,

XXVIII. Percy Bysshe Shelley, in 1819, by Amelia Curran.

Mary also saw Mrs. Godwin 'parade' before their windows and learned the next day that she had left home after a row and stayed out all night.[11]

Things were clearly becoming desperate. Then on the 21st Fanny told Mary and Shelley that Godwin was threatened with arrest by a creditor called Hogan. Once again, Shelley saved Godwin from the brink, and forwarded another £1,000 from a sum of £4,500 which he managed to winkle out of his father ostensibly to repay his own debts. Shelley was also given an annuity of £1,000, which, after settling an allowance of £200 on Harriet, left him comfortably off.

The presence of Clare was by now becoming intolerable, and she eventually decided to go to Lynmouth for several months. Charles also dropped out of their circle, for after a family quarrel he suddenly left Skinner Street for Europe. Shelley decided to buy a house in Bishopsgate, and settled down to write his second long poem *Alastor* in which the poet's search of an ideal vision of beauty leads him eventually to death. It was clearly a dramatization of his own predicament. He also wrote his *Essay on Life*, in which he moved towards Godwin's 'intellectual system' and the immaterialist position that 'nothing exists but as it is perceived'.[12]

Despite Shelley's largesse, Godwin in fact did not pay off the Hogan loan, and under the threat of a suit for collection broke his year-old silence to write directly to Shelley on 11 November. It marked the beginning of a voluminous correspondence in the following months which remained coldly formal and was almost entirely devoted to money matters. Even when Mary gave birth on 24 January 1816 to a son called William in honour of her father, Shelley merely added to the business letter of the day: 'Fanny & Mrs. Godwin will probably be glad to hear that Mary has safely recovered from a very favorable confinement, & that her child is well.'[13]

Whilst Shelley reread *Political Justice*, Godwin badgered him for more money to repay his debts. The poet replied on 7 January with a full account of the proceedings between himself and his father, and suggested that Godwin raise the money from well-wishers like Grattan, Mackintosh or Lord Holland on his security.[14] But Godwin was not to be put off so lightly, and insisted that Shelley pay him £200 which he had added, in a statement of his nominal debts for his father, to the £1,000 already forwarded. Shelley refused to send the money on, but agreed to sell an annuity to cover Hogan's loan.

When Shelley informed Godwin on 16 February, however, that he was thinking of settling in Italy, the philosopher was 'agitated, and almost driven to despair'.[15] He immediately recruited Thomas Turner, one of his young friends and husband of Cornelia Boinville, as a go-between, but Shelley took a dislike to him and suggested Mackintosh — 'He, I am informed, really desires to serve you . . .'[16] Mackintosh had in fact tried to obtain through Samuel Rogers some money from Byron who had been offered by John Murray a thousand guineas for the publication of *Parisina* and *The Siege of Corinth*. He described Godwin as a 'man of genius, likely, for his independence of thinking, to starve at the age of sixty'.[17] Although Byron agreed to give £600 to Godwin, Murray disapproved and in the resulting row the scheme fell through. But while they were friends once again, Mackintosh was the last man Godwin wanted to involve in his financial affairs.

Godwin's tone had perceptibly softened since Shelley threatened to go into exile, but he still refused to see him personally. In March, Shelley's patience at last broke, and he wrote in utmost fury what had been on his mind for some time:

> In my judgment neither I, nor your daughter, nor her offspring, ought to receive the treatment which we encounter on every side. It has perpetu-ally appeared to me to have been your especial duty to see that, so far as mankind value your good opinion, we were dealt justly by, and that a young family, innocent and benevolent and united, should not be confounded with prostitutes and seducers.[18]

Godwin was not to be roused. He answered coolly and stiffly: 'As long as understanding and sentiment shall exist in this form, I shall never cease from my disapprobation of that act of yours, which I regard as the great calamity of my life . . .'[19]

Fearful of another breach, Shelley quickly apologized for his violence and suggested that they confine their communication to business.[20] Godwin agreed, but still refused to see him when he called at Skinner Street once on 23 March and three times the next day. The philosopher also continued to refuse any cheque drawn by Shelley containing his name in order to keep their financial dealings a secret.

Shelley kept him informed of the progress of the Chancery suit he had taken out against his father over his inheritance, but when he learned of its failure he decided to sail secretly to Europe. On 3 May 1816 he wrote from Dover a valediction, reaffirming his indebtedness and loyalty:

> I respect you, I think well of you, better perhaps than of any other person whom England contains, you were the philosopher who first awakened, & who still as a philosopher to a very great degree regulate my under-standing. It is unfortunate for me that the part of your character which is least excellent should have been met by my convictions of what was right to do. But I have been too indignant, I have been unjust to you. — forgive me. — burn those letters which contain the records of my viol-ence, & believe that however what you erroneously call fame & honour separate us, I shall feel towards you as the most affectionate of friends.[21]

Shelley promised £300 to follow. Claire, as usual, accompanied Shelley and Mary, and about ten days later in Geneva met Byron, to whom she had already introduced herself.

Godwin in the meantime had gone on a tour to Scotland on 7 April, partly for a change of air and partly to do business. W. Simpkin agreed to publish a fourth edition of *Caleb Williams* and a second edition of *St. Leon*, and Godwin hoped that he could exploit the public interest with a new novel. He had approached Archibald Constable, to whom Charles had been apprenticed, and had received a favourable reply. Constable received him generously at his own home in Edinburgh and introduced him to James Ballantyne and Robert Cadell, the publishers, Francis Jeffrey, the editor and proprietor of the *Edinburgh Review*, and Dugald Stewart, the 'crack metaphysician of Great Britain'. The Earl of Buchan, elder brother of Lord Erskine, invited him to dinner. He even sat for a portrait by William Nicholson — not his old scientist friend, whose obituary he had written the previous year, but a local artist. It was all extremely kind and flattering, and Godwin wrote back to Skinner Street: 'I cannot well disappoint all the good people that have a desire to see the monster. And I firmly believe the connection will do me a world of good.'[22] The most memorable meeting for Godwin however was with Sir Walter Scott: he travelled with Constable and Ballantyne on 25 April to Abbotsford where they slept, and the next day he visited Melrose Abbey with the 'Great Unknown'. Unfortunately, he left no record of their meeting.

On his return journey, Godwin stayed with Wordsworth at Rydal Mount on 27 and 28 April, and met Derwent Coleridge there. Godwin found Derwent 'too forward and commonplace' and preferred his elder brother Hartley. He had however a high opinion of Wordsworth, and later told Maria Gisborne that he was in reality an 'enthusiastic admirer of nature', although he thought his poetry cold. He described his voice in speaking as hoarse: 'it is a horrible croaking, it is worse than croaking'.[23] But according to Crabb Robinson, Godwin left Wordsworth with 'very bitter and hostile feelings' because of their different political opinions. Godwin was also dissatisfied with his *Letter to a Friend of Robert Burns* (1816), which too readily disguised the 'infirmities of men of great intellectual powers'.[24]

After staying with the old republican Thomas Walker in Manchester, Godwin was a happy man when he arrived home on 7 May. He was 'all on fire' to resume writing his novel which was to be called *Mandeville. A Tale of the Seventeenth Century in England*.[25] Constable had advanced £200 and they had agreed to share the profits equally. He was therefore particularly disappointed to hear of Shelley's departure and only slightly reassured by the promise of more money and the message that no person could feel 'deeper interest for another, or venerate their character & talents more sincerely'.[26]

The death of Sheridan on 7 July also profoundly upset Godwin: it symbolized the passing of a whole era. He attended with his son William the funeral at Westminster Abbey and visited Sheridan's grave many times afterwards. Few friends visited Skinner Street now, and thoughts of death and bankruptcy weighed heavily on Godwin's mind. Fanny could not get him to talk about politics and she dreaded the effect of his morbid depression on his health — 'He cannot sleep at night, and is indeed very unwell'.[27]

Worse things were to follow. Shelley and Mary decided to return to England when they realized that seventeen-year-old Claire was pregnant by Byron. They settled in Bath so that Claire could have her baby clandestinely. Shelley went up to London to see money-lenders, and probably met Fanny, but his father threatened to cut off his annuity if he continued to misapply his fortune. He was forced to refuse Godwin on 2 October once and for all. 'Shelley's letter came like a thunderclap,' Fanny wrote to her sister. 'I watched Papa's countenance while he read it (not knowing the contents), and I perceived that Shelley had written in his most desponding manner.'[28]

But this was not all. Fanny had always been prone to depression, and the disastrous circumstances of the Skinner Street household deeply affected her. As the oldest in the family, she must have found her prospects dim in the gloomy house after the elopement of her sisters. She was painfully aware of her own illegitimacy and did not get on with her stepmother. Above all, she felt torn between her allegiance to Godwin and to the Shelleys; 'My heart is warm in your cause', she wrote to them, 'and I am *anxious, most anxious,* that Papa should feel for you as I do, both for your own and his sake.'[29] She was, to make matters more poignant, probably in love with Shelley; Godwin certainly thought so.[30]

At all events, Fanny suddenly left home on 7 October. Next day, she wrote from Bristol to Godwin that 'I depart immediately to the spot from which I hope never to remove' and sent a 'very alarming letter' to the Shelleys.[31] She may well have declared her hopeless love to Shelley as she passed through Bath, for he later wrote:

> Her voice did quiver as we parted,
>   Yet knew I not that heart was broken
> From which it came, and I departed
>   Heeding not the words then spoken.
>     Misery — O Misery,
>     This world is all too wide for thee.[32]

On receiving her letter on the 9th, he immediately set out to look for her, but returned at 2 a.m. without any news.

That night in a small upper room in the Mackworth Arms, Swansea, Fanny committed suicide by taking an overdose of laudanum. On a scrap of paper, she wrote:

I have long determined that the best thing I could do was to put an end to the existence of a being whose birth was unfortunate, and whose life has only been a series of pain to those persons who have hurt their health in endeavouring to promote her welfare. Perhaps to hear of my death will give you pain, but you will soon have the blessing of forgetting that such a creature ever existed as . . .'[33]

In a final act of consideration, Fanny tore off the signature. The report in the *Cambrian* on 12 October 1816 described her as a 'most respectable looking female' of about twenty-three years of age with long brown hair and a dark complexion. The only marks of identification were the letters 'M.W.' on her stays and a 'G' marked on her stockings.

Shelley went to Swansea on 11 October and returned next day with the 'worst account'.[34] On the 10th, Godwin took the Bristol coach but on reading the news of Fanny's suicide stopped off at Bath and spent the night in a hotel a quarter of a mile from Shelley's lodgings. He wrote to his wife, Shelley and Claire, and did his best to hush up the suicide. Fearful of yet another scandal, he forbad Shelley to claim Fanny's body or attend her funeral. 'Our feelings are less tumultous than deep,' he wrote to Mary on 13 October for the first time in two years. 'We have so conducted ourselves that not one person in our home has the smallest apprehension of the truth . . .'.[35] Although Shelley saw the corpse, he kept silent; Fanny was buried unclaimed in a pauper's grave. Relatives were at first told that she had gone to Ireland and died of a fever there.[36] Charles still did not know of her death by the following summer.

The year 1816 was to prove tragic for both the Shelley and Godwin households. A month after Fanny's suicide, Shelley's wife Harriet drowned herself on 9 November in the Serpentine. Her body, apparently far advanced in pregnancy, was not discovered until three weeks later. She had been cast out of her family's house and abandoned by a groom. Shelley felt 'a far severer anguish' on the death of Fanny, but he was furious with Harriet's callous family and his immediate concern was to obtain custody of his children Charles and Ianthe.[37]

Godwin was no less excited by the news from Shelley of Harriet's fate. He recorded retrospectively on 16 December the dates of her death and of the discovery of her corpse in his diary. He knew that the death of Harriet could mean at last the marriage of his daughter and long-awaited respectability. He wrote on the 17th to Shelley, who called next day and spent two hours with Mrs. Godwin for the first time at Skinner Street since the elopement. After more correspondence, Godwin and Shelley met on the 28th to get a marriage licence. The next day Mary joined them. Then on the 30th Godwin made the cryptic entry in his diary: 'Call on Mildred, ѡ. PBS, MWG & MJ: they dine & sup . . .'[38]

Mildred was in fact St. Mildred's Church, Bread Street, in the City, where the elopers were at last reconciled with the Godwins. Shelley wrote to Claire how this 'ceremony so magical in its effects' brought out Godwin's 'polished and cautious' attentions:

> He seems to think no kindness too great in compensation for what has past. I confess I am not entirely deceived by this, though I cannot make my vanity wholly insensible to certain attentions paid in a manner studiously flattering. Mrs. G. presents herself to me in her real attributes of affectation, prejudice, and heartless pride.[39]

Shelley made it clear in the same letter that he underwent for the second time a ceremony that he theoretically condemned in order to recover his children. He later told Byron however that it was principally for Mary's feelings for her father.[40]

Godwin was indeed delighted. He wrote about the marriage to his brother Hull in the New Year:

> Her husband is the eldest son of Sir Timothy Shelley, of Field Place, in the county of Sussex, Baronet. So that, according to the vulgar ideas of the world, she is well married, and I have great hopes the young man will make her a good husband. You will wonder, I daresay, how a girl without a penny of fortune should meet with so good a match. But such are the ups and downs of this world. For my part I care but little, comparatively, about wealth, so that it should be her destiny in life to be respectable, virtuous, and contented.[41]

The 'comparatively' spoke volumes. He neglected to mention Fanny's suicide or the birth of Claire's and Byron's illegitimate child Alba (later called Allegra) on 12 January 1817. He was also silent about his year-old grandson William. In the affair of Mary's marriage, Godwin hardly distinguished himself.

Godwin began to see Shelley regularly after the marriage. Early in 1817 he helped him with the court case at Chancery to obtain custody of his children. But it was not entirely motivated by altruism, for his own reputation was involved: Harriet's family accused Shelley of committing adultery with Mary Godwin whose father was 'the author of *Political Justice* & other *impious & seditious* writings'.[42] When Godwin learned that Harriet had been unfaithful four months before Shelley left England, the two decided to make full use of this in court. But despite the efforts of Basil Montagu and Leigh Hunt and even Dr. Parr, Shelley lost the case on 18 January.

Though the Shelleys spent most of February with the Hunts at

Hampstead, they constantly saw the Godwins, and for four nights at the beginning of the month slept at Skinner Street. Godwin and Shelley were on good terms once again, and the poet wrote to his father-in-law from his new abode in Marlow in March: 'Certain it is, that nothing gives me serener & more pure pleasure than your society . . .'[43] On a letter of Godwin's dated 29 April 1817, Shelley wrote the lines:

> Mighty eagle! thou that soarest
> O'er the misty mountain forest,
>   And amid the light of morning
> Like a cloud of glory liest,
> And when night descends defiest
>   The embattled tempests' warning![44]

He began raising money again for Godwin whose life was wearing away 'in lingering sorrow' at the endless delays in his affairs.[45] The philosopher now treated the 'blood horse', as he called him, with caution and could even joke, 'my bedchambers are by no means fit to receive a future ornament of the English Baronetage'.[46] The tables had clearly turned.

Whatever the morality of Godwin's dealings with Shelley, he was always ready to help those worse off than himself. When he heard that his old friend Marshal was unable to repay his debts, he immediately drew up a subscription address. After Shelley refused to help and Josiah Wedgwood ignored the appeal, Godwin turned once again to Francis Place who was on a visit to Jeremy Bentham in Somerset. 'I was cruelly disappointed', Godwin wrote,

> to find that you were just gone out of town . . . I hope however that the pleasures of the country, & the delight of Mr. Bentham's conversation (which, I assure you, I envy you, & have been twenty years trying to obtain) will not make you forget the good inclination I have often seen in you, to render yourself useful to another.[47]

Place agreed to help and soon repaid Marshal's debts. There was however a misunderstanding over Godwin's contribution of £13 which awakened all the old suspicions on both sides. When Godwin remarked on Place's 'incredible weakness' in keeping up a tone of hostility, he replied tersely: 'It is regret I feel, and never do I either see you, or think of you, without having that feeling excessively excited.'[48]

By now Godwin's financial situation had marginally improved. The sums raised by Shelley were enough to postpone his more pressing debts. A suit over rent, which the philosopher had refused to pay since 1807, was begun

XXIX. Godwin, aged 60, by William Nicholson, 1816. Engraved by W. H. Lizars for G. S. Mackenzie's *Illustrations of Phrenology*, 1820.

but showed no signs of immediate threat. The house at Skinner Street was also greatly reduced. Only young William, now fourteen, and their cook Esther lightened the echoing gloom. Fanny was dead, Mary and Claire were in Marlow with Shelley, and Charles was abroad.

Ever since the momentous row which had precipitated his departure in 1815, Charles had been travelling Europe — 'a butterfly of the best intentions—in the world', as he described himself.[49] Godwin considered that he had fallen in 'low profligacy', but Crabb Robinson for one felt he had behaved with 'great cruelty' to his stepson.[50] Charles himself felt guilty at abandoning his parents, and could not bring himself to write to them, let alone visit them. It was moreover his mother rather than his stepfather that kept him away. He wrote to Shelley from the Pyrenees that while his true feelings towards his mother were 'cold and inactive', Godwin's 'gentleness and rational treatment made an early and deep impression on me; I admire and love him infinitely'.[51]

Godwin in the meantime was hard at work on his new novel *Mandeville*, and felt the need to take a short holiday with the Shelleys at Marlow from 2 to 6 April. He met Peacock there and discussed 'novels & perfectibility' only to find himself later satirized as a philosopher of perfectibility in Peacock's novels. Hogg heard from Peacock how they had entertained '(altho' but inhospitably) a loquacious guest, who is alike hateful to gods & men, to birds, beasts & fishes'.[52] But for all his unusual loquacity, Godwin was afraid of upsetting Shelley. After informing him about some gossip on the levity of Harriet, for instance, he recounted to his wife:

> I knew that Shelley's temper was occasionally fiery, resentful, and indignant, and I passed this interval [from Friday to Monday] in no very enviable state. I thought perhaps I might have tried his temper too far. By the post-time on Monday my nerves were in a degree of flutter that I have very seldom experienced. But the letter came, and there was no harm: it was good-humoured.[53]

Preoccupied with his novel and debts, Godwin had urged his wife to visit her French friends in St. Etienne whom she had known twenty-five years before. But while Mrs. Godwin was away from 8 May to 10 July, Godwin merely vegetated at home. Mary, after completing her novel *Frankenstein; or, The Modern Prometheus* and taking advantage of her stepmother's absence, found him full of care during a week's visit at the end of May. 'I fear there is no way to relieve this,' she told Shelley.[54] Indeed, Godwin wrote to his wife that the wet spring weather seemed to turn his brain into a 'soft pulp', and he pictured himself as the 'fusty old fellow in Skinner Street, in his black morning coat, shivering over the half-extinguished embers of a

June fire'.[55] When he heard of his wife's early return, he tried to dissuade her: 'It is all prose here: life stripped of its romance, its fringe and its gilding, and not unmixed with sad realities.'[56] Her presence may well have made matters worse.

Godwin could at least take pride in Mary's developing talents. She published with Shelley in 1817 a *History of a Six Weeks' Tour*, a version of their elopement journey. This was then followed by her anonymous novel *Frankenstein* which she respectfully dedicated to her father. The *Quarterly Review* immediately spotted it as a product of his school: 'Mr. Godwin is the patriarch of a literary family, whose chief skill is in delineating the wanderings of the intellect, and which strangely delights in the most afflicting and humiliating of human miseries.'[57]

Godwin was not the only source and the novel was conceived as a ghost story to entertain Shelley, Claire and Byron during the wet summer of 1816 whilst they were staying near Geneva. It demonstrates however the central doctrine of *Political Justice* that the characters of men originate in their circumstances. As Shelley observed, the crimes and malevolence of the monster 'flow irresistibly from certain causes fully adequate to their production'.[58] It is the monster's harsh treatment and enforced solitude which corrupt him. He exclaims to his creator Frankenstein: 'I was benevolent and good; misery made me a fiend. Make me happy, and I shall again be virtuous.'[59]

At the same time, Mary recreates the nightmare world of *Caleb Williams* with its endless series of flights and pursuits and its dreadful fatality. She shows as in *St. Leon* a fascination with the occult and the dangers of an unchecked ambition: Frankenstein discovers the elixir of life only to dehumanize and isolate himself. And there is the same pessimism which haunts her father's fiction and which implies that life is a curse and that man is condemned to failure. Not surprisingly, Godwin found it 'the most wonderful book to have been written at twenty years of age that I ever heard of'.[60]

Throughout the summer of 1817, Godwin and Shelley corresponded regularly. They met each other eleven times in the autumn. On 19 October they went to Marlow together, where Godwin stayed for a few days — a visit which Mary thought would make her 'dreadfully melancholy', particularly as she had given birth to her third child Clara on 2 September, and was still in poor health.[61] On 2 November Shelley came up to London and slept at Skinner Street for six days. When Mary joined them on the 8th, the couple took lodgings but they continued to see Godwin nearly every day until their return to Marlow on the 24th. Claire came up especially for the last dinner. Shelley then reread *Political Justice* in the quiet of his Thameside retreat.[62]

Godwin in the meantime had fully recovered his spirits, had finished

*Mandeville,* and was on good terms with Shelley. All seemed propitious. He had no doubt been pleased by the moderation of Shelley's pamphlet *A Proposal for Putting Reform to the Vote throughout the Kingdom,* which, although advocating the use of the ballot, wanted like the Whigs to restrict the franchise to direct taxpayers. But when the two men discussed in November the death of Princess Charlotte and the hanging of three labourers after the Pentridge insurrection, there must have been considerable disagreement. Although partly inspired by Godwin's *Essay on Sepulchres,* Shelley in his *Address to the People on the Death of the Princess Charlotte* quotes Paine rather than Godwin on the title-page: 'We Pity the Plumage, but Forget the Dying Bird.'[63] Moreover, while locating the cause of political unrest in the exploitation of the producers of luxury, Shelley openly appeals to the People of England to develop an extra-parliamentary movement.

In the following month, Godwin read Shelley's long poem *Laon and Cynthia; or, The Revolution of the Golden City* (later renamed *The Revolt of Islam*). He must have been flattered by Shelley's tribute to him in the original dedication to Mary:

> One voice came forth from many a mighty spirit,
>     Which was the echo of three thousand years;
> And the tumultuous world stood mute to hear it,
>     As some lone man who in a desert hears
>     The music of his home: — unwonted fears
> Fell on the pale oppressors of our race,
>     And Faith, and Custom, and low-thoughted cares,
>   Like thunder-stricken dragons, for a space
> Left the torn human heart, their food and dwelling-place.[64]

In the preface, however, Shelley probably had Godwin in mind when he observed how many of the 'most ardent and tender-hearted of the worshippers of public good' had been 'morally ruined' by the failure of the French Revolution. It was therefore his intention to dispel the infectious 'gloom and misanthropy' of the age.[65] The result was one of the greatest, and longest, revolutionary poems in English: Cynthia unites with Laon to bring about a sexual and political revolution, and although their success is short-lived and they are burnt at the stake, in a final apotheosis they sail on a sunlit sea towards a visionary Hesperides.

The influence of Godwin is obvious. The aim of the poem is to demonstrate 'the transient nature of ignorance and error, and the eternity of genius and virtue'.[66] Shelley presents a world governed by Necessity and caught in the endless struggle between good and evil. He professes an openly anarchist creed and celebrates the Godwinian principles of liberty, equality, and universal benevolence. And there is even a note which asserts that Malthus's admission of moral restraint reduced his *Essay of Population* to a 'commentary illustrative of the unanswerableness of *Political Justice*'.[67]

Yet when Godwin read *Laon and Cynthhia* he was disappointed. He wrote to Shelley censuring the poem in particular and his poetic powers in general. Shelley, deeply hurt, wrote back on 11 December with a passionate defence of his power 'to apprehend minute & remote distinctions of feeling'. He was ready to accept his strictures on 'the economy of intellectual force', but was nothing less than appalled at Godwin's suggestion that his declaration for the Chancery case — 'a cold, forced, unimpassioned & insignificant piece of cramped & cautious argument' — and his 'little scrap' about *Mandeville* were better than his poem which grew from '"the agony & bloody sweat" of intellectual travail'.[68] A visit by Godwin and his son William to Marlow for a few days both in December and January did little to abate Shelley's indignation.

The critical failure of *Laon and Cynthia* finally made Shelley decide to leave for Italy. On hearing the unexpected news, Godwin became frantic once again. He begged Shelley to leave all his money in England under a joint account but his son-in-law would have none of it. He sold on 31 January 1818 another post-obit bond of £4,500 for £2,000, and gave Godwin about £750 of it. Shelley's largesse and his threatened departure brought home to Godwin the meanness of his overtures:

I am ashamed of the tone I have taken with you in all our late conversations. I have played the part of a supplicant, and deserted that of a philosopher. It was not thus I talked with you when I first knew you. I will talk so no more. I will talk principles; I will talk Political Justice; whether it makes for me or against me, no matter.[69]

Shelley however was in no mood for talking and throughout his last month in England he did not call on Godwin despite his steady stream of letters — on the 2, 3, 5 and 10 February, and then on the 17th, 22nd, 24th and 25th. On 6 March Godwin slipped in to see his daughter, and when Shelley returned, there followed a formal reconciliation. But there was little chance to discuss political justice and even less for Godwin to borrow money. The former atheist then attended on the 9th the mass christening of his three grandchildren — William, Clara and Allegra — at St. Giles-in-the-Fields. He saw Shelley for the last time on the following day. On the 11th, Shelley, Mary, Claire and their babies set off for Italy. As an afterthought, Shelley instructed his bankers from Dover to honour a bill of £150 for his father-in-law. It marked the unhappy ebb of the creative relationship between two great radical writers.

Although their relationship never fully recovered, Godwin and Shelley still wrote occasionally. In the summer, he told him of a plan for a book called 'The Lives of the Commonwealth's Men' and suggested Mary could undertake it:

> There is a strong and inveterate prejudice in this country in favour of what these heroes styled 'the government of a single person.' I would at least have it shown that ten men, some of them never surpassed in ability, perhaps none of them in integrity, in this island, devoted themselves in heart and soul, with all their powers, to a purer creed.[70]

Shelley replied that it was precisely the subject for Mary since he was himself 'little skilled' in English history and had been busy translating Plato's *Symposium*.[71] Indeed, Plato was speedily replacing Godwin as his principal philosophical oracle.

Godwin wrote to his daughter more often. When he heard the news of the death of her daughter Clara on 24 September 1818, he sincerely sympathized but characteristically called her to stoicism: 'it is only persons of a very ordinary sort, and of a pusillanimous disposition, that sink long under a calamity of this nature'.[72] It was good advice, for it seems that Claire gave birth to Shelley's child Elena on 27 December. He later registered her as Mary's child; she was to die shortly after her first birthday.

One tragedy was followed by another. After the death of his son William on the 7 June in the following year, Shelley felt compelled to break his year-long silence with Godwin to ask him to soothe Mary's mind. But the very next letter from Godwin apparently accused Shelley of being 'a disgraceful and flagrant person' who had promised to send more money. Shelley was disgusted, and wrote to Leigh Hunt: 'I have bought bitter knowledge with £4,700.'[73] Godwin did, however, try to help his daughter and urged her to accept her fate and to return to work, particularly as she was formed 'by nature' to belong to those who can 'advance their whole species one or more degrees in the scale of perfectibility'.[74]

Although Mary remained inconsolable, she continued to seek her father's approval. In the summer of 1819, whilst carrying her fourth child (Percy Florence, born in 12 November), she wrote a short novel called *Mathilda*. It treated the theme of incest and unconsciously reflected her feelings towards the two principal men in her life. While Godwin thought 'very highly' of some of its parts, he found the subject 'disgusting and detestable', and quietly put the manuscript in a drawer.[75] Three years later Mary was still trying to get it back, and the work was not published in her lifetime.

Shelley in the autumn also instructed his publisher to send a copy of his

*Prometheus Unbound* to Godwin. Although Shelley increasingly moved towards Platonism, the influence of Godwin remained strong throughout his life. Godwin had long argued that the imagination was the faculty of moral improvement, and in *Prometheus Unbound* Shelley intended 'to familiarise the highly refined imagination' with 'beautiful idealisms of moral excellence'.[76] As in Godwin's world, the universe of the poem is in the Manichean grip of an evil force represented by Jupiter, and a good power symbolized by Saturn. Just as Godwin was finding a tendency in nature which ensures the triumph of life (which he called 'Spirit' and presented as a personification of Necessity), so Shelley creates in Demogorgon a friendly power which brings about the golden age. And at the end of the third act, Shelley gives the most powerful expression to Godwin's ultimate vision of the reign of freedom:

> The loathsome mask has fallen, the man remains
> Sceptreless, free, uncircumscribed, but man
> Equal, unclassed, tribeless, and nationless,
> Exempt from awe, worship, degree, the king
> Over himself; just, gentle, wise . . .[77]

Although *Prometheus Unbound* was the most eloquent expression of his philosophy, Godwin told Maria Gisborne in 1820 that he did not think that he would read it through, for he hated to read books that are 'full of obscurities and puzzles'. Shelley never wrote, he added, 'with a calm proper tone, but rather with anger, bitterness, and violence'.[78]

He was however impressed with his verse tragedy *The Cenci*. It was based on a real story in sixteenth-century Italy of a sadistic patriarch, Count Cenci, who raped his daughter Beatrice, only to be killed by her with the help of his wife and son. It is easy to see why Godwin should have liked it. The central situation is very similar to that of *Caleb Williams*: both Falkland and Beatrice have a false notion of honour which compels them to revenge, while Beatrice and Caleb are victims of a relentless tyrant against whom they rebel.[79] And although both Beatrice and Caleb are destroyed by society, they demonstrate the power of truth over violence.[80] Godwin could thus write to Mary:

> I have read the tragedy of 'Cenci', and am glad to see Shelley at last descending to what really passes among human creatures. The story is certainly an unfortunate one, but the execution gives me a new idea of Shelley's powers. There are passages of great strength, and the character of Beatrice is certainly excellent.[81]

He would not have been so happy about the angry extremism of Shelley's political verse at the time. From Italy, the poet lamented the 'liberticide' of 'England in 1819', and the 'death-white shore/Of Albion' in 'Lines written during the Castlereagh Administration'. 'Men of England', he asked bitterly, 'wherefore plough/For the lords who lay ye low?'[82] In response to the Peterloo massacre, where armed yeomanry charged a defenceless crowd and killed eleven people, Shelley openly called in *The Masque of Anarchy* for class solidarity and mass demonstrations:

Rise like the Lions after slumber
In unvanquishable number —
Shake your chains to earth like dew
Which in sleep had fallen on you —
Ye are many — they are few.[83]

Nevertheless, in his more considered pamphlet *A Philosophical View of Reform*, Shelley offered a powerful restatement of Godwinian principles. He had told Peacock earlier in the year that he still considered 'Poetry very subordinate to moral & political science' and in the pamphlet acknowledged that Godwin had developed the latter with 'irresistible eloquence'.[84] At the outset, he calls Godwin and Bentham the leading philosophers of the age for having established 'the principle of utility as the substance and liberty and equality as for forms, according to which the concerns of human life ought to be administered'.[85] But he goes beyond Bentham to argue with Godwin that mankind has submitted to the 'mighty calamity' of government only to escape the worst evils of slavery, and to suggest that the ideal would be 'a just combination of the elements of social life' without government.[86] In his economics, moreover, he agrees with Godwin that labour is the sole source of wealth, that everyone has a 'sacred and indisputable right' to the fruits of one's own labour, and that the ultimate goal is the equality of possessions.[87]

While in theory Shelley is critical of the new aristocracy of capitalists, in practice he follows like Godwin the Whig programme of parliamentary reform. He not only thinks that the extension of the franchise to women is 'somewhat immature' but opposes the secret ballot on the Godwinian grounds that a popular assembly of electors would increase their political knowledge through 'the republican boldness of censuring and judging one another'.[88] He calls on the people to recognize that 'patience and reason and endurance' are the best means of progress.[89] Above all, he places his confidence in the irresistible force of public opinion, and looks to intellectuals like Godwin, Hazlitt, Bentham and Hunt to enlighten the people and to confound their oppressors — 'these, radiant and irresistible like the meridian sun, would strike all but the eagles who dared to gaze upon its beams, with blindness and confusion . . . it would be Eternity warning Time.'[90] Indeed, in a phrase which recalls Godwin in his *Life of Chaucer*, Shelley declares that poets and philosophers are the 'unacknowledged legislators of the world'.[91]

Apart from the imagery, nearly every word could have been written by Godwin. For all his youthful flirtation with conspiratorial groups, his call in moments of despair for mass insurrection, and his ethereal visions of heaven on earth, Shelley had learned from Godwin the practical need for the piecemeal reform of existing institutions through gradual education and enlightenment.

As Shelley was finishing the pamphlet in the spring of 1820 he reread *Political Justice*, and wrote to John and Maria Gisborne soon after: 'You know, that although I believe he is the only sincere enemy I have in the world, that added years only add to my admiration of his intellectual powers, & even the moral resources of his character.'[92] For all Godwin's importunity and hostility, Shelley could still write in the summer in his *Letter to Maria Gisborne*:

> You will see
> That which was Godwin, — greater none than he
> Though fallen — and fallen on evil times — to stand
> Among the spirits of our age and land,
> Before the dread tribunal of *to come*
> The foremost, — while Rebuke cowers pale and dumb.[93]

Shelley's last great works show him still to be under Godwin's sway. In *A Defence of Poetry* (1821), he celebrates like Godwin the value of chivalry for giving birth to the 'poetry of sexual love'.[94] In his celebrated distinction, he argues that 'Reason is to imagination as the instrument to the agent' but he gives equal place to the two faculties and insists that the imagination is the 'great instrument of moral good'.[95] On hearing the news of the Greek insurrection, Shelley also expressed in his verse drama *Hellas* his undying faith in the omnipotence of truth and his fervent hope that another Athens shall rise to

> Bequeath, like sunset to the skies,
>    The splendour of its prime;
> And leave, if nought so bright may live,
> All earth can take or Heaven can give.[96]

Thus while Shelley was never an uncritical disciple, he remained to the end faithful to the radiant vision of *Political Justice*. Ironically, he drew closer to Platonism as Godwin moved away from it, but their views of nature, perfectibility, imagination and love converged. For all their personal differences, the genius of Shelley ensured moreover that Godwin's dream of regenerated humanity reached a far wider audience. If Godwin is the greatest philosopher of anarchism, Shelley is its poet.

# CHAPTER XIX

# The Commonwealth Man

Godwin's importunity with Shelley and others was almost entirely due to the financial shakiness of the Juvenile Library. Yet he never regretted his involvement in the enterprise. After composing *Fleetwood* in 1805, his mind felt exhausted and the 'inglorious transactions of the shop below-stairs' kept him occupied whilst he gradually renewed his creative strength.[1] His mind however could not lie fallow for long. Despite the poor reception of his *Lives of Edward and John Philips*, which was enough to cure him of the 'intoxications of vanity', his long-standing interest in the Commonwealth was reawakened.[2] When he decided to try his hand at another novel, the seventeenth century therefore seemed an ideal setting. The result was *Mandeville. A Tale of the Seventeenth Century in England*, begun in May 1816 and after many interruptions completed for Constable in October of the following year.

Ironically, Godwin was partly inspired by Charles Brockden Brown's novel *Wieland* (1798) and Joanna Baillie's tragedy *De Montfort* (1800) which both betray the influence of *Caleb Williams*. As in Scott's early novels, he used the past to illuminate contemporary social and political problems. His plot however was his very own.

Mandeville relates how he witnesses at the age of three the massacre of both his parents during the Irish rebellion of 1641. His 'gloomy, unsocial and ferocious' temperament is then formed in his uncle's oppressive mansion by a harsh Calvinist tutor Hilkiah Bradford.[3] The dark atmosphere is only briefly relieved by the short visit of his angelic sister Henrietta.

As a boarder at Winchester School, Mandeville is unable to find friends, and becomes intensely envious of the popular and graceful Clifford. Their rivalry is intensified when Mandeville is replaced by Clifford as Sir Joseph Wagstaff's secretary and earns a reputation as a royalist spy. When Mandeville learns that his beloved sister wishes to marry his most hated rival, he is beside himself with sadistic jealousy. Urged on by the insidious lawyer Holloway, who becomes his guardian after the death of his uncle, he decides to abduct his sister. The plan misfires, and at the end of the novel Mandeville is horribly disfigured by Clifford in a fight.

It is the express purpose of the narrative, Mandeville declares, 'to show how a concurrence of a variety of causes operate to form a character'.[4] It is the original taint laid in Mandeville's character by his gloomy and isolated upbringing that makes it impossible for him to judge the real motives of himself and others. The principle of necessity however in Godwin's novel takes on the force of a supernatural destiny. Mandeville rebels hopelessly against his 'perverse and malignant' destiny; Clifford remains his 'evil genius'; and they are bound together with a chain 'the links of which could never be dissolved'.[5]

But although the novel dwells on the emotional state of Mandeville, Godwin places the narrative firmly in the religious and political context of the Commonwealth and tries to explain the failure of the Revolution.[6] The novel opens with the storming of the garrison of Charlemont by Sir Philim O'Neille during the Irish rebellion of 1641, and the narrator observes that the English were also ripe for the irresistible assertion of their rights.

Godwin does not offer a blatant plea for republicanism, but prefers to show how the background of his characters determines their political allegiance. Mandeville would seem to represent the progressive Presbyterian aristocracy, and although he listens to the democratic discourses of his sister, he is unable to transcend the prejudices of his class and time. His rival Clifford typifies the opportunist who, brought up in 'reverential ideas of kingship and prerogative', is ready to change his religion in order to realize his ambition in the royalist cause.[7] Colonel Penruddock, on the other hand, who leads the royalist rebellion, is presented as a noble cavalier, pure of intention and courageous in defeat, certainly not guilty of any crime which deserves the public scaffold. The republican side is only represented by Hilkiah, a man of great integrity but also of extremes: his evangelical religion is matched by levelling politics, and he hints darkly that the fifth-monarchy man might 'finally get the start of all, and level the proud fortunes of the noble and the gentleman with the dust'.[8]

Godwin's treatment of religion is equally subtle and discerning. Despite the purity of his heart, Hilkiah is portrayed as a bigoted and inflexible Calvinist. He considers the church of Rome as the 'spiritual Babylon' and regards 'light laughter, and merriment, and the frolics of youth, as indications of the sons of Belial and heirs of destruction'.[9] Mandeville adopts the religion of his tutor, and when he arrives at Oxford, he has cursing bouts with another misanthropic and royalist student, Lisle, against the Pope, the Cardinals, and the Jesuits. He exults to learn that Clifford has turned

Papist, for his apostasy means that he can at last hate him with a safe conscience. True to his upbringing, he looks upon Popery as 'the lowest pit of disgrace and calamity, into which human beings could fall'.[10]

But while Hilkiah and Mandeville are intended to show the force of religious prejudice in the seventeenth century and the dangers of extreme Calvinism, Godwin is not hostile to religion as such. Indeed, Mandeville expresses his mature opinion that

> Religion is the most important of all things, the great point of discrimination that divides the man from the brute. It is our special prerogative, that we can converse with that which we cannot see, and believe in that the existence of which is reported to us by none of our senses . . . Invisible things are the only realities . . .[11]

It is Henrietta, however, who is Godwin's most direct mouthpiece in the novel. To Hilkiah's 'religion of hatred', she opposes a 'religion of love' which is taken straight out of *Political Justice*. Firstly, she insists that by 'the very constitution of our being we are compelled to delight in society: "it is not good for man to be alone"'.[12] Secondly, she argues that man is a machine: 'He is just what his nature and his circumstances have made him: he obeys the necessities which he cannot resist.'[13] And finally, since Mandeville's acute sensibility makes him so misanthropic and jealous, she insists that his power resides in the rational part of his nature: 'I must be like a great military commander in the midst of a field of battle, calm, collected, vigilant, imperturbable: but the moment I am the slave of passion, my powers are lost . . .'[14]

Mandeville, however, is unwilling to accept all her teaching. He takes her point that all wealth resolves itself into 'a certain quantity of human labour' and that it is incumbent on him as a man of property 'to be munificent, without being either luxurious or prodigal'.[15] But when she draws a 'bewitching portrait of an obscure and rural life', he replies that man is not like an animal that can 'sleep away life on a sunny bank' — he can only be satisfied when engaged in some earnest pursuit.[16]

Similarly, in a discussion with Clifford, Mandeville objects to his view that the truly independent man has the fewest wants. Poverty, as well as wealth, has its drawbacks: 'I saw that poverty was environed on all sides with temptations, urging and impelling a man, to sell his soul, to sacrifice his integrity: to debase the clearness of his spirit, and to become the bond slave of a thousand vices.'[17] Godwin was clearly speaking from personal experience.

Although Godwin uses the characters to convey his mature philosophy, the overriding atmosphere, as in all his novels, is one of gloom and despondency. Mandeville's whole life demonstrates how easily motives can be misunderstood and how difficult it is to receive a fair verdict from one's fellows. It is the men like the obsequious Holloway (Hollow Way) and his fawning nephew Mallison (Son of Evil) who seem to succeed. Men who are intrinsically good, like Mandeville and his uncle, are condemned to suffer in the 'wild waste and harbourless desert of the world'.[18] Even the heavenly Henrietta is forced in the end to admit that for ever 'vice triumphs over virtue, and imbecility over strength'.[19] The motto on the title-page from Exodus, Chapter X — 'And the waters of that fountain were bitter, and they said, Let the name of it be called Marah' — suitably sets the tone of the thousand pages of the three-volume novel.

In *Mandeville*, the disintegrating tendencies already apparent in *St. Leon* and *Fleetwood* come to the fore. Only Mandeville stands out as a convincing and original portrait. The other characters are little more than extreme types, inevitably dominated by one passion, and incapable of much development. The plot not only meanders but at times disappears, as in the long history of Audley Mandeville in volume one, and Clifford's account of Sir Joseph Wagstaff in volume two. The lack of events means that most space is devoted to static and repetitive descriptions of states of mind. Where the whole plot in *Caleb Williams* conveyed the moral theme, here it is expressed in set speeches of moralizing.

Yet for all its faults, *Mandeville* remains a powerful and original work. There is much interesting debate and some passages of real spirit. Godwin gives a vivid portrait of seventeenth-century England and of the complex religious and political forces at work in the Civil War. Above all, he explores the misty borderline between the rational and the irrational and offers an astonishingly modern account of the social origins of madness.

The first critical reaction Godwin received was from Shelley. When a copy arrived on 1 December 1817, the day of publication, Mary was the first to read it. Shelley looked impatiently over her shoulder 'like a man on the brink of a precipice, or a ship whose sails are all lowered for the storm'.[20] Six days later, he wrote to Godwin from Marlow: 'In style & strength of expression Mandeville is wonderfully great, & the energy & the sweetness of the sentiments [are] scarcely to be equalled.'[21]

Godwin, only too conscious of his eclipse and with creditors knocking at the door, was naturally delighted. Never adverse to favourable publicity, he changed the personal pronoun to the impersonal and sent Shelley's comments to the *Morning Chronicle* where it was printed on 9 December as an 'Extract of a Letter from Oxfordshire'.

Shelley was gratified to see that Godwin valued his opinion so highly. He felt emboldened to write a more copious statement of his feelings which he sent to Leigh Hunt who published it in the *Examiner* on 28 December.

Shelley maintains that the interest of *Mandeville* is 'undoubtedly equal, in some respects superior' to that of *Caleb Williams*, although it contains no character like Falkland. Above all, he claims that the pleadings of Henrietta compose 'in every respect the most perfect and beautiful piece of writing of modern times'. It all goes to show that 'Godwin has been to the present age in moral philosophy what Wordsworth is in poetry.'[22] It was praise indeed.

*Mandeville* probably inspired Shelley's poems 'Love's Philosophy', which echoes the theme and even the phrasing of the epilogue to Henrietta's central speech, and his 'Ozymandias', where the poet views the monarch corrupted by his education as Mandeville sees Clifford.[23] But it proved an even greater subject for the satirists. Peacock in his novel *Nightmare Abbey* (1818) drew on it for his general setting, for his conception of Christopher Glowry's character, and for his treatment of misanthropy.[24] Indeed, there is even a direct reference: Mr. Flosky opens a novel called Devilman (play on the name Mandeville) and observes: 'Hm. Hatred — revenge — misanthropy — and quotations from the Bible. Hm. This is the morbid anatomy of black bile.'[25] An anonymous fourth volume entitled *Mandeville; or, The Last Words of a Maniac. A Tale of the Seventeenth Century in England, by Himself* also appeared in the same year: after more satirical bouts of loving and delirium, Mandeville and Clifford eventually kill each other and fall across Henrietta's grave.

Most readers felt that Godwin had gone too far. No notice appeared in the *Edinburgh Review* because its editor Francis Jeffrey distrusted Hazlitt and Mackintosh, whom Godwin suggested, and because Charles Lamb declined Constable's request for a review. Godwin also asked Elizabeth Inchbald to make marginal notes in her presentation copy but she failed to oblige.[26] In the *Scots Magazine*, however, Mackintosh rallied to the friend he had so abused and compared Godwin to Byron in their study of the 'dark recesses of the heart'.[27] John Lockhart in *Blackwood's Edinburgh Magazine* equally felt that both writers had given birth to 'a set of terrible personifications of pride, scorn, hatred, misanthropy, misery and madness' — although he admired Godwin's manly language and felt his conclusion equalled *King Lear*.[28] A correspondent to the editor found this far too encomiastic.[29] And so did the rest of the reviews: the *British Critic* dismissed the three 'tiresome' volumes; the *British Review and London Critical Journal* felt it was the dullest of his novels; and the *Quarterly Review* panned it as 'intolerably tedious and disgusting'.[30] It might have been a masterly picture of the wreck of a mind but the *Literary Journal and General Miscellany of Sciences* did not think it could be called a novel.[31]

Godwin did his best to reach as wide an audience as possible. A French translation appeared in Paris in 1818, and pirated editions in New York and Philadelphia in the same year. But when he approached Crabb Robinson about a German translation, Godwin received little encouragement: 'I did not add', wrote the diarist, 'that he has no great popularity in Germany'.[32] Unfortunately for Godwin, neither had he in England, and the sale of *Mandeville* only confirmed his conviction that he did not owe 'any considerable thanks to the kindness of my contemporaries'.[33]

Godwin's social life at this time was limited to a few friends and an occasional visit to the theatre. An exception was Ludwig Tieck, the German poet and critic, who called on 29 June 1817 to praise his writings.[34] He saw more of Mackintosh who was keen to make amends for his past harshness, but Coleridge had gradually dropped from his circle and was busy defending orthodoxy in religion and politics. Place was irretrievably estranged. The Lambs were still to be seen at Skinner Street, although their hostility to Mrs. Godwin remained undiminished.

The death of Curran on 14 October 1817 was a great blow and Godwin dedicated *Mandeville* to him as to 'the sincerest friend I ever had'. In an obituary published in the *Morning Chronicle* on 16 October, he praised him as not only the 'great ornament' of the Irish bar but as almost the last of 'that brilliant phalanx, the co[n]temporaries and fellow-labourers of Mr. Fox, in the cause of general liberty'.[35]

On the other hand, Godwin, through Shelley, was able to meet the writers of the next generation. He met Keats on 18 November 1817 and read his *Poems* (1817), but left no comment. Keats for his part read with enthusiasm *Caleb Williams, St. Leon,* and *Mandeville,* and agreed with Hazlitt's view that their effect was the result of an 'intense and patient study of the human heart'.[36] He was less taken with *Political Justice,* and thought that his 'Godwin–Methodist' friend Charles Wentworth Dilke would never come at a truth because he was 'always trying at it'.[37] Keats's publisher friend Cowden Clarke also considered Godwin 'a hard-judging, deep-sighted, yet strongly-feeling and strangely-imaginative author', although he disliked his 'snarly tone of voice' which exacerbated the effect of his 'sneering speeches and cutting retorts'.[38]

Godwin clearly did not get on with all of Shelley's contemporaries. When he was introduced to Byron on 4 August 1813, he apparently found him a 'very ugly man', and while he liked *Don Juan,* he could never read the third and fourth part of *Childe Harold*.[39] He thought even less of Leigh Hunt, and told Maria Gisborne that he was 'a man of factitious, though perfectly sincere character, made up out of notions derived from Italian poetry, and whims of various kinds'.[40]

Godwin still attracted the occasional disciple. On 11 June 1817 the nineteen-year-old American Joseph Bevan, a student of Godwin's old friend James Ogilvie, was introduced to him by Gulian Verplanck at the start of a tour of Scotland and Ireland. He asked the sixty-one-year-old philosopher for his advice on the course of studies it might be most advantageous for him to pursue. Godwin obliged and on 12 February 1818 sent him a long letter sketching a full curriculum. Since he was often asked for similar advice, he had it printed for his own distribution. When Constable saw a copy of his *Letter of Advice to a Young American,* he liked it so much that he had it inserted in the March 1818 issue of the *Scots Magazine.*[41]

The letter reflects Godwin's lifelong interest in education and his mature philosophical and literary opinions. As an educator, his principal aim is to make his fellow human beings independent and generous. But this is to be achieved not through the 'dry accumulation of science and natural facts', or even through the exercise of reason, but through the cultivation of the imagination. Morality, Godwin insists, depends 'agreeably to the admirable maxim of Jesus, upon our putting ourselves in the place of another, feeling his feelings, and apprehending his desires; in a word, doing to others, as we would wish, were we they, to be done unto'.[42]

In the curriculum, Godwin sees history as the most important subject for cultivating moral sentiments. He particularly recommends the history of Greece and Rome ('the bravest and sublimest fiction that it ever entered into the mind of man to create'); the age of chivalry (since it regarded woman 'as a being to be treated with courtship and consideration and fealty'); and the modern English period (as 'the English moral and intellectual character ranks the first of modern times').[43]

But Godwin would not neglect poetry. He suggests that Chaucer, Spenser, Shakespeare, and Milton are the best English poets. For prose, he singles out the Elizabethan writers and translators, and calls Bacon's language 'rather that of a God, than a man'.[44] To discipline the rational faculties, he believes metaphysics excels all other subjects and recommends those thinkers closest to him: Berkeley, Hume, Hartley and Andrew Baxter, as well as Jonathan Edwards on free will and Hutcheson and Hazlitt on benevolence. And since language is as necessary to the mind as hands are to the body, he urges the study of ancient and modern languages.

When it comes to method, Godwin stresses above all that early education should be directed at acquiring good habits and not at making 'parrots and monkies'.[45] It is not the memory but the imagination, the intellect, and the heart which are to be stimulated. He concludes by arguing that 'it is the truly enlightened man, that is best qualified to be truly useful'.[46]

In England, Godwin's *Letter of Advice to a Young American* was only reviewed by the *Monthly Repository*, which found it useful, and by Godwin's old friend and opponent Thelwall in the *Champion*, who thought it worth all that had been written on the subject in the last twenty years.[47] In America, it became one of Godwin's most reprinted works. In 1818, it appeared in the *Analectic Magazine* and *Robinson's Magazine* with praise and in the *Port Folio* with disapproval. Bevan arranged its publication in the *Georgia Journal* in the following year.[48]

In September 1819, the *Analectic Magazine* also issued a partial reprint of the pamphlet, together with five more of Godwin's letters to Bevan.[49] For political theory, Godwin directs Bevan to his *Political Justice* since 'If I had to write my work over again, I could correct many errors, but scarcely any thing that strikes my mind as fundamental.'[50] In practical politics, he is as moderate and wary as ever. He criticizes the French scheme of an electoral body, and the English reformers who wanted a national secret ballot on the same day. Instead, he prefers the traditional system of hustings and voting since it revives '(though, alas! but once in seven years)' the feeling that the people are 'freemen' and nourishes the love of 'what is right'. And yet he still wishes to avoid 'the sting, the terror, and the hot-blooded, savage, and dangerous feeling' of mass demonstrations.[51]

There were real grounds for Godwin's fear of tumult. After the Napoleonic wars, there had been a growing threat of revolution in England. The radical movement with its roots in the 1790s emerged with renewed vigour: Hampden clubs became hot-beds of disaffected rhetoric and Cobbett in his *Political Register*, Thelwall in the *Champion*, and Hunt in the *Examiner* thundered for parliamentary reform. 'Orator' Hunt attracted massive crowds at Spa Fields. On 2 December 1816, after one such meeting, a breakaway crowd broke into gunshops — including Beckwith's opposite Godwin's house — and marched to the Tower to urge troops to join them. The government responded by suspending Habeas Corpus and by hanging a rioter, John Cashman, at the scene of the crime at the junction of Skinner Street and Snow Hill. Godwin must have heard the cries of 'Murder!' and 'Shame!' through his study windows from the huge crowd which refused to disperse for several hours.[52] He also noted in his diary the 'outrage at Manchester' on 16 August 1819 which came to be known as the Battle of Peterloo. Six repressive Acts were quickly introduced which marked the beginning of the most sustained campaign of persecution in British history.

But despite the gravity and closeness of these events, Godwin held aloof from contemporary politics. When Lady Caroline Lamb, the former mistress of Byron and wife of William Lamb (the future Lord Melbourne), requested Godwin's support for her brother-in-law George at the Westminster election, he declined with the words:

> My creed is a short one. I am in principle a Republican, but in practice a Whig.
>
> But I am a philosopher: that is, a person desirous to become wise, and I aim at that object by reading, by writing, and a little by conversation.

> But I do not mix in the business of the world, and I am now too old to
> alter my course . . .[53]

Her insistence that she much admired *Political Justice* and the many subsequent invitations to stay at Brocket Hall failed to winkle Godwin out of his semi-retirement in Skinner Street.

Godwin was no less moderate in his dealings with a young disciple called Henry Blanch Rosser. Rosser felt that a reading of *Political Justice* in 1815 had moulded his character and enabled him to get to Cambridge. When Rosser however showed contempt for the Whigs, the philosopher insisted that they constituted the party to which a 'liberal-minded and enlightened man would adhere'.[54] Again, he shared Rosser's joy at the news of the Spanish Revolution but observed that since England was not yet ripe for universal suffrage ('the monarchy probably would not stand a year'), the medicine would be too strong for Spain.[55]

Above all, Godwin condemned his proselytizing atheism, arguing that while a man is right who does not believe in God, a 'man is wrong who is without religion'.[56] By a religious man, he meant a lover of nature:

> All that I see, the earth, the sea, the rivers, the trees, the clouds, animals, and, most of all, man, fills me with love and astonishment. My soul is full to bursting with the mystery of all this, and I love it the better for its mysteriousness. It is too wonderful for me; it is past finding out: but it is beyond expression delicious. This is what I call religion . . .[57]

In an unpublished 'Essay on Religion' written at this time, Godwin clarified his creed. He still believes that mankind could do very well without Christianity, and that in the Christian idea of God there is a tyrant perpetually controlling us who sits 'like Jeremy Bentham, perched on the top of his Panopticon, to spy into all our weaknesses'. But while Godwin is opposed to Christianity, he feels the emotional and imaginative springs of a religion are necessary for moral development:

> It is by dint of feeling & putting ourselves in fancy into the place of other men, that we can learn how we ought to treat them, & be moved to treat them as we ought. Man to express the thing in familiar language is a complex being, made up of a head & a heart. So far as we are employed in heaping up facts & in reasoning upon them merely, we are a species of machine; it is our impulses & our sentiments that are the glory of our nature.

He therefore proposes a religion based on the reverence of the works of man and of nature. An art gallery, for instance, could become a 'genuine temple of God', and instead of sermons, a noble lecture could be given 'on the beautiful structure of the universe, or the majesty of the human form in both mind and body'.[58] He never developed this 'religion' into a coherent system but remained faithful to its vision for the rest of his life.

But while Godwin was refusing to involve himself in practical politics and condemning atheism, he was not idle in philosophy. After completing *Mandeville*, he felt it was time to confront his chief opponent Malthus. While he had admitted the validity of Malthus's ratios in his *Thoughts* in 1801, a decade later he was no longer convinced that population in all old countries is always in excess of the means of subsistence. If anything, he wrote to a correspondent, it is the production of luxuries and the inequality of distribution which are responsible for poverty: if the rich abjured their wealth 'the instant effect, the effect for succeeding years, will be an excess of the means of subsistence'.[59] Malthus however continued to dominate public opinion. The popularity of his *Essay on the Principle of Population* warranted a fifth edition in 1817, and he considered Godwin sufficiently harmless to drop the chapter on him and to attack Owen in his place. Before quitting the world, Godwin therefore wished to refute him once and for all.

Godwin began writing his answer to Malthus on 14 December 1817. He thought he could complete it in six months, but it took him almost three years. He recruited the help of Rosser who sometimes acted as an amanuensis. His old friend the Scottish lexicographer David Booth offered the main argument of Book II on the powers of increase in the numbers of the world and helped Godwin with his statistics and illustrations. He also supplied the 'Dissertation on the Ratios of Increase in Population, and in the Means of Subsistence' which was annexed to the book. Godwin's own research and writing involved him in 'a world of difficulties' which required 'patience indescribable'.[60] It was not until 21 October 1820 that he finished the preface. On 1 November Longmans published, 'for the author', *Of Population. An Enquiry concerning the Power of Increase in the Numbers of Mankind, being an Answer to Mr. Malthus's Essay on that Subject*. It was the last of Godwin's works to make a public impact.

Godwin tried to turn the tables on Malthus, and adopted the polemical style which had been used against him. He will now have nothing to do with the 'most groundless paradoxes' of his *Essay on the Principle of Population*.[61] Where Malthus had presented himself as scientific and dismissed Godwin as a naive visionary, Godwin now accuses him of dwelling in 'abstractions and generalities' and places himself firmly in the empirical tradition of Bacon, who taught us 'to bring all nature to the tribunal of science'.[62] It is not to some perfect man or ideal society that Godwin refers, but to 'man as he is, and human societies as they are to be found'.[63]

In order to refute Malthus's ratios, Godwin first points to societies in the past, especially the republics of Greece and Rome, where there was no threat of overpopulation despite the absence of the checks of vice and misery. He then challenges Malthus's evidence for his claim that population when unchecked doubles itself every twenty-five years. Malthus had told Godwin in a letter dated 25 October 1818 that his chief authority for the geometrical ratio was the figures for the U.S.A., to which Godwin replies ironically that if America had not been discovered, it would never have been known.[64] The most reliable tables available, he maintains, are those for Sweden, where there are few immigrants and the sexes and ages of the population are known. Four children to every marriage is the average there, and since only two are likely to reproduce, population tends to remain constant.

Having refuted Malthus's geometrical ratio for population, Godwin turns his attention to the arithmetical ratio for the power of increase in the means of subsistence. Again, Godwin claims that there is simply no evidence to infer that population outgrows food supply. We live in an unpeopled world and there are vast tracts of land uncultivated. Each man is capable of producing more food than he can consume. It is the present civil institutions based on the inequality of mankind and the accumulation of property in the hands of a few which restrict the food supply.

Godwin's remedy is therefore to make more land available for cultivation and to improve the methods of agriculture. An initial period of extensive labour may be necessary, but the use of machinery will eventually increase 'the most valuable of human treasures, leisure'.[65] In the meantime, the seas remain largely untapped, vegetables could replace animals (thereby releasing more land for cultivation) and chemistry might offer a 'real infinite series of increase of the means of subsistence.[66]

But while Godwin devotes five out of his six books to refuting Malthus's ratios, he is clearly more at home discussing philosophical principles. Indeed, it is the chief object of his work to carry forward the great tradition of Solon, Plato, Montesquieu and Sidney, which Malthus had interrupted, and to return the science of politics to its just and legitimate purpose: 'the enquiring how mankind in society, by every means that can be devised, may be made happy'.[67]

The fundamental error of Malthus's system, Godwin argues, lies in his proposition 'That the passion between the sexes is necessary and will remain nearly in its present state'.[68] Although Malthus withdrew this premiss in his second edition, and admitted the check of moral restraint, he still argued that it operates with very inconsiderable force. Godwin, on the other hand, asserts that the sexual drive is not like hunger and can be easily controlled. Even women, whom he acknowledges to be the 'weaker vessel, and more a slave to passion', are as capable as men of self-government and generally marry to better their condition rather than to indulge their appetites.[69] In short, the power of moral restraint is 'immense'.[70]

Godwin next finds Malthus's doctrine to be one 'of quietism, and of negatively presenting a front of resistance against all improvements'.[71] The class nature of his recommendations are clear when he argues that the poor have 'no right to support' but the rich have a 'right to do what they will with their own'.[72] We are stewards, Godwin insists, not proprietors, of the good things of this life, and just as the rich man has a duty to help the poor man, so the poor man has a claim to his assistance. Again Malthus calls for the gradual abolition of the Poor Laws in order to dissuade the poor from marrying, and yet marriage is the 'grand holiday of our human nature'.[73] Ideally, the unfortunate would be looked after without intervention of the state, but the Poor Laws are better than no assistance at all. Finally, where Malthus advocates lower wages, Godwin maintains that higher wages would stimulate the economy and produce a redistribution of wealth so that 'the labourer would have more of those things which form the consolation of life, while the rich man would have fewer superfluities'.[74]

In his conclusion, Godwin focuses on the fundamental differences between himself and Malthus in their view of man and society. For Malthus the evils of which men complain do not lie within their reach to remove but 'come from the laws of nature, and the unalterable impulse of human kind'.[75] His code therefore consists principally of negatives: we must preach down private charity, frugality, and marriage. For Godwin, on the other hand, man is 'to a considerable degree the artificer of his own fortune', and there is 'no evil under which the human species can labour, that man is not competent to cure'.[76] It is human beings, not God or Nature, who are responsible for vice and misery. While Malthus could see no improvement in things as they are, Godwin therefore remains the great believer in individual and social progress.

In a nostalgic tone, Godwin compares the 'Old World' in which there was room 'for a generous ambition to unfold itself' with the new world ushered in by the *Essay on the Principle of Population* which appears like 'a city under the severe visitation of pestilence'.[77] To embrace Malthus's creed is to have a new religion, and a new God. Ironically, the former atheist of *Political Justice* now presents himself as a defender of Christianity, the religion of 'charity and love', and modestly hopes to have brought 'new arguments in aid of old truth'.[78]

Although some of Godwin's acquaintances had tried to discourage him, when *Of Population* appeared on 1 November 1820 most of them were impressed. Mackintosh felt that Godwin was 'somewhat intolerant' to Malthus, but at least agreed that the increase of mankind did not lead to 'any consequences unfavourable to their hopes'.[79] Crabb Robinson was convinced by Godwin and felt he had 'ably and eloquently exposed the abominable feelings' which made Malthus so popular.[80] Hazlitt, on the other hand, thought that Godwin 'judged ill' in trying to invalidate Malthus's principle, instead of pointing out the misapplication of it.[81] He also declined to write a review, complaining to Hunt that Godwin had stolen 'one half' of his work from his own *Reply to the Essay on Population* without acknowledgement.[82] Ironically, Hazlitt had written his *Reply* originally in defence of Godwin, and if anything the debt was from the younger to the older man.[83]

The liberal reviews were generally favourable. Thelwall's *Champion* declared that Godwin had annihilated Malthus's system.[84] The *Examiner* first reprinted the *Glasgow Chronicle*'s favourable notice and then argued that Godwin's main point was triumphantly proved.[85] The *London Magazine* spoke of Godwin's service to political economy, and the *Philosophical Magazine and Journal* agreed with his findings.[86] In the New Year, the *Monthly Magazine* approved of Godwin's exposure of Malthus; the *Monthly Review* gave its unqualified approbation; and the *Literary Chronicle and Weekly Review* added to their praise.[87] Reviewers, however, tended to stick to party lines in the Malthusian controversy, and not surprisingly the Tory *British Critic* observed that the 'querulous, conceited, vindictive, uncandid' nature of Godwin's work clearly showed that he was in his dotage.[88] F. S. Constancio did not agree, and his translation of Godwin's *Of Population* appeared in Paris in 1821.

Godwin was also pleased to hear that Lord Grenville was a convert and that the M.P.s W. Morgan, Francis Bartley and Dr. Rees supported him. Morgan in particular assured Godwin that he had given the 'death-blow' to Malthus's ratios.[89] In a parliamentary debate on the Poor Laws Amendment Bill on 7 June 1821, E. Harbord also argued that Godwin's excellent and elaborate answer had overthrown Malthus's doctrine. Even Courtenay, the Secretary to the Board of Control, assured Godwin that he would express his 'entire approbation' of his work in a subsequent stage of the Bill.[90]

Godwin had hoped, whilst writing his answer to Malthus's *Essay*, that the world would be 'delivered for ever from this accursed apology in favour of vice and misery, of hard-heartedness and oppression'.[91] At first, his principal opponents contented themselves with sending derisive notes to each other about his work. 'Have you seen Godwin against Malthus?', James Mill wrote to David Ricardo on 13 November 1820. 'To me it appears below contempt.'[92] Next John McCulloch wrote to Ricardo on 25 December: 'I do not think I ever saw a more miserable performance — It would be doing it far too much honour to take the least notice of it —.'[93] When Hutches

Trower wrote to Ricardo that 'It is intemperate and abusive; and with all the *pretence* of systematick investigation, it is a rambling disjointed performance,' Ricardo replied: 'Your view of Godwin's book exactly agrees with mine.'[94] And as for the chief opponent, Malthus wrote to Place on 19 February 1821: 'Mr. Godwin, in his last work, has proceeded to the discussion of the principles of population with a degree of ignorance of his subject which is really quite inconceivable.'[95] Godwin's disciple Rosser called on Place and Mill in January 1821, but he was unable to get a distinct statement of their objections to his book.[96]

The first public critique from the Malthus camp appeared in the *Huntingdon Gazette* on 13 January 1821. The reviewer complained that Godwin had failed to appreciate the role of capital and dismissed his book outright. Godwin was incensed by such criticism from a provincial journal and inserted on 22 January 1821 an advertisement in the *Morning Chronicle* that in a few days would be published 'A Reply to the Economists in Defence of the Answer to Mr. Malthus's Essay on Population by William Godwin' (Price: one shilling).

No copies of the pamphlet have survived, and it may never have been published. In the manuscript, however, Godwin complains that the political economists had formed a party against him, and the 'wise men of the North' had decided to pass over his work in silence. He repeats his main arguments against Malthus's ratios: we are ruined not by the increase in population as 'under the inexorable administration of Nature' but by the misuse of capital which enables one man 'to exercise dominion & authority over the industry of another'. The dominant tone is that of moral indignation: 'I have written a book in defence of human nature, & of all that is dear to the human heart: Mr. Malthus's essay is the bitterest libel upon God and man that ever was penned.'[97]

In the meantime, Godwin's *Of Population* had been cited in the parliamentary discussions on the Poor Laws, and its high price did not prevent it from falling into the hands of the 'labouring classes'.[98] Malthus was alarmed and at last forced to break his silence in the July 1821 issue of the *Edinburgh Review*. The serious part of the article attempted to refute the Swedish mortality lists, but Malthus resorted to insulting Godwin for his 'gross mistakes' and 'glaring misrepresentations'. 'It appears to us,' he declared bluntly, 'the poorest and most old-womanish performance that has fallen from the pen of a writer of name, since we have first commenced our critical career.'[99]

Godwin was hurt, particularly when he learned that the anonymous reviewer was his very opponent, and complained of the 'very scurrilous and abusive account' to his daughter.[100] Shelley, on first reading *Of Population*, told Claire that it was 'a dry but clever book, with decent interspersions of cant and sophistry'.[101] When he heard of the article in the *Edinburgh Review*, however, he wrote to John Gisborne that:

> Godwin's answer to Malthus is victorious & decisive, and that it should not be generally acknowledged as such is full evidence of the influence of successful evil & tyranny. What Godwin is compared to Plato & Lord Bacon we well know. But compared with these miserable sciolists he is a vulture (you know vultures have considerable appetites) to a worm.[102]

Godwin thought of replying to the *Edinburgh Review*, but left it to David Booth who published in 1823 *A Letter to the Rev. T.R. Malthus*. Rosser also wrote a pamphlet entitled *The Question of Population* which was 'A Tabulation of the Gross Blunders and Absurdities' of Malthus's article on Godwin's enquiry. Godwin's last contribution to the controversy was a letter, dated 29 December 1821 and signed 'L'Ami des Hommes', which he sent to the *Morning Chronicle*. Citing his own work, Godwin sarcastically denied that a recent census for Ireland supported Malthus's geometrical ratio: 'If Ireland, oppressed, rebellious, trampled upon, half-fed, half-starved, multiplies as fast as America, I am afraid all schemes for keeping down population are gone for ever.'[103] A shorter letter, dated 25 December and published in the *Examiner* on 6 January 1822, made the same point with greater asperity and revealed Godwin's hand.

Godwin's former disciple Place had become a recent ally of the political economists and felt it necessary to define his position. In an article he wrote for the *New Monthly Magazine*, he commended many of Godwin's arguments but objected to his defence of the Poor Laws since they discouraged exertion.[104] He sent the manuscript of his more considered *Illustrations and Proofs of the Principle of Population* (1822) to Ricardo, and specifically referred to it as a reply to Godwin.[105] But while firmly endorsing Malthus's ratios, he acknowledged his indebtedness to Godwin for his unshaken belief in social improvement and in education as a check to population.[106] He advocated, moreover, Godwin's doctrine of moral restraint with such enthusiasm — extending it to include birth control — that he earned the disapproval of the political economists and people even began to shun him.

Yet despite the friendly press and the enthusiastic efforts of his supporters, Godwin was unable to turn public opinion. The world indeed had changed since 1793 and political economy had triumphed over the older tradition of political philosophy. Alexander Everett came up in 1823 with some *New Ideas on Population with Remarks on the Theories of Malthus and Godwin*, claiming that Godwin was as wrong in expecting happiness to be achieved through the disappearance of all political institutions as Malthus was in holding their influence to be minimal. But the work had little effect, and Malthus felt sufficiently confident in 1826 to add only a brief reference to Godwin's book in the sixth edition of his *Essay*: 'I am quite sure every candid and competent inquirer after truth will agree with me in thinking that it does not require a reply.'[107]

As Godwin was making a last-ditch stand against Malthus, his life reached yet another crisis. Ever since 1807 he had withheld his annual rent of £150 for 41 Skinner Street because it was not clear who was the real owner following its disposal in a lottery. In August 1817, however, one Read managed to establish legal ownership, and issued a notice to quit on 23 June 1818. Godwin was deeply engaged in his work and the strain led to a slight stroke on 23 November. Although he dined out the following night, occasional attacks of numbness in his hands and legs returned. But this was not all. His publisher, Constable, threatened him in May 1819 with arrest for failing to redeem two promissory notes of £130 which could not be covered by the poor sales of *Mandeville*. Then on 19 October Godwin's landlord Read successfully obtained a court order for arrears of rent amounting to £1,500.

Despite their estrangement, Godwin's only recourse was to Shelley. At first the poet contemplated returning to England to raise the money, although according to Mary the journey would have been 'next door to death for him'.[108] As things turned out, Godwin managed to reach with Read a compromise sum of £500, although he still wrote to his daughter: 'If Shelley will not immediately send me such bills as I propose, or as you offer, my next request is, that he will let me alone, and not disturb the sadness of my shipwreck by holding out false lights, and deluding me with the appearance of relief, when no relief is at hand.'[109]

Shelley first asked Horace Smith to give Godwin £100 and requested the Gisbornes to lend the remaining £400 on his security. He made the proviso, however, that the money should go directly to the creditor, adding 'you know Godwin's implacable exactions; you know his boundless and plausible sophistry'.[110] On second thoughts, Shelley changed his mind. The dreadful effect Godwin's letters were having on Mary, who was in delicate health after the birth of Percy Florence in the previous November, and his own desperate financial situation made him refuse his father-in-law once and for all. On 7 August 1820, he wrote frankly:

> I have given you within a few years the amount of a considerable fortune, & have destituted myself, for the purpose of realising it of nearly four times the amount. Except for the *good will* which this transaction seems to have produced between you & me, this money, for any *advantage* that it ever conferred on you, might as well have been thrown into the sea.[111]

He ended by saying that he would intercept any letters which might disturb Mary and asked Godwin to discuss in future only literary or philosophical topics.

Godwin, in the meantime, had been complaining to the Gisbornes that

> S[h]elley would certainly be the death of him; that he had acted in the most equivocal and unmanly unintelligible manner, that he was perpetually leading him on to expectation, and never coming to any conclusion . . . there was as much mysticism in S[h]elley's conduct, as there was in the writings of Coleridge.[112]

When Godwin received Shelley's uncompromising letter on 25 August, Maria Gisborne noted that 'his tone of mind was deranged' and it took him some time before he could discuss the matter and justify his financial dealings with Shelley.[113]

In fact, the only real pleasure at this time for Godwin was the company of Maria Gisborne. He had of course once proposed to her when she was Maria Reveley, and had been 'extremely gratified' in 1818 to hear from Mary that they had become friends in Italy.[114] When they renewed their friendship in June 1820, Maria Gisborne found him 'much more corpulent' and since he lengthened out his sentences in order to speak 'with perfect correctness', she complained that 'he gets on very slowly'.[115]

At about the same time, Sir George Mackenzie included in his *Illustrations of Phrenology* (1820) an engraving of William Nicholson's portrait of Godwin (then in the possession of Archibald Constable), with an accompanying analysis of the unnamed 'Celebrated Literary Character'. In the portrait, a colleague of Mackenzie's discovered:

> the indications of a very powerful talent; a man of deep thought; such a one as might be an able lawyer, speaker and reasoner; and the development of imitation might assist to render his eloquence powerful, by giving it expression. Benevolence is strong; but there is very little veneration, and very little hope. Cautiousness is large, and so is destructiveness; ideality also is full. It is probable that this person is regular, or a man of order and method; but his reflections must have a gloomy taint; and his dissatisfaction with the world be considerable . . . He is a philanthropist, at least more so than a worshipper; though he probably believes in natural religion . . . This person may be respected for his talents, but is not to be envied for his whole development.[116]

The analysis suggests that objective science had been informed by literary gossip. Godwin later quoted it in an essay, but in order to argue that the 'thinking principle' is very different from the body in which it operates.[117]

However talented and benevolent Godwin may have appeared to Sir George Mackenzie, his reflections were certainly full of gloom. His landlord Read was still trying to eject him and recover the arrears in rent. On 24 July 1821, a jury decided unanimously against Godwin, but reserved the question whether he had a right to the established courtesy of a notice to quit which had not been properly adhered to. It was left to three Junior Judges of the King's Bench to decide the formality, but to Godwin's 'astonishment and utter confusion' they pronounced on 24 October in his favour.[118] It was a reprieve, but nothing more.

Godwin still could not get over the reception of his *Of Population*. He had submitted to many privations during its composition, confident that 'all would be ease and fruition', but when he made his accounts at the end of 1821 he found that his clear profits were only £40 7s 8d![119] To quell his anxiety and to earn some money he therefore decided to write a *History of the Commonwealth*, a much more ambitious project than the 'Lives of the Commonwealth's Men' he had recommended to his daughter in 1818. Henry Colburn agreed to pay £250 each for two volumes, and Godwin sat down with alacrity to write on 4 January 1822. He could not, however, entirely avoid 'things as they are', and on 16 April his landlord won a final verdict against him. He was ordered to pay £900 and vacate 41 Skinner Street. It seemed that his worst fears were about to be realized: at the age of sixty-six, he was threatened with homelessness and bankruptcy.

Shelley still believed that he was exaggerating, and complained to John Gisborne that the Godwins are 'for ever plotting & devising pretexts for money; none of which however they get: *1st* because I *can't*, & 2d because I *wont*'.[120] On 19 April, however, Godwin wrote pathetically to Mary: 'The die, so far as I am concerned, seems now to be cast, and all that remains is that I should entreat you to forget that you have a Father in existence. Why should your prime of youthful vigour be tarnished and made wretched by what relates to me?'[121]

He appealed on 1 May 1822 against the court order but was peremptorily refused. The same evening a writ of eviction and a bill of £135 were served upon him, and two men arrived to guard the house. He was given two days to clear out all his goods or they would be turned into the street. His son William wrote out overnight a catalogue of the best bound books to be auctioned in order to pay his landlord's costs, and his mother with her usual resourcefulness took a lodging in Pemberton Row, close to Gough Square, and a warehouse in Gunpowder Alley. On 3 May he made one final effort to extract some money from Shelley, but as he told his daughter, he realized it was a question 'of a drowning man, catching at a straw'.[122] On the following day he abandoned 41 Skinner Street, scene of so many tragic disappointments, forever.

Not wanting Mary, who was pregnant again for the fifth time in eight years, to be unduly alarmed, Shelley relented. But he preferred now to write to the detested Mrs. Godwin rather than her husband that he had asked Horace Smith to forward £400.[123] Unfortunately, Smith had given all his spare money to a relative, and suggested to Godwin that he declare himself bankrupt — 'the whole evil of which is six weeks' confinement'.[124]

Not all however was lost. Godwin's printer Macmillan and his stationer Curtis postponed bills and found enough money to enable Godwin to carry on the now profitable business, and Mrs. Godwin found better premises — albeit at the rent of £210 per annum — at 195 The Strand. The three remaining members of the Godwin family moved in on 26 June. Phoenix-like, the French and English Juvenile Library and School Library arose anew, and on 4 July Godwin opened the doors of the new shop with dreams of independence.

But news of disastrous events were to follow. On 16 June, Mary miscarried, and almost died through loss of blood. On 10 July Rosser, the Cambridge student who had become a close friend and ally in the Malthusian controversy, died. In the same week, on 8 July, Shelley was drowned whilst sailing in rough seas in the Gulf of Spezzia. Godwin only heard the news on 6 August and then indirectly through a letter from Leigh Hunt to his sister-in-law Bessey Kent in London. His immediate reaction was to suggest to Mary that

> This sorrowful event is perhaps calculated to draw us nearer to each other. I am the father of a family, but without children. I & my wife are falling fast into infirmity & helplessness; &, in addition to all our other calamities, we seemed destined to be left without connections & without aid. Perhaps now we and you shall mutually derive consolation from each other.[125]

Godwin made no direct comment about Shelley himself. Mary later wrote to Maria Gisborne however that he did not love his memory because he felt Shelley had 'injured' him and Claire.[126]

With the death of Shelley, Godwin's hopes of a large sum to cover his debts were destroyed. Other friends however came to the aid of the bankrupt. Lamb and Mackintosh started a private appeal and Benjamin Haydon, Crabb Robinson, John Murray, William Perry, Lord Gower, Lord Dudley and William Lamb all contributed. Even Walter Scott sent £10, although he insisted on remaining anonymous since 'I dissent from Mr. Godwin's theory of politics and morality as sincerely as I admire his genius'.[127]

On 23 December 1822, Godwin's landlord Read obtained another judgment for £373 6s 8d for rent between 1820 and 1822. Godwin's son William wrote to his sister early in the New Year: 'how we shall get on God only knows: I have some fear, it is true, but, like Pandora's box, I still find hope at the bottom'.[128] There was in fact none there and by July only £220 had been raised, of which already £100 had been spent. It seemed that Godwin's worst fears of 'being driven to sea on a plank' were about to be realized.[129] Lamb, Mackintosh and Crabb Robinson however decided to turn their private appeal into a public subscription for £600. Mackintosh wrote the document for the writer of 'great talents and reputation', and it was signed by a committee of Crabb Robinson, W. Ayrton, John Murray, Charles Lamb, Lord Gower, Lord Dudley, William Lamb and Mackintosh.[130] Lamb added a postscript on 1 October, pointing out that Godwin had made considerable progress in his *History of the Commonwealth*:

> His mind is at this moment so entirely occupied in this work, that he feels within himself the firmness and resolution that no *prospect* of evil or calamity shall draw him off from it or suspend his labours. But *the calamity itself*, if permitted to arrive, will produce the physical impossibility for him to proceed. His books and the materials of his work, as well as his present sources of income, will be taken from him.[131]

But despite the valiant efforts of Lamb, Mackintosh and Crabb Robinson, the subscription did not prove successful. Godwin put it down to the inefficiency and slowness of Murray, who was responsible for sending out the circular, but Crabb Robinson knew that only half the members of the committee bothered to attend meetings.[132] Many of Godwin's old connections, such as Basil Montagu and Sir Anthony Carlisle held back. In despair Godwin took the matter into his own hands. He wrote to Lady Caroline Lamb of his plight and she replied with a list of Whig politicians and yet another invitation to Brocket Hall.[133] He even wrote to a former school acquaintance Sergeant Lens who had once shown an act of kindness at a dancing-school in Norwich when he was twelve years old.[134]

Yet it was to no avail; only about half the necessary amount was raised. Fortunately, on 7 November 1823, Godwin reached a settlement with Read. His total claim was £430, of which Murray had paid £250, and for the remainder Godwin gave him four notes of £45 to be discounted at six-monthly intervals. Murray had in hand £41 5s., so there was a delay of a year before any fresh demand would be made. Godwin, for the moment at least, could breathe a little freer.

Despite his money worries, he still managed to continue his literary work. Early in 1822, Mary sent him the manuscript of her long novel *Valperga; or,*

*The Life and Adventures of Castruccio, Prince of Lucca*. She told him to make the best of it and to keep the proceeds from its publication. It was clearly written in his own manner. Against a vivid background of medieval Italy, Mary presents Castruccio as a man like St. Leon and Mandeville who sacrifices love for ambition. He neglects for plans of empire both Euthanasia, who is torn between her love for the tyrant and her passion for liberty, and Beatrice, a deeply religious woman who dies after being abandoned. But as Euthanasia asks: 'What is the world except what we feel?'[135]

Godwin was impressed. But while he felt it was a work of more genius than *Frankenstein*, he complained to Mary of its length: 'No hard blow was ever hit with a woolsack!'[136] He therefore set about cutting it extensively from April 1822 till the end of the year. When it was ready for publication in February 1823, he informed his daughter that he had taken great liberties with it but added that 'I need not tell you that all the merit of the book is exclusively your own.'[137]

After the death of Shelley, father and daughter did in fact grow closer in their mutual distress. He supervised her dealings with Sir Timothy Shelley in order to obtain provision for herself and her son Percy. He also urged her to write for a living like her mother had: 'You are now five-and-twenty, and, most fortunately, you have pursued a course of reading, and cultivated your mind, in a manner the most admirably adapted to make you a great and successful author. If you cannot be independent, who should be?'[138]

Although Mary felt her father slinked from disposing of her writings, he at least arranged a new edition of *Frankenstein* after its successful dramatization. He was in fact in comparatively good health and generally in high spirits. His research on the Commonwealth was going well. A second edition of *The Enquirer* appeared with the essay 'Of English Style' rewritten (literature, he now realized, does not progress like the sciences). In a modest preface, he asserted that he was half-inclined to despise the 'laborious trifles of his life's work' but it was more in jest than in earnest.[139] It was undoubtedly with renewed energy and hope that he went with his son William to meet his daughter and grandson at the wharf when they arrived back in England on 25 August 1823.

Mary had a 'very kind reception', she told Hunt, and everything was done to make her comfortable.[140] Though she found their new house in The Strand rather dismal, it was much better than the Skinner Street one. She took the precaution, however, of having her correspondence sent to the offices of the *Examiner* because of her meddling stepmother, and soon moved to her own lodgings. Godwin was delighted to be with her again, and apparently made her plan to return to Italy 'an affair of life and death with him'.[141]

Mary still looked to her father for advice on literary matters and sent him the manuscript of a tragedy in February 1824. He was not however prepared to humour her:

> To read your specimens, I should suppose that you had read no Tragedies but such as have been written since the date of your birth. Your personages are mere abstractions — the lines and points of a mathematical diagram — and not men and women. If A crosses B, and C falls upon D, who can weep for that?

And speaking from hard experience, he added that he was almost glad that she did not have dramatic talent: 'How many mortifications and heartaches would that entail on you.'[142] Mary wisely took his advice.

Instead, she returned to novel writing and came up with *The Last Man* (1826). It clearly marked a departure from the views of her father and dead husband. It opens in the twenty-first century as the republican dreams of Adrian are about to be realized. Yet egalitarianism is identified with the plague which is powerful enough to destroy civilization itself. 'Were the pride of ancestry,' Mary asks in true Burkean style, 'the patrician spirit, the gentle courtesies, and refined pursuits, splendid attributes of rank, to be erased among us?'[143] When they are, chaos prevails. The horrors of republican levelling are only superseded by the greatest leveller of them all, Death.

But while Mary was drawing the dangers of republicanism in the future, Godwin was celebrating the *History of the Commonwealth*. He undertook the task with great solemnity and care since 'in history we can only collect a dry outline, and timidly allow ourselves in a few uncertain conjectures, restrained at every moment by the majesty of truth, and the austerity of the school in which we have entered ourselves pupils'.[144] While drawing some inspiration from *A History of the British Empire from the Accession of Charles I to the Restoration* (1822) by George Brodie, he carefully examined all the available primary sources. He read the contemporary tracts in the British Museum, and consulted the journals of the Houses of Parliament and the Order Books of the Council of State. His many correspondents included Walter Scott and Isaac D'Israeli.[145] The result was a mammoth work of over two thousand pages which appeared in four volumes from 1824 to 1828.

Apart from narrating the main events of the Commonwealth in England, Godwin followed the doctrine of necessity and tried 'to assign the motives of the actors, and to trace up effects to the causes from which they sprung'.[146] At the same time, for all his stress on impartiality, he wished to be considered 'as feeling as well as thinking' and freely judged the characters and incidents under review.[147]

*Political Justice* had emerged from the great tradition of English republicanism, and it is clear on which side Godwin places himself. To allow one person, he writes in his introduction, to become the chief of a country is evidence of 'the infirmity of man'.[148] He also recognizes that the religious conflict during the Commonwealth was drawn on political and class lines. Although the Presbyterians hated the extension of royal power, their leaders were rich men and closely allied to the nobility, and therefore 'hated not less the fearlessness and masculine temper of mind which was growing up in the middling and lower orders of the community'.[149] While the Presbyterians were 'exclusive', the Independents practised the 'generous spirit of toleration'.[150]

Yet Godwin's account of the Levellers is not very enthusiastic. He feels that there was 'no true elevation' in Lilburne and while he agrees with the Levellers' call for a new parliament, he considers the army 'strikingly ill qualified to dictate to the peaceable and more numerous part of the community'.[151] As for Winstanley and the Diggers, whose doctrines were so close to his own, he thinks they were 'scarcely indeed worthy to be recorded'.[152]

Godwin reserves his greatest praise for the period of the Commonwealth from the abolition of the monarchy in 1649 to Cromwell's coup d'état in 1653. These five years may challenge any equal period of English history 'in the glory of its rule, and perhaps in the virtue and disinterestedness of many of its most distinguished leaders'.[153] Even so, Godwin has some difficulty in justifying their regicide and usurpation of power. Although he entertains an 'almost invincible abhorrence' to taking a man's life, and feels that the execution of Charles I was counter-productive, it at least demonstrated that no person, however high in station, could freely harm the welfare of the community.[154] Moreover, since natural justice promotes the general welfare, it is sometimes right to 'reinvest the community in the entire rights they possessed before particular laws were established'.[155] On these grounds, Strafford and Charles I were not judged amiss. Similarly, as the general welfare is paramount, there comes a point when 'submission ceases to be a duty, and resistance is a virtue': Fairfax and the army were therefore probably right in resisting a parliament in 1647 which wanted to disband them.[156]

Godwin confronts the problem of coercion and utility directly in his discussion of the Long Parliament which governed against the will of the majority of the people. In theory, he reaffirms his belief that it is wrong 'to impose the most unequivocal benefit upon a man, or a body of men, which he or they want the inclination to accept'. But in the complicated scene of human affairs, there is no theory that will fit all the cases. Appealing to the 'supreme law' of the 'general advantage', Godwin is therefore willing to allow that if a usurper succeeds, it is well: 'If he really effects all the good he proposes, if in the close of the affair he delivers up unlimited powers into the hands of a people now prepared for the wholesome use of them, and they become wise and manlike and virtuous and happy, Yes, — infallibly he did well.'[157] Godwin would therefore seem to countenance here a temporary and enlightened dictatorship on utilitarian grounds.

Godwin devoted his fourth volume to Cromwell. He finds him a man of great virtue, 'sincere in his religion, fervent in his patriotism, and earnestly devoted to the best interests of mankind'.[158] He approves of his wish to reform the law, to assist the poor against the oppression of the rich, to extend religious toleration, and to patronize learning. His fatal fault however was that he was 'drunk with the philtre of his power' which led him to declare himself Lord Protector.[159] But even here Godwin is ready to excuse him since 'the necessity of the situation in which he was placed impelled him'.[160]

In general, Godwin shows himself as cautious as ever in his politics. He infers from his study of the Commonwealth the need for a 'beneficent and sound constitution' in which 'the spirit of liberty should be combined with the venerableness of order'.[161] Ultimately, he valued a republic not for its liberty but for its tendency to attend to the interests of the whole, 'the preserving the character, the prosperity and welfare of the nation'. Liberty, like knowledge and virtue, is to be valued for 'the results with which it is pregnant, and not for its own sake alone'.[162] The supreme goal for Godwin is happiness. He remained a utilitarian to the end.

Harsh experience had taught Godwin, moreover, that

> It is comparatively easy for the philosopher in his closet to invent imaginary schemes of policy, and to shew how mankind, if they were without passions and without prejudices, might best be united in the form of a political community. But, unfortunately, men in all ages are the creatures of passions, perpetually prompting them to defy the rein, and break loose from the dictates of sobriety and speculation.[163]

It was an admission which threatened his whole scheme of perfectibility through gradual enlightenment and education. Indeed, the last of the great Commonwealth Men questioned in his old age whether the 'English intellect and moral feeling' will ever be ripe enough for a republican government.[164]

Godwin's *History of the Commonwealth* was the first substantial history written from the republican side. It was well-documented, original, and lucid. He successfully analyzed the motives of the leading protagonists and showed a masterly understanding of the period. But unlike his *Life of Chaucer* he paid more attention to statutes and battles than to the social and economic conditions of the people. At times, his style trips over dates and authorities, and the narrative flounders on the rocks of historical accuracy.

As usual, the critical response was drawn on party lines. The *British Critic* called it a silly book and quoted a paragraph for its wickedness, nonsense, and bad grammar.[165] The *Cambridge Quarterly and Academical Register* attacked Godwin's mask of impartiality and accused him of the grossest republican prejudices.[166] Despite the overweening pretensions and bombastic style, the *Monthly Review* at least found some merit in the fourth volume.[167]

On the other hand, the *Literary Chronicle* praised Godwin's inflexible integrity and philosophical mind; the *Eclectic Review* felt it was largely successful; and the *Monthly Magazine* called it a work of the highest value from a genuine patriot.[168] The *London Magazine* welcomed it as a much needed work.[169] Andrew Bisset in the *Westminster Review* liked the sharp and powerful style and the sincere desire for truth.[170] The *New Monthly Magazine* at first praised its impartiality, although the reviewer Cyrus Redding later thought it very adverse to the upper classes.[171] Godwin could at least draw some satisfaction from his indefatigable labours, and, unlike his most recent publications, his *History of the Commonwealth* sold well.

# CHAPTER XX

# Final Thoughts

Godwin, according to Hazlitt, had by 1825 sunk below the horizon, and enjoyed the 'serene twilight of a doubtful immortality'.[1] His personal life however was in crisis yet again for on 17 March 1825 he was forced to declare himself bankrupt. By enormous industry, by underhand jobbery, by plain doggedness, he had managed to postpone the inevitable for twenty years. But when it came, he was pleasantly surprised: his bankruptcy proved to be a liberation.

He left the expensive house and shop in The Strand on 30 May 1825 and retired to an obscure nook at 44 Gower Place. It cost only £40 per year. He lived there quietly with his library, his wife, and a servant called Jane, working hard at his books to cover his annual outgoings of £300 a year. His recreation was limited to the occasional game of whist or visit to the theatre.

His health was good, and he greatly enjoyed his writing. He saw his son William regularly, who after many false starts was forging ahead as a professional journalist and critic. He loved the company of his daughter Mary and grandson Percy Florence. When his wife left for a holiday in 1826, he had to reassure her that he still wanted her company and that 'Mrs. Shelley', as they called her, did not supply the deficiency.[2] 'How differently are you and I organized!' he wrote to Mary in the following year. 'In my seventy-second year I am all cheerfulness, and never anticipate the evil day with distressing feelings till to do so is absolutely unavoidable. Would to God you were my daughter in all but my poverty! But I am afraid you are a Wollstonecraft.'[3]

As he was finishing the fourth volume of his *History of the Commonwealth*, Godwin took a short holiday in the spring of 1828 with his daughter Mary in Hastings. In July, Charles Clairmont returned with a wife and two daughters from Vienna, where he had been a teacher of English despite the Austrian government's investigation of his subversive family background.

XXX. Godwin, aged 74, by Henry W. Pickersgill, 1830.

Claire also came back in October from Moscow where she had been a
governess. The Godwin family, so battered by disputes, was at last re-
united. But it was not to last for long: Charles, having failed to set up a
students' hostel for the new University College, returned to Vienna in
September 1829 to become a professor and eventually a tutor to the royal
family. Claire left in the same month to meet her charges in Dresden and to
lead a life full of regrets, other people's children, and increasing piety.

   In the meantime, Godwin was developing into a benign and comfortable
grandfather. Thomas Noon Talfourd, Lamb's friend, recalled that he
possessed 'a gracious suavity of manner which many "a fine old English
gentleman" might envy'.[4] When the young American novelist James

Fenimore Cooper called on him (brought by Mary's admirer John Howard Payne), they talked affably about American literature, and several times Cooper wished 'to pat the old man's bald head and tell him "he was a good fellow"'.[5] On the other hand, Robert Dale Owen, fresh from his New Harmony colony in America, found his father's mentor no match for Bentham: 'Feeble and bent, he had neither the bright eye nor the elastic step of the utilitarian philosopher.' His conversation gave the impression of 'intellect without warmth or heart; it touched on great principles, but was measured and unimpulsive'.[6]

But while Bentham was comfortably off, Godwin had to write for subsistence. In the autumn of 1828, he began a new novel eventually called *Cloudesley*. It was initially inspired by the true story of James Annesley who had been the subject of some *Memoirs of an Unfortunate Young Nobleman Returned from Thirteen Years Slavery in America* (1743). Once again, Godwin was also stimulated by folk tales and myths, and intended the novel to be a 'paraphrase' of the old ballad 'Babes in the Wood'. But he still believed that it was true to life; indeed, where biographies are merely guesses in the dark, 'fictitious history is more true and to be depended upon, when it has the fortune to be executed by a masterly hand, than that which is to be drawn from state papers, documents, and letters written by those who were actually engaged in the scene.'[7]

As a plot, it is perhaps the least successful of Godwin's novels. There are no central characters, and the action meanders all over Europe. The narrator Meadows opens with an account of himself in eighteenth-century Russia and then listens to the life story of Lord Danvers for more than six hundred pages — only to reappear briefly at the denouement. Cloudesley is first mentioned well into volume one and is killed off in the middle of volume three, and although the novel is named after him, he is eclipsed by Lord Danvers and his nephew Julian.

Lord Danvers's story is the substance of the novel. He relates how his brother Lord Alton married a passive and angelic Greek, Irene Colocotrini, only to be killed in a duel when her nationality was insulted. The widow dies in childbirth, but Danvers illegally assumes his brother's title and sends the rightful heir Julian to the continent with his secretary Cloudesley. Cloudesley brings him up in Italy as his own son.

He lives however to regret his dishonesty and decides to re-establish Julian's birthright. Danvers in the meantime has been consumed with guilt, and divine vengeance seems to strike with the death of his wife and all his children but one. But when Cloudesley goes to Ireland to plead Julian's cause, his ward joins the band of an aristocratic outlaw St. Elmo. Cloudesley eventually locates Julian on his return but is accidentally killed. It is left to Meadows, sent as an emissary from the expiring and penitent Danvers, to reveal Julian's identity and prevent him from being executed with the robber band.

Godwin remarks in his preface that he is interested in tracing 'the folds of the human heart, the endless intermixture of motive with motive'.[8] As always, he delights in showing how his characters interact with their circumstances. Meadows is a minister's son with a sound understanding and a romantic imagination — undoubtedly modelled on Godwin himself. Danvers, on the other hand, recalls Falkland, drunk with ambition and full of 'old notions' of 'title, and rank, and opulence'.[9] Cloudesley is one of Godwin's typical mixed characters: his original gentleness is turned into severe misanthropy by an unjust prison sentence but re-emerges under the influence of domestic affections. Julian betrays in every instant his high-born nature, but he too is misled by the generous spirit of the bandit leader St. Elmo and the harsh treatment of his temporary guardian Borromeo.

The two latter are perhaps the most interesting characters in the novel. St. Elmo is a 'compound of most irreconcilable qualities'.[10] A man of rank and education, he is forced to become an outlaw after an unsuccessful conspiracy against a tyrannical government. Like a Robin Hood who has read *Political Justice*, he regards civil society as 'a conspiracy against the inherent rights of man' and has sworn on 'the altars of immutable justice an everlasting war against all governments, and an open defiance to all law'.[11] He only takes from the rich their 'useless abundance' in order to give it to the poor.[12] While Godwin condemns his violence, he presents him as an essentially noble figure.

Borromeo — modelled according to Claire on Shelley's friend Edward Trelawny — is also a victim of a corrupt society.[13] His experience of slavery renders him a stern misanthrope who recognizes only the relative position of the bondsman and the lord. At the end of the novel, however, a surge of sympathy for the reprieved Julian converts him to universal benevolence.

Although Godwin fails to fuse his plot and characters into a unified whole, there are some powerful passages. He no doubt borrowed from his itinerant children Mary, Charles, and Claire the vivid scenes set in Italy, Vienna, and Russia. He lifted almost verbatim from one of Shelley's letters the description of the waterfall of Terni.[14] But as usual, Godwin intersperses the narrative with his own philosophical and social views.

There are some acute remarks on education. The once outlawed domestic affections are now considered the most important moral influence; indeed, there is a 'species of religion' in the relation between mother and child.[15] Even so, liberty is still the best school: it is only too easy to drive a child about like a beast, but childhood.

if we are kindly treated, if we are not galled with the iron yoke of despotism, if we are made to feel that we have a will of our own, if we are not thwarted and thrust aside from our innocent desires by the caprice of persons older than ourselves, is in many respects the happiest epoch of human existence.[16]

There are also bursts of his old radicalism. The main interest, he informed a correspondent, is designed 'to be for the oppressed and disowned, and not for the remorseful oppressor'.[17] He attacks the death penalty as 'the most audacious — I had nearly said, the most impious' of all the various acts of the human community.[18] In Rousseauist vein, he condemns the state of a king, of a noble, or of the rich: they adopt the 'artificial life, the inventions of vanity and grasping ambition, by which we have spoiled the man of nature, of pure, simple and undistorted impulses'.[19]

But Godwin no longer calls for a thorough transformation of society. His social answer is to choose an independent, simple but cultivated life. It is an 'obscure station' accompanied with the seeds of knowledge, emulation and applause which is most favourable to the growth of 'meditation, a deeprooted enthusiasm, sobriety and virtue'.[20] His moral answer is to practise universal love. At the end of the novel the real revolutionary St. Elmo is executed, Julian recovers his title and lands, and Borromeo draws the moral: 'The true key of the universe is love. That levels all inequalities, "makes low the mountain, and exalts the valley", and brings human beings of every age and station into a state of brotherhood.'[21] Godwin's final revolution is not on the barricades or even in the head but in the heart.

Although *Cloudesley* had neither the impetus of *Caleb Williams* nor the imaginative power of *Mandeville*, Godwin managed to persuade Henry Colburn and Richard Bentley to publish it on 4 March 1830. To their surprise, it immediately sold out and warranted a new edition. Godwin also contacted his old friend Washington Irving who arranged its publication in New York. A French translation by Jean Cohen appeared in Paris in the same year.

Godwin and his family awaited the reaction with trepidation. Mary probably wrote the review for *Blackwood's Edinburgh Magazine* in which Godwin is called a Nestor and his novel likened for its grace and dignity to a cathedral organ.[22] Hazlitt also took the opportunity to give a warm estimate of Godwin's works in the *Edinburgh Review*, and although he considered *Cloudesley* better written than *Caleb Williams*, declared it to be 'a palace of words built on nothing'.[23] It was one of the last things he wrote for he died on 18 September 1830.

Most of the other reviews were laudatory: the *Scotsman*, the *Monthly Magazine*, the *Monthly Review*, the *Examiner* and even the *Court Journal* all attested to its considerable power.[24] While the *Edinburgh Literary Journal* described Godwin as an almost forgotten novelist, the *Literary Gazette* recommended him as one who had left deep traces in English literature and the *Westminster Review* felt that he had combined the wisdom of old age with the simplicity of youth.[25] Only the *Athenaeum* thought it was a wretched novel.[26] The most enthusiastic was the *New Monthly Magazine* which called Godwin a sound veteran whose pages 'glow and seldom flag'.[27] Its editor Thomas Campbell became a close friend as a result.

In the same journal appeared an enthusiastic article on the novel signed 'The Lounger'. The author was Edward Lytton Bulwer, later Lord Lytton, who had first been introduced to Godwin by Lady Caroline Lamb in January 1826 whilst he was still a student at Cambridge. He wrote to his new friend: 'I am happy to hear on all sides the praises and increasing popularity of your book, "Cloudesley". Bentley told me it was selling surprisingly well, and I hear in another quarter that the sale has already far surpassed that of "Mandeville".'[28]

Bulwer had already published *Falkland* (1827) and *Pelham* (1828), which betrayed the influence of *Caleb Williams*. Godwin then suggested to him an adaptation of *The Beggar's Opera* to present-day conditions for his next novel.[29] When he read the resulting *Paul Clifford* in the spring of 1830, he was so impressed that he told Bulwer: 'There are many parts so divinely written that my first impulse was to throw my implements of writing in the fire, and to wish that I could consign all that I have published in the province of fiction to the same pyre.'[30] Godwin also gave Bulwer the notes for a projected novel on the scholarly murderer *Eugene Aram* which the young novelist duly wrote up and published in 1832. 'I can well conceive', he wrote in a later preface, 'what depth and power that gloomy record would have taken from the dark and inquiring genius of the author of *Caleb Williams*.'[31] Bulwer returned the favour in 1833 by arranging the publication in the *New Monthly Magazine* of Godwin's 'Fragment of a Romance' written in 1809.[32]

Godwin followed closely Bulwer's election campaign in 1830, and went on to meet at his house Augusta Leigh, Byron's notorious half-sister, the diarist Tom Moore, the young Benjamin Disraeli, and Ramohun Roy, a former ambassador from the court of Delhi. But although Godwin predicted 'a career of rectitude and honour' for his young friend, he did not quite live up to his expectations, for he remained a dandy and drifted towards Conservative politics.[33] Even so, Godwin probably remained the most important influence on Bulwer as a writer.

Godwin had observed in *Cloudesley* that when we grow old 'our desires are declining, our faculties have lost their sharpness, and we are reasonably contented "to close our eyes, and shut out daylight."'[34] He remained, however, as creative and busy as ever. After finishing *Cloudesley* on 16

January 1830, he sketched the next day the rough outline of another novel to be called *Deloraine*. At the same time, he finished a series of essays published in 1831 as *Thoughts on Man*. The fruit of thirty years' meditation, he considered them to be written in the 'full maturity' of his understanding and expected them to make a deep impression on the 'thinking part' of the public.[35] They are, like *The Enquirer*, reflections on the nature, productions and discoveries of mankind with the added bonus of autobiographical remarks. Addressed 'to plain men, and in clear and unambiguous terms', the dominant note is one of careful thinking and humanistic fervour.[36]

At the age of seventy-five, Godwin wished to sum up the principal changes in his philosophy since the first edition of *Political Justice*. In many of the essays, he is eager to draw more carefully the limits of knowledge based on experience. As he wrote in an unpublished one, the 'sceptic is the only consistent lover of truth'.[37] And just as he had drawn the distinction between theory and practice in politics, so he now applies the old axiom 'to think with the learned, and talk with the vulgar' to the whole scheme of human affairs.[38] It is, he argues, the natural tendency of human beings to reject rational demonstration and adhere to their senses. Thus while in 'the sobriety of the closet' he remains in his metaphysics an immaterialist and a necessitarian, he is willing to accept for practical purposes the apparent existence of matter and the illusory sense of liberty.[39]

Berkeley had been Godwin's principal mentor in immaterialism, but he prefers to extend Locke's denial of the secondary qualities of matter and Newton's suggestion that all the particles of the solar system might be contained in a nutshell in order to banish matter out of 'the theatre of real existences'.[40] Moreover, since there is no assignable analogy between the causes of sensation and the sensations themselves, the material world must be the 'mere creature' of our own minds.[41] Godwin does not however draw solipsistic conclusions. There may be no analogy between sensation and its cause, but there is a precise resemblance between the contents of my mind and those of others. If this were not the case, life would be reduced to a 'senseless mummery'.[42]

While Godwin argues that objects, if not other people, are creations of our minds, he is quick to add that such abstractions are 'too fine for the realities of life'.[43] He makes the same distinction in his treatment of necessity. It is still his unreserved conviction that 'man is a machine, that he is governed by external impulses'.[44] Yet he recognizes that we are fully penetrated with the notion that mind is endowed with an 'initiating power', or as Lord Kames put it in his *Essays on the Principles of Morality and Natural Religion* (1751), we possess a 'delusive sense of liberty'.[45] Far from rejecting such an idea, Godwin welcomes the delusion since it gives rise to the sentiment of conscience and fills us with moral enthusiasm. The great

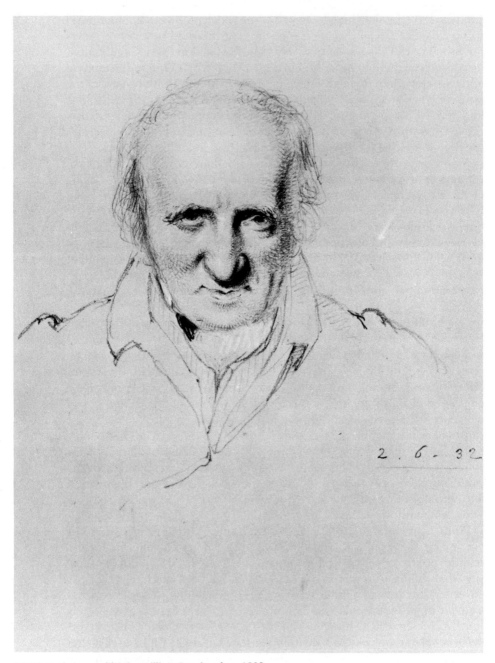

2 . 6 . 32

XXXI. Godwin, aged 76, by William Brockendon, 1832.

philosopher of necessity is therefore prepared at the end of his life to argue that free will is 'an integral part of the science of man, and may be said to constitute its most important chapter'.[46]

In his psychology, Godwin adopts a form of mental and not physical determinism. Man is the subject of sensible impressions, has the faculties of thinking and feeling, and is governed by the law of association. The latter gives rise to a sense of mental unity which in turn constitutes personal identity. How the mind is connected to the body remains 'utterly obscure and undefined', but Godwin insists that the mind has the body as 'its subject and its slave'.[47] Phrenology on the other hand reverses the order and exhibits us as 'the helpless victims of a blind and remorseless destiny'.[48]

At the same time, Godwin is well aware of the 'follies, extravagances and hallucinations' of the human intellect.[49] Rebelliousness may even be called our original sin. Nevertheless, we can still weigh arguments and evidence in the 'balance of an impartial and enlightened understanding' and reasoning itself can create a 'sudden and irresistible conviction'.[50] And while we cannot act without the impulse of desire or uneasiness, it is 'the thing upon which the mind is fixed that constitutes our motive'.[51] Despite Godwin's greater recognition of the irrational forces in human nature, reason therefore remains the supreme faculty.

Again, Godwin openly questions Helvétius's doctrine of the intellectual equality of human beings at birth and argues that we come into the world with various dispositions. It does not, however, substantially affect his belief in social progress and equality. Talents are not related to class — 'Nature distributes her gifts without any reference to the distinctions of artificial society' — nor are they in a limited supply — 'Nature never made a dunce.'[52] Putting idiots and extraordinary cases out of the question, every human being is endowed with talents, which, if rightly directed, would show him 'to be apt, adroit, intelligent and acute, in the walk for which his organisation especially fitted him'.[53] Such a creed, Godwin asserts, is more favourable than Helvétius's to a belief in human improvement since it provides the educator with a compass for his task.

Godwin feels moreover that inequality in the sense of difference can have positive value. Nothing is more certain, he argues, than the inequality of the sexes which endows one with 'softness and attractive grace' and the other with 'audacious, masculine and military qualities'.[54] He criticizes the Orientals who shut up their women like birds in cages, and the Greeks who treated them like slaves, but praises the age of chivalry for exalting and worshipping each sex for its different attributes. Love and friendship flourish best among unequals since it is only between them that genuine reciprocity and the 'unbending of the soul' can exist.[55] The greatest model of love therefore is between parents and children since it originates in the conscious feeling of the protector and the protected.

In his ethics, Godwin remains un uncompromising utilitarian. We are bound to employ every faculty we possess in a way 'which shall best conduce to the general advantage'.[56] But unlike Bentham, he has nothing but contempt for the French philosophy which makes self-love the basis of all our actions. Moreover, intention as well as tendency to do good are essential to virtue; indeed, Godwin adopts the extreme view that the 'most beneficent action that ever was performed, if it did not spring from the intention of good to others, is not of the nature of virtue'.[37]

Although Godwin celebrates friendship and domestic affections, he still holds firm to his doctrine of universal benevolence. He who for ever thinks that 'charity must begin at home' is in danger of becoming an 'indifferent citizen' and of losing those feelings of philanthropy which constitute 'the crowning glory of man'.[58] But while Godwin praises the self-denying patriotism of Greece and Rome, it is clear that his true inspiration is Christian. 'The end of the commandment', he quotes from the New Testament, '"is love."'[59] Sympathy is nothing less than the 'luminary of the moral world'.[60]

Godwin's attitude to education is as bold as ever. He suggests that schooling does more harm than good and that the pupil learns more in his hours of play. In school, all is mimicry and resembles the 'fresh-listed soldier at drill', while outside the child can engage in real discussion and be a genuine individual.[61] He therefore recommends the tutor to lead his pupil with a 'silken cord' and to help him learn for himself.[62] But Godwin's opposition to formal schooling does not lead him to the capricious indulgence of children. The ultimate business of education is to enable us to 'govern ourselves with steady severity, and by the dictates of an enlightened understanding'.[63]

In his social views, Godwin is no less radical. He complains of the great differences between the 'children of fashion' that stroll in St. James's and Hyde Park, and 'the care-worn hirelings' that amuse themselves with 'a little fresh air on a Sunday near Islington'.[64] Although the production of some civilizing 'refinements' might be worthwhile, the working-day should be greatly shortened.[65] Indeed, Godwin sees nothing but good coming from an increase in leisure for the lower classes. And as for their supposed lack of temperance, Godwin declares that the public house is the 'unrefined university' of the 'laborious classes'.[66] The more people are allowed to think, the less alcohol they will want to consume.

Surveying society as a whole, Godwin looks on his fellow species with a benevolent eye. To see history only as a tissue of crimes is to overlook the fact that the vast majority spend their lives in productive and peaceful activity. Godwin is struck more with the extent of human innocence than evil. Certainly there are men of strife like kings, ministers of state, and soldiers, but society for the greater part carries on its own organization. Indeed, Godwin is more than 'half tempted' to imagine like many anarchists after him that 'men might subsist very well in clusters and congregated bodies without the coercion of law'.[67]

Human beings, Godwin believes, are naturally gregarious and the censure of others would suffice to restrain them from acts of violence and crime. Yet Godwin does not want to replace the coercion of law by the tyranny of public opinion. We owe it to the 'sacred divinity of Truth' to try and correct our neighbours but we must be 'benevolent, sympathetic and affectionate' in our treatment and supply the materials for decision rather than decisions ready-made.[68]

In the beginning of his *Thoughts on Man*, Godwin calls his subject a 'godlike being' and the work as a whole is a sustained celebration of his achievements and possibilities.[69] Godwin's faith in the perfectibility of man may have been shaken in his long and difficult life, but it re-emerges stronger than ever. He ends his collection of essays with the confident belief that 'human understanding and human virtue will hereafter accomplish such things as the heart of man has never yet been daring enough to conceive'.[70]

In his old age, Godwin therefore keeps the main outlines of his philosophy intact. He remains a necessitarian and immaterialist in his metaphysics, a rationalist in his psychology, a utilitarian in his ethics, a libertarian in education, and an anarchist in politics. True he is prepared to think with the learned and talk with the vulgar, and accepts for practical purposes the delusive sense of liberty and the apparent existence of matter. He qualifies his view of equality and gives greater recognition to feeling. But this hardly adds up to 'the repudiation of the principles of a lifetime'.[71] Indeed, by rejecting the antithesis between head and heart, he manages to graft the insights of Romanticism on to his rational philosophy, thereby placing his case for political justice on firmer ground.

Godwin felt that his *Thoughts on Man* was a collection of 'new and interesting truths' in 'no unpopular style'.[72] Unfortunately, not everyone agreed. It was refused by nine publishers, including Murray, Cadell, Colburn, Lardner and Longmans, before being published by the obscure Effingham Wilson on 22 February 1831. Thomas Robinson wrote to his brother Henry Crabb that it was the 'sweepings of his study' and offered no abandonment of his 'revolting heresies'.[73] His brother was more forthright: he picked it up with interest and laid down with pain — 'a book of senilities', he wrote in his diary.[74] Mary Shelley, on the other hand, in the preface to Bentley's 1831 edition of *Caleb Williams*, argued that 'the divine charity' of the Sermon on the Mount found an echo in its pages.[75] Harriet Martineau in the *Monthly Repository* also saw in the essays the prophetic voice of socialist

AUTHOR OF "THOUGHTS ON MAN."

XXXII. Godwin, aged 78, by Daniel Maclise, 1834, for *Fraser's Magazine*.

philosophy calling for man to be employed according to his capacity and rewarded according to his need.[76]

The *Tatler* published several extracts, but pointedly observed that while the contest was between the aristocracy and the people, Godwin remained in his closet.[77] In an article which followed on his writings and character, however, he was called the 'most original writer of the present age', the brother of Owen and Bentham, the father of Shelley, an 'intellectual Rousseau' no less.[78] All the other reviews — the *Edinburgh Literary Journal*, *Fraser's Magazine*, the *Literary Gazette*, the *Monthly Magazine*, and the *Athenaeum* — were favourable, finding *Thoughts on Man* stimulating and original, and written in a terse and simple style.[79] The *Monthly Review* alone suggested that the essays should be read with caution since the author believed that reason and love were religion enough.[80]

Whilst composing his *Thoughts on Man*, Godwin had described himself half-jokingly to his daughter as a 'decrepit, superannuated old fellow'. But although seventy-six, he still found it necessary to write 'not for marble to be placed over my remains, but for bread to be put into my mouth'.[81] He planned books on Shakespeare and Burke but they came to nothing. He made notes for another novel. He wrote new prefaces for *Caleb Williams*, *St. Leon* and *Fleetwood* which Colburn and Bentley had decided to publish in their 'Standard Novels' series. He was even ready for the first time in forty years to try his hand again at journalism. On James Mackintosh's advice, he offered his services to Macvey Napier, the editor of the *Encyclopaedia Britannica* and the *Edinburgh Review*. Napier however remained unconvinced by Godwin's assurance that he would not embarrass others by his 'private singularities & extravagances' and turned down the idea of an article on two recent books on George III and Canning.[82]

Although he took no direct part, Godwin in the meantime was following political events closely. He was reassured by the July Revolution in France when the generous leaders — 'so much the reverse of the Revolution of 1789' — opted for a constitutional monarchy, thereby saying in effect to the rest of Europe: 'Be not alarmed: we will set no example of anarchy and the dissolution of government to the people over whom you reign.' But this was mainly because of his opposition to war: he felt it better to preserve peace than to win a war even for a just cause. He still continued to insist that 'I am a republican because I am a philanthropist. That form of society, perhaps, is the best which shall make individual man feel most generous and most noble.'[83]

In Britain, after decades of persecution and repression, the reformers were at last making some headway. The repeal of the Test and Corporation Acts — for which Godwin and his friends had fought in the 1790s — was achieved in 1828, followed a year later by Catholic emancipation.

Then the Whigs came into office in November 1830, with their leader Earl Grey determined to reform parliament. Godwin, who had defended their last coalition with North almost half a century before, was delighted. It meant that many of his acquaintances were now in power: he had seen the new Prime Minister as a young man at Sheridan's in 1786; the Home Secretary, Lord Melbourne, was Lardy Caroline Lamb's husband whom he had met in 1822; and the Chancellor of the Duchy of Lancaster was Lord Holland, who had supported his subscription in 1808. And then there was a Privy Councillor called Sir James Mackintosh, forever eager to make amends for past folly. It could only augur well.

But the Whigs had narrowly achieved power on the strident popular demands for annual elections, manhood suffrage, and a secret ballot. The growing trade union movement had reached fruition, albeit for a short time, in the National Association for the Protection of Labour. Demonstrations of more than 100,000 people, overwhelmingly composed of artisans and working men, were putting pressure on a weak parliament.

Godwin was worried, and he shared the Prime Minister's view that reform should be introduced to prevent the necessity for revolution. But while a widening of the franchise was welcome, Godwin baulked at the idea of a secret ballot. 'Little did I and my contemporaries of 1795 imagine', he wrote in *Thoughts on Man*, (which appeared only a fortnight before Lord John Russell introduced the first Reform Bill),

> that the *soi-disant* friends of liberty and radical reformers, when their turn of triumph came, would propose their Gagging Acts, recommending to the people to vote agreeably to their consciences, but forbidding them to give publicity to the honourable conduct they had been prevailed on to adopt![84]

Godwin met Bentham for the first time at James Northcote's on 6 July 1831 and no doubt made his view of his programme very clear.

Although the Whigs returned with an increased majority in June 1831, the reform Bill was defeated in the Lords in the autumn. There was a real threat of rebellion, with rioting in Derby, Bristol and Nottingham. Godwin was relieved at the passing of the first Reform Bill in the spring of 1832 which effectively enfranchised the middle classes and omitted the proposal for a secret ballot. He felt that at no other time since the first publication of *Political Justice* had its principles been more practised. He therefore considered issuing a new edition of his greatest work.

In the prospectus, he maintained that he had 'preserved undeviatingly' since 1793 'the principles to which the book owed its existence'. Any errors were 'mere excrescences', the 'lopping off of which will improve & not deteriorate the soundness & consistency of the whole'. He was confident, moreover, that 'the cause of improvement & equality would finally triumph'.[85] Unfortunately, however much Godwin felt *Political Justice* was in harmony with the spirit of the age, no publisher could be persuaded to share his enthusiasm.

At the same time, he wrote a prospectus for a 'History of the Protestant Reformation in England'. He saw it as the most important revolution since the birth of Christ. But while marking the 'dawn of intellectual liberty', it was a time when bigotry had never run to such enormous excesses.[86] The work would have been a fascinating history from one so steeped in the Dissenting tradition, but Godwin did not proceed with the plan.

As he was drawing up the prospectus, Godwin's only son William died of cholera on 8 September 1832 at the age of twenty-nine. After many false starts, he had become a parliamentary reporter on the *Morning Chronicle*, written an opera on the story of Robin Hood and a tragedy on the fate of Regulus, and had destroyed a novel. Two years before his death he had helped set up a club in commemoration of Shakespeare called 'The Mulberries' whose members were to include Dickens and Thackeray. Godwin had always been very fond of his son and never left his side during his short illness. He buried him in the Church of St. John the Evangelist, in the Waterloo Road near his house.

He later published a restrained but moving memoir with his son's novel *Transfusion; or, The Orphans of Unwalden* (1835). In the same tradition as *St. Leon* and *Frankenstein*, it has considerable psychological interest. The tribulations of the orphans Albert and Madeline at the hands of Count de Mara are traced until at the end of the novel the soul of Albert enters the dissolving organs of his sister. Albert is eventually left, in true Godwinian spirit, to acknowledge that his 'wretched destiny stung him with despair'.[87] Godwin also tried unsuccessfully to get his play 'The Sleeping Philosopher' performed. They both show that William Godwin Jr. had achieved his father's ambition for him to become a writer, and a good one at that.

Godwin however still had his beloved daughter Mary to comfort him in his twilight years. It was possibly his intense relationship with her that unexpectedly caused him to dry up after two and a quarter volumes of his novel *Deloraine* in the spring of 1832. At the end of the second volume, the hero replaces his love for his wife with that of his daughter, finding something in it 'that surpassed every thing that I had before witnessed in a human creature'.[88] Godwin may unconsciously have realized that he was touching on forbidden territory. At all events, after discussing it with Mary his mind like 'a train of gunpowder' was ignited and the third volume proved to be his best.[89]

The narrator Deloraine is yet another aristocrat who has become the 'most forlorn and odious of men', alone, hated and self-hating.[90] Brought up with every imaginable indulgence and by an exemplary tutor, he entered parliament and married the angelic Emilia Fitzcharles. Their union is bliss, consummated by the birth of a daughter Catherine. But whilst travelling on the continent Emilia is caught in a storm, miscarries and dies. Deloraine is inconsolable — until he meets and marries at the age of forty-two the young Margaret Borradale.

The marriage is without passion, and whilst his first wife was a woman of 'flesh and blood', the second is like a 'statue'.[91] In a long sub-plot, we learn that Margaret had been released from an arranged engagement to join her true-love William only to see him go down in a ship. William however miraculously escapes and re-appears after her marriage to Deloraine. When Deloraine sees them in a garden he mistakes him for a molester. He shoots: William is killed; Margaret faints and dies. The rest of the novel describes the exciting flight of Deloraine and his daughter Catherine from William's best friend Travers and Margaret's faithful servant Ambrose. As in *Caleb Williams*, Godwin rewrote the ending to ensure the triumph of truth and justice: Catherine persuades her father to confront his pursuers; Travers realizes the evils of revenge; and Deloraine is condemned by his conscience to a death-in-life.

The plot shows clear signs of weakness. There are too many sub-plots and the climax is slow in building up. Godwin always preferred to describe how his characters feel rather than what they do, but here his characterization remains sadly one-dimensional. Deloraine, whose leading feature is sensibility, goes from supreme joy in his first marriage, to the depths of despair in his second. His first wife Emilia is simply 'the most perfect specimen of female excellence that ever existed', and his second, Margaret, appears like 'a fairy vision'.[92] The soul of Catherine is purity itself, a model of filial love. Ambrose, on the other hand, is a picture of pure malevolence. Travers is perhaps the most interesting character who like so many of Godwin's heroes had been originally good but misled by a 'stubborn sense of honour'.[93]

But while Godwin's plot is uneven and his characterization unreal, he makes some acute philosophical remarks. The true self, he declares, is disembodied consciousness: 'Man, in the strictest sense, is nothing but a principle of thought, which no material force can arrest or imprisson, which bids defiance to all limits of space and time . . .'[94] It is by means of the 'vile incumbrance' of our body, however, that we are laid open to the tyranny of other men.[95] And if we try to present a false self to escape them, there can be considerable psychological damage. When Deloraine resorts to disguises, he recognizes that no other punishment could be so terrible. The 'essence of the nature of man', Godwin concludes, is to be 'as free as air' and lies in the 'spontaneous obedience of his limbs and his organs to the genuine impulse of his mind'.[96]

Godwin also demonstrates the moral implications of his revised view of necessity and free will. A friend of Deloraine argues that he cannot be held responsible for William's death because 'the act was an irresistible necessity, and flowed from an uncontrolable impulse'.[97] Deloraine, however, maintains uncompromisingly: 'Atrocious deeds are atrocious deeds, however circumstanced and however qualified.'[98] But although Godwin is uncertain whether the assassin is as irresponsible as his dagger, he is still critical of man-made laws. English law in the case of murder is like the application of 'a cloth-yard in a mercer's shop'.[99] In the long run, vice and virtue bring their own punishment and reward: 'Conscience is too true a monitor, to suffer her dictates to be baffled.'[100]

In his last novel, Godwin's radical purpose is as keen as ever. There are the same warnings against too isolated and indulgent an upbringing, and similar condemnation of the aristocratic code of honour. While the leading characters are corrupt nobles, Godwin supports plans in the West Indies 'to meliorate the conditions of the black cultivators of the soil, to imbue them with self-respect, and to hold out to them an ultimate prospect of independence'.[101] He also offers a final utopian picture of moderate and independent poverty in scattered hamlets which express 'an air of cheerfulness, neatness and salubrity' and suggest 'simple equality'.[102]

He had come to the conclusion, however, that the distinction of sex divides us no less effectively than the difference between species. While complaining about the wrongs of women he asserts that in the 'female bosom' there is 'a quickness, a truth, an intuition of feeling and taste' unknown to the 'sterner sex'.[103] Between man and man, the head still bears superior sway, but in the relationship between man and woman the heart is ever uppermost. In short, the companion of the first great feminist is able to declare at the end of his life: 'Man is the substantive thing in the terrestrial creation: woman is but the adjective, that cannot stand by itself . . . she is a frail flower; she wants a shelter, a protector, a pioneer . . . in forming his happiness, she forms her own.'[104]

In addition, while the sudden conversion of Travers by Catherine may be in keeping with the doctrine of *Political Justice*, the story suggests that error and prejudice always triumph. Deloraine is unable to control his passions and the whole world acts in a confederacy against him. Even the angelic Catherine is forced to lament to her father: 'Oh, why have not human creatures a confidence in the force of truth and justice?'[105] Significantly, the epigraph of the novel is the couplet from Pope: 'Why that bosom gored?/Why dimly gleans the visionary sword?' It is posed as a question, and Godwin offers no satisfactory answer.

Richard Bentley, impressed by the sales of Godwin's last novel, published *Deloraine* on 12 February 1833. After the heroic efforts of his friend John Howard Payne, a 'paltry edition' appeared in Philadelphia in the same year.[106] It was generally well received. Both the *Atlas* and the *Court Journal* were amazed that Godwin should write so vigorous a novel at his advanced age.[107] The *Age* was no less impressed by the profound moral reflections, while the *New Monthly Magazine* recommended its analysis of human passion.[108] Although the *Metropolitan Magazine* pronounced it a failure, it still called Godwin a tottering king.[109] Only the *Examiner* found the plot disagreeable and improbable, and the main character barbarous.[110]

Whilst writing *Deloraine* and immediately after the publication of his *Thoughts on Man*, Godwin considered composing a series of 'Lives of the English Philosophers'. He dropped the project however in favour of a work first planned in September 1830 on the history of superstition and magic. Ever since he was a child, he had been fascinated by mysteries, and he had already depicted in *St. Leon* a powerful portrait of a necromancer. His novels were inspired by myths, and he delighted to retell fables and legends in his children's books. His interest in the occult moreover shows that he was fully aware of the irrational forces at work in man. But he did not let it affect his confidence in reason, and he continued to the end the campaign of the Enlightenment to *écraser l'infâme* and to break the rod of the magician.

Godwin undertook his researches seriously. The result was not however a scientific treatise on natural magic, but a series of *Lives of the Necromancers; or, An Account of the Most Eminent Persons in Successive Ages, who have claimed for Themselves, or to whom have been imputed by Others, the Exercise of Magical Powers.* After considering the ambitious nature of man, he gives examples of Necromancy and Witchcraft from the Bible, then looks at Greece and Rome, the East, and Christianity, to end up with the Witch Trials in seventeenth-century New England. He also includes figures as disparate as Zoroaster, Pythagoras, Socrates, Nero, St. Dunstan, Macbeth, Thomas Aquinas, Faustus and Cellini.

Although Godwin wishes to exhibit the credulity of the human mind, his attitude to necromancy is ambivalent. As it originates from a wish to command future events, its history should teach us a 'useful pride in the abundance of our faculties'.[111] On the other hand, it shows the dangers of surrendering to the guidance of the imagination.

Man in his 'genuine and direct sphere' is a disciple of reason which prescribes that 'mind, as well as matter, is subject to fixed laws'.[112] Yet impatient man is not content with making use of his powers to improve his well-being, but boldly inquires into the invisible causes of things and peoples all nature with Gods and Devils. We thus become the 'passive and terrified slaves of the creatures of our imaginations'.[113]

Nevertheless, Godwin's prime purpose, as always, is moral. He condemns the way learning first became a monopoly of a select few, and was used to delude the many. He criticizes the sanguinary proceedings taken against witchcraft and the attempt of the Church to link it with heresy. He even discusses the English Law of High Treason to show how the language of Statute 25 Edward III reflected the widespread influence of witchcraft. In all, his aim is to demonstrate that all human beings are capable of changing themselves and are responsible for their own future. It is not therefore to the stars but to themselves that men must look for 'an account of what they shall do'.[114] Godwin often dwelt in the 'dreary abodes' of his wayward imagination yet he remained to the end a rationalist and a necessitarian in a world without God.[115]

As with his *Thoughts on Man*, Godwin had considerable difficulty in finding a publisher for his *Lives of the Necromancers*. Lardner was unwilling to offer him a reasonable price. Murray rejected it after reading the manuscript despite the intervention of Mary Shelley and John Lockhart. Colburn and Bentley were not interested, and even Cadell refused. In desperation, Godwin wrote to Walter Scott asking him to prevail on Cadell, but he merely offered to join a subscription to cover the expenses of the publication of any work 'not religious or political'.[116] This no doubt only added insult to injury. Fortunately, the obscure London publisher Frederick Mason at last agreed to accept it, and the *Lives of the Necromancers* appeared on 2 June 1834.

Although Scott's *Letters on Demonology and Witchcraft* (1830) had prepared the public, Godwin's work was not widely reviewed. A long article, probably by David Brewster, in the *Edinburgh Review* lamented Godwin's failure to furnish 'any clue through the intellectual labyrinth of Necromancy'.[117] The one paragraph which appeared in the *Gentleman's Magazine* found the style too condensed, and although the *Irish Monthly Magazine* praised Godwin's rich learning and ability, it declared that the work was disappointing.[118] When it appeared in America a year later the master of the occult Edgar Allan Poe, however, took the opportunity in the *Southern Literary Messenger* to say that Godwin's name meant excellence and that his style was finished and graceful.[119] The work was sufficiently in demand to be republished in New York in 1847 and 1876, and in London in 1876.

The *Lives of the Necromancers* was the last of Godwin's works to appear in his lifetime, but he was in fact never reduced to the penury he feared so much. In April 1833 Prime Minister Grey ceded to the demands of Mackintosh, Bulwer and others to offer a pension to the seventy-seven-year-old philosopher. Even Cobbett spoke up in his favour, declaring that Godwin had as much talent in his 'little finger' as Malthus had in his whole body.[120]

The author of *Political Justice*, who had roundly condemned pensions, duly accepted the post of 'Office Keeper and Yeoman Usher in the Receipt of the Exchequer'. It was worth £200 a year and included a residence at 13 New Palace Yard. He moved in with his wife and books on 4 May 1833. It was the supreme irony of Godwin's complicated life that the first great exponent of philosophical anarchism should spend his final days dependent on the beneficence of the State and in the shadow of Westminster Hall.

The post however was not a sinecure. Its duties included the payment of the tradesmen, the security of the Tally Court, and even the upkeep of the Fire Engine.[121] In July, Godwin wrote to his daughter despairingly: 'I am much tormented by my place, by my book, and hardly I suppose I shall ever be tranquil again.'[122] But he soon got used to his new abode. Harriet Martineau found the 'curious monument to a bygone state of society' in a small office under the roof of the Houses of Parliament with 'a salary, a dwelling, and coals and candle'. He appeared 'so comfortable that he had evidently no mind to die'.[123]

Godwin received few visits. Most of his old friends had died: Hazlitt in 1830, Marshal and Mackintosh in 1832, and Coleridge, Lamb and Thelwall in 1834. He had not seen Coleridge for many years, but on his death he thought of writing a memoir. Lamb had also kept his distance, although they renewed their friendship shortly before his death. He was not however completely neglected: Samuel Rogers would invite him over to Green Park, Trelawny or George Dyer would drop in, Holcroft's widow, now Mrs. James Kenney, was as hospitable as ever. He occasionally called on Lady Blessington. Wordsworth, on a rare visit to London on 2 March 1835, saw his former mentor.

The old philosopher also commanded sufficient interest to have his portrait made for posterity. In 1830 Henry Pickersgill sought him out. In 1832 William Brockedon sketched him and Sophia Gent painted him in watercolours. In the same year, he sat for one Joseph, probably George Joseph who painted Lamb's portrait. A caricature by Daniel Maclise also appeared in William Maginn's 'Gallery of Illustrious Literary Characters' in *Fraser's Magazine* in 1834. Harriet Martineau for one complained of its political prejudice — 'because the finest thing about him was his noble head, they put on a hat: and they presented him in profile because he had lost his teeth and his lips fell in'.[124] While Maginn liked Godwin's 'wonderful' books *Caleb Williams* and *St. Leon*, he felt his unfortunate personal history was a lesson for all.[125]

There were also some new friends. Claire introduced him to Daniel Gaskell, a radical M.P. whose wife Mary had been a disciple of Godwin in her youth. He was regularly invited to her house, an act which, according to Crabb Robinson, 'very few of her station & fortune would think of doing'.[126]

A young enthusiast like Frederick Reynolds could still dedicate his novel *Miserrimus* (1832) to the philospher, while a great mathematician like Charles Babbage continued to find him a welcome guest at his learned table.[127]

Thomas Carlyle, on a visit to London to arrange the publication of *Sartor Resartus*, left a vivid picture of Godwin at one of the Kenney soirées. He is, he wrote to his wife,

> a bald, bushy-browed, thick, hoary, hale little figure, taciturn enough, and speaking, when he does speak, with a certain *epigrammatic* spirit, wherein, except a little shrewdness, there is nothing but the most commonplace character. (I should have added that he wears spectacles, has full grey eyes, a very large blunt characterless nose, and ditto chin.)

Just as they began to discuss literary London, Godwin was summoned to take a hand at whist. The philosopher obliged, and sat playing cards amidst noisy dilettantes, a swarm of noisy children, chattering women, and the thunder of a piano duet.[128] Carlyle quietly retreated.

Another ardent and anonymous disciple sought Godwin out in New Palace Yard, one of the 'iron fortresses of Tyranny'. In their political discussions, Godwin expressed his satisfaction that modern radicals were 'less ferocious & sanguinary' than in his own day. He was also pleased to see his own principle of government becoming gradually recognized and partially practised. But when jokingly accused of conservatism, he made his political testament: 'In principle & theory I am avowedly a republican, but in practice a Whig. I abhor that bigotted adherence to old institutions, without reference to their fitness for present times which I understand by the term conservatism. But I also consider great & sudden changes injurious to a country.' The young man was so won over by the 'benignity of his smile, and the placid urbanity of his manners' that he considered Godwin 'the incarnation of justice itself'.[129]

The artist John Martin also found Godwin 'a quiet, retiring, unpretentious old gentleman' who preferred a game of whist in a cosy corner to conversation. But he was disappointed by his apparent change of principles. '"Mr. Godwin", said he, "you will admit that your 'Political Justice' was all for knocking down the aristocracy, and for throwing the whole power of the nation into the hands of the people?" "If I ever said so", said Godwin, "I must have been under a mistake".' When Martin argued that with the march of intellect the people begin to think, Godwin replied coolly, '"I doubt that a whole People *can* think". "Then," said Martin, "you throw up the democratic principle?" "Perhaps I do," said Godwin, making a trick.'[130] But although he grew less confident in the political wisdom of the people, he never gave up his republican feelings. Passing Buckingham Palace early in 1835 with Lady Blessington in a carriage, he declared to his aristocratic companion: 'There's a place worse than useless for a thing worse still!'[131]

Godwin knew now that he was approaching his end. In the summer of 1834, he had taken the opportunity of his wife's absence on holiday to write some reflections on a few loose sheets to be pasted on the last page of his diaries:

> With what facility have I marked these pages with the stamp of rolling weeks and months and years — all uniform, all blank! What a strange power is this! It sees through a long vista of time, and it sees nothing. All this at present is mere abstraction, symbols, not realities. Nothing is actually seen: the whole is ciphers, conventional marks, imaginary boundaries of unimagined things. Here is neither joy nor sorrow, pleasure nor pain. Yet when the time shall truly come, and the revolving year shall bring the day, what portentous events may stamp the page! what anguish, what horror, or by possibility what joy, what Godlike elevation of soul! . . .[132]

But despite his impending death, Godwin steadfastly refused to turn to the comforts of religion. Indeed, after finishing the *Lives of the Necromancers*, he began a collection of essays to be entitled after D'Holbach 'The Genius of Christianity Unveiled'. Although they were published posthumously, they completed a programme of reform undertaken forty years before. In *Political Justice*, he had tried to show the remedies for political evils, and now, at the end of his life, he wished to remove that 'oppressing weight of religious prejudice, which has exerted an influence no less fatal to the energies & independence of the intellectual part of our nature'.[133] Despite their repetitiveness and disorder, Godwin rightly considered these final essays to be a valuable legacy to his species.

They were not written easily: Godwin was perturbed by 'How much poetry, & reverential & profound feeling, piety, adoration, confiding hope, consolation in adversity & sorrow' his reasoning was calculated to destroy.[134] He overcame his scruples, however, and on 2 October 1835 wrote a bold preface calling the 'impartial and enlightened' to direct their attention to the 'world of realities'.[135]

Godwin is prepared to allow that a religious sense, which beholds the works of nature with wonder and awe, is necessary for the healthy mind, but religion encroaches too far when it 'proposes to deprive us of our senses, or prohibits in whatever direction the use of our reasoning powers'.[136] All systems which represent the cause of things to be an intelligent creator must therefore be only 'so many shades of anthropomorphism': man is not made in the image of God but the Christian God is made 'in the image of man'.[137] Christianity then is a system of falsehood derived solely from its human author and can only be a subject of historical recollection. If Christ were to return to nineteenth-century England, Godwin concludes, he would have little chance of winning converts.

But Godwin is not prepared to leave it at that and gives a careful examination of Christian doctrine. In the first place, the God depicted in the Scriptures must be a tyrant, whether he makes this life a state of probation or predestines the vast majority of mankind to eternal punishment. Secondly, the doctrine of original sin destroys 'all distinction between right and wrong, between conduct the most flagitious and the most exemplary'.[138] Thirdly, there could be no greater blasphemy than the system of rewards and punishments after death, which only encourages a 'servility, a fawning and cowardly prostration of soul'.[139]

Given the vast extent of suffering and calamity in the world, Godwin moreover can only doubt the alleged infinite power and benevolence of the Christian God. Indeed, he finds the Zoroastrian creed that there are two opposing forces of good and evil much superior an explanation. Where the 'great mystic' Coleridge is reported to have said in a moment of inspiration that the 'devil is God'. Godwin draws the literal inference and declares that 'God is the devil.'[140]

The historical Christ, Godwin is willing to admit, was undoubtedly a person of 'great genius, of profound contemplation, of exemplary purity, and the most exalted tone of feeling and thinking'.[141] But he was also considerably 'atrabilarious and saturnine' and perpetually surrounded his hearers with the four last things — death, judgment, heaven and hell.[142] The subsequent history of Christianity only made matters worse. An essentially intolerant creed, it led to bitter controversy and wars, imposed systematic falsehood, and rendered men abject and cowardly. The Church itself established a vast hierarchy, making kings at their pleasure and amassing a great part of the world's wealth. 'Oh', Godwin exclaims from the bottom of his old heart, 'when shall the mind of man again be free, shake off the chains that fasten it to its dungeon, and soar unrestrained in its native element? Who can tell, in the revolution of eighteen hundred years, what wonders it might not have effected?'[143]

It is clear that Godwin's opposition to Christianity stems from his confidence in freedom. For progress to occur, the whole community must be allowed 'to run the generous race for intellectual and moral superiority'.[144] They should not therefore have their understandings shackled by the fear of an all-seeing God and an afterlife of retribution: 'To be independent and erect is essential to the perfect man. To stand in awe of neither matter nor spirit. To fear (for fear we must) those things which in the world of realities we may encounter, and which may subdue us. But to fear nothing unnecessarily, and with superstition.'[145]

Similarly, while society calls forth our 'sweetest affections' and 'main virtues', it is not right that we should be content for our whole lives 'to dance in fetters'.[146] We love to revel in the unbounded freedom of thought, conscious that we are under no restraint either of man or God. Laws therefore should be as few as possible, forbidding nothing 'the indulgence of which would not, beyond question, be injurious to the common weal'.[147] The right of private judgment in everything beyond this should be sacred. Godwin thus remained true to the libertarian tradition of Dissent to the end.

Godwin's faith in social freedom was ultimately rooted in a kind of cosmic optimism. Just as he felt that humanity without restraints would thrive and progress, so he believed that nature left to itself would pursue a beneficial path. He defines nature in these last essays as the revolutions which occur in the world and which may be reduced to laws. There is a principle in nature, however, which is 'a secure alliance, a friend that, so far as the system of things extends, will never desert us'.[148] He will not call it 'Wisdom' or 'Providence', but he nevertheless places a certain confidence in the 'unseen hand' or in the 'mysterious power, the plastic nature' which sustains and gives harmony to the whole.[149]

While Godwin was writing his final essays, he was still not at ease in what his daughter called his 'tiny shabby place under Government'.[150] On 10 October his post was abolished by the reformed parliament, and six days later a great fire destroyed the Palace of Westminster. Godwin of course was responsible for the fire-fighting equipment, and should have made sure that the burning of the old tallies which caused the fire was done in the open air. It could well have had the appearance of a supreme gesture of contempt for a mouldy institution, but Godwin was quietly at the theatre watching Shakespeare's *Richard III* when the fire broke out. No one thought of accusing him of succeeding where Guy Fawkes had failed!

Godwin's house was untouched and he waited there anxiously for the worst news. His difficult situation was compounded by the return of the Tories in November. He immediately wrote to the Duke of Wellington, who said that he would look into the matter. When nothing came of it, he wrote again in January 1835 to the new Tory Prime Minister Sir Robert Peel, who graciously answered that he would do all that he could from a sense of justice as well as from a 'grateful Recollection of the Pleasure' derived from reading his books.[151] On 9 February 1835, the old radical learned that his government pension was secure.

Although Godwin's mind remained alert and vigorous, his body was beginning to show signs of decay. He suffered from his old fainting fits and his digestion was bad — 'deorsum', he noted regularly in his diary, as well as the remedy of castor oil and rhubarb pills. In the summer of 1835, he wrote to his daughter: 'I am now well — now nervous — now old — now young.'[152] One sign of age was his great horror of change. He refused to visit Mary in Harrow, preferring his own fireplace to the sight of green fields.

But still he was not left undisturbed. On 6 November, he was obliged to move to another public building, the Exchequer Office in Whitehall Yard. Yet he managed to continue the habits of forty years: a little reading in different languages, particularly Greek and Latin, some writing in the morning, and entertaining the odd friend in the afternoon. He still dined out occasionally and went to the theatre.

Only from the beginning of 1836 do his diary entries become intermittent. He had been troubled by severe colds for most of the winter, but felt strong enough to go to the opera to hear Zampa on 24 March. Two days later he made his last entry in his diary with his usual brevity: 'Sa. March 26 Constip. *Malfy*, fin. Call on Hudson, Trelawny calls, cough, snow.' He then carefully pasted in the reflections which he had written two years earlier. The cough brought a fever; he was ill about ten days; confined to his bed for five. Gradually his strength left him, until on 7 April 1836, he died. His daughter wrote to his old friend Mary Hays:

> I sat up several nights with him — and Mrs. Godwin was with him when I was not — as he had a great horror of being left to servants. His thoughts wandered a good deal but not painfully — he knew himself to be dangerously ill but did not consider his recovery impossible. His last moment was very sudden — Mrs. Godwin and I were both present. He was dozing tranquilly, when a slight rattle called us to his side, his heart ceased to beat, and all was over. This happened a little after 7 on the even[in]g of the 7 ins.[153]

He had just turned eighty.

In his will written in 1827, Godwin had characteristically requested his son and daughter to choose a book or set of books from his library as a memorial of his affection. He left his portrait by Northcote to both of them, Opie's portrait of Mary Wollstonecraft to his daughter, and hoped Opie's portrait of Holcroft would not be auctioned off. He asked Mary to look over his manuscripts and letters and to decide which of them were fit to be printed, and which should be consigned to the flames. His last desire was for his mortal remains to be deposited, as near as may be, to those of the 'author of a *Vindication of the Rights of Woman*' in St. Pancras Churchyard.[154]

Mary arranged for her mother's tomb to be opened in the quiet spot under the willow where Shelley had first declared his love. At a depth of twelve feet the coffin was found uninjured — the cloth still over it — and the plate tarnished but legible. Godwin's simple funeral on 14 April was restricted to a few friends: Mary and her sixteen-year-old son Percy Florence, Edward Trelawny, Thomas Campbell, James Kenney, Dr. David Uwins, and the Rev. John Hobart Caunter (who had adapted *St. Leon* for the stage a year before). Mary Jane Godwin was notably absent as her husband was lowered into the ground next to his first and greatest love. The small square monument that bore Mary Wollstonecraft's name was engraved with 'William Godwin, Author of "Political Justice". Born, March 3rd, 1756; Died, April 7th, 1836. Aged 80 years.'

When Mary Shelley died twenty-five years later, she also asked to be buried with her father and mother. Lady Jane Shelley preferred however to remove all their remains and deposit them with Shelley's heart in a vault in the churchyard of St. Peter's, Bournemouth, Hampshire, so as to be near them. They are still there today. In a public garden next to St. Pancras Church, there was until recently a square stone pedestal inscribed on three sides: 'To William Godwin, author of *Political Justice:* To Mary Wollstonecraft Godwin, author of a *Vindication of the Rights of Woman:* To Mary Jane, second wife of William Godwin.'

Godwin's widow Mary Jane was looked after by friends. The indefatigable philosopher only left £100 but his curious and valuable library was sold at Sotheby's. Thanks to the intervention of Sheridan's granddaughter Caroline Norton and later Edward Bulwer, Lord Melbourne gave her a pension until her death on 17 June 1841.

Mary had never got over the death of Shelley, and her novels after *The Last Man* showed a growing conservatism, as well as a marked decline in her creative powers. As requested, she began editing her father's 'Memoirs and Correspondence' for the publisher Henry Colburn. But after making some notes and enquiring after some letters to Crabb Robinson, Coleridge, Wordsworth and Hazlitt, her fear of becoming an 'object of scurrility and attacks' made her drop the project.[155] She also failed to publish his 'Genius of Christianity Unveiled'. The price of unorthodoxy had been too high for her.

She had a great deal to contend with during her eight-year relationship with Shelley. Of the five children she bore him in a life constantly on the move, only William and Percy Florence reached their third birthdays, and only Percy Florence survived. She had moreover to endure Shelley's love for Claire (with whom he seems to have had a child) and his impassioned pursuit, towards the end of his life, of the Platonic ideal as embodied in the women of their entourage. The fact that Mary managed to write so brilliantly in such difficult circumstances attests to her extraordinary strength and creativity.

XXXIII. Mary Shelley in 1841, by Richard Rothwell.

After the death of Shelley, however, she spent the rest of her life in growing isolation, writing uninspired biographies and educating Percy Florence. 'If talent descended, what ought he not be, he who is the blood of Godwin, Mrs. Wollstonecraft, Shelley and Mrs. Shelley!', mused Crabb Robinson in his diary.[156] But his mother wanted to forget their legacy. When a friend advised her to send her son to a school where they would teach him to think for himself, she exclaimed: 'For heaven's sake, let him learn to think like everyone else!'[157] She accordingly sent him to Harrow and Trinity College, and he later became a lawyer, an M.P. and an undistinguished patron of letters. He died in 1889, the last descendant of William Godwin.

# CONCLUSION

Throughout his long life, Godwin was obsessed with fame. But he was thrown up by the vortex of the French Revolution, and he sank when it subsided. The forces of reaction found in him a perfect victim and they rapidly transformed the sincere advocate of truth, the fearless defender of freedom, the calm man of universal benevolence and enlightenment, into a blood-thirsty monster. He was then quietly forgotten. Godwin in his lifetime therefore had no alternative but to look to posterity for a true recognition of his talents.

His friends did their best to put the record straight by publishing a sober obituary in the *Morning Chronicle*, the *Examiner* and the *Spectator* which observed that Godwin was the last of the revolutionary school of writers of any note and that *Political Justice* had attracted more attention than any other publication of the time.[1] The *New Monthly Magazine* further claimed that it was only in tragedy that he was unsuccessful.[2] But while the *Gentleman's Magazine* acknowedged that *Caleb Williams* was perhaps the 'most powerful novel in our language', it predictably dismissed Godwin's 'sour and unhealthy', opinions and concluded that 'it might have been better for mankind had he never existed'.[3] It was a view which was to be repeated many times.

Although Godwin as a man died in obscurity, his ideas were influencing the early socialists and slowly fermenting in the growing labour movement. William Thompson was 'saturated' with his spirit.[4] In *An Inquiry into the Principles of the Distribution of Wealth* (1824), Thompson adopted his radical utilitarianism and his system of 'voluntary equality of wealth'.[5] He looked forward moreover to a time when the advance of reason would enable mankind to live in a society without government, private property, marriage and the family.

As a utilitarian, Thomas Hodgskin followed Godwin rather than

Bentham in his defence of moral sentiments. He believed that the prosperity of every nation is in 'inverse proportion to the power and the interference of
its government' and that the greatest possible equality is the surest way to
promote the 'happiness of all'.[6] In his *Labour defended against the Claims of
Capital* (1825), he further argued like Godwin that the question of distribution
must be settled by the 'unfettered judgments of the labourers themselves'.[7]
Francis Place strongly disapproved of his 'wild speculations', especially his
Godwinian belief that 'all laws are and must be wholly mischievous and that
none should be allowed to exist'.[8]

Godwin's works were also often quoted in Owenite and Chartist journals.
Robert Dale Owen was spreading political justice in America, and the *New
Harmony Gazette* declared that Godwin was 'a mind of gigantic force, a
master-spirit'.[9] In his father's *Crisis, or, The Change from Error and Misery, to
Truth and Happiness*, Godwin was quoted in the early 1830s on the idle
upper classes, while at the end of the decade the *Working Bee*, the journal of
the Owenite Community at Manea Fea, regularly discussed his views,
especially on property and the relations between the sexes.[10] And since
Owen had borrowed so much from Godwin, it is not surprising that his
name should appear on a reading list for the Owenite social missionaries.[11]

After the Reform Act of 1832, the chief demand of the working class was
for the vote, but this also implied a desire for more social control over their
conditions of life and labour. Thus although Godwin condemned political
parties and saw in the secret ballot a symbol of slavery, the Chartists found
inspiration in his attack on property and the monarchy. James Watson, a
central figure in the National Union of Working Classes and speaker at
their weekly debates at the Rotunda, quoted Godwin on 6 and 20 April
1833 in the *Working Man's Friend and Political Magazine*. He published the
chapter in *Political Justice* on 'The Moral Effects of Aristocracy' with Hazlitt's essay *The Spirit of Monarchy* in a separate pamphlet two years later.
Henry Hetherington, another leader of the National Union of the Working
Classes, also quoted Godwin on property in the *Poor Man's Guardian* on 3
January 1835. Then at the height of the Chartist agitation from 1839 to
1843, their circulars in Scotland and England regularly quoted Godwin's
views on equality, anarchy, justice, law, property, and monarchy.[12]

Having issued *Political Justice* in eleven parts at sixpence each, James
Watson then published in one handy volume the entire third edition in
1842. It was enthusiastically reviewed by the *Union,* the *New Moral World,*
and the *People.*[13] W. J. Fox in his *Lectures addressed chiefly to the Working
Classes* (1845) warmly recommended it as a 'work full of noble-mindedness'
whose time was coming.[14] Abel Heywood also published in 1842 *An Essay on
Trades and Professions* from *The Enquirer.* In a glowing review, the *English
Chartist Circular* declared that few ages had produced a mind 'more com-

prehensive and penetrating' than Godwin's.[15]

Godwin's influence was therefore not only restricted to a small and highly educated group in Britain. While he was virtually forgotten by high society after his death, his works were being avidly discussed and read by the labour movement in the middle of the century. Engels's claim in 1844 that Godwin had become 'almost exclusively the property of the proletariat' was therefore fundamentally correct.[16] Four years later William Smyth was complaining in his *Lectures on the History of the French Revolution* that he had lived to see all the doctrines of Godwin revived.[17]

At the same time, Godwin continued to exert a real and lasting influence on isolated writers. George Henry Lewes, the companion of George Eliot, owned a rare copy of the first edition of *Political Justice* and made many careful annotations.[18] Douglas Jerrold, who had corresponded briefly with Godwin, promoted the radical cause in the pages of *Punch*. Dickens actually lodged in 1828 at Godwin's old home at 17, The Polygon, knew his son and daughter, and was impressed by his novels. He may have even partly modelled Harold Skimpole in *Bleak House* on him. The novelists Charles Reade and Wilkie Collins also admired Godwin.

Bulwer-Lytton continued to reveal his influence, and in his utopian novel *The Coming Race* (1860) combined Godwin's opposition to government, compulsion and wealth, with his own brand of patriarchal toryism. Although there is no clear evidence of indebtedness, Oscar Wilde's *The Soul of Man under Socialism* (1891) is pure Godwin. H. G. Wells's *Men like Gods* (1923) and more recently Aldous Huxley's *The Island* (1962) echo his anarchism. John Middleton Murry and Herbert Read both recognized a kindred spirit in the author of *Political Justice*.[19] Godwin therefore both reflected and helped form the powerful libertarian tradition in British history and thought.

In America, all of Godwin's major works appeared. His ward Thomas Cooper became a famous actor there, and Godwin was personally acquainted with Joel Barlow, William Austin, Aaron Burr, William Dunlap, Washington Irving, John Howard Payne, and James Fenimore Cooper. He had a powerful influence on radical thinkers like James Ogilvie, Bronson Alcott, Orestes Brownson and William Ellery Channing. He also impressed writers as diverse as John Daly Burke, Charles Brockden Brown, Edgar Allan Poe, William Gilmore Simms, and Nathaniel Hawthorne.

In France, all Godwin's novels except *Deloraine* were published, and Benjamin Constant only withheld his translation of *Political Justice* because of the adverse political situation. The *Bibliothèque Britannique* in Geneva summarized and translated many extracts from his works, thereby transmitting his ideas to Sismondi. Madame de Staël met Godwin, and Chénier, Chateaubriand, and Stendhal knew of his work. Balzac admired *Caleb*

*Williams* and it inspired Hugo's Jarvet in *Les Misérables*. An obituary in the *Revue Britannique* declared that in France the popularity of Godwin was only rivalled by Scott.[26]

It seems, however, that he had little influence on the major French social thinkers in the nineteenth century. Saint-Simon and Fourier worked out their ideas independently, and Proudhon, the first self-styled anarchist, only referred to Godwin once in his *Système des contradictions ou philosophie de la misère* (1846) as a communist of the same school as Owen. It was only early in the twentieth century after the biographies by Raymond Gourg and Henri Roussin appeared that socialists like Jean Jaurès showed a keen interest.[21]

In Germany, Godwin's three novels written at the turn of the century were translated and an abridged version of *Political Justice* appeared in 1803. The Romantic poet Ludwig Tieck praised Godwin's writings, but according to Crabb Robinson, by 1817 he had no great popularity.[22] Marx knew of Godwin through Engels, who recognized that he strove towards a communist position but came to an anti-social conclusion.[23] They decided however not to translate *Political Justice*, and merely referred to him as developing the theory of exploitation.[24]

Marx, of course, was not sympathetic to Godwin's undialectical immaterialism, his pervasive moral emphasis, and his opposition to organized politics. While Marx stressed the social being of man, Godwin saw him primarily as an individual. And where one looked to the urban proletariat as the agents of reform, the other favoured an intellectual elite. Nevertheless, through Owen, Thompson, and Hodgskin, Godwin's hope for the ultimate withering away of the state began to haunt the Marxist imagination.

At the turn of the century in Germany, Anton Menger and Paul Eltzbacher also made Godwin's economic and political views widely known and stimulated many studies.[25] In 1904 a new German translation of Book VIII 'Of Property' from *Political Justice* appeared. The anarchist Rudolf Rocker soon recognized that Godwin was the first to give a clear form to the anarchist conception of life.[26]

When a Russian translation of *Caleb Williams* appeared in St. Petersburg in 1838, it was, according to Belinsky, unanimously hailed as a masterpiece.[27] Godwin soon after became a favourite of the revolutionary novelist Chernyshevski: he thought *Political Justice* enchantingly written, and held *Of Population* to be a successful reply to Malthus.[28] Godwin does not, however, seem to have had a formative influence on the great Russian anarchists. There is no evidence that Bakunin read him. Tolstoy spoke of Godwin as providing an answer to the question of how a society could be established without a state authority, and quoted him on law, but he may not have read him directly.[29] Kropotkin, on the other hand, recognized that Godwin first stated 'in a quite definite form the political and economic principles of anarchism'.[30] Book VIII 'Of Property' and some other passages from *Political Justice* were translated into Russian in 1958 but understandably the editors of the Institute of Marxism–Leninism dismiss one of the founders of anarchism as a 'petty bourgeois publicist'.[31] *Caleb Williams* is also freely available in Russia and victims of state oppression continue to identify with the hero.[32]

Although Godwin may not have had a great influence on the nineteenth-century anarchist movement, he is now widely recognized as the founder of modern anarchism. Abridged versions of *Political Justice* have appeared in Los Angeles, New York, London, Tokyo, Bombay, Naples and Oxford. A complete Spanish translation was published in Buenos Aires in 1946, and Benjamin Constant's French translation appeared in Toronto in 1972. In 1953, the Belgian anarchist Hem Day (i.e. Marcel Dieu) significantly dedicated the first issue of his *Cahiers de Pensée et Action* to a collection of essays by an international symposium on 'Un Précurseur Trop Oublié'.[33] As governments become more powerful, authoritarian and secretive, Godwin's insights are being increasingly appreciated. Since the time of the French Revolution, his influence as a political thinker has never been so powerful as it is today.

As a philosopher, Godwin has been primarily remembered as a man who showed the dangers of excessive rationalism. He had, as Hazlitt so memorably put it, rendered an essential service to moral science 'by attempting (in vain) to pass the Arctic Circle and Frozen Regions, where the understanding is no longer warmed by the affections, nor fanned by the breeze of fancy!'[34] Certainly, Godwin believed until the end that 'Reason is our criterion — touchstone — surest guide — great distinction.'[35] It is the faculty which distinguishes between truth and falsehood, and a rational man can become satisfied with the truth of a proposition only when it is self-evident, deductive, or empirical. Everything else must rest upon authority, and should be regarded with the 'eye of scepticism and jealousy'.[36]

His philosophical method too is rational. He deliberately adopted the deductive approach of Hobbes rather than the empirical one of Aristotle. He wished to discover the one best mode of social existence for human beings deducible from their nature, and based his science of politics firmly on a science of ethics which in turn was based on a science of the mind. Indeed, it was the rigorously deductive nature of Godwin's philosophy which so exasperated his contemporaries. Godwin's friend and biographer Fenwick observed:

The principles contained in Political Justice had all the appearances and many of the effects of self-evident axioms. To understand the terms, and adopt the propositions of the work, were so nearly inseparable, that it was a fact that some very great and learned men, in expressing an abhorrence of its doctrines, could not conceal the secret that their detestation of Political Justice was chiefly occasioned by its subtlety in eluding their zeal to detect the radical error . . . Political Justice at once tortured their feelings and baffled their reason.[37]

Godwin was so pleased with these observations that he quoted them in his 1832 draft prospectus for a new edition of his *magnum opus*.

Godwin further looked to the improvement of reason as the means of improving our social condition. He based his theory of perfectibility on the following premisses: the characters of men originate in their circumstances; the voluntary actions of men originate in their opinions; immutable truth is omnipotent. It follows for Godwin that since human nature is malleable and rational motives necessarily terminate in action, enlightenment will suffice to make mankind free, virtuous and wise. While many would allow the inferences, it is Godwin's three fundamental premisses which have been most challenged and have led to the claim that he is a naive visionary.

In the first place, Godwin could be accused of having overestimated the influence of circumstances. Certainly, in the first edition of *Political Justice* he rejected innate ideas and original sin and maintained that human beings share a common nature and are intellectually equal at birth. Nevertheless, Godwin subsequently admitted the possibility of genetic differences: not only are we born with different dispositions, but there is, he suggested, some inevitable inequality between the sexes. Again, by rejecting original sin, he did not believe in natural goodness. We are born neither good nor evil, but have a potential for either. His doctrine of perfectibility did not therefore mean that all would become perfect but that human beings, regardless of sex, race or class, are potentially rational and virtuous. Godwin may have overlooked the interaction between nature and nurture, but he cannot be accused of crude environmentalism.

Secondly, it could be argued against Godwin that people do not always do what they think is right. There may be a wide gap between thought and action: something might be believed to be most desirable without necessarily being desired. It is true that in the first edition Godwin asserted that the will is the 'last act of the understanding'.[38] But under the influence of Hume, he soon transferred the motive power of action from reason to desire. Reason, he maintained, is not an independent principle but in a practical point of view 'merely a comparison and balancing of different feelings'.[39] Reason then can only evaluate ends and means; it cannot excite us to action.

Thirdly, it may be the case that there is no immutable truth independent of time and place, and that truth does not always triumph over error. Yet again, although Godwin may have talked of immutable truths in a Platonic way in his first edition of *Political Justice*, he stressed afterwards that by immutability he did not mean absolute truth but 'greater or less probability'.[40] He was also fully aware of the fragility of truth and the strength of prejudice and habit. He recognized that the history of mankind is 'little else than a record of crimes' and that it sufficiently shows that man is of all beings 'the most formidable enemy to man'.[41] Their education and upbringing had further blinded most of his contemporaries to things as they are, and had made them competitive and self-interested. Godwin may have shifted the responsibility for human weakness and depravity from 'Old Adam' to 'Positive Institutions' but he did not pretend that evil did not exist nor that it was easily eradicable.

Godwin's novels moreover show the disruptive power of the passions to such an extent that some have wondered whether they came from the same pen as that of the author of *Political Justice*.[42] But Godwin believed that the philosopher's task is to see things as they are, and in his novels he tried to portray reality as he saw it. They not only reveal the cruelties and injustices below the apparent order of his society but the spiritual terrors underlying the age of reason.

Throughout his major novels, Godwin developed the same theme: the perils of excessive ambition and honour, which, if unchecked, inevitably lead to disaster and despair. Unconscious fears and desires constantly overwhelm his characters' drive for wholeness and composure. Crippled by their upbringings, they cannot escape the prison of themselves. The apparent triumph of truth is always achieved with tragic consequences, and the lasting impression is one of a cruel world in which isolated beings constantly prey on each other. Whatever Godwin's faults, he is not guilty of psychological naïveté; if anything, he offers an astonishingly modern analysis of mental disorders.

Yet for all Godwin's profound awareness of the irrational forces in man, he believed to the end that reason perceives natural law in the world, judges morality, and decides what action is preferable. He also never relinquished the view that some evidence is irresistible and that we cannot really be convinced of the desirableness of an object without desiring it. His increasing admission of feeling as a motive power did not weaken but strengthened his philosophical system. He not only rejected Hume's antithesis between reason and passion but also saw them as inseparable. And contrary to what Don Locke argues, he never lived in a 'fantasy of reason', nor succumbed to a 'disease' of feeling.[43] Reason for Godwin is never a simple abstraction, a substitute deity, or an instrument of analysis. As a power of intuitive perception, it resembles not only Coleridge's view of Reason but Blake's concept of the Imagination.

Godwin's view of justice has been most responsible for earning him the reputation of having a 'great head full of cold brains'.[44] The rigour with which he applied the principles of utility and impartiality to condemn gratitude, promises, contracts, patriotism, exclusive friendships and family affections made him an original but also an exasperating moralist. But although he took reason for the rule of conduct and the general good for its end, it is not done in a heartless manner. Godwin had learned as a young man from Hutcheson that disinterested benevolence has 'its seat in the human heart'.[45] While the rational principle of impartiality in *Political Justice* is the 'beacon and regulator of virtue', it is not its inspiration.[46] It was Godwin's intense love of mankind that led him to try and absolve the narrow ties of self-interest and tribalism and to imagine himself in the place of others. Indeed, he went so far as to assert that moral principles begotten by reason 'will never be very strenuously espoused, till they are ardently loved'.[47]

It is precisely the peculiar blend of intense fervour and abstract lucidity which gives an incandescence to Godwin's stately prose and explains its extraordinary power. 'No book', Crabb Robinson wrote of *Political Justice*, 'ever made me feel more generously'. He later came to recognize that 'Godwin was in his early days an enthusiast of a high kind. There was a sort of religious and devotional spirit in his anti-religious prejudices, and while he disbelieved [in] a personal God, he worshipped a divine principle — the spirit of justice and truth . . .'[48] Godwin never relinquished his doctrine of universal benevolence, but, encouraged by Hume and Wollstonecraft, he increasingly stressed the value of the 'culture of the heart'.[49] At the end of his life he asserted simply that the 'true key of the universe is love'.[50] He remained without religion but Coleridge showed him the importance of a religious sense and he came to look on nature with awe and wonder. In all, it was a change of stress rather than direction, for Godwin can perhaps best be described without paradox as a rational Romantic.

It was Godwin's recognition of the demands of feeling which led him to distinguish like Hume between what the philosopher may accept in the 'sobriety of the closet' and what he may assume in 'actual life'.[51] While he remained a necessitarian and an immaterialist in theory, he came to think that a strict adherence to the doctrine of necessity would undermine the moral sentiments, and the denial of the independent existence of matter was counter to common sense. He therefore acted in practical life on the assumption of the existence of the external world and of free will. It was an unhappy compromise but he saw no other way out of the dilemma posed by the clash of his reason and feelings. Although it threatened, it did not however undermine the edifice of this thought.

Godwin's lifelong distinction between theory and practice in ethics and politics is perhaps less justifiable. Northcote accused him of being 'a profligate in theory, and a bigot in conduct' and the charge has often since been repeated.[52] He seemed to write against himself. A republican and anarchist in theory, he supported the Whigs in practice. He condemned the institution of marriage yet married twice. He advocated sincerity but was prepared to tell a lie. Godwin believed, however, that nothing could be more 'idle and shallow' than the competition set up between theory and practice, and felt that the distinction was both necessary and useful.[53]

He based his case on a general theory of knowledge and the supreme principle of utility. Human beings are beset with an inescapable contradiction: generalizations and abstractions are necessary in order to use language and to think, but true knowledge is of particulars. To rest in general rules is therefore sometimes inevitable but it can easily prevent us from seeing things as they are. We should go beyond them as much as possible and examine the particular case.

In ethics, it follows that we must always ascertain where the urgency of special circumstances is such as 'to supersede rules that are generally obligatory'.[54] Godwin therefore saw no contradiction in being a married opponent of marriage. While wishing to see the institution of marriage abolished in general, he married Mary Wollstonecraft because in the particular circumstances he judged that he would have done more harm by upholding rather than by breaking the general rule. In the same way, he argued that the rule of sincerity may be overlooked when the only means of avoiding instant destruction would be to utter a falsehood. Indeed, 'There is no maxim more clear than this, "Every case is a rule to itself."'[55] The belief in the uniqueness of every individual and action not only made Godwin an act-utilitarian but formed the basis of his anarchism.

In his politics, to be a republican in principle and a Whig in practice was not therefore inconsistent for Godwin. While he had a theoretical preference for republicanism, a study of the specific conditions of his time led him to support the Whig programme of parliamentary reform and to condemn the political associations and popular agitation of the radicals. He thought that his long-term goal of the dissolution of government and the equality of conditions would more likely be achieved by the gradual change of institutions and the calm enlightenment of the people than by any sudden and violent revolution. While believing that his theory was universally applicable and ultimately realizable, Godwin was thus willing to support any movement which seemed to be going in the right direction. His failure to find an adequate praxis contributed to his political disenchantment, but it was not due to any moral weakness or lack of philosophical rigour on his part. It resulted from his thoroughgoing utilitarianism.

Godwin's utilitarianism differed from that of Helvétius and Bentham in upholding the reality of altruism, the natural harmony of interests, and the moral importance of intentions. Unlike them, he further advocated the restraint of certain desires and made a qualitative distinction between pleasures. Yet these were innovations rather than departures from the utilitarian ethic, and he made a consistent attempt to subordinate his principles to the criteria of 'utility, pleasure, or happiness'.[56]

Certainly Godwin valued liberty, knowledge and virtue. This was not, however, for their own sake, but because liberty permits the most reliable execution of duty, knowledge best ensures the promotion of the general good, and virtue produces the most exquisite pleasure. Happiness for Godwin is always the supreme end, while liberty, knowledge, and virtue are only to be valued in ascending order as a means to that end. Godwin equally emphasized that intention is of no further value than as it leads to utility, that the restriction of certain pleasures would in the long run increase the total sum of pleasure. Although the pleasures of the mind are more exquisite than those of the body, the most desirable state of man is where he has access to all sources of pleasure and is 'in possession of a happiness the most varied and uninterrupted'.[57]

In fact, Godwin's bold application of the principle of utility led him to conclusions which many utilitarians would repudiate. Firstly, he outlaws domestic affections and gratitude since the only standard by which we should treat a person must be his or her importance to the general welfare. Secondly, he condemned promises, contracts, tests, and oaths because there exists always a prior and overriding obligation to utility. Thirdly, he opposed the positive rights of life and liberty on the grounds that we have duties to contribute to the 'greatest quantity of general good'.[58]

Because of his influence on British institutions Bentham has been remembered most, but Hazlitt was undoubtedly right when he observed that Godwin was 'the first *whole-length* broacher of the doctrine of *Utility*'.[59] Place moreover was in a good position to know that the abuse showered on *Political Justice* was 'mainly caused by its propagating utilitarian doctrines'.[60] It is Godwin's transformation of Christian ethics into an original system of utilitarianism which earns him not only an important place in the history of ethics but makes him an innovating moralist highly relevant to the modern world.

Godwin's aim in his politics was to place the principles of the subject on an immovable basis and to discover the 'one best method' of making people 'free, virtuous and wise'.[61] The French Revolution inspired him to collect whatever existed that was 'best and most liberal in the science of politics' and to systematize and develop it farther than had been done by any preceding writer.[62] In the outcome, he did more than simply re-arrange old principles. As an ex-Calvinist brought up in the culture of Rational Dissent, he assimilated the writings of the leading philosophers of the English and French Enlightenment to forge a political philosophy which was both new and revolutionary.

Godwin did not call himself an anarchist and understood the word 'anarchy' in the sense of disorder rather than as the positive state of freedom in the absence of government. Nevertheless, he still felt that even in its negative sense anarchy is preferable to despotism since it has a 'distorted and tremendous likeness, of true liberty' and 'awakens mind, diffuses energy and enterprize' through the community.[63] Like all subsequent anarchists, he made a fundamental distinction between society and government. Where the former grew out of mutual assistance and develops best when left unhindered, the latter originated in the errors of a few, is controlled by the rich, and checks improvement. Godwin saw the two as mutually opposed principles: government and authority are in stasis, while society and mind are in constant flux.

He therefore systematically rejected government and its coercive apparatus of standing armies, courts, and prisons. Although intended to suppress injustice, the effect of government has been to embody and perpetuate it. By concentrating the power of the community, it gives occasion to 'wild projects of calamity, to oppression, despotism, war and conquest'.[64] Its laws are primarily to defend inequality rather than to secure personal independence. Having encouraged robbery and defined crime, it then proceeds to punish deviants and tries to make them socially responsible by isolating them from society.

As for parliamentary democracy, Godwin thought it a sham. No one can be truly represented yet at elections the people are periodically asked to sign away their freedom. The practice of voting leads to the triumph of mediocrity and the tyranny of the majority. Truth, he insisted, cannot be decided by the casting of numbers. He therefore concluded that while the 'brute engine' of representative government may at present be a necessary evil, it is best when it governs least, and ultimately has 'mischiefs of various sorts incorporated with its substance' which are 'no otherwise removable than by its utter annihilation!'[65]

In place of government, Godwin proposed a decentralized and simplified society of independent face-to-face communities. In this pluralistic commonwealth, the basic unit would be the 'parish' or self-managing commune. Democracy would be direct and participatory so that the voice of reason could be heard. In a transitional period, there might be a need for popular juries to deal with injustices, and for a general assembly of the federated communes in times of emergency to organize defence or to arbitrate differences. But these would probably become superfluous as people grew used to governing themselves and would eventually give way to the spontaneously ordered society of anarchy. In his novels, he offered a glimpse of such a society with open families living simple but cultivated lives in harmony with nature.

Godwin believed that society is nothing more than an aggregate of individuals. At the same time, he maintained that man is a social being and that his best qualities are called forth by society. He therefore tried to establish the right balance between individual autonomy and collective living. He saw the growing threat of sclerotic institutions to personal independence and the danger of the individual losing himself in the arms and opinions of others. He knew the need for a 'sphere of discretion' or mental space for creative thought.[66] He therefore advocated that 'every man ought to rest upon his own centre, and consult his own understanding', and declared that co-operation is 'in some degree an evil'.[67]

The co-operation Godwin condemns, however, is the uniform group activity enforced by the division of labour or by those in power. Voluntary agreement and mutual aid, on the other hand, are the basis of his hopes for the future. Godwin's individualism does not exclude communal solidarity as John P. Clark suggests.[68] His whole system of ethics is inspired by a concern for others, while his novels show only too vividly the psychological and moral dangers of excessive solitude and isolation. In his regenerated society, there would be no conflict between autonomy and collectivity. Human beings would be at once more social and individual: 'each man would be united to his neighbour, in love and mutual kindness, a thousand times more than now: but each man would think and judge for himself'.[69] Godwin's anarchism is therefore closer to the communism of Kropotkin than the egoism of Stirner or the competition of Proudhon.

The political for Godwin is the personal. He saw an indissoluble connection between ethics and politics and recognized that political and economic change could only follow moral regeneration. He was as aware as Rousseau how modern society makes people wear masks and encourages them to appear what they are not. His characters in his novels are often tragically preoccupied with their reputation rather than with truth and conspicuously fail to communicate. Many of them actually resort to physical disguises to escape the tyranny of others. Society appears to be in a permanent state of civil war.

Godwin therefore first looked for a fundamental transformation in human relations. People should learn to free themselves from conceit, possession, and jealousy and allow others to be themselves and to follow their natural bent. At the same time, they should be ready to state their true feelings and opinions. In his cult of plain dealing and perfect sincerity, Godwin was trying to end unnecessary repression and release creative and intellectual energies. Above all, he felt that if our emotions were not checked, 'we should be truly friends with each other'.[70]

He also saw the practice of sincerity as an alternative to law in modifying the behaviour of others. But Godwin was careful to draw the dangers of mutual inspection and censorship and did not want to replace the oppression of government with the tyranny of public opinion. One should express one's view in a warm, affectionate, and sensitive way and always remember that every person is the ultimate judge of what he or she should do. Again, there is no tension between a sense of individuality and community: my neighbour may censure me freely and without reserve, but he should remember that 'I am to act by my deliberation and not his.'[71] Godwin remained a libertarian to the end.

Godwin's politics were ultimately based on the Greek notion of self-fulfilment. He also held firm to the classical liberal view that truth and enlightenment are achieved through pluralism and social diversity. But his own great contribution to political philosophy is the awareness of the inextricable connection between human happiness, freedom, rationality, and sincerity. By the intrepid deduction from first principles, he went beyond the radicalism of his age to become the first great theoretical exponent of anarchism and a major political thinker.

Like his politics, Godwin's economics are an extension of his ethics. He developed the labour theory of value to condemn the existing system of exploitation and to defend the right of the worker to the produce of his industry. While he was opposed to any enforced collectivization of wealth as an unacceptable interference with private judgment, he remained a communist. He argued that all property should be held in trust and distributed freely according to needs. He hoped that such voluntary distribution would lead to an equalization of conditions and that people would eventually be able to help themselves from a common storehouse.

In his view of population, Godwin correctly criticized the validity of Malthus's ratios. His general claim that an improvement in living standards would slow down rather than increase the growth in population seems to have been vindicated in advanced industrial societies. His advocacy of moral restraint and birth control has been widely adopted as the most suitable means to check population, and he rightly anticipated the potential of improved methods of agriculture in increasing the food supply. The problem still remains largely a question of the unequal distribution of resources rather than an excess in numbers.

Godwin wrote in the early days of the Industrial Revolution, and his vision of a free and equal society might appear essentially agrarian and atavistic. Individuals were to follow their inclinations and work at crafts or on the land, distributing freely rather than exchanging the surplus of their labour. Godwin, however, described the disastrous effects of 'accumulated property' or capital which turned society into warring classes of the rich and the poor and encouraged ruthless ambition and envy. He noted the close relationship between property and power. He was painfully aware of the alienation of the factory system in which men are reduced to machines.

But Godwin did not look back to some mythical Golden Age for a solution to this state of affairs. On the contrary, he looked forward to a more just and enlightened society in which the appropriate use of technology and science would increase leisure and personal independence. Although industrial development has so far tended to increase rather than diminish the division of labour, the new technology could potentially have the effect Godwin envisaged. His idea of an 'automatic plough', which so amused his contemporaries, has moreover been realized. And while mind may not yet be omnipotent over matter and the secret of immortality remains as elusive as ever, science has at least helped to eradicate disease and to prolong life considerably.

Having depicted a society torn by ideology and economic interest, Godwin did not appeal to class struggle but to gradual enlightenment and education. He was keenly aware of the authoritarian and repressive tendencies of revolutions. He also knew that means influence ends and that power cannot be used to abolish power. But he was no absolute pacifist. He countenanced the governmental use of coercion as a temporary expedient to maintain general security and in the final resort felt tyranny and violence should be resisted with force. Even so, it was always a confession of imbecility and never the proper means of enlightening the understanding. He preferred at all times a revolution in opinions rather than on the barricades.

Since he distrusted political parties, which make a part stand for the whole and seek to persuade by numbers, he advocated the formation of small, friendly circles of enlightened men and women who would coalesce into a wider movement. By cultivating sincerity and spreading truth, they would gradually undermine existing beliefs and practices and bring about the non-violent elimination of political institutions.

Although Godwin looked to an educated elite to act as catalysts, he is not the elitist Isaac Kramnick describes.[72] He did not believe that different social groups should be treated differently and rejected the notion that power should be related to intelligence. Unlike the French revolutionaries, he believed that all human beings, regardless of race or sex, are capable of improvement and self-government. And even if his firm faith in the ultimate triumph of truth was over-optimistic, he gave in his idea of loose groups of free and equal individuals the outline of all later anarchist organization.

Godwin counted on education and enlightenment as the best means of reform but it was not to be imposed by authoritarian teachers or political leaders. He saw in the newly proposed system of national education a more formidable alliance than Church and State, and correctly anticipated the dangers of totalitarian propaganda. Children, he insisted, should not be taught to venerate the commonwealth but truth. And since truth can be recognized only if it is made freely available and voluntarily acquired, he opposed any planned or centralized system of education.

While offering a radical critique of authority and punishment, he emphasized that learning should occur only through desire. Tutors should not inculcate a knowledge of facts but try to enlighten the understanding, develop the feelings, and cultivate the imagination. He attempted this with his own children and in the books he wrote for the Juvenile Library. He further encouraged small independent schools in which individual tuition could be tempered by social experience. He even suggested like the de-schoolers today that formal schooling does more harm than good and could be dispensed with altogether. Godwin thus became a pioneer of libertarian and progressive education.

Although he looked to education and enlightenment to bring about progress, Godwin did not think that it would be inevitable or sudden. He believed that there is a type of political society best adapted to every stage of improvement and suggested that the inequalities of property might perhaps constitute a state through which it is necessary to pass. But he is no histori-cist. He witnessed in history 'the appearance of flux and reflux' and thought progress could easily be reversed.[73] By perfectibility, moreover, he did not mean to imply that men would reach perfection, but that they have a progressive nature and are susceptible of perpetual improvement.

In fact, Godwin's sense of history was as developed as Burke's and his scholarship more painstaking. Although he saw history as philosophy teach-ing by examples and the highest form of history as biography, he tried to weigh the evidence impartially. His careful study of the past made him less optimistic about change than his fellow radicals who were inspired by the French Revolution. He did not rest his hopes on a cataclysmic upheaval but on the gradual reformation of the human personality which had been weighed down for centuries by superstition and ignorance. Far from being a mad incendiary, he interpreted the past in terms of slow, almost imper-ceptible progress and merely inferred that it would probably continue thus in the future.

Although Godwin's gradualism demonstrates that he is no naive utopian and is fully aware of the force of prejudice and habit, it gives a conservative turn to his practical politics. It left him with the dilemma of apparently abandoning generations to a life of suffering under a system of economic inequality and political authority, the disastrous effects of which he so eloquently portrayed. His reliance on informal enlightenment as a means of reform also throws up an inconsistency in his analysis of history. Throughout his work, he stressed how ideas and values are shaped by the environment, particularly by economic and political factors. He even admitted like Marx that the educator himself needs educating. But having demonstrated the interaction of ideas and circumstances, Godwin undialectically chose to tackle reform primarily in the realm of ideas instead of on both fronts. He was left with the problem that men cannot become wholly rational as long as government exists and yet government must exist while men remain irrational. It is a weakness in his system which he was unable to overcome.

While Godwin modified his philosophy as he grew older, he never abandoned his first principles and made the whole more coherent and subtle. His final essays were as vigorous as his first pamphlets. His lucid intelligence and penetrating argumentation improved rather than diminished with time. His philosophical style remained at once transparent, sinewy, and energetic. And while his histories could have been more disciplined and tighter, he was at his best in the imposed form of the essay.

In his fiction, however, Godwin showed a slow decline in old age. His three early novels were trials for his fledgeling wings, but in *Caleb Williams* he reached the height of his creative powers. He combined the sensibility of Richardson, the picaresque form of Cervantes, and his own doctrine of necessity to create a work of remarkable unity of spirit and design. The organic fusion of psychological insight, moral impetus, and historical narrative made it the best of the English Jacobin novels. It was not only the first thriller and psychological novel, but anticipates the anxieties of modern existentialism.

Although they reflected new tastes and different forms, Godwin did not change his theme in his five subsequent novels. An acutely sensitive hero, driven by ambition and honour, moves in tragic isolation from group to group in a series of disastrous adventures, until he is finally overwhelmed with guilt and remorse. No author, except perhaps Baudelaire, has dwelt so narrowly on one particular theme. But while his characters are crude compared with those of Jane Austen and his plots do not possess the coherence of Fielding, Godwin excelled in psychological drama. Inspired by myths and legends, his novels at their best have a profound mythic and symbolic power, and share the imaginative intensity of Poe.

*St. Leon* has more flowing eloquence than *Caleb Williams* but it lacks the dramatic interest. It still demonstrates how circumstances form character and mingles romance with social criticism, but there is more exploration of the feelings. This tendency culminated in *Fleetwood* which is a fully Roman-tic novel. But although Godwin made his style more evocative and subtle, he became too prolix and increasingly lost control of his form. Despite the prevailing gloom of *Mandeville*, it fails to achieve a unity of plot and character, and the meandering narrative is too often interrupted by tracts of moralizing. Godwin's last two novels are merely reworkings of earlier themes and situations and the disintegrating tendencies get the uppermost. The description of the mental states of his characters becomes too exagger-ated and mannered, and his women in particular are mere idealizations. Nevertheless, while *Caleb Williams* remains the pinnacle of Godwin's achievement, and there is a gradual decline thereafter in Godwin's imaginative powers, the later novels have been unduly neglected. Even so, he continued to experiment with different types of fiction and made a persistent attempt to discover an 'appropriate form'.[74] They are moreover undoubtedly worth reading for their compelling adventure, wild passion, and social comprehension.

As a man, Godwin was bold in theory but timid in life. The enforced isolation of his childhood, his painful experience of Calvinism, and the harsh treatment of his tutor, all combined to make him extremely nervous and sensitive to criticism. His concentrated studies only increased his spiritual agony. Although usually cheerful and even-tempered, he would suffer from bouts of depression which he believed were constitutional. His delicate health and fainting fits were undoubtedly symptoms of his inward struggle.

Behind the lucid precision of his style and logical firmness of his argu-ments, he was, as his novels and notes amply illustrate, full of self-doubt and guilt. He pulled God down from the heavens and stormed Church and State only to be horrified by his own boldness. His love of fame was the counterpart of his diffidence, and his cult of sincerity was in part a product of his social unease. It was precisely because Godwin had developed his reason to overcome the torture of his feelings that he appeared at once 'a cold formalist, and full of ardour and enthusiasm of mind'.[75] But it also meant that the dry logician could be a lover of the marvellous; the vigorous political philosopher, an imaginative writer of romances.

Despite the complexity of his character, Godwin attracted many friends. His simplicity, frankness and benevolence were well attested. He could be prickly but he bore no malice. His pedantry was tempered by a quiet sense of humour and an appreciation of irony. Although he was not a brilliant or expansive conversationalist, his original views, careful reasoning, and powerful insights drew the attention and sympathy of some of the greatest thinkers and artists of his day. There was something androgynous about him, and emancipated women in particular appreciated his understanding and manner. In many ways he was an authentic man in that he always tried to be honest and sincere. Far from dogmatic, he believed that moral rules should be abandoned in special cases. He welcomed confidence, and proved a great inspiration and help to many young disciples.

The greatest tragedy of Godwin's life was undoubtedly the death of Mary Wollstonecraft. For the first and last time, he met a woman who intimately shared his hopes and was ready to experiment in new forms of living. Under her influence, he began to lose his inhibitions and to become more fully himself. Unfortunately, her death blocked his further development and he was never able to overcome the loss. He increasingly looked for her idealized image in other women and created it in his fiction — a tendency which she would have been the first to stop. Persecution, obloquy and neglect followed soon after, and he spent the rest of his life in constant worry and chronic penury.

His second wife Mary Jane Clairmont proved a competent assistant in life's tasks but there was no real love between the two. Her jealousy and nagging tested his remarkable patience and only encouraged him to turn in on himself once again. Unlike Rousseau, he looked after his own and his step-children with great care and affection, and was deeply concerned with their education and well-being. His love was fully returned. And while he came to recognize that charity must begin at home, it never stopped there.

Godwin's involvement with the Juvenile Library proved the second great disaster in his life. It showed, however, his courage and stoicism in adversity rather than self-interest or double dealing. Crabb Robinson was right in that Godwin had 'no sense of *meum* and *tuum*', but Leslie Stephen's caricature of him as a 'venerable horseleech' is based on a misunderstanding of his philosophy.[76] Godwin believed that property is a trust which should be distributed according to need. He lent to those worse off when he could, and expected others to do the same. He may have been more on the receiving than the giving end, but this was a result of having a large family and an unsteady business rather than any personal profligacy. Indeed, he always lived in 'almost primitive simplicity' and had no expensive habits.[77]

Of all Godwin's actions, his harsh and importunate treatment of Shelley is perhaps the least excusable. Yet he took great pains to help his disciple and encouraged his moral and intellectual development. He was also deeply concerned about his daughters, and was misled by false promises of help. Shelley, for his part, often reacted to Godwin in love and hate as if he were a substitute father. If Godwin was unduly concerned about his reputation and over-insistent in his demands, Shelley was too impulsive and volatile. But whatever their respective failures, their financial dealings were at least in keeping with both their economic and moral views.

Godwin was not without his faults. His tenacity could easily be mistaken

XXXIV. Godwin, aged 76, by Sophia Gent, 1832.

for stubbornness, his moral fervour for priggishness, and his seriousness for dullness. He did not always know when to stop. In all his writings, he tended to dwell on one idea or push an argument to extremes. His resources of invention were not great: he modified rather than reconstructed his philosophy and developed rather than changed the basic formula in his novels.

Nevertheless, Godwin is a rare example of a man who excelled in both philosophy and literature: not only are his novels fused with ideas but his treatises are fired with feeling and imagination. He was never the cold, calculating rationalist of popular myth. As a contemporary wrote on his death:

> Godwin was versatile, he bore combin'd
> A woman's tenderness, a Cato's mind.
> Stern to himself, and rigidly severe,
> He play'd the stoic, while he shed the tear . . .[78]

A century and a half later, Godwin stands forth as an authentic human being, a truly creative writer, and one of the great humanists in the Western tradition.

# ABBREVIATIONS

## WORKS OF WILLIAM GODWIN

*P.J.*       *An Enquiry concerning Political Justice, and its influence on General Virtue and Happiness* (1793). In the second edition (1796) and in the third (1798), it was called *Enquiry concerning Political Justice, and its Influence on Morals and Happiness.* The third edition is referred to, unless otherwise stated.

*C.W.*       *Things as They Are; or, The Adventures of Caleb Williams* (1794). In the 1831 Bentley edition, Godwin changed the title to *Caleb Williams.*

*U.W.*       *Uncollected Writings (1785-1822)*, ed. Jack W. Marken and Burton R. Pollin (Gainesville, Florida, 1968).

## GENERAL

Ab. MSS.       Abinger Manuscripts.

B.L.       British Library.

D.W.L.       Dr. Williams's Library, London.

Paul       C. Kegan Paul, *William Godwin: His Friends and Contemporaries* (2 vols., 1876).

# NOTES

## NOTES TO INTRODUCTION

1. William Hazlitt, *The Spirit of the Age; or Contemporary Portraits* (1825) (Oxford, 1954), pp. 19–20.
2. Percy Bysshe Shelley to Godwin, 3 January 1812, *The Letters of Percy Bysshe Shelley*, ed. Frederick L. Jones (Oxford, 1964), I, 220.
3. Thomas de Quincey, *Collected Writings*, ed. David Masson (1897), III, 25.
4. Anton Menger, *The Right to the Whole Produce of Labour*, trans. M. E. Tanner, with an Introduction by H. S. Foxwell (1899), p.40.
5. Leslie Stephen, *History of English Thought in the Eighteenth Century* (New York, 1962), II, 238; 'William Godwin', *D.N.B.* (1890), XXII, 67.
6. Don Locke, *A Fantasy of Reason: The Life and Thought of William Godwin* (1980), p.349.
7. Ibid., p.352. See also my review in *Modern Language Review*, LXXVII, 4 (October 1982), 928–9.
8. Jean de Palacio, *William Godwin et son monde intérieur* (Lille, 1980), p.11. See also my review in *Etudes Anglaises*, XXXV, 3 (Juillet-Sept. 1982), 335–6.
9. *Thoughts on Man, his Nature, Productions and Discoveries* (1831), pp.260–1.
10. *Mandeville. A Tale of the Seventeenth Century in England* (1817), II, 282.
11. Ab. MSS.
12. *Thoughts on Man*, pp.239, 241.
13. Paul, I, 147.
14. *Thoughts on Man*, p.455.

## NOTES TO CHAPTER I

1. Anthony Lincoln, *Some Political & Social Ideas of English Dissent 1763–1800* (Cambridge, 1938), p.272.
2. Ab. MSS.
3. William Langford, *A Sermon occasioned by the Death of the Late Reverend Mr. Edward Godwin, preached at Little St. Helens, April 8, 1764* (1764), p. 30.
works, see the Appendix.
4. Ab. MSS. For a list of his works, see *Life and Times of Selina Countess of Huntingdon*, by a Member of the Houses of Shirley and Hastings (2nd edn. 1839), II, 371n.
5. Ab. MSS.
6. F. J. Gardiner, *History of Wisbech and Neighbourhood, during the last Fifty Years 1848–1898* (Wisbech, 1898), p.54.
7. See 'A Copy of a Manuscript Account of the Nonconformist Churches in Suffolk Compiled by the Rev'd Thomas Harmer of Wattisfield, with Additions (1774). Transcribed by Joseph Davey, December 1846'. D.W.L., Harmer MS. 76.1, ff.35–7.
8. See A. F. Thorpe, *Guestwick-Briston 1652–1952* (1952), p.2; C. Jolly, 'The Old Meeting House, Guestwick', *East Anglian Magazine*, XXXII (8 June 1973), 364–6.
9. See Naomi Riches, *The Agricultural Revolution in Norfolk* (Chapel Hill, 1937), p.238.
10. See *Guestwick Independent Church Book 1694–1854*, Norfolk Record Office, F.C.11/1.

11. Paul, I, 6.

12. See George Woodcock, *William Godwin: A Biographical Study* (1946), pp.6–7, 16–17.

13. See Palacio, *William Godwin et son monde intérieur*, op. cit., pp.30–1, 35.

14. Paul, I, 5.

15. Ibid., I, 9.

16. Ab. MSS.

17. Paul, I, 6.

18. Ann Godwin to William Godwin, 29 May 1788, Paul, I, 55.

19. *P.J.* (1793), I, 83.

20. Paul, I, 7.

21. Ann Godwin to William Godwin, 1798, Paul, I, 326.

22. Hannah Godwin to William Godwin, 29 May 1788, Paul, I, 55. Paul confused Godwin's sister Hannah with his niece Harriet (i.e. Joseph's daughter). For their identification, see *Shelley and his Circle*, ed. K. N. Cameron (Cambridge, Mass., 1961), I, 446–7.

23. See G. A. C., 'William Godwin', *Notes and Queries*, S.3., I (28 June 1862), 503. Today there is no trace of the Godwin family in the area.

24. Ann Godwin to William Godwin, 5 September 1792, Paul, I, 58.

25. Ab. MSS.

26. Paul, I, 7–8.

27. Ab. MSS.

28. Ibid.

29. Godwin to Percy Bysshe Shelley, 4 March 1812, Paul, II, 206.

30. Paul, I, 9.

31. Ab. MSS.

32. *Thoughts on Man*, p.143.

33. Ab. MSS.

34. Paul, I, 11.

35. See *The Enquirer. Reflections on Education, Manners, and Literature. In a Series of Essays* (1797), pp.153–4.

36. Ab. MSS.

NOTES TO CHAPTER II

1. See J. K. Edwards, 'The Economic Development of Norwich, 1750–1850, with Special Reference to the Worsted Industry' (unpublished Ph.D. thesis, University of Leeds, 1963), pp.87f.

2. See A. D. Bayne, *A Comprehensive History of Norwich* (1869), p.292.

3. See B. D. Hayes, 'Politics in Norfolk, 1750–1832' (unpublished Ph.D. thesis, University of Cambridge, 1957), pp.143f.

4. Ab. MSS.

5. See Bayne, *A Comprehensive History of Norwich*, op. cit., p.301.

6. See J. R. Burton, 'The Church over Water' (unpublished study, Norwich Central Library, 1976), IV, 651–72.

7. William Hull, 'A Brief Sketch of the Life and Character of the Rev'd Samuel Newton' in 'Church Book belonging to a Society of Christians who assemble at the Old Meeting House, Norwich, 1643–1839', *Norwich Old Meeting Congregational*, Norfolk Record Office, F.C. 19/1.

8. Ab. MSS.

9. Paul, I, 11.

10. *Thoughts on Man*, p.266.

11. *The Enquirer*, p.60.

12. Ab. MSS.

13. Cf. James Rieger, *The Mutiny Within: The Heresies of Percy Bysshe Shelley* (New York, 1967), pp.43–4.

14. *Mandeville*, I, 39, 150, 156.

15. Ab. MSS.

16. *Thoughts on Man*, pp.170–1.

17. Edward Baldwin (pseud.), *History of Greece* (1821), p.vii.

18. Note dated 18 November 1827, Ab. MSS.

19. For a list of Newton's works, see Hull, 'A Brief Sketch of the Life and Character of the Rev'd Samuel Newton', op. cit., Appendix.

20. See Newton to Godwin, 4 December 1793; 14 December 1793, Paul, I, 85–9.

21. Ibid., I, 13.

22. Newton, *The Leading Sentiments of the People called Quakers Examined* (1771), p.i.

23. For a biographical sketch of Sandeman, see his *Discourses on Passages of Scripture: with Essays and Letters*, ed. D.M. (2nd edn., Dundee, 1857), pp.v–xv.

24. See *The Causes and Reasons of the Present Declension among the Congregational Churches in London and the Country* (1766), pp.2–3, 49–61,

25. Hull, 'A Brief Sketch of the Life and Character of the Rev'd Samuel Newton', op. cit.

26. For a general account of the sect, see D. Bogue and J. Bennett, *History of Dissenters, from the Revolution in 1688, to the year 1808* (1812), IV, 107–25.
27. Ab. MSS.
28. *Essays Never Before Published* (1873), p.93.
29. Newton, *The Leading Sentiments of the People called Quakers Examined*, op. cit., p.222.
30. *C.W.*, pp.144, 305. Cf. B. J. Tysdahl, *William Godwin as Novelist* (1981), pp.160–1.
31. *Mandeville*, II, 51. Godwin's capital letters.
32. Ab. MSS.
33. *St. Leon: A Tale of the Sixteenth Century* (1799), IV, 252.
34. Bogue and Bennett, *History of Dissenters*, op. cit., IV, 119.
35. *Essays*, pp.123, 145.
36. Ab. MSS.
37. Paul, I, 359.
38. Hazlitt, *The Spirit of the Age*, op. cit., p.24. For a full account of the impact of Calvinism on Godwin, see my 'William Godwin: A Study of the Origins, Development and Influence of his Philosophy' (unpublished D.Phil. thesis, University of Sussex, 1976), ch. vi & vii.
39. Dated 10 March 1800, Ab. MSS.
40. Ibid.
41. Newton, *Syllabus of Christian Doctrines and Duties in the Catechetical Form* (Norwich, 1791), pp.iii, 162.
42. *P.J.* (1793), II, 833, 817.
43. Ab. MSS.
44. Sandeman, *Discourses on Passages of Scripture*, op. cit., p. vii.
45. *P.J.*, I, 59.
46. Ibid., I, ch. v.
47. Ab. MSS.
48. Newton, *A Letter to a Gentleman, containing an Account of the Terms and Manner of Admission into the Congregational Church at Norwich* (Norwich, 1775), p.6.
49. Hazlitt, *The Life of Thomas Holcroft*, (1816), ed. E. Colby (New York, 1968), II, 15–16.
50. *Letter of Advice to a Young American: on the Course of Studies it might be Most Advantageous for him to pursue* (1818), p.4.
51. Sandeman, *Discourses on Passages of Scripture*, op.cit., p.275.
52. *P.J.*, I, 313–14.
53. For Godwin's alleged indebtedness to Plato, see F. E. L. Priestley, 'Platonism in William Godwin's *Political Justice*', *Modern Language Quarterly*, IV (1943), 63–9.
54. Sandeman, *Discourses on Passages of Scripture*, op. cit., p.283.
55. *P.J.*, II, 3.
56. Bogue and Bennett, *History of Dissenters*, op. cit., IV, 113.
57. *P.J.*, II, 430.
58. Ibid., II, 429.
59. Ibid., II, 423.
60. Sandeman, *Discourses on Passages of Scripture*, op. cit., p.viii.
61. Newton to his congregation, March 1803, *Norwich Old Meeting Congregational*, op. cit.
62. *P.J.*, II, 429–30.
63. Ibid., II, 199.
64. Bogue and Bennett, *History of Dissenters*, op. cit., IV, 117.
65. Newton to Godwin, 4 December 1793, Paul, I, 85.
66. Godwin to Newton, n.d., Paul, I, 84.
67. See C. B. Jewson, *The Jacobin City: A Portrait of Norwich in its Reaction to the French Revolution 1788–1802* (1975), p. 137.
68. Godwin to Sergeant Lens, 24 September 1823, Paul, II, 287.
69. Paul, I, 12–13.
70. *Thoughts on Man*, p.268.
71. Newton to Godwin, 14 December 1793, Paul, I, 86–7.
72. Ab. MSS.
73. Ibid.
74. Ibid.

NOTES TO CHAPTER III

1. Joseph Priestley, *A Letter to the Right Honourable William Pitt* (1787), p.32.
2. See I. Parker, *Dissenting Academies in England* (Cambridge, 1914), pp.125–6.
3. *Proverbs*, XXII, 6.
4. Andrew Kippis, *A Sermon preached at the Old Jewry on 26th April, 1786, on occasion of a New Academical Institution* (1786), p.18.
5. *Memoirs of the Life of Gilbert Wakefield Written by Himself* (1792), p.366.

6. Priestley, *Autobiography* (1819), ed. J. Lindsay (Bath, 1970), p.76.

7. For Hoxton Academy, see H. McLachlan, *English Education under the Test Acts, being the History of the Non-conformist Academies, 1662–1820* (Manchester, 1931), pp.117–25.

8. Kippis, 'Doddridge', *Biographia Britannica; or, The Lives of the Most Eminent Persons who have flourished in Great Britain and Ireland* (1789), V, 283.

9. *Thoughts on Man*, p.333.

10. Paul, I, 355.

11. See Kippis, *Biographia Britannica*, op. cit., V, 283–4.

12. Ibid., V, 308.

13. See A. V. Murray, 'Doddridge and Education', *Philip Doddridge, 1702–51. His Contribution to English Education*, ed. G. F. Nuttall (1951), pp. 104–5.

14. Ab. MSS.

15. Edward Baldwin (pseud.), *The History of England* (1806), p.128.

16. Philip Doddridge, *A Course of Lectures on the Principal Subjects in Pneumatology, Ethics, and Divinity*, ed. S. Clark (1763), pp.121, 130.

17. Ab. MSS.

18. Doddridge, *Lectures*, op. cit., p.163.

19. Note dated 21 September 1799, Ab. MSS.

20. See *P.J.* (1793), I, 20.

21. See *Thoughts on Man*, Essays XII, XX, XXI.

22. Abraham Rees, *A Sermon preached at the Meeting-House, Westminster, on the 18th October 1795, upon the death of Rev. Andrew Kippis* (1795), p.38.

23. Kippis, 'Introductory Lectures to the Belles Lettres', D.W.L., Northampton MS. 69.6 f.1. The copies of these lectures were transcribed by Joseph Cornish, who signed them: 'New College, Hoxton, Decr. 21, 1769'.

24. Ab. MSS.

25. Paul, I, 355.

26. Ab. MSS.

27. See Godwin to Joseph Bevan, 27 April 1818, *Analectic Magazine*, XIV (1819), 238, (*U.W.* p.446).

28. Kippis, 'The History of Eloquence', D.W.L., Northampton MS. 69.6 f.12; 'A System of Chronology', ibid., f.116.

29. *P.J.*, I, 119.

30. *The Enquirer*, p.370.

31. Kippis, 'Notes on Professor Ward's System of Oratory', D.W.L., Northampton MS. 69.6 f.1.

32. Kippis, *Biographia Britannica*, op. cit., V, 307.

33. *The Enquirer*, pp.370, 480.

34. Ibid., p.374.

35. *P.J.*, I, 385.

36. *Mylius's School Dictionary of the English Language. To which is prefixed, A New Guide to the English Tongue by Edward Baldwin* (9th edn., 1819), pp.vii, lii–liii.

37. *The Enquirer*, p.47.

38. Paul, I, 355.

39. *Letter of Advice*, p.4.

40. Kippis, 'Introductory Lectures to the Belles Lettres', op. cit., f.15.

41. Kippis, 'A System of Chronology', op. cit., ff.115–16.

42. Paul, I, 361.

43. *Sketches of History, in Six Sermons* (1784), pp.67, 69.

44. 'Of Romance & History', Ab. MSS.

45. Ibid.

46. *P.J.*, I, 6; I, 457.

47. Ibid., I, 451.

48. *History of the Commonwealth of England* (1826), III, vi.

49. 'Of Romance & History', Ab. MSS.

50. *Letter of Advice*, p.9.

51. Paul, I, 15. Paul dates Godwin's 'autobiographical fragment' as 1800 (I, 2), but for its correct dating as 1808 or after, see Cameron, *Shelley and his Circle*, op. cit., II, 560–1.

52. Ab. MSS.

53. *The Herald of Literature; or, A Review of the Most Considerable Productions that will be made in the course of the ensuing Winter: With Extracts* (1784), p.86.

54. Andrew Baxter, *An Enquiry into the Nature of the Human Soul, wherein the Immateriality of the Soul is evinced from the Principles of Reason and Philosophy* (3rd ed., 1745), Summary of Contents.

55. Ab. MSS.

56. *Letter of Advice*, p.10.

57. Ab. MSS.

58. *P.J.*, I, 399–400, 400n.

59. Ab. MSS.

60. Ibid.

61. *P.J.*, I, 381n.

62. Ibid., I, 383.

63. Jonathan Edwards, 'Freedom of the Will,' *Works*, ed. P. Ramsey (New Haven, 1957), I, 370; *P.J.*, Bk.I, chap.v.

64. Priestley, *The Proper Objects of Education in the present State of the World: represented in a Discourse, delivered on Wednesday the 27th April, 1791* (1791), p.10.

65. *Gentleman's Magazine*, LXI (1791), 191.

66. Kippis, *A Sermon preached at the Old Jewry on the 26th April, 1786*, op.cit., pp.18, 9.

67. Rees, *The Advantages of Knowledge, illustrated and recommended in a Sermon, delivered on Wednesday the 30th April, 1788* (1788), p.31.

68. Paul, I, 14–15.

69. Ab. MSS.

70. Paul, I, 15.

71. Ibid., I, 16.

72. Joshua Toulmin, 'The Life of the Rev. Dr. Samuel Morton Savage', prefixed to his *Sermons on Several Evangelical and Practical Subjects* (Taunton, 1796), p.16.

73. Rees, *The Advantages of Knowledge*, op. cit., p.23.

74. Kippis, *An Address, delivered at the Interment of the late Rev. Dr. Richard Price, on the 26th of April, 1791* (1791), p.16.

75. Kippis, *A Sermon preached at the Old Jewry, on the 4th November, 1788, before the Society for commemorating the Glorious Revolution* (1788), p.25.

76. Kippis, *A Vindication of the Protestant Dissenting Ministers, with regard to their late Application to Parliament* (1722), p.26.

77. *P.J.*, II, 233.

78. Ibid., II, 331.

79. Ibid., II, 449.

80. Testimony, dated 25 May 1778, signed by Savage, Kippis, and Rees for Hoxton Academy and by Hugh Farmer and Thomas Taylor for the Coward Trust. Cameron, *Shelley and his Circle*, op. cit., I, 22–3.

81. *Thoughts on Man*, p.334.

82. *Mandeville*, I, 218.

83. Paul, I, 15; Ab. MSS.

84. *Damon and Delia. A Tale* (1784), p.103. The British Library has recently acquired the only known copy of this work and is publishing a facsimile reproduction of it.

85. Ab. MSS.

86. Paul, I, 16.


NOTES TO CHAPTER IV

1. *Sketches of History*, p.21.

2. Ibid., p.31.

3. Ibid., p.20.

4. Paul, I, 17.

5. Ibid., I, 17.

6. *Of Population: An Enquiry Concerning the Power of Increase in the Numbers of Mankind* (1820), p.233n.

7. Hazlitt, *The Life of Thomas Holcroft*, op.cit., II, 272.

8. Hazlitt, *The Spirit of the Age*, op. cit., pp.34–5.

9. Jonathan Edwards, *Two Dissertations* (Boston, 1765), p.117.

10. Ab. MSS.

11. Joseph Fawcett, *Sermons delivered at the Sunday-Evening Lecture, for the Winter-Season, at the Old Jewry* (1795), I, 144; Ab. MSS.

12. Fawcett, *The Art of War* (1795), p.7.

13. Ab. MSS.

14. Ibid.

15. Paul, I, 18.

16. Ibid., I, 19.

17. *The Enquirer*, p.291.

18. *P.J.*, II, 209n.

19. Godwin to Mary Hays, 2 September 1795, *The Love-Letters of Mary Hays, 1779–1780*, ed. A. F. Wedd (1925), p.231. For a fuller account of Swift's influence on Godwin, see J. A. Preu, *The Dean and The Anarchist* (Tallahassee, 1959).

20. Ab. MSS.

21. *P.J.*, II, 129n.

22. Godwin to Kippis (?), (March–April 1782), Cameron, *Shelley and his Circle*, op. cit., I, 31.

23. *Damon and Delia*, pp.103–5.

24. Godwin to Edmund Burke, 16 January 1783, in *The Correspondence of Edmund Burke*, ed. H. Furber and P. J. Marshall (Cambridge, 1965), V, 64.

25. *The History of the Life of William Pitt, Earl of Chatham* (1783), pp.x, xii.

26. Ibid., p.75.

27. Ibid., p.287.

28. Ibid., pp.141, 142.

29. *Gentleman's Magazine*, LIII (1783), 331.

30. *Critical Review*, LVIII (1783), 156; *Edinburgh Weekly Magazine*, LVII (1783), 277–9; *The New Annual Register for 1783* (1784), p.263.

31. Paul, I, 27.

32. Note dated 26 July 1811, Ab. MSS.

33. Ibid.

34. *A Defence of the Rockingham Party, in their Late Coalition with the Right Honourable Frederic Lord North* (1783), pp.3, 28.

35. Ibid., pp.13, 1.

36. Ibid., pp.33–4, 31.

37. See *Observations on a Pamphlet entitled, The Defence of the Rockingham Party* (1784); *Critical Review*, LV (1783), 405–6; *The New Annual Register for 1783* (1784), p.263.

38. *Monthly Review*, LXVIII (1783), 535; *London Magazine*, LII (1783), 243.

39. Godwin to Ann Godwin, n.d., Paul, I, 29.

40. Ab. MSS.

41. Hazlitt, *The Spirit of the Age*, op. cit., p.37.

42. *Thoughts on Man*, p.339.

43. Godwin to Ann Godwin, n.d., Paul, I.

NOTES TO CHAPTER V

1. *The Autobiography of Francis Place*, ed. M. Thrale (Cambridge, 1972), p.14.

2. G. S. Veitch, *The Genesis of Parliamentary Reform* (1913), p.68.

3. See M. D. George, *London Life in the Eighteenth Century* (New York, 1965), pp.380, 20n.

4. *An Account of the Seminary that will be opened on Monday the Fourth Day of August, at Epsom in Surrey, for the Instruction of Twelve Pupils in the Greek, Latin, French and English Languages* (1783), p.2.

5. Ibid., p.3.

6. Ibid., p.24.

7. Ibid., pp.48–9.

8. Ibid., p.37.

9. Ibid., pp.31–2.

10. Ibid., p.27.

11. Ibid., pp.46, 28.

13. *Monthly Review*, LXX (1784), 79.

14. *Gentleman's Magazine*, LIII (1783), 688.

15. Ab. MSS.

16. *Sketches of History*, pp.5, 20.

17. *English Review*, III (1784), 424–6; *European Magazine and London Review*, V (1784), 284–5.

18. *Monthly Review*, LXX (1784), 483–4.

19. *The Herald of Literature*, p.89.

20. Ibid., p.23.

21. Ibid., p.111.

22. Ibid., pp.106, 105.

23. *Critical Review*, LVII (1784), 24–6; *Monthly Review*, LXXI (1784), 69; *Gentleman's Magazine*, LIII (1783), 1037.

24. For Godwin's own account, see *The New Annual Register for 1784* (1785), pp.37–60. See also Marken, 'William Godwin's *Instructions to a Statesman*', *The Yale University Library Gazette*, IV (1959), 73–81.

25. *Instructions to a Statesman. Humbly inscribed to the Right Honourable George Earl Temple* (1784), p.16.

26. Ibid., pp.56–7.

27. Ibid., p.vi.

28. *Critical Review*, LVIII (1784), 70.

29. *Monthly Review*, LXX (1784), 70–1.

30. *Damon and Delia*, p.182.

31. Ibid., p.133. Cf. my 'Introduction' to *Damon and Delia* to be published by the British Library.

32. *English Review*, III (1784), 134.

33. *Critical Review*, LVII (1784), 473; *Westminster Magazine*, XII (1784), 380.

34. *Monthly Review*, LXXI (1784), 78.

35. *Italian Letters; or, The History of the Count de St. Julian* (1784), ed. Burton R. Pollin (Lincoln, Nebraska, 1965), p.4.

36. Ibid., p.12.

37. Ibid., pp.58–9.

38. Ibid., p.32.

39. Mary Shelley, quoted by Pollin, 'Introduction', *Italian Letters*, op. cit., p.xxxvi.

40. *Critical Review*, LVIII (1784), 211–13; *English Review*, IV (1784), 312.

41. *Monthly Review*, LXXI (1784), 386.

42. Mrs. Sothren to Godwin, 5 February 1796, Paul, I, 158.

43. *Gentleman's Magazine*, LV (1785), 117.

44. *Imogen: A Pastoral Romance. In Two Volumes. From the Ancient British* (1784), ed. J. W. Marken (New York, 1963), pp.21–3. Cf. I. Primer, 'Some Implications of Irony',

pp.118–21.

45. Ibid., p.47. In capitals in the original.

46. Ibid., p.25.

47. Ibid., p.35.

48. Ibid., p.46.

49. Cf. I. Kuczynski, 'Pastoral Romance and Political Justice', *Essays in Honor of William Gallacher* (Berlin, 1966), pp.105–6.

50. *Imogen*, p.52.

51. Ibid., p.67.

52. Ibid., pp.45, 83.

53. Ibid., p.59.

54. Ibid., p.83. Cf. Pollin, 'Primitivism in *Imogen*', ibid., p.117.

55. *Critical Review*, LVIII (1784), 312; *Monthly Review*, LXXII (1785), 234–5; *English Review*, IV (1784), 142.

56. L. A. H. de Cavitat, *An Early New York Library of Fiction* (New York, 1940), p.29.

57. Mary Shelley, quoted by Marken, 'Introduction', *Imogen*, p.18.

58. Paul, I, 47.

59. James Marshal to Godwin, 23 May 1784, Ab. MSS. Biographers have given Godwin's friend two 'ls', thinking Godwin dropped one as part of his programme to simplify spelling, but he signed himself 'Marshal' and Mary Shelley always referred to him as such.

60. Godwin to Joseph Priestley, ? 1785, Ab. MSS. For the articles on the Priestley controversy, see *English Review*, V (1785), 62–3, 105–24, 377–84; and for a commentary, see Martin Fitzpatrick, 'William Godwin and the Rational Dissenters', *The Price-Priestley Newsletter*, III (1979), 5–8.

61. Paul, I, 21.

62. Ab. MSS.

63. John Disney, *Memoirs of Thomas Brand Hollis* (1808), p.57.

64. Ab. MSS. There are over a hundred references to Barry in Godwin's diary from 1788 to 1805.

65. James Barry, 'A Letter to the Dilettante Society', *Works* (1809), II, 574.

66. *The New Annual Register for 1783* (1784), pp.172, 183. For Godwin's contributions, see also J. W. Marken, 'William Godwin's Writings for *The New Annual Register*', *Modern Language Notes*, LXVIII (1953), 477–9.

67. *The New Annual Register for 1783* (1784), p.187.

68. *The New Annual Register for 1784* (1785), pp.28, 65.

69. *The New Annual Register for 1790* (1791), p.75.

70. Ab. MSS.

71. Willis Webb to Godwin, 25 October 1787, Paul, I, 34.

72. Godwin to Richard Sheridan, 1786, Ab. MSS.

73. Godwin to Lord Holland, n.d., Ab. MSS.

74. For Godwin's identification as 'Mucius', see J. W. Marken, 'William Godwin and *The Political Herald, and Review*', *Bulletin of the New York Public Library*, LXV (1961), 517–33.

75. 'To the Right Honourable Edmund Burke', *The Political Herald, and Review*, I (December 1785), 329 (*U.W.*, p.17); 'To the Right Honourable William Pitt', ibid., II (May 1786), 246 (*U.W.*, p.32).

76. 'Memoirs of the Administration of the Government of Madras during the Presidency of Lord Macartney', ibid., III (September 1786), 82 (*U.W.*, p.61).

77. 'To the People of Ireland', ibid., III (November 1786), 26, 74 (*U.W.*, pp.52, 58).

78. Ibid., p.269 (*U.W.*, p.53).

79. 'To the Right Honourable William Pitt', ibid., II (May 1786), 242 (*U.W.*, p.28).

80. *History of the Internal Affairs of the United Provinces, from the year 1780, to the Commencement of Hostilities in June 1787* (1787), p. 332.

81. Ibid., p.345.

82. *English Review*, X (1787), 275; *The New Annual Register for 1787* (1788), pp.250–1.

83. Thomas Brand Hollis to Godwin, 10 January 1791, quoted by J. W. Marken, 'William Godwin's *History of the United Provinces*', *Philological Quarterly*, XLV (1966), 386.

84. Hannah Godwin to Godwin, 29 June 1784, Paul, I, 30–1.

85. Ab. MSS.

86. Paul, I, 25.

87. Thomas Holcroft to Godwin, 24 January 1800, Paul, II, 18.

88. Ab. MSS.

89. S. T. Coleridge to John Thelwall, 13 May 1796, *Collected Letters of Samuel Taylor Coleridge*, ed. E. L. Griggs (1956), I, 215.

90. Quoted by Thomas Ogle to Ralph Griffiths, 26 December 1792, Hazlitt, *The Life of*

*Thomas Holcroft*, op. cit., I, xxxiii.

91. Ab. MSS.

92. Ibid.

93. Thomas Holcroft, *The Family Picture; or, Domestic Dialogues on Amiable and Interesting Subjects; illustrated by Histories, Tales, Fables, Anecdotes, &c, intended to strengthen and inform the Mind* (1783), II, 209.

94. Holcroft to Godwin, 24 July 1788, Paul, I, 51.

95. Godwin to Holcroft, 5 August 1788, Paul, I, 54.

96. Paul, I, 37.

97. Ibid., I, 38–9.

98. Godwin to Thomas Cooper, 19 April 1790, Paul, I, 40.

99. William Dunlap, *A History of the American Theatre* (New York, 1832), pp.177, 182.

100. *The New Annual Register for 1788* (1789), p.42.

101. *An Abstract of the History and the Proceedings of the Revolution Society in London* (1789), p.14.

102. *The New Annual Register for 1788*, (1789), p.108.


NOTES TO CHAPTER VI

1. Ab. MSS.

2. Paul, I, 61.

3. Richard Price, *A Discourse on the Love of our Country* (1789), p.10.

4. Ibid., p.13.

5. Ibid., pp.49–50.

6. Paul, I, 62–3. Paul thought the address echoed Godwin's sentiments and style so closely that it was written by him.

7. Ab. MSS.

8. Godwin to Lord Robert Spencer, 24 January (? 1790), Ab. MSS.

9. Godwin to Sir Edward, n.d., B.L. Add. MS. 34,710 f.78.

10. Richard Watson to Godwin, 18 May 1790, Paul, I, 66. Locke (*A Fantasy of Reason*, op. cit., p.27), suggests this refers to an application made in 1787, but Godwin's diary records on 11 May 1790: 'Write to Watson & the abp.'; and on the 21st: 'Hear from Watson, read his letter to the abp'. Ab. MSS.

11. Ab. MSS.

12. *The New Annual Register for 1790* (1791), pp.74–5.

13. Godwin to Holcroft (?), n.d., Ab. MSS. M. Philp ('Godwin, Holcroft and the Rights of Man', in *Enlightenment and Dissent*, I (1982), 37–42) argues that the story of the committee is 'simply false' because Godwin did not know Paine at the time. Godwin's diary entries however cannot easily be dismissed and he later included in a list of his early works 'Paine's pamphlet, Feb. 22, 91', Ab. MSS. See also 'Godwin and the Publication of Thomas Paine's *Rights of Man*' in my thesis, op. cit., Appendix II, pp.352–4.

14. Holcroft to Godwin, n.d., Paul, I, 69.

15. For Godwin's account of his suicide, see *Tragical Consequences; or, A Disaster at Deal: being an unpublished letter of William Godwin, dated Wednesday, November 18th, 1789, and remarks thereon by Edmund Blunden* (1931).

16. Paul, I, 361.

17. Ab. MSS.

18. Paul, I, 76.

19. Ibid., I, 67.

20. *Of Population*, p. iv.

21. See Godwin's diary, Ab. MSS.

22. *P.J.*, (1793) I, viii, ix, x.

23. Godwin to Thomas Paine, 7 November 1791, Ab. MSS.

24. *Memoirs of the Author of a Vindication of the Rights of Woman* (1798), p.94.

25. Ibid., p.95.

26. *P.J.* (1793), I, 115.

27. Thomas Paine, *Common Sense* (1776), ed. I. Kramnick (Harmondsworth, 1976), p.65.

28. Paine, *The Rights of Man* (1791–2), ed. H. Collins (Harmondsworth, 1971), p.187.

29. For Godwin's references to James Mackintosh in his diary in 1792, see my thesis, op. cit., Appendix VI, p.362.

30. James Mackintosh, *Vindiciae Gallicae. Defence of the French Revolution and its English Admirers against the Accusations of the Right Hon. Edmund Burke; including some Strictures on the late Production of Mons. de Calonne* (2nd edn. 1791), p.116.

31. Ibid., p.307.

32. Ibid., pp.216–17.

33. For Godwin's references to Joel Barlow in his diary in 1792, see my thesis, op. cit., Appendix VII, p.363.

34. Joel Barlow, *Advice to the Privileged Orders in the Several States of Europe, resulting from the Necessity and Propriety of a General Revolution in the Principle of Government*, Part I (1792), p.116.

35. MS. of *Political Justice*, Vol. I, Victoria and Albert Museum Library, Forster MS. 222.

36. Godwin recorded in his diary that he wrote a 'memorial' of Nicholson on 19 June 1815, Ab. MSS.

37. For Godwin's references to William Nicholson in his diary from September 1791 to January 1793, see my thesis, op. cit., Appendix VIII, pp.364–5.

38. For Godwin's references to Holcroft in his diary at this time, see ibid., Appendix IX, pp.366–8.

39. Cf. John Binns, *Recollections of the Life of John Binns* (Philadelphia, 1854), p.54.

40. See *Monthly Review*, VI (1791), 324–9.

41. Hazlitt, *The Life of Thomas Holcroft*, op.cit., I, 284.

42. Ibid., II, 5.

43. Ibid., I, 299n.

44. See *Henry Crabb Robinson on Books and their Writers*, ed. E. J. Morley (1938), I, 3.

45. Holcroft, *Anna St. Ives* (1792), III, 156–7.

46. V. R. Stallbaumer, 'Holcroft's Influence on *Political Justice*', *Modern Language Quarterly*, XIV (1953), 25; *British Critic*, VI (1795), 315.

47. Quoted by Thomas Ogle to Ralph Griffiths, 26 December 1792, Hazlitt, *The Life of Thomas Holcroft*, op. cit., I, xxxii.

48. *P.J.* (1793), II, 862, 869, 872.

49. Holcroft, *Anna St. Ives*, op. cit., V, 56.

50. Godwin to Holcroft, n.d., Ab. MSS.

51. *P.J.* (1793), II, 850.

52. Holcroft, *Anna St. Ives*, op. cit., II, 25.

53. Ab. MSS.

54. *P.J.* (1793), I, 2.

55. Ibid., I, X; I, 166.

56. *Monthly Review*, X (1793), 312.

57. Holcroft, *The Adventures of Hugh Trevor* (1794–97), ed. S. Deane (1973), p.11.

58. Ab. MSS.

59. Paul, I, 71.

60. Elizabeth Inchbald to Godwin, 3 November 1792, Paul, I, 74.

61. Paul, I, 74.

62. Cf. Gwyn A. Williams, *Artisans and Sans-culottes: Popular Movements in France and Britain during the French Revolution* (1973), pp.70, 4.

63. Godwin to Thomas Erskine, n.d., quoted by Frederick Rosen, 'Progress and Democracy: William Godwin's Contribution to Political Philosophy' (unpublished Ph.D. thesis, University of London, 1965), Appendix C, pp.276–9.

64. Cf. *P.J.*, I, xi n.

65. 'To the Editor', *Morning Chronicle*, 1 February 1793 (*U.W.*, pp.112–14).

66. 'To Mr. Reeves', *Morning Chronicle*, 8 February 1793 (*U.W.*, p.116).

67. 'To Sir Archibald MacDonald, the Attorney General', *Morning Chronicle*, 26 March 1793 (*U.W.*, p.112).

68. 'To such Persons as may be appointed to serve upon Juries', *Morning Chronicle*, 30 March 1793 (*U.W.*, p.125).

69. *P.J.*, I, xi–xii.

## NOTES TO CHAPTER VII

1. Note dated 9 October 1832, Ab. MSS.

2. Note dated 10 October 1824, Ab. MSS.

3. *P.J.* (1793), I, 78. The first edition of *Political Justice* has continuous pagination throughout its two volumes.

4. Ibid., I, 306.

5. Ibid., I, ix.

6. Ibid., I, vii.

7. Ibid., I, 284n.

8. Ibid., I, 305.

9. Ibid., I, 286.

10. Ibid., I, 307.

11. Ibid., I, 320n.

12. Ibid., I, 319–20.

13. Ibid., II, 862, 869.

14. Ibid., II, 797.

15. Ibid., II, 502.

16. Ibid., I, 232.

17. Ibid., I, 58.

18. Ibid., I, 14, 12.

19. Ibid., I, 106, 105.

20. Ibid., I, 107.

21. Ibid., I, 5.

22. Ibid., I, 11.

23. Ibid., I, 325, 331.
24. Ibid., I, 343, 58.
25. Ibid., I, 57.
26. Ibid., I, 106.
27. Ibid., I, 324.
28. Ibid., Ibid., II, 889.
29. Ibid., II, 835; I, 254.
30. Ibid., I, 303.
31. Ibid., I, 63.
32. Ibid., I, 31; II, 453.
33. Cf. F. E. L. Priestley, 'Introduction' to the photographic facsimile of the third edition of *Political Justice* (Toronto, 1946), III, 18, 26.
34. *P.J.* (1793), I, vii, 80.
35. Ibid., I, 13.
36. Ibid., I, 121, 88.
37. Ibid., I, 98, 246.
38. Ibid., II, 766–7.
39. Ibid., II, 690.
40. Ibid., I, 314.
41. Ibid., I, 304.
42. Ibid., I, 309.
43. Ibid., I, 313.
44. Ibid., I, 311.
45. Ibid., I, 316–17.
46. Ibid., I, 121.
47. Ibid., I, 1–2.
48. Ibid., II, 801.
49. Ibid., II, 851.
50. Ibid., II, 852.
51. Ibid., I, 364; II, 833.
52. Ibid., I, 364.
53. Ibid., II, 796; I, 87.
54. Ibid., I, 117.
55. Ibid., I, 116.
56. Ibid., I, 151.
57. Ibid., I, 163.
58. Ibid., II, 796.
59. Ibid., I, 83.
60. Ibid., I, Cf. I, 253.
61. Ibid., II, 840.
62. Ibid., I, 171.
63. Ibid., I, 174.
64. Ibid., I, 238.
65. Ibid., I, 280.
66. Ibid., I, 242.
67. Hazlitt, *The Spirit of the Age*, op. cit., p.25.
68. *P.J.* (1793), I, 2.
69. Ibid., II, 856, 675.
70. Ibid., I, 241.
71. Ibid., I, 3, 237.
72. Ibid., I, 19.
73. Ibid., I, 79.
74. Ibid.
75. Ibid., I, 90.
76. Ibid., II, 583, 572.
77. Ibid., I, 157, 158.
78. Ibid., I, 162.
79. Ibid., I, 166.
80. Ibid., I, 2.
81. Ibid., I, 37.
82. Ibid., I, 32.
83. Ibid., I, 186.
84. Ibid., I, 182.
85. Ibid., II, 434.
86. Ibid., II, 458.
87. Ibid., II, 474.
88. Ibid., II, 487.
89. Ibid., II, 494.
90. Ibid., II, 553.
91. Ibid., II, 685.
92. Ibid., II, 571.
93. Ibid., II, 596–7.
94. Ibid., II, 603.
95. Ibid., II, 601.
96. Ibid., II, 621.
97. Ibid., II, 667–8.
98. Ibid., II, 689.
99. Ibid., II, 704.
100. Ibid., II, 694, 714.
101. Ibid., II, 734.
102. Ibid., II, 771.
103. Ibid., II, 720.
104. Ibid., II, 766–7.
105. Ibid., II, 752.
106. Ibid., II, 699.
107. Ibid., II, 653.
108. Ibid., II, 575.
109. Ibid., II, 576.
110. Ibid., II, 578–9.
111. Ibid., II, 809; 802.
112. Ibid., I, 35.
113. Ibid., II, 791.
114. Ibid., II, 857.
115. Ibid., II, 810.
116. Ibid., I, 71–2.
117. Ibid., II, 845.
118. Ibid., II, 813.
119. Ibid., I, 240.
120. Ibid., II, 565.
121. Ibid., II, 708.

122. Isaac Kramnick, 'Introduction', *Political Justice* (Harmondsworth, 1976), p.26.

123. *P.J.* (1793), II, 844.

124. Ibid., II, 845.

125. Ibid., II, 849.

126. Ibid., II, 850.

127. Ibid., II, 851.

128. Ibid., II, 856.

129. Clark, *The Philosophical Anarchism of William Godwin*, op. cit., p.84; Kramnick, 'Introduction', *Political Justice*, op. cit., p.52.

130. *P.J.* (1793), II, 854.

131. Ibid., I, x.

132. Ibid., I, 186.

133. Ibid., I, 69.

134. Ibid., I, 216.

135. Ibid., I, 208.

136. Ibid., I, xii.

137. Ibid., I, 203.

138. Ibid., I, 240.

139. Ibid., I, 207.

140. Ibid., II, 509.

141. Ibid., II, 831.

142. Stephen, *English Thought in the Eighteenth Century*, op. cit., II, 224.

143. *P.J.* (1793), II, 732.

144. Ibid., II, 774, 733.

145. Ibid., II, 738.

146. Ibid., II, 739.

147. Ibid., II, 826.

148. Ibid., I, xi.

149. Ibid., II, 894.

150. Ibid., I, xiii.

## NOTES TO CHAPTER VIII

1. Quoted by Ford K. Brown, *The Life of William Godwin* (1926), p.58.

2. John Fenwick, 'William Godwin', *Public Characters of 1799–1800* (1799), p.374.

3. Godwin to the National Convention, 26 January 1793, *Procès-Verbal de la Convention Nationale* (Paris, 1793), IX, 196–7.

4. See Godwin to John Fenwick, 15 February 1793, Cameron, *Shelley and his Circle*, op. cit., I, 117.

5. See Jean de Palacio, 'La fortune de Godwin en France. Le cas d'Elizabeth Hamilton', *Revue de Littérature Comparée*, XLI (1967), 321–41.

6. Henry Crabb Robinson, *Crabb Robinson in Germany 1800–1805*, ed. E. J. Morley (1929), p.135. For Constant's view of Godwin, see Godwin, *De la justice politique*, trans. B. Constant, ed. B. R. Pollin (Québec, 1972), 'Introduction', pp.27–47.

7. See Georg Forster to Theresa Forster, 23 July 1793, Max Nettlau, *Der Vorfrühling der Anarchie* (Berlin, 1925), p.72.

8. Henry Crabb Robinson to Thomas Robinson, 15 September 1802, Crabb Robinson Correspondence, D.W.L., MS. 1802 3A 26, 4.

9. See B. R. Pollin, 'Godwin's Letter to Ogilvie, Friend of Jefferson, and the Federalist Propaganda', *Journal of the History of Ideas*, XXVIII (1967), 432–44.

10. Benjamin Silliman, *Letters of Shah-Coolen, A Hindu Philosopher, residing in Philadelphia; to his Friend, El Hassan, an Inhabitant of Delhi* (Boston, 1802), p.14; *The Theories of Modern Philosophy in Religion, Government and Morals, contrasted with the Practical System of New England* (Hartford, 1802), pp.7–8.

11. *Monthly Review* X (1793), 311–20; X (1793), 435–45; XI (1793), 187–96.

12. See *Analytical Review*, XVI (1793), 121–30; XVI (1793), 388–404.

13. *The New Annual Register for 1793* (1794), pp.218–19.

14. *Literary and Biographical Magazine and British Review* X (1793), 224–6; X (1793), 306–10.

15. *Critical Review* VII (1793), 361–72; VIII (1793), 290–6; IX (1793), 149–54.

16. *British Critic* I (1793), 307–18.

17. Mary Shelley (Paul, I, 80) claims that *Political Justice* sold for three guineas but it was in fact for £1 16s 0d (see *Analytical Review*, xvi (1793), 121; *British Critic*, I (1793). 309).

18. Fenwick, *Public Characters*, op. cit., p.364.

19. See H. D. Symonds, *Manual of Liberty; or, Testimonies on behalf of the Rights of Mankind* (1795), pp.4–5, 46–7, 80–2, 87, 121–2, 177–8, 238–9, 292–3, 283–8; Thomas Spence, *Pig's Meat, or Lessons for the Swinish Multitude* I (1793), 200–1, 219–20; II (1794), 137–9, 188–94; and Daniel Isaac Eaton, *Politics for the People: or, A Salmagundy for Swine* I, 6 (1793), 86–9; I, 12 (1793), 168–72; II, 5

(1794), 6–7.

20. See M. D. George, *Catalogue of Prints and Drawings in the British Museum* (1942), VII, 502–3.

21. William Hamilton Reid, *The Rise and Dissolution of the Infidel Societies in this Metropolis* (2nd edn., 1800), pp.32, 116.

22. Paul, I, 118.

23. Note dated 23 March 1793, in Godwin's 'Supplement to Journal', Paul, I, 116.

24. Samuel Newton to Godwin, 4 December 1793, Paul, I, 85.

25. Gilbert Wakefield, *A Letter to William Wilberforce* (1797), pp.64–5.

26. Paul, I, 116.

27. Robert Bisset, *The Life of Edmund Burke* (2nd edn., 1800), II, 429.

28. Paul, I, 80. For the real price see n.17.

29. For Horseman and his friends Stoddart and Dibdin, see A. Koszul, 'Un disciple inconnu de Godwin', *Etudes Anglaises*, VI '1953), 239–49.

30. *Henry Crabb Robinson on Books and their Writers*, op. cit., I, 3; Crabb Robinson to William Pattison, 25 April 1795; ibid., III, 841; *Cambridge Intelligencer* CVII (1975), 4.

31. Charles Lloyd and Charles Lamb, *Blank Verse* (1798), p.11n.

32. Arthur H. Houston, *Daniel O'Connell: His Early Life, and Journal, 1795–1802* (1906), pp.107, 119, 102.

33. F. W. Hackwood, *William Hone; His Life and Times* (1912), p.51.

34. Godwin to Francis Place, 11 September 1814, Graham Wallas, *The Life of Francis Place 1771–1854* (1898), p.60; John Thelwall, *The Tribune*, II (1796), vii.

35. See Robert Southey to Horace Walpole Bedford, 12 December 1793, *New Letters of Robert Southey*, ed. Kenneth Curry (New York, 1965), I, 40.

36. Southey to Grosvenor Charles Bedford, 27 September 1794, ibid., I, 79.

37. Southey to Thomas Southey, 6 November 1794, ibid., I, 86.

38. Coleridge to Godwin, 29 March 1811, *Collected Letters*, op. cit., III, 316.

39. Southey to Grosvenor Bedford, 1 October 1795, *The Life and Correspondence of Robert Southey*, ed. Cuthbert C. Southey (1849), I, 247.

40. Southey to Grosvenor Bedford, 21 November 1795, ibid., I, 256.

41. Southey to Grosvenor Bedford, 26 June 1796, ibid., I, 282.

42. Southey to John Rickman, July 1805, *New Letters*, I, 389.

43. *The Notebooks of Samuel Taylor Coleridge*, ed. Kathleen Coburn (1957), I, 1658.

44. Southey to William Taylor, 12 March 1799, *The Life and Correspondence of Robert Southey*, op. cit., II, 13.

45. Samuel Taylor Coleridge, 'To William Godwin, Author of "Political Justice"', *Poetical Works*, ed. Ernest H. Coleridge (1969), p.86.

46. Coleridge to Southey, 13 July 1794, *Collected Letters*, op. cit., I, 86.

47. Coleridge to Southey, 11 September 1794, ibid., I, 102.

48. Coleridge to Southey, 21 October 1794, ibid., I, 115.

49. See Coleridge, *Notebooks*, op. cit., I, 81n.

50. Coleridge to James Perry, 5 February 1818, *Collected Letters*, op. cit., IV, 830n. Coleridge's memory is not entirely accurate here, for he had read Godwin in October 1794 before their meeting.

51. Coleridge to Southey, 17 December 1794, ibid., I, 138.

52. Coleridge to John Thelwall, 13 May 1796, ibid., I, 215.

53. Coleridge, 'A Moral and Political Lecture', *The Collected Works of Samuel Taylor Coleridge*, ed. L. Patton and P. Mann (1971), I, 12–13.

54. Coleridge, 'A Political Lecture at Bristol, 1795', *The Friend*, ibid., IV, 1, 334, 338.

55. Coleridge, *Conciones ad Populum* (1795), ibid., I, 46.

56. See Coleridge, *Lectures on Revealed Religion, its Corruption and Political Views* (1795), ibid., I, 164 and note, 228 and note.

57. Coleridge, *Notebooks*, op. cit., I, 174 (16).

58. Coleridge to Thelwall, 13 May 1796, *Collected Letters*, op. cit., I, 214.

59. Coleridge to Thelwall, 22 June 1796, ibid., I, 221.

60. Coleridge, 'Modern Patriotism', *The Watchman*, *Works*, op. cit., II, 99–100.

61. 'Caius Gracchus' to the Editor of the *Bristol Gazette*, 24 March 1796, quoted in *Collected*

*Letters*, I, 197–8n; Coleridge to 'Caius Grac-chus', 2 April 1796, ibid., I, 200.

62. Coleridge to Thelwall, 13 May 1796, ibid., I, 212. Thelwall's letter, which Col-eridge quotes, is lost.

63. Coleridge to Benjamin Flower, 2 November 1796, ibid., I, 247.

64. Coleridge to Thelwall, 13 November 1796, ibid., I, 253.

65. Coleridge to Flower, 11 December 1796, ibid., I, 267–8.

66. Coleridge to Thelwall, 6 February 1797, ibid., I, 306.

67. Coleridge, *Notebooks*, op. cit., I, 621.

68. Paul, I, 17.

69. Coleridge to Godwin, 29 March 1811, *Collected Letters*, op. cit., III, 315.

70. Coleridge to Godwin, 26 March 1811, ibid., III, 313–14.

71. Coleridge, *Notebooks*, op. cit., I, 910.

72. Hazlitt, 'Memorabilia of Mr. Coleridge', *The Round Table, Complete Works*, ed. P. P. Howe (1934), XX, 216–17.

73. Coleridge, 'The Landing Place', *The Friend, Works*, op. cit., IV, 1, 156.

74. 'On Genius and Novelty', ibid., p.108.

75. Cf. Lucyle Werkmeister, 'Coleridge and Godwin on the Communication of Truth', *Modern Philology*, LV (1958), 170–7.

76. Cf. Priestley, 'Introduction', *Political Jus-tice*, op. cit., III, 105–6.

77. For an opposing view, see C. W. Roberts, 'The Influence of Godwin on Wordsworth's *Letter to the Bishop of Llandaff*', *Studies in Philology*, XXIX (1932), 588–606.

78. William Wordsworth to William Mathews, 8 June 1794, *The Letters of William and Dorothy Wordsworth; The Early Years 1787–1805*, ed. E. de Selincourt, revised by Chester L. Shaver (Oxford, 2nd edn., 1967), pp.124–5.

79. *P.J.* (1793), II, 735–6; Wordsworth to Mathews, 8 June 1794, *Letters*, op. cit., p.125. Cf. C. W. Roberts, 'Wordsworth, *The Philan-thropist* and *Political Justice*', *Studies in Philol-ogy*, XXXI (1934), 84–91.

80. Wordsworth to Francis Wrangham, 20 November 1795, *Letters*, op. cit., p.159.

81. Cf. Stephen C. Gill, 'Adventures on Salisbury Plain and Wordsworth's Poetry of Protest 1795–1797', *Studies in Romanticism*,

XII (1972), 48–65.

82. Ab. MSS.

83. Hazlitt, *The Spirit of the Age*, op. cit., p.20.

84. Basil Montagu to R. J. Mackintosh, n.d., *Memoirs of the Life of the Right Honourable Sir James Mackintosh*, ed. R. J. Mackintosh (1835), I, 149–50.

85. Wordsworth, *The Prelude*, ed. E. de Selincourt (1969), Bk.X, ll.820–30.

86. Ibid., ll.808–9, 818, 876–7, 879.

87. Ibid., l.900.

88. Ibid., ll.890–9. Cf. Alan Grob, 'Word-sworth and Godwin: A Reassessment', *Studies in Romanticism*, VI (1966), 111–13.

89. Ernest de Selincourt, 'Preface to Word-sworth's *Borderers*', *The Nineteenth Century*, C (1926), 731, 733.

90. Wordsworth, *Poetical Works*, ed. T. Hutchinson, rev. E. de Selincourt (1969), p.50.

91. Cf. Robert Osborn, 'Meaningful Obscur-ity: The Antecedents and Character of Riv-ers', *Bicentenary Wordsworth Studies*, ed. J. Wordsworth (1970), pp.403–11. Rivers was called Oswald in the final draft of 1842.

92. Wordsworth, *The Prelude*, op. cit., Bk.XI, ll.124, 135–7.

93. Ibid., Bk.X, ll.667–70.

94. Wordsworth, *Poetical Works*, op. cit., pp.734–5.

95. Ibid., p.444, ll.98–101.

96. Ibid., p.18, ll.60–4. Cf. Mary Jacobus, *Tradition and Experiment in William Word-sworth's Lyrical Ballads (1798)* (Oxford, 1976), p.22.

97. Wordsworth to Charles James Fox, 14 January 1801, *Letters*, op. cit., p.315.

98. Wordsworth to William Mathews, 21 March 1796, ibid., pp.170–1.

99. Geoffrey Little, 'An Incomplete Words-worth Essay upon Moral Habits', *Review of English Literature*, II (1961), 11–13.

100. Locke (*A Fantasy of Reason*, op. cit., p.90) is clearly mistaken in asserting that Wordsworth was 'never an acolyte'.

101. Wordsworth to Coleridge, 24–27 December 1799, *Letters*, op. cit., pp.276–7.

102. Wordsworth, *The Prelude*, op. cit., Bk.X, ll.840–3.

103. *Thoughts on Man*, p.337.

104. Paul, I, 123.

105. Godwin to Joseph Gerrald, 23 January 1794, ibid., I, 126–8.

106. *The Trial of Joseph Gerrald* (Edinburgh, 1794), p.232.

107. Cf. E. P. Thompson, *The Making of the English Working Class* (Harmondsworth, 1970), p.141.

108. *American Universal Magazine*, II (1797), 161–2.

109. See Godwin to Charles Sinclair, 15 December 1794, Rosen, 'Progress and Democracy', op. cit., Appendix E, pp.284–5.

110. *The Charge delivered by the Right Honourable Sir James Eyre* (1794), p.12 (*U.W.*, p.140).

111. *Cursory Strictures on the Charge delivered by Lord Chief Justice Eyre to the Grand Jury, October 2, 1794* (1794), p.10 (*U.W.*, 154).

112. Ibid., p.14 (*U.W.*, p.158).

113. Ibid., p.22 (*U.W.*, p.166). For Mary Shelley's interesting analysis of the pamphlet, see Paul, I, 129–33.

114. Quoted by Brown, *The Life of William Godwin*, op. cit., p.95.

115. *Answer to Cursory Strictures on a Charge delivered to the Grand Jury, October 2, 1794, by Lord Chief Justice Eyre. Said to be written by Judge Thumb* (1794), p.2 (*U.W.*, p.178).

116. Ibid., p.7–8 (*U.W.*, p.183–4).

117. *A Reply to an Answer to Cursory Strictures, supposed to be wrote by Judge Buller, by the Author of Cursory Strictures* (1794), pp.4–5 (*U.W.*, pp.188–9).

118. Ibid., pp.5, 6 (*U.W.*, pp.189, 90).

119. Godwin to Mrs. Holcroft, 9 October 1794, Ab. MSS.

120. See Holcroft to Godwin, 24 November 1794, Hazlitt, *The Life of Thomas Holcroft*, op. cit., II, 60–1.

121. Godwin to Sir James Eyre, n.d., Ab. MSS.

122. Hazlitt, *The Spirit of the Age*, op. cit., p.34.

123. Dr. Samuel Parr to Godwin, 10 November 1794, Paul, I, 137.

124. Paul, I, 147.

125. Charles Cestre, *John Thelwell* (1906), p.131; John Thelwall, *The Tribune*, II (1796), viii.

126. Cf. B. Sprague Allen, 'William Godwin's Influence on John Thelwall', *Publications of the Modern Language Association*, XXXVII (1922), 662–82.

127. Cf. Thompson, *The Making of the English Working Class*, op.cit., pp.175–6.

128. Godwin to Thelwall, 18 September 1794, Cestre, *John Thelwall*, Ibid., pp.201–2.

129. Mrs. Thelwall, *Life of John Thelwall* (1837), p.367.

130. See *The Autobiography of Francis Place*, op.cit., pp.136–7, 143, 217–18.

131. Place, B.L. Add. MS. 35, 143, f.15.

132. Place, B.L. Add. MS. 27, 815, f.165.

133. Thompson, *The Making of the English Working Class*, op.cit., p.158.

134. *Considerations on Lord Granville's and Mr. Pitt's Bills, concerning Treasonable and Seditious Practices, and Unlawful Assemblies, by a Lover of Order* (1795), p.1 (*U.W.*, p.195).

135. Ibid., p.83 (*U.W.*, p.277).

136. Ibid., p.17 (*U.W.*, p.211); p.21 (*U.W.*, p.215).

137. Ibid., p.21 (*U.W.*, p.215).

138. Ibid., pp.17–18 (*U.W.*, pp.211–12). Isaac Kramnick wrongly asserted that Godwin was 'defending Pitt' in his attack on Thelwall, 'On Anarchism and the Real World: William Godwin and Radical England', *American Political Science Review*, LXVI (1972), 125. See John P. Clark's reply, 'On Anarchism in an Unreal World: Kramnick's View of Godwin and the Anarchists', ibid., LXIX (1975), 162–7. Kramnick continued to misrepresent Godwin as repudiating 'reform politics' in his edition of *Political Justice*, op. cit., p.33.

139. *Considerations on Lord Grenville's and Mr. Pitt's Bills*, op. cit., p.22 (*U.W.*, p.216).

140. Thelwall to Godwin, 28 November 1795, Cestre, *John Thelwall*, op. cit., pp.137–8.

141. Godwin to Thelwall, 28 November 1795, ibid., p.203.

142. Godwin to Thelwall, 29 November 1795, ibid., p.204.

143. See Thelwall, *The Tribune* (1796), II, xv.

144. See Godwin to Thelwall, *The Tribune*, III (1796), 101–13.

145. See *The Tribune*, III (1796), 103–5.

146. See Coleridge to Thelwall, 13 May 1796, *Collected Letters*, op. cit., I, 212–13.

Coleridge quotes Thelwall's letter which is lost.

147. Thomas Amyot to Henry Crabb Robinson, 16 August 1796, Crabb Robinson Correspondence, D.W.L., MS. 1796, 78, 2.

NOTES TO CHAPTER IX

1. Paul, I, 79.
2. Ibid., I, 77.
3. Ibid., I, 78.
4. Dunlap, *A History of the American Theatre*, op. cit., p.182.
5. Amelia Alderson to Mrs. Taylor, 1794, Cecilia Lucy Brightwell, *Memorials of the Life of Amelia Opie* (Norwich, 2nd edn., 1854), p.42.
6. Paul, I, 82–3.
7. Godwin to George Robinson, 29 March 1793, Ab. MSS.
8. Paul, I, 78.
9. *C.W.*, Appendix II, p.338.
10. Note dated 10 October 1824, Ab. MSS.
11. *C.W.*, p.337.
12. Tysdahl (*William Godwin as Novelist*, op.cit., p.3) claims that *Caleb Williams* is 'one of the most profoundly ambiguous novels in the English language'.
13. *C.W.*, p.339.
14. Ibid., p.2.
15. Ibid., p.303. Cf. P. N. Furbank, 'Godwin's Novels', *Essays in Criticism*, V (1955), 217–18.
16. Cf. Rudolph F. Storch, 'Metaphors of Private Guilt and Social Rebellion in Godwin's *Caleb Williams*', *English Literary History*, XXXIV (1967), 189–90, 194–5.
17. *C.W.*, p.340.
18. Ibid., p.3.
19. Ibid., p.96.
20. Ibid., p.107.
21. Ibid., p.251.
22. Ibid., p.340.
23. Ibid., p.146.
24. *P.J.*, I (1793), I, 176–7.
25. 'Of History & Romance', Ab. MSS.
26. *C.W.*, p.1.
27. Ibid., p.326. Cf. Jean de Palacio, 'William Godwin, Ariosto, and the Grand Tour; or *Caleb Williams* Reconsidered', *Revista di Litterature Moderne e Comparate*, XXIII (1970),

111–20.
28. Cf. David McCracken, '*Godwin's Caleb Williams*: A Fictional Rebuttal of Burke', *Studies in Burke and his Time*, XI (1969–70), 1446–52. Marilyn Butler ('Godwin, Burke and *Caleb Williams*', *Essays in Criticism*, XXXII (1982), 252) also identifies Falkland as Burke and suggests that the novel is 'about hierarchy'.
29. *C.W.*, p.159.
30. Ibid., p.114.
31. Ibid., p.340.
32. Cf. B. R. Pollin, 'The Significance of Names in the Fiction of William Godwin', *Revue des Langues Vivantes*, XXXVIII (1971), 390–1.
33. Cf. Gary Kelly, *The English Jacobin Novel, 1780–1805* (Oxford, 1976), p.207.
34. *British Critic*, IV (1794), 70.
35. Ibid., VI (1795), 94.
36. *C.W.*, p.73.
37. Ibid., pp.277–8.
38. Ibid., p.181. Godwin refers in his footnote to the reformer John Howard, *The State of the Prisons in England and Wales 1777–80* (4th edn. 1792).
39. *C.W.*, p.210.
40. Ibid., pp.332, 4.
41. Cf. D. Gilbert Dumas, 'Things as They Were: The Original Ending of *Caleb Williams*', *Studies in English Literature*, VI (1966), 593.
42. *C.W.*, p.310.
43. Ibid., p.323.
44. Ibid., p.325.
45. Ibid., pp. 338–9. See also James Marshal to Godwin, 31 May 1793, Paul, I, 90.
46. *C.W.*, p.339.
47. Elizabeth Inchbald to Godwin, n.d., Paul, I, 139.
48. *C.W.*, p.341.
49. *Henry Crabb Robinson on Books and their Writers*, op. cit., I, 345.
50. Anna Seward to M. Powys, 1 June 1796, *The Letters of Anna Seward*, ed. Archibald Constable (1811), IV, 211.
51. See *British Critic*, IV (1794), 70.
52. *Analytical Review*, XXI (1795), 166; *Monthly Review*, XV (1794), 149.
53. See *Critical Review*, XI (1794), 290–6.
54. Hazlitt, *The Spirit of the Age*, op. cit., p.32.

55. Ab. MSS.

56. Mackintosh, Review of *The Lives of Edward and John Philips, Edinburgh Review*, XXV (1815), p.486.

57. *Henry Crabb Robinson on Books and their Writers*, op. cit., I, 377.

58. See B. Sprague Allen, 'William Godwin and the Stage', *Publications of the Modern Language Association*, XXXV (1920), 358–74.


NOTES TO CHAPTER X

1. Ab. MSS.

2. Joseph Ritson to the editor, 26 February 1796, *The Letters of Joseph Ritson, Esq. Edited chiefly from Originals in the Possession of his Nephew* (1833), II, 117.

3. Godwin to ?, n.d., Ab. MSS.

4. *C.W.*, p.292.

5. *The Enquirer*, p.27.

6. *P.J.* (1796), I, 95.

7. Ibid., I, 27n.

8. Ibid., I, 25n.

9. Ibid., I, 66.

10. Ibid., I, 72.

11. Ibid., I, 82.

12. Ibid., I, 85.

13. Ibid., I, 71.

14. Ibid., I, 86–7.

15. Ibid., I, 453, 455.

16. Ibid., II, 485.

17. Ibid., I, 241.

18. Ibid., II, 519.

19. Ibid., I, 93.

20. Ibid., I, 55n.

21. Note dated 10 March 1800, Ab. MSS.

22. Godwin to George Dyson, n.d., Paul, I, 48.

23. *P.J.* (1796), I, 203.

24. Ibid., I, 441.

25. Ibid., II, 488.

26. Ibid., I, 428.

27. Ibid., II, 487.

28. Ibid., I, 449.

29. Ibid., I, 443.

30. Ibid., I, 448.

31. Ibid., I, 150.

32. Ibid., I, 157.

33. Ibid., I, 51, 17.

34. Ibid., I, 357.

35. Ab. MSS.

36. *P.J.* (1796), I, 60.

37. David Hume, *A Treatise of Human Nature* (1739–40), ed. L. A. Selby-Bigge (1968), p.413.

38. Ibid., p.415.

39. *P.J.* (1796), I, 425.

40. Ibid., II, 488n.

41. Ab. MSS.

42. Hume, *A Treatise of Human Nature*, op. cit., pp.618, 602.

43. *P.J.* (1796), I, 427.

44. Ibid., II, 499, 502.

45. *P.J.* (1793), I, 2.

46. *P.J.* (1796), I, 5.

47. Ibid., I, 50–1.

48. *P.J.* (1793), I, 73; *P.J.* (1796), I, 108; *P.J.* (1793), I, 71; *P.J.* (1796), I, 106.

49. Ibid., I, 258.

50. Ibid., I, 259.

51. Ibid., I, 261.

52. Ibid., I, 269.

53. Ibid., I, 168.

54. Ibid., I, 169.

55. Ibid., II, 425.

56. Ibid., II, 428.

57. Ibid., II, 442, 3.

58. Ab. MSS.

59. De Quincey, *Collected Writings*, op.cit., XI, 328.

60. *P.J.* (1796), I, xv.

61. *The Enquirer*, p.vi.

62. Ibid., p.viii.

63. Ibid., p.ix–x.

64. Ab. MSS.

65. Note dated 26 September 1799, Ab. MSS.

66. *The Enquirer*, p.11.

67. Godwin to James Ogilvie, 1797, first printed in the *National Intelligencer and Washington Advertiser*, II, 225 (16 April 1802), 3.

68. *The Enquirer*, p.6.

69. Ibid., p.24.

70. Ibid., p.59.

71. Ibid., p.58.

72. Ibid., p.64.

73. Ibid., p.80.

74. Ibid., p.31.

75. Ibid., pp.46, 47.

76. Ibid., p.89.

77. Ibid., p.106.
78. Ibid., p.125.
79. Ibid., p.309.
80. Ibid., p.105.
81. Ibid., p.306.
82. Ibid., p.315.
83. Ibid., p.340.
84. Ibid., p.347.
85. Ibid., p.281.
86. Ibid., p.167.
87. Ibid., pp.243, 242.
88. Ibid., p.244.
89. Ibid., p.177.
90. Ibid., p.178.
91. Ibid., p.181.
92. Ibid., pp.189, 194n, 193.
93. Ibid., p.199.
94. Ibid., p.209.
95. Ibid., p.219.
96. Ibid., pp.223, 224, 222.
97. Ibid., p.227.
98. Ibid., p.236.
99. Ibid., p.322.
100. Ibid., p.232.
101. Ibid., p.213.
102. Ibid., pp.362, 476.
103. Ibid., p.370.
104. Paul, I, 357.
105. See *Monthly Magazine*, IV (1797), 119; *Monthly Review*, XXIII (1797), 291–302; *Monthly Visitor*, I (1797), 381–4, 457–9; *Scots Magazine*, LIX (1797), 751–2.
106 See *Analytical Review*, XXV (1797), 395–404; ibid., XXVII (1798), 481–90; *Critical Review*, XX (1797), 58–64.
107. See *British Critic*, XI (1798), 20–7.
108. See *The New Annual Register for 1797* (1799), 220–1.
109. See *English Chartist Circular*, II, 61 (1842), 36.

NOTES TO CHAPTER XI

1. Hazlitt, Review of *Cloudesley*, *Edinburgh Review*, LI (1830), 144.
2. Paul, I, 359.
3. *The Enquirer*, p.vii.
4. Hazlitt, 'The Plain Speaker', *Works*, op. cit., XII, 198; *The Spirit of the Age*, op. cit., p.36.
5. See Paul, I, 360.
6. Holcroft to Godwin, 22 July 1795, Paul, I, 150.
7. Ab. MSS.
8. See Coleridge to John Thelwall, 13 May 1796, *Collected Letters*, op. cit., I, 214.
9. Brightwell, *Memorials of the Life of Amelia Opie*, op. cit., pp.56–7.
10. Mary Shelley, Paul, I, 161.
11. Godwin to ?, 29 October 1797, Ab. MSS.
12. William Frend to Mary Hays, 1794, Frida Knight, *University Rebel: The Life of William Frend (1757–1841)* (1971), p.201.
13. Hays to Godwin, 14 October 1794, *The Love-letters of Mary Hays*, op. cit., pp.227–9. Cf. M. Ray Adams, 'Mary Hays, Disciple of William Godwin', *Publications of the Modern Language Association*, LV (1940), 472–83.
14. *The Love-letters of Mary Hays*, op. cit., p.9.
15. Godwin to Mary Wollstonecraft, 17 August 1796, *Godwin & Mary. Letters of William Godwin and Mary Wollstonecraft*, ed. Ralph M. Wardle (Lawrence, 1967), p.17.
16. Hays to Godwin, 8 March 1796, *The Love-letters of Mary Hays*, op. cit., p.233.
17. Godwin to Hays, January 1796, ibid., p.232.
18. Wollstonecraft, *An Historical and Moral View of the Origin and Progress of the French Revolution* (1794), pp.72, 73.
19. Wollstonecraft, *Thoughts on the Education of Daughters: with Reflections on Female Conduct, in the More Important Duties of Life* (1787), p.12.
20. Wollstonecraft, *Mary, A Fiction and The Wrongs of Woman*, ed. Gary Kelly (1976), p.68.
21. Wollstonecraft, *Vindication of the Rights of Woman: With Strictures on Political and Moral Subjects (1792)*, ed. M. B. Kramnick (Harmondworth, 1975), p.91.
22. *Memoirs of the Author of a Vindication of the Rights of Woman* (1798), pp.80, 83, 82.
23. John Knowles, *The Life and Writings of Henry Fuseli* (1831), I, 164.
24. Mary Hays, *Annual Necrology* (1797–8), p.460.
25. *Memoirs*, p.83.
26. Southey to Joseph Cottle, 13 March 1797, *The Life and Correspondence of Robert Southey*, op. cit., I, 306n.

27. *Memoirs*, p.149.

28. Ibid., p.129.

29. Wollstonecraft to Godwin, 1 July 1796, quoted by Brown, *The Life of William Godwin*, op. cit., p.116.

30. *Memoirs*, pp.151–2.

31. Godwin to Wollstonecraft, 13 July 1796, *Godwin & Mary*, op. cit., p.8.

32. Claire Tomalin, *The Life and Death of Mary Wollstonecraft* (1974), p.205.

33. *Memoirs*, pp.150–3.

34. Wollstonecraft to Godwin, 17 August 1796, *Godwin & Mary*, op. cit., p.15.

35. Godwin to Wollstonecraft, 17 August 1796, ibid., p.16.

36. Godwin to Wollstonecraft, 19 August 1796, ibid., p.22.

37. Wollstonecraft to Godwin, 7 December 1796, ibid., p.54.

38. Wollstonecraft to Godwin, 10 September 1796, ibid., p.31; 4 October 1796, ibid., p.42.

39. Wollstonecraft to Godwin, 13 September 1796, ibid., p.33.

40. Wollstonecraft to Godwin, 10 September 1796, ibid., p.30.

41. Wollstonecraft, *Mary, A Fiction and The Wrongs of Woman*, op. cit., p.73.

42. Ibid., p.153.

43. 'Conclusion, by the Editor' (i.e. Godwin), ibid., p.204.

44. Wollstonecraft to Godwin, 10 September 1796, *Godwin & Mary*, op. cit., p.31.

45. Wollstonecraft to Godwin, 4 October 1796, ibid., p.41.

46. See Tomalin, *The Life and Death of Mary Wollstonecraft*, op. cit., p.212n.

47. Wollstonecraft to Godwin, 31 December 1796, *Godwin & Mary*, op. cit., p.60.

48. Wollstonecraft to Godwin, 1 January 1797, ibid., p.61.

49. *P.J.* (1793), II, 850; Wollstonecraft to Ruth Barlow, 27 April 1794, *Four New Letters of Mary Wollstonecraft and Helen M. Williams*, ed. B. P. Kurtz and C. C. Autrey (Berkeley, Calif., 1937), p.41.

50. Godwin to Mary Hays, 10 April 1797, quoted by Ralph M. Wardle, *Mary Wollstonecraft: A Critical Biography* (Lincoln, 1967), p.287.

51. Godwin to Thomas Wedgwood, 19 April 1797, Paul, I, 235. Cf. Godwin's justification in his *Memoirs*, pp.157–8.

52. Godwin to ?, n.d., Ab. MSS.

53. Holcroft to Godwin, 6 April 1797, Paul, I, 240.

54. Ann Godwin to Godwin, 3 May 1797, Paul, I, 237.

55. Mary Shelley, Paul, I, 239.

56. Elizabeth Inchbald to Godwin, 11 April 1797, Paul, I, 240.

57. Godwin to Inchbald, 13 September 1797, Paul, I, 278.

58. Amelia Alderson to Mrs. Taylor, n.d., Brightwell, *Memorials of the Life of Amelia Opie*, op.cit., p.61.

59. Anna Barbauld to Mrs. Beecroft, quoted by Wardle, *Mary Wollstonecraft*, op. cit., p.289.

60. Wollstonecraft to Alderson, n.d., Brightwell, *Memorials of the Life of Amelia Opie*, op. cit., pp.60–1.

61. Wollstonecraft to Godwin, 21 May 1797, *Godwin & Mary*, op. cit., p.76; Paul, I, 361.

62. Wollstonecraft to Godwin, 6 June 1797, *Godwin & Mary*, op.cit., p.82; Godwin to Wollstonecraft, 10 June 1797, Paul, p.89.

63. Godwin to Wollstonecraft, 5 June 1797, Paul, p.79.

64. Godwin to Wollstonecraft, 10 June 1797, Paul, p.91.

65. Godwin to Wollstonecraft, 15 June 1797, Paul, p.102.

66. Godwin to Wollstonecraft, 17 June 1797, Paul, pp.104–5.

67. Godwin to Wollstonecraft, 10 June 1797, Paul, p.90.

68. Eliza Fenwick to Everina Wollstonecraft, 12 September 1797, Paul, I, 283.

69. For Godwin's diary entries during his wife's illness, see Paul, I, 274–5.

70. Godwin to Holcroft, 10 September 1797, Paul, I, 275–6.

71. Godwin to ?, n.d., quoted by Kelly, *The English Jacobin Novel*, op. cit., p.226.

72. Godwin to Elizabeth Inchbald, 10 September 1797, Paul, I, 276.

73. Inchbald to Godwin, 26 October 1797, Paul, I, 279.

74. Godwin to Mrs. Cotton, 24 October 1797, Paul, I, 280–1.

75. *Memoirs*, p.112.

76. Ibid., p.163.

77. *Memoirs* (2nd edn., 1798), pp.204–5.

78. *Memoirs* (1st edn.), p.135.

79. Ibid., p.166; Wollstonecraft to Godwin, 31 December 1796, *Godwin & Mary*, op. cit., p.56.

80. *Memoirs* (2nd edn.), p.53, 91.

81. See *Analytical Review*, XXVII (1798), 235–40.

82. See *Monthly Magazine*, V (1798), 493–4.

83. *Monthly Review*, XXVII (1798), 321–2.

84. *Anti-Jacobin Review and Magazine; or, Monthly Political and Literary Censor*, I (1798), 94–102. Thereafter referred to as *Anti-Jacobin Review*.

85. *European Magazine and London Review*, XXXIII (1798), 251.

86. Quoted by Wardle, *Mary Wollstonecraft*, op. cit., p.317.

87. Anna Seward to H. Repton, 13 April 1798, *The Letters of Anna Seward*, op. cit., V, 73–4.


NOTES TO CHAPTER XII


1. Cf. Palacio, *William Godwin et son monde intérieur*, op. cit., p.61.

2. Paul, I, 357.

3. Wedgwood to Godwin, 6 January 1798, Paul, I, 311.

4. R. B. Litchfield, *Tom Wedgwood. The First Photographer* (1903), p.208.

5. Wedgwood to Godwin, 31 July 1797, David Erdman, 'Coleridge, Wordsworth and the Wedgwood Fund, 1', *Bulletin of the New York Public Library*, LX (1956), 430–2.

6. Wedgwood to Godwin, 15 April 1804, Paul, II, 126.

7. Godwin to John Arnot, 23 November 1798, Paul, I, 319.

8. Arnot to Godwin, 4 August 1799, Ab. MSS.

9. Arnot to Godwin, 5 July 1799, Ab. MSS.

10. James Losh Diaries, March 1798, quoted by Locke, *A Fantasy of Reason*, op. cit., p.150.

11. Godwin to Harriet Lee, 2 June 1798, Paul, I, 300.

12. Godwin to Lee (June 1798), Paul, I, 303, 304.

13. Godwin to Lee (June 1798), Paul, I, 305.

14. Lee to Godwin, 31 July 1798, Paul, I, 308.

15. Godwin to Lee (August 1798), Paul, I, 309.

16. Godwin to Maria Reveley (July 1799), Paul, I, 333–4.

17. Godwin to Reveley (August 1799), Paul, I, 335.

18. Godwin to Reveley (September 1799), Paul, I, 336–7. Cf. Marthe Severn Storr, 'L'Amour et le mariage chez Godwin', *Revue Anglo-Americaine*, XII (1932), 31–45.

19. Preface dated July 1797, *P.J.*, I, xviii.

20. Ab. MSS.

21. Godwin to Wedgwood, 29 April 1797, Ab. MSS.

22. See *P.J.*, I, 25n.

23. *P.J.* (1793), I, 292; *P.J.* (1798), I, 370; *P.J.* (1793), I, 286; *P.J.* (1798), I, 364.

24. *P.J.* (1793), I, 285; *P.J.* (1798), I, 363.

25. *P.J.* (1796), I, 58; *P.J.* (1798), I, 57.

26. *P.J.* (1798), I, xxvi.

27. Ab. MSS.

28. Locke, *A Fantasy of Reason*, op. cit., p.140.

29. Ab. MSS.

30. *P.J.*, I, xxvi.

31. Ibid., II, 87.

32. Ibid., I, xxiii.

33. Ibid., I, xxvii.

34. Ibid., II, 146, 510.

35. Ibid., I, xxiv.

36. Ibid., I, xxvi.

37. Ibid., II, 516.

38. Ibid., II, 518.

39. Locke, *A Fantasy of Reason*, op. cit., p.140.

40. Paul, I, 294–5.

41. Ibid., I, 295.

42. Ibid., I, 296.

43. Coleridge, *Biographia Literaria*, (1817), ed. George Watson (1962), p.169; *St. Leon*, I, vi.

44. Cf. W. A. Flanders, 'Godwin and Gothicism: *St. Leon*', Texas Studies in Literature and Language, VIII (1967), 534; and Tysdahl, *William Godwin as Novelist*, op. cit., pp.81–90.

45. *St. Leon*, III, 28.

46. Ibid., III, 115–16.

47. Ibid., I, ix.

48. Wollstonecraft, *Vindication of the Rights*

*of Woman*, op. cit., p.141.

49. *St. Leon*, I, 105.

50. Ibid., IV, 216–17.

51. Ibid., III, 74.

52. Ibid., I, 219.

53. Ibid., III, 6–7.

54. According to his diary, Godwin consulted *The Necromancer* (by Lorenz Flammenberg, trans. Peter Teuthold, 1794), on 24 July 1795. Ab. MSS.

55. *St. Leon*, IV, 187.

56. Thomas Holcroft to Godwin, 19 July 1799, Paul, I, 343.

57. *St. Leon*, I, 67.

58. Ibid., II, 17.

59. Ibid., II, 149.

60. Ibid., III, 198.

61. Ibid., III, 246–7.

62. Ibid., II, 27.

63. Ibid., II, 299, 305.

64. Ibid., II, 234.

65. Ibid., IV, 56.

66. Ibid., IV, 112.

67. Ibid., II, 204.

68. Ibid., I, 229.

69. See *Monthly Magazine*, VIII (1800), 1054–5; *Monthly Mirror*, IX (1800), 25–30.

70. See *Monthly Review*, XXXIII (1800), 23–9; *New London Review*, II (1799), 519–26; *Critical Review*, XXVIII (1800), 40–8.

71. See *British Critic*, XV (1800), 47–52; *Anti-Jacobin Review*, V (1800), 23–8, 145–53.

72. Godwin's note, Ab. MSS.

73. Hazlitt, *The Spirit of the Age*, op. cit., p.31.

74. Quoted by William Maginn, 'William Godwin', *Fraser's Magazine*, X (1834), 463.

75. Godwin's note, dated 3 January 1800, Ab. MSS.

76. Coleridge, *Notebooks*, op. cit., I, 254.

77. Holcroft to Godwin, 9 September 1800, Paul, II, 25.

78. Anna Seward to Thomas Park, 30 January 1800, *Letters of Anna Seward*, op. cit., V, 275.


NOTES TO CHAPTER XIII

1. Godwin to Harriet Lee, June 1798, Paul, I, 303.

2. *Thoughts. Occasioned by the Perusal of Dr.*

*Parr's Spital Sermon, preached at Christ Church, April 15, 1800: being a Reply to the Attacks of Dr. Parr, Mr. Mackintosh, the Author of an Essay on Population, and Others* (1801), pp.21–2 (*U.W.*, p.310).

3. See letter from 'A.V.', *Cambridge Intelligencer*, CV (18 July 1795), 4.

4. See letter from 'Philo Godwin', ibid., CVII (1 August 1795), 4.

5. Thomas Amyot to Crabb Robinson, 3 February 1796, Crabb Robinson Correspondence, D.W.L., MS. 1796, 70, 1.

6. Isaac D'Israeli, *Vaurien; or Sketches of the Times: Exhibiting Views of the Philosophies, Religion, Politics, Literature, and Manners of the Age* (1797), I, 50, 71.

7. Ibid., I, 71n.

8. Crabb Robinson to Thomas Robinson, 18 December 1797, Crabb Robinson Correspondence, D.W.L., MS. 1797, 102, 3.

9. *Anti-Jacobin: or Weekly Examiner*, II, 23 (1798), 180.

10. Ibid., II, 36 (1798), 286.

11. Fabricius (i.e. George Canning), 'The Anarchists', *Anti-Jacobin Review*, I (1798), 366.

12. For a general treatment of the reaction against Godwin, see B. Sprague Allen, 'The Reaction against William Godwin', *Modern Philology*, XVI (1918), 57–75; and B. R. Pollin, 'Verse Satires on William Godwin in the Anti-Jacobin Period', *Satire Newsletter*, II (1964), 31–40.

13. Thomas James Mathias, *The Shade of Alexander Pope on the Banks of the Thames* (2nd edn., Dublin, 1799), pp.48n, 44–50.

14. Mathias, *The Pursuits of Literature. A Satirical Poem in Four Dialogues. With Notes* (9th edn., Dublin, 1799), pp.210–12.

15. Ibid., pp.371n, 377n.

16. See Thomas Dutton, *The Literary Census. A Satirical Poem* (1798), p.71.

17. Charles Lloyd, *Lines suggested by the Fast appointed on Wednesday, February 27, 1799* (Birmingham, 1799), pp.3, 7. See also *Anti-Jacobin Review*, II (1799), 429–32.

18. Charles Lamb, 'Living Without God', in Lloyd's *Lines suggested by the Fast*, op. cit., p.3n.

19. *Anti-Jacobin Review*, IX (1801), 518.

20. John Ferriar, 'A Dialogue in the Shades',

*Illustrations of Sterne: With Other Essays and Verses* (1798), reprinted in A. E. Rodway, *Godwin and the Age of Transition* (1952), p.217. See also *Anti-Jacobin Review*, III (1799), 165–8.

21. Charles Lloyd, *Edmund Oliver* (1798), II, 149.

22. Ibid., II, 288.

23. Lloyd, *Letter to the Anti-Jacobin Reviewers* (Birmingham, 1799), p.20.

24. See Sophia King, *Waldorf; or, The Dangers of Philosophy. A Philosophical Tale* (1798), I, 33, 107.

25. *Historical, Biographical, Literary and Scientific Magazine*, I (1799), 26–32.

26. George Walker, *The Vagabond* (1799), II, 88.

27. Ibid., II, 255. Cf. Hugh H. MacMullan, 'Satire of George Walker's *Vagabond* (1799) on Rousseau and Godwin', *Publications of the Modern Language Association*, LIII (1937), 215–29.

28. See Mary Ann Burges, *The Progress of the Pilgrim of Good-Intent, in Jacobinical Times* (5th edn., 1801), pp.24–5, 48, 81–3.

29. Count Reginald de St. Leon (i.e. Edward Dubois), *St. Godwin: A Tale of the Sixteenth, Seventeenth, and Eighteenth Century* (1800), p.78.

30. Ibid., p.203.

31. Ibid., p.233.

32. Ibid., p.235.

33. Robert Bisset, *Life of Edmund Burke* (1798), I, 552.

34. Bisset, *Douglas; or, The Highlander* (1800), I, xxiv.

35. Ibid., III, 44.

36. See ibid., III, 88–97.

37. Ibid., III, 102.

38. See Elizabeth Hamilton, *Memoirs of Modern Philosophers* (1800), II, 36–42.

39. Ibid., III, 225.

40. *Dorothea; or, A Ray of New Light* (2nd edn., 1802), I, 148.

41. Charles Lucas, *The Infernal Quixote* (1801), II, 298.

42. Ibid., IV, 362.

43. *Thoughts*, p.10 (*U.W.*, p.299).

44. *Jane Austen's Letters to her Sister Cassandra and Others*, ed. R. W. Chapman (2nd edn., 1952), I, 133.

45. De Quincey, *Collected Writings*, op. cit., III, 25.

46. *Thoughts*, p.51 (*U.W.*, p.341).

47. Thomas Green, *An Examination of the Leading Principle of the New System of Morals* (2nd edn., Cambridge, 1799), p.iv.

48. Ibid., pp.32, 38.

49. Ibid., p.51.

50. William C. Proby, *Modern Philosophy and Barbarism; or, A Comparison between the Theory of Godwin and the Practice of Lycurgus* (1798), pp.6, 9, 11.

51. Ibid., p.21.

52. Ibid., p.79.

53. George Hutton, *A Sermon, preached in the Cathedral-Church at Lincoln on Sunday September 16, 1798* (Lincoln, 1798), p.10.

54. George Gleig, *Sermons preached occasionally in the Episcopal Chapel, Stirling, during the Eventful Period from 1793 to 1803* (Edinburgh, 1803), pp.253–4.

55. Robert Fellowes, *A Picture of Christian Philosophy; or, A Practical Illustration of the Character of Jesus* (2nd edn., 1799), p.iv.

56. Ibid., p.81.

57. *Memoirs of James Mackintosh*, op. cit., I, 94.

58. Mackintosh, *A Discourse on the Study of the Law of Nature and Nations* (1799), pp.25, 36.

59. Ibid., p.40.

60. Godwin to Mackintosh, 27 January 1799, *Thoughts*, pp.13–15 (*U.W.*, pp.302–4). Paul (I, 328) and subsequent biographers have mistakenly thought that the letter has not survived. The original is in B.L. Add. MS. 52, 451 ff.32–3.

61. Mackintosh to Godwin, 30 January 1799, Paul, I, 329.

62. Godwin to Mackintosh, 3 February 1799, Ab. MSS.

63. Mackintosh to George Moore, 6 January 1800, *Memoirs of James Mackintosh*, op.cit., I, 125.

64. Mackintosh ibid., I, 112–13.

65. *Thoughts*, p.19 (*U.W.* p.308).

66. Hazlitt, *The Spirit of the Age*, op. cit., p.150.

67. Godwin to Samuel Parr, 3 January 1800, Paul, I, 376–7.

68. See *Thoughts*, pp.18–20 (*U.W.*, pp.307–8).

69. Hazlitt, *The Spirit of the Age*, op. cit., p.150; Coleridge to Godwin, 23 June 1802, *Collected Letters*, op. cit., II, 737; *The Works of Charles and Mary Lamb*, ed. E. V. Lucas (1903), V, 102.

70. Coleridge to Godwin, 13 October 1800, *Collected Letters*, op. cit., I, 636.

71. Hazlitt, *The Spirit of the Age*, op. cit., p.149.

72. Mackintosh to Sharp, 9 December 1804, *Memoirs of James Mackintosh*, op. cit., I, 135.

73. Godwin to Parr, 24 April 1800, Paul, I, 378.

74. Crabb Robinson to Robert Hall, 30 August 1798, Crabb Robinson Correspondence, D.W.L., MS. 1798, 116, 2.

75. Hall to Crabb Robinson, 13 October 1798, ibid., 1798, 118, 3.

76. Hall, *Modern Infidelity considered with Respect to its Influence on Society; in a Sermon preached at the Baptist Meeting, Cambridge* (Cambridge, 1800), pp.iii–iv.

77. Ibid., p.53.

78. *Thoughts*, p.10 (*U.W.*, p.299).

79. See John Bowles, *Reflections on the Political and Moral State of Society, at the Close of the Eighteenth Century* (1800), pp.127, 134; William Hamilton Reid, *The Rise and Dissolution of the Infidel Societies in this Metropolis*, op. cit., pp.32, 116.

80. Charles Findlater, *Liberty and Equality: A Sermon, or Essay: Being the Substance of what was delivered from the Pulpit at Newlands, upon the Fast-Day, 13th March 1800* (Edinburgh, 1800), p.24n.

81. Ibid., p.49.

82. Godwin to Mary Wollstonecraft, 7 June 1797, Paul, I, 253.

83. Godwin to Samuel Parr, 3 January 1800, Paul, I, 376.

84. Parr to Mackintosh, n.d., *Memoirs of James Mackintosh*, op. cit., I, 105–6.

85. Parr, *A Spital Sermon, preached at Christ Church, upon Easter Tuesday, April 15, 1800; to which are added Notes* (1801), p.2.

86. Ibid., pp.9, 10–11.

87. See ibid., pp.72, 74.

88. Ibid., p.139.

89. *Edinburgh Review*, I (1802), 22.

90. Dugald Stewart to Parr, 30 May 1801, *The Works of Samuel Parr*, ed. John Johnstone

(1828), I, 720.

91. Godwin to Parr, 24 April 1800, Paul, I, 378.

92. Parr to Godwin, 29 April 1800, Paul, I, 383.

93. See Parr to Godwin, 28 October 1800, Paul, I, 386.

94. See Paul, I, 383–6.

95. Godwin to Parr, n.d., Paul, I, 386–7.

96. *Thoughts*, p.28 (*U.W.*, p.317).

97. Ibid., p.34 (*U.W.*, p.323).

98. Ibid., p.32 (*U.W.*, p.321).

99. Ibid., p.43 (*U.W.*, p.333).

100. Thomas Malthus, *An Essay on the Principle of Population, as it affects the Future Improvement of Society, with Remarks on the Speculations of Mr. Godwin, M. Condorcet, and other Writers* (1798), ed. Anthony Flew (Harmondsworth, 1970), pp.132–3.

101. Ibid., p.70.

102. Ibid., p.144.

103. Ibid., p.176.

104. Malthus to Godwin, 20 August 1798, Paul, I, 323–4.

105. *Thoughts*, pp.55–6 (*U.W.*, pp.345–6).

106. Ibid., p.65 (*U.W.*, p.357).

107. Ibid., p.73 (*U.W.*, p.365).

108. Ibid., pp.8–9 (*U.W.*, pp.297–8).

109. Ibid., p.7 (*U.W.*, p.293).

110. Ibid., p.6 (*U.W.*, pp.290–1).

111. Ibid., p.81 (*U.W.*, p.373).

112. Paul, II, 71.

113. Southey to Charles Biddlecombe, 17 August 1801, *New Letters*, op. cit., I, 246.

114. *U.W.*, p.xxix.

115. Coleridge to Godwin, 22 September 1801, *Collected Letters*, op. cit., II, 761.

116. Coleridge to Godwin, 23 June 1802, ibid., II, 736.

117. See *Monthly Mirror*, X (1801), 183; *Monthly Review*, XXXVII (1802), 254–6; *Edinburgh Review*, I (1802), 24–6.

118. See *Monthly Magazine*, XII (1802), 578–9.

119. See *Anti-Jacobin Review*, X (1801), 394–9; *British Critic*, XVIII (1801), 184–92.

120. Godwin to the editor, 10 November 1801, *Monthly Magazine*, XII (1801), 387–88 (*U.W.*, pp.375–8).

121. See *Monthly Magazine*, XII (1802), 484.

122. Malthus, *Essay on the Principle of*

*Population* (2nd edn., 1803), p.380.

123. See *Massouf; or, The Philosophy of the Day. An Eastern Tale* (1802), pp.131–6, 172–9, 204–5.

124. Philip Smyth, *Rhyme and Reason, Short and Original Poems* (1803), pp.124–25.

125. See Thomas Belsham, *Elements of the Philosophy of the Mind, and of Moral Philosophy* (1801), pp.439–47.

126. See Edward Maltby, *Illustrations of the Truth of the Christian Religion* (1802), pp.285–325.

127. Robert Hall, *Sentiments Proper to the Present Crisis. A Sermon preached at Bridge Street, Bristol, October 19, 1803* (1803), p.35.

128. *Christian Observer*, II (1803), 156. Reprinted by B. R. Pollin, 'Verse Satires on William Godwin in the Anti-Jacobin Period', *Satire Newsletter*, op. cit., pp.36–7.

129. Amelia Opie, *Adeline Mowbray, or The Mother and Daughter. A Tale* (3rd edn., 1810), III, 208.

130. See Isaac D'Israeli, *Flim-Flams! or, The Life and Errors of my Uncle, and the Amours of my Aunt* (1805), III, 67–8, 140.

131. Ibid., III, 246.

132. *Edinburgh Review*, I (1802), 88.

133. Thomas Robinson to Crabb Robinson, 16 August 1802, Crabb Robinson Correspondence, D.W.L., MS. 1802, 51, 2.

134. Bisset, *Modern Literature: A Novel* (1804), II, 186–7.


NOTES TO CHAPTER XIV

1. Godwin to ?, 29 August 1801, *Monthly Magazine*, XII (1801), 388. (*U.W.*, p.378).

2. Coleridge to Southey, 24 December 1799, *Collected Letters*, op. cit., I, 553.

3. James Ballantyne to Godwin, 14 November 1799, Paul, I, 352.

4. Hazlitt, *The Life of Thomas Holcroft*, op. cit., II, 231.

5. Ibid., p.232.

6. Holcroft to Godwin, 19 July 1799, Paul, I, 345.

7. Godwin to Holcroft, 13 September 1799, Paul, I, 346.

8. Holcroft to Godwin, 24 January 1800, Paul, II, 18.

9. Godwin to Holcroft, May 1800, Paul, II, 21.

10. Holcroft to Godwin, 13 June 1800, Paul, II, 24.

11. Godwin to Elizabeth Inchbald, 28 November 1799, *Memoirs of Mrs. Inchbald*, ed. James Boaden (1833), II, 29.

12. Inchbald to Godwin, 4 December 1799, Paul, I, 350.

13. John Philpot Curran to Godwin, 8 June 1800, Paul, I, 363.

14. *Morning Chronicle*, 16 October 1817 (*U.W.*, p.464).

15. William Henry Curran, *The Life of the Right Honourable John Philpot Curran* (1819), II, 201–2.

16. Godwin to James Marshal, 11 July 1800, Paul, I, 365.

17. Godwin to Marshal, 2 August 1800, Paul, I, 367.

18. Curran to Godwin, 8 June 1800, Paul, I, 363.

19. Godwin to Marshal, 2 August 1800, Paul, I, 369.

20. Godwin to Coleridge, n.d., Paul, II, 5.

21. Godwin to Marshal, 2 August 1800, Paul, I, 369.

22. Godwin to Marshal, 14 August 1800, Paul, I, 373–4.

23. Godwin to Marshal, 2 August 1800, Paul, I, 368.

24. Coleridge to Southey, 24 December 1799, *Collected Letters*, op. cit., I, 553.

25. Coleridge to Godwin, 8 January 1800, *Collected Letters*, op. cit., I, 560.

26. Coleridge to Godwin, 3 March 1800, *Collected Letters*, op. cit., I, 580.

27. Coleridge to Godwin, 21 May 1800, *Collected Letters*, op. cit., , I, 588.

28. Paul, I, 357–8.

29. Coleridge, *Biographia Literaria*, op. cit., p.112; 'Fears in Solitude', *Poetical Works*, op. cit., p.257.

30. Note dated February 1800, Ab. MSS.

31. Basil Willey, *The Eighteenth-Century Background* (Harmondsworth, 1972), pp.196–8.

32. Coleridge to Godwin, 8 September 1800, *Collected Letters*, op. cit., I, 620; Charles Lamb to Coleridge, 16 or 17 April 1800, *The Letters of Charles and Mary Anne Lamb*, ed.

Edwin W. Marrs Jr. (1975), I, 200.

33. Coleridge to Godwin, 22 September 1800, *Collected Letters*, op. cit., I, 625.

34. Coleridge to Godwin, 13 October 1800, *Collected Letters*, op. cit., I, 636.

35. Lamb to Coleridge, 6 July 1796, *Letters*, op. cit., I, 40.

36. E. V. Lucas, *The Life of Charles Lamb* (3rd edn., 1906), I, 179.

37. Lamb to Thomas Manning, 8 February 1800, *Letters*, op. cit., I, 183.

38. Lamb to Manning, 18 February 1800, *Letters*, op. cit., I, 185–6.

39. Lamb to Coleridge, 28 July 1800, *Letters*, op. cit., I, 216.

40. Lamb to Manning, 3 November 1800. *Letters*, op. cit., I, 244.

41. Holcroft to Godwin, 22 November 1799, Paul, I, 348.

42. Godwin to John Kemble, n.d., Paul, II, 45.

43. Coleridge to Godwin, 6 December 1800, *Collected Letters*, op. cit., I, 653.

44. Lamb, *Works*, op. cit., V, 121.

45. Ab. MSS.

46. *Antonio: A Tragedy in Five Acts* (1800), p.26.

47. Ibid., p.52.

48. Lamb, *Works*, op. cit., II, 293.

49. *Morning Post*, 15 December 1800.

50. See Coleridge to Godwin, 17 December 1800, *Collected Letters*, op. cit., I, 656.

51. Holcroft to Godwin, 26 December 1800, Paul, II, 26.

52. See Kemble to Godwin, 14 December 1800, Paul, II, 49.

53. Lamb to Manning, 15 December 1800, *Letters*, op. cit., I, 259.

54. Lamb to Manning, ?19 December 1800, *Letters*, op. cit., I, 261.

55. Anna Seward to Thomas Park, 5 January 1801, *Letters of Anna Seward*, op. cit., V, 344.

56. See *Critical Review*, XXXIII (1801), 23–7.

57. See *London Chronicle*, LXXXVIII (1800), 579; *Monthly Review*, XXXIV (1801), 438; *British Critic*, XVII (1801), 364–71.

58. *Anti-Jacobin Review*, VIII (1801), 61.

59. Elizabeth Inchbald to Godwin, 5 January 1801, Paul, II, 77.

60. Coleridge to Godwin, 17 December 1800, *Collected Letters*, I, 657.

61. Lamb to Manning, 27 December 1800, *Letters*, op. cit., I, 263.

62. Coleridge to Godwin, 25 March 1801, *Collected Letters*, op. cit., II, 713–14.

63. Coleridge to Godwin, 8 July 1801, *Collected Letters*, op. cit., II, 742–3.

64. Godwin to Sheridan, 10 September 1801, Paul, II, 65.

65. Godwin to Kemble, 28 September 1801, Paul, II, 67–8.

66. Lamb to Godwin, 17 September 1801, Paul, II, 87.

NOTES TO CHAPTER XV

1. Holcroft to Godwin, 26 December 1800, Paul, II, 26.

2. Paul, I, 13.

3. Ibid., I, 358–60.

4. Ibid., II, 58.

5. Godwin to Mary Jane Godwin, 24 September 1812, quoted by Herbert Huscher, 'The Clairmont Enigma', *Keats-Shelley Memorial Bulletin*, XI (1960), 16.

6. See Huscher, 'Charles Gaulis Clairmont', *Keats-Shelley Memorial Bulletin*, , VIII (1957), 10–12.

7. See Claire Clairmont to Lord Byron, 1816, quoted by R. G. Grylls, *Claire Clairmont, Mother of Byron's Allegra* (1939), p.55. In Godwin's family, Mary Jane Clairmont was called Jane, but when she left home she renamed herself Claire.

8. *Henry Crabb Robinson on Books and their Writers*, op. cit., I, 235.

9. See Huscher, 'The Clairmont Enigma', *Keats-Shelley Memorial Bulletin*, op. cit., pp.10–12.

10. Godwin to Mary Jane Godwin, 1812, quoted by R. G. Grylls, *William Godwin and his World* (1953), p.167.

11. Lamb to John Rickman, 16 September 1801, *Letters*, op. cit., II, 22. Lamb added in a postscript that the lady was a 'very disgusting woman'.

12. Godwin to Mary Jane Clairmont, 9 October 1801, Paul, II, 76–7.

13. Ab. MSS.

14. Lamb to Thomas Manning, 15 February 1802, *Letters*, op. cit., II, 55.

15. Lamb to Manning, 24 September 1802, *Letters*, op. cit., II, 70.

16. Ann Godwin to Godwin, 15 November 1803, Paul, II, 100.

17. Godwin to Mary Jane Godwin, 28 October 1803, Paul, II, 98–9.

18. Holcroft to Godwin, 1 January 1802, Paul, II, 109–10.

19. Lady Mountcashel to Godwin, 21 February 1802, Paul, II, 115.

20. Coleridge to Godwin, 22 January 1802, *Collected Letters*, op. cit., II, 782, 783.

21. Coleridge to Godwin, 4 June 1803, *Collected Letters*, op. cit., II, 946–7.

22. See Godwin to David Booth, 27 December 1802, Bodleian Library, MS. Eng. Letters, d.74, ff.122–3.

23. Thomas Robinson to Henry Crabb Robinson, 8 November 1803, Crabb Robinson Correspondence, D.W.L., MS. 1803, 107, 4, 3.

24. William Austin, *Letters from London: written during the Years 1802 and 1803* (Boston, 1804), p.203.

25. From the diary of Joseph Carrington Cabell, quoted by Marcia Allentuck, 'An Unpublished Account of Encounters with William Godwin in 1804', *Keats-Shelley Journal*, XX (1971), 20.

26. Coleridge to Godwin, n.d., Ab. MSS.

27. *Life of Geoffrey Chaucer, the Early English Poet: including the Memoirs of his Near Friend and Kinsman, John of Gaunt, Duke of Lancaster: with Sketches of the Manners, Opinions, Arts, and Literature of England in the Fourteenth Century* (2nd edn., 1804), I, x–xi.

28. Ibid., I, iv.

29. Ibid., I, ii–iii.

30. Ibid., I, 320–1.

31. Ibid., I, 28.

32. Ibid., I, 70.

33. Ibid., II, 56.

34. *Edinburgh Review*, III (1804), 449, 440.

35. *The Annual Review and History of Literature for 1803*, II (1804), 470, 472.

36. Robert Southey to William Taylor, 11 April 1804, J. W. Robberds, *A Memoir of the Life and Writings of the Late William Taylor of Norwich* (1843), I, 500.

37. Taylor to Southey, 20 May 1804, ibid., I, 505.

38. Southey to Taylor, 1 July 1804, ibid., I, 507–8.

39. Coleridge to Godwin, 26 March 1811, *Collected Letters*, op. cit., III, 314.

40. Lamb to Godwin, 8 November 1803, *Letters*, op. cit., II, 126.

41. Lamb to Godwin, 10 November 1803, *Letters*, op. cit., II, 127–8.

42. See *Literary Journal*, III (1804), 11–19, 65–79; *Imperial Review*, I (1804), 1–13, 185–206.

43. See *Critical Review*, III, 1 (1804), 60–5, 144–50, 324–42; *European Magazine and London Review*, XLIV (1803), 441–6; XLV (1804), 44–8, 121–30, 201–11, 281–93.

44. See *Monthly Review*, XLVI (1805), 113–30, 287–302; *Monthly Magazine*, XVI )1804), 627–8.

45. See *Monthly Mirror*, XVII (1804), 253–8, XVIII (1804), 173–6.

46. See *British Critic*, XXIII (1804), 226–33; *Anti-Jacobin Review*, XVIII (1804), 220–41. See also *Anti-Jacobin Review*, XVIII, 337–50; XIX (1804), 30–44, 154–67, 249–63.

47. Sir Walter Scott to George Ellis, 19 March 1804, *The Letters of Sir Walter Scott*, ed. H. J. C. Grierson (1932), I, 216.

48. Wedgwood to Godwin, 15 April 1804, Paul, II, 126.

49. Horne Tooke to Godwin, 6 December 1803, Paul, II, 105.

50. See Godwin to Flaxman, 17 October 1803, B.L. Add. MS. 39, 781 f.40; 16 July 1804, ibid., f.44.

51. Coleridge to Southey, 20 February 1804, *Collected Letters*, op. cit., II, 1072.

52. Coleridge to Godwin, 3 February 1804, *Collected Letters*, op. cit., II, 1056.

53. Coleridge to Mrs. S. T. Coleridge, 4 February 1804, *Collected Letters*, op. cit., II, 1057; Coleridge to Wordsworth, 8 February 1804, ibid., II, 1059.

54. Coleridge to Southey, 20 February 1804, *Collected Letters*, op. cit., II, 1073.

55. Southey to Coleridge, February 1804, *The Life and Correspondence of Robert Southey*, op. cit., II, 266.

56. Holcroft to Godwin, 25 September 1804, Paul, II, 126.

57. Cf. F. Rosen, 'Godwin and Holcroft', *English Language Notes*, V (1968), 183–6.

58. Paul, I, 296.

59. *Fleetwood: or, The New Man of Feeling* (1805), I, vii. Preface dated 14 February 1805.

60. Ibid., I, viii–ix.

61. Ibid., I, 18.

62. Ibid., I, 3.

63. Ibid., II, 189; III, 155. Cf. Tysdahl, *William Godwin as Novelist*, op. cit., p.118.

64. *Fleetwood*, II, 218.

65. Ibid., I, xii.

66. Ibid., II, 193.

67. Ibid., III, 34.

68. Ibid., II, 207.

69. Ibid., I, 143.

70. Ibid., II, 133.

71. Ibid., II, 128.

72. Ibid., II, 132.

73. Ibid., I, 244.

74. Ibid., I, 247–8.

75. Ibid., I, 248.

76. Hazlitt, *The Spirit of the Age*, op. cit., pp.33–4.

77. Mackintosh to Amelia Opie, 30 September 1805, Brightwell, *Memorials of the Life of Amelia Opie*, op. cit., p.89.

78. See *Edinburgh Review*, VI (1805), 182–93.

79. See *Monthly Review*, XLIX (1806), 102.

80. See *Critical Review*, IV (1805), 383–91.

81. See *Anti-Jacobin Review*, XXI (1805), 337–58.

82. See *British Critic*, XXVI (1805), 189–94.

83. See *Imperial Review*, IV (1805), 576–86.

84. See *The Annual Review and History of Literature for 1805*, IV (1806), 649–50.

85. *Monthly Magazine*, XIX (1805), 585.

86. Godwin to ?, n.d., Ab. MSS.

## NOTES TO CHAPTER XVI

1. Godwin to ?, n.d., Ab. MSS.

2. Cameron, *Shelley and his Circle*, op. cit., II, 545.

3. See Godwin to Dr. Matthew Raine, 12 April 1808, Paul, II, 166.

4. Godwin to William Cole, 2 March 1802, Paul, II, 118.

5. Claire to Mrs. Jefferson Hogg, 1 February 1833, *Shelley and Mary*, ed. Lady Jane Shelley (1882), IV, 1175.

6. Edward Baldwin, *Fables, Ancient and Modern* (1805), p.iii.

7. Ibid., p.92.

8. Ibid., p.165.

9. Ibid., p.141.

10. See *Anti-Jacobin Review*, XXII (1805), 420–1; *British Critic*, XXVI (1805), 578–9.

11. See *The Guardian of Education*, V (1806), 282–96.

12. See *Critical Review*, VIII (1806), 334–5; *European Magazine and London Review*, L (1806), 130; *Literary Journal*, II, 10 (1806), 112; *Anti-Jacobin Review*, XXV (1806), 424.

13. *The Pantheon: or Ancient History of the Gods of Greece and Rome. Intended to facilitate the Understanding of the Classical Authors, and of the Poets in General* (1806), p.vii.

14. Ibid., p.x.

15. See *Monthly Mirror*, I (1807), 184; *British Critic*, XXIX (1807), 452; *Eclectic Review*, III (1807), 922–3.

16. Edward Baldwin, *The History of England* (1806), p.viii.

17. Ibid., p.114.

18. Ibid., p.142.

19. See *Anti-Jacobin Review*, XXV (1806), 423.

20. See *British Critic*, XXVIII (1806), 98; *Critical Review*, VIII (1806), 332; *Monthly Review*, LI (1806), 205.

21. Theophilus Marcliffe, *The Life of Lady Jane Grey, and Lord Guildford Dudley, Her Husband* (1806), p.v.

22. Ibid., p.109–10.

23. See *Anti-Jacobin Review*, XXV (1806), 423.

24. See *Literary Journal*, II (1806), 112.

25. *London Chronicle*, 22 November 1806, p.499 (*U.W.*, pp.457–62).

26. Ab. MSS.

27. Ab. MSS.

28. Mary Lamb to Sarah Stoddart, 28 November 1807, *Letters*, op. cit., II, 262.

29. Coleridge to Southey, 14 December 1807, *Collected Letters*, op. cit., III, 43.

30. *Faulkener: A Tragedy* (1807), p.37.

31. Ibid., p.vii.

32. Ibid., p.22.

33. Ibid., p.4.

34. Ibid., p.76.

35. Ibid., p.77.

36. *European Magazine and London Review*, LII (1807), 466–7.

37. *London Chronicle*, 17 December 1807, p.587.

38. *Satirist or Monthly Meteor*, I (1808), 437.

39. See *Critical Review*, XIII (1808), 415–20; *Literary Panorama*, VII (1808), 993–5; *Monthly Review*, LVII (1808), 100.

40. *Morning Chronicle*, 5 April 1809 (*U.W.*, p.467).

41. Godwin to Mary Jane Godwin, 5 June 1806, Paul, II, 148–9.

42. See F. K. Brown, 'Notes on 41 Skinner Street', *Modern Language Notes*, LIV (1939), 326–32.

43. W. Thornbury and E. Walford, *Old and New London* (1873), II, 490.

44. Eliza Fenwick to Mary Hays, 5 November 1807, A. F. Wedd, *The Fate of the Fenwicks* (1927), p.20.

45. Charles Lamb to William Wordsworth, 29 January 1807, *Letters*, op. cit., II, 256.

46. Godwin to Lamb, 10 March 1808, *Letters*, op. cit., II, 278.

47. Lamb to Godwin, ? 10 March 1808, *Letters*, op. cit., II, 279.

48. Godwin to Lamb, 11 April 1808, *Letters*, op. cit., II, 283.

49. Lamb to Godwin, 11 April 1808, *Letters*, op. cit., II, 283.

50. Godwin to Lamb, 12 April 1808, *Letters*, op. cit., II, 284n.

51. Godwin to Mary Jane Godwin, 8 May 1808, Paul, II, 172.

52. Godwin to Dr. Ash, 21 May 1808, Paul, II, 173–4.

53. Godwin to Marshal, 9 June 1808, Paul, II, 159.

54. Godwin to Marshal, 11 June 1808, Paul, II, 160.

55. Edward Baldwin, *History of Rome: from the Building of the City to the Ruin of the Republic* (1809), p.iii.

56. Ibid., p.39.

57. See *Monthly Review*, LXIII (1810), 206–7; *European Magazine and London Review*, LVI (1809), 378–9; *Critical Review*, XVIII (1809), 322.

58. Godwin to Archibald Constable, 12 July 1809, Thomas Constable, *Archibald Constable and his Literary Correspondents* (Edinburgh, 1873), II, 50.

59. Godwin to David Booth, 6 September 1809, Cameron, *Shelley and his Circle*, op. cit., II, 558.

60. Ab. MSS.

61. Godwin to Crabb Robinson, Crabb Robinson Correspondence, D.W.L. MS. 1809, 13a; 13b.

62. *Mylius's School Dictionary of the English Language. To which is prefixed A New Guide to the English Tongue, by Edward Baldwin* (1809), pp.vi, vii.

63. See word entries in the dictionary.

64. *A New Guide to the English Tongue*, op. cit., pp.lii–liii.

65. See *Anti-Jacobin Review*, XXXIV (1809), 197; *European Magazine and London Review*, LVI (1809), 378; *Monthly Review*, LXIV (1811), 97–8.

66. See W. F. Mylius, *The Junior Class Book; or, Reading Lessons for Every Day of the Year* (1809), p.129; and *The Enquirer*, p.422.

67. Godwin to Hazlitt, 4 August 1807, Ab. MSS.

68. Hazlitt to Godwin, 6 August 1807, Ab. MSS.

69. Hazlitt to Godwin, ? June 1809, H. Baker, *William Hazlitt* (1962), p.171.

70. Hazlitt to Godwin, n.d., Paul, II, 175.

71. Godwin to Archibald Constable, 23 November 1809, *Archibald Constable and his Literary Correspondents*, op. cit., II, 53.

72. Lamb to Thomas Manning, 2 January 1810, *Letters*, op. cit., III, 37.

73. See *Anti-Jacobin Review*, XXXVI (1810), 320–1; *Critical Review*, XXI (1810), 109; *Monthly Review*, LXIII (1812), 211–12.

74. *Essay on Sepulchres: or, A Proposal for erecting some Memorial of the Illustrious Dead in All Ages on the Spot where their Remains have been interred* (1809), p.iii.

75. Ibid., pp.60–1.

76. Ibid., pp.5–6.

77. Ibid., pp.75–76n.

78. Ibid., p.23.

79. Ibid., pp.23, 25.

80. Ibid., p.vi.

81. See *British Critic*, XXXV (1810), 535; *Critical Review*, XIX (1810), 29–34; *European Magazine and London Review*, LVIII (1810), 48–50; *Literary Panorama*, VI (1809), 887–9; *Monthly Review*, LVI (1810), 111.

82. Charles Lamb to Coleridge, 7 June 1809, *Letters*, op. cit., III, 14.

83. Mary Lamb to Sarah Stoddart Hazlitt, 10 December 1808, *Letters*, op. cit., II, 287.

84. 'Essay on Death', dated 6 October 1810, Ab. MSS.

85. *Mandeville*, I, viii.

86. 'Fragment of a Romance', *New Monthly Magazine*, XXXVII (1833), 37.

87. Ibid., pp.38, 34. Cf. B. R. Pollin, 'William Godwin's Fragment of a Romance', *Comparative Literature*, XVI (1964), 40–54.

88. Godwin to Elizabeth Inchbald, 18 February 1805, Victoria and Albert Museum Library, Forster MS. 226.

89. Inchbald to Amelia Opie, 7 December 1809, Brightwell, *Memorials of the Life of Mrs. Opie*, op. cit., p.139.

90. Hazlitt, *The Life of Thomas Holcroft*, op. cit., II, 310.

91. Godwin to Mrs. Holcroft, n.d., Paul, II, 176–7.

92. The brick stack still stands today next to the disused Meeting House in Guestwick.

93. Godwin to Mary Jane Godwin, 21 August 1809, Paul, II, 180.

94. J. Parton, *The Life and Times of Aaron Burr* (14th edn., New York, 1861), p.155.

95. Aaron Burr to Theodosia Burr, 21 November 1808, *The Correspondence of Aaron Burr and his Daughter, Theodosia*, ed. M. Van Doren (New York, 1929), p.264.

96. Robert Lloyd to Hannah Lloyd, March 1809; Robert Lloyd to Hannah Lloyd, Easter 1809, E. V. Lucas, *Charles Lamb and the Lloyds* (1898), pp.154, 158.

97. De Quincey, *Collected Writings*, op. cit., III, 23–5.

98. Godwin to Patrick Patrickson, 18 December 1810, Paul, II, 193.

99. Crabb Robinson to William Pattison, 26 May 1795, *Henry Crabb Robinson on Books and their Writers*, op. cit., III, 842.

100. *Henry Crabb Robinson on Books and their Writers*, op. cit., I, 14.

101. Ibid., I, 25.

102. Ibid., I, 14.

103. Ibid., I, 55.

104. Ibid., I, 61.

105. Ibid., I, 29.

106. Coleridge to Godwin, 29 March 1811, *Collected Letters*, op. cit., III, 315.

107. See Mary Lamb to Sarah Stoddart Hazlitt, 7 November 1809, *Letters*, op. cit., III, 32.

108. Charles Lamb to Thomas Manning, 29 March 1809, *Letters*, op.cit., III, 4.

109. Charles Lamb to William Hazlitt, 28 November 1810, *Letters*, op.cit., III, 68.

110. Lamb, *Works*, op. cit., I, 277.

111. Charles Lamb to Godwin, ? November or December 1810, *Letters*, op. cit., III, 70.

112. Mary Lamb to Sarah Stoddart Hazlitt, 30 March 1810, *Letters*, op. cit., III, 49.

113. William Wordsworth to Godwin, 9 March 1811, *Letters*, op. cit., II, 467–8.

114. Mylius, *The Poetical Class Book: or, Reading Lessons for Every Day of the Year, selected from the Most Popular English Poets, Ancient and Modern* (1810), p.v.

115. Mylius, *The First Book of Poetry. For the Use of Schools. Intended as Reading Lessons for the Younger Classes* (1811), pp.iii–iv.

116. Baldwin, *History of Greece from the Earliest Records of that Country to the Time in which it was reduced into a Roman Province* (1821), p.iv.

117. Palacio (*William Godwin et son monde intérieur*, op. cit., p.83), mistakenly attributes the *Dramas* to Godwin. The author of the Juvenile Library's version of Jauffret's work is given however as 'The Editor of Tabart's Popular Tales', i.e. Mary Jane Godwin, editor of *Tabart's Collection of Popular Stories for the Nursery*.

118. State Papers, Public Record Office, Domestic, Geo. III, 1813, January to March, No.217.

119. *Henry Crabb Robinson on Books and their Writers*, op. cit., I, 175.

120. Thomas Noon Talfourd, *Final Memorials of Charles Lamb* (1848), II, 149–50.

121. See Place Papers, B.L. Add. MS. 35, 145, ff.32–3.

122. *Henry Crabb Robinson on Books and their Writers*, op. cit., I, 43.

123. Mary Jane Godwin to Godwin, 14 August 1811, Paul, II, 187.

124. Godwin to Mary Jane Godwin, 31 August 1811, Paul, II, 189.

125. Godwin to Mary Jane Godwin, 1812, quoted by Grylls, *William Godwin and his World*, op. cit., pp.167–8.

NOTES TO CHAPTER XVII

1. In a note to Trelawny on Shelley's letter of 30 December 1816, quoted by Grylls, *Claire Clairmont, Mother of Byron's Allegra* op. cit.op.cit., p.274.

2. *The Private Journal of Aaron Burr* (Rochester, 1903), II,. 326.

3. Godwin to ?, n.d., Paul, II, 214.

4. Mary Shelley to Jane Williams, 1822, quoted by E. Nitchie, *Mary Shelley, Author of 'Frankenstein'* (New Brunswick, 1953), p.89.

5. Mary Shelley to Mary Gladstone, 30 October 1834, *The Letters of Mary W. Shelley*, ed. Frederick L. Jones (Norman, 1944), II, 88.

6. Frederick L. Jones, 'Mary Shelley to Maria Gisborne: New Letters, 1818–1822', *Studies in Philology*, LII (1955), 68.

7. Mary Shelley to Marianne Hunt, 5 March 1819, *Letters of Mary W. Shelley*, op. cit., I, 23; Mary Shelley to Percy Bysshe Shelley, 26 September 1817, ibid., I, 32.

8. Godwin to William Baxter, 8 June 1812, Cameron, *Shelley and his Circle*, op. cit., III, 101–2.

9. See Godwin to Mary Jane Godwin, 24 May 1811, Paul, II, 185.

10. Godwin to Archibald Constable, 28 September 1811, *Archibald Constable and his Literary Correspondents*, op. cit., II, 56.

11. Ibid., II, 60.

12. *Transfusion: by the late William Godwin, Jun. With a Memoir of his Life and Writings by his Father* (1835), I, xvii–xviii.

13. Percy Bysshe Shelley to Thomas Jefferson Hogg, 8 May 1811, *Letters*, op. cit., I, 80.

14. Shelley to Godwin, 16 January 1812, *Letters*, op. cit., I, 231.

15. Timothy Shelley to William Whitton, 27 October 1811, *Letters*, op. cit., I, 166n.

16. Shelley to Godwin, 3 January 1812, *Letters*, op. cit., I, 220.

17. Shelley to Godwin, 10 January 1812, *Letters*, op. cit., I, 227–8.

18. Godwin to Shelley, 13 January 1812, quoted by Shelley to Elizabeth Hitchener, ? 16 January 1812, *Letters*, op. cit., I, 233.

19. Shelley to Godwin, 16 January 1812, *Letters*, op. cit., I, 230–1.

20. Shelley to Elizabeth Hitchener, ? 16 January 1812, *Letters*, op. cit., I, 232.

21. Shelley to Godwin, ? 26 January 1812, *Letters*, op. cit., I, 242–3.

22. Shelley to Godwin, 24 February 1812, *Letters*, op. cit., I, 260.

23. *Shelley's Prose: or, The Trumpet of Prophecy*, ed. D. L. Clark (Albuquerque, 1954), p.51.

24. Ibid., p.49.

25. Shelley to Elizabeth Hitchener, 26 January 1812, *Letters*, op. cit., I, 239.

26. *Shelley's Prose*, op. cit., p.55.

27. Godwin to Shelley, 4 March 1812, Paul, II, pp.204–6.

28. Shelley to Godwin, 8 March 1812, *Letters*, op. cit., I, 267.

29. *Shelley's Prose*, op. cit., p.68.

30. Godwin to Shelley, 14 March 1812, *Letters*, op. cit., I, 269–70n.

31. Shelley to Godwin, 18 March 1812, *Letters*, op. cit., I, 277–8.

32. Godwin to Shelley, 30 March 1812, *Letters*, op. cit., I, 278–9n.

33. Shelley to Godwin, 3 June 1812, *Letters*, op. cit., I, 303.

34. Shelley to Godwin, 11 June 1812, *Letters*, op. cit., I, 306–7.

35. Godwin to Shelley, c.4 July 1812, *Letters*, op. cit., I, 313n.

36. Shelley to Godwin, 7 July 1812, *Letters*, op. cit., I, 314.

37. Harriet Shelley to Catherine Nugent, 4 August 1812, *Letters*, op. cit., I, 320n.

38. Shelley to Godwin, 29 July 1812, *Letters*, op. cit., I, 316–17.

39. Godwin to Mary Jane Godwin, 19 September 1812, Paul, II, 212.

40. Harriet Shelley to Catherine Nugent, ? October–November 1812, *Letters*, op. cit., I, 327n.

41. See Godwin's diary, Ab. MSS.

42. Harriet Shelley to Catherine Nugent, ? October–November 1812, *Letters*, op. cit., I, 327n.

43. Godwin to Francis Place, 27 November 1812, Place Papers, B.L., Add. MS. 35, 145, f.41.

44. Place to Godwin, 28 November 1812, B.L., Add. MS. 35, 145, f.44.

45. Mrs. Julian Marshall, *The Life & Letters of Mary Wollstonecraft Shelley* (1889), I, 33–4.ᵖ

46. Godwin to Shelley, 10 December 1812, *Letters*, op. cit., I, 340–1n.

47. Harriet Shelley to Catherine Nugent, 16 January 1813, *Letters*, op. cit., I, 350n.

48. Shelley, *Poetical Works*, ed. Thomas Hutchinson and G. M. Matthews (Oxford, 1970), p.776, IV, ll.104–7.

49. Ibid., p.786, VI, ll.197–8.

50. Ibid., p.796, VIII, ll.225–9.

51. See ibid., pp.802, 806, 826.

52. Ibid., pp.811, 832, 807.

53. *Shelley's Prose*, op. cit., pp.186, 182.

54. Ibid., pp.202, 212.

55. Ibid., p.214.

56. Quoted by Brown, *The Life of William Godwin*, op. cit., p.276.

57. Thomas Jefferson Hogg, *Life of Percy Bysshe Shelley* (1858), II, 463.

58. Ibid., II, 445–7.

59. Godwin to Place, 5 September 1813, Place Papers, B.L., Add. MS. 35, 145, f.39.

60. For the negotiations, see Cameron, *Shelley and his Circle*, op. cit., III, 335–8. From October to April, Godwin wrote to Shelley twenty-six times. See *Letters*, op. cit., I, 381n, 386n.

61. Shelley, Dedication to 'The Revolt of Islam', *Poetical Works*, op. cit., pp.39, XII, ll.100–1.

62. Shelley to Hogg, 4 October 1814, *Letters*, op. cit., I, 402.

63. Shelley, *Poetical Works*, op. cit., p.522.

64. Quoted by Richard Holmes, *Shelley: The Pursuit* (1976), p.230.

65. Godwin to John Taylor, 27 August 1812, *The Elopement of Percy Bysshe Shelley and Mary Wollstonecraft Godwin as narrated by William Godwin with Commentary by H. Buxton Forman* (1911), p.10.

66. Diary, Ab. MSS.

67. Shelley to Harriet Shelley, ? 14 July 1814, *Letters*, op. cit., I, 390.

68. Mary Jane Godwin to Lady Mountcashel, 20 August 1814, Edward Dowden, *The Life of Percy Bysshe Shelley* (1866), II, Appendix A, p.544.

69. Harriet Shelley to Catherine Nugent, 20 November 1814, *Letters*, op. cit., I, 421n.

70. See Mary Jane Godwin to Lady Mountcashel, 15 November 1815, Dowden, *The Life of Percy Bysshe Shelley*, op. cit., II, Appendix A, p.546.

71. Godwin to Patrick Patrickson, 30 July 1814, Paul, II, 198.

72. Patrickson to Godwin, 9 August 1814, Paul, II, 199.

73. Place to Godwin, 1 September 1814, Place Papers, B.L. Add. MS. 35, 145, ff.49–50.

74. Godwin to Place, 2 September 1814, Place Papers, B.L. Add. MS. 35, 145, ff.51–2.

75. Place to Godwin, 3 September 1814, Place Papers, B.L. Add. MS. 35, 145, f.53.

76. Godwin to Place, 3 September 1814, Place Papers, B.L. Add. MS. 35, 145, f.55.

77. Place to Godwin, 9 September 1814, Place Papers, B.L. Add. MS. 35, 145, f.57.

78. Godwin to Place, 11 September 1814, Place Papers, B.L. Add. MS. 35, 145, ff.58–9.

79. See Godwin to Place, 14 October 1814, Place Papers, B.L., Add. MS. 35, 152, f.95.

80. Place Papers, B.L., Add. MS. 35, 145, f.36.

81. Ab. MSS.

82. See *Life of Robert Owen written by Himself* (1857), p.212; F. Podmore, *Robert Owen, A Biography* (1923), p.647.

83. Robert Owen, *A New View of Society* (1813/14), ed. V. A. C. Gatrell (Harmondsworth, 1970), p.108.

84. Ibid., p.99.

85. Fanny Godwin to Mary Shelley, 29 July 1816, *Shelley and Mary*, op. cit., I, 107.

86. See Hackwood, *William Hone, His Life and Times*, op. cit., p.51.

87. *The Examiner*, 4 August 1816, pp.493–5. See also John Brown, *Remarks on the Plans and Publications of Robert Owen, Esq., of New Lanark* (Edinburgh, 1817), p.39.

88. See M. D. George, *Catalogue of Prints and Drawings in the British Museum*, op. cit., IX, 11941.

89. Horatio Smith, *Horace in London, consisting of Imitations of the First Two Books of the Ideas of Horace* (2nd edn., 1813), pp.80–2.

90. Charles Lamb to Thomas Manning, 25 December 1815, *Letters*, op. cit., III, 205.

91. *Lives of Edward and John Philips, Nephews and Pupils of Milton. Including Various Particulars of the Literary and Political History of their Times* (1815), p.v.

92. Ibid., p.157.

93. Ibid., p.319.

94. Ibid., p.267.

95. Ibid., p.255.

96. Ibid., p.247.

97. Mary and Charles Lamb to Mrs. Morgan and Charlotte Brent, 22 May 1815, *Letters*, op. cit., III, 161.

98. *Monthly Review*, LXXVIII (1815), 414–24.

99. See *British Critic*, XLVII (1816), 257–69; *British Review and London Critical Journal*, VII (1816), 375–421.

100. *Edinburgh Review*, XXV (1815), 485–501.

101. See *Henry Crabb Robinson on Books and their Writers*, op. cit., I, 114.

102. Baker, *William Hazlitt*, op. cit., p.194n.

103. *Letters of Verax, to the Editor of the Morning Chronicle, on the Question of a War to be commenced for the Purpose of putting an End to the Possession of the Supreme Power in France by Napoleon Bonaparte* (1815), p.iii (*U.W.*, p.381). For the background to the pamphlet, see B. R. Pollin, 'Godwin's *Letters of Verax*', *Journal of the History of Ideas*, XXVIII (1967), 432–44.

104. *Letters of Verax*, pp.34, 33, 28 (*U.W.*, pp.416, 415, 410).

105. Ibid., p.45 (*U.W.*, p.427).

106. *Monthly Magazine*, XXXIX (1815), 547.

107. *Henry Crabb Robinson on Books and their Writers*, op. cit., I, 171.

108. See *Diary, Reminiscences, and Correspondence of Henry Crabb Robinson*, ed. Thomas Sadler (1869), I, 491.


NOTES TO CHAPTER XVIII

1. Shelley to Harriet, 26 September 1814, *Letters*, op. cit., I, 397; Shelley to Harriet, 27 September 1814, ibid., I, 398.

2. *Mary Shelley's Journal*, ed. Frederick L. Jones (Norman, 1947), p.21.

3. Shelley to Hogg, 4 October 1814, *Letters*, op. cit., I, 403.

4. Shelley to Mary, 24 October 1814, *Letters*, op. cit., I, 408.

5. *Mary Shelley's Journal*, op. cit., p.23.

6. Mary to Shelley, 28 October 1814, *Mary Shelley's Letters*, op. cit., I, 4.

7. Godwin to John Taylor, 8 November 1814, quoted by B. R. Pollin, 'Godwin's Account of Shelley's Return in September 1814, A Letter to John Taylor', *Keats-Shelley Memorial Bulletin*, XXI (1970), 23.

8. See *The Journals of Claire Clairmont*, ed. M. K. Stocking. With the assistance of D. M. Stocking (Cambridge, Mass., 1968), p.59.

9. See John Taylor to Place, 16 December 1824, Place Papers, B.L. Add. MS. 35, 145 f.67.

10. *Mary Shelley's Journal*, op. cit., p.42.

11. Ibid., p.43.

12. *Shelley's Prose*, op. cit., p.173.

13. Shelley to Godwin, 25 January 1816, *Letters*, op. cit., I, 447.

14. See Shelley to Godwin, 7 January 1816, *Letters*, op. cit., I, 439–40.

15. Godwin to Shelley, 23 February 1816, *Letters*, op. cit., I, 454n.

16. Shelley to Godwin, 26 February 1816, *Letters*, op. cit., I, 456.

17. Mackintosh to Samuel Rogers, 1816, P. W. Clayden, *Rogers and his Contemporaries* (1889), I, 211.

18. Shelley to Godwin, 6 March 1816, *Letters*, op. cit., I, 459.

19. Godwin to Shelley, 6 March 1816, quoted by Brown, *The Life of William Godwin*, op. cit., p.304.

20. See Shelley to Godwin, 7 March 1816, *Letters*, op. cit., I, 460.

21. Shelley to Godwin, 3 May 1816, *Letters*, op. cit., I, 472–3.

22. Godwin to Mary Jane Godwin, 14 April 1816, Paul, II, 235–6. For Godwin's diary entries during his tour, see ibid., II, 231–4.

23. *Maria Gisborne and Edward E. Williams, Shelley's Friends: Their Journals and Letters*, ed. Frederick L. Jones (Norman, 1951), pp.40, 45.

24. *Henry Crabb Robinson on Books and their Writers*, op. cit., I, 183–4.

25. Godwin to Mary Jane Godwin, 30 April

1816, Paul, II, 236–7.

26. Shelley to Godwin, 24 June 1816, *Letters*, op. cit., I, 478.

27. Fanny to Mary, 29 July 1816, *Shelley and Mary*, op. cit., I, 112.

28. Fanny to Mary, 3 October 1816, *Shelley and Mary*, op. cit., I, 145.

29. Ibid.

30. See *Maria Gisborne*, op. cit., p.39.

31. Godwin to Mary, 13 October 1816, *Shelley and Mary*, op. cit., I, 148; *Mary Shelley's Journal*, op. cit., p.66.

32. Shelley, *Poetical Works*, op. cit., p.546.

33. Paul, II, 242. For a discussion of Fanny's motives, see B. R. Pollin, 'Fanny Godwin's Suicide Re-examined', *Etudes Anglaises*, XVIII (1965), 528–68.

34. *Mary Shelley's Journal*, op. cit., p.66.

35. Godwin to Mary, 13 October 1816, *Shelley and Mary*, op. cit., I, 148.

36. See Godwin to Thomas Cooper, 16 December 1817, *Shelley and his Circle*, ed. D. H. Reiman (Cambridge, Mass., 1973), V, 354–5.

37. Shelley to Byron, 17 January 1817, *Letters*, op. cit., I, 530.

38. Ab. MSS.

39. Shelley to Claire, 30 December 1816, *Letters*, op. cit., I, 525.

40. See Shelley to Byron, 23 April 1817, *Letters*, op. cit., I, 540.

41. Godwin to Hull Godwin, 21 February 1817, Paul, II, 246.

42. Shelley to Mary, 11 January 1817, *Letters*, op. cit., I, 527.

43. Shelley to Godwin, 9 March 1817, *Letters*, op. cit., I, 535.

44. See Godwin to Shelley, 29 April 1817, *Shelley and his Circle*, op. cit., V, 203.

45. Godwin to Shelley, 15 April 1817, *Shelley and Mary*, op. cit., I, 201A.

46. Godwin to Shelley, 12 May 1817, *Shelley and Mary*, op. cit., I, 201B.

47. Godwin to Place, 18 August 1817, Place Papers, B.L. Add. MS. 35, 145, f.61.

48. Godwin to Place, 2 January 1818, Place Papers, B.L. Add. MS. 35, 145, f.64; Place to Godwin, 3 January 1818, ibid., f.66.

49. Charles Clairmont to Shelley, 8 August 1816, *Shelley and Mary*, op. cit., I, 115.

50. Godwin to Mary, 30 January 1821, *Shelley and Mary*, op. cit., III, 580B; *Henry Crabb Robinson on Books and their Writers*, op. cit., I, 198.

51. Charles Clairmont to Shelley, 26 January 1817, *Shelley and Mary*, op. cit., I, 186.

52. Hogg to Shelley, 25 April 1817, *Letters*, op. cit., I, 542n.

53. Godwin to Mary Jane Godwin, 14 May 1817, Paul, II, 249.

54. Mary to Shelley, 29 May 1817, *Mary Shelley's Letters*, op. cit., I, 25.

55. Godwin to Mary Jane Godwin, 22 May 1817, Paul, II, 250; Godwin to Mary Jane Godwin, 2 June 1817, Paul, II, 250.

56. Godwin to Mary Jane Godwin, 9 July, Paul, II, 251.

57. *Quarterly Review*, XVIII (1818), 382.

58. *Shelley's Prose*, op. cit., p.307.

59. Mary Shelley, *Frankenstein; or, The Modern Prometheus* (1817), ed. R. E. Dowse and D. J. Palmer (1967), p.101.

60. Godwin to Mary, 18 February 1823, *Shelley and Mary*, op. cit., IV, 915.

61. Mary to Shelley, 16 October 1817, *Mary Shelley's Letters*, op. cit., I, 43.

62. See *Mary Shelley's Journal*, op. cit., pp.85–7.

63. Cf. William H. Davenport, 'Shelley and Godwin's "Essay on Sepulchres"', *Notes & Queries* (1952), 124–5.

64. Shelley, *Poetical Works*, op. cit., p.40, XIII, ll.109–117.

65. Ibid., p.33.

66. Ibid., p.32.

67. Ibid., p.34n.

68. Shelley to Godwin, 11 December 1817, *Letters*, op. cit., I, 577–8.

69. Godwin to Shelley, 31 January 1818, *Letters*, op. cit., I, 597–8n.

70. Godwin to Shelley, 8 June 1818, *Shelley and Mary*, op. cit., II, 282, 283.

71. Shelley to Godwin, 25 July 1818, *Letters*, op. cit., II, 21.

72. Godwin to Mary, 27 October 1818, *Shelley and Mary*, op. cit., II, 338A.

73. Shelley to Leigh Hunt, 15 August 1819, *Letters*, op. cit., II, 109.

74. Godwin to Mary, 9 September 1819, *Shelley and Mary*, op. cit., II, 410B.

75. *Maria Gisborne*, op. cit., p.44.

76. Shelley, *Poetical Works*, op. cit., p.207.

77. Ibid., p.253, II, iv, ll.193–7.
78. *Maria Gisborne*, op. cit., p.45.
79. Cf. William H. Marshall, '*Caleb Williams* and *The Cenci*', *Notes & Queries*, N.S., VII (1960), 261.
80. Cf. R. P. Lessenich, 'Godwin and Shelley: Rhetoric versus Revolution', *Studia Neophilologica,* XLVII (1975), 52.
81. Godwin to Mary, 30 March 1820, Paul, II, 272.
82. Shelley, *Poetical Works*, op. cit., pp.575, 571, 572.
83. Ibid., p.344.
84. Shelley to Peacock, 23–24 January 1819, *Letters*, op. cit., II, 71; *Shelley's Prose*, op. cit., p.253.
85. *Shelley's Prose*, p.234.
86. Ibid., pp.237, 252.
87. Ibid., p.251.
88. Ibid., pp.254–5.
89. Ibid., p.253.
90. Ibid., p.259.
91. Ibid., p.240. Cf. *Life of Chaucer* (1803), I, 370.
92. Shelley to John and Maria Gisborne, 26 May 1820, *Letters*, op. cit., II, 202–3.
93. Shelley, *Poetical Works*, op. cit., p.367, ll.196–201.
94. *Shelley's Prose*, op. cit., p.289.
95. Ibid., pp.277, 283.
96. Shelley, *Poetical Works*, op. cit., p.477, ll.1086–89.

NOTES TO CHAPTER XIX

1. Godwin to Mary Shelley, 30 March 1820, Paul, II, 271.
2. *Mandeville*, pp.xi–xii.
3. Ibid., II, 164.
4. Ibid., I, 220.
5. Ibid., I, 263; I, 305; II, 102.
6. Cf. Marion Omar Farouk, '*Mandeville: A Tale of the Seventeenth Century* — Historical Novel or Psychological Study?', *Essays in Honour of William Gallacher*, op. cit., pp.111–17.
7. *Mandeville*, I, 270.
8. Ibid., I, 152.
9. Ibid., I, 39, 119.
10. Ibid., III, 43.
11. Ibid., III, 48.
12. Ibid., II, 140.
13. Ibid., II, 143.
14. Ibid., II, 150.
15. Ibid., II, 133.
16. Ibid., II, 129, 130.
17. Ibid., I, 256–8.
18. Ibid., II, 294.
19. Ibid., III, 266.
20. Shelley to Godwin, 1 December 1817, *Letters*, op. cit., I, 570.
21. Shelley to Godwin, 7 December 1817, *Letters*, op. cit., I, 574.
22. *Shelley's Prose*, op. cit., pp.309, 310.
23. Cf. B. R. Pollin, 'Godwin's *Mandeville* in the Poems of Shelley', *Keats-Shelley Memorial Bulletin*, XIX (1968), 33–40.
24. Cf. John Colmer, 'Godwin's *Mandeville* and Peacock's *Nightmare Abbey*', *Review of English Studies*, XXI (1970), 331–6.
25. Thomas Love Peacock, *Nightmare Abbey* (1818) (New York, 1964), p.26.
26. See Godwin to Elizabeth Inchbald, 1 December 1817, Victoria and Albert Museum Library, Forster MS. 226.
27. *Scots Magazine*, II (1818), 57–65.
28. *Blackwood's Edinburgh Magazine*, II (1817), 268–79.
29. See ibid., II (1818), 402–3.
30. See *British Critic*, LI (1818), 325–30; *British Review and London Critical Journal*, XI (1818), 108–20; *Quarterly Review*, XVIII (1817), 176–7.
31. See *Literary Journal and General Miscellany of Sciences*, VIII (1818), 117–18.
32. *Henry Crabb Robinson on Books and their Writers*, op. cit., I, 206.
33. *Mandeville*, I, xi.
34. See *Henry Crabb Robinson on Books and their Writers*, op. cit., I, 208.
35. *Morning Chronicle*, 16 October 1817 (*U.W.*, p.463).
36. John Keats to George and Georgiana Keats, 2 January 1819, *The Letters of John Keats 1814–1821*, ed. Hyder Edward Rollins (Cambridge, Mass., 1958), II, 25.
37. Keats to George and Georgiana Keats, 24 September 1819, *Letters of John Keats,* op. cit., II, 213.
38. Charles and Mary Cowden Clarke, *Recollections of Writers* (1878), p.37.
39. *Maria Gisborne*, op. cit., p.39.

40. Ibid., p.42.

41. See *Scots Magazine*, II (1818), 209–13.

42. *Letter of Advice*, p.4 (*U.W.*, p.432).

43. Ibid., pp.5, 8, 13 (*U.W.*, pp.433, 436, 441).

44. Ibid., p.12 (*U.W.*, p.440).

45. Ibid., p.11 (*U.W.*, p.439).

46. Ibid., p.15 (*U.W.*, p.443).

47. See *Monthly Repository*, XIII (1818), 580; *Champion*, No. 276 (19 April 1818), 250–1.

48. See *Analectic Magazine*, XII (1818), 128–35; *Robinson's Magazine*, XI (1818), 262–8; *Port Folio*, IV, 6 (1818), 170–83; *Georgia Journal* (29 June 1819), pp.1–2.

49. See *Analectic Magazine*, XIV (1819), 230–43. Cf. J. W. Marken, 'Joseph Bevan and William Godwin', *Georgia Historical Quarterly*, XLIII (1959), 302–18.

50. Godwin to Bevan, 19 March 1818, *U.W.*, p.445.

51. Godwin to Bevan, 29 June 1818, *U.W.*, p.447.

52. See Thompson, *The Making of the English Working Class*, op. cit., p.664.

53. Godwin to Lady Caroline Lamb, 25 February 1819, Paul, II, 266.

54. Godwin to Rosser, 7 March 1820, Paul, II, 263.

55. Godwin to Rosser, 27 March 1820, Paul, II, 265.

56. Godwin to Rosser, 7 March 1820, Paul, II, 263.

57. Godwin to Rosser, 27 March 1820, Paul, II, 264.

58. 'Essay on Religion', dated 7 May 1818, Ab. MSS.

59. Godwin to J. F. Newton, 3 August 1811, B.L. Add. MS. 37, 232 f.38.

60. Godwin to Mary Shelley, 30 March 1820, Paul, II, 271.

61. *Of Population*, p.487.

62. Ibid., pp.572, 312.

63. Ibid., p.166.

64. See Malthus to Godwin, 25 October 1818, ibid., pp.122–3; 139–40.

65. Ibid., p.496.

66. Ibid., p.500.

67. Ibid., p.112.

68. Malthus, *Essay on the Principle of Population* (1st edn.), op. cit., p.70.

69. *Of Population*, p.532.

70. Ibid., p.534.

71. Ibid., p.539.

72. Ibid., p.549.

73. Ibid., p.555.

74. Ibid., p.606.

75. Ibid., p.621.

76. Ibid., p.615.

77. Ibid., pp.619–620.

78. Ibid., pp.623, 626.

79. Mackintosh to Godwin, 6 September 1821, Paul, II, 274–5.

80. *Henry Crabb Robinson on Books and their Writers*, op. cit., I, 263.

81. Hazlitt, *The Spirit of the Age*, op. cit., p.173.

82. Hazlitt to Leigh Hunt, 21 April 1821, quoted by P. P. Howe, *The Life of William Hazlitt* (1949), p.321.

83. Cf. W. P. Albrecht and C. E. Pulos, 'Godwin and Malthus', *Publications of the Modern Language Association*, LXX (1955), 552–6.

84. See *Champion*, No. 414 (10 December 1820), 322.

85. See *Examiner* (24 December 1820), pp.826–7; (1 April 1821), p.206; (12 August 1821), pp.503–4; (9 September 1821), pp.562–4.

86. See *London Magazine* 1 (1820), 654–60; *Philosophical Magazine and Journal*, XLVI (1820), 445–7.

87. See *Monthly Magazine*, L (1821), 559–60; *Monthly Review*, XCIV (1821), 113–36; *Literary Chronicle and Weekly Review*, No.89 (27 January 1821), 49–52.

88. *British Critic*, LVII (1821), 247–60.

89. W. Morgan to Godwin, 6 November 1820, Paul, II, 272.

90. See Godwin to Mary Shelley, 29 June 1821, *Shelley and Mary*, op. cit., III, 698A–C.

91. Godwin to Mary Jane Godwin, 31 August 1819, Paul, II, 260.

92. James Mill to David Ricardo, 13 November 1820, *The Works and Correspondence of David Ricardo*, ed. P. Sraffa and M. H. Dobb (Cambridge, 1952), VIII, 291–2.

93. John McCulloch to Ricardo, 25 December 1820, ibid., p.326.

94. Hutches Trower to Ricardo, 1 April 1821, ibid., p.361; Ricardo to Trower, 21 April 1821, ibid., p.368.

95. Malthus to Place, 19 January 1821, quoted by Kenneth Smith, *The Malthusian Controversy* (1951), p.123.

96. See Rosser to Godwin, 9 January 1821, Paul, II, 273.

97. Ab. MSS.

98. See *Edinburgh Review*, XXV (1821), 363.

99. Ibid., pp.373–4, 362.

100. Godwin to Mary Shelley, 10 October 1821, *Shelley and Mary*, op. cit., III, 698D.

101. Shelley to Claire Clairmont, 16 June 1821, *Letters*, op. cit., II, 303.

102. Shelley to John Gisborne, 22 October 1821, *Letters*, op. cit., II, 364.

103. *Morning Chronicle*, 11 January 1822 (*U.W.*, pp.487–8).

104. See *New Monthly Magazine*, I (1821), 195–205.

105. See Place to Ricardo, *c.*3 September 1821, *Works and Correspondence of David Ricardo,* op. cit., IX, 48.

106. See Place, *Illustrations and Proofs of the Principle of Population; being an Examination of the Proposed Remedies of Mr. Malthus and a Reply to the Objections of Mr. Godwin and Others* (1822), pp.39, 165.

107. Malthus, *An Essay on the Principle of Population* (6th edn., 1826), Appendix, p.498.

108. Mary Shelley to Maria Gisborne, 9 November 1819, *Letters*, op. cit., II, 159n.

109. Godwin to Mary Shelley, 13 June 1820, quoted by Brown, *The Life of William Godwin*, op. cit., p.343.

110. Shelley to John and Maria Gisborne, 30 June 1830, *Letters*, op. cit., II, 208.

111. Shelley to Godwin, 7 August 1820, *Letters*, op. cit., II, 225.

112. *Maria Gisborne*, op. cit., p.43.

113. Ibid., p.47.

114. Godwin to Mary Shelley, quoted by Mary Shelley to Maria Gisborne, 17 August 1818, *Mary Shelley's Letters*, op. cit., I, 55.

115. *Maria Gisborne*, op. cit., pp.35, 39.

116. Sir George S. Mackenzie, *Illustrations of Phrenology. With Engravings* (Edinburgh, 1820), pp.257–9. For a discussion, see B. R. Pollin, 'Nicholson's Lost Portrait of William Godwin', *Keats-Shelley Journal*, XVI (1967), 57–60.

117. *Thoughts on Man*, p.102.

118. Godwin to Mary Shelley, 30 October 1821, *Shelley and Mary*, op. cit., III, 704C.

119. Godwin to Mary Shelley, 31 January 1822, *Shelley and Mary*, op. cit., III, 734.

120. Shelley to John Gisborne, 10 April 1822, *Letters*, op. cit., II, 409–10.

121. Godwin to Mary Shelley, 19 April 1822, *Letters*, op. cit., II, 423n.

122. Godwin to Mary Shelley, 3 May 1822, *Letters*, op. cit., II, 424n.

123. See Shelley to Mary Jane Godwin, 29 May 1822, *Letters*, op. cit., II, 428–9.

124. See Horace Smith to Shelley, 5 June 1822, *Letters*, op. cit., II, 425–6.

125. Godwin to Mary Shelley, 6 August 1822, *Letters*, op. cit., II, 460.

126. Mary Shelley to Maria Gisborne, 11 June 1835, *Mary Shelley's Letters*, op. cit., II, 99.

127. Sir Walter Scott to Benjamin Haydon, October 1822, *Letters of Sir Walter Scott*, op. cit., VII, 252.

128. William Godwin Jr. to Mary Shelley, 25 February 1823, Paul, II, 277.

129. Godwin to Mary Shelley, 15 November 1822, *Shelley and Mary*, op. cit., III, 904B.

130. Subscription appeal, dated 8 July 1823, Paul, II, 283.

131. Postscript, dated 1 October 1823, quoted by Brown, *The Life of William Godwin*, op. cit., p.353.

132. See Crabb Robinson to James Masquerier, 25 June 1823, Crabb Robinson Correspondence, D.W.L. MS. 1823, 8, 43.

133. See Godwin to Lady Caroline Lamb, 20 September 1823, Paul, II, 283–4; Lady Caroline Lamb to Godwin, n.d., Paul, II, 285–6.

134. See Godwin to Sergeant Lens, 24 September 1823, Paul, II, 286–8.

135. Mary Shelley, *Valperga; or, The Life and Adventures of Castruccio, Prince of Lucia* (1823), I, 193.

136. Godwin to Mary Shelley, 15 November 1822, *Shelley and Mary*, op. cit., III, 904B–C.

137. Godwin to Mary Shelley, 14 February 1823, *Shelley and Mary*, op. cit., IV, 915.

138. Godwin to Mary Shelley, 18 February 1823, *Shelley and Mary*, op. cit., IV, 915.

139. *The Enquirer* (2nd edn., 1823), p.vii.

140. Mary Shelley to Leigh Hunt, 9 Sep-

tember 1823, *Mary Shelley's Letters*, op. cit., I, 258.

141. Mary Shelley to Leigh Hunt, 18 September 1823, *Mary Shelley's Letters*, op. cit., I, 265.

142. Godwin to Mary Shelley, 27 February 1824, *Shelley and Mary*, op. cit., IV, 1016B.

143. Mary Shelley, *The Last Man* (1826), ed. H. J. Luke Jr. (Lincoln, 1965), p.161.

144. *History of the Commonwealth of England. From its Commencement, to the Restoration of Charles the Second* (1824–8), IV, 531.

145. See Walter Scott to Godwin, 22 November 1824, Paul, II, 292–4; Isaac D'Israeli to Godwin, 12 July 1828, Paul, II, 294–5.

146. *History of the Commonwealth*, III, v.

147. Ibid., I, vii.

148. Ibid., I, 3.

149. Ibid., II, 336.

150. Ibid., I, 343–4.

151. Ibid., III, 79; III, 68.

152. Ibid., III, 82.

153. Ibid., III, vi.

154. Ibid., I, 93.

155. Ibid., I, 90.

156. Ibid., II, 333.

157. Ibid., III, 120.

158. Ibid., IV, vii.

159. Ibid., IV, 599.

160. Ibid., IV, 597.

161. Ibid., IV, 602.

162. Ibid., III, 189.

163. Ibid., IV, 579.

164. Ibid., I, 6.

165. See *British Critic*, LX (1824), 1–20.

166. See *Cambridge Quarterly Review and Academical Register*, I (1824), 183–208.

167. See *Monthly Review*, IX (1828), 474–89. See also ibid., CIV (1824), 242–51; III (1826), 146–62; VI (1827), 287–303.

168. See *Literary Chronicle*, VI (1824), 145–8, 165–7; VIII (1826), 465–8, 488–92, 520–3; I (1827), 401–4, 418–19, 434–6; *Eclectic Review*, XXIII (1824), 193–205; *Monthly Magazine*, LV (1824), 440–1; III (1827), 81–2; VII (1829), 82–4.

169. See *London Magazine*, X (1824), 57–60.

170. See *Westminster Review*, XVI (1827), 328–51.

171. See *New Monthly Magazine*, X (1824),

570–5; XXV (1829), 119–27.

NOTES TO CHAPTER XX

1. Hazlitt, *The Spirit of the Age*, op. cit., p.19.

2. Godwin to Mary Jane Godwin, 6 April 1826, Paul, II, 296.

3. Godwin to Mary Shelley, 9 October 1827, Paul, II, 299.

4. Talfourd, *Final Memories of Charles Lamb* op. cit., II, 140.

5. H. W. Boynton, *James Fenimore Cooper* (New York 1931), p.176.

6. Robert Dale Owen, *Threading My Way. Twenty-Seven Years of Autobiography* (1874), p.180.

7. *Cloudesley*, I, vi.

8. Ibid., I, ix.

9. Ibid., II, 3.

10. Ibid., III, 106.

11. Ibid., III, 109.

12. Ibid., III, 107.

13. See *Journals of Claire Clairmont*, op. cit., pp.416–17.

14. Compare *Cloudesley*, III, 138–9, and Shelley to Peacock, 20 November 1818, *Letters*, op. cit., II, 55–6.

15. *Cloudesley*, II, 240.

16. Ibid., II, 256.

17. Godwin to Charles Ollier, 1 March 1830, Catalogue of Autograph Letters, Magg Bros. (1922), item 3276, p.90.

18. *Cloudesley*, III, 296.

19. Ibid., III, 208.

20. Ibid., III, 334.

21. Ibid., III, 342.

22. See *Blackwood's Edinburgh Magazine*, XXVII (1830), 711–16.

23. *Edinburgh Review*, LI (1830), 144–59.

24. See *The Scotsman: or, Edinburgh Political and Literary Journal*, XIV (1830), 297; *Monthly Magazine*, IX (1830), 466–7; *Monthly Review*, XIII (1830), 596–604; *Examiner*, 25 April 1830, pp.258–60; *Court Journal*, L (1830), 236–7, LI (1830), 252–3.

25. See *Edinburgh Literary Journal*,, III (1830), 201; *Literary Gazette*, no.685 (6 March 1830), 151–2; *Westminster Review*, XII (1830), 491–4.

26. See *Athenaeum*, no.125 (20 March 1830),

162–4.

27. *New Monthly Review*, XXVIII (1830), 368–73.

28. Edward Lytton Bulwer to Godwin, 1 April 1830, Paul, II, 306.

29. See Michael Sadleir, *Bulwer: A Panorama. Edward and Rosina 1803–1836* (1931), p.224.

30. Godwin to Bulwer, 13 May 1830, Paul, II, 306.

31. Bulwer-Lytton, *Eugene Aram* (1854), p.v.

32. Godwin to Bulwer, 16 September 1830, Paul, II, 307.

33. Cf. Tysdahl, *Godwin as Novelist*, op. cit., p.163.

34. *Cloudesley*, III, 286.

35. Godwin to Mary Shelley, 15 April 1830, *Shelley and Mary*, op. cit., IV, 1172A.

36. *Thoughts on Man*, p.iv.

37. 'Essay on Scepticism', Ab. MSS.

38. *Thoughts on Man*, p.240.

39. Ibid., p.239.

40. Ibid., p.437.

41. Ibid., p.445.

42. Ibid., p.448.

43. Ibid., p.439.

44. Ibid., p.240.

45. Ibid., pp.230–1.

46. Ibid., p.239.

47. Ibid., pp.365, 7.

48. Ibid., p.373.

49. Ibid., p.244.

50. Ibid., pp.259, 251.

51. Ibid., p.212.

52. Ibid., pp.29, 52.

53. Ibid., p.25.

54. Ibid., p.292.

55. Ibid., p.287.

56. Ibid., p.300.

57. Ibid., p.209.

58. Ibid., p.222.

59. Ibid., p.205.

60. Ibid., p.234.

61. Ibid., p.169.

62. Ibid., p.264.

63. Ibid., p.109.

64. Ibid., p.185.

65. Ibid., p.174.

66. Ibid., pp.178, 177.

67. Ibid., pp.112–13.

68. Ibid., pp.305, 302.

69. Ibid., p.9.

70. Ibid., p.471.

71. Locke, *A Fantasy of Reason*, op. cit., p.327.

72. Godwin to Mary Shelley, 15 April 1830, *Shelley and Mary*, op. cit., IV, 1172A.

73. Thomas Robinson to Crabb Robinson, 19 July 1831, Crabb Robinson Correspondence, D.W.L., MS. 1831, 135, 4, 1.

74. *Henry Crabb Robinson on Books and their Writers*, op. cit., I, 418.

75. *Caleb Williams* (1831), p.xii. In the 1832 Paris edition of the novel, the memoirs of Godwin in the preface are signed by Mary Shelley.

76. See *Monthly Repository*, V (1831), 433–40.

77. See *Tatler*, no.141 (15 February 1831), 561; no.145 (19 February 1831), 577–8; no.146 (21 February 1831), 381–2; no.169 (19 March 1831), 674.

78. *Tatler,* no.287 (4 August 1831), 117–18; no.305 (25 August 1831), 189–90; no.306 (26 August 1831), 194.

79. See *Edinburgh Literary Journal*, V (1831), 145–6; *Fraser's Magazine*, III (1831), 569–86; *Literary Gazette*, no.736 (26 February 1831), 135; no.743 (16 April 1831), 246–7; *Monthly Magazine*, XI (1831), 531–4; *Athenaeum*, no.171 (5 February 1831), 82–4.

80. See *Monthly Review*, I (1831), 515–33.

81. Godwin to Mary Shelley, 22 July 1830, *Shelley and Mary*, op. cit., IV, 1172B–C.

82. Godwin to Macvey Napier, 7 March 1831, B.L. Add. MS. 34, 615, f.53.

83. Godwin to W. Cross, 31 January 1831, Paul, II, 329.

84. *Thoughts on Man*, p.327.

85. Prospectus dated 9 October 1832, Ab. MSS.

86. Prospectus dated 22 September 1832, Ab. MSS.

87. William Godwin Jr., *Transfusion; or, The Orphans of Unwalden* (1835), III, 312.

88. *Deloraine* (1833), II, 202.

89. Godwin to Mary Shelley, 13 April 1832, *Shelley and Mary*, op. cit., IV, 1162. Cf. Palacio, *William Godwin et son monde intérieur*, op. cit., pp.192–3.

90. *Deloraine*, I, 3.

91. Ibid., I, 267, 282.

92. Ibid., I, 35; 266.

93. Ibid., III, 29.

94. Ibid., III, 12.

95. Ibid., III, 13.

96. Ibid., III, 268.

97. Ibid., III, 231.

98. Ibid., III, 236.

99. Ibid., II, 168.

100. Ibid., III, 307.

101. Ibid., II, 266.

102. Ibid., III, 41–2.

103. Ibid., I, 38.

104. Ibid., I, 70.

105. Ibid., III, 303.

106. John Howard Payne to Godwin, 30 November 1833, Paul, II, 326.

107. See *Atlas*, (17 March 1833), p.163; *Court Journal*, no.202 (9 March 1833), 123.

108. See *Age*, IX (10 March 1833), 74; *New Monthly Magazine*, XXXVII (1833), 503–4.

109. See *Metropolitan Magazine*, VI (1833), 114.

110. See *Examiner* (17 March 1833), p.164.

111. *Lives of the Necromancers; or, An Account of the Most Eminent Persons in Successive Ages, who have claimed for themselves, or to whom has been imputed by Others, the Exercise of Magical Power* (1834), p.v.

112. Ibid., pp.vii, 1.

113. Ibid., p.x.

114. Ibid., p.425.

115. Ibid., p.464.

116. Scott to Godwin, 24 February 1831, Paul, II, 313.

117. *Edinburgh Review*, LX (1834), 37–54.

118. See *Gentleman's Magazine*, IV (1835), 630; *Irish Monthly Magazine of Politics and Literature*, III (1834), 408–20.

119. See *Southern Literary Messenger*, II (1835), 65. For Godwin's influence on Poe, see B. R. Pollin, 'Poe and Godwin', *Nineteenth Century Fiction*, XX (1965), 237–53.

120. *Weekly Register*, 18 June 1831.

121. For a full list of his duties, see Public Records Office, E 403/2499.

122. Godwin to Mary Shelley, July 1833, *Shelley and Mary*, op. cit., IV, 1180.

123. Harriet Martineau, *Autobiography* (1877), I, 403.

124. Ibid., I, 399.

125. *Fraser's Magazine*, X (1834), 463.

126. Henry Crabb Robinson to Thomas Robinson, 21 April 1843, Crabb Robinson Correspondence, D.W.L., MS. 1843, 36a, 5, 2.

127. See Godwin to Charles Babbage, 20 March 1835, B.L. Add. MS. 37, 189, f.55.

128. Thomas Carlyle to Mrs. Carlyle, 17 August 1831, James A. Froude, *Thomas Carlyle. A History of the First Forty Years of his Life 1795–1835* (1882), II, 172.

129. 'Recollections of William Godwin', unsigned, Ab. MSS.

130. Charles MacFarlane, *Reminiscences of a Literary Life* (1917), p.99.

131. *The Diary of Benjamin Robert Haydon*, ed. Willard Bissell Pope (Cambridge, Mass., 1963), IV, 270.

132. Dated 21 August 1834, Paul, II, 331.

133. Ab. MSS.

134. Note dated 30 September 1835, Ab. MSS.

135. Prospectus dated 2 October 1835, Ab. MSS.

136. *Essays*, p.13.

137. Ibid., p.244.

138. Ibid., p.213.

139. Ibid., pp.253–4.

140. Ibid., p.243.

141. Ibid., p.151.

142. Ibid., p.178.

143. Ibid., p.208.

144. Ibid., p.6.

145. Ibid., pp.284–5.

146. Ibid., pp.218, 219.

147. Ibid., p.68.

148. Ibid., p.268.

149. Ibid., pp.85, 87.

150. Mary Shelley to Maria Gisbourne, 17 July 1834, *Mary Shelley's Letters*, op. cit., II, 83.

151. Sir Robert Peel to Godwin, 3 January 1835, B.L. Add. MS. 40, 409 f.98.

152. Mary Shelley to Maria Gisbourne, 11 June 1835, *Mary Shelley's Letters*, op. cit., II, 97.

153. Mary Shelley to Mary Hays, 20 April 1836, *Mary Shelley's Letters*, op. cit., II, 114.

154. Quoted by Brown, *The Life of William Godwin*, op. cit., p.372.

155. Mary Shelley to Trelawny, 27 January 1837, *Mary Shelley's Letters*, op. cit., II, 119.

156. *Henry Crabb Robinson on Books and their Writers*, op. cit., II, 569.

157. Quoted by R. G. Grylls, *Mary Shelley: A Biography* (1938), p.xiii.

NOTES TO CONCLUSION

1. See *Morning Chronicle*, 9 April 1836; *Examiner*, 10 April 1836; and *Spectator*, IX (9 April 1836), 337–8.

2. *New Monthly Magazine*, XLVII (1836), 133–4.

3. *Gentleman's Magazine*, V (1836), 666–8.

4. H. S. Foxwell, 'Introduction' to Anton Menger, *The Right to the Whole Produce of Labour*, op. cit., p.xxxix.

5. See William Thompson, *An Inquiry into the Principles of the Distribution of Wealth most conducive to Human Happiness; applied to the newly Proposed System of Voluntary Equality of Wealth* (1824), ch.i and vi.

6. Thomas Hodgskin, *Travels in the North of Germany* (1820), I, 417; II, 461.

7. Hodgskin, *Labour defended against the Claims of Capital* (1825), ed. G. D. H. Cole (1922), p.85.

8. Place to Dr. Burbeck, 11 June 1825, Place Papers, B.L. Add. MS. 27, 823 f.369.

9. *New Harmony Gazette*, III, 27 (30 April 1828), 214.

10. *Crisis, or, The Change from Error and Misery, to Truth and Happiness*, I (18 August 1832), 95; II (6 July 1833), 204. For the many references to Godwin in the *Working Bee*, see B. R. Pollin, *Godwin Criticism: A Synoptic Bibliography* (Toronto, 1967), pp.341–2.

11. See J. F. C. Harrison, *Robert Owen and the Owenites in Britain and America: The Quest for a New Moral World* (1969), p.219n.

12. For references to Godwin in the *Chartist Circular* (Glasgow) and *English Chartist Circular and Temperance Record*, see Pollin, *Godwin Criticism*, op. cit., pp.253–6; 261–3.

13. See *Union: A Monthly Record of Moral, Social and Educational Progress*, I, 2 (1 May 1842), 64; *New Moral World*, IV, 35 (25 February 1843), 284; and *People: Their Rights and Liberties, their Duties and their Interests*, III, 139 (1850), 276–8.

14. W. J. Fox, *Lectures addressed chiefly to the Working Classes* (1845), II, 340.

15. *English Chartist Circular and Temperance Record*, II, 61 (1842), p.36.

16. Frederick Engels, *The Condition of the Working Class in England* (1845), introd. by Eric Hobsbawm (Frogmore, 1974), pp.265–6.

17. William Smyth, *Lectures on the History of the French Revolution* (2nd edn., 1855), II, 211.

18. The copy is now held in Dr. Williams's Library.

19. See John Middleton Murry, *Times Literary Supplement*, (4 April 1936), pp.285–6; Herbert Read, 'Foreword' to Woodcock, *William Godwin*, op. cit., pp.vii–ix.

20. See *Revue Britannique*, XXIX (1836), 376–80.

21. See Jean Jaurès, *Histoire socialiste de la révolution française* (Paris, 1923), V, 420–64.

22. *Henry Crabb Robinson on Books and their Writers*, op. cit., I, 208, 206.

23. See Frederick Engels to Karl Marx, 17 March 1845, quoted by Max Nettlau, *Der Vorfrühling der Anarchie*, op. cit., p.73.

24. See Marx and Engels, *The German Ideology*, ed. C. J. Arthur (1970), p.112.

25. See Anton Menger, *The Right to the Whole Produce of Labour*, op. cit., pp.40–6; Paul Eltzbacher, *Anarchism* (1906), trans. S. T. Byington (New York, 1908), pp.40–64.

26. See Rudolf Rocker, *Anarchism and Anarcho-syndicalism* (1938), p.6.

27. See V. G. Belinsky, *Complete Works* (Moscow, 1953), III, 111–12.

28. See N. G. Chernyshevski, *Complete Works* (Moscow, 1951), X, 738–42.

29. See Leo Tolstoy, *Complete Works* (Moscow, 1935), XXXV, 205–6; XXXVII, 222; XLIV, 159.

30. Peter Kropotkin, *Modern Science and Anarchism* (1912), pp.13–14.

31. Name Index to Engels, *The Condition of the Working Class in England*, op. cit., p.328.

32. See Michael Agoursky, '*Caleb Williams* in Mojaisk', *Times Literary Supplement*, (25 March 1977), p.371.

33. See *Cahiers de Pensée et Action*, I (1953), 1–80.

34. Hazlitt, *The Spirit of the Age*, op. cit., p.30.

35. Ab. MSS.

36. *Essays*, p.277.

37. Fenwick, *Public Characters*, op. cit., p.373.

38. *P.J.* (1793), I, 303.

39. Ibid. (1798), I, xxvi.

40. Ibid. (1796), I, 55n.

41. Ibid. (1798), I, 6–7.

42. Cf. Tysdahl, *William Godwin as Novelist*, op. cit., p.90.

43. Locke, *A Fantasy of Reason*, op. cit., pp.11, 140.

44. *Life, Letters, and Journals of George Ticknor*, ed. G. S. Hillard (1876), I, 294.

45. *An Account of the Seminary*, p.49.

46. *P.J.*, II, 493.

47. Ibid., I, 81.

48. *Henry Crabb Robinson on Books and their Writers*, op. cit., I, 3, 345.

49. *St. Leon*, I, ix.

50. *Cloudesley*, III, 342.

51. *Thoughts on Man*, pp.239, 242.

52. Hazlitt, 'Conversations of James Northcote', *Works*, op. cit., XI, 235.

53. *P.J.*, I, 344.

54. Ibid., I, 347.

55. Ibid., II, 399.

56. Ibid., I, 345.

57. Ibid., I, xxiii.

58. Ibid., I, 135.

59. Hazlitt, Review of *Cloudesley, Edinburgh Review*, op. cit., p.146.

60. Place Papers, B.L. Add. MS. 351, 45, f.109.

61. *P.J.*, I, 314.

62. *Of Population*, p.iv.

63. *P.J.* (1793), II, 738, 737.

64. Ibid. (1798), I, xxiv.

65. Ibid., II, 212.

66. Ibid., I, 167.

67. Ibid. (1793), II, 854, 844.

68. See Clark, *The Philosophical Anarchism of William Godwin*, op. cit., p.299.

69. *P.J.*, II, 466.

70. Ibid., I, 335.

71. Ibid., I, 168.

72. See Kramnick, 'Introduction', *Political Justice,* op. cit., p.48.

73. *P.J.*, I, 281.

74. Tysdahl, *William Godwin as Novelist,* op. cit., p.157.

75. Hazlitt, 'Conversations of James Northcote, *Works*, op. cit., XI, 235.

76. *Henry Crabb Robinson on Books and their Writers*, op. cit., II, 491; Stephen, 'William Godwin', *D.N.B.* (1890), XXII, 67.

77. Horace Smith, 'A Graybeard's Gossip about a Literary Acquaintance', *New Monthly Magazine*, LXXXVIII (1848), 339.

78. From a 'Monody on the death of William Godwin', Ab. MSS. This long poem is in Mary Shelley's hand and may have been written by her.

# SELECT BIBLIOGRAPHY

The following contains a list of Godwin's complete works and the main commentaries. It corrects and updates Burton R. Pollin's *Godwin Criticism: A Synoptic Bibliography* (Toronto: University of Toronto Press, 1967). The place of publication is London unless otherwise stated.

## I MANUSCRIPT COLLECTIONS

*Bodleian Library, Oxford.* The Abinger collection, owned by Lord Abinger, is being transferred on loan to the library. It includes Godwin's diaries and memoirs as well as the bulk of his manuscripts, notes and correspondence. Available on microfilm, uncatalogued, from the library.

*Victoria and Albert Museum Library, London.* The Forster Collection contains the MSS. of *Political Justice* (with revisions for different editions), *Caleb Williams* (with the original ending), *Life of Geoffrey Chaucer*, and *History of the Commonwealth of England*, as well as miscellaneous correspondence.

*Pforzheimer Library, New York.* The collection includes the MS. of *Fleetwood*, revisions of *St. Leon*, drafts, notes and miscellaneous correspondence. It has been edited by K. N. Cameron, *Shelley and his Circle* (vols. I–IV, Cambridge, Mass: Harvard U.P., 1961–70) and D. H. Reiman, ibid. (vols. V–VI, 1973).

*British Library, Reference Division.* Miscellaneous correspondence and the Francis Place Papers.

*Public Records Office, London.* Report on Godwin's Juvenile Library, State Papers, Domestic, Geo. III, 1813 January to March, No.217. File on Godwin's appointment as 'The Officer Keeper and Yeoman Usher in the Receipt of the Exchequer', E403/2499.

*Keats–Shelley Memorial House, Rome.* 'The Library Catalogue of William Godwin in his own Handwriting in 1817'. Available on microfilm from Keats House, London.

'The Catalogue of the Curious Library of that Very Eminent and Distinguished Author William Godwin (1836), compiled by Sotheby and Son', printed in *Sale Catalogues of Libraries of Eminent Persons*, ed. A. N. L. Munby (London: Mansell with Sotheby Parke Bernet Publications, 1973), VIII, 277–318.

## II THE WORKS OF WILLIAM GODWIN

### (i) BOOKS AND PAMPHLETS

These include anonymous, pseudonymous and substantially revised works in chronological order. The first edition of each work and the editions referred to in the text are given.

*The History of the Life of William Pitt, Earl of Chatham* (G. Kearsley, 1783; 2nd ed., G. Kearsley, 1783).

*A Defence of the Rockingham Party, in their Late Coalition with the Right Honourable Frederic Lord North* (J. Stockdale, 1783).

*An Account of the Seminary that will be opened on Monday the Fourth Day of August, at Epsom in Surrey, for the Instruction of Twelve Pupils in the Greek, Latin, French and English Languages* (T. Cadell, 1783).

*The Herald of Literature; or, A Review of the Most Considerable Productions that will be made in the Course of the Ensuing Winter: With Extracts* (J. Murray, 1784).

*Sketches of History, in Six Sermons* (T. Cadell, 1784).

*Instructions to a Statesman. Humbly inscribed to the Right Honourable George Earl Temple* (J. Murray, J. Debrett & J. Sewell, 1784).

*Damon and Delia: A Tale* (T. Hookham, 1784; to be republished by the British Library).

*Italian Letters; or, The History of the Count de St. Julian* (2 vols., G. Robinson, 1784; ed. B. R. Pollin, Lincoln: Univ. of Nebraska Press, 1965).

*Imogen: A Pastoral Romance. In Two Volumes. From the Ancient British* (2 vols., W. Lane, 1784; ed. J. W. Marken, New York: New York Public Library, 1963).

*History of the Internal Affairs of the United Provinces, from the Year 1780, to the Commencement of Hostilities in June 1787* (G. G. & J. Robinson, 1787).

*An Enquiry concerning Political Justice, and its influence on General Virtue and Happiness* (2 vols., G. G. & J. Robinson, 1793).

*Enquiry concerning Political Justice, and its Influence on Morals and Happiness* (2nd ed., 2 vols., G. G. & J. Robinson, 1796; 3rd ed., 2 vols., G. G. & J. Robinson, 1798; J. Watson, 1842).

*Godwin's Political Justice. A Reprint of the Essay on 'Property' from the Original Edition*, ed. H. S. Salt (Swan Sonnenschein, 1890).

*Enquiry concerning Political Justice and its Influence on Morals and Happiness by William Godwin. Photographic facsimile of the third edition corrected, edited with variant readings of the first and second editions and with a critical introduction and notes* by F. E. L. Priestley (3 vols., Toronto: Univ. of Toronto Press, 1946).

*Enquiry concerning Political Justice by William Godwin. With Selections from Godwin's Other Writings*, abridged and edited by K. Codell Carter (O.U.P., 1971).

*De la justice politique*, trans. Benjamin Constant, ed. B. R. Pollin (Québec: Les Presses de l'Université de Laval, 1972).

*Enquiry concerning Political Justice*, ed. Isaac Kramnick (Harmondsworth: Pelican Books, 1976).

*Things as They Are; or, The Adventures of Caleb Williams* (3 vols., B. Crosby, 1794; 2nd ed., 3 vols., G. G. & J. Robinson, 1796; 3rd ed., 3 vols., G. G. & J. Robinson, 1797; 4th ed., 3 vols., W. Simpkin & R. Marshal, 1816).

*Caleb Williams* (H. Colburn & R. Bentley, 1831; trans., Paris: Baudry, 1832; ed. G. Sherburn, New York: Reinhart, 1960; ed. D. McCracken, O.U.P., 1970).

*Cursory Strictures on the Charge delivered by Lord Chief Justice Eyre to the Grand Jury, October 2, 1794* (D. I. Eaton, 1794).

*A Reply to an Answer to Cursory Strictures, supposed to be wrote by Judge Buller. By the Author of Cursory Strictures* (D. I. Eaton, 1794).

*Considerations on Lord Grenville's and Mr. Pitt's Bills, concerning Treasonable and Seditious Practices, and Unlawful Assemblies. By a Lover of Order* (J. Johnson, 1794).

*The Enquirer. Reflections on Education, Manners, and Literature. In a Series of Essays* (G. G. & J. Robinson, 1797; 2nd ed., Edinburgh: John Anderson, London: W. Simpkin & R. Marshal, 1823).

*Memoirs of the Life of Simon Lord Lovat. Written by Himself, in the French Language and now First translated, from the Original Manuscript* (G. Nichol, 1797). Trans. by Godwin in 1784.

*Memoirs of the Author of a Vindication of the Rights of Woman* (J. Johnson, G. G. & J. Robinson, 1798; 2nd ed., J. Johnson, 1798).

*Memoirs of Mary Wollstonecraft*, ed. W. Clark Durrant (London: Constable & Co., New York: Greenberg, 1927).

*Posthumous Works of the Author of a Vindication of the Rights of Woman*, ed. Godwin (4 vols., J. Johnson, 1798).

*St. Leon: A Tale of the Sixteenth Century* (4 vols., G. G. & J. Robinson, 1799; 2nd ed., 4 vols., G. G. & J. Robinson, 1800; 3rd ed., 4 vols., W. Simpkin & R. Marshal, 1816; H. Colburn & R. Bentley, 1831).

*Antonio: A Tragedy in Five Acts* (G. G. & J. Robinson, 1800).

*Thoughts. Occasioned by the Perusal of Dr. Parr's Spital Sermon, preached at Christ Church, April 15, 1800: being a Reply to the Attacks of Dr. Parr, Mr. Mackintosh, the Author of an Essay on Population, and Others* (G. G. & J. Robinson, 1801).

*Life of Geoffrey Chaucer, the Early English Poet, including the Memoirs of his Near Friend and Kinsman, John of Gaunt, Duke of Lancaster: With Sketches of the Manners, Opinions, Arts and Literature of England in the Fourteenth Century* (2 vols., R. Phillips, 1803; 2nd ed., 4 vols., R. Phillips, 1804).

*Fleetwood: or, The New Man of Feeling* (3 vols., R. Phillips, 1805; 2nd ed., R. Bentley, 1832).

*Fables, Ancient and Modern. Adapted for the Use of Children*. By Edward Baldwin (T. Hodgkins, 1805).

*The Looking Glass. A True History of the Early Years of an Artist; Calculated to awaken the Emulation of Young Persons of Both Sexes, in the Pursuit of Every laudable Attainment: particularly in the Cultivation of the Fine Arts*. By Theophilus Marcliffe (T. Hodgkins, 1805).

*The Life of Lady Jane Grey, and of Lord Guildford Dudley, her Husband*. By Theophilus Marcliffe (T. Hodgkins, 1806).

*The History of England. For the Use of Schools and Young Persons*. By Edward Baldwin (T. Hodgkins, 1806).

*The Pantheon: or Ancient History of the Gods of Greece and Rome. Intended to facilitate the Understanding of the Classical Authors, and of the Poets in General*. By Edward Baldwin (T. Hodgkins, 1806).

*Rural Walks* (1806). Lost.

*Scripture Histories, given in the Words of the Original*. By Edward Baldwin (2 vols., ? 1806). Lost.

*Faulkener: A Tragedy* (R. Phillips, 1807).

*Essay on Sepulchres: or, A Proposal for erecting some Memorial of the Illustrious Dead in All Ages on the Spot where their Remains have been interred* (W. Miller, 1809).

*The History of Rome: From the Building of the City to the Ruin of the Republic*. By Edward Baldwin (M. J. Godwin & Co., 1809).

*Mylius's School Dictionary of the English Language. To which is prefixed A New Guide to the English Tongue by Edward Baldwin* (M. J. Godwin & Co., 1809; 9th ed., M. J. Godwin & Co., 1819). Godwin extensively revised Mylius's School Dictionary.

*The Junior Class-Book; or, Reading Lessons for Every Day in the Year*. By William Frederic Mylius (M. J. Godwin & Co., 1809). Probably Godwin's work.

*Outlines of English Grammar, partly abridged from Hazlitt's New and Improved Grammar of the English Tongue*. By Edward Baldwin. (M. J. Godwin & Co., 1810).

*The Poetical Class-Book; or, Reading Lessons for Every Day of the Year, selected from the Most Popular English Poets, Ancient and Modern*. By W. F. Mylius (M. J. Godwin & Co., 1810). Probably Godwin's work.

*The First Book of Poetry. For the Use of Schools. Intended as Reading Lessons for the Younger Classes*. By W. F. Mylius (M. J. Godwin & Co., 1811). Probably Godwin's work.

*Lives of Edward and John Philips. Nephews and Pupils of Milton. Including Various Particulars of the Literary and Political History of their Times* (Longman, Hurst, Rees, Orme & Brown, 1815).

*Letters of Verax, to the Editor of The Morning Chronicle, on the Question of a War to be commenced for the Purpose of putting an End to the Possession of Supreme Power in France by Napoleon Bonaparte* (R. & A. Taylor, 1815).

*Mandeville. A Tale of the Seventeenth Century in England* (3 vols., Edinburgh: A. Constable & Co.; London: Longman, Hurst, Rees, Orme & Brown, 1817).

*Letter of Advice to a Young American: on the Course of Studies it might be Most Advantageous for him to pursue* (M. J. Godwin & Co., 1818).

*Of Population. An Enquiry concerning the Power of Increase in the Numbers of Mankind, being an Answer to Mr. Malthus's Essay on that Subject* (Longman, Hurst, Rees, Orme & Brown, 1820).

*A Reply to the Economists in Defence of the Answer to Mr. Malthus's Essay on Population by William Godwin* (1821). Lost.

*History of Greece: From the Earliest Records of that Country to the Time in which it was reduced into a Roman Province.* By Edward Baldwin (M. J. Godwin & Co., 1821).

*Valperga; or, The Life and Adventures of Castruccio, Prince of Lucca.* By Mary Shelley (3 vols., G. & B. W. Whittaker, 1823). Extensively revised by Godwin.

*History of the Commonwealth of England. From its Commencement, to the Restoration of Charles the Second* (4 vols., H. Colburn, 1824–8).

*Cloudesley. A Tale* (3 vols., H. Colburn & R. Bentley, 1830).

*Thoughts on Man, his Nature, Productions and Discoveries. Interspersed with Some Particulars respecting the Author* (Effingham Wilson, 1831).

*Deloraine* (3 vols., R. Bentley, 1833).

*Lives of the Necromancers: or, An Account of the Most Eminent Persons in Successive Ages, who have claimed for themselves, or to whom has been imputed by Others, the Exercise of Magical Power* (F. J. Mason, 1834).

'The Moral Effects of Aristocracy' in *The Spirit of Monarchy*, by William Hazlitt (Wakelin, 1835).

*An Essay on Trades and Professions by William Godwin, containing a Forcible Exposure of the Demoralizing Tendences of Competition* (Manchester: Heywood; London: Hetherington; Finsbury: Watson; Liverpool: Stewart; Birmingham: Guest; and others, 1842).

*Essays Never Before Published*, ed. C. Kegan Paul (H. S. King, 1873).

*Four Early Pamphlets (1783–1784)*, ed., B. R. Pollin (Gainesville, Florida: Scholars' Facsimiles & Reprints, 1966).

*Uncollected Writings (1785–1822)*, ed. J. W. Marken & B. R. Pollin (Gainesville, Florida: Scholars' Facsimiles & Reprints, 1968).


(ii)  PUBLISHED ARTICLES AND LETTERS

'British and Foreign History Section', *The New Annual Register, or General Repository of History and Politics, and Literature, for the years 1783 to 1790* (1784–91).

'Character of Chatham', *The New Annual Register for 1783* (1784), 19–24.

Unsigned articles, *English Review, or an Abstract of English and Foreign Literature*. These probably include the review of *Imogen, a Pastoral Romance*, ibid., IV (1784), 142; and the articles covering the controversy inspired by Joseph Priestley's *History of the Corruptions of Christianity* (1782), ibid., V (1785), 52–4, 105–24, 377–84.

Letter 'To the Right Hon. William Wyndham Grenville, Joint Paymaster of his Majesty's Forces', signed 'Mucius', *Political Herald, and Review*, I, 3 (October 1785), 165–82.

Letter 'To the Right Honourable Edmund Burke', signed 'Mucius', *Political Herald, and Review* I, 5 (December 1785), 321–9.

Letter 'To the Right Honourable William Pitt', *Political Herald, and Review*, II, 10 (May 1786), 175–83; ibid. (March 1786), 241–9.

Letter 'To the Right Honourable Henry Dundas, Treasurer of the Navy', *Political Herald, and Review*, II, 11 (June 1786), 402–11.

Article on 'Modern Characters, by the Right Honourable William Pitt', *Political Herald, and Review*, II, 13 (August 1786), 19–24.

Letter I 'To the People of Ireland', *Political Herald, and Review*, III, 16 (November 1786), 268–75.

Review of Thomas Holcroft's translation of *The Posthumous Works of Frederic II, King of Prussia*, *Monthly Review*, VI (November 1791), 324–9.

Letter to Richard B. Sheridan, dated 29 April 1791. Publication unknown.

Letter to the National Convention, dated 26 January 1793, *Procès-Verbal de la Convention Nationale* (Paris, 1793), IX, 196–7.

Review of Mrs. Inchbald's *Every One has a Fault*, *European Magazine and London Review*, XXIII (February 1793), 148–9.

Letter I 'To the Editor', signed 'Mucius', *Morning Chronicle*, 1 February 1793.

Letter II 'To Mr. Reeves, Chairman of the Society for Protecting Liberty and Property against Republicans and Levellers', signed 'Mucius', *Morning Chronicle*, 8 February 1793.

Letter III 'To Sir Archibald MacDonald Attorney General', signed 'Mucius', *Morning Chronicle*, 26 March 1793.

Letter IV 'To Such Persons as may be appointed to serve upon Juries for the Trial of Seditious and Treasonable Words', signed 'Mucius', *Morning Chronicle*, 30 March 1793.

Letter to the Editor on Muir and Palmer, *Morning Chronicle* (1793) (Given in Paul, I, 121–3).

'Cursory Strictures on the Charge delivered by Lord Chief Justice Eyre to the Grand Jury, October 2, 1794', *Morning Chronicle*, 21 October 1794.

'A Reply to An Answer to Cursory Strictures, supposed to be wrote by Judge Buller', *The Times*, 25 October 1794.

Letter to the Editor on *Caleb Williams*, dated 7 June 1795, *British Critic*, VI (July 1795), 94–5.

Letter to John Thelwall, dated 23 October 1795, *The Tribune, a Periodical Publication, consisting chiefly of the Political Lectures of John Thelwall*, III (1796), 101–5.

Letter to the Editor on infanticide, dated 10 November 1801, *Monthly Magazine*, XII (December 1801), 387–8.

Letter to James Ogilvie, dated 1797, *National Intelligencer and Washington Advertiser,* II, 225 (16 April 1880), 3.

'Biographical Sketch of the late Joseph Ritson', *Monthly Magazine*, XVI (November 1803), 375–6. Reprinted in *Monthly Mirror*, XIX (May 1805), 291–4.

Letter to the Editor, dated 21 June 1805, requesting materials for a History of England, *Monthly Magazine*, XIX (July 1806), 585.

Letter to the Editor, and a 'Character of Mr. Fox', dated 21 October 1806, *London Chronicle* (22–25 November 1806), p.499.

Letter to the Editor on Kemble's acting, signed 'Aristarchus', dated 3 April 1809, *Morning Chronicle*, 5 April 1809.

Letter to the Editor on the question of a war against Napoleon Bonaparte, signed 'Verax', *Morning Chronicle*, 25 May 1815.

Memoir of William Nicholson, 19 June 1815, publication unknown.

Memoir of John Philpot Curran, *Morning Chronicle*, 16 October 1817.

'A Letter of Advice to a Young American', *Scots Magazine*, N.S. II (January 1818), 57–65.

'A Letter of Advice to a Young American', *Analectic Magazine* (Philadelphia), XII (August 1818), 128–35. Reprinted in *Port Folio* (Philadelphia), IV, 6 (September 1818), 170–83; *Robinson's Magazine* (Baltimore), XI (November 1818), 262–8; and *Georgia Journal* (Milledgeville), (29 June 1819), pp.1–2.

'Further Letters of Advice to a Young American', *Analectic Magazine* (Philadelphia), XIV (September 1819), 230–43.

Letter to the Editor on Population, dated 25 December 1821, *Examiner* (6 January 1822), pp.3–4. Probably Godwin's.

Letter to the Editor on Population, signed 'L'Ami des Hommes', dated 29 December 1821, *Morning Chronicle*, 11 January 1822.

'Fragment of a Romance', *New Monthly Magazine*, XXXVII (January 1833), 32–41.

'Memoir of the Life and Writings of William Godwin, Jun.', prefixed to his novel, *Transfusion* (1835), I, vi–xix.

*The Elopement of Percy Bysshe Shelley and Mary Wollstonecraft Godwin. As narrated by William Godwin. With Commentary by H. Buxton Forman* (Privately printed, 1811).

'Letter of William Godwin to Charles Ollier', 1 March 1830', *Catalogue of Autograph Letters* (Maggs Bros., 1922), item 3276, p.90.

*Tragical Consequences; or, A Disaster at Deal: being an unpublished letter of William Godwin, dated Wednesday, November 18th, 1789, and remarks thereon by Edmund Blunden* (Fytton Armstrong, 1931).

'Letter of William Godwin to David Booth. Author of the *Analytical Dictionary,* of December 27, 1812', *Bodleian Library Record,* I (1940), 223.

'Letter of William Godwin to William Botwright', *A Catalogue of Autograph Letters* (Winifred A. Myers, 1965), item 215, p.41.

*Godwin & Mary: Letters of William Godwin and Mary Wollstonecraft,* ed. Ralph M. Wardle (Lawrence: Kansas U.P., 1967).


III  SECONDARY WORKS ON WILLIAM GODWIN

    (i)  UNPUBLISHED WORKS (Ph.D. theses, unless otherwise stated)

ABREU, John Warren, 'Philosophy into Fiction: The Novels of William Godwin' (City University of New York, 1978).

ALLEN, B. Sprague, 'William Godwin: His Life, his Works, and his Influence on Shelley' (Harvard University, 1913).

CLARK, John Philip, 'The Social and Political Philosophy of William Godwin' (Tulane University, 1974).

DUMAS, Donald Gilbert, *'Caleb Williams:* Doctrine into Art' (University of California, Berkeley, 1968).

EARLE, Osborne, 'The Reputation and Influence of William Godwin in America' (Harvard University, 12938).

FLANDERS, Jane Townsend, 'Charles Brockden Brown and William Godwin: Parallels and Divergences' (University of Wisconsin, 1965).

FLEISHER, David, 'William Godwin: His Background, Thought and Influence on Shelley's Formative Period' (Harvard University, 1941).

JUROE, James, *'St. Leon: A Tale of the Sixteenth Century* by William Godwin. A Critical and Annotated Edition' (Northwestern University, 1950).

KRANCIK, John Jnr., 'The Hero of Feeling in William Godwin's Fiction' (University of Michigan, 1968).

LEWISOHN, David, 'The Political Philosophy of William Godwin' (M.A. thesis, University of Sussex, 1967).

MARKEN, Jack W., 'The Early Works of William Godwin' (University of Indiana, 1953).

MARSHALL, Peter H., 'William Godwin: A Study of the Origins, Development, and Influence of his Philosophy' (D.Phil. thesis, University of Sussex, 1976).

McCELVEY, George Edward, 'William Godwin's Novels: Theme and Craft' (Duke University, 1969).

McCRACKEN, James David, 'Politics and Propaganda in Godwin's Novels' (University of Chicago, 1967).

MIKHALCHEV, Teodor, 'Wandlungen and Windersprüche in der Philosophie Godwins' (Hamburg University, 1937).

MYERS, Mitzi, 'Aspects of William Godwin's Reputation in the 1790s' (Rice University, 1969).

PETERSON, Carrol David, 'The Development of William Godwin's Thought after 1793' (University of Arkansas, 1972).

PREU, James A., 'The Importance of Jonathan Swift in the Genesis of William Godwin's *Political Justice'* (Tulane University, 1952).

PRIESTLEY, F. E. L., 'A Critical Edition of William Godwin's *Enquiry concerning Political Justice'* (University of Toronto, 1940).

RIEGER, James H., 'The Gnostic Prometheus: A Study of Godwin and the Shelleys' (Harvard University, 1963).

ROEMER, Donald, 'William Godwin's *Caleb Williams:* The Ideologue as Novelist' (Brandeis University, 1971).

ROSEN, Frederick, 'Progress and Democracy: William Godwin's Contribution to Political Philosophy' (University of London, 1965).

ROSENTHAL, William A., 'A Critical Edition of William Godwin's *The Enquirer*' (Northwestern University, 1949).

THOMAS, James Andrew, 'The Philosophical Anarchism of William Godwin: His Philosophy of Man, State, and Society' (University of Southern California, Los Angeles, 1964).

WEEKES, Harold Victor, 'William Godwin as a Novelist' (University of Toronto, 1961).

WILLIAMS, Dennis A., 'William Godwin's Problem of Autonomy, 1791–1797 (University of Kentucky, 1974).

(ii) BOOKS AND PAMPHLETS

(a) *Before 1900*

BULLER, Sir Francis, *Answer to Cursory Strictures. On a Charge delivered to the Grand Jury, October 2, 1794, by Lord Justice Eyre. Said to be written by Judge Thumb. In the Ministerial Paper called The Times, October 25, 1794* (D. I. Eaton, 1794).

EVERETT, Alexander H., *New Ideas on Population: With Remarks on the Theories of Malthus and Godwin* J. Muller, 1823).

GREEN, Thomas, *An Examination of the Leading Principle of the New System of Morals, as that Principle is stated and applied in Mr. Godwin's Enquiry, in a Letter to a Friend* (1799) (2nd ed., T. N. Longman, 1799).

MALTHUS, Thomas, *An Essay on the Principle of Population, as it affects the Future Improvement of Society, with Remarks on the Speculations of Mr. Godwin, M. Condorcet, and other Writers* (1798), ed. A. Flew (Harmondsworth: Penguin Books, 1970).

*Observations on a Pamphlet entitled, The Defence of the Rockingham Party* (1784).

PARR, Samuel, *A Spital Sermon, preached at Christ Church, upon Easter Tuesday, April 15, 1800; to which are added Notes* (J. Mawman, 1801).

PAUL, C. Kegan, *William Godwin: his Friends and Contemporaries* (2 vols., Henry S. King, 1876).

PLACE, Francis, *Illustrations and Proofs of the Principle of Population; including an Examination of the Proposed Remedies of Mr. Malthus and a Reply to the Objectoions of Mr. Godwin and Others* (Longman, Hurst, Rees, Orme & Brown, 1822).

PROBY, William C., *Modern Philosophy and Barbarism: or, A Comparison between the Theory of Godwin and the Practice of Lycurgus* (R. H. Westley, 1798).

(b) *After 1900*

ARGENTON, Alberto, *La Concezione pedagogica di William Godwin* (Bologna: Patrón, 1977).

BRAILSFORD, H. N., *Shelley, Godwin and their Circle* (O.U.P., 1913).

BRODTMANN, Catherina N., *William Godwin, der Theoretiker des Individualisischen Anarchismus* (Meeuws: Kaldenkirchen, 1931).

BROWN, Ford K., *The Life of William Godwin* (J. M. Dent & Son, 1926).

CLARK, John P., *The Philosophical Anarchism of William Godwin* (Princeton, New Jersey: Princeton U.P., 1977).

DAY, Hem, pseud. (i.e. Marcel Dieu), *A l'école de Godwin. La non-violence comme technique de libération* (Paris-Bruxelles: Pensée et Action, 1953).

DETRE, Jean, *A Most Extraordinary Pair: Mary Wollstonecraft and William Godwin* (New York: Doubleday & Co., 1975).

ELSNER, Paul, *Percy Bysshe Shelleys Abhangigkeit von William Godwins Political Justice* (Berlin: Mayer & Muller, 1906).

FLEISHER, David, *William Godwin: A Study in Liberalism* (G. Allen & Unwin, 1951).

GOURG, Raymond, *William Godwin (1756–1836): sa vie, ses oeuvres principales, 'La Justice politique'* (Paris: Felix Alcan, 1908).

HUGHES, Dean Thomas, *Romance and Psychological Realism in William Godwin's Novels* (New York: Arno Press, 1980).

GRYLLS, Rosalie G., *William Godwin and his World* (Odhams Press, 1953).

JENSEN, Albert, *William Godwin, Anarkismens Forste Vetenskaplige Teoretiker och Apostel* (Falkoping, 1916).

KAYMER, Gunter, *Der Gesellschaftliche Optimismus William Godwins in Seiner Literarischen Darlegung* (Cologne, 1958).

LOCKE, Don, *A Fantasy of Reason: The Life and Thought of William Godwin* (Routledge & Kegan Paul, 1980).

MICHALTSCHEFF, Teodor, *Grundzuge, Stellung, und Entwicklung der Philosophie William Godwins* (Hamburg, 1935).

MEYER, Johannes, *William Godwins Romane. Ein Beitrang zur Geschichte des Englischen Romans* (Weida i. Th: Thomas & Hubert, 1906).

MONRO, D. H., *Godwin's Moral Philosophy: An Interpretation of William Godwin* (O.U.P., 1953).

PALACIO, Jean de, *William Godwin et son monde intérieur* (Lille: Presses Universitaires de Lille, 1980).

POLLIN, Burton R., *Education and Enlightenment in the Works of William Godwin* (New York: Las Americas, 1962).

POWERS, Catherine Richardson, *The Influence of William Godwin on the Novels of Mary Shelley* (New York: Arno Press, 1980).

PREU, James A., *Antimonarchism in Swift and Godwin* (Tallahassee: Florida State U.P., 1955).

———, *The Dean and the Anarchist* (Tallahassee: Florida State U.P., 1959).

RAMUS, Pierre, pseud. (i.e. Rudolf Grossman), *William Godwin, der Theoretiker des Kommunistischen Anarchismus: Eine Biographische Studie mit Auszugen aus seinen Schriften* (Leipzig: Mit Geleitwort von W. Borgius, Fee Dietrich, 1907).

ROBINSON, Victor, *Lives of Great Altrurians: William Godwin and Mary Wollstonecraft* (New York: The Altrurians, 1907).

RODWAY, A. E., *Godwin and the Age of Transition* (G. G. Harrap, 1952).

ROUSSIN, Henri, *William Godwin* (Paris: Plon-Nourrit, 1913).

SAITZEFF, Helene, *William Godwin und die Anfänge des Anarchismus im XVIII. Jahrhundert. Ein Beitrag zur Geschichte des Politischen Individualismus* (Berlin: Verlag von O. Haring, 1907).

SCHEUERMANN, Mona, *The Novels of William Godwin and Those of his Contemporaries* (New York: Arno Press, 1980).

SHIRAI, Atsushi, *William Godwin Kenkyu* (Tokyo, 1964).

SIMON, Helene, *William Godwin und Mary Wollstonecraft: Eine Biographisch-Soziologische Studie* (Munich: C. H. Beck, 1909).

SMITH, Elton Edward and Esther Greenwell, *William Godwin* (New York: Twayne, 1965).

TYSDAHL, B. J., *William Godwin as Novelist* (Athlone Press, 1981).

WÖHLER, Eva, *Das Bevölkerungsproblem bei Malthus in seinem Gegensatz zu den Theorien von Godwin* (Hamburg, 1938).

WOODCOCK, George, *William Godwin. A Biographical Study* (Porcupine Press, 1946).

ZACCARIA, Césare, *William Godwin: Le constructeur. Fédérations de personnes* (Paris-Bruxelles: Pensée et Action, 1953).

(iii) ARTICLES AND CHAPTERS

(a) *Before 1900*

ANON., 'Biographical Sketch of William Godwin', *Monthly Mirror*, XIX (1805), 5–7, 85–93.

———, 'An Estimate of the Literary Character of William Godwin', *Monthly Magazine*, XLV (1818), 299–302.

———, 'On the Writings and Character of Godwin', *Tatler*, 287 (4 August 1831), 117–18; 288 (5 August 1831), 121–2; 291 (9 August 1831), 133–4; 300 (19 August 1831), 169–70; 305 (25 August 1831), 189–90; 306 (26 August 1831), 194; 308 (29 August 1831), 201–2.

———, Obituaries of William Godwin, *Morning Chronicle* (9 April 1836); *Spectator*, IX (9 April 1836), 337–8; *Examiner* (10 April 1836), p.230; *Atlas* (10 April 1836), p.229; *Athenaeum* (16 April 1836), p.273; *Gentleman's Magazine*, V (1836), 666–8; *New Monthly Magazine*, XLVII (1836), 133–4.

————, 'William Godwin', *The Penny Encyclopaedia of the Society for the Diffusion of Useful Knowledge*, XI (1838), 290–1.

BELSHAM, Thomas, 'Godwin's Account of Virtue'. *Elements of the Philosophy of the Mind, and of Moral Philosophy* (J. Johnson, 1801), pp.439–47.

CONSTANCIO, F. S., 'William Godwin', *Biographie universelle*, ed. L. G. Michaud (1852–66), XVII, 40–2.

CONSTANT, Benjamin, 'De Godwin, et de son ouvrage sur la justice politique', *Mercure de France*, II (1817), 161–73.

DEANE, G. F., 'William Godwin', *London Magazine*, I (August 1820), 163–9.

DE QUINCEY, Thomas, 'Notes on Gilfillan's Gallery of Literary Portraits', *Tait's Edinburgh Magazine*, VII (1845), 724.

DOWDEN, Edward, 'Godwin and Mary Wollstonecraft', *The French Revolution and English Literature* (New York: Scribner, 1897), pp.46–89.

FENWICK, John, 'William Godwin', *Public Characters of 1799–1800* (R. Phillips, 1799), 358–76.

GILFILLAN, George, 'William Godwin', *A Gallery of Literary Portraits* (Edinburgh: W. Tait, 1845), pp.15–36.

HAZLITT, William, 'William Godwin', *The Spirit of the Age; or, Contemporary Portraits* (1825) (O.U.P. 1954), pp.19–39.

————, Review of *Cloudesley* and Estimate of Other Works, *Edinburgh Review*, LI (1830), 144–59.

HOLCROFT, Thomas, Review of *Political Justice, Monthly Review*, N.S. X (1793), 311–20; ibid., 435–45; ibid., XI (1793), 187–96.

HANCOCK, Albert E., 'William Godwin, the English Radical', *The French Revolution and the English Poets* (New York: H. Holt & Co., 1899), pp.30–9.

HUNT, Leigh, Review of *Caleb Williams, Tatler*, No.185 (7 April 1831), 737.

JEAFFRESON, J. C., 'William Godwin', *Novels and Novelists, from Elizabeth to Victoria*, (Hurst & Blackett, 1858) I, 369–88.

'K', 'Godwin's and Phillips' School Books', *Christian Remembrancer; or, The Churchman's Biblical, Ecclesiastical, and Literary Miscellany*, III (1831), 457–8.

MACKINTOSH, James, Review of *The Lives of Edward and John Philips, Edinburgh Review*, XXV (1815), 485–501.

————, Review of *Mandeville, Scots Magazine*, N.S. II (January 1818), 57–65.

MALTBY, Edward, 'Mr. Godwin's Misrepresentations of the Christian Religion and the Character of its Founder Examined', *Illustrations of the Truth of the Christian Religion* (Cambridge, 1802), pp.285–325.

MALTHUS, Thomas R., Review of *Of Population, Edinburgh Review*, XXXV (1821), 362–77.

MARTINEAU, Harriet, Review of *Thoughts on Man, Monthly Repository*, N.S. V (1831), 433–50.

OLIPHANT, Margaret, 'William Godwin', *The Literary History of England at the End of the Eighteenth and Beginning of the Nineteenth Century* (Macmillan, 1882) II, 207–67.

PLACE, Francis, 'On the Theories of Malthus and Godwin', *New Monthly Magazine*, N.S. I (1821), 195–205.

POE, Edgar Allan, Review of *Lives of the Necromancers, Southern Literary Messenger*, II (December 1835), 65.

ROBINSON, Henry Crabb, Letter to the Editor from 'Philo-Godwin', *Cambridge Intelligencer*, CVII (1 August 1795), 4.

SALT, H. S., 'Godwin's *Political Justice*', *Time. A Monthly Magazine*, N.S. III (1890), 508–19.

————, 'William Godwin', *Today. A Monthly Magazine of Scientific Socialism*, VIII (1887), 13–23.

SCOTT, Sir Walter, Review of *Life of Chaucer, Edinburgh Review*, III (1804), 437–52.

————, Review of *Fleetwood, Edinburgh Review*, VI (April, 1805), 182–93.

SHELLEY, Mary Wollstonecraft, Review of *Cloudesley*, *Blackwood's Edinburgh Magazine*, XXVII (1830), 711–16.

——, 'Memoirs of William Godwin', *Caleb Williams* (H. Colburn & R. Bentley, 1831), Preface, pp.i–xiii.

SHELLEY, Percy Bysshe, Letter on *Mandeville*, inserted by Godwin as a 'Letter from Oxfordshire', *Morning Chronicle* (9 December, 1817).

——, Review of *Mandeville*, *Examiner* (28 December, 1817), 826–7.

SMITH, Horace, 'A Graybeard's Gossip about his Literary Acquaintance', *New Monthly Magazine*, LXXXII (1848), 338–9.

SMYTH, William, 'William Godwin', *Lectures on the History of the French Revolution* (H. G. Bohn, 1855) II, 208–29.

SOUTHEY, Robert, Review of *Life of Chaucer*, *The Annual Review, and History of Literature for the Year 1803*, II (1804), 462–73.

STEPHEN, Leslie, 'Godwin and Shelley', *Cornhill Magazine*, XXXIX (1879), 281–302.

——, 'William Godwin', *D.N.B.* XXII (1890), 64–8.

——, 'William Godwin's Novels', *National Review*, XXXVIII (1902), 908–23.

——, 'William Godwin', *History of English Thought in the Eighteenth Century* (1876) (New York: Harcourt, Brace & World, 1962), II, 224–39.

TALFOURD, T., 'The Living Novelists', *New Monthly Magazine*, XIV (1820), 54–7.

THELWALL, John, 'On William Godwin', *The Tribune, a Periodical Publication, consisting chiefly of the Political Lectures of John Thelwall*, II (1796), vi–xviii; ibid., III (1796), 101–5.

(b) *After 1900*

ADAMS, M. Ray, 'Mary Hays, Disciple of William Godwin', *Publications of the Modern Language Association*, LV (1940), 472–83.

AGOURSKY, Michael, '*Caleb Williams* in Mojaisk', *Times Literary Supplement* (25 March 1977), p.371.

ALBRECHT, W. P. and PULOS, C. E., 'Godwin and Malthus', *Publications of the Modern Language Association*, LXX (1955), 552–6.

ALDRIDGE, A. O., 'Jonathan Edwards and William Godwin on Virtue', *American Literature*, XVIII (1947), 308–18.

ALLEN, B. Sprague, 'The Reaction against William Godwin', *Modern Philology*, XVI (1918), 57–75.

——, 'William Godwin as a Sentimentalist', *Publications of the Modern Language Association*, XXIII (1918), 1–29.

——, 'William Godwin and the Stage', *Publications of the Modern Language Association*, XXXV (1920), 358–74.

——, 'Godwin's Influence on John Thelwall', *Publications of the Modern Language Association*, XXXVII (1922), 662–82.

——, 'Minor Disciples of Radicalism in the Revolutionary Era', *Modern Philology*, XXI (1924), 277–301.

ALLEN, Walter, 'Introduction', *The Adventures of Caleb Williams* (Cassell, 1966), pp.vi–xv.

ALLENTUCK, Marcia, 'An Unpublished Account of Encounters with William Godwin in 1804', *Keats–Shelley Journal*, XX (1971), 19–21.

'Answer to Query about William Godwin', *Notes and Queries*, III, 3 (2 August, 1862), 94.

ARVON, Henri, 'William Godwin', *L'Anarchisme* (Paris: Presses Universitaires de France, 1951), pp.22–30.

BARKER, Gerard, 'Justice to *Caleb Williams*', *Studies in the Novel*, VI (1974), 377–88.

——, 'Ferninando Falkland's Fall: Grandison in Disarray', *Papers on Language and Literature,* XVI (1980), 376–86.

BECKETT, Juliet, 'Introduction' to Godwin's *St. Leon* (New York: Arno, 1971), ix–xxix.

BLUNDEN, Edmund, 'Godwin's Library Catalogue', *Keats–Shelley Memorial Bulletin, Rome*, IX (1950), 27–9.

————, *Tragical Consequences; or a Disaster at Deal: being an Unpublished Letter of William Godwin dated Wednesday, November 18, 1789, and Remarks thereon* (Fytton Armstrong, 1931).

BOULTON, James T., 'William Godwin, Philosopher and Novelist', *The Language of Politics in the Age of Wilkes and Burke* (Routledge & Kegan Paul, 1963), pp.207–49.

BRAILSFORD, H. N., 'William Godwin', *Great Democrats*, ed. A. Barratt Brown (I. Nicholson & Watson, 1934), pp.321–66.

BROWN, Ford K., 'Notes on 41 Skinner Street', *Modern Language Notes*, LIV (1939), 326–32.

BUTLER, Marilyn, *'Caleb Williams', Jane Austen and the War of Ideas* (O.U.P., 1975), pp.57–75.

————, 'Godwin, Burke and *Caleb Williams*', *Essays in Criticism*, XXXII (1982), 237–57.

BUXTON FORMAN, H., *The Elopement of Percy Bysshe Shelley and Mary Wollstonecraft Godwin, as narrated by William Godwin, with Commentary* (privately printed, 1911).

CELLO, Jean, 'Godwin contre Rousseau', *Cahiers de Pensée et Action*, I (1953), 37–47.

CHANDLER, S. B., 'Manzoni e William Godwin', *Rivista di Letteratura Moderne e Comparate*, XXIII (1975), 271–7.

CLARK, John P., 'On Anarchism in an Unreal World: Kramnick's View of Godwin and the Anarchists', *American Political Science Review*, LXIX (1975), 162–7.

————, 'Rejoinder to Comment by Isaac Kramnick', *American Political Science Review*, XIX (1975), 169–70.

CLIFFORD, Gay, *'Caleb Williams* and *Frankenstein:* First Person Narrative and "Things as They Are"', *Genrex* (1977), 601–17.

CLOGAN, Paul M., 'Literary Criticism in William Godwin's *Life of Chaucer*', *Medievalia et Humanistica*, VI (1975), 189–98.

COBB, Joan P., 'Godwin's Novels and *Political Justice*', *Enlightenment Essays*, IV (1973), 15–28.

COLLINS, H., 'William Godwin', *Socialist Review*, VIII (1961), 6.

COLLINS, John Churton, 'William Godwin and Mary Wollstonecraft', *The Posthumous Essays of John Churton Collins* (J. M. Dent & Sons, 1912), pp.68–98.

COLMER, John, 'Godwin's *Mandeville* and Peacock's *Nightmare Abbey*', *Review of English Studies*, XXI (1970), 331–6.

COOK, Wayne, 'Two Letters of William Godwin', *Keats–Shelley Journal*, XV (1966), 9–13.

CORRADO, Adriana, 'Ipotesi di Lettura di *Caleb Williams*', *Studi di Letteratura e di Linguistica*, III (1983), 46–122.

CRUTWELL, Patrick, 'On *Caleb Williams*', *Hudson Review*, XI (1958), 87–95.

DAVENPORT, William H., 'Shelley and Godwin's "Essay on Sepulchres"', *Notes and Queries*, CXCVII (1952), 124–5.

DAY, Hem, pseud. (i.e. Marcel Dieu), 'La Non-violence comme technique de libération', *Cahiers de Pensée et Action*, I (1953), 68–74.

————, 'El Valor Literario de William Godwin I–II', *Cenit*, III (August 1953), 982–4; III (September 1953), 1020–2.

DEEN, Floyd H., 'The Genesis of *Martin Faber* in *Caleb Williams*', *Modern Language Notes*, LIX (1944), 315–17.

DEEN, L. W., 'Coleridge and the Sources of Pantisocracy: Godwin, the Bible, and Hartley', *Boston University Studies in English*, V (1961), 234–45.

DIXSAUT, Jean, 'Le discours troué: du bon usage des citations dans *Caleb Williams*', *Langues Modernes*, LXXII (1978), 612–6.

DOLLEANS, Edouard, 'Un Essai de psychologie historique: William Godwin', *Revue de Métaphysique et de Morale*, XXIII, 2 (March 1916), 363–95.

–————, 'Mary Wollstonecraft et William Godwin', *Drames intérieurs* (Paris, 1944), pp.83–109.

DRIVER, C. H., 'William Godwin', *The Social and Political Ideas of Some Representative Thinkers of the Revolutionary Era*, ed. F. J. C. Hearnshaw (George Harrap & Co., 1931), pp.160–71.

DUERKSEN, R. A., *'Caleb Williams, Political Justice* and *Billy Budd*', *American Literature*, XXXVIII (1966), 372–6.

DUMAS, D. Gilbert, 'Things as They Were: The Original Ending of *Caleb Williams*', *Studies in English Literature*, VI (1966), 575–97.

ELTZBACHER, Paul, 'Godwin's Teaching', *Anarchism*, trans. S. T. Byington (New York: Benj. R. Tucker, 1908), pp.40–64.

ENGLAND, Martha, 'Felix Culpa' (on *Imogen*), *Bulletin of the New York Public Library*, LXVII (1963), 115–18. Reprinted in *Imogen: A Pastoral Romance*, ed. J. W. Marken (New York, 1963), pp. 109–112.

ERDMAN, D. V., 'Blake Entries in Godwin's Diary', *Notes and Queries*, CXCVIII (August 1953), 354–6.

———, 'Blake and Godwin', *Notes and Queries*, CXCIX (February 1954), 66–7.

EVANS, Frank B., 'Shelley, Godwin, Hume and the Doctrine of Necessity', *Studies in Philology*, XXXVII (1940), 632–40.

EWEN, D. R., 'Godwin and Shelley', *Times Literary Supplement* (6 April 1951), p.213.

FAIRCHILD, H. N., 'Burke and Godwin', *The Romantic Quest* (New York: Columbia U.P., 1931), pp.16–33.

FAROUK, Marion Omar, '*Mandeville: A Tale of the Seventeenth Century* — Historical Novel or Psychological Study?', *Essays in Honor of William Gallacher* (Berlin: Humboldt-Universitat, 1966), pp.111–17.

FEDELI, Ugo, 'William Godwin I–II', *Umanita Nova*, XXXI (15 July 1951), 3; (22 July 1951), 3.

FITZPATRICK, Martin, 'William Godwin and the Rational Dissenters', *The Price–Priestley Newsletter* III (1979), 4–28.

FLANDERS, W. A., 'Godwin and Gothicism: *St. Leon*', *Texas Studies in Literature and Language*, VII (1967), 533–45.

FLEISHER, David, 'On Godwin and Shelley', *Times Literary Supplement* (27 April 1951), p.261.

FURBANK, P. N., 'Godwin's Novels', *Essays in Criticism*, V (1955), 214–28.

FYKADA, Hiroshi, 'William Godwin's Anarchism', *Annual Report of Research* (Faculty of Letters, University of Tokyo) No.6 (1955), 327–43.

G. A. C., 'William Godwin', *Notes and Queries*, 3, I (28 June 1862), 503.

GARCES, Fortun, 'La Vuelta a Godwin', *Cenit*, I (1951), 163–6.

GARRETT, Roland, 'Anarchism or Political Democracy: The Case of William Godwin', *Social Theory and Practice*, I (1971), 111–20.

GARROD, H. W., 'Godwin and Godwinism', *Wordsworth; Lectures and Essays* (O.U.P., 1913), pp.57–72.

GEORGE, Margaret, 'The Married Woman,' *One Woman's Situation. A Study of Mary Wollstonecraft* (Urbana, Chicago, London: Univ. of Illinois Press, 1970) pp.149–68.

GLASHEEN, Adaline E., 'Shelley's First Published Review of *Mandeville*', *Modern Language Notes*, LIX (1944), 172–3.

GOLD, Alex, Jr., 'It's Only Love: The Politics of Passion in Godwin's *Caleb Williams*', *Texas Studies in Literature and Language*, XIX (1977), 135–60.

GRAY, Alexander, 'William Godwin', *The Socialist Tradition: Moses to Lenin* (Longmans, 1963), pp.114–35.

GREEN, David B., 'Letters of Godwin and Thomas Holcroft to William Dunlap', *Notes and Queries*, CCI (october 1956), 441–3.

GREGORY, Allene, 'William Godwin', *The French Revolution and the English Novel* (New York: G. P. Putnam's Sons, 1915), pp.86–119.

GRIFFITH, Ben W., 'An Experiment on the American Bookseller: Two Letters from Irving to Godwin', *Nineteenth Century Fiction*, XII (1957), 237–9.

GROB, Alan, 'Wordsworth and Godwin: A Reassessment', *Studies in Romanticism*, VI (1966), 99–119.

GROSS, Harvey, 'The Pursuer and the Pursued: A Study of *Caleb Williams*', *Texas University Studies in Literature and Language*, I (1959), 401–11.

HALEVY, Elie, 'William Godwin', *The Growth of Philosophic Radicalism* (1928), trans. M. Morris (Faber & Faber, 1972), pp.191–203.

HALLER, William, 'Political Justice, 1793 and 1919', The Review, I (1919), 514–15.

HARPER, George M., 'Rousseau, Godwin and Wordsworth', Atlantic Monthly, CIX (1912), 639–50.

HARVEY, A. D., 'The Nightmare of Caleb Williams', Essays in Criticism, XXVI (1976), 236–49.

———, Frankenstein and Caleb Williams, Keats–Shelley Journal, XXVIII (1980), 236–49.

HODGART, Matthew, 'Politics and Prose Style in the Late Eighteenth Century: The Radicals', Bulletin of the New York Public Library, LXV (1962), 464–9.

———, 'Radical Prose in the Late Eighteenth Century', The English Mind: Studies in the English Moralists presented to Basil Willey, ed. H. S. Davies and G. Watson (C.U.P., 1964), pp.149–52.

HOGLE, Jerrold E., 'The Texture of the Self in Godwin's Things as They Are', Boundary, VII, 2 (1979), 261–81.

HUNTER, Parks C. Jr., 'William Godwin's Lengthy Preoccupation with Antonio, Keats-Shelley Journal, XXIII (1974), 21–4.

JAURES, Jean, 'William Godwin', Histoire socialiste de la révolution française (Paris: Editions de la Librairie de l'Humanité, 1922–3), V, 420–64.

JOHNS, D. S., 'William Godwin — Sentimentalist', Congregational Quarterly, XIV (1936), 195–205.

JOLL, James, 'William Godwin', The Anarchists (Eyre & Spottiswoode, 1964), pp.31–9.

KAREYEV, N. I., 'William Godwin and his Political Justice', Uchenyye Zapiski (Moscow), III (1929), 327–40.

KELLY, Gary D., 'Godwin, Wollstonecraft and Rousseau', Women and Literature, III, 2 (1975), 21–6.

———, 'History and Fiction: Bethlem Gabor in Godwin's St. Leon', English Language Notes, XIV (1976), 117–20.

———, 'William Godwin', The English Jacobin Novel 1780–1805 (O.U.P., 1976), pp.179–260.

KERMODE, Frank, 'On Caleb Williams, Observer Magazine, (18 November 1979), p.130.

KIELY, Robert, 'Caleb Williams', The Romantic Novel in England (Cambridge, Mass., Harvard U.P., 1972), pp.81–97.

KINGSLAND, William G., 'Shelley and Godwin', Poet-Lore, X (1898), 389–97.

KOSZUL, A., 'Un disciple inconnu de Godwin', Etudes Anglaises, VI (1953), 239–49.

KOSZUL, A. and BRESCH, G., 'Une Lettre de William Godwin', Revue Anglo-Americaine, VI (1929), 430–2.

KOVAČEVIČ, Ivanka, 'William Godwin', Fact into Fiction: English Literature and the Industrial Scene 1750–1850 (Leicester: Leicester U.P., 1975), pp. 177–210.

KRAMNICK, Isaac, 'On Anarchism and the Real World: William Godwin and Radical England', American Political Science Review, LXVI (1972), 114–28.

———, 'Introduction', Enquiry concerning Political Justice (Harmondsworth: Pelican Books, 1976), pp. 7–54.

KROPF, C. R., 'Caleb Williams and the Attack on Romance', Studies in the Novel, VIII (1976), 81–7.

KUCZYNSKI, Ingrid, 'Pastoral Romance and Political Justice', Essays in Honor of William Gallacher (Berlin: Humboldt-Universitat, 1966), pp.101–10.

KUIČ, Ranka, Revolucionarna Misao Persija Biša Šelija u Njegovim Proznim i Poetskim Delima: Njeni Izvori, Razvoj i Odnos Prema Idejama Viljema Godvina i Tomasa Peina (Belgrade: Univ. of Belgrade, 1968), pp.83–119.

LAMOINE, Georges, 'Caleb Williams, le mythe de Faust, et l'intention morale', Bulletin de la Société d'Etudes Anglo-Americaines des XVIIe et XVIIIe Siècles, IX (1979), 91–110.

LESSENICH, Rolf P., 'Godwin and Shelley: Rhetoric versus Revolution', Studia Neophilogica, XLVII (1975), 40–52.

LOOMIS, Emerson Robert, 'The Godwins in the Letters of Shah-Coolen', Nineteenth Century Fiction, XVII (1962), 78–80.

LOVEMAN, Samuel, 'Godwin and Shelley', Times Literary Supplement (23 March 1951), p.181.

LUND, Mary G., 'Mary Shelley's Father', *Discourse*, XI (1969), 130–5.

MACMULLAN, Hugh H., 'Satire of George Walker's *Vagabond* (1799) on Rousseau and Godwin', *Publications of the Modern Language Association*, LIII (1937), 215–29.

MARKEN, Jack W., 'William Godwin's Writings for *The New Annual Register*', *Modern Language Notes*, LXVIII (1953), 477–9.

———, 'The Canon and Chronology of William Godwin's Early Works', *Modern Language Notes*, LXIX (1954), 176–80.

———, 'Joseph Bevan and William Godwin', *Georgia Historical Quarterly*, XLIII (1959), 302–18.

———, 'William Godwin's *Instructions to a Statesman*', *Yale University Library Gazette*, XXXIV (1959), 73–81.

———, 'William Godwin and *The Political Herald, and Review*', *Bulletin of the New York Public Library*, LXV (1961), 517–33.

———, 'Introduction to *Imogen*', *Bulletin of the New York Public Library*, XLVII (1963), 7–16.

———, 'William Godwin's *History of the United Provinces*', *Philological Quarterly*, XLV (1966), 379–86.

MARSHALL, Peter H., 'William & Mary', *New Statesman* (10 December 1976), p.842.

———, Review of Don Locke, *A Fantasy of Reason: The Life and Thought of William Godwin* (1980), *Modern Language Review*, LXXVII, 4 (October, 1982), 928–9.

———, Review of Jean de Palacio, *William Godwin et son monde intérieur* (1980), *Etudes Anglaises*, XXXV, 3 (Juillet-Sept., 1982), 335–6.

———, 'Introduction' to William Godwin's *Damon and Delia*, to be published by the British Library.

MARSHALL, William H., '*Caleb Williams* and *The Cenci*', *Notes and Queries*, N.S. VII (1960), 260–3.

McCRACKEN, David, 'Godwin's *Caleb Williams*: A Fictional Rebuttal of Burke', *Studies in Burke and his Time*, XI (1969–70), 1442–52.

———, 'Godwin's Literary Theory: The Alliance between Fiction and Political Philosophy', *Philological Quarterly*, XLIX (1970), 113–33.

———, 'Godwin's Reading in Burke', *English Language Notes*, VII (1970), 264–70.

———, 'Introduction', *Caleb Williams* (O.U.P., 1970), pp.vii–xxvi.

MERCHANT, W. M., 'Wordsworth's Godwinian Period', *Comparative Literature Studies*, IV (1942), 18–23.

MILLER, Jacqueline T., 'The Imperfect Tale: Articulation, Rhetoric, and Self in *Caleb Williams*', *Criticism*, XX (1978), 366–82.

MIYOSHI, Masao, '*Caleb Williams*', *The Divided Self* (New York and London, 1969), pp.23–9.

MYERS, Mitzi, 'Godwin's Changing Conception of *Caleb Williams*', *Studies in English Literature*, XII (1972), 591–628.

MONRO, D. H., 'William Godwin', *Encyclopaedia of Philosophy*, ed. P. Edwards (8 vols., Collier-Macmillan, 1967), III, 358–62.

———, 'Godwin, Oakeshott and Mrs. Bloomer', *Journal of the History of Ideas*, XXXV (1974), 611–24.

MURRY, John Middleton, 'William Godwin: Apostle of Universal Benevolence', *Times Literary Supplement* (4 April 1936), pp.285–6.

———, 'The Protestant Dream', *Heaven—and Earth* (Jonathan Cape, 1938), pp.254–68.

NETTLAU, Max, 'William Godwin', *Der Vorfrühling der Anarchie: Ihre Historische Entwicklung von den Anfangen bis Zum Jahre* (Berlin: Fritz Kater, 1925), pp.67–72.

———, 'William Godwin', *Volonta*, XX (1967), 417–22.

NEWTON, A. Edward, 'The Ridiculous Philosopher', *The Amenities of Book-Collecting and Kindred Affections* (John Lane, 1920), pp.226–48.

———, 'Skinner Street News', *The Greatest Book in the World and Other Papers* (Boston: Little, Brown and Company, 1925), pp.343–407.

OUSBY, Ian, '"My Servant Caleb": Godwin's *Caleb Williams* and the Political Trials of the 1790s', *University of Toronto Quarterly*, XLIV (1974), 47–55.

PALACIO, Jean de, 'L'Etat présent des études Godwiniennes', *Etudes Anglaises*, XX (1967), 149–59.

——, 'La fortune de Godwin en France: le cas d'Elizabeth Hamilton', *Revue de Littérature Comparée*, XLI (1967), 321–41.

——, 'Encore du nouveau sur Godwin', *Etudes Anglaises*, XX (1969), 49–57.

——, 'William Godwin, Ariosto, and the Grand Tour; or, *Caleb Williams* Reconsidered', *Rivista di Letterature Moderne e Comparate*, XXIII (1970), 111–20.

——, 'Godwin et la tentation de l'autobiographie (William Godwin et J.-J. Rousseau)', *Etudes Anglaises*, XXVII (1974), 143–57.

PARTINGTON, W., 'End Papers of Marginalia: *Letter of Advice to a Young American*', *Bookman* (New York), LXXIII (1931), 669–71.

PATTON, Lewis, 'The Shelley–Godwin Collection of Lord Abinger', *Duke University Library Notes*, XXVII (1953), 11–17.

PESTA, John, '*Caleb Williams*: A Tragedy of Wasted Love', *Tennessee Studies in Literature*, XVI (1971), 67–76.

PHILP, M., 'Godwin, Holcroft and the Rights of Man', *Enlightenment and Dissent*, I (1982), 37–42.

PLAMENATZ, John, 'Godwin: A Radical Utilitarian', *The English Utilitarians* (Oxford: Basil Blackwell, 1949), pp.88–96.

POLLIN, Burton R., 'Primitivism in *Imogen*', *Bulletin of the New York Public Library*, LXVII (1963), 186–90. Reprinted in *Imogen: A Pastoral Romance*, ed. J. W. Marken (New York, 1963), pp.113–17.

——, 'Godwin's *Letters of Verax*', *Journal of the History of Ideas*, XXV (1964), 353–73.

——, 'Verse Satires on William Godwin in the Anti-Jacobin Period', *Satire Newsletter*, II (1964), 31–40.

——, 'William Godwin's Fragment of a Romance', *Comparative Literature*, XVI (1964), 40–54.

——, 'Fanny Godwin's Suicide Re-Examined', *Etudes Anglaises*, XVIII (1965), 258–68.

——, 'Poe and Godwin', *Nineteenth-Century Fiction*, XX (1965), 237–53.

——, 'A Federalist Farrago, or "The Enlightened Eighteenth Century"', *Satire Newsletter*, IV (1966), 29–32.

——, 'Godwin's Letter to Ogilvie, Friend of Jefferson and the Federalist Propaganda', *Journal of the History of Ideas*, XXVIII (1967), 432–44.

——, 'Nicholson's Lost Portrait of William Godwin', *Keats–Shelley Journal*, XVI (1967), 57–60.

——. 'Godwin's *Mandeville* in the Poems of Shelley', *Keats – Shelley Memorial Bulletin*, XIX (1968), 33–40.

——, 'Godwin's Account of Shelley's Return in September 1814: A Letter to John Taylor', *Keats–Shelley Memorial Bulletin*, XXI (1970), 21–31.

——, 'The Significance of Names in the Fiction of William Godwin', *Revue des Langues Vivantes*, XXXVIII (1971), 388–99.

PREU, James, 'Swift's Influence on Godwin', *Journal of the History of Ideas*, XV (1954), 371–83.

PRIESTLEY, F. E. L., 'Platonism in William Godwin's *Political Justice*', *Modern Language Quarterly*, IV (1943), 63–9.

——, 'Introduction', *Enquiry concerning Political Justice* (Toronto: Univ. of Toronto Press, 1946), III, 3–113.

——, 'William Godwin and History', *Essays in Legal History in Honor of Felix Frankfurter*, ed. M. D. Forkosch (Indianapolis: Bobbs-Merrill, 1966), pp.423–37.

PRIMER, Irwin, 'Some Implications of Irony' (on *Imogen*), *Bulletin of the New York Public Library*, LXVII (1963), 237–60. Reprinted in *Imogen: A Pastoral Romance*, ed. J. W. Marken (New York, 1963), pp.118–21.

PRUNIER, André, 'William Godwin, el Anarquista Pacifico', *Cenit*, I (1951), 210–13.

——, 'William Godwin 1–3', *Umanita Nova*, XXXI (4 March 1951), 3; (11 March 1951), 3; (18 March 1951), 3.

——, 'L'Anarchiste pacifique', *Cahiers de Pensée et Action*, I (1953), 8–13.

——, 'Godwin, était-il communiste?', ibid., 22–5.

READ, Herbert, 'Foreword', *William Godwin. A Biographical Study* by George Woodcock (Porcupine Press, 1946), pp.vii–ix.

RIEGER, James, 'Godwin's *Caleb Williams*', *The Mutiny Within: The Heresies of Percy Bysshe Shelley* (New York: G. Braziller, 1967), pp.34–48.

RITTER, Alan, 'Godwin, Proudhon, and the Anarchist Justification of Punishment', *Political Theory*, III (1975), 69–87.

ROBERTS, Charles W., 'The Influence of Godwin on Wordsworth's *Letter to the Bishop of Llandaff*', *Studies in Philology*, XXIX (1932), 588–606.

——, 'Wordsworth, *The Philanthropist*, and *Political Justice*', *Studies in Philology, XXXI (1934), 84–91*.

ROEMER, Donald, 'The Achievement of Godwin's *Caleb Williams: The Proto-Byronic Squire Falkland*', *Criticism*, XVIII (1976), 81–7.

ROGERS, A. K., 'Godwin and *Political Justice*', *International Journal of Ethics*, XXII (1911), 50–68.

ROGERS, Deborah D., '*Caleb Williams:* Things as They Are Not', *American Notes and Queries*, XIII (1975), 133.

ROSEN, Frederick, 'Godwin and Holcroft', *English Language Notes*, V (1968), 183–6.

——, 'The Principles of Population as Political Theory: Godwin's *Of Population* and the Malthusian Controversy', *Journal of the History of Ideas*, XXXI (1970), 33–48.

ROTHSTEIN, Eric, 'Allusion and Analogy in the Romance of *Caleb Williams*', *University of Toronto Quarterly*, XXXVII (1967), 18–30.

——, '*Caleb Williams*', *Systems of Order and Inquiry in Later Eighteenth-Century Fiction* (Berkeley: Univ. of California Press, 1975), pp.208–42.

RUTHERFORD, Mark (i.e. William Hale White), 'Godwin and Wordsworth', *More Pages from a Journal, with Other Papers* (O.U.P., 1910), pp.205–14.

SAINTSBURY, George, 'William Godwin', *The English Novel* (J. M. Dent, 1913), pp.167–70.

——, 'Bolshevism in its Cradle: The Life and Opinions of William Godwin', *New World*, I (1919), 547–56.

SARTIN, Max, 'William Godwin I–III', *Volonta*, VI (1952), 328–38; 528–33; 598–602.

SCHEUERMANN, Mona, 'From Mind to Society: *Caleb Williams* as a Psychological Novel', *Dutch-Quarterly Review of Anglo-American Letters,* VII (1977), 115–27.

SCHIAVINA, Raffaele, 'William Godwin', *Volonta*, IV (1950), 645–50.

SCHIER, Donald, 'A Contemporary French Critique of *Caleb Williams*', *Revue de Littérature Comparée*, XLVII (1973), 412–18.

SCRIVENER, Michael H., 'Godwin's Philosophy: A Revaluation', *Journal of the History of Ideas*, XXXIX (1978), 615–26.

SEDELOW, Walter A. Jr., 'New Interest in William Godwin', *American Journal of Economics and Sociology*, XXIX (1970), 108–12.

SEN, Amiyakumar, 'Godwin and Shelley', *Journal of the Department of Letters* (Calcutta University), XIX (1930), 1–23.

SERGENT, Alain and HARMEL, Claude, 'William Godwin', *Histoire de l'anarchie* (Paris: Le Portulau, 1949), pp.89–109.

SHARROCK, Roger, 'Godwin on Milton's Satan', *Notes and Queries*, CCVII (1962), 463–5.

SHERBURN, George, 'Introduction', *The Adventures of Caleb Williams* (New York: Reinhart, 1960), pp.i–xxx.

——, 'Godwin's Later Novels', *Studies in Romanticism*, I (1962), 65–82.

SHIRAI, Otsushi, 'Life and Thought of Godwin', *Annual Report of Economics* (Keio University, Tokyo), IV (1961), 95–176.

————, 'On William Godwin', *Keio Economic Studies* (Tokyo), III (1965), 39–64.

————, 'Robert Owen and William Godwin', *Mita Journal of Economics* (Keio University, Tokyo), LVIII, 1 (1965), 5–6; ibid., 2 (1965), 2–4; ibid., LIX (1966).

————, 'The Impact on Japan of William Godwin's Ideas', *American Journal of Economics and Sociology*, XXIX (1970), 89–96.

SILVER, Harold, 'William Godwin', *The Concept of Popular Education. A Study of Ideas and Movements in the Early Nineteenth Century* (MacGibbon & Kee, 1965), pp.84–95.

SIMON, Helene, 'Godwin's Ethik', *Zukunft* (Berlin), XVII (1909) 381–5.

STALLBAUMER, V. R., 'Holcroft's Influence on *Political Justice*', *Modern Language Quarterly*, XIV (1953), 21–30.

STAMPER, Rexford, '*Caleb Williams:* The Bondage of Truth', *Southern Quarterly*, XII (1972), 39–50.

STARR, G. A., 'Henry Brooke, William Godwin, and "Barnabas Tirrell/Tyrrell"', *Notes and Queries*, XXV (1978), 67–8.

STEEVES, Harrison R., 'Social Justice in the Novel', *Before Jane Austen: The Shaping of the English Novel in the Eighteenth Century* (Allen & Unwin, 1966), pp.296–310.

STONE, E., '*Caleb Williams* and *Martin Faber*: A Contrast', *Modern Language Notes*, LXII (1947), 480–3.

STORCH, Rudolf F., 'Metaphors of Private Guilt and Social Rebellion in Godwin's *Caleb Williams*', *English Literary History*, XXXIV (1967), 188–207.

STORR, Marthe Severn, 'L'Amour et le mariage chez Godwin', *Revue Anglo-Americaine*, XII (1932), 31–45.

TAYLOR, S., 'M. J. Godwin and Co.; Juvenile Library and Publication House in the Early Nineteenth Century', *Hornbook*, XX (1944), 78–87.

TOMALIN, Claire, 'Godwin', *The Life and Death of Mary Wollstonecraft* (Weidenfeld and Nicolson, 1974), pp.205–17.

TOZAWA, Tetsuhiko, 'William Godwin', *Kokka No Shorai* (Tokyo, 1955), pp.87–171.

UPHAUS, Robert W., '*Caleb Williams:* Godwin's Epoch of Mind', *Studies in the Novel* IX (1977), 279–96.

WALTON, James, 'Mad feary father': *Caleb Williams* and the novel form', *Salzburg Studies in English Literature*, XLVII (1975), 1–61.

WARDLE, Ralph M., 'Fulfillment', *Mary Wollstonecraft: A Critical Biography* (Lawrence: Univ. of Kansas Press, 1951), pp.258–308.

WATKINS, Frederick M., 'Godwin's *Enquiry concerning Political Justice*', *Canadian Journal of Economics and Political Science*, XIV (1948), 107–12.

WERKMEISTER, Lucyle, 'Coleridge and Godwin on the Communication of Truth', *Modern Philology*, LV (1958), 170–7.

WHITNEY, Lois, 'William Godwin', *Primitivism and the Idea of Progress in English Popular Literature of the Eighteenth Century* (Baltimore: Johns Hopkins Press, 1934), pp.84–95, 207–19.

WILCOX, Stewart C., 'A Hazlitt Borrowing from Godwin', *Modern Language Notes*, LVIII (1943), 69–70.

WILLEY, Basil, 'Nature in Revolution and Reaction', *The Eighteenth Century Background: Studies on the Idea of Nature in the Thought of the Period* (Chatto & Windus, 1940), pp.205–39.

WILSON, Angus, 'The Novels of William Godwin', *World Review*, XXVIII (1951), 37–41.

WOODCOCK, George, 'William Godwin', *Politics*, III, 8 (1946), 260–7.

————, 'William Godwin: L'Oeuvre méconnue', *Cahiers de Pensée et Action*, I (1953), 1–7.

————, 'William Godwin', *University Libertarian*, III (1957), 4–6.

————, 'The Man of Reason', *Anarchism: A History of Libertarian Ideas and Movements* (Harmondsworth: Penguin Books, 1975), pp.56–86.

————, 'Things as They Might Be: Things as They Are: Notes on the Novels of William Godwin', *Dalhousie Review*, LIV (1975), 685–97.

————, 'The Libertarian Virtues', *Times Literary Supplement* (28 April 1978), 477–8.

ZACCARIA, Césare, 'William Godwin 1–3', *L'Adunata* (New York) IV, 37 (12 September 1925), 2; IV, 38 (19 September 1925) 2–3; IV, 39 (26 September 1925), 1–2; IV, 41 (10 October 1925), 1.

———, 'William Godwin: Fédérations de personnes', *Cahiers de Pensée et Action*, I (1953), 48–67.

# INDEX